Rick Steves, Rick
Rick Steves' Budapest

BUDAPEST

Rick Steves & Cameron Hewitt

CONTENTS

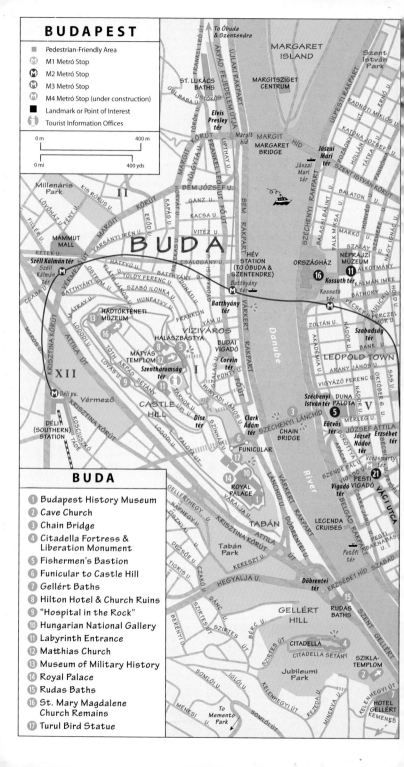

BUDAPEST

- ■ Pedestrian-Friendly Area
- Ⓜ M1 Metró Stop
- Ⓜ M2 Metró Stop
- Ⓜ M3 Metró Stop
- Ⓜ M4 Metró Stop (under construction)
- ■ Landmark or Point of Interest
- 🛈 Tourist Information Offices

0 m   400 m
0 mi   400 yds

BUDA

1 Budapest History Museum
2 Cave Church
3 Chain Bridge
4 Citadella Fortress & Liberation Monument
5 Fishermen's Bastion
6 Funicular to Castle Hill
7 Gellért Baths
8 Hilton Hotel & Church Ruins
9 "Hospital in the Rock"
10 Hungarian National Gallery
11 Labyrinth Entrance
12 Matthias Church
13 Museum of Military History
14 Royal Palace
15 Rudas Baths
16 St. Mary Magdalene Church Remains
17 Turul Bird Statue

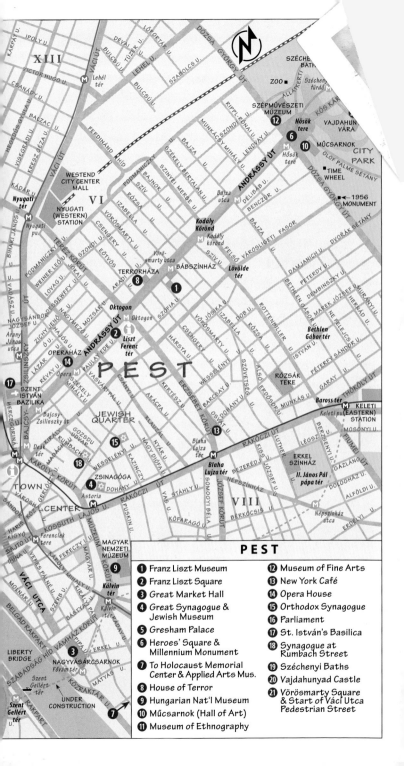

PEST

1. Franz Liszt Museum
2. Franz Liszt Square
3. Great Market Hall
4. Great Synagogue & Jewish Museum
5. Gresham Palace
6. Heroes' Square & Millennium Monument
7. To Holocaust Memorial Center & Applied Arts Mus.
8. House of Terror
9. Hungarian Nat'l Museum
10. Műcsarnok (Hall of Art)
11. Museum of Ethnography
12. Museum of Fine Arts
13. New York Café
14. Opera House
15. Orthodox Synagogue
16. Parliament
17. St. István's Basilica
18. Synagogue at Rumbach Street
19. Széchenyi Baths
20. Vajdahunyad Castle
21. Vörösmarty Square & Start of Váci Utca Pedestrian Street

Memento Park

Hungarian Parliament

Széchenyi Baths

Great Market Hall

Old Town Sopron

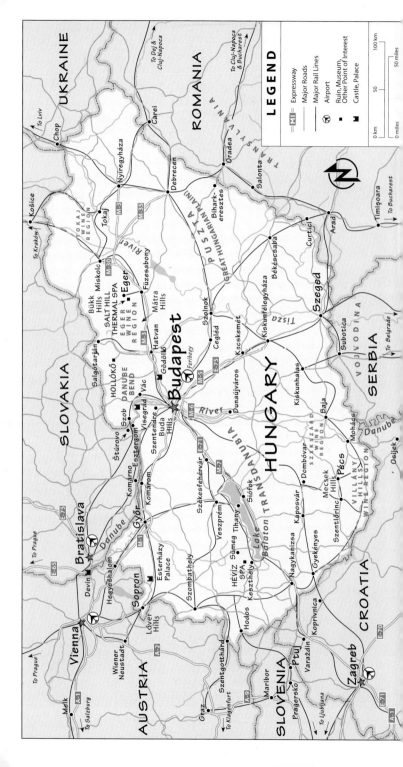

Rick Steves'

BUDAPEST

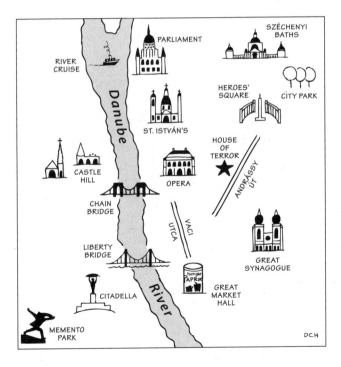

SZÉCHENYI BATHS

PARLIAMENT

RIVER CRUISE

HEROES' SQUARE

CITY PARK

Danube

ST. ISTVÁN'S

HOUSE OF TERROR

CASTLE HILL

OPERA

ANDRÁSSY ÚT

CHAIN BRIDGE

VACI UTCA

GREAT SYNAGOGUE

LIBERTY BRIDGE

CITADELLA

River

Hungar APRIL

GREAT MARKET HALL

MEMENTO PARK

DCH

INTRODUCTION

Budapest (locals say "BOO-daw-pesht") is a unique metropolis at the heart of a unique nation. Here you'll find experiences like nothing else in Europe: Feel your stress ebb away as you soak in hundred-degree water, surrounded by opulent Baroque domes...and by Speedo- and bikini-clad Hungarians. Ogle some of Europe's most richly decorated interiors, which echo a proud little nation's bygone glory days. Open your ears to a first-rate performance at one of the world's top opera houses—at bargain prices. Ponder the region's bleak communist era as you stroll amidst giant Soviet-style statues designed to evoke fear and obedience. Try to wrap your head around Hungary's colorful history...and your tongue around its notoriously difficult language. Dive into a bowl of goulash, the famous paprika-flavored peasant soup with a kick. Go for an after-dinner stroll along the Danube, immersed in a grand city that's bathed in floodlights.

Budapest excites good travelers...and exasperates bad ones. I love this city for its flaws as much as for its persistent personality. As a tour guide, for years I've introduced travelers to Budapest: walked them step-by-step through the byzantine entry procedure at the thermal baths; handed them a glass of local wine with an unpronounceable name and an unforgettable flavor; and taught them to greet their new Hungarian friends with a robust *"Jó napot kívánok!"* I've watched them struggle to understand—and gradually succumb to the charms of—this fascinating but beguiling place. And I've taken careful notes. This book represents the lessons I've learned on my own and, with them, organized to help you experience Budapest with the wisdom of a return visitor.

INTRODUCTION

Map Legend

⚲	Viewpoint	✈	Airport	)▨(	Tunnel
♠	Entrance	Ⓣ	Taxi Stand	▭	Pedestrian Zone
👥	Tourist Info	Ⓜ	Metró Stop	------	Railway
WC	Restroom	Ⓣ	Tram Stop	O╫╫╫╫O	Funicular
♖	Castle	Ⓑ	Bus Stop	├─┼─┤	Tram
⛪	Church	⚓	Boat Stop	⫿⫿⫿⫿	Stairs
☪	Mosque	Ⓟ	Parking	......	Walk/Tour Route
✡	Synagogue			------	Trail

Use this legend to help you navigate the maps in this book.

About This Book

Think of *Rick Steves' Budapest* as a personal tour guide in your pocket. Better yet, it's actually two tour guides in your pocket: The co-author of this book is Cameron Hewitt, who writes and edits guidebooks for my travel company, Rick Steves' Europe Through the Back Door. Inspired by Hungary's epic past, charming people, and delightfully spicy cuisine, Cameron has spent more than a decade closely tracking the exciting changes in this part of the world. Together, Cameron and I keep this book up-to-date and accurate (though, for simplicity, from this point on "we" will shed our respective egos and become "I").

Here's what you'll find in the following chapters:

Hungary offers an introduction to this mesmerizing land, including a crash course in its notoriously difficult language.

Orientation to Budapest includes specifics on public transportation, helpful hints, local tour options, easy-to-read maps, and tourist information. The "Planning Your Time" section suggests a day-to-day schedule for how to best use your limited time.

Sights in Budapest describes the top attractions and includes their cost and hours.

The **Thermal Baths** chapter offers step-by-step instructions for enjoying Budapest's quintessential activity like a local.

The **Self-Guided Walks and Tours** cover Budapest's Leopold Town (the banking and business district), Pest Town Center (the down-and-dirty downtown urban zone), Andrássy út (the main boulevard, lined with fine architecture and great sightseeing), Heroes' Square and City Park (the city's playground, including a Who's Who lesson in Hungarian history), and Castle Hill (the city's historic center). The tours lead you through three of Budapest's most compelling sights: the House of Terror Museum, the Great Synagogue and Jewish Quarter, and Memento Park.

Key to This Book

Updates
This book is updated regularly, but things change. For the latest, visit www.ricksteves.com/update, and for a valuable list of reports and experiences—good and bad—from fellow travelers, check www.ricksteves.com/feedback.

Abbreviations and Times
I use the following symbols and abbreviations in this book:
Sights are rated:

▲▲▲	**Don't miss**
▲▲	**Try hard to see**
▲	**Worthwhile if you can make it**
No rating	**Worth knowing about**

Tourist information offices are abbreviated as **TI**, and bathrooms are WCs. To categorize accommodations, I use a **Sleep Code** (described on page 226).

Like Hungary, this book uses the **24-hour clock** for schedules. It's the same through 12:00 noon, then keep going: 13:00, 14:00, and so on. For anything over 12, subtract 12 and add p.m. (14:00 is 2:00 p.m.).

When giving **opening times**, I include both peak season and off-season hours if they differ. So, if a museum is listed as "May-Oct daily 9:00-16:00," it should be open from 9 a.m. until 4 p.m. from the first day of May until the last day of October (but expect exceptions).

If you see a ✪ in a sight listing, it means that the sight is covered in much more detail in one of the tour chapters.

For **transit or tour departures**, I first list the frequency, then the duration. So, a train connection listed as "2/hour, 1.5 hours" departs twice each hour, and the journey lasts an hour and a half.

Sleeping in Budapest describes my favorite hotels, from good-value deals to cushy splurges.

Eating in Budapest outlines one of Hungary's top attractions—its delicious cuisine—and serves up a range of options, from inexpensive take-out joints to fancy restaurants.

Budapest with Children includes my top recommendations for keeping your kids (and you) happy in Budapest.

Shopping in Budapest gives you tips for shopping painlessly and enjoyably, without letting it overwhelm your vacation or ruin your budget.

Entertainment in Budapest is your guide to fun, from a low-key stroll along the Danube embankment to Budapest's most cutting-edge nightspots...and everything in between (opera, tourist concerts, music pubs, river cruises, and more).

Budapest Connections lays the groundwork for your smooth arrival and departure, outlining your options for traveling to destinations by train, bus, plane, car, and Danube riverboat.

Day Trips from Budapest includes the opulent Gödöllő Palace, the folk village of Hollókő, and the "Danube Bend" river towns of Szentendre, Visegrád, and Esztergom.

The **Beyond Budapest** section includes in-depth chapters on Hungary's best attractions outside of Budapest: the towns of **Eger, Pécs,** and **Sopron.** I've also thrown in the nearby Slovak capital of **Bratislava.**

Hungary: Past and Present is an overview of this nation's epic and illustrious history, and a survey of contemporary Hungary.

The **appendix** is a traveler's tool kit, with telephone tips, useful phone numbers, recommended books and films, a festival list, climate chart, handy packing checklist, hotel reservation form, and Hungarian survival phrases.

Browse through this book and select your favorite sights. Then have a great trip! Traveling like a temporary local, and taking advantage of the information here, you'll enjoy the absolute most of every mile, minute, and dollar. I'm happy that you'll be visiting places I know and love, and meeting some of my favorite Hungarians.

Planning

This section will help you get started on planning your trip—with advice on trip costs, when to go, and what you should know before you take off.

Travel Smart

Your trip to Budapest is like a complex play—easier to follow and really appreciate on a second viewing. While no one does the same trip twice to gain that advantage, reading this book in its entirety before your trip accomplishes much the same thing.

Design an itinerary that enables you to visit sights at the best possible times. Note holidays, festivals, specifics on sights, and days when sights are closed. For example, most Hungarian museums close on Mondays. To get between destinations smoothly, read the tips in this book's appendix on taking trains and buses, and renting a car and driving. A smart trip is a puzzle—a fun, doable, and worthwhile challenge.

Be sure to mix intense and relaxed periods in your itinerary. To maximize rootedness, minimize one-night stands. If you're venturing outside Budapest, it's worth taking a long drive after dinner (or a train ride with a dinner picnic) to get settled in a town for two nights. Every trip—and every traveler—needs slack time (laundry, picnics, people-watching, and so on). Pace yourself. Assume you will return.

Reread this book as you travel, and visit local tourist information offices (abbreviated as TI in this book). Upon arrival in a new town, lay the groundwork for a smooth departure; get the schedule for the train, bus, or boat that you'll take when you depart. Drivers can study the best route to their next destination.

Get online at Internet cafés or at your hotel, and carry a mobile phone (or use a phone card) to make travel plans: You can find tourist information, learn the latest on sights (special events, tour schedules, etc.), book tickets and tours, make reservations, reconfirm hotels, research transportation connections, check weather, and keep in touch with your loved ones.

Enjoy the hospitality of the Hungarian people. Connect with the culture. Set up your own quest for the best thermal bath, bowl of goulash, nostalgic Golden Age interior, or atmospheric café. Slow down and be open to unexpected experiences. Ask questions—most locals are eager to point you toward their idea of the right direction. Keep a notepad in your pocket for noting directions, organizing your thoughts, and confirming prices. Wear your money belt, learn the currency, and figure out how to estimate prices in dollars. Those who expect to travel smart, do.

Trip Costs

Traveling in Budapest (and throughout Hungary) is a good value. While Budapest has Westernized at an astonishing rate since the Iron Curtain fell, it's still cheaper than most Western European capitals.

Five components make up your trip costs: airfare, surface transportation, room and board, sightseeing and entertainment, and shopping and miscellany.

Airfare: A basic round-trip flight from the US to Budapest can cost, on average, about $800-1,400 total, depending on where you fly from and when (cheaper in winter).

Surface Transportation: For a typical one-week visit, figure about $100. That includes $22 for a week-long Budapest transit pass, $70 for side-trips to other Hungarian towns (e.g., about $30 round-trip to Eger and $40 round-trip to Pécs), plus an extra $8 for miscellaneous taxi rides. Add around $20 per person for each transfer between the airport and downtown Budapest (cheaper but slower if you take public transportation). If you rent a car for a few days of side-tripping, figure about $100 per day (cheaper per day for longer rentals).

Room and Board: You can thrive in Budapest on an average of $100 a day per person for room and board. A $100-a-day budget per person allows $10 for lunch, $25 for dinner, and $65 for

INTRODUCTION

lodging (based on two people splitting the cost of a $130 double room that includes breakfast). If you're on a tighter budget, settle for a $100 double room (still plenty comfortable) to bring the per-person average down to $85 per day. Students and tightwads can enjoy Budapest for as little as $40 a day ($20 per hostel bed, $20 for meals). If you're traveling beyond Budapest, accommodations cost much less in smaller Hungarian towns and cities (a comfortable double typically costs no more than $90, bringing your budget down to $80 per day per person for two people traveling together).

Sightseeing and Entertainment: You'll pay about $8-17 for major sights (House of Terror, Memento Park, touring the Parliament or Opera House), $3-6 for minor ones, and $15-25 for splurge experiences (soaking in a thermal bath, taking a nighttime boat cruise on the Danube, going to a tourist concert or opera). You can hire your own private guide for four hours for around $120—a great value when divided between two or more people. An overall average of $20-35 a day works for most people. Don't skimp here. After all, this category is the driving force behind your trip—you came to sightsee, enjoy, and experience Budapest.

Shopping and Miscellany: Figure $1-2 per postcard, coffee, beer, or ice-cream cone. Shopping can vary in cost from nearly nothing to a small fortune. Good budget travelers find that this category has little to do with assembling a trip full of lifelong and wonderful memories.

Sightseeing Priorities

Depending on the length of your trip, assuming you're using public transportation, and taking geographic proximity into account, here are my recommended priorities.

3 days:	Budapest
5 days, add:	Eger and one more day in Budapest
7 days, add:	Pécs and another day in Budapest, or choose a day trip
10 days, add:	Bratislava, Sopron, and additional day trips
More days, add:	More time in Budapest and more day trips

Note that Bratislava fits well on the way if you're going between Budapest and Vienna. For more tips, see "Planning Your Time" on page 36.

When to Go

The "tourist season" runs roughly from May through September. Book ahead for festivals and national holidays that occur throughout the year (for a list, see the appendix).

Summer (July and August) has its advantages: very long days, the busiest schedule of tourist fun and special festivals, and virtually no business travelers to compete with for hotel rooms. However, because Hungary has a practically Mediterranean climate, summer temperatures can skyrocket to the 80s or 90s (choose a hotel with air-conditioning). And many cultural events (such as the opera) are on summer vacation.

In spring and fall—May, June, September, and early October—travelers enjoy fewer tourist crowds and milder weather. This is my favorite time to visit Budapest. However, it's also prime convention time (especially September), when hotels tend to fill up and charge their top rates.

Winter travelers find concert season in full swing, with absolutely no tourist crowds, but some accommodations and sights are either closed or run on a limited schedule. Confirm your sightseeing plans locally, especially when traveling off-season. The weather can be cold and dreary, and night will draw the shades on your sightseeing before dinnertime. For weather specifics, see the climate chart in the appendix.

Know Before You Go

Your trip is more likely to go smoothly if you plan ahead. Check this list of things to arrange while you're still at home.

You need a **passport**—but no visa or shots—to travel in Hungary. You may be denied entry into certain European countries if your passport is due to expire within three to six months of your ticketed date of return. Get it renewed if you'll be cutting it close. It can take up to six weeks to get or renew a passport (for more on passports, see www.travel.state.gov). Pack a photocopy of your passport in your luggage in case the original is lost or stolen.

Book rooms well in advance if you'll be traveling at busy convention times (Sept-Oct) or during any major holidays (see page 476).

Call your **debit- and credit-card companies** to let them know the countries you'll be visiting, to ask about fees, to request your PIN code (it will be mailed to you), and more. See page 12 for details.

Do your homework if you want to buy **travel insurance.** Compare the cost of the insurance to the likelihood of your using it and your potential loss if something goes wrong. Also, check whether your existing insurance (health, homeowners, or renters) covers you and your possessions overseas. For more tips, see www.ricksteves.com/insurance.

If you're planning on **renting a car** in Hungary, bring your driver's license and an International Driving Permit (see page 303).

If you plan to hire a **local guide,** reserve ahead by email. Popular guides can get booked up.

If you're bringing a **mobile device,** download any apps you might want to use on the road, such as translators, maps, and transit schedules. Check out **Rick Steves Audio Europe,** featuring hours of travel interviews and other audio content about Hungary (via www.ricksteves.com/audioeurope, iTunes, Google Play, or the Rick Steves Audio Europe free smartphone app; for details, see page 472).

Check the **Rick Steves guidebook updates** page for any recent changes to this book (www.ricksteves.com/update).

Since **airline carry-on restrictions** are always changing, visit the Transportation Security Administration's website (www.tsa. gov) for an up-to-date list of what you can bring on the plane with you...and what you have to check.

Attitude Adjustment

Americans sometimes approach Hungary—for so long part of the "Evil Empire"—expecting grouchy service, crumbling communist infrastructure, and grimy, depressing landscapes. But those who visit are pleasantly surprised at the color, friendliness, safety, and ease of travel here. Many Hungarians speak excellent English and are forever scrambling to impress their guests. Any remaining rough edges simply add to the charm and carbonate the experience.

The East-West stuff still fascinates us, but to locals, the Soviet regime is old news, Cold War espionage is the stuff of movies, and oppressive monuments to Stalin are a distant memory. More than two decades after the fall of the Iron Curtain, Hungarians think about communism only when tourists bring it up. Freedom is a generation old, and—for better or for worse—McDonald's, MTV, and mobile phones are every bit as entrenched here as anywhere else in Europe.

When Hungary and seven other former Soviet Bloc countries joined the European Union in 2004—followed by two more in 2007—the geographical center of Europe shifted from Brussels to Prague. The Hungarians have put the communist days behind them and have embraced the EU: Hungary has already waived passport checks along its borders with fellow EU members (see "Practicalities," next), and may adopt the euro currency in the future. Now more than ever, Hungarians bristle at the idea that they live in "Eastern" Europe (which implies a connection to Russia); to them, it's *Central* Europe. They're looking to the future...and hope you will, too.

Practicalities

Emergency and Medical Help: The all-purpose emergency number in Hungary is 112. You can also call 107 for police, 104 for ambulance, or 105 for fire. If you come down with a minor ailment, do as the Hungarians do and go to a pharmacy (*gyógyszertár* or *patika*) for advice. Or ask at your hotel for help; they know of the nearest medical and emergency services. Embassies can recommend English-speaking doctors (see contact information on page 470).

Theft or Loss: To replace a passport, you'll need to go in person to an embassy or consulate (see page 470). If your credit and debit cards disappear, cancel and replace them (see "Damage Control for Lost Cards" on page 13). File a police report, either on the spot or within a day or two; you'll need it to submit an insurance claim for lost or stolen railpasses or travel gear, and it can help with replacing your passport or credit and debit cards. For more information, see www.ricksteves.com/help. Precautionary measures can minimize the effects of loss—back up your photos and other files frequently.

Borders: There are no passport checks when traveling between Hungary and the 25 other open-borders Schengen Agreement countries (including neighbors Slovakia, Austria, and Slovenia). At airports, by car, or by train, you'll simply zip through the border without stopping. (Hungary's southern and eastern neighbors—Croatia, Serbia, Romania, and Ukraine—have not yet joined Schengen, so you'll need to show your passport when entering any of those places...although Romania may qualify in 2013.) Even as borders fade, when you change countries, you must still change telephone cards, postage stamps, and underpants.

Time Zones: Hungary is generally six/nine hours ahead of the East/West Coasts of the US. The exceptions are the beginning and end of Daylight Saving Time: Hungary and Europe "spring forward" the last Sunday in March (two weeks after most of North America), and "fall back" the last Sunday in October (one week before North America). For a handy online time converter, try www.timeanddate.com/worldclock.

Business Hours: Most stores are open Monday through Friday (roughly 10:00-18:00), with a late night on Thursday (until 20:00 or 21:00). On Saturday, shops are usually open only from 10:00 to 13:00 or 14:00. Sundays have the same pros and cons as they do for travelers in the US: Sightseeing attractions are generally open; shops, banks, and markets are closed; public-transportation options are fewer; and city traffic is light. Rowdy evenings are rare on Sundays.

Many businesses, as well as many museums, close on Good Friday, Easter, and New Year's Day. On Christmas, virtually everything closes down. Museums are also generally closed December 24 and 26; smaller shops are usually closed December 26.

Watt's Up? Europe's electrical system is 220 volts, instead of North America's 110 volts. Most newer electronics (such as laptops, battery chargers, and hair dryers) convert automatically, so you won't need a converter, but you will need an adapter plug with two round prongs, sold inexpensively at travel stores in the US. Avoid bringing older appliances that don't automatically convert voltage; instead, buy a cheap replacement in Europe.

Discounts: Discounts aren't listed in this book. However, many Hungarian sights offer discounts for youths (under 18) and students with proper identification cards (www.isic.org). Always ask. Some discounts are available only for EU citizens.

Money

This section covers advice on how to pay for purchases on your trip (including getting cash from ATMs and paying with plastic), dealing with lost or stolen cards, VAT (sales tax) refunds, and tipping.

What to Bring

Bring both a credit card and a debit card. You'll use the debit card at cash machines (ATMs) to withdraw local cash for most purchases, and the credit card to pay for larger items. Some travelers carry a third card, in case one gets demagnetized or eaten by a temperamental machine.

I also carry a few hundred dollars in hard cash as an emergency backup (in $20 bills rather than hard-to-exchange $100 bills).

Cash

Cash is just as desirable in Hungary as it is at home. Small businesses (hotels, restaurants, and shops) prefer that you pay your bills with cash. Some vendors will charge you extra for using a credit card, and some won't take credit cards at all. Cash is the best—and often only—way to pay for bus fare, taxis, and local guides.

Throughout Hungary, ATMs are the standard way for travelers to get cash. In Hungary, ATMs are called *bankjegy-automata* (BONK-yedge OW-toh-maw-taw). Most Hungarians also recognize the international term *Bankomat*. Stay away from "independent" ATMs such as Travelex, Euronet, and Forex, which charge huge commissions and have terrible exchange rates.

To withdraw money from an ATM, you'll need a debit card (ideally with a Visa or MasterCard logo for maximum usability), plus a PIN code. Know your PIN code in numbers; there are only numbers—no letters—on European keypads. For security, it's best to shield the keypad when entering your PIN at an ATM. Although you can use a credit card for ATM transactions, it's generally more expensive (and only makes sense in an emergency), because it's considered a cash advance rather than a withdrawal. Try to withdraw large sums of money to reduce the number of per-transaction bank fees you'll pay.

Avoid using currency exchange booths, which generally offer

Exchange Rates

Hungary still uses its traditional currency, the **forint** (abbreviated Ft, or sometimes HUF).

200 Ft = about $1

To figure dollars, divide by two and drop the last two digits. For example, 1,000 Ft = about $5, 5,000 Ft = about $25, and 10,000 Ft = about $50. Note that the exchange rate has fluctuated wildly in recent years, and these are just rough estimates. To get the latest rates and print a cheat sheet, see www.oanda.com.

While Hungary is on track to adopt the Europe-wide **euro** currency, it likely won't happen for several years. However, you might already see some prices (especially hotel rates in Budapest) listed in euros for the convenience of international visitors. Even when you see prices listed in euros, locals gladly accept (and sometimes prefer) payment in forints.

Hungary's neighbors Slovakia (whose capital, Bratislava, is included in this book), Austria, and Slovenia all use the euro:

1 euro (€) = about $1.30

To roughly convert prices in euros to dollars, add 30 percent: €20 is about $26, €50 is about $65, and so on. (Check www.oanda.com for the latest exchange rates.)

So, that 1,500-Ft canister of paprika costs $7.50, that €25 meal in Bratislava is about $33, and that 13,000-Ft taxi ride through Budapest is...uh-oh.

lousy rates and/or charge excessive fees. One exception is if you are traveling between countries that have different currencies (say, from Hungary to Slovakia or Croatia). Coins can't be exchanged once you leave the country, so try to spend them before you cross the border. But bills are easy to convert to the "new" country's currency. Regular banks have the best rates. Post offices and train stations usually change money if you can't get to a bank.

Pickpockets target tourists. To safeguard your cash, wear a money belt—a pouch with a strap that you buckle around your waist like a belt and tuck under your clothes. Keep your cash, credit cards, and passport secure in your money belt, and carry only a day's spending money in your front pocket.

Credit and Debit Cards

For purchases, Visa and MasterCard are more commonly accepted than American Express. Just like at home, credit or debit cards work easily at larger hotels, restaurants, and shops, but most prefer cash—and small vendors require it. I typically use my debit card to withdraw cash to pay for most purchases. I use my credit card only in a few specific situations: to book hotel reservations by phone, to cover major expenses (such as car rentals, plane tickets, and hotel stays), and to pay for things near the end of my trip (to avoid another visit to the ATM). While you could use a debit card to make most large purchases, using a credit card offers a greater degree of fraud protection (because debit cards draw funds directly from your account).

Ask Your Credit- or Debit-Card Company: Before your trip, contact the company that issued your debit or credit cards.

• Confirm that your card **will work overseas,** and alert them that you'll be using it in Europe; otherwise, they may deny transactions if they perceive unusual spending patterns.

• Ask for the specifics on transaction **fees.** When you use your credit or debit card—either for purchases or ATM withdrawals—you'll often be charged additional "international transaction" fees of up to 3 percent (1 percent is normal) plus $5 per transaction. If your card's fees seem high, consider getting a different card just for your trip: Capital One (www.capitalone.com) and most credit unions have low-to-no international fees.

• If you plan to withdraw cash from ATMs, confirm your daily **withdrawal limit,** and if necessary, ask your bank to adjust it. Some travelers prefer a high limit that allows them to take out more cash at each ATM stop (saving on bank fees), while others prefer to set a lower limit in case their card is stolen. Note that foreign banks also set maximum withdrawal amounts for their ATMs.

• Get your bank's emergency **phone number** in the US (but not its 800 number, which isn't accessible from overseas) to call collect if you have a problem.

• Ask for your credit card's **PIN** in case you need to make an emergency cash withdrawal or encounter Europe's "chip-and-PIN" system; the bank won't tell you your PIN over the phone, so allow time for it to be mailed to you.

Chip and PIN: While much of Europe is shifting to a "chip-and-PIN" system for credit and debit cards, Hungary still uses the old magnetic-swipe technology. (European chip-and-PIN cards are embedded with an electronic chip, and require the purchaser to punch in a PIN rather than sign a receipt.) If you happen to encounter chip and PIN, it will probably be at automated payment machines, such as those at toll roads or self-serve gas pumps. On the outside chance that a machine won't take your card, find a cashier who can make your card work (they can print a receipt for you to sign), or find a machine that takes cash. But don't panic. Most travelers who are carrying only magnetic-stripe cards never encounter any problems.

Dynamic Currency Conversion: If merchants offer to convert your purchase price into dollars (called dynamic currency conversion, or DCC), refuse this "service." You'll pay even more in fees for the expensive convenience of seeing your charge in dollars.

Damage Control for Lost Cards

If you lose your credit, debit, or ATM card, you can stop people from using it by reporting the loss immediately to the respective global customer-assistance centers. Call these 24-hour US numbers collect: Visa (tel. 303/967-1096), MasterCard (tel. 636/722-7111), and American Express (tel. 336/393-1111). European toll-free numbers (listed by country) can be found at the websites for Visa and MasterCard.

At a minimum, you'll need to know the name of the financial institution that issued you the card, along with the type of card (classic, platinum, or whatever). Providing the following information will allow for a quicker cancellation of your missing card: full card number, whether you are the primary or secondary cardholder; the cardholder's name exactly as printed on the card; billing address; home phone number; circumstances of the loss or theft; and identification verification (your birth date, your mother's maiden name, or your Social Security number—memorize this, don't carry a copy). If you are the secondary cardholder, you'll also need to provide the primary cardholder's identification-verification details. You can generally receive a temporary card within two or three business days in Europe.

If you report your loss within two days, you typically won't be responsible for any unauthorized transactions on your account, although many banks charge a liability fee of $50.

Tipping

A decade ago, tipping was unheard of in Hungary. But then came the tourists. Today, while tipping is on the rise, it isn't as automatic or as generous as in the US—but for special service, tips are appreciated, if not expected. As in the US, the proper amount depends on your resources, tipping philosophy, and the circumstances, but some general guidelines apply.

Restaurants: Tipping is an issue only at restaurants that have table service. If you order your food at a counter, don't tip.

Most Budapest restaurants automatically tack on a 10 to 12 percent service charge. Check for it as a line-item at the end of bill: Look for "service," "tip," *felszolgálási díj*, or *szervízdíj*. If you see this charge, an additional tip is not necessary. However, if the service charge isn't included, most servers expect about a 10 percent tip (though a bit less is fine, if it rounds to a convenient total). More than 10 percent is reserved only for exemplary service, and

15 percent verges on extravagant. For example, for a 3,650-Ft bill, I'd hand over 4,000 Ft (that's a 350-Ft tip, or a bit more than 9 percent—perfectly acceptable). If you're not sure whether your bill includes the tip, just ask. In smaller cities and towns outside Budapest, it's very rare for the service charge to be tacked on—rounding the bill up 10 percent is more than enough.

Taxis: To tip the cabbie, round up about 10 percent (for a 1,350-Ft fare, pay 1,500 Ft). If the cabbie hauls your bags and zips you to the airport to help you catch your flight, you might want to toss in a little more. But if you feel like you're being driven in circles or otherwise ripped off, skip the tip.

Special Services: In general, if someone in the service industry does a super job for you, a small tip (200-400 Ft) is appropriate, but not required. If you're not sure whether (or how much) to tip for a service, ask your hotelier or the TI.

Getting a VAT Refund

Wrapped into the purchase price of your Hungarian souvenirs is a Value-Added Tax (VAT) of about 25 percent. You're entitled to get most of that tax back if you purchase more than 45,000 Ft (about $225) worth of goods at a store that participates in the VAT-refund scheme. Typically, you must ring up the minimum at a single retailer—you can't add up your purchases from various shops to reach the required amount.

Getting your refund is usually straightforward and, if you buy a substantial amount of souvenirs, well worth the hassle. If you're lucky, the merchant will subtract the tax when you make your purchase. (This is more likely to occur if the store ships the goods to your home.) Otherwise, you'll need to:

Get the paperwork. Have the merchant completely fill out the necessary refund document, called a "Tax-Free Shopping Cheque." You'll have to present your passport. Get the paperwork done before you leave the store to ensure you'll have everything you need (including your original sales receipt).

Get your stamp at the border or airport. Process your VAT document at your last stop in the European Union (such as at the airport) with the customs agent who deals with VAT refunds. Before checking in for your flight, find the local customs office, and be prepared to stand in line. Keep your purchases readily available for viewing by the customs agent (ideally in your carry-on bag—don't make the mistake of checking the bag with your purchases before you've seen the agent). You're not supposed to use your purchased goods before you leave. If you show up at customs wearing your new communist-kitsch T-shirt, officials might look the other way—or deny you a refund.

Collect your refund. You'll need to return your stamped

document to the retailer or its representative. Many merchants work with a service, such as Global Blue or Premier Tax Free, that has offices at major airports, ports, or border crossings (either before or after security, probably strategically located near a duty-free shop). These services, which extract a 4 percent fee, can refund your money immediately in cash or credit your card (within two billing cycles). If the retailer handles VAT refunds directly, it's up to you to contact the merchant for your refund. You can mail the documents from home, or more quickly, from your point of departure (using an envelope you've prepared in advance or one that's been provided by the merchant). You'll then have to wait—it can take months.

Customs for American Shoppers
You are allowed to take home $800 worth of items per person duty-free, once every 30 days. You can also bring in one liter of alcohol duty-free. As for food, you can take home many processed and packaged foods: sealed bags of paprika, vacuum-packed cheeses, dried herbs, jams, baked goods, candy, chocolate, oil, vinegar, mustard, and honey. Fresh fruits and vegetables and most meats are not allowed. Any liquid-containing foods must be packed in checked luggage, a potential recipe for disaster. To check customs rules and duty rates, visit www.cbp.gov.

Sightseeing

Many of Budapest's museums are dusty and a bit old-fashioned. But with patience and imagination, and a solid background in the topic (provided by this book's descriptions, self-guided tours, in-depth sidebars, and the Hungary: Past and Present chapter), Budapest's museums come to life and become genuinely enthralling.

Sightseeing can be hard work. Use these tips to make your visits to Budapest's big sights meaningful, fun, efficient, and painless.

Plan Ahead
Set up an itinerary that allows you to fit in all your must-see sights. For a one-stop look at opening hours, see "Budapest at a Glance" on pages 58-59. Most sights keep stable hours, but you can easily confirm the latest by asking the local TI.

Don't put off visiting a must-see sight—you never know when a place will close unexpectedly because of strikes or renovation. On holidays (see list on page 476), expect reduced hours or closures.

To get the most out of the self-guided tours and sight descriptions in this book, reread them the night before your visit. A walk through the communist relics at Memento Park, for instance, is more meaningful if you've read up on the Soviet era the night before. When you arrive at the sight, use the overview map to get the lay of the land and the basic tour route.

When possible, visit key museums first thing (when your energy is best) and save other activities for the afternoon. Hit a sight's highlights first, then see the rest if you have the stamina and time. Going at the right time can also help you avoid crowds. This book offers specific tips on a few of Budapest's most crowded sights.

At Sights

Here's what you can typically expect:

Some sights (including the Parliament, Great Synagogue, and Holocaust Memorial Center) have metal detectors that will slow your entry, while others require you to check daypacks and coats. To avoid checking a small backpack, carry it under your arm like a purse as you enter. From a guard's point of view, a backpack is generally a problem while a purse is not.

At churches—which often offer interesting art and a cool, welcome seat—a modest dress code (no bare shoulders or shorts) is encouraged.

Flash photography is sometimes banned, but taking photos without a flash is normally allowed. Flashes damage oil paintings and distract others in the room. At some places, you'll have to buy a pricey "photo ticket" for permission. Even without a flash, a hand-held camera will take a decent picture (or buy postcards or posters at the museum bookstore).

Museums may have special exhibits in addition to their permanent collections. Some exhibits are included in the entry price; others come at an extra cost (which you may have to pay even if you don't want to see the exhibit).

Once inside, you'll generally follow a confusing one-way tour route through a maze of rooms with squeaky parquet floors, monitored by grumpy grannies who listlessly point you in the right direction.

While most museums label exhibits in English, most don't post full descriptions; you'll have to buy a book or borrow laminated translations. In some cases, neither option is available.

Expect changes—items can be on tour, on loan, out sick, or shifted at the whim of the curator. To adapt, pick up any available free floor plans as you enter, and ask museum staff if you can't find a particular item.

Some Budapest museums rent audioguides, which generally offer dry recorded descriptions in English. If you bring your own earbuds, you can enjoy better sound and avoid holding the device to your ear. To save money, bring a Y-jack and share one audioguide with your travel partner.

Important sights may have an on-site café or cafeteria (usually

How Was Your Trip?

Were your travels fun, smooth, and meaningful? If you'd like to share your tips, concerns, and discoveries, please fill out the survey at www.ricksteves.com/feedback. I value your feedback. Thanks in advance—it helps a lot.

a handy place to rejuvenate during a long visit). The WCs at sights are usually free and generally clean.

Many places sell postcards that highlight their attractions. Before you leave, scan the postcards and thumb through the biggest guidebook (or skim its index) to be sure you haven't overlooked something that you'd like to see.

Most sights stop admitting people 30-60 minutes before closing time, and some rooms may close early (often about 45 minutes before the actual closing time). Guards usher people out, so don't save the best for last.

Every sight and museum offers more than what is covered in this book. Use the self-guided tours in this book as an introduction—not the final word.

Traveling as a Temporary Local

We travel all the way to Europe to enjoy differences—to become temporary locals. You'll experience frustrations. Certain truths that we find "God-given" or "self-evident," such as cold beer, ice in drinks, bottomless cups of coffee, "first" names first, cigarette smoke being irritating, and bigger being better, are suddenly not so true. One of the benefits of travel is the eye-opening realization that there are logical, civil, and even better alternatives. A willingness to go local ensures that you'll enjoy a full dose of local hospitality.

Fortunately for you, hospitality is a Hungarian forte. The warmth of the Hungarians seems only to have been enhanced during the communist era: Tangible resources were in short supply, so an open door and a genial conversation were all that people had to offer. Even so, some people—hardened by decades of being spied on by neighbors and standing in long lines to buy food for their family—seem brusque at first. In my experience, all it takes is a smile and a little effort to befriend these residents of the former "Evil Empire."

Europeans generally like Americans. But if there is a negative aspect to the image Europeans have of Americans, it's that we are

loud, wasteful, ethnocentric, too informal (which can seem disre-
spectful), and a bit naive.

While Hungarians look bemusedly at some of our Yankee ex-
cesses—and worriedly at others—they nearly always afford us individual travelers all the warmth we deserve.

Judging from all the happy feedback I receive from travelers,
it's safe to assume you'll enjoy a great, affordable vacation—with
the finesse of an independent, experienced traveler.

Thanks, and *jó utat*—happy travels!

Back Door Travel Philosophy

From Rick Steves' *Europe Through the Back Door*

Travel is intensified living—maximum thrills per minute and one of the last great sources of legal adventure. Travel is freedom. It's recess, and we need it.

Experiencing the real Europe requires catching it by surprise, going casual..."through the Back Door."

Affording travel is a matter of priorities. (Make do with the old car.) You can eat and sleep—simply, safely, and enjoyably—anywhere in Europe for $120 a day plus transportation costs. In many ways, spending more money only builds a thicker wall between you and what you traveled so far to see. Europe is a cultural carnival, and time after time, you'll find that its best acts are free and the best seats are the cheap ones.

A tight budget forces you to travel close to the ground, meeting and communicating with the people. Never sacrifice sleep, nutrition, safety, or cleanliness to save money. Simply enjoy the local-style alternatives to expensive hotels and restaurants.

Connecting with people carbonates your experience. Extroverts have more fun. If your trip is low on magic moments, kick yourself and make things happen. If you don't enjoy a place, maybe you don't know enough about it. Seek the truth. Recognize tourist traps. Give a culture the benefit of your open mind. See things as different, but not better or worse. Any culture has plenty to share.

Of course, travel, like the world, is a series of hills and valleys. Be fanatically positive and militantly optimistic. If something's not to your liking, change your liking.

Travel can make you a happier American, as well as a citizen of the world. Our Earth is home to seven billion equally precious people. It's humbling to travel and find that other people don't have the "American Dream"—they have their own dreams. Europeans like us, but with all due respect, they wouldn't trade passports.

Thoughtful travel engages us with the world. In tough economic times, it reminds us what is truly important. By broadening perspectives, travel teaches new ways to measure quality of life.

Globetrotting destroys ethnocentricity, helping us understand and appreciate other cultures. Rather than fear the diversity on this planet, celebrate it. Among your most prized souvenirs will be the strands of different cultures you choose to knit into your own character. The world is a cultural yarn shop, and Back Door travelers are weaving the ultimate tapestry. Join in!

HUNGARY

Magyarország

Hungary is an island of Asian-descended Magyars in a sea of Slavs. Even though the Hungarians have thoroughly integrated with their Slavic and German neighbors in the millennium-plus since they arrived, there's still something about the place that's distinctly Magyar (MUD-jar). Here in quirky, idiosyncratic Hungary, everything's a little different from the rest of Europe—in terms of history, language, culture, customs, and cuisine—but it's hard to put your finger on exactly how.

Travelers to Hungary notice many endearing peculiarities. Hungarians list a person's family name first, and the given name is last—just as in many other Eastern cultures (think of Kim Jong Il). So the composer known as "Franz Liszt" in German is "Liszt Ferenc" in his homeland. (To help reduce confusion, many Hungarian business cards list the surname in capital letters.) Hungarians have a charming habit of using the English word "hello" for both "hi" and "bye," just like the Italians use "ciao." You might overhear a Hungarian end a telephone conversation with a cheery "Hello!" Hungarians even drove on the left side of the road until 1941.

Just a century ago, this country controlled half of one of Europe's grandest realms: the Austro-Hungarian Empire. Today, perhaps clinging to their former greatness, many Hungarians remain old-fashioned and nostalgic. With their dusty museums and bushy moustaches, they love to remember the good old days. Buildings all over the country are marked with plaques boasting *MŰEMLÉK* ("historical monument").

Thanks to this focus on tradition, the Hungarians you'll encounter are generally polite, formal, and professional. Hungarians have class. Everything here is done with a proud flourish. People in the service industry seem to wear their uniforms as a badge of honor rather than a burden. When a waiter comes to your table

in a restaurant, he'll say, *"Tessék parancsolni"*—literally, "Please command, sir." The standard greeting, *"Jó napot kívánok,"* means "I wish you a good day." Women sometimes hear the even more formal greeting, *"Kezét csókolom"*—"I kiss your hand." And when your train or bus makes a stop, you won't be alerted by a mindless, blaring beep—but instead, by peppy music. (You'll be humming these contagious little ditties all day.) Perhaps thanks to this artful blending of elegance and formality, Hungarians have a cultural affinity for the French.

Hungarians are also orderly and tidy...in their own sometimes unexpected ways. Yes, Hungary has its share of litter, graffiti, and crumbling buildings, but you'll find great reason within the chaos. The Hungarian railroad has a long list of discounted fares—for seniors, kids, dogs...and monkeys. Just in case. (It could happen.) My favorite town name in Hungary: Hatvan. This means "Sixty" in Hungarian...and it's exactly 60 kilometers from Budapest. You can't argue with that kind of logic.

This tradition of left-brained thinking hasn't produced many great Hungarian painters or poets who are known outside their homeland. But the Hungarians, who are renowned for their ingenuity, have made tremendous contributions to science, technology, business, and industry. Hungarians of note include Edward Teller (instrumental in creating the A-bomb), John von Neumann (a pioneer of computer science), Andy Grove (who, as András Gróf, emigrated to the US and founded Intel), and George Soros (the billionaire investor famous—or notorious—for supporting left-wing causes). A popular local joke claims that Hungarians

HUNGARY

Hungary Almanac

Official Name: Simply Magyarország (Hungary).

Snapshot History: Settled by the Central Asian Magyars in A.D. 896, Hungary became Catholic in the year 1000, and went on to become Christian Europe's front line in fighting against the Ottomans (Muslims from today's Turkey) in the 16th-17th centuries. After serving as co-capital of the vast Austro-Hungarian Empire and losing World Wars I and II, Hungary became a Soviet satellite until achieving independence in 1989.

Population: Hungary's 10 million people (similar to Michigan) are 92 percent ethnic Hungarians who speak Hungarian. One in 50 is Roma (Gypsy). Half the populace is Catholic, with 20 percent Protestant and 25 percent listed as "other" or unaffiliated. Of the world's approximately 12 million ethnic Hungarians, one in six lives outside Hungary (mostly in areas of Romania, Slovakia, Serbia, and Croatia that were once part of Hungary).

Latitude and Longitude: 47°N and 20°E; similar latitude to Seattle, Paris, and Vienna.

Area: 36,000 square miles, similar to Indiana or Maine.

Geography: Hungary is situated in the Carpathian Basin, bound on the north by the Carpathian Mountains and on the south by the Dinaric Mountains. Though it's surrounded by mountains, Hungary itself is relatively flat, with some gently rolling hills. The Great Hungarian Plain—which begins on the east bank of the Danube in Budapest—stretches all the way to Asia. Hungary's two main rivers—the Danube and Tisza—run north-south through the country, neatly dividing it into three regions.

Biggest Cities: Budapest (the capital on the Danube, nearly 2 million), Debrecen (in the east, 205,000), and Miskolc (in the north, 170,000).

are so clever that they can enter a revolving door behind you and exit in front of you.

Perhaps the most famous Hungarian "scientist" invented something you probably have in a box in your basement: Ernő Rubik, creator of the famous cube. Hungarians' enjoyment of a good mind-bending puzzle is also evident in their fascination with chess, which you'll see played in cafés, parks, and baths.

Like their Viennese neighbors, Hungarians know how to enjoy the good life. Favorite activities include splashing and soaking in their many thermal baths (see the Thermal Baths chapter). "Taking the waters," Hungarian-style, deserves to be your top priority while you're here. Though public baths can sound intimidating, they're a delight. In this book I recommend my three favorite baths in Budapest, a fine bath in Eger, and another just outside of Eger. For each one, I've included careful instructions to help you enjoy the warm-

Economy: The Gross Domestic Product is $198 billion (a third of Poland's), but the GDP per capita is $19,800 (only slightly less than Poland's). Thanks to its progressive "goulash communism," Hungary had a head start on many other former Soviet Bloc countries and is now thriving, privatized...and largely foreign-owned. In the 1990s, many communist-era workers (especially women) lost their jobs. Today, the workforce is small (only 57 percent of eligible workers) but highly skilled. Grains, metals, machinery, and automobiles are major exports, and about one-quarter of trade is with Germany.

Currency: 200 forints (Ft, or HUF) = about $1.

Government: The single-house National Assembly (200 seats) is the only ruling branch directly elected by popular vote. The legislators in turn select the figurehead president (currently János Áder) and the ruling prime minister (Viktor Orbán); both belong to the right-of-center Fidesz party.

Flag: Three horizontal bands, top to bottom: red (representing strength), white (faithfulness), and green (hope). It's identical to the Italian flag, but flipped 90 degrees counterclockwise. It often includes the Hungarian coat of arms: horizontal red-and-white stripes (on the left); the patriarchal, or double-barred, cross (on the right); and the Hungarian crown (on top).

The Average János: The typical Hungarian eats a pound of lard a week (they cook with it). The average family has three members, and they spend almost three-fourths of their income on (costly) housing. According to a recent condom-company survey, the average Hungarian has sex 131 times a year (behind only France and Greece), making them Europe's third-greatest liars.

water fun like a pro. (To allay your first fear: Yes, you can wear your swimsuit the entire time.)

Hungarians have also revived an elegant, Vienna-style café culture that was dismantled by the communists. Whiling away the afternoon at a genteel coffeehouse, as you nurse a drink or a delicate dessert, is a favorite pastime. (For the best options in Budapest, see "Budapest's Café Culture" on page 263.)

Classical music is revered in Hungary, perhaps as nowhere else outside Austria. Aside from scientists and businessmen, the best-known Hungarians are composers: Béla Bartók, Zoltán Kodály, and Franz Liszt. (For more on these figures, see "Hungarian Music" on page 284-285.)

While one in five Hungarians lives in Budapest, the countryside plays an important role in Hungary's economy—this has always been a highly agricultural region. You'll pass through fields of wheat and corn, but the grains are secondary to Hungarians' (and tourists') true love: wine. Hungarian winemaking standards plummeted under the communists, but many vintner families are now reclaiming their land, returning to their precise traditional methods, and making wines worth being proud of once more. (For details, see "Hungarian Wines" on page 252.)

Somehow Hungary, at the crossroads of Europe, has managed to become cosmopolitan while remaining perfectly Hungarian. In the countryside, where less mixing has occurred, traditional Magyar culture is more evident. But in the cities, the Hungarians—like Hungary itself—are a cross-section of Central European cultures: Magyars, Germans, Czechs, Slovaks, Poles, Serbs, Jews, Ottomans, Romanians, Roma (Gypsies), and many others. Still, no matter how many generations removed they are from Magyar stock, there's something different about Hungarians—and not just the language. Look a Hungarian in the eye, and you'll see a glimmer of the marauding Magyar, stomping in from the Central Asian plains a thousand years ago.

Hungarian Language

Even though Hungary is surrounded by Slavs, Hungarian is not at all related to Slavic languages (such as Polish, Czech, or Croatian). In fact, Hungarian isn't related to *any* European language, except for very distant relatives Finnish and Estonian. It isn't even an Indo-European language. English is more closely related to Hindi, Russian, and French than it is to Hungarian.

Hungarian is agglutinative, which means that you start with a simple root word and then start tacking on suffixes to create meaning—sometimes resulting in a pileup of extra sounds. The emphasis always goes on the first syllable, and the following syllables are droned in a kind of a monotone—giving the language a distinctive cadence that Hungary's neighbors love to tease about.

While the language is overwhelming for tourists, one easy word is *"Szia"* (SEE-yaw), which means both hello and goodbye (like "ciao" or "aloha"). Confusingly, sometimes Hungarians simply say the English word "hello" to mean either "hi" or "bye." Another handy word that Hungarians (and people throughout Central Europe) will understand is *Servus* (SEHR-voos, spelled *Szervusz* in Hungarian)—the old-fashioned greeting from the days of the Austro-Hungarian Empire. If you draw a blank on how to say hello, just offer a cheery, *"Servus!"*

Hungarian pronunciation is straightforward, once you remember a few key rules. The trickiest: *s* alone is pronounced "sh," while *sz* is pronounced "s." This explains why you'll hear in-the-know travelers pronouncing Budapest as "BOO-daw-pesht." You might catch the *busz* up to Castle Hill—pronounced "boose." And

"Franz Liszt" is easier to pronounce than it looks: It sounds just like "list." To review:

s sounds like "sh" as in "shirt"

sz sounds like "s" as in "saint"

Hungarian has a set of unusual palatal sounds that don't quite have a counterpart in English. To make these sounds, gently press the thick part of your tongue to the roof or your mouth (instead of using the tip of your tongue behind your teeth, as we do in English):

gy sounds like "dg" as in "hedge"

ny sounds like "ny" as in "canyon" (not "nee")

ty sounds like "tch" as in "itch"

cs sounds like "ch" as in "church"

As for vowels: The letter *a* almost sounds like o (aw, as in "hot"); but with an accent *(á)*, it brightens up to the more standard "ah." Likewise, while *e* sounds like "eh," *é* sounds like "ay." An accent *(á, é, í, ó, ú)* indicates that you linger on that vowel, but not necessarily that you stress that syllable. Like German, Hungarian has umlauts *(ö, ü)*, meaning you purse your lips when you say that vowel: roughly, *ö* sounds like "ur" and *ü* sounds like "ew." A long umlaut *(ő, ű)* is the same sound, but you hold it a little longer. Words ending in *k* are often plural.

Here are a few other letters that sound different in Hungarian than in English:

c and **cz** both sound like "ts" as in "cats"

zs sounds like "zh" as in "leisure"

j and **ly** both sound like "y" as in "yellow"

OK, maybe it's not *so* simple. But you'll get the hang of it...and Hungarians will appreciate your efforts.

For a complete list of Hungarian survival phrases, see page 483 in the appendix.

BUDAPEST

ORIENTATION TO BUDAPEST

Europe's most underrated big city, Budapest is as challenging as it is enchanting. The sprawling Hungarian capital on the banks of the Danube is, in so many ways, the capital of Central Europe. It's a city of nuance and paradox—cosmopolitan, complicated, and tricky for the first-timer to get a handle on. Like a full-bodied Hungarian wine, Budapest can overwhelm visitors...even as it intoxicates them with delights.

Think of Budapest as that favorite Hungarian pastime, chess: It's simple to learn...but takes a lifetime to master. This chapter is your first lesson. Then it's your move.

Budapest: A Verbal Map

Budapest is huge, with nearly two million people. Like Vienna, the city was built as the head of a much larger empire than it currently governs—which can make it feel a bit too grandiose for the capital of a small country. But the city is surprisingly easy to manage once you get the lay of the land and learn the excellent public transportation network. Those who are comfortable with the Metró, trams, and buses have the city by the tail (see "Getting Around Budapest" on page 45).

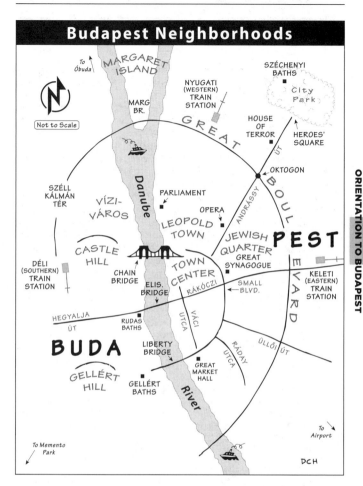

Budapest Neighborhoods

To Óbuda

MARGARET ISLAND

N

Not to Scale

MARG BR.

NYUGATI (WESTERN) TRAIN STATION

SZÉCHENYI BATHS

City Park

GREAT

HOUSE OF TERROR

HEROES' SQUARE

OKTOGON

SZÉLL KÁLMÁN TÉR

VÍZI-VÁROS

Danube

PARLIAMENT

OPERA

ANDRASSY

BOULEVARD

PEST

CASTLE HILL

LEOPOLD TOWN

JEWISH QUARTER

DÉLI (SOUTHERN) TRAIN STATION

CHAIN BRIDGE

ELIS. BRIDGE

TOWN CENTER

GREAT SYNAGOGUE

RÁKÓCZI

SMALL BLVD.

KELETI (EASTERN) TRAIN STATION

HEGYALJA ÚT

RUDAS BATHS

VÁCI UTCA

BUDA

LIBERTY BRIDGE

GREAT MARKET HALL

RÁDAY UTCA

ÜLLŐI ÚT

GELLÉRT HILL

GELLÉRT BATHS

River

To Memento Park

To Airport

DCH

The city is split down the center by the Danube River. On the east side of the Danube is flat **Pest** (pronounced "pesht"), and on the west is hilly **Buda**. A third part of the city, **Óbuda,** sits to the north of Buda.

Buda and Pest are connected by a series of characteristic bridges. From north to south, there's the low-profile **Margaret Bridge** (Margit híd, crosses Margaret Island), the famous **Chain Bridge** (Széchenyi lánchíd), the white and modern **Elisabeth Bridge** (Erzsébet híd), and the green **Liberty Bridge** (Szabadság híd). These bridges are fun to cross by foot, but it's faster to go under the river (on the M2/red Metró line), or to cross over it by tram or bus. (Four more bridges lie beyond the tourist zone: the Petőfi and Rákóczi bridges to the south, and Árpád and Megyeri bridges to the north.)

Snapshot History of Budapest

When describing the story of this grand metropolis, it's tempting to fall back on the trusty onion metaphor: Budapest, which has been adored and destroyed by many different groups across the centuries, is layered with history...sometimes stinky, sometimes sweet. The Hungary: Past and Present chapter—and many other tidbits throughout this book—will help you peel back those layers, step-by-step. But here's the quick version:

Budapest is hot—literally. The city sits on a thin layer of earth above thermal springs, which power its many baths. Even the word "Pest" comes from a Slavic word for "oven." Two thousand years ago, the Romans had a settlement (called Aquincum) on the northern edge of today's Budapest. Several centuries later, in A.D. 896, a mysterious nomadic group called the Magyars arrived from the steppes of Central Asia and took over the Carpathian Basin (roughly today's Hungary). After running roughshod over Europe for a time, the Magyars—the ancestors of today's Hungarians—settled down, adopted Christianity, and became fully European. The twin towns of Buda and Pest emerged as the leading cities of Hungary.

In the 16th century, the Ottomans invaded and occupied the region for nearly a century and a half. The Habsburgs (monarchs of neighboring Austria) finally forced them out, but Buda and Pest were in ruins. The cities were rebuilt in a more Austrian style.

After many decades of Hungarian uprisings, the Compromise of 1867 granted Hungary an equal stake in the Austro-Hungarian Empire. Six years later, the cities of Buda, Pest, and Óbuda united to form the capital city of Budapest, which governed a huge chunk of Eastern Europe. For the next few decades, Budapest boomed, and Hungarian culture enjoyed a Golden Age.

Budapest uses a **district** system (like Paris and Vienna). There are 23 districts *(kerület)*, identified by Roman numerals. For example, Castle Hill is in district I and City Park is in district XIV. Notice that the district number does not necessarily indicate how central a location is: Districts II and III are to the north of Buda, where few tourists go, while the heart of Pest is district V. Addresses often start with the district number (as a Roman numeral). Budapest's four-digit postal codes also give you a clue as to the district: The first digit (always 1) represents Budapest, then a two-digit number represents the district (such as "05" for district V), then a final digit gives more specific information about the location.

As you navigate Budapest, remember these key Hungarian terms: *tér* (pronounced "tehr," square), *utca* (OOT-zaw, street), *út* (oot, boulevard), *körút* (KUR-root, ring road), *híd* (heed, bridge), and *város* (VAH-rohsh, town). To better match what you'll see lo-

The expansion reached its peak with a flurry of construction surrounding the year 1896—Hungary's 1,000th birthday.

But with Hungary's defeat in World War I, the city's fortunes reversed. World War II left Budapest in ruins...and in the hands of the Soviets. A bold uprising in 1956 was brutally dealt with, but before long a milder "goulash communism" emerged in Hungary. Budapest, though still oppressed, was a place where other Eastern Europeans could come to experiment with "Western evils"... from Big Macs to Nikes.

Since communism's graceful exit in 1989, Budapest has once again been forced to reinvent itself. During this time of transition, the city has struggled with whether to cling to its past glory days, or to leave all that behind and create something new. The architectural tendency here has been to renovate stately old buildings exactly as they were (rather than incorporating modern elements, as is the trend in much of the world). Budapest is one of Europe's most nostalgic places—although to many locals, the city sometimes feels trapped by its own sentimentality. Investors and city planners are increasingly attempting to jolt Budapest into the future with some modern flourishes. It will be fascinating to see which of these influences wins out in the end, as this dynamic, living city continues to grow.

Through it all, Budapest—atmospherically shot through with the crumbling elegance of former greatness—remains the heart and soul of Central Europe. It's a rich cultural stew made up of Hungarians, Germans, Slavs, and Jews, with a dash of Turkish paprika—simmered for centuries in a thermal bath. Each group has left its mark, but through it all, something has remained that is distinctly...Budapest.

cally, in this book I've mostly used these Hungarian terms (instead of the English equivalents).

Let's take a tour through the places where you'll be spending your time, neighborhood by neighborhood. This section—like all of the sightseeing, sleeping, eating, and other advice in this book— is divided between Pest and Buda. (It might help to think of these as two separate cities...which, after all, they once were.)

Pest

Pest—the real-world commercial heart of the city—is where most tourists spend the majority of their time.

"Downtown" Pest (district V), just across the river from Castle Hill, is divided into two sections:

The more genteel northern half, called **Leopold Town** (Lipótváros), surrounds the giant red-domed, riverside Parliament building. This is the governmental, business, and banking district, with

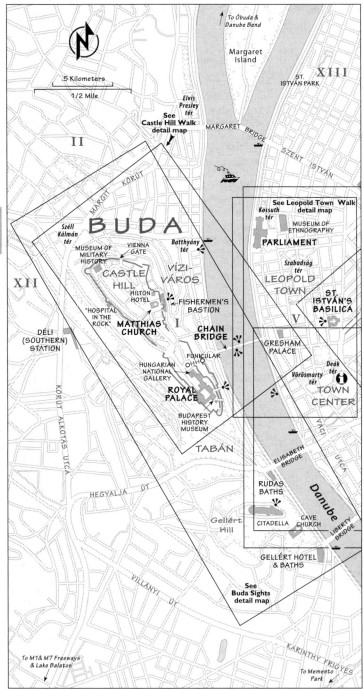

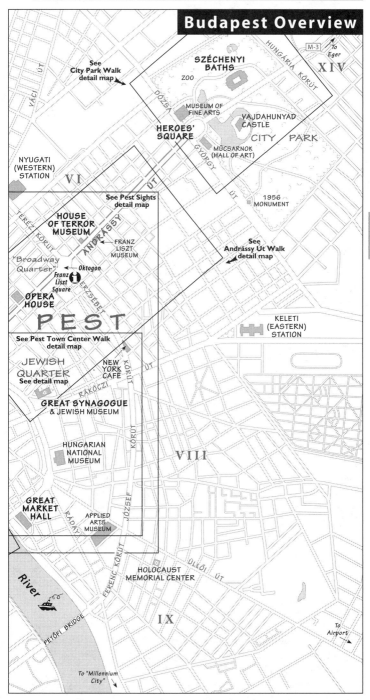

Budapest Overview

VÁCI ÚT

See City Park Walk detail map

SZÉCHENYI BATHS

ZOO

DÓZSA

MUSEUM OF FINE ARTS

HEROES' SQUARE

HUNGÁRIA KÖRÚT

M-3 To Eger

XIV

VAJDAHUNYAD CASTLE

CITY PARK

GYÖRGY

MŰCSARNOK (HALL OF ART)

NYUGATI (WESTERN) STATION

VI

See Pest Sights detail map

TERÉZ KÖRÚT

HOUSE OF TERROR MUSEUM

ANDRÁSSY ÚT

FRANZ LISZT MUSEUM

"Broadway Quarter"

Oktogon

Franz Liszt Square

ERZSÉBET KÖRÚT

OPERA HOUSE

1956 MONUMENT

See Andrássy Út Walk detail map

KELETI (EASTERN) STATION

P E S T

See Pest Town Center Walk detail map

JEWISH QUARTER See detail map

NEW YORK CAFÉ

KÖRÚT

RÁKÓCZI

GREAT SYNAGOGUE & JEWISH MUSEUM

HUNGARIAN NATIONAL MUSEUM

KÖRÚT

VIII

GREAT MARKET HALL

RÁDAY

APPLIED ARTS MUSEUM

JÓZSEF

River

FERENC KÖRÚT

HOLOCAUST MEMORIAL CENTER

ÜLLŐI ÚT

PETŐFI BRIDGE

IX

To Airport

To "Millennium City"

several fine monuments and grand buildings. Leopold Town is sleepy after hours.

The southern half, the grittier and more urban-feeling **Town Center** (Belváros, literally "Inner Town"), is a thriving shopping, dining, nightlife, and residential zone that bustles day and night. The main pedestrian artery through the Town Center is the famous (and overrated) Váci utca shopping street, which runs parallel to the fine and scenic Danube promenade one block inland. At the southern end of the Town Center is the vast Great Market Hall, with the café street Ráday utca just beyond.

The Town Center is hemmed in by the first of Pest's four concentric **ring roads** *(körút)*. The innermost ring is called the Kiskörút, or "Small Boulevard." The next ring, several blocks farther out, is called the Nagykörút, or "Great Boulevard." These ring roads change names every few blocks, but they are always called *körút*. Historically, the Nagykörút is subdivided into sections named for Habsburg monarchs, such as Lipótkörút ("Leopold Boulevard"); each of these sections also defines a neighborhood, such as Lipótváros ("Leopold Town"). Beyond the Nagykörút are two more ring roads—the Hungária körút highway, and the partially unfinished M-0 expressway—that few tourists see.

Arterial **boulevards,** called *út,* stretch from central Pest into the suburbs like spokes on a wheel. One of these boulevards, **Andrássy út,** provides a useful spine for reaching some of outer Pest's best sights, restaurants, and accommodations. It begins at the Small Boulevard (near Deák tér) and extends past several key sights (including the Opera and the House of Terror museum) and dining zones (such as the "Broadway Quarter" and Franz Liszt Square) out to **City Park.** The park has its own collection of attractions, including the monumental Heroes' Square and Budapest's top experience: soaking in the Széchenyi Baths.

Various key sights lie along the **Small Boulevard** ring road (connected by trams #47 and #49), including (from north to south) the Great Synagogue (marking the start of the **Jewish Quarter,** which feels a bit run-down but features several Jewish sights as well as a hopping nightlife zone with cool "ruin pubs"), the National Museum, and the Great Market Hall.

Several other points of interest are spread far and wide along the **Great Boulevard** ring road (circled by trams #4 and #6). From north to south, it passes Margaret Island (the city's playground, in the middle of the Danube); the Nyugati/Western train station; the prominent Oktogon intersection, where it crosses Andrássy út; the opulent New York Café, with the Keleti/Eastern train station just up the street; and the intersection with Üllői út, near the Holocaust Memorial Center and the Applied Arts Museum.

Buda

Sleepy Buda looks pretty (and gets first billing in the city's name), but most tourists spend less time here than in exciting Pest. The Buda side is domi-nated by two hills: **Castle Hill,** topped by the green  dome of the Royal Palace and the spiny Neo-Gothic spire of the Matthias Church; and to the south, the taller, wooded **Gellért Hill,** capped by a 150-year-old fortress and the Liberation Monument.

The **Castle District,** atop Castle Hill (in district I), is historic but fairly dull. It's packed with tourists by day, and dead at night. The pleasant **Víziváros** (VEE-zee-vah-rohsh) residential neigh-borhood, or "Water Town," is squeezed between the castle and the river. The square called Batthyány tér, roughly at the north end of Víziváros, is a hub for the neighborhood, with a handy Metró stop (M2/red line), tram stops, market hall, and eateries. Just north of Castle Hill (and Víziváros) is **Széll Kálmán tér,** another transit hub for Buda, with a Metró station (M2/red line), several tram stops, and the giant Mammut shopping mall.

Tucked to the south of **Gellért Hill** is another fine residential district. Here you'll find the Gellért Hotel, with its famous ther-mal baths; the Rudas Baths are also at the base of Gellért Hill, but farther to the north.

Central Buda is surrounded by a ring road, and the busy Heg-yalja út rumbles through the middle of the tourists' Buda (between Castle and Gellért Hills). Behind Castle and Gellért Hills is a low-lying neighborhood of little interest to tourists (except for the Déli/Southern train station), and beyond that rise the **Buda Hills,** a scenic and upscale residential area.

Outer Budapest

The city doesn't end there. This book also includes tips for the Óbuda district north of central Buda; sights on the outskirts of town (but accessible on the suburban transit network), including Memento Park, Gödöllő Palace, and the small riverside town of Szentendre; and more.

Planning Your Time

Visitors attempting to "do" Budapest in just one day leave dazed, exhausted...and yearning for more. Two days are the bare minimum, and force you to tackle the city at a breakneck pace (and you still won't see everything). Three days work, but assume you'll go fast and/or skip some things. Four days are ideal, and a fifth day (or even sixth) gives you time for various day-trip options.

Budapest is quite decentralized: Plan your day ahead to minimize backtracking, and refer to your map frequently. Just about everything is walkable, but distances are far, and public transit can save valuable time.

Each of this book's self-guided walks acts as a sightseeing spine for a particular neighborhood or area: Pest's **Leopold Town,** Pest's **Town Center,** Pest's **Andrássy út,** Pest's **Heroes' Square and City Park,** and Buda's **Castle Hill.** Each walk offers an orientation overview, with several in-depth sightseeing opportunities along the way. If you're ambitious, you can do several of these walks in a single day—but you'll have to skip most of the museums. To take your time and dip into each sight, spread the walks over several days.

When divvying your time between Buda and Pest, consider that (aside from the Gellért and Rudas Baths) Buda's sightseeing is mostly concentrated on Castle Hill, and can easily be seen in less than a day, while Pest deserves as much time as you're willing to give it. Start by getting your bearings in Pest (where you'll likely spend most of your time), then head for relatively laid-back Buda when you need a break from the big city.

Below are some possible plans, depending on the length of your trip. Note that these very ambitious itineraries assume you want to sightsee at a speedy pace. In the **evening,** you have a wide range of options (many of which are outlined in the Entertainment in Budapest chapter): enjoying good restaurants, taking in an opera or concert, snuggling on a romantic floodlit river cruise, relaxing in a thermal bath, exploring the city's unique "ruin pubs," or simply strolling the Danube embankments and bridges.

Budapest in Two Days

Your time will be full but memorable. Spend Day 1 in Pest. Start with the Leopold Town Walk, then the Pest Town Center Walk. From the Great Market Hall (at the end of that walk), circle around the Small Boulevard to Deák tér and consider the Andrássy út and Heroes' Square/City Park walks. Or, if you're exhausted already, just take the M1/yellow Metró line to Hősök tere, ogle the Heroes' Square statues and Vajdahunyad Castle, and reward yourself with a soak at Széchenyi Baths. (Note that this schedule leaves virtually no time for entering any museums—though you might be able to

Daily Reminder

Monday: Most of Budapest's museums are closed on Mondays. But you can still take advantage of plenty of other sights and activities: all three major baths, Memento Park, Great Synagogue and Jewish Quarter, Matthias Church on Castle Hill, St. István's Basilica, Parliament tour, Great Market Hall, Opera House tour, City Park (and Zoo), Danube cruises, concerts, and bus, walking, and bike tours. Monday is also a great day to do the Leopold Town and Pest Town Center walks, since their major sights are virtually unaffected.

Tuesday: All major sights are open.

Wednesday: All major sights are open.

Thursday: Some shops are open later (until 20:00 or 21:00), as is the Műcsarnok (Hall of Art, until 20:00).

Friday: All major sights are open. The Great Synagogue, Orthodox Synagogue, and Synagogue at Rumbach Street close early (usually around 12:30 or 13:30).

Saturday: The Great Synagogue, Orthodox Synagogue, and Synagogue at Rumbach Street are closed today. Most shops close early (usually 13:00 or 14:00), and the Great Market Hall closes at 15:00. The Petőfi Csarnok flea market is hopping (8:00-14:00).

Sunday: The Great Market Hall and Franz Liszt Museum are closed today, as are most shops, though large shopping malls remain open. The Petőfi Csarnok flea market is open (8:00-14:00), and the Szimpla ruin pub hosts a morning farmers market (9:00-14:00).

fit in one or two big sights, such as the Parliament, Opera House, Great Synagogue, or House of Terror.)

On the morning of Day 2, tackle any Pest sights you didn't have time for yesterday (or take the bus out to Memento Park). After lunch, ride bus #16 from Deák tér to Castle Hill and follow the Castle Hill Walk. Head back to Pest for some final sightseeing and dinner.

Budapest in Three or Four Days

Your first day is for getting your bearings in Pest. Choose between touring the Parliament or the Opera House; for the Parliament, buy your tickets in the morning before starting your day. Then do the Leopold Town Walk, followed by the Andrássy út and Heroes' Square/City Park walks, ending with a soak at the Széchenyi Baths.

On Day 2, delve deeper into Pest, starting with the Pest Town Center Walk. After visiting the Great Market Hall, consider crossing

ORIENTATION TO BUDAPEST

Budapest Essentials

English	Hungarian	Pronounced
Pest Town Center	Belváros	BEHL-vah-rohsh
Pest's Leopold Town	Lipótváros	LEE-poht-vah-rohsh
Pest Town Center's Main Pedestrian Street	Váci utca	VAHT-see OOT-zaw
Pest Town Center's Main Square	Vörösmarty tér	VEW-rewsh-mar-tee tehr
Pest's Grand Boulevard	Andrássy út	AWN-drah-shee oot
Heroes' Square	Hősök Tere	HEW-shewk TEH-reh
City Park	Városliget	VAH-rohsh-lee-geht
(Buda) Castle	(Budai) Vár	BOO-die vahr
Castle Hill	Várhegy	VAHR-hayj
Buda's "Water Town"	Víziváros	VEE-zee-vah-rohsh
Chain Bridge	Széchenyi Lánchíd	SAY-chehn-yee LAHNTS-heed
Liberty Bridge (green, a.k.a. Franz Josef Bridge)	Szabadság Híd	SAW-bawd-shahg heed
Elisabeth Bridge (white, modern)	Erzsébet híd	EHR-zay-beht heed
Margaret Bridge (crosses Margaret Island)	Margit híd	MAWR-geet heed
Danube River	Duna	DOO-naw
Eastern Train Station	Keleti pályaudvar	KEH-leh-tee PAH-yuh-uhd-vawr
Western Train Station	Nyugati pályaudvar	NYOO-gaw-tee PAH-yuh-uhd-vawr
Southern Train Station	Déli pályaudvar	DAY-lee PAH-yuh-uhd-vawr
Suburban Train System	HÉV	hayv

the river for a soak at the Gellért or Rudas Baths (if you want more spa time), or circle around the Small Boulevard to see the National Museum and/or Great Synagogue and Jewish Quarter.

On Day 3, use the morning to see any remaining sights, then ride the 11:00 bus out to Memento Park. On returning, grab a quick lunch and take bus #16 from Deák tér to Castle Hill, where you'll do the Castle Hill Walk.

With a fourth day, spread the Day 1 tours over more time, and circle back to any sights you've missed so far.

If you've got five or more days, consider some of these tempting destinations...

Beyond Budapest

Eger, at the heart of a popular wine region and packed with offbeat sights, is an easy day trip from Budapest (2.5 hours by train or 2 hours by bus each way). **Pécs,** with a gorgeously colorful streetscape and engaging sightseeing, is a bit farther away (3 hours by train), but arguably even more interesting. Roughly between Budapest and Vienna, the small town of **Sopron** (historic and charming) and the Slovak capital of **Bratislava** (big, bustling, and on the move) are both worthy stopovers. Each of these is covered in its own chapter. While any of these could be done as long day trips from Budapest, it's much more satisfying to spend the night (especially in Eger and Pécs).

The Day Trips from Budapest chapter covers excursions that are less appealing than the farther-flung towns mentioned above— but easier to do in a day from Budapest: The **Danube Bend** comprises three towns north of Budapest: the charming, Balkan-flavored artists' colony of **Szentendre;** the castle at **Visegrád;** and Hungary's most impressive church at **Esztergom.** (The Danube Bend is also doable by car on the way to Bratislava or Vienna.) To the east are **Gödöllő Palace** (dripping with Habsburg history, and a very easy side-trip from Budapest) and the more distant village of **Hollókő,** an open-air folk museum come to life (by car, these two can be combined into a single rewarding day, and you'll be back in Budapest in time for dinner).

Overview

Tourist Information

The city of Budapest runs several TIs (www.budapestinfo.hu, tel. 1/438-8080). The main branch is a few steps from the M2 and M3 Metró station at **Deák tér** (daily 8:00-20:00, free Wi-Fi, Sütő utca 2, near the McDonald's, district V). Other locations include **Franz Liszt Square,** a block south of the Oktogon on Andrássy út (daily March-Oct 10:00-20:00, Nov-Feb 10:00-18:00, free Wi-Fi, Liszt

Ferenc tér 11, district VII, M1: Oktogon, tel. 1/322-4098), and in both terminals at the **airport** (TI at Terminal 2A open daily 8:00-23:00; TI at Terminal 2B open daily 10:00-22:00). The helpfulness of Budapest's TIs can vary, but all offer a nice variety of free, useful publications, including a good city map, the information-packed *Budapest Guide* booklet, and various events planners: *Budapest Panorama*, *Servus*, and the youthful *Budapest Funzine*. At any TI, you can collect a pile of other free brochures (for sights, bus tours, and more) and buy a Budapest Card.

Sightseeing Passes: The **Budapest Card** includes free use of all public transportation, free walking tours of Buda and Pest, a few free museum admissions (Budapest History Museum, Museum of Fine Arts, Museum of Ethnography, Hungarian National Gallery), and 10-50 percent discounts on many other major museums and attractions (4,500 Ft/24 hours, 7,500 Ft/48 hours, 8,900 Ft/72 hours; includes handy 100-page booklet with maps, updated hours, and brief museum descriptions; www.budapest-card.com). If you take advantage of the included walking tours, the Budapest Card could be a good value for a very busy sightseer—do the arithmetic.

TourInform: The Hungarian National Tourist Office operates a small TI on Castle Hill. It's located in the circular, white building in the park across from Matthias Church (daily 10:00-18:00, maps and bus tickets).

Discover Budapest: Ben Frieday, an American in love with Budapest (and one of its women), runs this agency, which specializes in answering questions Americans (especially backpackers) have about Budapest and Hungary. It's conveniently located near Andrássy út, behind the Opera House at Lázár utca 16 (district VI, M1: Opera). At their office, you can use the Internet (150 Ft/15 minutes at a terminal, free Wi-Fi) or rent a bike (May-Oct daily 9:00-20:00, shorter hours off-season, tel. 1/269-3843, www.discoverbudapest.com). This location also houses the Tree Hugger Dan secondhand bookstore (described later, under "Helpful Hints") and is the meeting point for Ben's various tours: Absolute Walking Tours and Yellow Zebra bike and Segway tours (all described later in this chapter).

Arrival in Budapest

For a comprehensive rundown on Budapest's train stations, bus stations, airport, driving tips, and boat connections, see the Budapest Connections chapter.

Helpful Hints

Navigation Note: In 2010, Budapest renamed several of its city-center squares, streets, and Metró stations. While this book's maps are up-to-date, if you're using an older source you may find references to the old names. Here's a decoder:

Old Name	New Name
Roosevelt tér	**Széchenyi István tér**
Moszkva tér	**Széll Kálmán tér**
Köztársaság tér	**II. János Pál pápa tér** ("John Paul II Square")
Lágymányosi híd (bridge)	**Rákóczi híd**
Ferenc körút (Metró stop)	**Corvin-negyed**
Ferihegy Airport	**Liszt Ferenc (Franz Liszt) Airport**

Construction Alert: Budapest is a city in transition, with constant urban beautification work going on. In 2013 and 2014, several city-center zones are likely to be affected, including Ferenciek tere (in Pest's Town Center), Kossuth tér (near the Parliament), and along Pest's Danube embankment and Váci utca. While these areas will become more inviting in the future, in the short term construction can wreak havoc on walking routes and public transportation. Be prepared to run into some hassles during your visit; stay patient and ask locals for advice on getting around the obstacles.

Rip-Offs: Budapest feels—and is—safe, especially for a city of its size. While there's little risk of violent crime, and I've rarely had someone try to rip me off here, you might run into a petty crook or two (such as con artists or pickpockets). As in any big city, it's especially important to secure your valuables and wear a money belt in crowded and touristy places, particularly on the Metró and in trams. Keep your wits about you and refuse to be bullied or distracted. Any deal that seems too good to be true...probably is.

Restaurants on the Váci utca shopping street are notorious for overcharging tourists. Here or anywhere in Budapest, don't eat at a restaurant that doesn't list prices on the menu, and always check your bill carefully. Increasingly, restaurants are adding a (legitimate) service charge of 10 to 12 percent to your bill; if you don't notice this, you might accidentally double-tip (for more on tipping, see page 13).

If you're a male in a touristy area and a gorgeous local girl takes a liking to you, avoid her. She's a *konzumlány* ("consumption girl"), and the foreplay going on here will climax in your grand rip-off. You'll wind up at her "favorite bar," with astronomical prices enforced by a burly bouncer.

Budapest's biggest crooks? Unscrupulous cabbies. For tips on outsmarting them, see "Getting Around Budapest—By Taxi" on page 51. Bottom line: Locals *always* call for a cab, rather than hail one on the street or at a taxi stand. If you're not comfortable making the call yourself, ask your hotel or restaurant to call for you.

Emergency Numbers: The default emergency telephone number in Hungary is 112. You can also dial 107 for police, 104 for ambulance, or 105 for fire.

Medical Help: Near Buda's Széll Kálmán tér, **FirstMed Centers** is a private, pricey, English-speaking clinic (by appointment or urgent care, call first, Hattyú utca 14, 5th floor, district I, M2: Széll Kálmán tér, tel. 1/224-9090, www.firstmedcenters. com). Hospitals *(kórház)* are scattered around the city. Ambulances usually head for the Országos Baleseti Intézet, just south of Pest's Keleti/Eastern train station (Fiumei út 17, district VIII).

Pharmacies: The helpful **Dorottya Gyógyszertár** pharmacy is dead-center in Pest, between Vörösmarty and Széchenyi squares. Because they cater to clientele from nearby international hotels, they have a useful directory that lists the Hungarian equivalent of US prescription medicines (Mon-Fri 8:00-20:00, closed Sat-Sun, Dorottya utca 13, district V, M1: Vörösmarty tér, for location see map on pages 236-237, tel. 1/317-2374). Each district has one pharmacy that stays open 24 hours (these should be noted outside the entrance to any pharmacy).

Calling Mobile Numbers: In Hungary, mobile numbers (generally beginning with 0620, 0630, or 0670) are dialed differently, depending on where you're calling from. I've listed them as you'd dial them from a fixed line within Hungary. From another country, or from a mobile phone in Hungary, omit the initial 06, and replace it with the international access code (011 from the US, 00 from Europe, or + on a mobile phone), then 36, then the number. For more tips on calling, see page 463.

Train Tickets: Ticket-buying lines can be long at train stations, particularly for long-distance international trains. If you want to buy your ticket in advance, **MÁV** (Hungarian Railways) has a very convenient ticket office right in the heart of downtown Pest. They generally speak English and sell tickets for no additional fee (Mon-Fri 9:00-18:00, closed Sat-Sun, just up from the Chain Bridge and across from Erzsébet tér at József Attila utca 16, district V, M1: Vörösmarty tér, for location see map on pages 236-237).

Internet Access: Most hotels have Wi-Fi or cable Internet in the rooms for travelers with their own laptops (usually free, sometimes for a fee). Internet cafés are everywhere—just look for signs or ask your hotel. In Pest, I like **Discover Budapest,** with fast access and good prices (free Wi-Fi, Internet termi-

Tonight We're Gonna Party Like It's 1896

Visitors to Budapest need only remember one date: 1896. For the millennial celebration of their ancestors' arrival in Europe, Hungarians threw a huge blowout party. In the thousand years between 896 and 1896, the Magyars had gone from being a

nomadic Central Asian tribe that terrorized the Continent to sharing the throne of one of the most successful empires Europe had ever seen.

On the morning of New Year's Day, 1896, church bells clanged endlessly through the streets of Buda and Pest. In June of that year, Emperor Franz Josef and Empress Sisi were two of the 5.7 million people who came to enjoy the Hungarian National Exhibition at City Park. At Vérmező Park (behind Castle Hill), whole oxen were grilled on the spit to feed commoners.

Much as the year 2000 saw a fit of new construction worldwide, Budapest used its millennial celebration as an excuse to build monuments and buildings appropriate for the co-capital of a huge empire, including:

- **Heroes' Square** and the **Millennium Monument**
- **Vajdahunyad Castle** (in City Park)
- The riverside **Parliament** building (96 meters tall, with 96 steps at the main entry)
- **St. István's Basilica** (also 96 meters tall)
- The M1/yellow Metró line, a.k.a. *Földalatti* ("Underground")—the first subway on the Continent
- The **Great Market Hall** (and four other market halls)
- **Andrássy út** and most of the fine buildings lining it
- The **Opera House**
- A complete rebuilding of **Matthias Church** (on Castle Hill)
- The **Fishermen's Bastion** decorative terrace (by Matthias Church)
- The green **Liberty Bridge** (then called Franz Josef Bridge, in honor of the ruling Habsburg emperor)

Ninety-six is the key number in Hungary—even the national anthem (when sung at the proper tempo) takes 96 seconds. But after all this fuss, it's too bad that the date was wrong: A commission—convened to establish the exact year of the Magyars' debut—determined it happened in 895. But city leaders knew they'd never make an 1895 deadline, and requested the finding be changed to 896.

nals-150 Ft/15 minutes; for location, hours, and contact information, see "Discover Budapest" listing on page 40).

Post Offices: These are marked with a smart green *posta* logo (usually open Mon-Fri 8:00-18:00, Sat 8:00-12:00, closed Sun).

Laundry: Budapest doesn't have a handy coin-op, self-serve launderette. But two places in Pest can do your laundry for a reasonable price. Your best option is **Laundromat-Mosómata,** just behind the Opera House (2,400 Ft to wash and dry a big load, generally takes 3-5 hours, Mon-Fri 10:00-18:00, Sat 10:00-14:00, closed Sun; walk straight behind the Opera House and turn right on Ó utca, then look left for signs at #24-26, district VI, M1: Opera, for location see map on page 232; mobile 0670-340-0478). Another option—closer to the Town Center, but with more difficult communication—is **Patyolat Gyorstisztító.** They say it's "self-service," but usually you can just drop off your clothes with the monolingual laundry ladies in the morning and pick them up in the afternoon (borrow the English information sheet; allow 2,700 Ft to wash and dry a small load, 5,000 Ft for a big load; Mon-Fri 7:00-19:00, Sat 7:00-13:00, closed Sun; just up from Váci utca at the corner of Vármegye utca and Városház utca, district V, M3: Ferenciek tere, for location see map on pages 236-237).

English Bookstores: The **Central European University Bookshop** offers the best selection anywhere of scholarly books about this region (and beyond). They also sell guidebooks, literary fiction, and some popular American magazines—all in English (Mon-Fri 10:00-19:00, Sat 10:00-14:00, closed Sun, just down the street in front of St. István's Basilica at Zrínyi utca 12, district V, for location see map on pages 236-237, tel. 1/327-3096).

Tree Hugger Dan, which bills itself as a "local bookstore with a global conscience," is crammed with 18,000 second-hand English books (in the Discover Budapest office just behind the Opera House—see hours on page 40).

Bestsellers has a fine selection of new books, mostly in English; it's just around the corner from CEU Bookshop, near St. István's Basilica (Mon-Fri 9:00-18:30, Sat 10:00-17:00, Sun 10:00-16:00, Október 6 utca 11, tel. 1/312-1295).

Red Bus Bookstore has a decent selection of used books in English (also buys used books, Mon-Fri 11:00-18:00, Sat 10:00-15:00, closed Sun, Semmelweis utca 14, district V, M2: Astoria, for location see map on pages 236-237, tel. 1/337-7453).

Local Guidebook: András Török's fun, idiosyncratic *Budapest: A Critical Guide* is the best guidebook by a local writer. Its quirky walking tours do a nice job of capturing the city's spirit (available in English at some souvenir stands and bookshops).

Bike Rental: You can rent a bike at **Yellow Zebra,** part of Discover Budapest (2,000-3,000 Ft/all day, 3,000-4,500 Ft/24 hours, price depends on type of bike; for location, hours, and contact information, see "Discover Budapest" listing on page 40).

Drivers: Friendly, English-speaking **Gábor Balázs** can drive you around the city or into the surrounding countryside (3,600 Ft/hour, 3-hour minimum in city, 4-hour minimum in countryside—good for a Danube Bend excursion, mobile 0620-936-4317, bgabor.e@gmail.com).

 József Király runs a 10-car company, Artoli (20,000 Ft/4 hours within town, 40,000 Ft/8 hours to Danube Bend, these prices for up to 4 people—more for bigger groups, tel. 1/240-4050, mobile 0620-369-8890, www.artolibus.com, artoli@t-online.hu).

 Note that these are drivers, not tour guides. For tour guides who can drive you to outlying sights, see "Tours in Budapest," later.

Best Views: Budapest is a city of marvelous vistas. Some of the best are from the Citadella fortress (high on Gellért Hill), the promenade in front of the Royal Palace and the Fishermen's Bastion on top of Castle Hill, and the embankments or many bridges spanning the Danube (especially the Chain Bridge). Don't forget the view from the tour boats on the Danube—lovely at night.

Updates to this Book: For news about changes to this book's coverage since it was published, see www.ricksteves.com/update.

Getting Around Budapest

Budapest sprawls. Connecting your sightseeing just on foot is tedious and unnecessary. It's crucial to get comfortable with the public transportation system—Metró lines, trams, buses, trolley buses, and boats that can take you virtually anywhere you want to go. Budapest's well-planned cityscape and thoughtfully coordinated transit network combine to make it one of the easiest big European cities to zip around.

The same tickets work for the entire system. Buy them at kiosks, Metró ticket windows, or machines. The new machines are slick and easy (with English instructions). The old orange ones are tricky: Put in the appropriate amount of money, then wait for your ticket or press the

ORIENTATION TO BUDAPEST

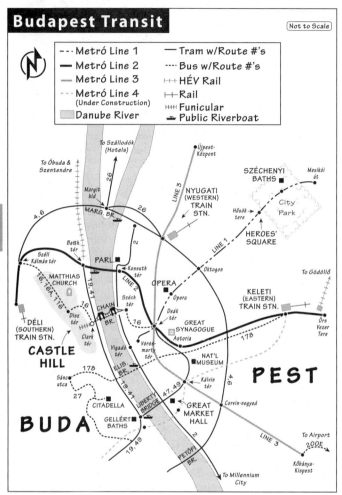

button. As it can be frustrating to find a ticket machine (especially when you see your tram or bus approaching), I generally invest in a multi-day ticket to have the freedom of hopping on at will.

Your options are as follows:

• **Single ticket** (*vonaljegy,* for a ride of up to an hour on any means of transit; transfers allowed only within the Metró system)—350 Ft (or 450 Ft if bought from the driver)

• **Short single Metró ride** (*Metrószakaszjegy,* 3 stops or fewer on the Metró)—300 Ft

• **Transfer ticket** (*átszállójegy*—allowing up to 90 minutes, including one transfer between Metró and bus)—530 Ft

• **Pack of 10 single tickets** *(10 darabos gyűjtőjegy),* which can be shared—3,000 Ft (that's 300 Ft per ticket, saving you 50 Ft per ticket; note that these must stay together as a single pack—they can't be sold separately)

• Unlimited multi-day travel cards for Metró, bus, and tram, including a **24-hour travel card** (*24 órás jegy*, 1,650 Ft), **three-day ticket** (*72 órás jegy*, 4,150 Ft/72 hours), and **weekly ticket** (*hetijegy*, 4,950 Ft/7 days)

• **24-hour group travel card** (*csoportos 24 órás jegy*, 3,300 Ft), covering up to five adults—a great deal for groups of three to five people

• The **Budapest Card,** which combines a multi-day ticket with sightseeing discounts (but it's generally a bad value—see page 40)

Always validate single-ride tickets as you enter the bus, tram, or Metró station (stick it in the elbow-high box). On older buses and trams that have little red validation boxes, stick your ticket in the black slot, then pull the slot toward you to punch holes in your ticket. Multi-day tickets need be validated only once. The stern-looking people with blue-and-green armbands waiting as you enter or exit the Metró want to see your validated ticket. Cheaters are fined 6,000 Ft on the spot, and you'll be surprised how often you're checked (inspectors are most commonly seen at train stations and along the touristy M1/yellow line). All public transit runs from 4:30 in the morning until 23:10. A useful route-planning website is www.bkv.hu.

Handy Terms: *Á ___ félé* means "in the direction of ___." *Megálló* means "stop" or "station," and *Végállomás* means "end of the line."

By Metró

Riding Budapest's Metró, you really feel like you're down in the efficient guts of the city. There are three working lines:

• **M1/yellow**—The first Metró line on the Continent, this shallow line runs under Andrássy út from the center to City Park (see "Millennium Underground of 1896" on page 142).

• **M2/red**—Built during the communist days, it's 115 feet deep and designed to double as a bomb shelter. This line has undergone a thorough renovation, leaving its stations new and shiny. The only line going under the Danube to Buda (for now), M2 connects the Déli/Southern train station, Széll Kálmán tér (where you catch bus #16, #16A, or #116 to the top of Castle Hill), Batthyány tér (where you catch the HÉV train to Óbuda or Szentendre), Kossuth tér (behind the Parliament), Astoria (near the Great Synagogue on the Small Boulevard), and the Keleti/Eastern train station.

• **M3/blue**—This line makes a broad, boomerang-shaped swoop north to south on the Pest side. It hasn't been renovated and is noticeably older, but its number will come up soon. Key stops include the Nyugati/Western train station, Ferenciek tere (in the heart of Pest's Town Center), Kálvin tér (near the Great Market Hall and many recommended hotels), and Corvin-negyed (near the Holocaust Memorial Center).

• **M4/green (under construction)**—Possibly opening in 2014, this brand-new line will run from southern Buda to the Gellért Baths, under the Danube to Fővám tér (behind the Great Market Hall) and Kálvin tér (where it will cross the M3/blue line), then up to Keleti/Eastern train station (where it will cross the M2/red line). The city-center portion of this line may open sometime in 2014; as stations farther out are finished, the line will get longer and longer. To check progress, see www.metro4.hu.

The three original lines—M1, M2, and M3—cross only once: at the **Deák tér** stop (often signed as *Deák Ferenc tér*) in the heart of Pest, near where Andrássy út begins.

Aside from the historic M1 line, most Metró stations are at intersections of ring roads and other major thoroughfares. You'll usually exit the Metró into a confusing underpass packed with kiosks, fast-food stands, and makeshift markets. Directional signs (listing which streets, addresses, and tram or bus stops are near each exit) help you find the right exit. Or do the prairie-dog routine: Surface to get your bearings, then head back underground to find the correct stairs up to your destination.

Metró stops themselves are usually very well-marked, with a list of upcoming stops on the wall behind the tracks. Digital clocks either count down to the next train's arrival, or count up from the previous train's departure; either way, you'll rarely wait more than five minutes during peak times.

You'll ride very long, steep, fast-moving escalators to access the M2 and M3 lines. Hang on tight, enjoy the gale as trains below shoot through the tunnels...and don't make yourself dizzy by trying to read the Burger King ads.

Note: The city is due to upgrade the M3/blue line soon. They usually do work in "low season" for business, which is peak season for tourists: July and August. If a particular stretch of Metró line is closed, buses run the same route instead. This can extend the length of your journey—allow plenty of time. For the latest on which stations are closed, ask your hotel or the TI, or check www. bkv.hu.

By HÉV

Budapest's suburban rail system, or HÉV (pronounced "hayv," stands for Helyiérdekű Vasút, literally "Railway of Local Interest"), branches off to the outskirts and beyond. Of the four lines, tourists are likely to use only two: the **Szentendre line,** which begins at Batthyány tér in Buda's Víziváros neighborhood (at the M2/red line stop of the same name) and heads through Óbuda to the charming Danube Bend town of Szentendre; and the **Gödöllő line,** which begins at Örs vezér tere (in outer Pest, at the end of the M2/red line) and heads to the town of Gödöllő, with its Habsburg palace. (Szentendre and Gödöllő are both described in the Day Trips from Budapest chapter.)

The HÉV is covered by standard transit tickets and passes for rides within the city of Budapest (such as to Óbuda). But if going beyond—such as to Szentendre or Gödöllő—you'll have to pay more. Tell the ticket-seller (or punch into the machine) where you're going, and you'll be issued the proper ticket. If you have a transit pass, you'll pay only the difference.

By Tram

Budapest's trams are handy and frequent, taking you virtually anywhere the Metró doesn't. Here are some trams you might use (note that all of these run in both directions):

Tram **#2:** Follows Pest's Danube embankment, parallel to Váci utca. From north to south, it begins at the Great Boulevard (near Margaret Bridge) and passes the Parliament, Széchenyi István tér and the Chain Bridge, Vigadó tér, and the Great Market Hall. From there, it continues southward to the Petőfi Bridge, then all the way to the "Millennium City" complex near Rákóczi Bridge. (Note that a similar route might also be operated by tram **#2A.**)

Trams **#19** and **#41:** Run along Buda's Danube embankment from Batthyány tér (with an M2/red Metró station, and HÉV trains to Óbuda and Szentendre). From Batthyány tér, these trams run (north to south) through Víziváros to Clark Ádám tér (the bottom of the Castle Hill funicular, near the stop for bus #16 up to Castle Hill), then under Elisabeth Bridge (get off at Döbrentei stop for the Rudas Baths) and around the base of Gellért Hill to the Gellért Hotel and Baths (Gellért tér stop).

Trams **#4** and **#6:** Zip around Pest's Great Boulevard ring road (Nagykörút), connecting Nyugati/Western train station and the Oktogon with the southern tip of Margaret Island and Buda's Széll Kálmán tér (with M2/red Metró station).

Trams **#47** and **#49:** Connect the Gellért Baths in Buda with Pest's Small Boulevard ring road (Kiskörút), with stops at the Great Market Hall, the National Museum, the Great Synagogue (Astoria stop), and Deák tér (end of the line).

By Bus and Trolley Bus

I use the Metró and trams for most of my Budapest commuting. But some buses are useful for shortcuts within the city, or for reaching outlying sights. Note that the transit company draws a distinction between gas-powered "buses" and electric "trolley buses" (which are powered by overhead cables). Unless otherwise noted, you can assume the following are standard buses:

Buses **#16, #16A,** and **#116:** All head up to the top of Castle Hill (get off at Dísz tér, near the Royal Palace). You can catch any of these three at Széll Kálmán tér (on M2/red Metró line). When coming from the other direction, bus #16 makes several handy stops in Pest (Deák tér, Széchenyi István tér), then crosses the Chain Bridge for more stops in Buda (including Clark Ádám tér, at Buda end of Chain Bridge on its way up to the castle).

Trolley buses **#70** and **#78:** Zip from near the Opera House (intersection of Andrássy út and Nagymező utca) to the Parliament (Kossuth tér).

Bus **#178:** Goes from Keleti/Eastern train station to central Pest (Astoria and Ferenciek tere Metró stops), then over the Elisabeth Bridge to Buda.

Bus **#26:** Begins at Nyugati/Western train station and heads around the Great Boulevard to Margaret Island, making several stops along the island.

Bus **#27:** Runs from either side of Gellért Hill to just below the Citadella fortress at the hill's peak (Búsuló Juhász stop).

Bus **#200E:** Connects Liszt Ferenc Airport to the Kőbánya-Kispest M3/blue Metró station.

Buses **#54** and **#55:** Head from Boráros tér (at the Pest end of the Petőfi Bridge) to the Ecseri Flea Market.

By Boat

Budapest's public transit authority recently introduced a system of Danube riverboats *(hajójárat)* that connect strategic locations throughout the city. The riverboat system has drawbacks: Frequency is sparse (1-2/hour on weekdays, hourly on weekends), only a handful of city-center stops are of interest to tourists, and it's typically slower than hopping on the Metró or a tram. But it's also a romantic, cheap alternative to pricey riverboat cruises, and can be a handy way to connect some sightseeing points.

A 400-Ft ticket covers any trip; on weekdays, it's also covered by a 24-hour, 48-hour, or one-week transit pass (but not by the Budapest Card; on weekends, you have to buy a ticket regardless of your pass).

Four stops fall within downtown Budapest:
• **Jászai Mari tér,** at the Pest end of Margaret Bridge;
• **Batthyány tér,** on the Buda embankment in Víziváros;
• **Petőfi tér,** on the Pest embankment next to the Danube Legenda riverboats (dock 8); and
• **Szent Gellért tér,** at the Buda end of Liberty Bridge, next to the Gellért Baths.

Boats may not run in winter, and some stops may be closed if the river level gets very low; as this is a new service, expect changes. For details, see www.bkv.hu or call 1/258-4636.

By Taxi

Budapest's public transportation is good enough that you probably won't need to take many taxis. But if you do, you're likely to run into a dishonest driver. Arm yourself with knowledge: Cabbies are not allowed to charge more than a drop rate of 300 Ft, and then 240 Ft/kilometer. (The prices go up at night, between 22:00 and 6:00 in the morning: 420 Ft drop, 350 Ft/kilometer.) The big companies charge even less than these rates. Prices are per ride, not per passenger. A 10 percent tip is expected. A typical ride within central Budapest shouldn't run more than 2,000 Ft. Despite what some slimy cabbies may tell you, there's no legitimate extra charge for crossing the river.

Instead of hailing a taxi on the street, do as the locals do and call a cab from a reputable company—it's cheaper and you're more likely to get an honest driver. Try **City Taxi** (tel. 1/211-1111), **Taxi 6x6** (tel. 1/266-6666), or **Főtaxi** (1/222-2222). Most dispatchers speak English, but if you're uncomfortable calling, you can ask your hotel or restaurant to call for you. (Request that they call a "City Taxi"—otherwise, they might call a pricier company to get a bigger kickback.)

Many cabs you'd hail on the streets are there only to prey on rich, green tourists. Avoid unmarked taxis (nicknamed "hyenas" by locals), as well as any cabs that wait at tourist spots and train stations. If you do wave down a cab on the street, choose one that's marked with an official company logo and telephone number, and has a yellow license plate (if the plate's not yellow, it's not official). Ask for a rough estimate before you get in—if it doesn't sound reasonable, walk away. If you wind up being dramatically overcharged for a ride, simply pay what you think is fair and go inside. If the driver follows you (unlikely), your hotel receptionist will defend you.

On a recent trip to Budapest, I arrived late at night at the Keleti/Eastern train station. The lone, unmarked taxi out front wanted 4,000 Ft for the ride to my hotel. Following my own advice, I called a legitimate company and ordered a taxi from the English-speaking dispatcher. A few minutes later, an honest cabbie picked me up and whisked me to my hotel...for 1,500 Ft.

Tours in Budapest

By Foot

▲▲▲**Local Guides**—Budapest has an abundance of enthusiastic, hardworking, young guides who speak perfect English and enjoy showing off their city. Given the rea-

sonable fees and efficient use of your time, hiring your own personal expert is an excellent value. While they might be available last-minute, it's better to reserve in advance by email. I have two favorites, either of whom can do half-day or full-day tours, and can also drive you into the countryside: **Péter Pölczman** is an exceptional guide who really puts you in touch with the Budapest you came to see (€90/4 hours, €150/8 hours, mobile 0620-926-0557, www.budapestyourself.com, polczman@freestart.hu or peter@budapestyourself.com). **Andrea Makkay** is also great, with professional polish (same rates as Péter, mobile 0620-962-9363, www.privateguidebudapest.com, andrea.makkay@gmail.com—arrange details by email; if Andrea is busy, she can arrange to send you with another guide).

Elemér Boreczky, a semi-retired university professor, leads walking tours with a soft-spoken, scholarly approach, emphasizing Budapest's rich tapestry of architecture as "frozen music." Elemér is ideal if you want a walking graduate-level seminar about the easy-to-miss nuances of this grand metropolis (€25/hour, tel. 1/386-0885, mobile 0630-491-1389, www.culturaltours.mlap.hu, boreczky.elemer@gmail.com).

Péter, Andrea, and Elemér have all been indispensable help to me in writing and updating this book.

Walking Tours—Budapest has several backpacker-oriented walking-tour companies. While most travelers can get by with the self-guided walks and tours in this book—and I highly recommend hiring one of the excellent local guides listed above—these outfits are handy for those who want a live guide without paying for a private tour.

Budapest's best-established outfit is **Absolute Walking Tours,** run by Oregonian Ben Frieday and offering tours that are informal but informative. Travelers with this book get a 500-Ft discount on any tour. The Absolute Walk gives you a good overview of Budapest (4,500 Ft, daily at 10:00, 3.5 hours). The Hammer & Sickle Tour includes a walk through Castle Hill (with an emphasis on WWII history), sites related to the 1956 Uprising, and a visit to a mini-museum of communist artifacts (4,500 Ft, 2-3/week, 3.5 hours). The Hungro Gastro Food and Wine Tasting Tour gives you information on traditional recipes and ingredients, and a chance to taste several specialties at a local restaurant (9,000 Ft, 4/week, 1/week in winter, 2.5 hours, reservations required). In the evening, consider the Night Stroll, which includes a one-hour cruise on the Danube (8,000 Ft, 4/week March-Oct, 2/week Nov-Feb, 3 hours); or the Nightlife Dinner and/or rowdier Pub Crawl, which sometimes continues late into the night (9,500 Ft for dinner and pub crawl, 5,000 Ft for pub crawl only, dinner begins at 19:00, pub crawl departs at 21:00, 4/week April-Oct, 2/week Nov-March, at least 3 hours). They also offer a fashion and shopping tour, a Christmas Market tour (Dec only), and an "Alternative Budapest" tour that visits artsy, edgy, off-the-beaten path parts of town (for details on any of their tours, see www.absolutetours.com or contact the Discover Budapest office at tel. 1/269-3843). All tours (except the "Alternative" tour) depart from the Discover Budapest office behind the Opera House (see the "Discover Budapest" listing on page 40); the "Alternative" tour departs from the blocky, green-domed Lutheran church at Deák tér, near the Metró station. If you pre-book online, you're still eligible for a Rick Steves discount (enter coupon code RICK to get 10 percent off), and you'll also have the option of booking a 1,000-Ft transfer from your hotel to your walk's starting point.

You'll also see various companies advertising **"free" walking tours.** While there is no set fee to take these tours, guides are paid only if you tip (they're hoping for 2,000 Ft/person). There's a basic 2.5-hour introduction to the city (departing daily at 10:30, and again at 14:00 or 14:30), as well as itineraries focusing on the communist era and the Jewish Quarter. Because they're working for tips, the generally good-quality, certified guides are highly motivated to impress their customers. But because the "free" tag attracts very large groups, these tours tend to be less intimate than paid tours, and (especially the introductory tours) take a once-over-lightly "infotainment" approach. Still, these "free" tours get rave reviews from travelers and offer an inexpensive introduction to the city. As this scene is continually evolving, look for local fliers to learn about the options and meeting points.

By Boat

▲▲**Danube Boat Tours**—Cruising the Danube, while touristy, is a fun and convenient way to get a feel for the city's grand layout. The most established company, **Danube Legenda,** is a class act that runs well-maintained, glassed-in panoramic boats day and night. All cruises include a free drink and headphone commentary. By night, TV monitors show the interiors of the great buildings as you float by.

I've negotiated a special discount with Legenda for my readers (but you must book direct in person and ask for the Rick Steves price). By **day,** the one-hour cruise costs 2,800 Ft for Rick Steves readers, or pay 3,600 Ft to also include a one-hour walking tour around Margaret Island (6/day May-Aug, 5/day April and Sept, 4/day March and Oct, 1/day Nov-Feb). By **night,** the one-hour cruise (with no Margaret Island visit) costs 4,400 Ft for Rick Steves readers (4/day March-Oct, 1/day Nov-Feb). Note: These special prices are for 2013, and may be slightly higher in 2014.

The Legenda dock is in front of the Marriott on the Pest embankment (find pedestrian access under tram tracks at downriver end of Vigadó tér, district V, M1: Vörösmarty tér, tel. 1/317-2203, www.legenda.hu). Competing river-cruise companies are nearby, but given the discount, Legenda offers the best value.

Margaret Island Shuttle—If you just want to get out on the water, but don't care for a full tour with commentary, consider Mahart's cheap hop from Vigadó tér to Margaret Island (490 Ft one-way, 990 Ft round-trip, 4/day, 45 minutes, June-Aug daily, Sept and May Sat-Sun only, none Oct-April, boat dock directly in front of Vigadó tér). Mahart's standard sightseeing cruises pale in comparison to Legenda's.

On Wheels

Bike and Segway Tours—Various companies offer **bike tours** around the city; as the most interesting part of town (Pest) is quite flat and spread out, this is a good way to see the place. The best-established option is Yellow Zebra, a sister company of Absolute Walking Tours (6,000 Ft, 3.5 hours; July-Aug daily at 11:00 and 17:00; April-June and Sept-Oct daily at 11:00; Nov and March only Fri-Sun at 11:00—cancelled in below-freezing temperatures; no tours Dec-Feb).

The same company also offers tours of the city by **Segway** (stand-up electric scooter). Although expensive, it's a unique way to see Budapest while trying out a Segway. Each tour begins with a 30- to 45-minute training; my readers get a 10 percent discount

(17,000 Ft/2.5 hours, daily at 10:00 and 14:00, also an evening tour April-Sept daily at 14:30). You can reserve and prepay online (www.yellowzebratours.com, enter coupon code RICK).

The bike and Segway tours both meet at the Discover Budapest office behind the Opera House (see page 40; tel. 1/269-3843, www.yellowzebratours.com).

Bus Tours—Various companies run hop-on, hop-off bus tours, which make 12 to 16 stops as they cruise around town on a two-hour loop with headphone commentary (generally 5,000/24 hours, 6,000 Ft/48 hours). Most companies also offer a wide variety of other tours, including dinner boat cruises and trips to the Danube Bend. Pick up fliers about all these tours at the TI or in your hotel lobby.

RiverRide—This company offers a bus tour with a twist: Its amphibious bus can actually float on the Danube River, effectively making this a combination bus-and-boat tour (7,500 Ft, 2 hours, live guide in English and German, 4/day April-Oct, 3/day Nov-March, departs from Széchenyi tér, tel. 1/332-2555, www.riverride.com).

ORIENTATION TO BUDAPEST

SIGHTS IN BUDAPEST

The sights listed in this chapter are arranged by neighborhood for handy sightseeing. When you see a ✪ in a listing, it means the sight is covered in much more depth in one of my walks or self-guided tours. This is why Budapest's most important attractions get the least coverage in this chapter—we'll explore them later in the book. For tips on sightseeing, see page 15.

Budapest boomed in the late 19th century, after it became the co-capital of the vast Habsburg Empire. Most of its finest buildings (and top sights) date from this age. To appreciate an opulent interior—a Budapest experience worth ▲▲▲—I strongly recommend touring either the Parliament or the Opera House, depending on your interests. The Opera tour is more crowd-pleasing, while the Parliament tour is a bit drier (with a focus on history and parliamentary process)—but the spaces are even grander. Seeing both is also a fine option. "Honorable mentions" go to the interiors of St. István's Basilica, the Great Synagogue, New York Café, and both the Széchenyi and the Gellért Baths. This diversity—government and the arts, Christian and Jewish, coffee-drinkers and bathers—demonstrates how the shared prosperity of the late 19th century made it a Golden Age for a broad cross-section of Budapest society.

Remember, most sights in town offer a discount if you buy a Budapest Card (described on page 40). If you have a Budapest Card, always ask about discounts when you buy your ticket.

City leaders have secured EU funding to consolidate several Budapest museums (including the National Gallery, the Museum of Fine Arts, the Ethnographic Museum, the Ludwig Museum, and more) in a brand-new, custom-built facility near City Park. As of this book's publication, this project is still on the drawing board—but it may be underway by 2014.

Pest

Most of Pest's top sights cluster in four neighborhoods: **Leopold Town** and the **Town Center** (together forming the city's "downtown," along the Danube); along **Andrássy út;** and at **Heroes' Square and City Park.** Each of these areas is covered by a separate self-guided walk (as noted by ☉ below). The **Jewish Quarter** is covered in the Great Synagogue and Jewish Quarter Tour. But several other excellent sights are not contained in these areas, and are covered in greater depth in this chapter: along the **Small Boulevard** (Kiskörút); along the **Great Boulevard** (Nagykörút); and along the boulevard called **Üllői út.**

Leopold Town (Lipótváros)

☉ Most of these sights are covered in detail in the Leopold Town Walk chapter. If a sight is covered in the walk, I've listed only its essentials here. These are listed north to south.

▲▲Hungarian Parliament (Országház)

With an impressive facade and an even more extravagant interior, the oversized Hungarian Parliament stakes its claim on the Danube. A hulking Neo-Gothic base topped by a soaring Neo-Renaissance dome, it's one of the city's top landmarks. Touring the building offers the chance to stroll through one of Budapest's best interiors. On the 45-minute tour, you'll first pass through a security checkpoint, then climb up a 96-step staircase. Stops include the monumental entryway, the Hungarian crown (under the ornate gilded dome—described on page 107), and the legislative chamber of the now-disbanded House of Lords. Your guide will explain the history and symbolism of the building's intricate decorations and offer a lesson in the Hungarian parliamentary system. You'll find out why a really good speech was nicknamed a "Havana" by cigar-aficionado parliamentarians.

Cost and Hours: 3,500 Ft, free for EU citizens if you show your passport; English tours usually daily at 10:00, 12:00, and 14:00—but there can be more tours with demand and fewer for no apparent reason, so confirm in advance; on Mondays when parliament is in

Budapest at a Glance

In Pest

▲▲▲**Széchenyi Baths** Budapest's steamy soaking scene in City Park—the city's single best attraction. **Hours:** Swimming pool—daily 6:00-22:00, thermal bath—daily 6:00-19:00. See page 70.

▲▲**Hungarian Parliament** Vast riverside government center with remarkable interior. **Hours:** English tours usually daily at 10:00, 12:00, and 14:00. See page 57.

▲▲**Great Market Hall** Colorful Old World mall with produce, eateries, souvenirs, and great people-watching. **Hours:** Mon 6:00-17:00, Tue-Fri 6:00-18:00, Sat 6:00-15:00, closed Sun. See page 64.

▲▲**Great Synagogue** The world's second-largest, with fancy interior, good museum, and memorial garden. **Hours:** March-Oct Sun-Thu 10:00-17:30, Fri 10:00-15:30; Nov-Feb Sun-Thu 10:00-15:30, Fri 10:00-13:30; always closed Sat and Jewish holidays. See page 66.

▲▲**Hungarian State Opera House** Neo-Renaissance splendor and affordable opera. **Hours:** Lobby/box office open Mon-Sat from 11:00 until show time—generally 19:00; Sun open 3 hours before performance—generally 16:00-19:00, or 10:00-13:00 if there's a matinee; English tours nearly daily at 15:00 and 16:00. See page 67.

▲▲**House of Terror** Harrowing remembrance of Nazis and communist secret police in former headquarters/torture site. **Hours:** Tue-Sun 10:00-18:00, closed Mon. See page 67.

▲▲**Heroes' Square** Mammoth tribute to Hungary's historic figures, fronted by art museums. **Hours:** Square always open. See page 68.

▲▲**City Park** Budapest's backyard, with Art Nouveau zoo, Transylvanian Vajdahunyad Castle replica, amusement park, and Széchenyi Baths. **Hours:** Park always open. See page 69.

▲▲**Vajdahunyad Castle** Epcot-like replica of a Transylvanian castle and other historical buildings. **Hours:** Always viewable. See page 69.

▲▲**Holocaust Memorial Center** Excellent memorial and museum honoring Hungarian victims of the Holocaust. **Hours:** Tue-Sun 10:00-18:00, closed Mon. See page 71.

▲**St. István's Basilica** Budapest's largest church, with a saint's withered fist and great city views. **Hours:** Mon 9:00-16:30, Tue-Fri 9:00-17:00, Sat 9:00-13:00, Sun 13:00-17:00; panorama terrace daily July-Sept 10:00-19:00, Oct-June 10:00-17:00. See page 61.

▲**Hungarian National Museum** Expansive collection of fragments from Hungary's history. **Hours:** Tue-Sun 10:00-18:00, closed Mon. See page 65.

▲**Margaret Island** Budapest's traffic-free urban playground, with spas, ruins, gardens, a game farm, and fountains, set in the middle of the Danube. **Hours:** Park always open. See page 75.

In Buda

▲▲**Matthias Church** Landmark Neo-Gothic church with gilded history-book interior and revered 16th-century statue of Mary and Jesus. **Hours:** Mon-Sat 9:00-17:00—possibly also 19:00-20:00 in summer, Sun 13:00-17:00, may close Sat after 14:30 for weddings. See page 78.

▲▲**Gellért Baths** Touristy baths in historic Buda hotel. **Hours:** Daily 6:00-20:00. See page 83.

▲▲**Rudas Baths** Half-millennium-old Turkish dome over a series of hot-water pools. **Hours:** Daily 6:00-20:00. See page 83.

▲▲**Memento Park** Larger-than-life communist statues collected in one park, on the outskirts of town. **Hours:** Daily 10:00-sunset. See page 88.

▲**Hungarian National Gallery** Top works by Hungarian artists, housed in the Royal Palace. **Hours:** Tue-Sun 10:00-18:00, closed Mon. See page 78.

▲**"Hospital in the Rock"** Fascinating underground network of hospital and bomb-shelter corridors from WWII and the Cold War. **Hours:** Daily 10:00-20:00. See page 80.

In Óbuda

▲**Vasarely Museum** Mind-bending works by Op Art founder. **Hours:** Tue-Sun 10:00-17:30, closed Mon. See page 85.

▲**Imre Varga Collection** Evocative works by Hungary's top sculptor. **Hours:** Tue-Sun 10:00-18:00, closed Mon. See page 87.

session—generally Sept-May—the
only English tour is generally at
10:00; Kossuth tér 1-3, district V,
M2: Kossuth tér, tel. 1/441-4904,
www.parlament.hu.

Getting Tickets: There are
two lines at the security barrier behind the building: one to buy tickets and get your appointed time,
the other to meet your tour guide and begin your tour. The ticket
office opens each day at 8:00 (tickets sold for same-day tours only).
On busy days, ticket-buyers line up, and tours can sell out (especially if a tour group has reserved a large block of tickets, which
individuals can't do). If your heart is set on getting in, buy your
tickets early (for morning tours, I'd try to arrive by 9:00; the ticket-
buying line is longest around 10:30). Behind the Parliament, follow signs to the entry marked "X" (slightly right of center as you
face the back of the giant building), and find the line at the fence
marked *For Buying Tickets*. Wait for the guard to let you enter door
X, pay the cashier to get your English tour ticket and time, and
return to the mob to wait for your tour.

Near the Parliament

Kossuth (Lajos) Tér—This giant square behind the Parliament
is peppered with monuments honoring great Hungarian statesmen (Lajos Kossuth, Ferenc Rákóczi, Imre Nagy), artists (Attila
József), and anonymous victims of past regimes (you'll see two
different memorials to the 1956 Uprising, during which protesters
were gunned down on this very square).

For more details about Kossuth tér, ✪ see the Leopold Town
Walk chapter.

The square is fronted by the...

Museum of Ethnography (Néprajzi Múzeum)—This museum,
housed in one of Budapest's majestic venues, feels deserted. Its fine
collection of Hungarian folk artifacts (mostly from the late 19th
century) takes up only a small corner of the cavernous building. The
permanent exhibit, with surprisingly good English explanations,
shows off costumes, tools, wagons, boats, beehives, furniture, and
ceramics of the many peoples who lived in pre-WWI Hungary
(which also included much of today's Slovakia and Romania). The
museum also has a collection of artifacts from other European and
world cultures, which it cleverly assembles into good temporary
exhibits.

Cost and Hours: 1,400 Ft, includes worthwhile special exhibitions, Tue-Sun 10:00-18:00, closed Mon, Kossuth tér 12, district
V, M2: Kossuth tér, tel. 1/473-2200, www.neprajz.hu.

Between the Parliament and Town Center

For more details on all of the following sights, ❂ see the Leopold Town Walk chapter.

▲**Szabadság Tér ("Liberty Square")**—One of Budapest's most genteel squares, this space is marked by a controversial monu-

ment to the Soviet soldiers who "liberated" Hungary at the end of World War II, and ringed by both fancy old apartment blocks and important buildings (such as the former Hungarian State Television headquarters, the US Embassy, and the National Bank of Hungary). A fine café, fun-filled playgrounds, and statues of prominent Americans (Ronald Reagan and Harry Hill Bandholtz) round out the square's many attractions. More architectural gems—including the quintessentially Art Nouveau Bedő-Ház and the Postal Savings Bank in the Hungarian national style—are just a block away.

▲**St. István's Basilica (Szent István Bazilika)**—Budapest's biggest church is one of its top landmarks. The grand interior cel-

ebrates St. István, Hungary's first Christian king. You can see his withered, blackened, millennium-old fist in a gilded reliquary in the side chapel. Or you can zip up on an elevator (or climb up stairs partway) to a panorama terrace with views over the rooftops of Pest. The skippable treasury has ecclesiastical items, historical exhibits, and artwork.

Cost and Hours: Interior—free but 200-Ft donation strongly suggested, open to tourists Mon 9:00-16:30, Tue-Fri 9:00-17:00, Sat 9:00-13:00, Sun 13:00-17:00, open slightly later for worshippers; panorama terrace—500 Ft, daily July-Sept 10:00-19:00, Oct-June 10:00-17:00; treasury-400 Ft, same hours as terrace; Szent István tér, district V, M1: Bajcsy-Zsilinszky út or M3: Arany János utca.

▲**Gresham Palace**—This stately old Art Nouveau building, long neglected, has now been renovated to its former splendor. Overlooking Széchenyi tér, it once held the offices of a life-insurance company; today it houses one of Budapest's top hotels. Even if you're not a guest, ogle its glorious facade and stroll through its luxurious lobby (lobby open 24 hours daily, Széchenyi tér 5-6, district V, M:1 Vörösmarty tér or M:2 Kossuth tér, www.fourseasons.com/budapest).

SIGHTS IN BUDAPEST

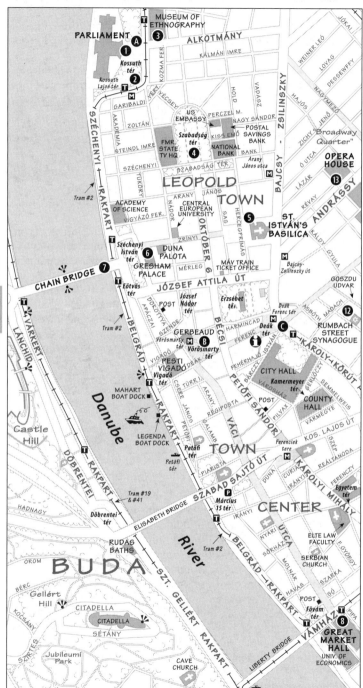

Pest Sights

1. Hungarian Parliament
2. Kossuth (Lajos) Tér
3. Museum of Ethnography
4. Szabadság Tér
5. St. István's Basilica
6. Gresham Palace
7. Chain Bridge
8. Great Market Hall
9. Hungarian National Museum
10. Great Synagogue
11. Orthodox Synagogue
12. Synagogue at Rumbach Street
13. Hungarian State Opera House
14. House of Terror
15. Franz Liszt Museum
16. New York Café
17. To Holocaust Memorial Center
18. Applied Arts Museum

Start of Pest Walks

A. Leopold Town Walk
B. Pest Town Center Walk
C. Andrássy Út Walk
D. Jewish Quarter Walk

(See detail maps in appropriate chapters)

SIGHTS IN BUDAPEST

▲**Chain Bridge (Lánchíd)**—The city's most beloved bridge stretches from Pest's Széchenyi tér to Buda's Adam Clark tér (named for the bridge's designer). The gift of Count István Széchenyi to the Hungarian people, the Chain Bridge was the first permanent link between the two towns that would soon merge to become Budapest.

Pest Town Center (Belváros)

✪ All of these sights are covered in detail in the Pest Town Center Walk chapter. I've listed only the essentials here.

▲**Vörösmarty Tér**—The central square of the Town Center, dominated by a giant statue of

the revered Romantic poet Mihály Vörösmarty and the venerable Gerbeaud coffee shop, is the hub of Pest sightseeing. Within a few steps of here are the main walking street, Váci utca (described below), the delightful Danube promenade, the "Fashion Street" of Deák utca, and much more.

Váci Utca—In Budapest's Golden Age, Váci Street was where well-heeled urbanites would shop, then show off for one another. During the Cold War, it was the first place in the Eastern Bloc where you could buy a Big Mac or Adidas sneakers. And today, it's an overrated, overpriced tourist trap disguised as a pretty street. I'll admit that I have a bad attitude about Váci utca. It's because more visitors get fleeced by dishonest shops, crooked restaurants, and hookers masquerading as lonely hearts here than anywhere else in town. Like moths to a flame, tourists can't seem to avoid this strip. And I can't blame them. Walk Váci utca to satisfy your curiosity. But then venture off it to discover the real Budapest.

▲▲**Great Market Hall (Nagyvásárcsarnok)**—"Great" indeed is this gigantic marketplace on three levels: produce, meats, and other foods on the ground floor; souve-

nirs upstairs; and fish and pickles in the cellar. The Great Market Hall has somehow succeeded in keeping local shoppers happy, even as it's evolved into one of the city's top tourist attractions. Goose liver, embroidered tablecloths, golden Tokaji Aszú wine, pickled peppers, communist-kitsch T-shirts, savory *lángos* pastries, patriotic green-white-and-red flags, kid-pleasing local candy bars, and paprika of every degree of spiciness...if it's

SIGHTS IN BUDAPEST

Hungarian, you'll find it here. Come to shop for souvenirs, to buy a picnic, or just to rattle around inside this vast, picturesque, Industrial Age hall.

Hours and Location: Mon 6:00-17:00, Tue-Fri 6:00-18:00, Sat 6:00-15:00, closed Sun, Fővám körút 1-3, district IX, M3: Kálvin tér.

Along the Small Boulevard (Kiskörút)

These two major sights are along the Small Boulevard, between the Liberty Bridge/Great Market Hall and Deák tér. (Note that the Great Market Hall, listed earlier, is also technically along the Small Boulevard.)

▲Hungarian National Museum (Magyar Nemzeti Múzeum)

One of Budapest's biggest museums features all manner of Hungarian historic bric-a-brac, from the Paleolithic age to a more recent infestation of dinosaurs (the communists). Artifacts are explained by good, if dry, English descriptions. The first floor (one flight down from the entry) focuses on the Carpathian Basin in the pre-Magyar days, with ancient items and Roman remains. The basement features a lapidarium, with medieval tombstones and more Roman ruins. Upstairs, 20 rooms provide a historic overview from the arrival of the Magyars in 896 up to the 1989 revolution. The museum adds substance to your understanding of Hungary's story—but it helps to have a pretty firm foundation first (read this book's Hungary: Past and Present chapter). The most engaging part is room 20, with an exhibit on the communist era, featuring both pro- and anti-Party propaganda. The exhibit ends with video footage of the 1989 end of communism—demonstrations, monumental parliament votes, and a final farewell to the last Soviet troops leaving Hungarian soil. Another uprising—the 1848 Revolution against Habsburg rule—was declared from the steps of this impressive Neoclassical building.

Cost and Hours: 1,100 Ft, audioguide-750 Ft/hour, Tue-Sun 10:00-18:00, closed Mon, last entry 30 minutes before closing, near Great Market Hall at Múzeum körút 14-16, district VIII, M3: Kálvin tér, tel. 1/327-7773, www.hnm.hu.

Jewish Quarter (Zsidónegyed)

✪ The Great Synagogue and other sights in this area are described in far greater detail in the Great Synagogue and Jewish Quarter Tour.

▲▲**Great Synagogue (Zsinagóga)**—Thanks to the unusual history of Pest's Jewish community, this synagogue feels more like a Christian house of worship than a Jewish one.

The gorgeously restored, intricately decorated interior is one of Budapest's finest. Attached to the synagogue is a small but well-presented Jewish Museum, and behind it is an evocative memorial garden with the powerful *Tree of Life* monument to Hungarian victims of the Holocaust, as well as a symbolic grave for Swedish diplomat Raoul Wallenberg, who worked to save the lives of Hungarian Jews during World War II. The synagogue is also a starting point for various tours both of the building itself, and of the surrounding Jewish sights.

Cost and Hours: 2,250 Ft for Great Synagogue and Jewish Museum, 500 Ft extra to take photos, *Tree of Life* and memorial garden are always free; March-Oct Sun-Thu 10:00-17:30, Fri 10:00-15:30; Nov-Feb Sun-Thu 10:00-15:30, Fri 10:00-13:30; always closed Sat and Jewish holidays, last entry 30 minutes before closing. Dohány utca 2, district VII, near M2: Astoria or the Astoria stop on trams #47 and #49. Tel. 1/344-5131, www.dohanyutcaizsinagoga.hu.

Hungarian Jewish Archives and Family Research Center— At the back of the Great Synagogue's memorial garden, this facility houses a small exhibit about the Jewish Quarter and an archive of Jewish birth, marriage, and death records.

Cost and Hours: Exhibit covered by Great Synagogue ticket, 1,000 Ft to use archives, Mon-Thu 10:00-17:00, Fri 10:00-15:00, closed Sat-Sun, Wesselényi utca 7, best to call or email ahead to arrange help with archives, tel. 1/413-5547, www.milev.hu, family@milev.hu.

Orthodox Synagogue—Recently renovated and reopened to the public, this colorfully decorated space is Budapest's second-most-interesting Jewish sight, just two blocks behind the Great Synagogue.

Cost and Hours: 1,000 Ft, Sun-Thu 10:00-15:00, Fri 10:00-12:30, closed Sat, enter down little alley, Kazinczy utca 27, district VII, M2: Astoria.

Synagogue at Rumbach Street—Still rough around the edges, this house of worship awaits a more thorough restoration. In the meantime, it's open for visitors to walk around the Moorish-style interior, designed by Otto Wagner.

Cost and Hours: 500 Ft, Sun-Thu 10:00-15:30, Fri 10:00-

13:30, closed Sat, from the *Tree of Life* it's two blocks down Rumbach utca toward Andrássy út, district VII, M2: Astoria.

Andrássy Út

○ All of these sights are covered in detail in the Andrássy Út Walk chapter, with the exception of the House of Terror, which is further described in the House of Terror Tour chapter. I've listed only the essentials here.

▲▲**Hungarian State Opera House (Magyar Állami Operaház)**—This sumptuous temple to music is one of Europe's finest opera houses. Built in the late 19th century by patriotic Hungarians striving to thrust their capital onto the European stage, it also boasts one of Budapest's very best interiors.

You can drop in whenever the box office is open to ogle the ostentatious **lobby** (Mon-Sat from 11:00 until show time—generally 19:00, or until 17:00 if there's no performance; Sun open 3 hours before the performance—generally 16:00-19:00, or 10:00-13:00 if there's a matinee; Andrássy út 22, district VI, M1: Opera).

The 45-minute **tours** of the Opera House are a must for music-lovers, and enjoyable for anyone, though the guides can be hit-or-miss: Most spout plenty of fun, if silly, legends, but some can be quite dry. You'll see the main entryway, the snooty lounge area, some of the cozy but plush boxes, and the lavish auditorium. You'll find out why secret lovers would meet in the cigar lounge, how the Opera House is designed to keep the big spenders away from the nosebleed-seats rabble, and how to tell the difference between real marble and fake marble (2,900 Ft, 500 Ft extra to take photos, 500 Ft extra for 5-minute mini-concert of two arias after the tour, tours nearly daily at 15:00 and 16:00, tickets are easy to get—just show up right before the tour; buy ticket in opera shop—enter the main lobby and go left, shop open daily 11:00-18:00—or until the end of the second intermission during performances, Oct-March closed for lunch 13:30-14:00; tel. 1/332-8197). Since the real appeal is the chance to see the interior, skip the tour if you're going to an opera performance.

▲▲**House of Terror (Terror Háza)**—The building at Andrássy út 60 was home to the vilest parts of two destructive regimes: first the Arrow Cross (the Gestapo-like enforcers of Nazi-occupied Hungary), then the ÁVO and ÁVH secret police (the insidious KGB-type wing of the Soviet satellite government). Now re-envisioned as the "House of Terror," this building uses high-tech, highly conceptual, bombastic exhibits to document (if not proselytize about) the ugliest moments in Hungary's difficult 20th century. Enlightening and well-presented, it rivals Memento Park as Budapest's best attraction about the communist age.

Cost and Hours: 2,000 Ft, possibly more for special exhibits, audioguide-1,500 Ft, Tue-Sun 10:00-18:00, closed Mon, last entry 30 minutes before closing, Andrássy út 60, district VI, M1: Vörösmarty utca—*not* the Vörösmarty tér stop, tel. 1/374-2600, www.terrorhaza.hu.

○ See the House of Terror Tour chapter.

Franz Liszt Museum—In this surprisingly modest apartment where the composer once resided, you'll find a humble but appealing collection of artifacts. A pilgrimage site for Liszt fans, it's housed in the former Academy of Music, which also hosts Saturday-morning concerts.

Cost and Hours: 1,300 Ft; dry English audioguide with a few snippets of music-700 Ft, otherwise scarce English information—borrow the information sheet as you enter; Mon-Fri 10:00-18:00, Sat 9:00-17:00, closed Sun, Vörösmarty utca 35, district VI, M1: Vörösmarty utca—*not* Vörösmarty tér stop, tel. 1/322-9804, www.lisztmuseum.hu.

Heroes' Square and City Park

○ All of these sights are covered in detail in the Heroes' Square and City Park Walk chapter, with the exception of Széchenyi Baths, which are described in the Thermal Baths chapter. I've listed only the essentials here. To reach this area, take the M1/yellow Metró line to Hősök tere (district XIV).

▲▲**Heroes' Square (Hősök Tere)**—Built in 1896 to celebrate the 1,000th anniversary of the Magyars' arrival in Hungary, this

vast square culminates at a bold Millennium Monument. Standing stoically in its colonnades are 14 Hungarian leaders who represent the whole span of this nation's colorful and illustrious history. In front, at the base of a high pillar, are the seven original Magyar chieftains, the Hungarian War Memorial, and young Hungarian skateboarders of the 21st century.

SIGHTS IN BUDAPEST

It's an ideal place to appreciate Budapest's greatness and to learn a little about its story. The square is also flanked by a pair of museums (described below).

For a statue-by-statue self-guided tour of Heroes' Square, ✪ see the Heroes' Square and City Park Walk chapter.

Museum of Fine Arts (Szépművészeti Múzeum)—This collection of Habsburg art—mostly Germanic, Dutch, Belgian, and Spanish, rather than Hungarian—is Budapest's best chance to appreciate some European masters.

Cost and Hours: 1,800 Ft, may be more for special exhibits, audioguide-1,500 Ft, WC and coat check downstairs, Tue-Sun 10:00-17:30, closed Mon, last entry one hour before closing, Dózsa György út 41, tel. 1/469-7100, www.szepmuveszeti.hu.

Műcsarnok ("Hall of Art")—Facing the Museum of Fine Arts from across Heroes' Square, the Műcsarnok shows temporary exhibits by contemporary artists—of interest only to art-lovers. The price varies depending on the exhibits and on which parts you tour. The Ernst Museum wing features up-and-coming artists.

Cost and Hours: 1,800 Ft, or 1,900 Ft with Ernst Museum; Tue-Wed and Fri-Sun 10:00-18:00, Thu 12:00-20:00, closed Mon; Ernst Museum open Tue-Sun 11:00-19:00, closed Mon; Dózsa György út 37, tel. 1/460-7000, www.mucsarnok.hu.

▲▲**City Park (Városliget)**—This particularly enjoyable corner of Budapest, which sprawls behind Heroes' Square, is endlessly en-

tertaining. Explore the fantasy castle of Vajdahunyad (described next). Visit the animals and ogle the playful Art Nouveau buildings inside the city's zoo, ride a roller-coaster at the amusement park, or enjoy a circus under the big top (all described in the Budapest with Children chapter). Go for a stroll, rent a rowboat, eat some cotton candy, or challenge a local Bobby Fischer to a game of chess. Or (best of all) take a dip in Budapest's ultimate thermal spa, the Széchenyi Baths (described later). This is a fine place to just be on vacation.

▲▲**Vajdahunyad Castle (Vajdahunyad Vára)**—An elaborate pavilion that the people of Budapest couldn't bear to tear down after their millennial celebration ended a century ago, Vajdahunyad Castle has become a fixture of City Park. Divided into

four parts—representing four typical, traditional schools of Hungarian architecture—this "little Epcot" is free and always open to explore. It's dominated by a fanciful replica of a Renaissance-era Transylvanian castle. Deeper in the complex, a curlicue-covered Baroque mansion houses (unexpectedly) the **Museum of Hungarian Agriculture,** noteworthy for its grand interior (Magyar Mezőgazdasági Múzeum; 1,100 Ft; April-Oct Tue-Sun 10:00-17:00; Nov-March Tue-Fri 10:00-16:00, Sat-Sun 10:00-17:00; closed Mon year-round; last entry 30 minutes before closing, tel. 1/363-1117, www.mezogazdasagimuzeum.hu).

▲▲▲**Széchenyi Baths (Széchenyi Fürdő)**—My favorite activity in Budapest, the Széchenyi Baths are an ideal way to reward yourself for the hard work of sightseeing and call it a culturally enlightening experience. Soak in hundred-degree water, surrounded by portly Hungarians squeezed into tiny swimsuits, while jets and cascades pound away your tension. Go for a vigorous swim in the lap pool, giggle and bump your way around  the whirlpool, submerge yourself to the nostrils in water green with minerals, feel the bubbles from an underwater jet gradually caress their way up your leg, or challenge the locals to a game of Speedo-clad chess. And it's all surrounded by an opulent yellow palace with shiny copper domes. The bright blue-and-white of the sky, the yellow of the buildings, the pale pink of the skin, the turquoise of the water...Budapest simply doesn't get any better.

Cost and Hours: 3,400 Ft for locker (in gender-segregated locker room), 400 Ft more for personal changing cabin, cheaper after 19:00, 150 Ft more on weekends; admission includes outdoor swimming pool area, indoor thermal baths, and sauna; swimming pool generally open daily 6:00-22:00, thermal bath daily 6:00-19:00, may be open later on summer weekends, last entry one hour before closing, Állatkerti körút 11, district XIV, M1: Széchenyi fürdö, tel. 1/363-3210, www.szechenyibath.com.

○ See the Thermal Baths chapter.

On the Great Boulevard (Nagykörút)

▲**New York Café**—My vote for the most over-the-top extravagant coffeehouse in Budapest, if not Europe, this restored space ranks up there with the city's most impressive old interiors. Springing for a pricey cup of coffee here (consider it the admission fee) is worth it simply to soak in all the opulence.

Cost and Hours: Free to take a quick peek, pricey coffee and meals, daily 9:00-24:00, Erzsébet körút 9-11, district VII, M2: Blaha Lujza tér, tel. 1/886-6167. For more details, see page 264 of the Eating in Budapest chapter.

South of Downtown Pest

These two areas of Pest—a short commute to the south from the center of Pest (10-15 minutes by tram or Metró)—offer a peek at some worthwhile, workaday areas where relatively few tourists venture.

Museums near Üllői Út

These two museums are near the city center, on the boulevard called Üllői út. You could stroll there in about 10 minutes from the Small Boulevard ring road (walking the length of the Ráday utca café street gets you very close), or hop on the M3/blue Metró line to Corvin-negyed (just one stop beyond Kálvin tér).

▲▲**Holocaust Memorial Center (Holokauszt Emlékközpont)**—This sight honors the nearly 600,000 Hungarian victims of the Nazis...one out of every ten Holocaust victims. The impressive modern complex (with a beautifully restored 1920s synagogue as its centerpiece) is a museum of the Hungarian Holocaust, a monument to its victims, a space for temporary exhibits, and a research and documentation center of Nazi atrocities. Interesting to anybody, but essential to those interested in the Holocaust, this is Budapest's—and one of Europe's—best sights about that dark time. (For background on the Hungarian Jewish experience, see page 184.)

Cost and Hours: 1,400 Ft, Tue-Sun 10:00-18:00, closed Mon, Páva utca 39, district IX, M3: Corvin-negyed, tel. 1/455-3333, www.hdke.hu.

Getting There: From the Corvin-negyed Metró stop, use the exit marked *Holokauszt Emlékközpont* and take the left fork at the exit. Walk straight ahead two long blocks, then turn right down Páva utca.

Visiting the Center: You'll pass through a security checkpoint to reach the courtyard. Once inside, a black marble wall is etched with the names of victims. Head downstairs to buy your ticket.

The excellent permanent exhibit, called "From Deprivation of Rights to Genocide," traces in English the gradual process of disenfranchisement, marginalization, exploitation, dehumanization, and eventually extermination that befell Hungary's Jews as World War II wore on. From the entrance, a long hallway with shuffling feet on the soundtrack replicates the forced march of prisoners. The one-way route through darkened halls uses high-tech exhibits, including interactive touch screens and movies, to tell the story. By demonstrating that pervasive anti-Semitism existed here long before World War II, the pointed commentary casts doubt on the widely held belief that Hungary initially allied itself with the Nazis partly to protect its Jews. While the exhibit sometimes acknowledges Roma (Gypsy) victims, its primary focus is on the fate of the Hungarian Jews. Occasionally the exhibit zooms in to tell the story of an individual or a single family, following their personal story through those horrific years. One powerful room is devoted to the notorious Auschwitz-Birkenau concentration camp, where some 430,000 Hungarian Jews were sent—most to be executed immediately upon arrival. The main exhibit ends with a thoughtful consideration of "Liberation and Calling to Account," analyzing the impossible question of how a society responds to and recovers from such a tragedy.

The finale is the interior of the synagogue, now a touching memorial filled with glass seats, each one etched with the image of a Jewish worshipper who once filled it. Up above, on the mezzanine level, you'll find temporary exhibits and an information center that helps teary-eyed descendants of Hungarian Jews track down the fate of their relatives.

Applied Arts Museum (Iparművészeti Múzeum)—This remarkable late-19th-century building, a fanciful green-roofed castle that seems out of place in an otherwise dreary urban area, was designed by Ödön Lechner (who also did the Postal Savings Bank—see page 116). The interior is equally striking: Because historians of the day were speculating about possible ties between the Magyars and India, Lechner decorated it with Mogul

motifs (from the Indian dynasty best known for the Taj Mahal). Strolling through the forest of dripping-with-white-stucco arches and columns, you might just forget to pay attention to the exhibits... which would be a shame. This is the third-oldest applied arts institution in the world (after ones in London and Vienna). The small but excellent permanent collection upstairs, called "Collectors and Treasures," displays furniture, clothes, ceramics, and other everyday items, with an emphasis on curvy Art Nouveau (all described in English). This and various temporary exhibits are displayed around a light and airy atrium. If you're visiting the nearby Holocaust Memorial Center, consider dropping by here for a look at the building.

Cost and Hours: Ticket price varies with exhibits, but

generally around 1,800 Ft, Tue-Sun 10:00-18:00, closed Mon, Üllői út 33-37, district IX, M3: Corvin-negyed, tel. 1/456-5100, www.imm.hu.

Getting There: From the Corvin-negyed Metró stop, follow signs to *Iparművészeti Múzeum* and bear right up the stairs.

Millennium City Center

Along the Danube riverbank at the Rákóczi Bridge, you'll find a cutting-edge cultural complex with some of Budapest's best modern venues for music and theater. While there's not much

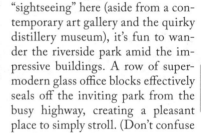

"sightseeing" here (aside from a contemporary art gallery and the quirky distillery museum), it's fun to wander the riverside park amid the impressive buildings. A row of supermodern glass office blocks effectively seals off the inviting park from the busy highway, creating a pleasant place to simply stroll. (Don't confuse this with the similarly named Millenáris Park, at the northern edge of Buda.)

Getting There: Though it looks far on the map, this area is easy to reach: From anywhere along the Pest embankment (including Kossuth tér by the Parliament, Vigadó tér in the heart of Pest's Town Center, or Fövam tér next to the Great Market Hall), hop on tram #2 and ride it south about 10-15 minutes to the Millenniumi Kulturális Központ stop.

National Theater (Nemzeti Színház)—This facility anchors the complex with an elaborate industrial-Organic facade, studded with statues honoring the Hungarian theatrical tradition. The surrounding park is a lively people zone laden with whimsical art—Hungarian theater greats in stone, a vast terrace shaped like a ship's prow, a toppled colonnade, and a stone archway that evokes an opening theater

curtain. Twist up to the top of the adjacent, yellow-brick ziggurat tower for fine views over the entire complex and all the way to downtown Budapest.

Palace of Arts (Művészetek Palotája)—With a sterner facade, this gigantic facility houses the 1,700-seat Béla Bartók National Concert Hall and the smaller 460-seat Festival Theater (free to enter the building, open daily 10:00-20:00 or until end of last performance, www.mupa.hu). The complex is also home to the Ludwig Museum, Budapest's premier collection of contemporary art, with mostly changing exhibits of today's biggest names (price varies depending on exhibits, Tue-Sun 10:00-18:00, closed Mon, Komor Marcell utca 1, tel. 1/555-3444, www.ludwigmuseum.hu).

Zwack Museum—The Zwacks' earnest little distillery exhibit is best for those who already have an affinity for all things Hungarian. This

museum and visitors center is housed in a corner of the sprawling distillery complex that produces Unicum, the abundantly flavored liquor that's Hungary's favorite spirit (described on page 251). The Zwack clan, the family behind its production, is a Hungarian institution—like the Anheuser-Busch clan in the US. The museum offers a doting look at the family and their company, headquartered right here since 1892 (with a 45-year break during communism).

Cost and Hours: 1,800 Ft, Mon-Fri 10:00-17:00, closed Sat-Sun, Soroksári út 26, enter around the corner on Dandár utca, tel. 1/476-2383.

Getting There: It's near the Haller utca stop on tram #2 (the stop just before Millennium Park); from the tram stop, walk back a block and head up Dandár utca.

Visiting the Museum: The visit begins with a 20-minute film in English (more about the family than about their products), continues through the museum upstairs (glass display cases jammed with old ads, documents, and—up in the gallery—thousands of tiny bottles), and ends with a tasting of three Zwack products, including Unicum. The Zwacks' story is a fascinating case study in how communism affected longstanding industry—privatization, exile, and a triumphant return. And, while the museum feels a bit like a shrine to their own ingenuity, it's worthwhile for Unicum fans.

The Danube (Duna)

The mighty river coursing through the heart of the city defines Budapest. Make time for a stroll along the delightful riverfront embankments of both Buda and Pest. For many visitors, a highlight is taking a touristy but beautiful boat cruise up and down the Danube—especially at night (see "Tours in Budapest" on page 52). Or visit the river's best island...

▲Margaret Island (Margitsziget)

In the Middle Ages, this island in the Danube (just north of the Parliament) was known as the "Isle of Hares." In the 13th century, a desperate King Béla IV swore that if God were to deliver Hungary from the invading Tatars, he would dedicate his youngest daughter Margaret to the Church. Hungary was spared...and Margaret was shipped to a nunnery here. But, the story goes, Margaret embraced her new life as a castaway nun, and later refused her father's efforts to force her into a politically expedient marriage with a Bohemian king. She became St. Margaret of Hungary, and this island was named for her.

The island remained largely undeveloped until the 19th century, when a Habsburg aristocrat built a hunting palace here and turned it into his playground. It gradually evolved into a lively garden district, connected to Buda and Pest by a paddleboat steamer. Eventually a bath and hotel complex was built (to take advantage of the island's natural thermal springs), and Margaret Island was connected to the rest of the city in 1901 by the Margaret Bridge. In the genteel age of the late 19th century, a small entrance fee was charged to frolic on the island, to keep the rabble away.

Today, Margaret Island remains Budapest's playground. Budapesters come to relax in this huge, leafy park...in the midst of the busy city, yet so far away (no cars are allowed on the island—just public buses). The island rivals City Park as the best spot in town for strolling, jogging, biking, and people-watching. Margaret Island is also home to some of Budapest's many baths, one of which (Palatinus Strandfürdő) is like a mini-water park. Rounding out the island's attractions are an iconic old water tower, the remains of Margaret's convent, a rose garden, a game farm, and a "musical fountain" that performs to the strains of Hungarian folk tunes.

Perhaps the best way to enjoy Margaret Island is to rent some wheels. **Bringóhintó** ("Bike Castle"), with branches at both ends of the island, rents all manner of wheeled entertainment (open daily year-round until dusk; location at Margaret Bridge opens

at 10:00, at opposite end opens at 8:00; tel. 1/329-2746, www.bringohinto.hu). The main office is a few steps from the bus stop called "Szállodák (Hotels)." For two or more people, consider renting a fun bike cart—a four-wheeled carriage with two sets of pedals, a steering wheel, handbrake, and canopy (bikes—690 Ft/30 minutes, 990 Ft/1 hour, then 200 Ft/hour; bike carts—1,980 Ft/30 minutes, 2,980 Ft/1 hour; 20,000-Ft deposit

or leave your ID). Because they have two locations, you can take bus #26 to the northern end of the island, rent a bike and pay the deposit, bike one-way to the southern tip of the island, and return your bike there to reclaim your deposit. Follow this route (using the helpful map posted inside the bike cart): water tower, monastery ruins, rose garden, past the game farm, along the east side of the island to the dancing fountain; with more time, go along the main road or the west side of the island to check out the baths.

Getting There: Bus #26 begins at Nyugati/Western train station, crosses the Margaret Bridge, then drives up through the middle of the island—allowing visitors to easily get from one end to the other (3-6/hour). **Trams** #4 and #6, which circulate around the Great Boulevard, cross the Margaret Bridge and stop at the southern tip of the island, a short walk from some of the attractions. From Vigadó tér (along the Pest embankment), you can catch a Mahart shuttle **boat** to the island (see page 54).

Buda

Nearly all of Buda's top sights are concentrated on or near its two riverside hills: Castle Hill and Gellért Hill.

Castle Hill (Várhegy)

✪ Most of these sights are covered in detail in the Castle Hill Walk chapter. If a sight is covered in the walk, I've listed only its essentials here.

Royal Palace and Nearby
Royal Palace (Királyi Palota)—While imposing and grand-seeming from afar, the palace perched atop Castle Hill is essentially a shoddily rebuilt shell. But the terrace out front

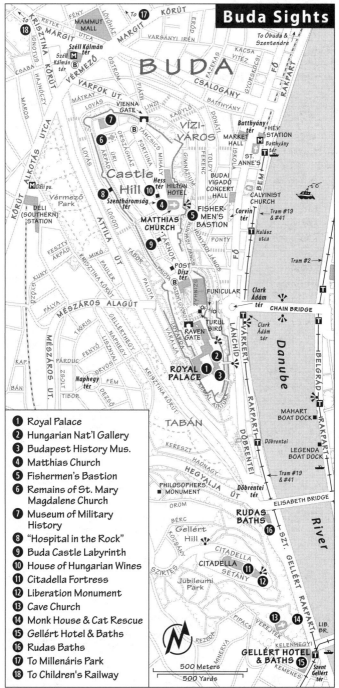

Buda Sights

1. Royal Palace
2. Hungarian Nat'l Gallery
3. Budapest History Mus.
4. Matthias Church
5. Fishermen's Bastion
6. Remains of St. Mary Magdalene Church
7. Museum of Military History
8. "Hospital in the Rock"
9. Buda Castle Labyrinth
10. House of Hungarian Wines
11. Citadella Fortress
12. Liberation Monument
13. Cave Church
14. Monk House & Cat Rescue
15. Gellért Hotel & Baths
16. Rudas Baths
17. To Millenáris Park
18. To Children's Railway

500 Meters
500 Yards

SIGHTS IN BUDAPEST

offers glorious Pest panoramas, there are signs of life in some of its nooks and crannies (such as a playful fountain depicting King Matthias' hunting party), and the complex houses two museums (described below).

▲**Hungarian National Gallery (Magyar Nemzeti Galéria)**— The best place in Hungary to appreciate the works of homegrown artists, this art museum offers a peek into the often-morose Hungarian worldview. The collection includes a remarkable group of 15th-century, wood-carved altars from Slovakia (then "Upper Hungary"); piles of gloomy canvases dating from the dark days after the failed 1848 Revolution; several works by two great Hungarian Realist painters, Mihály Munkácsy and László Paál; and paintings by the troubled, enigmatic, and recently in-vogue Post-Impressionist Tivadar Csontváry Kosztka, including the huge *Theater at Taormina*.

Cost and Hours: 1,200 Ft, may be more for special exhibits, 500 Ft extra to take photos, Tue-Sun 10:00-18:00, closed Mon, required bag check for large bags, café, in the Royal Palace—enter from terrace by Eugene of Savoy statue, district I, mobile 0620-439-7325, www.mng.hu.

For a self-guided tour of the Hungarian National Gallery, ✪ see the Castle Hill Walk chapter.

Budapest History Museum (Budapesti Történeti Múzeum)—This earnest but dusty collection strains to bring the history of this city to life. The dimly lit fragments of 14th-century sculptures, depicting early Magyars, allow you to see how Asian those original Hungarians truly looked. The "Budapest: Light and Shadow" exhibit deliberately but effectively traces the union between Buda and Pest. Rounding out the collection are exhibits on prehistoric residents and a sprawling cellar that unveils fragments from the oh-so-many buildings that have perched on this hill over the centuries.

Cost and Hours: 1,500 Ft, audioguide-1,200 Ft, some good English descriptions posted; March-Oct Tue-Sun 10:00-18:00,Nov-Feb Tue-Sun 10:00-16:00, closed Mon year-round; last entry 30 minutes before closing, district I, tel. 1/487-8800, www.btm.hu.

For more details about the Budapest History Museum, ✪ see the Castle Hill Walk chapter.

Matthias Church and Nearby

▲▲**Matthias Church (Mátyás-Templom)**—Arguably Budapest's finest church inside and out, this historic house of worship—with a frilly Neo-Gothic spire and gilded Hungarian historical motifs slathered on every interior wall—is Castle Hill's best sight. From the humble Loreto Chapel (with a tranquil statue of

the Virgin that helped defeat the Ottomans), to altars devoted to top Hungarian kings, to a replica of the crown of Hungary, every inch of the church oozes history. Unfortunately, parts of the interior will be closed for refurbishment through 2014.

Cost and Hours: 1,000 Ft, includes Museum of Ecclesiastical Art (unless closed for renovation), audioguide may be available, Mon-Sat 9:00-17:00—possibly also open 19:00-20:00 in summer, Sun 13:00-17:00, may close Sat after 14:30 for weddings, Szentháromság tér 2, district I, tel. 1/488-7716, www.matyas-templom.hu.

For a self-guided tour of the Matthias Church, ✪ see the Castle Hill Walk chapter.

Fishermen's Bastion (Halászbástya)—Seven pointy domes and a double-decker rampart run along the cliff in front of Matthias Church. Evoking the original seven Magyar tribes, and built for the millennial celebration of their arrival, the Fishermen's Bastion is one of Budapest's top landmarks. This fanciful structure adorns Castle Hill like a decorative frieze or wedding-cake flowers. While some suckers pay for the views from here, parts of the rampart are free and always open. Or you can enjoy virtually the same view through the windows next to the bastion café for free.

Cost and Hours: 600 Ft, buy ticket at ticket office along the park wall across the square from Matthias Church, daily mid-March-mid-Oct 9:00-21:00; after closing time and off-season, no tickets are sold, but bastion is open and free to enter; Szentháromság tér 5, district I.

House of Hungarian Wines (Magyar Borok Háza)—The slopes of Castle Hill were once blanketed with vineyards, producing wines

that aged in cellars burrowed inside the castle walls. Across the street from Matthias Church, this sprawling network of cellars comes with a well-presented survey of Hungary's 22 wine-growing regions. If they're not too busy, your tasting will include a little tour of the exhibit and a lesson in Hungarian winemaking. While Hungarian wines are well worth a taste, I'd rather do it in a trendy urban wine bar like DiVino (see page 257). But if you'd like to lubricate your castle visit, this place is handy.

Cost and Hours: 3,000 Ft/3 wines, 10,000 Ft/7 "exclusive" wines, 12,000 Ft/6 premium reds, daily 12:00-20:00, Szentháromság tér 6, tel. 1/201-4062, www.magyarborokhaza.com.

North Castle Hill

Remains of St. Mary Magdalene Church—Standing like a lonely afterthought at the northern tip of Castle Hill, St. Mary Magdalene was the crosstown rival of the Matthias Church. After the hill was recaptured from the Ottomans, only one church was needed, so St. Mary sat in ruins. But ultimately they rebuilt the church tower—which today evokes the rich but now-missing cultural tapestry that was once draped over this hill (free, always viewable).

Museum of Military History (Hadtörténeti Múzeum)—This fine museum explains various Hungarian military actions through history in painstaking detail. Watch military uniforms and weaponry evolve from the time of Árpád to today. With enough old uniforms and flags to keep an army-surplus store in stock for a decade, but limited English information, this place might interest military and history buffs.

Cost and Hours: 1,100 Ft, April-Sept Tue-Sun 10:00-18:00, Oct-March Tue-Sun 10:00-16:00, closed Mon year-round, Tóth Árpád sétány 40, district I, tel. 1/325-1600.

Under Castle Hill

The hill is honeycombed with caves and passages, which are accessible to tourists in two different locations: The better option ("Hospital in the Rock") comes with a fascinating tour illustrating how the caves were in active use during World War II and the Cold War; the Labyrinth offers a quicker visit with only a lightweight, quasi-historical exhibit.

▲**"Hospital in the Rock" Secret Military Hospital and Nuclear Bunker (Sziklakórház és Atombunker)**—Bring your Castle Hill visit into modern times with this engaging tour. Sprawling beneath Castle Hill is a 25,000-square-foot labyrinthine network of hospital and fallout-shelter corridors built during the mid-20th century. (Hidden access points are scattered throughout the tourist zone, aboveground.) While pricey, this visit is a must for doctors, nurses, and World War II buffs. I enjoy this as a lively interactive experience to balance out an otherwise sedate Castle Hill visit.

Cost and Hours: 3,600 Ft for required 1.25-hour tour, 10 percent discount with Matthias Church ticket, daily 10:00-20:00, English tours at the top of each hour, last tour departs at 19:00, gift shop like an army-surplus store, Lovas utca 4C, district I, mobile 0670-701-0101, www.hospitalintherock.com.

Getting There: To find the hospital, stand with your back to

Matthias Church and the Fishermen's Bastion. Walk straight past the plague column and down the little street (Szentháromság utca), then go down the covered steps at the wall. At the bottom of the stairs, turn right on Lovas utca, and walk 50 yards to the well-marked bunker entrance.

Background: At the outbreak of World War II, in 1939, the Hungarian government began building a secret emergency surgical hospital here in the heart of Budapest. When the war finally reached Hungary, in 1945, the hospital was in heavy use. While designed for 200 patients, eventually it held more than triple that number. Later, the forgotten hospital was used for two months to care for those injured in the 1956 Uprising. Then, as nuclear paranoia grew intense in the late 1950s and early 1960s, it was expanded to include a giant bomb shelter and potential post-nuclear-holocaust hospital.

Visiting the Hospital and Bunker: After decades in mothballs, the complex opened its doors to tourists a few years ago. First you'll watch an eight-minute movie (with English subtitles) about the history of the place. Then, on the required tour (about one hour in the hospital, then 15 minutes in the bunker), your guide leads you through the tunnels to see room after room of perfectly preserved WWII and 1960s-era medical supplies and equipment, most still in working order. More than a hundred wax figures engagingly bring the various hospital rooms to life: giant sick ward, operating room, and so on. On your way to the fallout shelter, you'll pass the decontamination showers, and see primitive radiation detectors and communist propaganda directing comrades how to save themselves in case of capitalist bombs or gas attacks. In the bunker, you'll also tour the various mechanical rooms that ventilated and provided water to this sprawling underground city.

Labyrinth of Buda Castle (Budavári Labirintus)—Armchair spelunkers can explore these dank and hazy caverns, with some wax figures in period costume, sparse historical information in English, a few actual stone artifacts, and a hokey Dracula exhibit (based on likely true notions that the "real" Dracula, the Transylvanian Duke Vlad Țepeș, was briefly imprisoned under Buda Castle). As this is indeed a labyrinth, expect to get lost—but don't worry; eventually you'll find your way out. After 18:00, they turn the lights out and give everyone gas lanterns. The exhibit loses something in the dark, but it's nicely spooky and a fun chance to startle amorous Hungarian teens—or be startled by mischievous ones. Even so, this hokey tourist trap pales in comparison to the other "underground" option.

Cost and Hours: 2,000 Ft, daily 10:00-19:30, last entry at 19:00, entrance between Royal Palace and Matthias Church at Úri utca 9, district I, tel. 1/212-0207, www.labirintus.com.

Gellért Hill (Gellérthegy) and Nearby

The hill rising from the Danube just downriver from the castle is Gellért Hill. When King István converted Hungary to Christi-

anity in the year 1000, he brought in Bishop Gellért, a monk from Venice, to tutor his son. But some rebellious Magyars had other ideas. They put the bishop in a barrel, drove long nails in from the outside, and rolled him down this hill...tenderizing him to death. Gellért became the patron saint of Budapest and gave his name to the hill that killed him. Today the hill is a fine place to commune with nature on a hike or jog, followed by a restorative splash in its namesake baths. The following sights are listed roughly from north to south.

Monument Hike—The north slope of Gel-lért Hill (facing Castle Hill) is good for a low-impact hike. You'll see many monuments, most notably the big memorial to Bishop Gel-lért himself (you can't miss it as you cross the Elisabeth Bridge on Hegyalja út). A bit far-ther up, seek out a newer monument to the world's great philosophers—Eastern, West-ern, and in between—from Gandhi to Plato to Jesus. Nearby is a scenic overlook with a king and a queen holding hands on either side of the Danube.

Citadella—This strategic, hill-capping fortress was built by the Habsburgs after the 1848 Revolution to keep an eye on their Hun-garian subjects. There's not much to do up here (no museum or exhibits), but it's a good destination for an uphill hike, and provides the best panoramic view over all of Budapest.

The hill is crowned by the **Liberation Monument,** featuring a woman holding aloft a palm branch. Locals call it "the lady with the big fish" or "the great bottle opener." A heroic Soviet soldier, who once inspired the workers with a huge red star from the base of the monument, is now in Memento Park (see page 88).

Getting There: It's a steep hike up from the river to the Cita-della. Bus #27 cuts some time off the trip, taking you up to the Búsuló Juhász stop (from which it's still an uphill hike to the for-tress). You can catch bus #27 from either side of Gellért Hill. From the southern edge of the hill, catch this bus at the Móricz Zsig-mond körtér stop (easy to reach: ride trams #19 or #41 south from anywhere along Buda's Danube embankment, or trams #47 or #49 from Pest's Small Boulevard ring road; you can also catch any of these trams at Gellért tér, in front of the Gellért Hotel). Alternatively, on the northern edge of the hill, catch bus #27 along the busy highway (Hegyalja út) that bisects Buda, at the intersection with Sánc utca (from central Pest, you can get to this stop on bus #78 from Astoria or Ferenciek tere).

Cave Church (Sziklatemplom)—Hidden in the hillside on the south end of the hill (across the street from Gellért Hotel) is Budapest's atmospheric cave church—burrowed right into the rock face. The communists bricked up this church when they came to power, but now it's open for visitors once again (500 Ft, unpredictable hours, closed to sightseers during frequent services). The little house at the foot of the hill (with the pointy turret) is where the monks who care for this church reside.

You might see something else in need of care here—stray cats, who are watched after by a local charity. Started by an American, this volunteer organization spays, neuters, and feeds the many stray cats who call Gellért Hill home (www.gellerthillcats.webeden. co.uk). They encourage visitors to drop by (best around dusk) and call to the cats to say hello.

▲▲Gellért Baths—Located at the famous and once-exclusive Gellért Hotel, right at the Buda end of the Liberty Bridge, this elegant bath complex has long been the city's top choice for a swanky, hedonistic soak. It's also awash in tourists, and the Széchenyi Baths beat it out for pure fun...but the Gellért Baths' mysterious (and gender-segregated) thermal spa rooms, and its giddy outdoor wave pool, make it an enticing thermal bath option.

Cost and Hours: 4,100 Ft for a locker, 300 Ft more for a personal changing cabin, cheaper after 17:00; open daily 6:00-20:00, last entry one hour before closing; Kelenhegyi út 4-6, district XI, tel. 1/466-6166, ext. 165, www.gellertbath.com.

۞ See the Thermal Baths chapter.

▲▲Rudas Baths—Along the Danube toward Castle Hill from Gellért Baths, Rudas (ROO-dawsh) offers Budapest's most old-fashioned, Turkish-style bathing experience. In fact, the main pools sit under a 500-year-old Ottoman dome. On weekdays, it's a nude, gender-segregated experience, as bathers move from pool to pool to tweak their body temperature. It becomes more accessible (and mixed) on weekends, when men and women put on swimsuits and mingle beneath that historic dome.

Cost and Hours: 2,900 Ft, 300 Ft more on weekends, cheaper weekdays 9:00-12:00; thermal baths open daily 6:00-20:00; men-only Mon and Wed-Fri, women-only Tue, both genders Sat-Sun, Döbrentei tér 9, district I, tel. 1/375-8373, www.rudasbaths.com.

۞ See the Thermal Baths chapter.

The Rest of Buda

There's not much of interest to tourists in Buda beyond Castle and Gellért Hills.

The **Víziváros** area, or "Water Town," is squeezed between Castle Hill and the Danube. While it's a great home base for sleeping and eating (see those chapters for details), and home to the Budai Vigadó concert venue (see the Entertainment in Budapest chapter), there's little in the way of sightseeing. The riverfront Batthyány tér area, at the northern edge of Víziváros, is both a transportation hub (M2/red Metró line, HÉV suburban railway to Óbuda and Szentendre, and embankment trams) and a shopping and dining center.

To the north of Castle Hill is **Széll Kálmán tér,** a transportation hub (for the M2/red Metró line, several trams, and buses #16, #16A, and #116 to Castle Hill) and shopping center (featuring the giant Mammut supermall, and many smaller shops that cling to it like barnacles to a boat). This unpretentious zone, while light on sightseeing, offers a chance to commune with workaday Budapest. Its one attraction is **Millenáris Park,** an inviting play zone for adults and kids that combines grassy fields and modern buildings. Though not worth going out of your way for, this park might be worth a stroll if the weather's nice and you're exploring the neighborhood (a long block behind Mammut mall).

Rózsadomb ("Rose Hill"), rising just north of Széll Kálmán tér, was so named for the rose garden planted on its slopes by a Turkish official 400 years ago. Today it's an upscale residential zone.

To the south, the district called the **Tabán**—roughly between Castle Hill and Gellért Hill—was once a colorful, ramshackle neighborhood of sailor pubs and brothels. After being virtually wiped out in World War II, now it's home to parks and a dull residential district.

Beyond riverfront Buda, the terrain becomes hilly. This area—the **Buda Hills**—is a pleasant getaway for a hike or stroll through wooded terrain, but still close to the city. One enjoyable way to explore these hills is by hopping a ride on the Children's Railway (see the Budapest with Children chapter).

Two other major attractions—the part of town called **Óbuda** ("Old Buda") and **Memento Park**—are on the Buda side of the river but away from the center, and described in the following sections.

Outer Budapest

The following sights, while technically within Budapest, take a little more time to reach.

Óbuda

Budapest was originally three cities: Buda, Pest, and Óbuda. Óbuda ("Old Buda") is the oldest of the three—the first known residents of the region (Celts) settled here, and today it's still littered with ruins from the next occupants (Romans). Despite all the history, the district ranks relatively low on the list of Budapest's sightseeing priorities: Aside from a charming small-town ambience on its main square, it offers a pair of good museums on two important 20th-century Hungarian artists, and—a short train ride away—some Roman ruins.

Getting There: To reach the first three sights listed here, go to Batthyány tér in Buda (M2/red Metró line) and catch the HÉV suburban train north to the Szentlélek tér stop. The Vasarely Museum is 50 yards from the station (exit straight ahead, away from the river; it's on the right, behind the bus stops). The town square is 100 yards beyond that (bear right around the corner), and 200 yards later (turn left at the ladies with the umbrellas), you'll find the Imre Varga Collection. Aquincum is three stops farther north on the HÉV line.

▲**Vasarely Museum**—This museum features two floors of eye-popping, colorful paintings by Victor Vasarely, the founder of Op

Art. If you're not going to Vasarely's hometown of Pécs, which has an even better museum of his works (see page 387), this place gives you a good taste. The exhibition—displayed in a large, white hall with each piece labeled in English—follows his artistic evolution from his youth as a graphic designer to the playful optical illusions he was most famous for. You'll find most of these trademark works (as well as temporary exhibits of other artists) upstairs. Sit on a comfy bench and stare into Vasarely's mind-bending world. Let yourself get a little woozy. Think of how this style combines right-brained abstraction with an almost rigidly left-brained, geometrical approach. It makes my brain hurt (or maybe it's just all the wavy lines). Vasarely and the movement he pioneered helped to inspire the trippy styles of the 1960s. If the art gets you pondering Rubik's Cube, it will come as no surprise that Ernő Rubik was a professor of mathematics here in Budapest.

SIGHTS IN BUDAPEST

Cost and Hours: 800 Ft, Tue-Sun 10:00-17:30, closed Mon, Szentlélek tér 6, district III, tel. 1/388-7551, www.vasarely.hu. The museum is immediately on the right as you leave the Szentlélek tér HÉV station.

Óbuda Main Square (Fő Tér)—If you keep going past the Vasarely Museum and turn right, you enter Óbuda's cute Main Square. The big, yellow building was the Óbuda Town Hall when this was its own city. Today it's still the office of the district mayor. While still well within the city limits of Budapest, this charming square feels like its own small town.

To the right of the Town Hall is a whimsical, much-pho-

tographed statue of **women with umbrellas.** Replicas of this sculpture, by local artist Imre Varga, decorate the gardens of wealthy summer homes on Lake Balaton. Varga created many of Budapest's distinctive monuments, including the *Tree of*

Life behind the Great Synagogue and a major work that's on display at Memento Park. His museum is just down the street (turn left at the umbrella ladies).

▲**Imre Varga Collection (Varga Imre Gyűjtemény)**—Imre Varga, who worked from the 1950s through the 2000s, is one of Hungary's most prominent artists, and probably its single best sculptor. This humble museum—crammed with his works (originals, as well as smaller replicas of Varga statues you'll see all over Hungary), and with a fine sculpture garden out back—offers a good introduction to the man's substantial talent. Working mostly with steel, his pieces can appear rough and tangled at times, but are always evocative and lifelike. Unfortunately, English information is virtually nonexistent here. If you're planning a visit, try to be here on Saturday morning. That's when Varga himself, now in his 80s, drops by at 10:00 to chat with visitors. He speaks English and he enjoys explaining his art.

Cost and Hours: 800 Ft, Tue-Sun 10:00-18:00, closed Mon, Laktanya utca 7, district III, Szentlélek tér HÉV station, tel. 1/250-0274, www.budapestgaleria.hu.

Visiting the Museum: The first room holds a replica of a sculpture of St. István approaching the Virgin Mary, the original of which is in the Vatican. The next room has several small-scale copies of famous Varga works from around the country, including some you might recognize from Budapest (such as the *Tree of Life* from behind the Great Synagogue).

Pause at the statue with the headless, saluting soldier wearing medals. Through the communist times, there were three types of artists: banned, tolerated, and supported. Varga was tolerated, and works like this subtly commented on life under communism. In fact, the medallions nailed to the figure's chest were Varga's own, from his pre-communist military service. Anyone with such medallions was persecuted by communists in the 1950s...so Varga disposed of his this way.

Nearby is the exit to the garden out back, with a smattering of life-size portraits (including three prostitutes leaning against a wall, illustrating the passing of time). The rest of the museum is predominantly filled with portraits (mostly busts) of various important Hungarians. You'll see variations on certain themes that intrigued Varga, including a reclining ballerina.

Aquincum Museum—Long before Magyars laid eyes on the Danube, Óbuda was the Roman city of Aquincum. Here you can explore the remains of the 2,000-year-old Roman town and amphitheater. The museum is proud of its centerpiece, a water organ.

Cost and Hours: 1,500 Ft; May-Sept Tue-Sun 9:00-18:00, closed Mon; Oct and late April Tue-Sun 9:00-17:00, closed Mon; Nov-mid-April Tue-Sun 9:00-16:00, closed Mon; Szentendrei út 139, district III, HÉV north to Aquincum stop, tel. 1/250-1650, www.aquincum.hu.

Getting There: From the HÉV stop, cross the busy road and turn to the right. Go through the railway underpass, and you'll see the ruins ahead and on the left as you emerge.

▲▲Memento Park (a.k.a. Statue Park)

Little remains of the communist era in Budapest. To sample those drab and surreal times, head to this motley collection of statues, which seem to be preaching their Marxist ideology to each other in an open field on the outskirts of town. You'll see the great figures of the Soviet Bloc, both international (Lenin, Marx, and Engels) and Hungarian (local bigwig Béla Kun) as well as gigantic, stoic figures representing Soviet ideals. This stiff dose of Socialist Realist art, while time-consuming to reach, is rewarding for those curious for a taste of history that most Hungarians would rather forget.

Cost and Hours: 1,500 Ft, daily 10:00-sunset, six miles southwest of city center at the corner of Balatoni út and Szabadka út, district XXII, tel. 1/424-7500, www.mementopark.hu.

Getting There: A handy bus goes from Deák tér in downtown Pest to the park (year-round daily at 11:00, July-Aug also at 15:00; round-trip takes 2.5 hours total, including a 1.5-hour visit to the park, 4,900-Ft round-trip includes park entry). You can also get there by public transit, but it's more complicated.

○ See the Memento Park Tour chapter.

Beyond Budapest

For information on the village of **Szentendre** and the Royal Palace at **Gödöllő** (both just outside the city limits), as well as some places farther afield (the royal castles at Visegrád, the great church at Esztergom, and the folk village of Hollókő), see the Day Trips from Budapest chapter.

THERMAL BATHS

Fürdő

Splashing and relaxing in Budapest's thermal baths is the city's top attraction. Though it might sound daunting, bathing with the Magyars is far more accessible than you'd think. The first two thermal baths I've described in this chapter (Széchenyi and Gellért) are basically like your hometown swimming pool—except the water is 100 degrees, there are plenty of jets and bubbles to massage away your stress, and you're surrounded by scantily clad Hungarians. If you want a more "authentic" and naked experience, I've also described one of those (Rudas).

All this fun goes way back. Hungary's Carpathian Basin is essentially a thin crust covering a vast reservoir of hot water. The Romans named their settlement near present-day Budapest Aquincum—meaning "abundant waters"—and took advantage of those waters by building many baths. Centuries later, the occupying Ottomans revived the custom. And today, thermal baths are as Hungarian as can be.

Locals brag that if you poke a hole in the ground anywhere in Hungary, you'll find a hot-water spring. Judging from Budapest, they could be right: The city has 123 natural springs and some two dozen thermal baths *(fürdő)*. The baths, which are all operated by the same government agency, are actually a part of the health-care system. Doctors regularly prescribe treatments that include massage, soaking in baths of various heat and mineral compositions, and swimming laps. For these patients (who you might see carrying a blue ticket), a visit to the bath is subsidized.

But increasingly, there's a new angle on Hungary's hot water:

entertainment. Adventure water parks are springing up all over the country, and even the staid old baths have some enjoyable jets and currents. Overcome your jitters, follow my instructions, and dive in...or miss out on *the* quintessential Budapest experience.

Orientation

American tourists often feel squeamish at the thought of bathing with Speedo-clad, pot-bellied Hungarians. Relax! It's less intimidating than it sounds—and the fun you'll have far outweighs the jitters. I was nervous on my first visit, too. But now I feel like a trip to

Hungary just isn't complete without a splish-splash in the bath.

While Budapest has several mostly nude, gender-segregated Turkish baths (such as Rudas), my favorites—Széchenyi and Gellért—are less intimidating: Men and women are usually together, and you can keep your swimsuit on the entire time. (Even at mixed baths, there generally are a few clothing-optional, gender-segregated areas, where locals are likely to be nude—or wearing a *kötény*, a loose-fitting loincloth.)

Bring along these items, if you have them: a swimsuit, towel, flip-flops, soap and shampoo for a shower afterward, a comb or brush, and maybe sunscreen and leisure reading. Hotels typically frown on guests taking their room towels to the baths. Try asking nicely if they have some loaner towels just for this purpose (they'll probably tell you to rent one there...but what they don't know won't hurt them). At Budapest's baths, you can usually rent a towel or swimsuit (for men, Speedos are always available, trunks sometimes).

Each bath complex has multiple pools, used for different purposes. Big pools with cooler water are for serious swimming, while

the smaller, hotter thermal baths (*gyógyfürdő*, or simply *gőz*) are for relaxing, enjoying the jets and current pools, and playing chess. The water bubbles up from hot springs at 77° Celsius (170° Fahrenheit), then is mixed with cooler water to achieve the desired temperatures. Most pools are marked with the

THERMAL BATHS

water temperature in Celsius (cooler pools are about 30°C/86°F; warmer pools are closer to 36°C/97°F or 38°C/100°F, about like the hot tub back home; and the hottest are 42°C/108°F...yowtch!). Locals hit the cooler pools first, then work their way up to the top temps.

While the lap pools are chlorinated, most of the thermal baths are only lightly chlorinated, or not at all. Unlike swimming pools in the US—where the water is recycled back into the pool—water here is slowly drained out and replaced with fresh water from the hot springs. Locals figure this makes chemicals unnecessary. Still, total germophobes may not be entirely comfortable at the baths; either convince yourself to go with the flow, or skip the trip.

You'll also usually find a dry sauna, a wet steam room, a cold plunge pool (for a pleasurable jolt when you're feeling overheated), and sunbathing areas (which may be segregated and clothing-optional). Some baths have fun flourishes: bubbles, whirlpools, massage jets, wave pools, and so on.

The most challenging part of visiting a Hungarian bath is the inevitably complicated entrance procedure. This is one of today's best time-travel experiences to communist Eastern Europe. Things have gotten much easier in recent years, but you'll still be confronted with a complex payment scheme, lengthy menus of massages and other treatments, and occasionally monolingual staff. While it seems confusing at first, it's more logical than you might think—and, thankfully, English translations of your ticket options and directions to various parts of the complex are posted. Although I've carefully outlined the specifics for each bath, they can change from year to year. Some general tips: Keep track of any receipt or slip of paper you're given, as you may be asked to show it later (for example, to get your towel deposit back). Hang in there, go where people direct you, and enjoy this unique cultural experience. Remember, they're used to tourists—so don't be afraid to act like one. If you can make it through those first few confusing minutes, you'll soon be relaxing like a pro.

Advance tickets for the baths are sold in hotel lobbies and other sales outlets all over town. But as there's rarely a line to buy a bath ticket, prebooking makes little sense—just buy your tickets when you arrive at the bath.

Budapest's baths recently upgraded to a system that uses a plastic, watch-like wristband as your ticket. When you enter, touch the wristband to the entry turnstile, then again to be assigned a changing cabin or to access a locker, then again each time you want to unlock your cabin or locker. When you're done, drop the wristband into a slot as you exit the turnstile. This wristband system frees you up to enjoy and explore the baths, since you don't have to rely on a grumpy attendant to direct you, or lock and unlock your cabin.

While enjoying the baths, you can leave your clothing and other belongings in your locked cabin or locker. Although I've found these to be safe, and bath employees assure me that thefts are rare (a cabin is safer than a locker), it's at your own risk. Another option is to leave valuables in a safe (generally costs 500 Ft, ask when you buy ticket). Many locals bring plastic shopping bags to hold their essentials: towels, leisure reading, and sunscreen.

Be aware that the jets, bubbles, waves, waterfalls, and whirlpools sometimes take turns running. For example, a current pool runs for 10 minutes, then a series of jets starts up and the current pool stops for 10 minutes, then the current pool starts up again, and so on. If a particularly fun feature of the pool doesn't seem to be working, just give it a few minutes.

Here are some useful phrases:

English	Hungarian	Pronounced
Bath	*Fürdő*	FEWR-dur
Men	*Férfi*	FAYR-fee
Women	*Női*	NUR-ee
Changing Cabin	*Kabin*	KAH-been
Locker	*Szekrény*	SEHK-rayn
Ticket Office	*Pénztár*	PAYNZ-tar
Thermal Bath	*Gyógyfürdő,*	JODGE-fewr-dur,
	Gőz	gorz

Please trust me, and take the plunge. My readers almost unanimously report that the thermal baths were their top Hungarian experience. If you go into it with an easygoing attitude and a sense of humor, I promise you'll have a blast.

The Baths

Budapest's two-dozen baths *(fürdő)* were taken over by the communist government, and they're all still owned by the city. The three baths listed here are the best-known, most representative, and most convenient for first-timers: The Széchenyi Baths are more casual and popular with locals; the Gellért Baths are touristy, famous, and genteel; and the Rudas Baths are old-school Turkish, with more nudity and less "fun" (unless you find public nudity fun...but that's a whole other book). To me, Széchenyi is second to none, but some travelers prefer the Gellért or Rudas experience. As they're all quite different, doing more than one is an excellent option. For more information on all of Budapest's baths, see www.budapestgyogy-furdoi.hu or www.spasbudapest.com.

▲▲▲Széchenyi Baths (Széchenyi Fürdő)

To soak with the locals, head for this bath complex—the big, yellow, copper-domed building in the middle of City Park.

Széchenyi (SAY-chehn-yee) is the best of Budapest's many bath experiences. Relax and enjoy some Hungarian good living. Magyars of all shapes and sizes stuff themselves into tiny swimsuits and strut their stuff. Housewives float blissfully in the warm water. Intellectuals and Speedo-clad elder statesmen stand in chest-high water around chessboards and ponder their next moves. This is Budapest at its best.

Cost: 3,400 Ft for locker (in gender-segregated locker room), 400 Ft more for personal changing cabin, 150 Ft more on weekends, cheaper if you arrive after 19:00. The price includes the outdoor swimming pool area and the indoor thermal bath and sauna (but note that the indoor sections close earlier—see below). Couples can share a changing cabin: One person pays the cabin rate, the other pays the locker rate, but both use the same cabin.

Hours: Swimming pool (the best part, outdoors) open daily 6:00-22:00, indoor thermal bath and sauna open daily 6:00-19:00, last entry one hour before closing. On some summer weekends, the baths may be open later (see "Night Bathing," later).

Location and Entrances: In City Park at Állatkerti körút 11, district XIV, M1: Széchenyi fürdő. The huge bath complex has three entrances. The busiest one—technically the **"thermal bath entrance"**—is the grand main entry, facing south (roughly toward Vajdahunyad Castle). I avoid this entrance—there's often a line during peak times, and it's a bit more confusing to find your way once inside. Instead, I prefer the **"swimming pool entrance,"** facing the zoo on the other side of the complex—it's faster and more user-friendly, has shorter lines, and is open later. A third, smaller **"medical entrance,"** to the right as you face the zoo entry (near the Metró station), provides access to either the thermal bath changing rooms or the swimming pool changing rooms, but can also have long lines (tel. 1/363-3210, www.szechenyibath.com).

Massage: A wide array of massages and other special treatments are offered—find the English menu in the lobby. If you're interested in this, set up an appointment and pay at the office near

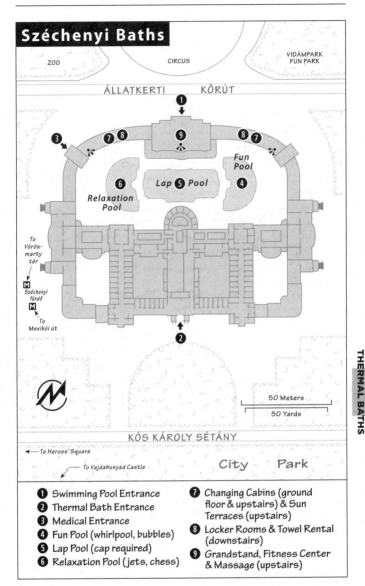

Széchenyi Baths

ZOO
CIRCUS
VIDÁMPARK
FUN PARK

ÁLLATKERTI   KÖRÚT

1

3

7 **8**

9

8 **7**

Fun
Pool

6

Lap **5** Pool

4

Relaxation
Pool

To
Vörös-
marty
tér

M
Széchenyi
fürdő
M
To
Mexikói út

2

50 Meters

50 Yards

KÓS KÁROLY SÉTÁNY

← To Heroes' Square

To Vajdahunyad Castle

City   Park

1 Swimming Pool Entrance
2 Thermal Bath Entrance
3 Medical Entrance
4 Fun Pool (whirlpool, bubbles)
5 Lap Pool (cap required)
6 Relaxation Pool (jets, chess)

7 Changing Cabins (ground
floor & upstairs) & Sun
Terraces (upstairs)
8 Locker Rooms & Towel Rental
(downstairs)
9 Grandstand, Fitness Center
& Massage (upstairs)

THERMAL BATHS

the towel-rental desk (3,000-4,900 Ft, expect 15-30-minute wait for your appointment when it's busy). Note that these massages are medicinal—not the mellow, soothing variety you might expect back home. You'll pay more for something more hedonistic. There are two other options: a Thai massage parlor at the upper level of the complex (above the swimming pool entrance—just follow the signs) and a separate "information" desk just inside the swimming-pool entrance where you can book a "V.I.P. massage" (either option costs 11,000-14,000 Ft/1 hour).

Night Bathing: The baths are a joy in the evening, when both the price and the crowds are reduced. In cool weather, or even rain or snow, the pools maintain their hot temperatures—making this a delightful after-hours activity. Busy sightseers can be extremely efficient by closing down the museums, then heading to the baths. The only caveat: The indoor (and less appealing) thermal bath sections close after 19:00.

Additionally, Széchenyi is open late into the night on summer weekends, for an event called *Szecska* ("Chaff"), with a nightclub atmosphere (4,000 Ft, late June-early Sept Sat 22:00-4:00 in the morning, www.szecska.hu); also in summer, Széchenyi may periodically host a late-night weekend "sparty" called Cinetrip, where the bath complex basically becomes one big hot-water dance club (for schedule and details, see www.cinetrip.hu). As these late-night hours are a fairly recent addition, confirm that the baths are open before making the trip.

Entry Procedure: While the following details might seem intimidating, it's easier than it sounds. Take your time and you'll eventually find your way. These instructions assume that you're using the swimming pool entrance (from this entrance, there are parallel facilities in each direction).

First, in the grand lobby, pay the cashier. You'll be given a waterproof, watch-like wristband with an electronic chip inside. Touch your wristband to the panel on the turnstile to enter the complex. Just after the turnstile, pause to get oriented: Straight ahead is a row of private changing cabins. At the start of this row is a stairwell. If you go **up the stairs,** you'll find another floor of changing cabins (as well as the Thai massage area, gender-segregated "solarium" sun terraces, and a fun grandstand overlooking the main pool—these are ideal vantage points to snap some photos before you change). If you go **down the stairs,** you'll find a long hallway lined with hairdryers and mirrors; the locker rooms are at each end (remember, men are *férfi* and women are *női*). Also downstairs, you'll find the counter where you can rent a towel or swimsuit (do this before you change, as you'll need money: towel-600 Ft plus refundable 1,000-Ft deposit; swimsuit-1,000 Ft plus refundable 5,000-Ft deposit). Renting a small safe for your valuables costs 500 Ft.

Report to the area that you paid for (private cabin or locker room). If you paid for a **cabin,** look for an electronic panel on the

wall, and hold your wristband against this panel for a few seconds—you'll automatically be assigned a number for a cabin. Go
find your cabin. When you touch your wristband to the lock, the
light turns blue and the door unlocks. The door should lock automatically when you close it (but test it to be sure). You can reopen
your cabin as often as you like. If you forget the number of your
cabin, just touch your wristband to the panel in the hall, and it'll
remind you.

If you paid for a **locker,** you can head for the locker room and
choose any open one. Once you hold your wristband against it to
lock it, it can only be unlocked by that same wristband.

If you get confused, the attendants (who usually speak a few
words of English) can help you find your way.

Phew. Now that you've changed into your swimsuit and stored
your belongings, let's have some fun.

Taking the Waters: The bath complex has two parts, outside
and inside.

For most visitors, the
best part is the swimming
pool area **outside.** Orient
yourself to the three pools
(facing the main, domed
building): The pool to the
left is for fun (cooler water—
30°C/86°F, warmer in win-
ter, lots of jets and bubbles,

lively and often crowded, includes circular current pool); the pool
on the right is for relaxation (warmer water—38°C/100°F, mellow atmosphere, a few massage jets, chess); and the main pool in
the center is all business (cooler water—28°C/82°F in summer,
26°C/79°F in winter, people doing laps, swimming cap required).
You get extra credit for joining the gang in a chess match. Stairs
to saunas (with cold plunge pools, cold showers, and even an ice
maker) are below the doors to the indoor thermal bath complex.

There's a basic **snack bar** right in the middle of the complex,
but you're allowed to bring in your own food if you munch dis-
creetly.

For good **views**—or to use the well-equipped **fitness center**—
climb up the stairs near the front of the changing-cabin hallways.
There you'll find the grandstand area overlooking the main pool,
with the fitness center just above it.

If you're feeling waterlogged and need a break from the
baths, it's fun just to explore the sprawling complex. It's a bit of
a maze, but don't be afraid to poke around (but keep in mind
that several areas—such as the solarium sun terraces up top—are

gender-segregated; again, men are *férfi* and women are *női*). Go for a photo safari, and don't miss the grandstand.

Inside the main building is the thermal bath section, a series of mixed-gender indoor pools; each of these is designed for a specific medical treatment. You'll notice each one is labeled with the temperature (ranging from 28°C/82°F to 36°C/97°F to 38°C/100°F; you'll also find steam rooms with a 18°C/64°F cold plunge pool nearby). The pools also have varying types and amounts of healthy minerals—some of which can make the water quite green and/or stinky. Hungarians who use Széchenyi Baths medicinally have worked out a specific regimen for moving from pool to pool. But if all of this smelly water is lost on you (as it is on many foreigners), it's totally fine to focus on the fun outdoor pools. (I've had many great visits to Széchenyi Baths without ever going inside the thermal bath complex.)

Exit Procedure: When you leave, be sure to leave your locker open. If you rented a towel or swimsuit, return it to the desk where you got it to reclaim your deposit. Then, as you exit the complex, insert your wristband into the little slot at the turnstile to exit. Then continue your sightseeing...soggy, but relaxed.

If you're heading to the **Metró,** the station is very close, but easy to miss: It's basically a pair of nondescript stairwells in the middle of the park, roughly toward Heroes' Square from the thermal bath entrance (look for the low-profile, yellow *Földalatti* sign; to head for downtown, take the stairwell marked *a Vörösmarty tér felé*).

▲▲Gellért Baths (Gellért Fürdő)

Using the baths at Gellért (GEH-layrt) Hotel costs a bit more than the Széchenyi Baths, and you won't run into nearly as many locals; this is definitely a more upscale, touristy, spa-like scene. Because most of the warmest pools are in gender-segregated areas (except on weekends), it's not ideal for opposite-sex couples or families who want to spend time together. But if you want a soothing, luxurious bath experience in an elegant setting, this is the place. And if it's fun you're looking for, the Gellért Baths have something that Széchenyi doesn't: a huge, deliriously enjoyable wave pool that'll toss you around like a queasy surfer (summer only).

Cost: 4,100 Ft for a locker, 300 Ft more for a personal changing cabin, cheaper if you arrive after 17:00.

Hours: Daily 6:00-20:00, last entry one hour before closing.

Note that on Saturdays and Sundays, the thermal bath areas are mixed; on weekdays, they're gender-segregated.

Location: It's on the Buda side of the green Liberty Bridge (trams #47 and #49 from Deák tér in Pest, or trams #19 and #41 along the Buda embankment from Víziváros below the castle, Gellért tér stop). The entrance to the baths is under the white dome opposite the bridge (Kelenhegyi út 4-6, district XI, tel. 1/466-6166, ext. 165, www.gellertbath.com).

Entry Procedure: The grand entry hall is fully open to visitors, so feel free to poke around to get the lay of the land before buying your ticket (good views from the gallery up above). The entrance doors are flanked by ticket windows, and on the left is a window where you can deposit valuables in the safe (500 Ft). Halfway down the hall on the right is an information booth that usually has English-speaking staff.

In the summer, they sell two different tickets based on which changing area you'll use (same price for either ticket). With a **thermal bath ticket,** you'll change in a large, gender-segregated area that connects directly to the also-segregated thermal baths (so some people walk nude directly from their cabins to the bath); opposite-sex couples can't share a changing cabin here. With a **swimming pool ticket,** you'll go to a mixed area where opposite-sex couples can share a cabin (this area also has gender-segregated locker rooms). Both tickets allow you to move freely between the thermal baths and swimming pool areas once you're inside. I prefer the swimming pool section, which has more secure lockers. Couples who want to share a cabin should ask for "swimming pool ticket, one cabin, one locker."

A dizzying array of **massages** and other treatment options are also sold at the ticket windows. Most are available only with a doctor's note, but some massages are for anyone (generally 3,200

Ft/20 minutes, 4,200 Ft/30 minutes, 5,200 Ft/40 minutes; arrange a time when you buy your ticket). Upstairs, you can also book a Thai massage.

Buy your ticket (and, if you like, pay for a massage), and you'll be issued a plastic wristband that acts as your ticket. Then glide through the swanky lobby. The indoor swimming pool is on your right, about halfway down the main hall. Looking through the window to the pool, visualize the perfectly symmetrical bath complex: The men's thermal bath, changing cabins, and lockers are on the left, while the identical women's facilities are on the right. The two sections meet at this shared pool in the center.

If you bought a swimming pool ticket, you'll touch your wristband to the turnstile and enter here: Men/*férfi* go down the stairs on the left, and women/*nôi* on the right (either way, you'll head down a long hallway, then up stairs to the changing areas—a mixed-gender area for cabins down below, with a segregated locker area up above). If you have a thermal bath ticket, the entrances are a bit farther away: women to the right, closer to the entrance; and men to the left, at the end of the hall.

If you want to rent a towel (600 Ft) or swimsuit (1,000 Ft; both with a 4,000-Ft deposit, cash only), look for the desk near the entrance to the changing cabin area.

Once inside the changing area, if you bought a cabin ticket, hold your wristband against the electronic panel to be assigned a changing cabin number. Once you track it down, touch your wristband to the cabin to open it. The door locks automatically behind you (but test it just to be sure). If you bought a locker ticket, you can choose any open locker, then lock it with your wristband. It can only be unlocked using that same wristband.

Taking the Waters: Once you've changed, you can spend your time either indoors or out. From the locker room, look for signs *to the effervescent bath-pool* (for the indoor section) or *to the swimming-pool with artificial waves* (for the outdoor section).

Inside, the central, mixed-gender, genteel-feeling hall is home to a cool-water swimming pool (swimming cap required—free loaners available) and a crowded hot-water pool (36°C/97°F). On sunny days, they crank open the retractable roof; for nice views down onto the pool, find the stairs up near the locker rooms. Back toward the main hall are doors to the gender-segregated, clothing-optional massage rooms and thermal baths (easy to miss—walk to far end of pool and look for signs). These grand old halls, slathered with colorful porcelain decorations, have big pools at either end: 36°C (97°F) and 38°C (100°F). Notice that these temperatures perfectly flank the normal temperature of the human body, allowing you to toggle your temp at will. At the far end of the bath are a steam room (45-50°C/113-122°F) and a cold plunge pool (18°C/64°F). Back out near the changing cabins is a dry sauna (a.k.a. "dry sweating rooms," 50-70°C/122-158°F). If you paid for a massage, report to the massage room in this section at your appointed time—or just show up and see if they can take you.

Outside, you'll find several sunbathing areas and a warm

Welcome to Chisago Lakes Area Library!
You checked out the following items:

1. Rick Steves' Budapest
   Due: 7/6/17 11:59 PM
   Barcode: 32050006896937

2. Frommer's Germany 20
   Due: 7/6/17 11:59 PM
   Barcode: 32050007016576

3. The hate u give
   Due: 7/6/17 11:59 PM
   Barcode: 32050008152578

4. How about a hug?
   Due: 7/6/17 11:59 PM
   Barcode: 32050006553538

EC-CL 2017-06-15 16:37
You were helped by Kirsten

thermal pool (hiding up the stairs on the right). But the main attraction is the big, unheated wave pool in the center (generally closed Oct-April, weather-dependent). Not for the squeamish, this pool thrashes fun-loving swimmers around like driftwood. The swells in the deeper area are fun and easy to float on, but the crashing waves at the shallow end are vigorous, if not dangerous. If there are no waves, just wait around for a while (you'll hear a garbled message on the loudspeaker five minutes before the tide comes in).

Exit Procedure: When you're finished, return your towel and swimsuit to reclaim your deposit, then insert your wristband into the slot at the exit turnstile. If you had a locker, remember to leave it unlocked when you leave (otherwise, when you try to exit they'll send you back to unlock it).

▲▲Rudas Baths (Rudas Fürdő)

To get to the Turkish roots of Budapest's obsession with thermal baths, head for Rudas (ROO-dawsh). The most historic, local, and potentially intimidating of the three baths I list, Rudas feels more

like the classic Turkish baths of yore: On most days, it's men-only, and those men wander around nude or in flimsy loin-cloths under a 500-year-old dome first built by the Otto-man Turks. These baths are not about splashy fun—there are

no jets, bubbles, or whirlpools. Instead, Rudas is about history, and about serious temperature modulation—stepping your body temperature up and down between very hot and very cold. While not for the skittish, Rudas offers adventurous travelers and bath connoisseurs another facet of the Budapest baths experience. Be aware that all of Budapest's single-sex, nude baths are (to varying degrees) a popular meeting point for the local gay community—though Rudas is less so than some others (such as Király Baths). Rudas becomes far more widely accessible to all visitors on weekends (Sat-Sun), when men and women mingle together in swimsuits under the fine old dome; then, at nighttime (Fri-Sat only), this old chamber becomes a modern nightclub until the wee hours.

Cost: The thermal bath costs 2,900 Ft, 300 Ft more on weekends, cheaper weekdays 9:00-12:00; the swimming pool has a separate ticket for 1,900 Ft, but there's no point coming here for the swimming pool (boring and modern; the ones at Széchenyi and Gellért are better).

Hours: The thermal baths (the part you're interested in) are open daily 6:00-20:00, last entry one hour before closing. The baths are open only to men Mon and Wed-Fri; only to women Tue; and to both men and women Sat-Sun.

Location: It's in a low-profile building at the foot of Gellért Hill, just south of the white Elisabeth Bridge (Döbrentei tér 9, district I, tel. 1/375-8373, www.rudasbaths.com). From the Döbrentei stop on trams #19 and #41 (along the Buda riverfront, between the Gellért Baths and Batthyány tér), walk under the off-ramps for the big white bridge, pass the statue of Elisabeth, and go through the tunnel. The baths are straight ahead.

Night Bathing: In addition to normal opening hours, the baths are open—to both men and women, in swimsuits—with a dance hall ambience Fri-Sat 22:00-4:00 in the morning (3,600 Ft). Additionally, Rudas may host special late-night Cinetrip parties on some weekends (for details, see www.cinetrip.hu).

Entry Procedure: Buy your ticket, and if you want, rent a towel (300 Ft for a "bath sheet," plus 1,000-Ft refundable deposit) or a swimsuit (1,000 Ft plus 4,000-Ft deposit), or book a massage. You can choose between two types: The "aroma relax massage" is a gentle, quiet experience more typical of an American-style massage (though still more medicinal than hedonistic), while the "water massage with soap" is rougher (for exfoliating) and in a noisy, busy room (either type costs 3,000 Ft/20 minutes, 4,000 Ft/30 minutes, 4,900 Ft/40 minutes).

You'll be issued a plastic wristband, which you'll use to go through the turnstile into the changing area (two floors of private cabins—there are no lockers in the thermal bath section). If you paid to rent a towel or swimsuit, give your receipt to the attendant to claim it now. Hold your wristband against the electronic panel on the wall for a few seconds to be assigned a cabin number, then find that cabin and touch your wristband to the lock in order to open it. After you change and are ready to explore the complex, the cabin should lock automatically when you close the door (but test it just to be sure).

If you're here on a mixed day (Sat-Sun), the dress code is swimsuits. On other days, bathers can go nude, and many of the men wear a flimsy loincloth called a *kötény* (issued as you enter). If you're a self-conscious, gawky tourist (it happens to the best of us), you can wear your swimsuit...although you might get some funny looks.

Taking the Waters: This historic complex was thoroughly renovated a few years go, making the outer section feel almost institutional. But the innermost section transports you half a millennium back.

Rudas is all about modulating your body temperature—pushing your body to its limit with heat, then dousing off quickly with a bucket of cold water, then heating up again, and so on. The different temperatures are designed to let you do this as gradually or quickly as you like.

The central chamber, under an original 35-foot-high Turkish dome supported by eight pillars, is the historic core of the baths. The main, octagonal pool in the center is surrounded by four smaller pools, each in its own corner. Working clockwise from the right as you enter, the four corner pools get progressively hotter: 28°C (82°F), 30° C (86°F), 33°C (91°F), and 42°C (108°F). While the hottest pool feels almost scalding at first, you can ease your way into it, the same way you would into cold water. Conveniently, the largest, central pool—at 36°C (97°F)—is not too hot, not too cold...juuuust right.

Along one wall are entrances to the wet sauna (*nedves gőzkamra*, to the left), with 50°C (122°F) scented steam; and the dry sauna (*hőlégkamra*, to the right), with three progressively hotter rooms ranging from 45°C (113° F) to 72°C (161°F). Near the entrance to each one is a shower or—if you don't want to beat around the bush—a bucket of frigid water (pull the rope for immediate relief if you're feeling overheated).

Surrounding this central chamber are hallways with other areas: resting rooms, tanning beds (*szolarium*, costs extra), massage rooms, a cold plunge pool, and a scale to see how much sweat you've lost.

Float on your back for a while in the main octagonal pool, pondering the faintly glittering translucent tiles embedded in the old Turkish dome. You'll notice that the voices echoing around that dome are mostly Hungarians—there are very few tourists here. You might see people stretching, moving from pool to pool very purposefully, or even doing chin-ups from the metal supports; some are athletes, training for their next event.

Exit Procedure: After changing, return your rental towel and swimsuit to the attendant and get your receipt; present this at the front desk (along with your original towel receipt) to get your deposit back. Then drop your wristband through the little slot at the turnstile, head out the door, and stumble along the Danube...as relaxed as you'll ever be.

Aaaaahhh.

LEOPOLD TOWN WALK

Lipótváros, from the Parliament to the Chain Bridge

The Parliament building, which dominates Pest's skyline, is the centerpiece of a banking and business district that bustles by day, but for the most part is relatively quiet at night and on weekends. Called Lipótváros ("Leopold Town"), this area is one of Budapest's most genteel quarters, and features some of the best of Budapest's many monuments. This walk also takes in several of the city's most grandiose landmarks: the Parliament, St. István's Basilica, the Gresham Palace, and the Chain Bridge.

Note: If you're planning to tour the Parliament interior, get tickets before you begin this walk (as explained on page 60). Then do the first part of this walk while waiting for your Parliament tour to begin.

Orientation

Length of This Walk: Allow 1.5 hours, not including time to enter the sights.

Getting There: We'll begin on Kossuth tér, behind the Parliament. You can take the M2/red line to the Kossuth tér stop; or, from southern Pest (such as the Great Market Hall—at the end of the Pest Town Center Walk; or Vigadó tér near Vörösmarty tér), take tram #2 along the Danube embankment, and hop off at the looming Parliament building.

Construction Warning: Kossuth tér, where this walk starts, is slated for some construction work in the near future; you may have to improvise (using this chapter's map) if my recommended route is interrupted.

Parliament: 3,500 Ft; English tours usually daily at 10:00, 12:00, and 14:00—confirm in advance; Kossuth tér 1-3, tel. 1/441-4904, www.parlament.hu.

St. István's Basilica: Interior—free, but 200-Ft donation strongly suggested, open to tourists Mon 9:00-16:30, Tue-Fri 9:00-17:00, Sat 9:00-13:00, Sun 13:00-17:00, open slightly later for worshippers; panorama terrace—500 Ft, daily July-Sept 10:00-19:00, Oct-June 10:00-17:00; treasury—400 Ft, same hours as terrace; Szent István tér, district V, M1: Bajcsy-Zsilinszky út or M3: Arany János utca.

Starring: Grand buildings, fine facades, and monuments, monuments, monuments.

Nearby Eateries: For restaurants in Leopold Town, see page 257.

The Walk Begins

(See "Leopold Town Walk" map, page 106.)
• *Start in the large square—half-paved, half-grassy—on the non-river side of the gigantic, can't-miss-it, red-domed...*

Hungarian Parliament (Országház)

The Parliament was built from 1885 to 1902 to celebrate the Hungarian millennium year of 1896 (see sidebar on page 43). Its elegant, frilly spires and riverside location were inspired by its counterpart in London (where the architect studied). When completed, the Parliament was a striking and cutting-edge example of the mix-and-match Historicist style of the day—just as Frank Gehry's undulating buildings are examples of today's bold new aesthetic. Like the Hungarian people, this building is at once grandly ambitious and a somewhat motley hodgepodge of various influences—a Neo-Gothic palace topped with a Neo-Renaissance dome, which

once had a huge, red communist star on top of the tallest spire. Fittingly, it's the city's top icon. The best views of the Parliament are from across the Danube—especially in the late-afternoon sunlight.

The enormous building—with literally miles of stairs—was appropriate for a time when Budapest ruled much of Eastern Europe. The Parliament was built in an exuberant age, when Hungary was part of the Dual Monarchy—the "Austro-Hungarian Empire"—and triple the size it is today. Look at the Parliament with an 1896 Hungarian state of mind. The building is a celebration

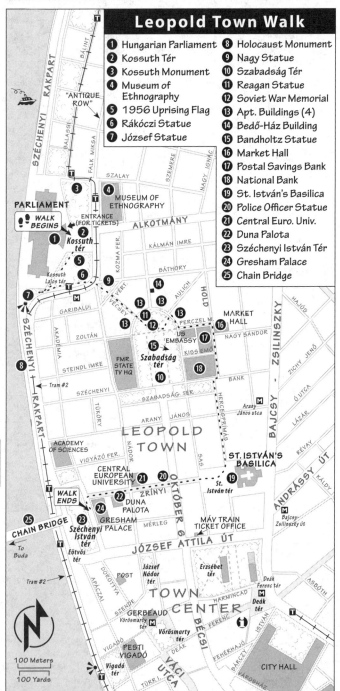

Leopold Town Walk

1. Hungarian Parliament
2. Kossuth Tér
3. Kossuth Monument
4. Museum of Ethnography
5. 1956 Uprising Flag
6. Rákóczi Statue
7. József Statue
8. Holocaust Monument
9. Nagy Statue
10. Szabadság Tér
11. Reagan Statue
12. Soviet War Memorial
13. Apt. Buildings (4)
14. Bedő-Ház Building
15. Bandholtz Statue
16. Market Hall
17. Postal Savings Bank
18. National Bank
19. St. István's Basilica
20. Police Officer Statue
21. Central Euro. Univ.
22. Duna Palota
23. Széchenyi István Tér
24. Gresham Palace
25. Chain Bridge

of Hungary, built with Hungarian hands and of Hungarian materials. But now it feels just plain too big—the legislature only occupies an eighth of the space. Like Britain's Parliament, this building used to be home to a House of Lords and a House of Commons. The Lords are long gone, and their vacated territory is what visitors usually tour (but you sometimes might see the House of Commons, if Parliament is not in session).

The interior—decorated with 84 pounds of gold—is even more glorious than the facade. Apart from all that opulence, it also holds the **Hungarian crown** (directly under the dome—surrounded, as if at a tribal summit, by over a thousand years' worth of Hungary's great kings). This quintessential symbol of Hungarian sovereignty is supposedly the original one that Pope Sylvester II sent to Hungary to crown István on Christmas Day in the year 1000. Since then the crown has been hidden, stolen, lost, and found again and again...supposedly bending the cross on top in the process. That original, simple crown has been encrusted with jewels and (as a gift from a Byzantine emperor) adorned with a circlet. This makes the crown look like a hybrid of East and West—perhaps appropriately, as for much of history Budapest was seen as the gateway to the Orient. In modern times, the crown actually spent time in Fort Knox, Kentucky, where the US government kept it safe between the end of World War II and 1978, when Jimmy Carter returned it to Hungary.

• *The vast square behind the Parliament is studded with attractions.*

Kossuth Tér

This square is sprinkled with interesting monuments and packed with Hungarian history. Stand by the tall, silver-colored flagpole (which flies a flag only for special occasions), facing **entrance "X"** at the back of the building. Waiting patiently are two lines of visitors ready to tour the Parliament (one line to buy tickets, the other waiting for their tour time). If you'd like to take the tour, get in the line marked *For Buying Tickets* and wait for your turn to buy tickets now (English tours several times daily; for details, see page 57).

Just to the right, notice the big black box that seems to be melting like a candle. The **eternal flame** flickering at the top honors the victims of the 1956 Uprising, many of whom died in this square (see the "1956" sidebar).

Turn 90 degrees to the right. At the far end of the grassy park, a statue of the square's namesake, **Lajos Kossuth,** rallies the people of Hungary to arms, as leader of the 1848 Revolution against the

Habsburgs. Below him, on the left, a family gazes adoringly at Kossuth as they send their soldier son off to war; on the right, we see that people of all walks of life joined the (ultimately unsuccessful) rebellion.

The street that leaves this square behind Kossuth's right shoulder is Falk Miksa utca, Budapest's **"antique row"**—a great place to browse for nostalgic souvenirs (see page 276).

Walk halfway across the big, empty asphalt lot behind the Parliament. Look back and across the street to see the **Museum of Ethnography.** While its collection of Hungarian folk artifacts is good (closed Mon, see page 60), the building is even more notable. The design was actually the first runner-up for the Parliament building, so they built it here, where it originally housed the Supreme Court.

• *Now continue through the lot to the opposite end. At the edge of the grassy park, find the Hungarian flag with a hole cut out of the center.*

This **flag** commemorates the 1956 Uprising, when protesters removed the communist seal the Soviets had added to their flag. Two days into that revolt, on October 25, the ÁVH (communist police) and Soviet troops on the rooftop above opened fire on demonstrators gathered in this square—massacring many and leaving no doubt that Moscow would not tolerate dissent. For more on this tragic chapter of Hungarian history, see the "1956" sidebar.

Now imagine this same park in the **fall of 2006,** when it became the site of a new wave of demonstrations—initially impromptu, then carefully choreographed—against Hungary's prime minister, Ferenc Gyurcsány. Using particularly colorful language in a speech intended only for his own party members, Gyurcsány admitted to lies, deceit, and deception in the way he'd run the government and the recent election. When the tape was leaked to the media, Hungarians showed up here to (unsuccessfully) demand Gyurcsány's resignation. While a few of the demonstrations turned violent, most remained peaceful. For more about these events, see page 460.

LEOPOLD TOWN WALK

City of Monuments

There's a reason why Budapest is so monument-crazy. In 1897,

German Emperor Wilhelm II came to visit his ally and rival, Habsburg Emperor Franz Josef, here in Budapest. Wilhelm commented on how few monuments graced the city streets, prompting a jealous Franz Josef to fund the immediate creation of 10 new statues around town. The Budapesters' enjoyment of a good monument continues today. Here are a few favorites, scattered around the city:

- **Attila József,** the brooding young poet, on the riverbank by the Parliament (see page 110).
- **Imre Nagy,** the brave anti-communist leader, standing pensively on a bridge just behind Parliament (see page 111).
- **Empty Shoes** lining the Danube riverbank between the Parliament and the Chain Bridge, honoring Jews who stood there before being executed by the Nazis (see page 110).
- **Anonymous,** the first scribe to chronicle the history of the Hungarian people, in City Park's Vajdahunyad Castle (see page 180).
- **George Washington,** minding his own business deep in City Park near Vajdahunyad Castle (see page 180).
- **1956,** a gigantic rusted-metal hull in City Park, honoring the way Hungarians came together to attempt to throw off Soviet rule (see page 177).
- **Heroes' Square,** where 21 Hungarian leaders (and one angel) stand sternly as a Who's Who of Hungarian history (see page 167).
- **Memento Park,** a collection of surviving communist-era statues and monuments that evoke the Red old days (see page 215).

In the field behind this flag, you'll see a monument to yet another rebel: **Ferenc Rákóczi,** who valiantly (but unsuccessfully) led the Hungarians in their War of Independence (1703-1711) against the Habsburgs. (For more on this leader, see page 174.)

• Now walk along the path between the Parliament and the park toward the river. When you reach the tram tracks, turn right and continue past the little guardhouse toward the Danube. Ahead and on the left, you'll see (with his back to you)...

Attila József (1905-1937)

This beloved modern poet lived a tumultuous, productive, and short life before he killed himself by jumping in front of a train at age 32. József's poems of life, love, and death—mostly written in the 1920s and 1930s—are considered the high point of Hungarian literature. His birthday (April 11) is celebrated as National Hungarian Poetry Day.

Here József re-enacts a scene from one of his best poems, "At the Danube." It's a hot day—his jacket lies in a heap next to him, his shirt-sleeves are rolled up, and he cradles his hat loosely in his left hand. "As I sat on the bank of the Danube, I watched a watermelon float by," he begins. "As if flowing out of my heart, murky, wise, and great was the Danube." In the poem, József uses the Danube as a metaphor for life—for the way it has interconnected cities and also times—as he reflects that his ancestors likely pondered the Danube from this same spot. Looking into his profound eyes, you sense the depth of an artist's tortured inner life.

• *Continue straight down toward the Danube, surveying the panorama from the top of the big staircase over the busy road. From here, you enjoy sweeping views across to Buda, dominated by Castle Hill.*

If you visually trace the Pest riverbank to the left about 100 yards, just before the tree-filled, riverfront park, you can just barely see several low-profile dots lining the embankment. This is a...

Holocaust Monument

Consisting of 50 pairs of bronze shoes, this monument commemorates the Jews who were killed when the Nazis' puppet government, the Arrow Cross, came to power in Hungary in 1944. While many Jews were sent to concentration camps, the Arrow Cross massacred some of them right here, shooting them and letting their bodies fall into the Danube.

You can't walk to the shoes directly from here (there's no safe crosswalk over the embankment road). For a slightly better view of the Holocaust Monument, you can walk along the tram tracks to another viewpoint just downriver; but to reach the shoes themselves, you'll have to access the embankment from near the Chain

Bridge, then walk back up this way along the water (you can do this at the end of this walk).

• *Backtrack past Attila József, cross the tram tracks and the street, turn left, and walk along the ugly building (with an entrance to the Metró) up to the back corner of Kossuth tér. Across the street in a little park (at Vértanúk tere), you'll see a monument to...*

Imre Nagy (1896-1958)

The Hungarian politician Imre Nagy (EEM-ray nodge), now thought of as an anti-communist hero, was actually a life-long communist. In the 1930s, he alleg-edly worked for the Soviet secret police. In the late 1940s, he quickly moved up the hierarchy of Hungary's communist government, becoming prime minister during a period of reform in 1953. But when his proposed changes alarmed Moscow, Nagy was quickly demoted.

When the 1956 Uprising broke out on October 23, Imre Nagy was drafted (reluctantly, some say) to become the head of the move-ment to soften the severity of the communist regime. Because he was an insider, it briefly seemed that Nagy might hold the key to finding a middle path (represented by the bridge he's standing on) between the suffocating totalitarian model of Moscow and the freedom of the West. Some suspect that Nagy himself didn't fully grasp the dramatic sea change represented by the uprising. When he appeared at the Parliament building on the night of October 23 to speak to the reform-craving crowds for the first time, he began by addressing his countrymen—as communist politicians always did—with, "Dear comrades..." When the audience booed, he amended it: "Dear friends..."

But the optimism was short-lived. The Soviets violently put down the uprising, arrested and sham-tried Nagy, executed him, and buried him disgracefully, face-down in an unmarked grave. The regime forced Hungary to forget about Nagy.

Later, when communism was in its death throes in 1989, the Hungarian people rediscovered Nagy as a hero. His body was lo-cated, exhumed, and given a ceremonial funeral at Heroes' Square. And today, thanks to this monument, Nagy keeps a watchful eye on today's lawmakers in the Parliament across the way.

• *Go up the short, diagonal street behind Nagy, called Vécsey utca. After just one block, you emerge into...*

1956

The year 1956 is etched into the Hungarian psyche. In that year, the people of Budapest staged the first major uprising against the communist regime. It also marked the first time that the Soviets implicitly acknowledged, in brutally putting down the uprising, that the people of Eastern Europe were not "communist by choice."

The seeds of revolution were sown with the death of a tyrant: Josef Stalin passed away on March 5, 1953. Suddenly the choke-hold that Moscow had held on its satellite states loosened. During this time of "de-Stalinization," Hungarian premier Imre Nagy presided over two years of mild reform, before his political opponents (and Moscow) became nervous and demoted him. (For more on Nagy, see page 111.)

In 1955, Austria declared its neutrality in the Cold War. This thrust Hungary to the front line of the Iron Curtain, and raised the stakes both for Hungarians who wanted freedom and for Soviets who wanted to preserve their buffer zone. When Stalin's successor, Nikita Khrushchev, condemned Stalin's crimes in a "secret speech" to communist leaders in February of 1956, it emboldened the Soviet Bloc's dissidents. A workers' strike in Poznań, Poland, in October inspired Hungarians to follow their example.

On October 23, 1956, the Hungarian uprising began. A student union group gathered in Budapest at 15:00 to articulate a list of 16 demands against the communist regime. Then they marched toward Parliament, their numbers gradually swelling. One protester defiantly cut the Soviet-style insignia out of the center of the Hungarian flag, which would become the uprising's symbol.

By nightfall, some 200,000 protesters filled Kossuth tér behind Parliament, calling for Imre Nagy, the one communist leader they believed could bring change. Nagy finally appeared around 21:00. Ever the pragmatic politician, he implored patience. Following the speech, a large band of protesters took matters into their own hands, marched to City Park, and tore down the hated Stalin statue that stood there (see page 177).

Another group went to the National Radio building to read their demands on the air. The ÁVH (communist police) refused to let them do it, and eventually opened fire on the protesters. The peaceful protests evolved into an armed insurrection, as frightened civilians gathered weapons and supplies.

Overnight, Moscow decided to intervene. Budapesters awoke on October 24 to find Red Army troops occupying their city. That morning, Imre Nagy—who had just been promoted again to prime minister—promised reforms and tried to keep a lid on the simmering discontent.

The next day, October 25, a huge crowd gathered on Kossuth tér behind the Parliament to hear from Nagy. In the hubbub, shots rang out as Hungarian and Soviet soldiers opened fire on the (mostly unarmed) crowd. At least 70 protesters were killed and more than 100 injured.

The Hungarians fought back with an improvised guerilla resistance. They made use of any guns they could get their hands on, as well as Molotov cocktails, to strike against the Soviet occupiers. Many adolescents (the celebrated "Pest Youth") participated. The fighting tore apart the city, and some of the fallen were buried in impromptu graves in city parks.

Political infighting in Moscow paralyzed the Soviet response, and an uneasy ceasefire fell over Budapest. For 10 tense days, it appeared that the Soviets might allow Nagy to push through some reforms. Nagy, a firmly entrenched communist, had always envisioned a less repressive regime...but within limits. While he was at first reluctant to take on the mantle of the uprising's leadership, he gradually began to echo what he was hearing on the streets. He called for free elections, the abolishment of the ÁVH, the withdrawal of Soviet troops, and Hungary's secession from the Warsaw Pact.

But when the uprisers attacked and killed ÁVH officers and communist leaders in Budapest, it bolstered the case of the Moscow hardliners. On November 4, the Red Army launched a brutal counterattack in Budapest that left the rebels reeling. At 5:20 that morning, Imre Nagy's voice came over the radio to beg the world for assistance. Later that morning, he sought asylum at the Yugoslav Embassy across the street from City Park. He was never seen alive in public again.

János Kádár—an ally of Nagy's who was palatable to the uprisers, yet firmly loyal to Moscow—was installed as prime minister. The fighting dragged on for about another week, but the uprising was eventually crushed. By the end, 2,500 Hungarians and more than 700 Soviets were dead, and 20,000 Hungarians were injured. Communist authorities arrested more than 15,000 people, of whom at least 200 were executed (including Imre Nagy). Anyone who had participated in the uprising was blacklisted; fearing this and other forms of retribution, some 200,000 Hungarians fled to the West.

Though the 1956 Uprising met a tragic end, within a few years Kádár did succeed in softening the regime, and the milder, so-called "goulash communism" emerged. And today, even though the communists are long gone, the legacy of 1956 pervades the Hungarian consciousness. Some Budapest buildings are still pockmarked with bullet holes from '56, and many Hungarians who fled the country in that year still have not returned. October 23 remains Hungary's most cherished holiday.

Szabadság Tér (Liberty Square)

"Liberty Square"—one of Budapest's most inviting public spaces—was so named when a Habsburg barracks here was torn down after the Hungarians gained some autonomy in the late 19th century.

• *The first person you'll see as you enter the square, striding confidently and charismatically away from the Parliament, is an actor-turned-politician you may recognize...*

Ronald Reagan is respected in Hungary for his role as a Cold Warrior. But don't take this monument as a sign that he's universally adored by Hungarians; in truth, this statue, the result of a political stunt, was erected in 2011 to deflect attention from a brewing scandal. When the right-wing Fidesz party took power in Hungary in 2010, they quickly began rolling back previous democratic reforms and placing alarming constraints on the media. Many international observers—including the US government—spoke out against what they considered an infringement on freedom of the press. In an effort to appease American concerns, Prime Minister Viktor Orbán erected this statue on one of his capital's main squares—and then, perhaps not quite grasping the subtleties of American political divisions, invited Secretary of State Hillary Clinton to the unveiling. While Reagan certainly played a role in ending the Cold War, many patriots here are offended at the overstated commentary on the adjacent touchscreen, claiming that Reagan "almost single-handedly won the soul-destroying Cold War"—a statement that insultingly ignores the contributions and sacrifices of so many other important figures, including Imre Nagy. Either way, it's fun to watch the steady stream of passersby (both Hungarians and tourists) do a double-take, chuckle, then snap a photo with The Gipper.

• *Walk around the stout obelisk to the center of the square. Stand facing the obelisk.*

This is the **Soviet War Memorial,** commemorating "Liberation Day": April 4, 1945, when the Soviets officially forced the Nazis out of Hungary. As a very rare reminder of the Soviet days—you almost never see hammers-and-sickles in the streets of Hungary anymore—it has often been defaced, which is why a fence surrounds it. Some Budapesters feel that the memorial should be removed. Ponder for a moment this complex issue: Soviet troops did liberate Hungary from the Nazis. Does their leaders' later oppression of the Hungarians make these soldiers' sacrifice less worthy of being honored?

There's a certain irony now that Ronald Reagan stands just a few yards from the Soviet War Memorial (perhaps a fittingly schizophrenic metaphor for this city's complex history and allegiances). Maybe someday the Soviet War Memorial could be replaced by a statue honoring that *other* important figure in ending Eastern European communism—who'd also be palatable to Russians—Mikhail Gorbachev.

Ringing the top of Szabadság tér (behind the memorial) are **four ornate apartment buildings,** typical of high-class townhouses from Budapest's Golden Age in the late 1800s. While each one is strikingly different from the next, they are all typical of Historicism—the mix-and-match aesthetic that was popular at the time. Like residential buildings throughout Pest, the ground  floor has particularly high ceilings. But the second and third floors were more desirable—up away from the rabble of street life, but with relatively few stairs (in a time before elevators were common). Notice that in each of these buildings, those are the only floors with balconies.

Here's an optional detour for architecture buffs: If you go up the middle street between these buildings (Honvéd utca, straight  ahead from the middle of Szabadság tér), a few doors down on the right you'll find one of Budapest's finest Art Nouveau buildings, **Bedő-Ház.** The curvy green facade is a textbook example of the Hungarian Secession style. Built in 1903, the building was dilapidated for decades before a studs-out restoration in 2007. Inside is a small café and three floors with a modest but interesting exhibit of Art Nouveau items (mostly elegantly delicate furniture, plus some dishes and other household items; 1,500 Ft, Mon-Sat 10:00-17:00, closed Sun, Honvéd utca 3, tel. 1/269-4622).

For just a peek, duck into the next-door Secessió Café & Delikat, which occupies part of the building (Mon-Fri 8:00-19:00, Sat 10:00-17:00, closed Sun).

• *Back in the middle of Szabadság tér, turn with your back to the Soviet memorial, and look down to the far end of the square.*

On the right is a giant building that once housed the stock exchange and, later, **Hungarian State Television,** or MTV—not music television, but Magyar television. As a symbol of government-run media, it was one of the few buildings damaged in the 2006 riots. Now the building has been converted into luxury offices and apartments.

The genteel open-air **café** in the middle of the park is an inviting place for a coffee break.

Across the square (on the left, behind subtle but effective car-bomb barriers), the yellow corner building is the **US Embassy.** This is where Cardinal József Mindszenty holed up for 15 years during the Cold War to evade arrest by the communist authorities (see page 341). A hundred yards down the left side of the square (and worth a detour for military buffs) stands a statue of **Harry Hill Bandholtz,** a US officer from World War I who prevented treasured Hungarian art from being taken by Romania. This statue stood inside the US Embassy for 40 chilly years (1949-1989), but now it's back out in the open.

• *We're headed down Perczel Mór utca, the street next to the US Embassy—but you'll have to detour a bit to the left (and tiptoe around some barricades) to get there. After one block on Perczel Mór utca, you run into...*

Hold Utca

Look for the big yellow *Vásárcsarnok* sign. This **market hall** was built around the same time as the Great Market Hall, but it's smaller and less touristy—worth poking around inside. If you're hungry, sit down at one of several dirt-cheap market eateries, or gather a picnic here to eat at nearby Szabadság tér (Mon 6:30-17:00, Tue-Fri 6:30-18:00, Sat 6:30-14:00, closed Sun).

Exit the market building and turn left onto Hold utca. As you walk down this street, keep your eyes high on the green-and-yellow roofline of the building on the right. This **Postal Savings Bank,** designed by Ödön Lechner in the late 19th century, combines traditional folk motifs with cutting-edge Art Nouveau in an attempt to forge a new, distinctly Hungarian national style. A key element of this emerging style was the use of colorful mosaic tiles to decorate the roof. (In its truest form, this style uses pyrogranite ceramic

tiles from the famous Zsolnay porcelain factory in the city of Pécs—see pages 388-389.) The beehives along the rooftop are an appropriate symbol for a bank—where people store money as bees store honey. When asked why he lavished such attention on the rooftop, which few people can see, Lechner said, "To please the birds." (To get a better look without wings, you can pay 1,500 Ft at the Hotel President across the street to ride an elevator to their sixth-floor observation deck.)

Walking farther along Hold utca, you pass the grand **National Bank of Hungary,** with entertaining reliefs tracing the history of money.

• *Walk to the end of the giant bank building, then continue two blocks straight ahead up Hercegprímás utca. You'll emerge into a broad plaza in front of Budapest's biggest Catholic church....*

St. István's Basilica (Szent István Bazilika)

The church is only about 100 years old—like most Budapest landmarks, it was built around the millennial celebrations of 1896. Designed by three architects over more than 50 years, St. István's is particularly eclectic. Each architect had a favorite style: Neoclassical, Neo-Renaissance, and Neo-Baroque. Construction was delayed for a while when the giant dome collapsed midway through.

Head up the grand stairs to get oriented. To the right is the ticket desk, the elevator to the treasury, and the entrance to the church. To the left is the elevator to the panoramic tower.

The church's **interior** is dimly lit but gorgeously restored; all the gilded decorations glitter in the low light. Pick up the handy self-guided-tour brochure as you enter. You'll see not Jesus, but St. István (Stephen), Hungary's first Christian king, glowing above the high altar.

The church's main claim to fame is the **"holy right hand" of St. István.** The sacred fist—a somewhat grotesque, 1,000-year-old withered stump—is in a jeweled box in the chapel to the left of the main altar (follow signs for *Szent Jobb Kápolna*, chapel often closed). Pop

in a 200-Ft coin for two minutes of light. Posted information describes the hand's unlikely journey to this spot (chapel open April-Sept Mon-Sat 9:00-16:30, Sun 13:00-16:30; Oct-March Mon-Sat 10:00-16:00, Sun 13:00-16:30).

On your way out, in the back-right corner of the church, you'll find a small exhibit about the building's history.

There are two other attractions at St. István's, each covered by a separate ticket. The **panoramic tower** offers views over Budapest's rooftops that are pretty distant (and disappointing without a good zoom lens), but it does provide a good sense of the sprawl of the city. You have various options: You can walk up the entire way (302 steps); or you can take an elevator to midlevel (with WCs), where you can follow signs to another elevator (plus 42 steps) or climb 137 steps to the top. To the right as you face the church, an elevator zips up to the skippable church

treasury, a small collection of vestments, ecclesiastical gear, a model of the building, exhibits about its construction, a porcelain replica of the Hungarian crown, and a fine Murillo *Holy Family*—all well-described in English.

The church also hosts regular **organ concerts** (advertised near the entry).

• *The square in front of the church is called, logically...*

St. István Tér

This grand plaza is a classic example of how Budapest has spiffed up its once-gloomy downtown. A decade ago, this space was an ugly parking lot. Then, a few years back, a German engineering firm created an experimental, cutting-edge parking garage beneath this square. Instead of finding a parking space, drivers simply leave their car on a pallet and walk up to the square—while the car-loaded pallet is moved with a series of giant elevators and conveyor belts to a parking space. This futuristic system is all going on underfoot. Meanwhile, over the last couple of years, the streets around this plaza—once sleepy—have been transformed into one of Budapest's trendiest nightlife zones, with lots of bars, restaurants, and cafés catering to local yuppies. The **DiVino wine bar,** at the bottom of the square, is a perfect place to sample a variety of Hungarian vintages by the glass; this and other nearby eateries are recommended on page 257.

• *From here, you have two options. If you'd like to skip ahead to my* **Andrássy Út Walk,** *you're very close: Walk around the right side of the* *basilica, turn right on busy Bajcsy-Zsilinszky út, and you're one block from the start of Andrássy út (across the street, on your left).*

Or you can complete this walk to Vörösmarty tér, where you can begin the **Pest Town Center Walk**. For this option, walk straight ahead from St. István's main staircase down...

Zrínyi Utca

Recently pedestrianized Zrínyi utca is a fine people zone, and a handy way to connect St. István's to the river. Plans are in the works to redevelop other central Pest streets to be as pedestrian-friendly as this one.

At the bottom of the plaza, you'll cross **Sas utca,** home to several good and trendy restaurants (including the recommended Café Kör to the right, and the recommended Borkonyha to the left). Consider window-shopping here and reserving a place for dinner tonight.

At the next corner (on the right), look for the costumed, bushy-mustachioed **police officer** statue, evoking the grand old days of the Austro-Hungarian Empire (just before World War I). There's no particular story for this character: he's just for fun. In keeping with their rich tradition of monuments, the local district sponsors a contest each year to come up with the best statues.

Farther down this block, on the right-hand corner, is **Central European University.** Offering graduate study for Americans and students from all over Central and Eastern Europe, this school is predominantly funded by George Soros, a Hungarian who escaped communism by emigrating to the US, then became a billionaire through shrewd investments. Today Soros is loved by the left and loathed by the right as a major contributor to liberal campaigns. But he hasn't forgotten worthy causes back home. In addition to funding this university, he is at the forefront of a movement for Central Europeans to better protect the rights of their huge Roma (Gypsy) population. The university's CEU Bookshop, a few steps up Zrínyi utca toward the basilica, is the best place in town to find academic books about the region in English (listed on page 44).

Continue down Zrínyi utca. After crossing Nádor utca, on the left you'll see **Duna Palota** ("Danube Palace")—a former casino, and today a venue and ticket office for Hungária Koncert's popular tourist shows. If you're up for a crowd-pleasing show of either classical or folk music, drop in here to check your options (see page 281 in the Entertainment in Budapest chapter).

Zrínyi utca dead-ends at the big traffic circle called **Széchenyi István tér**. For decades, this was called Roosevelt tér, in honor of the American statesman who helped defeat the Nazis in World War II—even though the statues here actually depict Hungarians. But in 2010, the parliament renamed the square for the Hungarian statesman whose statue stands on the right: István Széchenyi, the early 19th-century nobleman who, among other deeds, built the Chain Bridge and founded the Hungarian Academy of Sciences (both of which face this square). On the left is the statesman Ferenc Deák, who fought for Hungarian autonomy using peaceful means.

• *Turn left and walk a half-block to the entrance (on the left) of the...*

Gresham Palace

The Gresham Palace was Budapest's first building in the popular Historicist style, and also incorporates elements of Art Nouveau.

Budapest boomed at a time when architectural eclecticism—mashing together bits and pieces of different styles—was in vogue. But because much of the city's construction was compressed into a short window of time, even these disparate styles enjoy an unusual harmony. Damaged in World War II, the building was an eyesore for decades. (Reportedly, an aging local actress refused to move out, so developers had to wait for her to pass on before they could reclaim the building.) In 1999, the Gresham Palace was meticulously restored to its former glory. Even if you can't afford to stay here (see page 238 in the Sleeping in Budapest chapter), saunter into the lobby and absorb the gorgeous details. For example, not only did they have to re-create the unique decorative tiles—they had to rebuild the original machines that made the tiles.

• *Grandly spanning the Danube from this spot is the...*

Chain Bridge (Széchenyi Lánchíd)

One of the world's great bridges connects Pest's Széchenyi tér and Buda's Clark Ádám tér. This historic, iconic bridge, guarded by lions (symbolizing power), is Budapest's most enjoyable and convenient bridge to cross on foot.

Until the mid-19th century, only pontoon barges spanned the Danube between Buda and Pest. In the winter, the pontoons had

to be pulled in, leaving locals to rely on ferries (in good weather) or a frozen river. People often walked across the frozen Danube, only to get stuck on the other side during a thaw, with nothing to do but wait for another cold snap.

Count István Széchenyi was stranded for a week trying to get to his father's funeral. After missing it, Széchenyi commissioned Budapest's first permanent bridge—which was also a major symbolic step toward another of Széchenyi's pet causes, the unification of Buda and Pest. The Chain Bridge was built by Scotsman Adam Clark between 1842 and 1849, and it immediately became an important symbol of Budapest. Széchenyi—a man of the Enlightenment—charged both commoners and nobles a toll for crossing his bridge, making it an emblem of equality in those tense times. Like all of the city's bridges, the Chain Bridge was destroyed by the Nazis at the end of World War II, but was quickly rebuilt.

• Our walk is over. From Széchenyi tér, you can catch bus #16 from in front of the Hungarian Academy of Sciences (at the right end of the square) to Castle Hill, or simply walk across the Chain Bridge for great views. For a better look at the empty-shoes Holocaust Monument, you can safely cross from here to the embankment, then follow it back toward the Parliament.

If you'd like to wind up in the heart of Pest, Vörösmarty tér (and the start of my **Pest Town Center Walk**—see next chapter) is just two long blocks away: Turn left out of the Gresham Palace, and walk straight on Dorottya utca.

PEST TOWN CENTER WALK

Belváros, from Vörösmarty Tér to the Great Market Hall

Pest's Belváros ("Inner Town") is its gritty urban heart—simultaneously its most beautiful and ugliest district. You'll see fancy facades, some of Pest's best views from the Danube embankment, genteel old coffee houses that offer a whiff of the city's Golden Age, inviting oasis parks tucked between densely populated streets, and a cavernous, colorful market hall filled with Hungarian goodies. But you'll also experience crowds, grime, and pungent smells like nowhere else in Budapest. Remember: This is a city in transition. Local authorities plan to ban traffic from more and more Town Center streets in the coming years. If construction and torn-up pavement (common around here) impede your progress, be thankful that things will be nicer for your next visit. Within a decade, all of those rough edges will be sanded off...and tourists like you will be nostalgic for the "authentic" old days. (If you want the sanitized version today, stick with the other tourists on Váci utca.)

Even if this whole walk doesn't appeal to you, don't miss the spectacular Great Market Hall, described on page 134.

Orientation

Length of This Walk: Allow 1.5 hours.

Getting There: Take the M1/yellow Metró line to the Vörösmarty tér stop.

Construction Alert: Several of the areas covered by this walk—including Váci utca, the Danube embankment, and Ferenciek tere—are slated for renovation in the next few years. Expect construction chaos and confusion during your visit, and use this chapter's map to navigate around any potential mess.

Károlyi Park: Free, open daily May-Aug 8:00-21:00, April and Sept 8:00-19:00, Oct-March 8:00-17:00.

Great Market Hall: Free, Mon 6:00-17:00, Tue-Fri 6:00-18:00, Sat 6:00-15:00, closed Sun, Fővám körút 1-3.

Starring: The urban core of Budapest, a gorgeous riverfront promenade, several of the city's top cafés, and a grand finale at the Great Market Hall.

Nearby Eateries: For restaurants in Pest's Town Center, see page 254.

The Walk Begins

(See "Pest Town Center Walk" map, page 125.)

• *Start on the central square of the Town Center, Vörösmarty tér (at the M1 Metró stop of the same name). Face the giant, seated statue in the middle of the square.*

Vörösmarty Tér

As we begin exploring the central part of Pest, consider its humble history. In the mid-1600s, Pest was under Ottoman occupation and nearly deserted. By the 1710s, the Habsburgs had forced out the Ottomans, but this area remained a rough-and-tumble, often-flooded quarter just outside the Pest city walls. Peasants came here to enjoy bearbaiting (watching brutal, staged fights between bloodhounds and bears—like cockfights, only bigger and angrier, with more fur and teeth). The rebuilding of Pest was gradual; most of the buildings you'll see on this walk are no older than 200 years.

Today this square—a hub of activity in the Town Center—is named for the 19th-century Romantic poet **Mihály Vörösmarty** (1800-1855), whose statue dominates the little park at the square's center. Writing during the time of reforms in the early 19th century, Vörösmarty was a Romantic whose poetry still stirs the souls of patriotic Hungarians—he's like Byron, Shelley, and Keats rolled into one. One of his most famous works is a patriotic song whose popularity rivals the national anthem's: "Be faithful to your country, all Hungarians." At Vörösmarty's feet, as if hearing those inspiring words chiseled into the stone, figures representing the Hungarian people rise up together. During Vörösmarty's age, the peasant Magyar tongue was, for the very first time, considered worthy of literature. The people began to think of themselves not merely as "subjects of the Habsburg Empire"...but as Hungarians.

• *Survey the square with a spin tour. First, facing the statue of Vörösmarty, turn 90 degrees to the left.*

At the north end of the square is the landmark **Gerbeaud café** and pastry shop. Between the World Wars, the well-to-do ladies of

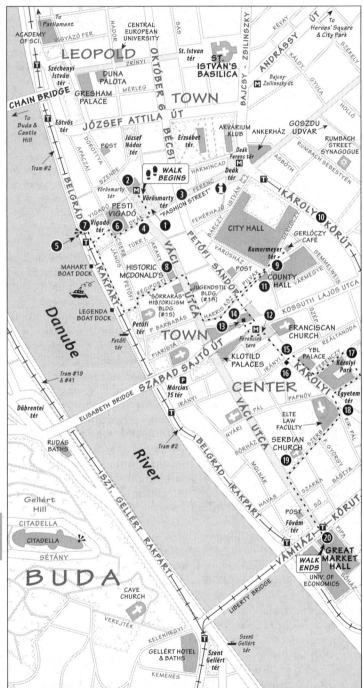

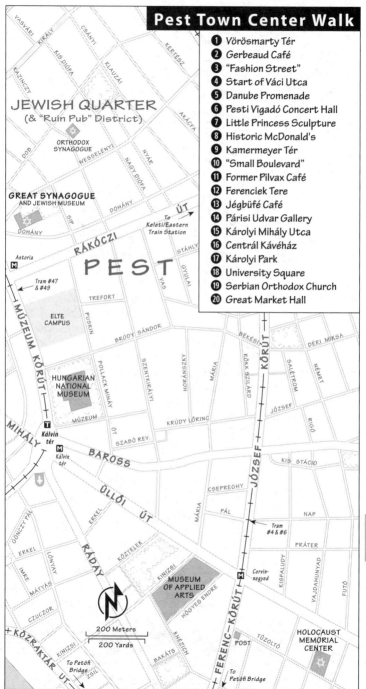

Pest Town Center Walk

1. Vörösmarty Tér
2. Gerbeaud Café
3. "Fashion Street"
4. Start of Váci Utca
5. Danube Promenade
6. Pesti Vigadó Concert Hall
7. Little Princess Sculpture
8. Historic McDonald's
9. Kamermeyer Tér
10. "Small Boulevard"
11. Former Pilvax Café
12. Ferenciek Tere
13. Jégbüfé Café
14. Párisi Udvar Gallery
15. Károlyi Mihály Utca
16. Centrál Kávéház
17. Károlyi Park
18. University Square
19. Serbian Orthodox Church
20. Great Market Hall

JEWISH QUARTER
(& "Ruin Pub" District)

ORTHODOX SYNAGOGUE

GREAT SYNAGOGUE
AND JEWISH MUSEUM

To Keleti/Eastern Train Station

Astoria

RÁKÓCZI ÚT

PEST

Tram #47 & #49

ELTE CAMPUS

HUNGARIAN NATIONAL MUSEUM

Kálvin tér

BAROSS

ÜLLŐI ÚT

MUSEUM OF APPLIED ARTS

Tram #4 & #6

Corvin-negyed

HOLOCAUST MEMORIAL CENTER

POST

200 Meters
200 Yards

To Petőfi Bridge

To Petőfi Bridge

Budapest would meet here after shopping their way up Váci utca. Today it's still *the* meeting point in Budapest (for tourists, at least). Consider stepping inside to appreciate the elegant old decor, or for a cup of coffee and a slice of cake (but meals here are overpriced). Better yet, hold off for now—more appealing cafés await later on this walk.

The yellow **M1 Metró stop** between Vörösmarty and Gerbeaud is the entrance to the shallow *Földalatti,* or "underground"—the first subway on the Continent (built for the Hungarian millennial celebration in 1896). Today, it still carries passengers to Andrássy út sights, running under that street all the way to City Park (it basically runs beneath the feet of people following my Andrássy Út Walk).

• *Turn another 90 degrees to the left.*

This super-modern **glass building** is the newest addition to Vörösmarty tér. If you think its appearance is jarring, then you should have seen the communist-style eyesore it replaced. Downstairs is upscale shopping; higher up are offices; and at the top are luxury apartments. Early plans called for a Mediterranean garden spiraling up inside this building, but it never materialized—so now it's just a beautiful waste of space.

• *Turn another 90 degrees to the left, and walk to the beginning of the Váci utca pedestrian street. Look up the street that's to your left (with the yellow, pointy-topped building at the end).*

This street (Deák utca) was recently pedestrianized as a **"Fashion Street,"** lined with top-end shops. This is the easiest and most pleasant way to walk to Deák tér (where the three Metró lines converge) and, beyond it, through Erzsébet tér to the boulevard called Andrássy út (❷ see the Andrássy Út Walk chapter).

• *Extending straight ahead from Vörösmarty tér is a broad, bustling, pedestrianized shopping street. For now, look—but do not walk—down this street; we'll stroll a different stretch of it later on this walk.*

Dating from 1810-1850, **Váci utca** (VAHT-see OOT-zah) is one of the oldest streets of Pest. Váci utca means "street to Vác"—a town 25 miles to the north. This has long been the street where the elite of Pest

would go shopping, then strut their stuff for their neighbors on an evening promenade. Today, the tourists do the strutting here—

and the Hungarians go to American-style shopping malls. On the right at the start of this street, just past the Hard Rock Café, is the brand-new, top-of-the-line Váci 1 shopping mall—where few locals can afford to shop.

This boulevard—Budapest's tourism artery—was a dreamland for Eastern Bloc residents back in the 1980s. It was here that they fantasized about what it might be like to be free, while drooling over Nikes, Adidas, and Big Macs before any of these "Western evils" were introduced elsewhere in the Warsaw Pact region.

Ironically, this street—once prized by Hungarians and other Eastern Europeans because it felt so Western—is what many Western tourists today mistakenly think is the "real Budapest." Visitors mesmerized by this people-friendly stretch of souvenir stands, Internet cafés, and upscale boutiques are likely to miss some more interesting and authentic areas just a block or two away.

Don't fall for this trap. You could have a fun and fulfilling trip to this city without setting foot on Váci utca. In fact, this walk is designed to give you only the briefest taste of Váci utca's tackiness. (If you're dying to saunter down Váci utca, this walk concludes at its far end—it takes about 20 minutes to walk back to its start.) Instead, we'll zigzag through the heart of Pest's Town Center for a look at the *real* "real Budapest."

• *Head for the river: Take the street that runs along the left side of the big glass building at the bottom of Vörösmarty tér. Cross the street and continue all the way to the railing and tram tracks. Swing about 30 yards to the right along the tracks, pausing by the statue of the girl with the dog. You're on the most colorful stretch of the...*

Danube Promenade (Dunakorzó)

Some of the best views in Budapest are from this walkway facing Castle Hill—especially this stretch, between the white Elisabeth Bridge (left) and the iconic Chain Bridge (right). This is a favorite place to promenade *(korzó)*, strolling aimlessly and greeting friends. Imagine the days before World War II, when—instead of mid-century monstrosities Marriott and InterContinental—this strip was lined with elegant grand hotels: Hungaria, Bristol, Carlton.

Take in the views of Buda, across the river (left to right): Gellért Hill, topped with its distinctive Liberation Monument; the green-domed Royal Palace, capping Castle Hill; and, farther along the hilltop, the colorful tile roof and spiny spire of the Matthias Church, surrounded by the cone-shaped decorations of the Fishermen's Bastion.

Behind you (fronting the little park) is a big concert hall, which dominates this part of the promenade. This is the Neo-Ro-

mantic-style **Pesti Vigadó**— built in the 1880s, and recently restored. Charmingly, the word *vigadó*—used to describe a concert hall—literally means "joyous place." In front, the playful statue of **the girl with her dog** captures the fun-loving spirit

along this drag. At the gap in the railing, notice the platform to catch **tram #2,** which goes frequently in each direction along the promenade—a handy and scenic way to connect riverside sights in Pest. (You can ride it to the right, to the Parliament and the start of my Leopold Town Walk; or to the left, to the Great Market Hall—where this walk ends.)

• *About 30 more yards toward the Chain Bridge, find the little statue wearing a jester's hat. She's playing on the railing, with the castle behind her.*

The **Little Princess** is one of Budapest's symbols and a favorite photo-op for tourists. While many of the city's monuments have interesting back-stories, more recent statues (like this one) are simply whimsical and fun.

• *Now walk down the promenade to the left (toward the white bridge). Directly in front of the corner of the Marriott Hotel, watch for the easy-to-miss stairs leading down under the tram tracks, to a crosswalk that leads safely across the busy road to the riverbank. From the top of these stairs, look along the river.*

Lining the **embankment** are several long boats: Some are excursion boats for sightseeing trips up and down the Danube (especially pleasant at night), while others are overpriced (but scenic) restaurants. Kiosks along here dispense info and sell tickets for the various boat companies—look for Danube Legenda (their dock is just downstream from here—go down the stairs, cross the road, then walk 100 yards left; for details, see page 54).

• *For now, continue walking downstream (left) along the promenade, passing in front of the blocky, dirty-white Marriott. When you reach the end of the Marriott complex, at the little parking lot, turn inland (left), cross the street, and walk up the street called Régi Posta utca. Head for the Golden Arches. You deserve a break today.*

Historic McDonald's

The fancy McDonald's (on the left) was a landmark in Eastern Europe—the first McDonald's behind the Iron Curtain. Budapest has

always been a little more rebellious, independent, and cosmopolitan than other Eastern European cities, whose citizens flocked here during the communist era. Váci utca (which we'll see next) was a showcase street during those grim times, making this a strategic location for Ronald McDonald and Co. Since you had to wait in a long line—stretching around the block—to get a burger, it wasn't "fast food"...but at least it was "West food." Váci utca also had a "dollar store," where you could buy hard-to-find items as long as you had Western currency. During the Cold War, Budapest was sort of the "Sin City" of the Eastern Bloc. (What happened in Budapest, stayed in Budapest. Unless the secret police were watching...which they always were...uh-oh.)

• *After the McDonald's, Régi Posta utca crosses...*

Váci Utca

We'll follow this crowded drag for two blocks to the right. As we stroll, be sure to look up. Along this street and throughout Pest, spectacular facades begin on the second floor, above a plain entryway (in the 1970s, the communist government made ground-floor shop windows uniformly dull). Locals like to say these buildings are "wearing socks." Pan up above the knees to see some of Pest's best architecture. These were the townhouses of the aristocracy whose mansions dotted the countryside. You might notice that some of the facades are plain. Many of these used to be more ornate, like their neighbors, but were destroyed by WWII bombs and rebuilt in the stripped-down style of the austere years that followed.

As you head to the right down Váci utca, notice two buildings in particular. The second building on the right, at #15 (marked *Sörörrás*), features beautiful carved wood on the bottom and tile-and-stone decorations on the top. Combining everything that was typically thought of as "beautiful" in the late 19th century, this building exemplifies Historicism. Across the street and down one door (at #18), we see another architect's response to that facade: stern *Jugendstil* (Vienna's answer to Art Nouveau). Based in a movement called "The Secession" for the way it broke away from past conventions, this building almost seems to be having a conversation with the one across the street: "Dude, tone it down. Be cool."

Continue strolling down the street. Here and elsewhere along Váci utca, you'll see restaurants touting Hungarian fare. Avoid these places. Any restaurant along this street is guaranteed to be at least half as good and twice as expensive as other eateries nearby. (For better options—some just a few steps from Váci utca—see the Eating in Budapest chapter.)

• *After about two blocks, turn left up the lane called Harris köz (passing the entrance to the underground Hungarian Shopping Market). Cross Petőfi Sándor utca and keep going straight for two more blocks, until you dead-end at a little square with an appealing café.*

Kamermeyer Tér

Two monumental buildings flank this square: To the left, the extremely long, pink-and-yellow building is the **City Hall** (Városház). Notice it's flying three flags: EU (blue with a circle of yellow stars), Hungary (red, white, and green), and Budapest (red, yellow, and blue; with a griffin and lion holding the city seal). The green building to the right is the **Pest County Hall.**

On this spot, a local entrepreneur is trying to capture some of the Parisian-style elegance that once pervaded this fine city. The highly recommended **Gerlóczy Café** does a fine job reviving the refined café culture of Budapest's Golden Age. This is a great place for a sit-and-sip coffee stop or a full meal (described on page 254)...though additional coffee stops are coming up soon.

Looking down the street to the left of the café, the brick apartment building marks Pest's **Small Boulevard**—once its city wall, now its inner ring road (and here named Károly körút). The Great Synagogue and Jewish Quarter are less than a 10-minute walk away (to detour there now, head to the Small Boulevard, then go right; see the ✪ Great Synagogue and Jewish Quarter Tour chapter).

On your right is Jack Doyle's Irish pub. But this was once yet another historic café. Look up to see the *Pilvax* label, dating from the time when this was the **Pilvax Café.** On the morning of March 15, 1848, a collection of local intellectuals and artists—who came to be known as the "Pest Youth"—gathered here to listen to their friend Sándor Petőfi (sort of the Hungarian Lord Byron) read a new poem. Petőfi's call to arms so inspired the group that they decided to revolt against their Habsburg oppressors...right away. Later that day, Petőfi read his poem again on the steps of the National Museum, rebels broke a beloved patriot out of jail at the castle, the group printed their list of 12 demands at a nearby print shop...and the 1848 Revolution had begun. To this day, March 15 remains an important national holiday. For more on 1848, see page 450.

• *Backtrack two short blocks to Petőfi Sándor utca, cross it, then take an immediate left and follow Petőfi street to the end of the block. Stand at the busy highway and survey the area called...*

Ferenciek Tere

"Franciscan Square"—so named for the church across the highway—will likely be under construction during your visit, as it re-

ceives a desperately needed and long-overdue renovation. For years this has been the perfect place to take in some of Pest's best "diamond in the rough" architecture...fantastic facades that stand grim and caked with soot. The boulevard was developed (like so much of Budapest) in the late 19th century, to connect the Keleti/Eastern train station (to the left, not visible from here) with the Elisabeth Bridge (to the right). Looking toward the Elisabeth Bridge, you'll see that the busy highway is flanked by twin apartment blocks called the **Klotild Palaces.** While the right one has been turned into a hotel, the left one—and the big building next to it—are still soot-caked. Imagine this area before 20th-century construction routed a major thoroughfare through it, when people could stroll freely amidst these elaborate facades. Someday, you might not have to imagine. But for now, breathe in the real Budapest.

Head toward the bridge, noticing (on your right) another artifact of communism: the unique **Jégbüfé.** This recommended communist-era *bisztró* serves stand-up coffee and cakes to urbanites on the go. For more details on this place, including how and what to order, see page 265.

Continue about 30 yards past Jégbüfé. On the right (at Kossuth Lajos út 11) is the low-profile entrance to the **Párisi Udvar** ("Parisian Courtyard")— a grand, hidden gallery with delicate woodwork, fine mosaics that glitter evocatively in the low light, and a breathtaking stained-glass dome. Like

the streets around it, this fine space sat neglected for decades, rotting all around its tenants. Now everybody has moved out, and it's up for sale. While it's likely closed for your visit, peek (or, if possible, walk) through the gate to appreciate a grand space...and daydream about the day when it's returned to its former glory.

This gallery is a reminder that if you only experience what's on the main streets in Budapest, you'll miss a big part of the story. Behind most of Pest's once-grand, now-crumbling facades, you'll find cozy courtyards where residents carry out much of their lives. These courtyards, shared among neighbors and ringed by a common balcony, stay cool through the summer. Poking into some of these courtyards (which are generally open to the public, offering a handy shortcut through city blocks) is an essential Back Door experience for understanding the inner life of Budapest.

• *Facing the gallery door, turn 180 degrees and head straight down the stairs into the pedestrian underpass. Surfacing on the other side, turn left, walk to the end of the block, then (at the church) turn right and walk along...*

Károlyi Mihály Utca

As you walk up the street, appreciate the pretty corner spires on the buildings. The yellow one marks the university library.

PEST TOWN CENTER WALK

At the end of the block, cross Irányi utca, and you'll be face-to-face with the entrance to the recommended **Centrál Kávéház** (on the right-hand corner)—another of Budapest's newly rejuvenated, old-style café/restaurants (see page 265). Step inside to be transported to another time. If you haven't taken a coffee break yet, now's a good time.

Just past Centrál Kávéház, on the left (at #12), is the recently restored **Ybl Palace.** Designed by and named for the prominent architect Miklós Ybl (who also did the Opera House), its inner courtyard hosts a restaurant/café called Egy Kettő ("One, Two")—poke in to see the impressive remodel job (closed Sun).

• *Continue along Károlyi Mihály utca to the end of the block, then take the first left up Ferenczy István utca. After the long building, dip through the green fence on the right, into...*

Károlyi Park (Károlyi Kert)

This delightful, flower-filled oasis offers the perfect break from loud and gritty urban Pest. Once the private garden of the aristocratic Károlyi family from eastern Hungary (whose mansion

it's behind), it's now a public park beloved by people who live, work, and go to school in this neighborhood. The park is filled with tulips in the spring, potted palm trees in the summer, and rich colors in the fall. On a sunny summer day, locals escape here to read books, gossip with neighbors, or simply lie in the sun. Many schools are nearby. Teenagers hang out here after school, while younger kids enjoy the playground. (If you need a break after all that coffee, a pay WC is in the green pavilion in the far-right corner.)

• *Exit the park straight ahead from where you entered, and turn right down Henszimann utca. At the end of the street, you'll come to a church with onion-dome steeples. The big plaza in front of it is...*

University Square (Egyetem Tér)

This square is one of Budapest's most recent to enjoy a makeover. An initiative called the "Heart of the City" is targeting EU and

Hungarian funds at city-center streets and squares like this one (as well as Károlyi Mihály utca, which we were walking down earlier). Traffic is carefully regulated. Notice the automatic bollard that goes up and down to let in approved vehicles: buses, taxis, and local residents only. The modern lampposts and barriers are an interesting (and controversial) choice in this nostalgic city, where the priority is usually on re-creating the city exactly as it was a century ago. The idea in this case is to keep the original buildings, but surround them with a modern streetscape.

The colonnaded building on the left is the law school for ELTE University (Hungary's biggest, with 30,000 students and colleges all over the city). The letters stand for "Eotvös Lorand Technical University," named for an influential physicist. As in much of the former Soviet Bloc, the university system in Hungary is still heavily subsidized by the government. It's affordable to study here...*if* you can get in (competition is fierce).

• *Facing the university building, turn left, then take the first right down Szerb utca. After one long block, on the right, in the park behind the yellow fence, is a...*

Serbian Orthodox Church

This used to be a strongly Serbian neighborhood—there's still some Cyrillic writing on some of the buildings nearby. The church is rarely open, but if it is, step inside to be transported to the far-eastern reaches of Europe...heavy with incense and packed with icons.

The Serbs are just one of many foreign groups that have coexisted here. Traditionally, Hungary's territory included most of Slovakia and large parts of Romania, Croatia, and Serbia—and people from all of those places (along with Austrians, Jews, and Roma/Gypsies) flocked to Buda and Pest. And yet, most of the residents of this cosmopolitan city still speak Hungarian. Throughout centuries of foreign invasions and visitors, new arrivals have undergone a slow-but-sure process of "Magyarization"—"becoming" Hungarian (often against their will). This has made Budapest one of the greatest "melting pot" cities in Europe, if not the world.

• *Continue down Szerb utca, until it runs into Váci utca. Turn left, and set your sights on the colorful tiled roofs two blocks directly ahead. Across the street is the...*

Great Market Hall (Nagyvásárcsarnok)

This market hall (along with four others) was built—like so much of Budapest—around the millennial celebration year of 1896 (see page 43). Appreciate the colorful Zsolnay tiles lining the roof—frostproof and harder than stone, these were an integral part of the Hungarian national style that emerged in the late 19th century. Tunnels connect this hall to the Danube, where goods could be unloaded at the customs house (now Budapest Corvinus University of Economics, formerly Karl Marx University, next door) and easily transported into the market hall.

To the right, the green **Liberty Bridge**—formerly named for Habsburg Emperor Franz Josef—spans the Danube to the Gellért Baths, in the shadow of Gellért Hill. And to the left, the Small Boulevard (here named Vámház körút) curls around toward Deák tér, passing along the way Kálvin tér, the National Museum, and the Great Synagogue.

Step inside the market and get your bearings: The cavernous interior features three levels. The ground floor has produce stands,

PEST TOWN CENTER WALK

bakeries, butcher stalls, heaps of paprika, goose liver, and salamis. Upstairs are stand-up eateries and souvenirs. And in the basement are a supermarket, a fish market, and piles of pickles.

Main Floor

Before exploring, take this guided stroll along the market's "main drag" (straight ahead from the entry). Notice the floor slopes slightly downhill to the left. Locals say that the vendors along the right wall are (appropriately enough) higher-end, with more specialty items, while the ones along the left wall are cheaper. Just inside the door, to the right as you enter, notice the small electronic scale—so shoppers can double-check to be sure the merchants didn't cheat them.

In the first "block" of stalls, the corner showcase on the left explains how this stall has been in the same family since 1924, and includes photos of three generations. At the end of this set of stalls, in the dairy case, they sell **Túró Rudi** (TOO-roh ROO-dee), a semi-sweet cottage cheese covered in chocolate (in the red-and-white polka-dot wrapper). This is a favorite treat for young Hungarians—mothers get their kids to behave here by promising to buy them one. Across the "street," the corner showcase on the right (at the end of this block) displays some favorite **Hungarian spirits:** Tokaji Aszú, colored (and priced) like gold and called "the wine of kings, and the king of wines" (see page 253); Unicum, the

secret-recipe herbal liquor beloved by Hungarians and un-
drinkable to everyone else (see
page 251); and the local version
of schnapps, *pálinka*, in several
fruit flavors.

In the second block, meat
is on the right, and produce is
on the left. At the end of this

section on the left, you have a good opportunity to sample home-made **strudels** *(rétesek)* of various flavors for 230 Ft.

In the third block, you'll see overpriced paprika on both sides. To save a few forints, turn left before entering this block, go down

the street, then turn right at the next corner. The **Csárdi és Csárdi** stall (on the right) lets you sample both types of paprika: sweet (*édes,* used for flavor) and hot (*csipós,* used sparingly to add some kick). Note the difference, choose your favorite, and buy some to take home (for more information, see

"Paprika Primer" on page 250). They also sell fun little wooden spice spoons.

Back on the main paprika drag, just after the stairs on the right, hung high amidst the paprika (at the Kmetty & Kmetty stall), is a photo of **Margaret Thatcher** visiting this market in 1989. She expected atrocious conditions compared to English markets, but was pleasantly surprised to find this place up to snuff. This was, after all, "goulash communism" (Hungary's pragmatic mix, which allowed a little private enterprise to keep people going). On the steps of this building, she delivered a historic speech about open society, heralding the impending arrival of the market economy.

At the fourth block, on the right, the corner showcase features another favorite Hungarian food: **goose liver** *(libamáj)*—not to be confused with the cheaper and less typical duck liver *(kacsamáj);* see the geese standing above the case. Goose liver comes in various forms: most traditional is packaged whole (*naturel* or *blokk*), others are pâté (*parfé* or *püré*). Hungary is, after France, the world's second-biggest producer of foie gras.

In the fifth block, on the left, look for another local favorite: Hungarian **szalámi** (Pick, a brand from the town of Szeged, is a favorite here).

Reaching the sixth block, above the corner showcase on the right, you'll see a poster showing two types of uniquely Hungarian **livestock:** *Mangalica* is a hairy pig that almost went extinct, but became popular again after butchers discovered it makes great ham—and has a lower fat content than other types of pork (look for this on local menus). *Szürkemarha* are gray longhorn cattle. Keeping an eye on all that livestock, but not pictured here, is the distinctive *Puli* (or larger *Komondor*)—a Hungarian sheepdog with tightly curled hair that resembles dreadlocks.

• *Head up the escalator at the back of the market (on the left).*

Upstairs

Along the upstairs back wall are historic photos of the market hall (and pay WCs).

If you're in the mood for some shopping, this is a convenient (if pricey) place to look—with a great selection of souvenirs both traditional (embroidery) and not-so-traditional (commie-kitsch T-shirts). For tips on shopping here, see the Shopping in Budapest chapter.

The left wall (as you face the front) is lined with fun, cheap, stand-up, Hungarian-style fast-food joints and six-stool pubs. About two-thirds of the way along the hall (after the second bridge), the **Lángos** stand is the best eatery in the market, serving up the deep-fried snack called *lángos*—similar to elephant ears, but savory rather than sweet. The most typical version is *sajtos tejfölös*— with sour cream and cheese. You can also add garlic *(fokhagyma)*. The **Fakanál Étterem** cafeteria above the main entrance is handy but pricey.

• *For a less glamorous look at the market, head down the escalators to the...*

Basement

In addition to the handy supermarket down here, the basement is pungent with tanks of still-swimming carp, catfish, and perch, and piles of pickles (along  the left side). Stop at one of the pickle stands and take a look. Hungarians pickle just about anything: peppers and cukes, of course, but also cauliflower, cabbage, beets, tomatoes, garlic, and so on. They use particularly strong vinegar, which has a powerful flavor but keeps things very crispy. Until recently—before importing fruits and vegetables became more common—most "salads" out of season were pickled items like these. Vendors are usually happy to give you a sample; consider picking up a colorful jar of mixed pickled veggies for your picnic.

• *When your exploration is finished...so is this walk. Exit the hall the way you came in. Near the Great Market Hall, you have several sight-seeing options. If you'd like to stroll back to Vörösmarty tér—this time along the fashionable Váci utca—you can walk straight ahead from the market. The green Liberty Bridge next to the market leads straight to Gellért Hotel, with its famous hot-springs bath, at the foot of Gellért Hill (see the Thermal Baths chapter; trams #47 and #49 zip you right there).*

*Convenient trams connect this area to the rest of Budapest: **Tram #2** runs from under the Liberty Bridge along the Danube directly back to Vigadó tér (at the promenade by Vörösmarty tér), the Chain Bridge, and the Parliament (where my **Leopold Town Walk** begins). **Trams #47** and **#49** (catch them directly in front of the market) zip to the right around the Small Boulevard to the National Museum (see page 65) and, beyond that, the Great Synagogue (for my **Great Synagogue and Jewish Quarter Tour**) and Deák tér (the starting point of my **Andrássy Út Walk**)—or you can simply walk around the Small Boulevard to reach these sights in about 10-15 minutes.*

ANDRÁSSY ÚT WALK

From Deák Tér to Heroes' Square

Connecting downtown Pest to City Park, Andrássy út is Budapest's main boulevard, lined with plane trees, shops, theaters, cafés, and locals living well. Budapesters like to think of Andrássy út as the Champs-Elysées and Broadway rolled into one. While that's a stretch, it is a good place to stroll, get a feel for today's urban Pest, and visit a few top attractions (most notably the Opera House and the House of Terror) on the way to Heroes' Square and City Park.

Orientation

Length of This Walk: Allow an hour, not including time to enter the sights.

Overview: Andrássy út is divided roughly into thirds. The most interesting first section (from Deák tér to the Oktogon) is the focus of this walk. The middle section (between the Oktogon and Kodály körönd) features one major sight, the House of Terror. The final third (Kodály körönd to Heroes' Square), while pleasant and comparatively low-key, offers fewer sight-seeing opportunities.

Shortcut: The M1/yellow Metró line runs every couple of minutes just under the street—so it's easy to skip several blocks ahead, or to backtrack (stops marked by yellow signs).

Getting There: The walk begins at Deák tér—easy to reach from anywhere in the city, as it's on all three Metró lines. If you're coming from Vörösmarty tér in central Pest, simply hop the M1/yellow Metró line one stop, or walk five minutes up Deák utca. If you want to skip to the start of Andrássy út itself, you can ride the M1 to the Bajcsy-Zsilinszky út stop and start this walk at the "Millennium Underground of 1896" section.

Opera House: Lobby free to enter Mon-Sat 11:00 until show time—generally 19:00, or until 17:00 if there's no performance, on Sun open 3 hours before the performance—generally 16:00-19:00, or 10:00-13:00 if there's a matinee; tours-2,900 Ft, 500 Ft extra for 5-minute mini-concert following the tour, in English nearly daily at 15:00 and 16:00—buy tickets at shop inside lobby and to the left, shop has slightly shorter hours than lobby; Andrássy út 22, tel. 1/332-8197.

House of Terror: 2,000 Ft, possibly more for special exhibits, audioguide-1,500 Ft, Tue-Sun 10:00-18:00, closed Mon, last entry 30 minutes before closing, Andrássy út 60, tel. 1/374-2600, www.terrorhaza.hu.

Franz Liszt Museum: 1,300 Ft, audioguide-700 Ft, Mon-Fri 10:00-18:00, Sat 9:00-17:00, closed Sun, Vörösmarty utca 35, tel. 1/322-9804, www.lisztmuseum.hu.

Starring: Budapest's most elegant drag, with fine architecture, upscale shopping, great restaurants, and top-notch sightseeing—from opulent (Opera House) to sobering (House of Terror).

Nearby Eateries: For restaurants near Andrássy út, see page 258.

The Walk Begins

(See "Andrássy Út Walk" map, page 140.)
• *Begin in the middle of the paved square (near the M2 and M3 Metró entrances) called...*

Deák Tér

This modest square seems more important than it is, since it's the place where the three Metró lines intersect. (All Metró tracks lead to Deák.) The square is named for **Ferenc Deák** (1803-1876), a statesman who pushed for persistent international pressure on the Habsburgs to im-

prove Hungary's status after his rabble-rousing compatriots failed in the 1848 Revolution. (The peace-loving Deák was sort of a Hungarian Jimmy Carter.) It worked. With the Compromise of 1867, Hungary was granted a good measure of autonomy in the empire.

Sitting unassumingly on the square is the blocky, typically austere **Lutheran church,** with its Neoclassical colonnade entry and shallow green dome. Looming over the square across the street is the landmark, but sadly neglected, yellow office block called the **Ankerház.** Like the square it dominates, this building isn't as important as it might seem.

On the upper part of the square (up the stairs) is a memorial

Andrássy Út Walk

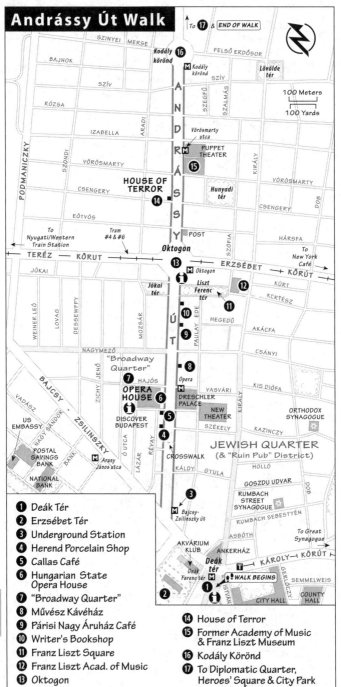

To ⑰ & END OF WALK

SZINYEI MERSE

BAJNOK

Kodály ⑯
körönd

FELSŐ ERDŐSOR

Ⓜ Kodály
körönd

SZÍV

Lövölde
tér

SZÍV

RÓZSA

ARADI

SZEGFŰ

SZALMÁS

100 Meters

100 Yards

IZABELLA

SZONDI

VÖRÖSMARTY

Vörösmarty
utca

Ⓜ PUPPET
THEATER

KIRÁLY

VÖRÖSMARTY

PODMANICZKY

CSENGERY

HOUSE OF
TERROR

⑭

⑮

Hunyadi
tér

CSENGERY

DOB

EÖTVÖS

To
Nyugati/Western
Train Station

Tram
#4 & #6

POST

SZÓFIA

HÁRSFA

TERÉZ — KÖRUT

Oktogon

⑬

ERZSÉBET

KÖRÚT

To
New York
Café

JÓKAI

Ⓜ Oktogon

ⓘ

KÜRT

WEINER LEÓ

LOVAG

DESSEWFFY

MOZSÁR

Jókai
tér

Liszt
Ferenc
tér

⑫

KERTÉSZ

⑪

⑩

HEGEDŰ

AKÁCFA

Ⓤ

⑨

PAULAY EDE

NAGYMEZŐ

CSÁNYI

BAJCSY - ZSILINSZKY

ZICHY JENŐ

"Broadway
Quarter"

⑦ HAJÓS

⑧

Opera

KIS DIÓFA

VADÁSZ

NAGY SÁNDOR

OPERA HOUSE

⑥

ⓘ

VASVÁRI

KIRÁLY

ORTHODOX
SYNAGOGUE

US
EMBASSY

DISCOVER
BUDAPEST

⑤

DRESCHLER
PALACE

NEW
THEATER

POSTAL
SAVINGS
BANK

BANK

Ⓜ Arany
János utca

ÓUTCA

LÁZÁR

RÉVAY

④

SZÉKELY

KAZINCZY

JEWISH QUARTER
(& "Ruin Pub" District)

NATIONAL
BANK

CROSSWALK

KÁLDY

GYULA

HOLLÓ

GOSZDU UDVAR

DOB

③

Ⓜ Bajcsy-
Zsilinszky út

RUMBACH
STREET
SYNAGOGUE

RUMBACH SEBESTYÉN

To Great
Synagogue

ASBÓTH

AKVÁRIUM
KLUB

ANKERHÁZ

KÁROLY

KÖRÚT

Deák
Ferenc tér

Deák
tér

Ⓜ Ⓣ

ⓘ WALK BEGINS

②

①

GERLÓCZY

ISTVÁN

SEMMELWEIS

CITY HALL

COUNTY
HALL

❶ Deák Tér
❷ Erzsébet Tér
❸ Underground Station
❹ Herend Porcelain Shop
❺ Callas Café
❻ Hungarian State
   Opera House
❼ "Broadway Quarter"
❽ Művész Kávéház
❾ Párisi Nagy Áruház Café
❿ Writer's Bookshop
⓫ Franz Liszt Square
⓬ Franz Liszt Acad. of Music
⓭ Oktogon

⓮ House of Terror
⓯ Former Academy of Music
   & Franz Liszt Museum
⓰ Kodály Körönd
⓱ To Diplomatic Quarter,
   Heroes' Square & City Park

to **Gábor Sztehlo,** a Lutheran pastor who rescued approximately 2,000 local Jews from the Arrow Cross regime during the Holocaust. Hungarian officials understandably love to celebrate these (relatively rare) "righteous Gentiles" who came to the rescue of the Jews. (For more on the Holocaust in Hungary, see page 184.)

• *From Deák tér, cross Harmincad street— the one with all the bus stops (including one to Memento Park, explained on page 216)—and head for...*

Erzsébet Tér

This pretty, leafy park is named for one of Deák's contemporaries: Elisabeth, the wife of the Habsburg Emperor Franz Josef. While Deák pressed Franz Josef with diplomacy, Empress Elisabeth (a.k.a. Sisi) pressured him at home...Hungarian autonomy was one of her pet issues (for more on this "royal and imperial" couple, see page 316).

The park was long marred by the presence of a gloomy, polluting, communist-era international bus station. A few years ago, locals reclaimed the space as a welcoming public zone. Notice there are two parts to Erzsébet tér: the more traditional park behind the bus-station skeleton, and a sleek, modern new area in front of it. Recently the government planned to build a new national theater in this spot, and they even began to dig the foundation. But when the parliament changed hands, construction was aborted—leaving a giant hole that locals called "The National Ditch."

Eventually they came up with a creative use for the space: an underground parking garage and a unique café/nightclub. Walk closer to the wall and look down (at the end facing Deák tér): A long series of terraces filled with café tables leads down into the **Akvárium** nightclub. On balmy summer nights, outdoor performances take place here, and this whole area is filled with young locals. The incline leads to the indoor, underground part of the café. Walk a little farther through the park to reach the artificial pond that covers part of the ditch. Look closely: Especially at night, you can see through the glass floor of the very shallow pond and spot people walking around in the underground nightclub. (For more, see page 286.)

ANDRÁSSY ÚT WALK

• *At the far corner of Erzsébet tér (past the ditch), cross the busy Small Boulevard (here called Bajcsy-Zsilinszky út) to the beginning of Andrássy út. For now, stay on the right side of the boulevard. A few steps up from where the street begins,* look for the yellow railings on either side of the street with the low-profile Földalatti *sign. This marks the Bajcsy-Zsilinszky út Metró stop. Go down the steps and back more than 100 years (if they ask you for your Metró ticket, just take a peek, then head back up).*

Millennium Underground of 1896

Built to get the masses conveniently out to Heroes' Square for the festivities, this fun and extremely handy little Metró line follows Andrássy út from Vörösmarty tér (Pest's main square) to City Park. It was originally dubbed the "Franz Josef Underground Line"— in honor of the then-emperor—but later simply became known as the Underground *(Földalatti)*. Just 20 steps below street level, it's so shallow that you must follow the signs on the street (listing end

points—*ua Mexikói út felé* takes you toward City Park) to gauge the right direction, because there's no underpass for switching platforms. The first underground on the Continent (London's is older), it originally had horse-drawn cars. Trains depart every couple of minutes. Though recently renovated, the M1 line retains its 1896 atmosphere, along with fun black-and-white photos of the age.

• *From the top of the stairs here, notice the great view across the street to St. István's Basilica. Now continue...*

Strolling up Andrássy Út

This grand boulevard—140 feet wide and nearly 2 miles long—was begun in 1871, when city bigwigs decided that on-the-rise Budapest needed an answer to Paris' Champs-Elysées. But instead of leading to an Arc de Triomphe, Andrássy út culminates at the similarly triumphal Heroes' Square. The boulevard also provided a convenient link between the dense urban center of Pest and the green expanse of City Park, allowing city-dwellers to zip out for a break from the bustle without plodding along congested narrow streets. The boulevard was officially inaugurated with much fanfare in 1885. Because most of the buildings were built within about 15

Gyula Andrássy
(1823-1890)

A key player in the 1848 Revolution, Count Gyula (Julius) Andrássy went on to help forge (along with Ferenc Deák) the
Dual Monarchy of the Austro-Hungarian Empire. As Budapest
boomed, Andrássy also served as an urban planner who championed the idea of building a grand boulevard from downtown
to City Park. Andrássy was also the Hungarian prime minister and Austro-Hungarian foreign minister (1871-1879). Eventually he was forced to step down after his unpopular campaign to appropriate Bosnia-Herzegovina (and consequently
boost the Slav population of the empire, which destabilized its
delicate ethnic balance). But to most Hungarians, Andrássy is
best known for his alleged relationship with Empress Sisi, who
adored all things Hungarian (see page 316). Her third daughter—believed to be the count's—was known as the Little Hungarian Princess.

years, Andrássy út enjoys a pleasant architectural harmony. Historicism—a creative merging of various complementary styles—was
all the rage at the time, and many of the structures also employ the
urban Germanic Neoclassical style known as *Gründerzeit*. Look up
as you stroll to see the heroic statuary adorning the tops of buildings.

Since being built, this boulevard—and the major intersections
along its length—have constantly changed names with the tenor
of the times. Originally called Radial Boulevard (Súgarút), it was
later christened for Count Andrássy, who had strongly promoted
its construction (see sidebar). When the Soviets moved in, they renamed it Sztálin út; after the 1956 Uprising, it was briefly called
Hungarian Youth Boulevard, before they re-dubbed it People's
Republic Boulevard. And finally, with the fall of communism, it
regained its historical name: Andrássy út.

Running parallel to Andrássy út, two blocks to the right, is
Király utca, which is lined with home-improvement shops (a hot
commodity in this city, where so many people are fixing up flats
long neglected by the communists). This area—formerly the Jewish
Quarter, and now more seedy than most parts of central Pest—is
also home to the city's distinctive "ruin pubs" (described on page
287).

• *At your first opportunity—about a block and a half up from the underground station—cross to the left side of Andrássy út to find the next
few attractions. As you cross, look right to the far end of the street, where
a heroic statue marks Heroes' Square. The studs between the curb and
parked cars define the bike lane.*

This first stretch of Andrássy út is being developed as the city's cancan of big-money stores featuring international brands, such as Gucci and Louis Vuitton. But there are still some local shops—on the left, at #16, is a **Herend** shop, selling very expensive pieces of Hungary's top porcelain (see page 275).

Upscale as it has become, Andrássy út remains an artery for the city, often clogged with traffic...except during "critical mass," when 80,000 bikers take back the street twice a year (though these days it's occurring more and more often—generally on weekends). During these times, the street is closed to traffic for a full day and given over to cyclists, in-line skaters, skateboarders, and pedestrians...a tempting taste of what could be.

On the left side of the street, on the corner at #20, look for the recommended **Callas café,** with sumptuous *Jugendstil* decor (for details, see page 266).

It was along this stretch of Andrássy út that Steven Spielberg filmed much of *Munich,* since the street has fine architecture that can stand in for many great European cities.

• *On the left, just after Callas, is the can't-miss-it...*

Hungarian State Opera House (Magyar Állami Operaház)

The Neo-Renaissance home of the Hungarian State Opera features performances (almost daily except during outdoor music season, late June-early Sept) and delightful tours. The building dates from the 1890s, not long after Budapest had become co-capital of the Habsburg Empire. The Hungarians wanted to put their city on the map as a legitimate European capital, and that meant they needed an opera house. Emperor Franz Josef pro-

vided half the funds...on the condition that it be smaller than the opera house in his hometown of Vienna. And so, Miklós Ybl designed a building that would exceed Vienna's famous Staatsoper in opulence, if not in size. (Franz Josef was reportedly displeased.) It was built using almost entirely Hungarian materials. After being damaged in World War II, it was painstakingly restored in the early 1980s. Today, with lavish marble-and-gold-leaf decor, a gorgeous gilded interior slathered with paintings of Greek myths, and high-quality performances at bargain prices, this is one of Europe's finest opera houses.

You have a few options for seeing this place. To just get a taste, slip in the front door when the box office is open and check out the sumptuous entryway. For the full story (and to get into the remarkable auditorium), take one of the 45-minute guided tours in English (usually every day at 15:00 and 16:00—see page 67). To see the Opera House in action, take in an excellent (and refreshingly affordable) performance—for specifics, see page 280.

• *The Opera House marks the beginning of an emerging dining-and-nightlife zone dubbed the...*

"Broadway Quarter"

The street just behind the Opera House, **Hajós utca,** is traffic-free and a budding outdoor-dining zone with a smattering of trendy restaurants...and more soon to appear.

• *Cross to the right side of Andrássy út for the next few sights.*

Across the street from the Opera House, and echoing its shape (although in a different style), is the **Dreschler Palace.** It

was co-designed by Ödön Lechner, a leading architect whose works also include the Postal Savings Bank (see page 116). In this building's late-19th-century heyday, one of Budapest's top cafés filled its gallery. More recently, it housed the Ballet Institute. And not long ago, the beautiful but neglected building was purchased by a luxury hotel chain...but the plans fell through, and it's still waiting for a new tenant. Tucked behind it is the **New Theater** (Új Szinház, with a fine *Jugendstil* facade), one of many popular venues around here for Hungarian-language plays (Paulay Ede utca 35, tel. 1/269-6021, www.ujszinhaz.hu).

A few steps up Andrássy út on the right (at #29) is another fine historic café, **Művész Kávéház.** As it's a hangout for actors and musicians, this is your best chance to rub elbows with actual drama queens and divas (described on page 266).

The next major cross-street, **Nagymező utca,** features a chic cluster of restaurants, bars, and theaters. This is an enjoyable place to stroll on a summer evening. While you might be tempted to attend a show along Budapest's answer to Broadway, note that most of the plays and musicals here are in Hungarian only. So unless you want to hear "Music of the Night" sung in Hungarian (as it was meant to be), keep looking. (The Entertainment in Budapest chapter offers several more accessible alternatives.)

Continue straight across Nagymező utca, staying on the right side of Andrássy út. A half-block down on the right (at #39) is

a grand old early-20th-century building marked **Párisi Nagy Áruház** (Paris Department Store), with a fine recommended café inside. One of the city's first department stores, this was a popular shopping stop for years, even through communism (many young adults remember their parents bringing them here as kids). But as was common in Budapest, the store closed down and sat deserted and glum for years until investors came along to rescue it. The new owners, the Alexandra bookstore chain, turned the main area into a great bookshop, created office space above, and—inside, up the escalator at the back—fully restored the sumptuous Lotz Hall to create an excellent café with tinkling-piano ambience and reasonable prices. Dip inside to check it out (free entry, daily 10:00-22:00; for more details, see page 265). Upstairs is an art gallery and antiques shop.

At the end of the block on the right (at #45) is a much humbler (but arguably more historic) bookstore: the **Writer's Bookshop** (Írók Boltja). During Budapest's late-19th-century glory days, the Japan Café at this spot was the haunt of many of the great artistic minds that populated the city, including architect Ödön Lechner and poet Attila József. Today the management still encourages loitering (and sells some English books).

• *Just after the bookshop is Budapest's outdoor-dining mecca...*

Franz Liszt Square (Liszt Ferenc Tér)

This leafy square is surrounded by hip, expensive cafés and restaurants. (The best is the recommended, kitschy, communist-themed restaurant **Menza**.) This is *the* scene for Budapest's yuppies.

Strangely, neither the statue on this square nor the one facing it, across Andrássy út, is of Franz Liszt. But deeper in the park, you'll find a modern statue of Liszt dramatically playing an imaginary piano. And at

the far end of the square is the **Franz Liszt Academy of Music,** founded by and named for this half-Hungarian, half-Austrian composer who had a Hungarian name and passport. Liszt loved his family's Magyar heritage (though he didn't speak Hungarian) and spent his last six years in Budapest. His Academy of Music, while undergoing a renovation, still teaches students and hosts concerts (for details, see page 282; for more on Liszt, see page 284).

• *One block up from Franz Liszt Square is the gigantic crossroads known as the...*

Oktogon

This vast intersection with its corners snipped off—where Andrássy út meets the Great Boulevard ring road (Nagykörút)—was called Mussolini tér during World War II, then November 7 tér in honor of the Bolshevik Revolution.

Today kids have nicknamed it American tér for the fast-food joints littering the square and streets nearby. Standing (carefully) in the center of Andrássy út, you can already see the column of Heroes' Square at the end of the boulevard.

From here, if you have time to delve into workaday Budapest, consider a trip on tram #4 or #6, which trundle in both directions around the ring road. If you've got time for a short detour to the most opulent coffee break of your life, head for the recommended **New York Café** (see page 264): Just hop on a tram to the right (tram #6 toward Móricz Zsigmond körtér or tram #4 toward Fehérvári út), and get off at the Wesselényi utca stop.

• *There's one more major sight between here and Heroes' Square. Walk two more blocks up Andrássy út to reach the...*

House of Terror (Terror Háza)

The building at Andrássy út 60 (on the left) has been painted a lifeless blue-gray, and the word "TERROR" is carved into the overhanging eaves. This is the place where two evil regimes tortured their Hungarian subjects. Now a modern museum documenting the terror of Hungary's "double occupation"—first at the hands of the Nazis, then the Soviets—this is essential sightseeing for those intrigued by Budapest's dark 20th century, and interesting to anyone. ☺ See the House of Terror Tour chapter.

• *Two significant buildings stand across the boulevard from the House of Terror (on the right side of Andrássy út, just behind the Metró stop).*

Former Academy of Music (Franz Liszt Museum) and Puppet Theater

The yellow building on the corner of Vörösmarty utca (at Andrássy #67) is the **former Academy of Music**—founded by Franz Liszt and later moved to the building we just saw on his square. Upstairs is the small but endearing **Franz Liszt Museum,** in the old flat where the composer spent much of his time for the last six years of his life. This dusty collection might interest classical music buffs but will probably underwhelm most others. After putting on shoe covers, you glide through three rooms filled with period furniture and pianos (including ones custom-made for Liszt, and a "composing desk" with a small three-octave keyboard built by famous piano-maker Ludwig Bösendorfer). Liszt's bedroom (to the right as you enter) contains his actual bed and a little personal altar where he knelt to pray. Look for the lithographs of Liszt sitting in this very room. The cupboard contains personal belongings, including a plate that belonged to writer (and Liszt friend) George Sand, and locks of the composer's hair that were saved by his fans. In his heyday, Liszt was as adored as much as today's biggest-name rock stars.

On Saturdays at 11:00, **performances** take place in the building's small concert hall (included in admission; details might change when renovation of the main Academy of Music, back on Franz Liszt Square, is finished).

The next building is the **Puppet Theater** (Bábszinház), a venue for top-notch puppet shows (see page 272 for details).

• *While you can hoof it from here to Heroes' Square (visible in the distance, about a 15-minute walk), there's less to see along the rest of Andrássy út. If you prefer, hop on the Metró here (from right in front of the Puppet Theater) and ride it three stops to Hősök tere.*

Or, if you continue walking up Andrássy út, after four blocks you'll reach the grand intersection called...

Kodály Körönd

This circular crossroads—which seems to echo the octagonal one we passed through earlier—is named for another great Hungarian composer, Zoltán Kodály (who lived in a mansion here, at #1, now a museum; for more on Kodály, see page 285). During the Nazi occupation, it had the jarring name Hitler tér.

Standing in the four wedge-shaped parks—overshadowed by the stately mansions surrounding them—are statues of four Hungarian heroes who fought against Ottoman invaders. Think of these as rejects from the Millennium Monument at Heroes' Square just up the boulevard. In fact, two of the original statues from Kodály körönd were eventually "promoted" to the colonnade there, and their spots here were taken by two different heroes.

• *After Kodály körönd, Andrássy út enters its final third, the...*

Diplomatic Quarter

Continuing up the street, notice that the buildings lining Andrássy út shrink and pull back from the busy boulevard, huddling behind trees. Instead of boasting bulky four- and five-story apartment blocks, it turns into a sleepy, leafy residential zone. These villas were formerly occupied by aristocrats, diplomats, and wealthy Jews. Today this is where many foreign states maintain their embassies. If you'd like to skip the final stretch, you can hop on the Metró at Kodály körönd. Or, to complete your stroll, keep going.

• *Andrássy út terminates at Heroes' Square. See* **Heroes' Square and City Park Walk** *chapter.*

HOUSE OF
TERROR TOUR

Terror Háza

Along one of the prettiest stretches of urban Budapest, in the house at 60 Andrássy Boulevard, some of the most horrific acts in Hungarian history took place. The former headquarters of two of the country's darkest regimes—the Arrow Cross (Nazi-occupied Hungary's version of the Gestapo) and the ÁVO/ÁVH (communist Hungary's secret police)—is now, fittingly, an excellent museum that recounts those times of terror. The high-tech, conceptual, and sometimes over-the-top exhibits attempt to document the atrocities endured by Hungary during the 20th century. This is a powerful experience, particularly for elderly Hungarians who knew both victims and perpetrators and have personal memories of the terrors that came with Hungary's "double occupation."

Orientation

Cost: 2,000 Ft, possibly more for special exhibitions.

Hours: Tue-Sun 10:00-18:00, closed Mon, last entry 30 minutes before closing.

Getting There: It's located at Andrássy út 60, district VI, near the Vörösmarty utca stop of the M1/yellow Metró line. Note that this is Vörösmarty utca, not Vörösmarty tér (which is a different stop). Outside, an overhang casts the shadow outline of the word "TERROR" onto the building.

Audioguide and Information: The 1,500-Ft English audioguide is good but almost too thorough, and can be difficult to hear over the din of Hungarian soundtracks in each room. You can't fast-forward through the dense and sometimes long-winded commentary. As an alternative, my self-guided tour covers the key points. A silver plaque in each room provides the basics (in English), and each room is stocked with free English fliers providing more in-depth information (very similar to what's covered by the audioguide). Tel. 1/374-2600, www.terrorhaza.hu.

Length of This Tour: 1.5-2 hours.

Services: Café, good bookshop, and WCs.

Photography: Not allowed inside.

Starring: Fascism, communism, and the resilient Hungarian spirit.

Nearby Eateries: For more restaurants near the House of Terror, see page 258.

Background

In the lead-up to World War II, Hungary initially allied with Hitler—both to retain a degree of self-determination and to try to regain its huge territorial losses after World War I's devastating Treaty of Trianon (see page 453). As the rest of Europe fell into war, Hungary tiptoed between supporting the Nazis and, wherever possible, charting its own course. The Hungarians found themselves in the unenviable position of providing a buffer between Nazi Germany to the west and the Soviet Union to the east. They did just enough to stay in the Nazis' good graces (the Hungarian Second Army invaded the Soviet Union in 1941), while attempting to maintain what autonomy they could.

Hitler finally got fed up with Hungary's less-than-wholehearted support, and in March of 1944, the Nazi-affiliated Arrow Cross Party was forcibly installed as Hungary's new government. The Arrow Cross immediately set to work exterminating Budapest's Jews (most of whom had survived until then, although they had suffered under the earlier regime's anti-Semitic laws). The Nazi surrogates deported nearly 440,000 Jewish people to Auschwitz, murdered thousands more on the streets of Budapest, and executed hundreds in the basement of this building. (For more on this ugly time, see page 184.)

The Red Army entered Hungary from the USSR in late August of 1944. After a hard-fought battle (and a devastating siege), they took Budapest on February 13, 1945, and forced the last Nazi soldier out of Hungary on April 4. Although the USSR characterized this as the "liberation" of Hungary, it soon became clear that the Hungarians had merely gone from the Nazi frying pan into the Soviet fire. Here in Budapest, the new communist leaders took over the same building as headquarters for their secret police (the ÁVO, later renamed ÁVH). To keep dissent to a minimum, the secret police terrorized, tried, deported, or executed anyone suspected of being an enemy of the state.

Critics of this museum point out that it doesn't draw a very fine distinction between these two very different phases of the "double occupation." As you tour the exhibits, remember that as similar as their methods might seem, the Nazis and the communists represented opposite extremes of the political spectrum. Hungarians, like so many others in the 20th century, got caught in the cross fire.

The Tour Begins

• *Buy your ticket (and rent an audioguide, if you wish) and head into the museum.*

Atrium

The atrium features a Soviet T-54 tank, symbolizing the looming threat of violence that helped keep both regimes in power. Tanks like this one rolled into Hungary to crush the 1956 Uprising. Behind the tank, stretching to the ceiling, is a vast wall covered with 3,200 portraits of people who were murdered by the Nazis or the communists in this very building.

• *The one-way exhibit begins two floors up, then spirals down to the cellar—just follow signs for* Kiállítás/Exhibition. *To begin, you can either take the elevator (to floor 2), or walk up the red stairwell nearby, decorated with old Socialist Realist sculptures from the communist days (including, near the base of the stairs, two subjects you won't find at Memento Park: Josef Stalin and Mátyás Rákosi, the most severe communist leader of Hungary).*

Once upstairs, the first room gives an overview of the...

Double Occupation (Kettős Megszállás)

The video by the entrance sets the stage for Hungary's 20th century: its territorial losses after World War I; its alliance with, then invasion by, the Nazis; and its "liberation," then occupation, by the USSR (described earlier, under "Background").

The TV screens on the partition in the middle of the room show grainy footage of both sides of the "double occupation": the Nazis on the black side and the Soviets (appropriately) on the red side. Do a slow counterclockwise loop, starting with the black (Nazi) side. See Hitler speaking and saluting in occupied Hungary, and Nazis goose-stepping down Andrássy út. The giant, ironic quote reads, "Last night I dreamed that the Nazis were gone...and nobody else came."

But come they did. The giant picture of the destroyed Chain

Bridge (on the far wall) shows the passing of the torch between the two regimes and is a chilling reminder that these two equally brutal groups, which employed similar means of terror, were sworn enemies: As the Soviets' Red Army approached from the east to liberate Hungary, the Nazis made a last stand in Budapest (Hitler, who considered the Danube a natural border, ordered them never to retreat). The Nazis destroyed all of the bridges across the Danube (some without warning, while they were filled with civilians), then holed up on Castle Hill. The Soviets laid siege for 100 days, gradually devastating the city.

Circling around to the red (Soviet) side, you see Budapest in the aftermath of World War II and the early days of Soviet rule. The telephones on the wall play Hungarian sound clips from the time.

• *Go through the* **Passage of Hungarian Nazis,** *decorated with the words of a proclamation by Arrow Cross leader Ferenc Szálasi (there's also a WC). Continue into the room of...*

Hungarian Nazis (Nyilas Terem)

The table is set with Arrow Cross china, bearing a V-for-victory

emblem with a laurel wreath. At the head of the table stands an Arrow Cross uniform. Examine the armband: The red and white stripes are an old Hungarian royal pattern, dating from the days of St. István, and the insignia combines arrows, a cross, and an "H" for Hungary. On the loudspeaker, Arrow Cross leader Ferenc Szálasi preaches about reclaiming a "Greater Hungary" and about fighting against the Jews and the insidious influence of their Bolshevism. On the far wall, the footage of the frozen river shows where many of those Jews ended up: unceremoniously shot into the icy Danube. Listen for the sickening, periodic splash...splash...splash....

• *As you leave the room, the exhibit subtly (perhaps too subtly) turns the page from the Nazi period to the communist one.*

Gulag

After the Red Army drove the Nazis out of Hungary, they quickly set to work punishing people who had backed their enemies. Being sent to a gulag was one particularly hard fate.

The word "gulag" refers to a network of secret Soviet prison camps, mostly in Siberia. These were hard-labor camps where potential and actual dissidents were sent in order to punish them, remove their dangerous influence from society, and make an example of those who would dare to defy the regime. The Soviets euphemistically told them they were going away for "a little work" *(malenki robot)*. It was an understatement.

On the carpet, a giant map of the USSR shows the locations of some of these camps, where an estimated 600,000-700,000

Hungarian civilians and prisoners of war were sent...about half of whom never returned. And that only represents a tiny fraction of the millions of people from throughout Europe and the USSR thought to have perished in the gulag system. The lighted cones locate specific camps, with artifacts from those places. Video screens show grainy footage of transfer trains clattering through an icy countryside, gruesome scenes from the camps, and prisoner testimony. (For more on the atrocious conditions in the gulag, see sidebar on page 162.)

People of Germanic heritage living in Hungary were targeted for deportation, but—due to a strict Moscow-imposed quota system—nobody was immune. Among the gulag victims was the Swedish diplomat Raoul Wallenberg, who had rescued many Hungarian Jews from the Nazis (see page 190).

Those who survived their experience with "corrective forced labor" were often not allowed to return to their families, and if they did, were sworn to secrecy...never allowed to tell of the horrors of the gulag until after 1989. The last Hungarian gulag prisoner, András Toma, finally returned from Siberia in 2000, having been interned in a mental hospital for decades after the gulags were dissolved—two years in a gulag followed by 53 years in an asylum. The doctors, unfamiliar with his tongue-twisting Hungarian language, assumed he was simply mad.

Changing Clothes (Átöltözés)

This locker room—with rotating figures dressed alternately in Arrow Cross and communist uniforms—satirizes the readiness of many Hungarians to align with whoever was in power. The sped-up video shows turncoat guards changing their uniforms. While it seems absurd that someone's allegiance could shift so quickly, many of these people were told that they'd be executed if they did not switch...or they could "change clothes," admit their mistake in joining the Arrow Cross, and pledge allegiance to the new communist regime. For most, it was an easy choice. Many people (including Cardinal József Mindszenty) were imprisoned by both regimes—and it's entirely plausible that they saw the same guards dressed in both uniforms.

The Fifties ('50-es Évek)

Of course, the transition was not always so straightforward. The insinuation of the communist regime into the fabric of Hungary was a gradual process. From the Red Army's "liberation" in 1945 until 1948, a power struggle raged between pro-democracy factions and the Soviet-backed communist puppet leaders. The voting booths at the beginning of this room symbolize that, at first, the Soviets fostered an illusion of choice for the Hungarian people. Elections were held throughout the Soviet satellite states in the mid-1940s, with the assumption that the communist Hungarian Workers' Party would sweep into power. But in the 1945 parliamentary elections, the communists won only 17 percent of the vote. After this, the Soviets gradually eliminated opposition leaders by uncovering "plots," then executing the alleged perpetrators. In the following two elections, they also stacked the deck by allowing workers to vote as often as they liked—often five or six times apiece (using the blue ballot cards you'll see in the voting booths). Even so, in the 1947 election, the communists still had to disqualify 700,000 opposition votes in order to win. (And you thought "hanging chads" were aggravating.)

Once in power, the Hungarian Workers' Party ruled with an iron fist and did away with the charade of elections entirely. Hungary became a "People's Republic" and was reorganized on the Soviet system. Private property was nationalized, the economy became fully socialistic, and the country fell into poverty.

Not that you'd know any of this from the sanitized, state-sponsored images of the time. In the voting booths, screens show a loop of communist propaganda from the 1950s. Lining the walls

are glossy communist-era paintings, celebrating the peasants of the "people's revolution" (farmers, soldiers, and sailors looking boldly to the future), idyllic scenes of communities coming together, and romanticized depictions of communist leaders (Lenin as the brave sailor; Mátyás Rákosi—the portly, bald communist leader of Hungary—as the kindly grandfather, gladly receiving flowers from a sweet young girl). Imagine the societal schizophrenia bred by the communists' good-cop, bad-cop methods: pretending to be a bunch of nice guys while at the same time terrorizing the people.

The distorted stage separates these two methods of people-control. The stretched-out images of Lenin, Rákosi, and Stalin imply the falsehood of everything we've just seen; backstage is the dark underbelly of the regime—the constant surveillance that bred paranoia among the people. The cases at the end display documentation for show trials. We'll learn more about these means of terror as we progress.

Soviet "Advisors" (Szovjet Tanácsadók)

These "advisors" were more like supervisors. On the wall plaque is a list of the Soviet ambassadors to Hungary, who wielded ter-

rific influence over the communist leaders here. Yuri Andropov, the ambassador during the 1956 Uprising, helped set up the ÁVH secret police and later became the Soviet premier. So shocked was Andropov at how quickly the uprising had escalated, that he later advocated for cracking down violently at the first signs of unrest in the empire (think of the Soviet tanks rolling into Czechoslovakia during the 1968 Prague Spring).

The desk displays items from the ambassador's office, and the video screens show footage of the ambassador garnering goodwill by visiting families, factories, and so on. A portrait of Stalin slyly surveys the scene.

In the passage, a TV plays an idyllic propaganda video of happy and productive farmers, with swelling music to rouse the Hungarian patriotic spirit.

Resistance (Ellenállás)

It wasn't all upbeat and shiny. This room—empty aside from three very different kitchen tables—symbolizes the way that resistance to the regime emerged in every walk of life. Each table and chair represents a different social class: countryside peasant, middle-class urbanite, and bourgeoisie. On each table is a propaganda message that was printed by that dissident (and now used as evidence in

their interrogation). Notice that, like the furniture, these messages evolve in sophistication from table to table. A screen facing each table shows footage of an accused person from that class, labeled with how many years *(év)* each one spent in prison.

• *Go down the stairs, and enter the room about...*

Resettlement and Deportation (Kitelepítés)

The creation of small nations from sprawling empires at the end of World War I had also created large minority groups, which could upset the delicate ethnic balance of a new country. Having learned this lesson, the Soviets strove to create homogenous states without minorities. Ethnic cleansing on a staggering scale—or, in the more pleasant parlance of the time, "mutual population exchange"—took place throughout Central and Eastern Europe in the years following World War II (for example, three million ethnic Germans were forced out of Czechoslovakia). In Hungary, 230,000 Germans were uprooted and deported. Meanwhile, Hungarians who had become ethnically "stranded" in other nations after the Treaty of Trianon were sent to Hungary (100,000 from Slovakia, 140,000 from Romania, and 70,000 from Yugoslavia). Most have still not returned to their ancestral homes.

Notice the doorbell on the plaque at the beginning of the room. Press the white button to hear the jarring sound that hundreds of thousands of people heard in the middle of the night, when authorities showed up at their doorstep to tell them they had to pack up and move. These people were forced to sign an "official agreement of repatriation" (see the deportation paperwork on the wall), and then were taken away by the ÁVO. They were strictly limited in the number of belongings they could bring; the rest was left behind, carefully inventoried, and folded into the wealth of the upwardly mobile Party bureaucrats—represented by the fancy black sedan with plush hammer-and-sickle upholstery draped in black in the middle of the room.

In the hallway at the end of this section (after the WCs), peer into the haunting **torture cell**. Inside you'll see original items used to beat and torture prisoners.

Surrender of Property and Land (Beszolgáltatás)

With the descent of the communist cloak, people were forced to surrender their belongings to the government. Land was redistributed. Even those who came out ahead in this transaction—formerly landless peasants—found that it was a raw deal, as they were now expected to meet often-impossible production quotas. The Soviet authorities terrorized the peasant class in order to pry as many people as possible away from their old-fashioned farming lifestyles (not to mention deeply held Hungarian traditions), and embrace the industrialization of the new regime. Some 72,000 wealthy peasants called *kulaks*, who did not want to turn over their belongings, ended up on a list to be deported; all told, some 300,000 people were eventually ejected. (Eventually the regime sidestepped the peasant-farmer "middleman" completely, as farms were simply collectivized and run as giant units.)

Of the produce grown in Hungary, a significant amount was sent to other parts of the Soviet Bloc, leading to rampant shortages. The Hungarian people had to survive on increasingly sparse rations. Enter the labyrinth of pork-fat bricks, which remind old-timers of the harsh conditions of the 1950s (lard on bread for dinner). Look for the ration coupons, which people had to present before being allowed to buy even these measly staples. The pig hiding out in the maze is another symbol of these tough times. Traditionally, peasants would slaughter a pig in order to sustain themselves through the winter. But the communist authorities could seize that pig for their own uses, leaving the farmers to rely on the (unreliable) government to provide for their families. To avoid this, many farmers would slaughter their pigs illegally in the cellar, instead of out in the open.

ÁVO

The communist secret police (State Security Department, or ÁVO, later called the State Security Authority, or ÁVH) began as a means to identify and try war criminals. But the organization quickly mutated into an apparatus for intimidating the common people of Hungary—equivalent to the KGB in the Soviet Union. Before they were finished, the ÁVO/ÁVH imprisoned, abused, or murdered one person from every third Hungarian family. On the wall are pictures of secret police leaders and a Rákosi quote: "The ÁVH is the fist of the Party." This organization infiltrated every walk of Hungarian life. Factory workers and farmers, writers and singers, engineers and doctors, teenagers and senior citizens, even Party leaders and ÁVO/ÁVH officers were vulnerable. Their power came from enlisting untold numbers of civilians as informants (see sidebar, next page).

Victims and Victimizers

The foot soldiers of the secret police were civilians—workaday people who informed on their friends and neighbors in vast numbers. Anything could be cause for suspicion, even just not clapping quite hard enough at a Hungarian Workers' Party rally. The regime routinely turned family members against one another. They were just as likely to compel you to implicate your father or brother as your neighbor or co-worker. Pavlik Morozov, a Soviet boy, was the literal poster child for this, after he informed on his own father. It was common to simultaneously be an informant and be informed upon by someone else.

Imagine being a man or woman on the street in 1950s Budapest. Like most people on this planet, you are basically apolitical—you couldn't care less who's in charge, as long as you can raise your family in peace and prosperity. One day on your way to work, a black van pulls up next to you, and in a blur, you're pulled inside. An intimidating agent asks you to report on your friends' water-cooler conversation—particularly any statements against the regime, no matter how casual.

 When you hesitate, the agent says, "Your son András is so very bright. It would be a shame if he could not attend university." Or maybe, "You appear to have a promising career in engineering ahead of you. And yet, it is so difficult to find employment in your chosen field. Well, there's always ditch-digging."

The decision about whether to collaborate with the secret police suddenly becomes muddled. (Which would you choose? Are you *sure*?) Some people refused and endured years or decades of misery. Others capitulated, enjoyed relatively fulfilling lives, but regretted selling out their friends and even their families. In post-communist Hungary, both groups wonder if they made the right choice.

Gábor Péter's Office

Gábor Péter was the first director of the ÁVO/ÁVH. Like many former communist leaders, Péter wound up a prisoner himself (notice the prison motif lurking around the edges of the room). It became an almost expected part of the life cycle of a communist bigwig to eventually be fingered as an enemy...the more power you gained, the better an example you became. (In Péter's case, it didn't help that he was Jewish—anti-Semitism didn't leave Hungary when the Arrow Cross left.) It was abundantly clear that nobody was safe. Péter went to his grave in 1993 without remorse for his participation in the Soviet regime.

"Justice" (Igazságszolgálatás)

This room explores the concept of "show trials"—high-profile, loudly publicized, and completely choreographed trials of people

who had supposedly subverted the regime. The burden of proof was on the accused, not on the accuser, and coerced confessions were fair game. From 1945 until the 1956 Uprising, more than 71,000 Hungarians were accused of political crimes, and 485 were executed.

The TV screen shows various show trials, including the one for Imre Nagy (leader of the 1956 Uprising—see page 112) and his associates. Nagy was found guilty and executed in 1958.

In some cases—as in Nagy's—the defendants had defied the regime. But in many cases, the accused were innocent. (The authorities simply wanted to make an example of someone—innocence was irrelevant.) For example, if there was a meat shortage, they'd arrest and try slaughterhouse workers, ferreting out the ones who "didn't do their best." They might even execute the foreman. Not only did this intimidate all of the others to work harder, it also kept people who had gained some small measure of power in check.

The area behind the stage names the judges of these trials, with photos of some of them. Looking at these people, consider that it was not unusual for judges who had conducted show trials to later go on trial themselves.

Propaganda

Next you'll encounter another, more upbeat method for controlling the people: bright, cheery communist propaganda. The motivational film (on the right) extols the value of pro-

ductivity. Find the chalkboard where workers would keep track of the "work competition" *(munkaverseny hiradó)* by noting the best workers and how far above the average productivity they achieved.

The next room shows how advertising became more colorful in the 1970s and 1980s. (Because there was no real competition in the marketplace, glossy posters were relatively rare.) Look at a few of the posters: Several tout Bambi Narancs, the first Hungarian soft drink (from a time when Coke and Pepsi were pipe dreams). The poster about the Amerikai Bogár warns of the threat of the "American Beetle" (from Kolorádó), which threatened Hungarian crops. When the communists collectivized traditional family farm plots, they removed the trees and hedgerows that separated them—thereby removing birds that had kept pest populations in check. When a potato beetle epidemic hit, rather than acknowledging their own fault, the communists blamed an American conspiracy.

"The Hungarian Silver" (A Magyar Ezüst)

This was a nickname for aluminum, which was produced in large quantities from local bauxite (the pile of rocks in the middle of the room). The items that line the walls, made of this communist equivalent of "silver," lampoon the lowbrow aesthetic of that era.

Religion (Felekezetek)

In 1949, nearly 7 out of every 10 Hungarians identified themselves as Catholics. Over the next four decades, that number declined precipitously. The communist regime infiltrated church leadership, and bishops, priests, monks, and nuns filled Hungarian prisons. Many people worshipped in private (hence the glowing cross hidden under the floorboards). Those who were publicly faithful were discriminated against, closely supervised by the secret police, and often arrested. As things mellowed in the 1960s and 1970s, it was easier to be openly religious, but people of faith were still considered an "enemy of the class" and risked being blacklisted (they might have difficulty finding a job, or their children

Gulag and Work Camps

The stories that later emerged from the Soviet gulag system and the equivalent Hungarian work camps are unthinkably nauseating. Prisoners lived in makeshift barracks with wide gaps between the boards, allowing freezing winter winds to howl through. They were forced to do backbreaking manual labor (such as quarrying stone) and were punished when they failed to meet their impossible daily quotas. Nutrition was laughable—prisoners would become walking skeletons in short order. While the gulags were not formally "death camps," many prisoners died of exposure, overwork, accidents, punishment, and disease. Two unlucky prisoners, who had served time both at the Nazi-run Dachau Concentration Camp and at the communist Recsk work camp in Hungary, reported that conditions had been better at Dachau.

It's particularly appalling to think that many innocent people were sent to work camps. One prisoner explained that he was accidentally arrested because his name was similar to a suspect's; however, by the time the mistake was sorted out, it was too late to let him go...so off he went to the camp. Another prisoner was

could be denied an education). Hungarians had to choose between church and success. The loudspeakers at the end of the room, which belched communist propaganda, stand at odds with the vestments.

The next hallway contains a tribute to **Cardinal József Mind-szenty,** who was arrested and beaten by the communists and later sought refuge in the US embassy for 15 years (see sidebar on page 341).

• *Now head down to the basement in a creepy...*

Elevator

The elevator gradually lowers into the cellar. As it descends, you'll watch a three-minute video of a guard explaining the grotesque execution process.

• *When the door opens, you're in the...*

Prison Cellar (Pincebörtön)

As you exit the elevator, a movie shows this cellar when it was first reclaimed in the 1980s. It's chilling to think of this space's history: In the early 1950s, it was the scene of torture; in 1956, it became

recruited by the secret police to make a list of the people he knew to be dissidents. Instead he made a list of the people he disliked the most, then signed his own name at the bottom. Later, a black van pulled up to him on the street and he was thrown in the back—face-to-face with all of the people he'd turned in.

And yet, for some prisoners, their time in a work camp was strangely enjoyable. They were surrounded by other intelligent people, with nothing to do all day but engage in enlightening conversation while they worked. Think of the Greek myth of Sisyphus, who is condemned to spend eternity rolling a stone up a hill again and again. Some philosophers optimistically believe that the only thing Sisyphus could do was to resolve to be happy. (One good book about the work camp experience, by George Faludy, has the insightful title *My Happy Days in Hell*.)

One university professor was not actually imprisoned but became unemployable because he was outspoken. He could find work only as a ditch-digger...and looked forward to going to his job every day, so he could engage in long conversations with his fellow ousted professors, who dug ditches alongside him.

Hungary's work camps were closed soon after Stalin's death in 1953. The regime denied their existence, and the topic was taboo through the 1980s. People whose relatives had perished in these camps could not speak of it for decades. Only after 1989 have these families been allowed to mourn publicly.

a clubhouse of sorts for the local communist youth. It has been reconstructed and now looks as it might have circa 1955.

Wander through **former cells** used for different purposes. On the right side of the hall are a "wet cell" (where the prisoner was

forced to sit in water) and a cramped "foxhole cell" (where the prisoner was forced to crouch). On the left side are a "standing cell" (where the prisoner was forced to stand 24 hours a day) and a padded cell. On both sides, you'll also see standard cells with photos of the men who once filled them.

In the large room after the cells, you'll see a stool with a lamp; nearby are the **torture** devices: hot pads and electrical appliances. The bucket and hose were used to revive torture victims who had blacked out. Interrogations would normally happen at night, after food, water, and sleep had been withheld from the prisoner for days. Communist interrogators employed techniques still beloved by some torture connoisseurs today, such as "stress positions"...though waterboarding was still just a glimmer in some young sadist's eye. Simple beatings, however, were commonplace.

After the torture room, a small room on the right contains a **gallows** that was used for executions (described earlier on your journey, in the elevator video).

As you think of the people who were imprisoned and murdered here, feel the vibration of traffic on Andrássy út just outside—these victims were so close to the "normal" world, yet so far away.

Internment (Internálás)

While the most notorious gulag network was in Siberia, a similar system also emerged in the Soviet satellites, such as Hungary, which had its own network of prison camps (including a secret one at a quarry overlooking the village of Recsk, not far from Eger—symbolized by the pile of rocks in the center of the room). In just three years (1945-1948), more than 40,000 people were sent to such camps, and the practice continued until 1953. The subtitled video shows a wealthy woman talking about her own experience being sent to one such camp to "learn how to work."

1956 Uprising ('56 Forradalom)

This room commemorates the 1956 Uprising (see page 112). The Hungarian flag with a hole cut out of the middle (a hastily removed Soviet emblem) and the slogan *Ruszkik Haza!* ("Russkies go home!") are important

symbols of that time. The clothes and bicycle recall the "Pest Youth," teenagers and preteens who played a major role in the uprising. The Molotov cocktail—a bottle of flammable liquid with a cloth wick—was a weapon of choice for the uprisers. Screens show the events of '56.

In the next room **(Megtorlás)** stand six symbolic gallows—actually used for executions (though not in this building). Children's voices quietly read aloud the names of some of those killed in the aftermath of 1956. Some 230 were formally executed, while another 15,000 were indicted. (On the gallows, see the legal paperwork for execution.)

Emigration (Kivándorlás)

More than 200,000 Hungarians simply fled the country after the uprising. A wall of postcards commemorates these emigrants, who flocked to every corner of the Western world. Once they reached Austrian refugee camps, these desperate Hungarians could choose where to go—the US offered to fly them anywhere in America to get them started. A video screen shows people leaving Hungary and arriving at their destination, with the help of the United States. Only 11,000 of them would eventually return to their homeland.

Hall of Tears (Könnyek Terme)

This somber memorial commemorates all of the victims of the communists from 1945 to 1967 (when the final prisoners were released from this building).

Room of Farewell (Búcsú Terme)

This room shows several color video clips that provide a (relatively) happy ending: the festive and exhilarating days in 1991 when the Soviets departed, making way for freedom; the reburial of the Hungarian hero, Imre Nagy, at Heroes' Square; and the dedication of this museum. In the film that shows the Soviets' goodbye, watch for the poignant moment when the final Russian officer crosses the bridge on foot, with a half-hearted salute and a look of relief.

Victimizers (Tettesek)

The chilling finale: walls of photographs of the "victimizers"—members and supporters of the Arrow Cross and ÁVO, many of whom are still living and who were never brought to justice. The Hungarians have a long way to go to reconcile everything  they lived through in the 20th century. For many of them, this museum is an important first step.

HEROES' SQUARE AND CITY PARK WALK

Hősök Tere és Városliget

The grand finale of Andrássy út, at the edge of the city center, is also one of Budapest's most entertaining quarters. Here you'll find the grand Heroes' Square, dripping with history (both monumental and recent); the vast tree-filled expanse of City Park, dressed up with fanciful buildings that include a replica Transylvanian castle and an Art Nouveau zoo; and, tucked in the middle of it all, Budapest's finest thermal spa and single best experience, the Széchenyi Baths. If the sightseeing grind gets you down, take a mini-vacation from your busy vacation like the Budapesters do...and escape to City Park.

Orientation

Length of This Walk: One hour, not including museum visits or the baths.

What to Bring: If taking a dip in the Széchenyi Baths, bring your swimsuit and a towel from your hotel (or rent these items there). You may also want to bring flip-flops, sunscreen, and soap and shampoo to shower afterward.

Getting There: If you walk the full length of Andrássy út (see the Andrássy Út Walk chapter), you'll run right into Heroes' Square. But most visitors hightail it out here on the M1/yellow Metró line, and hop off at the Hősök tere stop. You'll exit the Metró in the middle of busy Andrássy út. Cross the street three times (making three-quarters of a circle) to work your way to the middle of Heroes' Square, with a great view of the Millennium Monument. (If you're heading directly for the baths, you could ride the M1 line one stop farther, to the Széchenyi fürdő stop.)

Museum of Fine Arts: 1,800 Ft, audioguide-1,500 Ft, Tue-Sun

10:00-17:30, closed Mon, last entry one hour before closing, Dózsa György út 41, tel. 1/469-7100, www.szepmuveszeti.hu.

Műcsarnok ("Hall of Art"): 1,800 Ft, or 1,900 Ft with Ernst Museum; Tue-Wed and Fri-Sun 10:00-18:00, Thu 12:00-20:00, closed Mon; Ernst Museum open Tue-Sun 11:00-19:00; closed Mon; Dózsa György út 37, tel. 1/460-7000, www.mucsarnok.hu.

Museum of Hungarian Agriculture (in Vajdahunyad Castle): 1,100 Ft; April-Oct Tue-Sun 10:00-17:00; Nov-March Tue-Fri 10:00-16:00, Sat-Sun 10:00-17:00; closed Mon year-round; tel. 1/363-1117, www.mezogazdasagimuzeum.hu.

Széchenyi Baths: 3,400 Ft for locker (in gender-segregated locker room), 400 Ft more for personal changing cabin, cheaper after 19:00, 150 Ft more on weekends; admission includes outdoor swimming pool area, indoor thermal baths, and sauna; swimming pool generally open daily 6:00-22:00, thermal bath daily 6:00-19:00, may be open later on summer weekends, last entry one hour before closing, Állatkerti körút 11, district XIV, tel. 1/363-3210, www.szechenyibath.com.

Starring: A lineup of looming Hungarian greats, a faux-Transylvanian castle, Budapest's best baths, and the city's most enticing green patch.

The Walk Begins

• *Stand in the middle of...*

Heroes' Square (Hősök tere)

Like much of Budapest, this Who's Who of Hungarian history at the end of Andrássy út was commissioned to celebrate the country's 1,000th birthday in 1896 (see page 43). Ironically, it wasn't finished until 1929—well after Hungary had lost World War I and two-thirds of its historical territory, and was facing its darkest hour. Today, more than just the hottest

place in town for skateboarding, this is the site of several museums and the gateway to City Park.

• *The giant colonnades and tall column that dominate the square make up the...*

Millennium Monument

Step right up to meet the world's most historic Hungarians (who look to me like their language sounds). Take a moment to explore this monument, which offers a step-by-step lesson in the story of the Hungarians. (Or, to skip the history lesson, you can turn to "Museum of Fine Arts" on page 175.)

Central Column: The Magyars

The granddaddy of all Magyars, **Árpád** stands proudly at the bottom of the pillar, peering down Andrássy út. He's surrounded by six other chieftains; all together, seven Magyar tribes first arrived in the Carpathian Basin (today's Hungary) in the year 896. Remember that these ancestors of today's Hungarians were from Central Asia and barely resembled the romanticized, more European-looking figures you see here. (Only one detail of these statues is authentically Hungarian: the bushy moustaches.) Magyar horsemen were known and feared for their speed: They rode sleek Mongolian horses (rather than the powerful beasts shown here), and their use of stirrups—revolutionary in Europe at the time—allowed them to ride fast and turn on a dime in order to quickly overrun their battlefield opponents. Bows and spears were their weapons of choice; they'd have had little interest in the chain mail and heavy clubs and battle axes that Romantic sculptors gave them. They used these skills to run roughshod over the Continent, laying waste to Europe.

The 118-foot-tall pillar supports the archangel **Gabriel** as he offers the crown to Árpád's great-great-grandson, István (as we'll learn, he accepted it and Christianized the Magyars).

In front of the pillar is the **Hungarian War Memorial** (fenced in to keep skateboarders from enjoying its perfect slope).

The **sculptures** on the top corners of the two colonnades represent, in order from left to right: Work and Welfare, War, Peace, and the Importance of Packing Light.

Each statue in the two colonnades represents a great Hungarian leader, with a relief below showing a defining moment in his life. Likewise, each one represents a trait or trend in the colorful story of this dynamic people. (For all the details, see the Hungary: Past and Present chapter.)

• *Behind the pillar, look to the...*

First (Left) Colonnade

The first colonnade features rulers from the early glory days of Hungary.

St. István (c. 967-1038)

After decades of terrorizing Europe, the Magyars were finally defeated at the Battle of Augsburg in 955. King Géza realized that unless they could learn to get along with their neighbors, the Magyars' military might only garner them short-term prosperity. Géza decided to baptize his son, Vajk, gave him the Christian name István (Stephen), and married him off to a Bavarian princess. On Christmas Day in the year 1000, commissioners of the pope (pictured in the relief below) brought to István the same crown that still sits under the Parliament dome. To historians, this event marks the beginning of the Christian (and therefore European) chapter of Magyar history. (For more on István, see page 211.)

St. László I (c. 1040-1095)

Known as Ladislas in English, László was a powerful knight/king who carried the Christian torch first taken up by his cousin István. Joining the drive of his fellow European Christian leaders, he led troops into battle to expand his territory into today's Croatia. Don't let the dainty chain-mail skirt fool you... that axe ain't for chopping wood. In the relief below, see László swing the axe against a pagan soldier who had taken Christian women hostage. László won a chunk of Croatia, then lost it...but was sainted anyway (hence the halo). László's story is the first of many we'll hear about territorial expansion and loss—a crucial issue to Hungarian leaders across the centuries (and even today).

Kálmán (c. 1070-1116)

Kálmán (Coloman) traded his uncle László's bloody axe for a stack of books. Known as "the Book-Lover," Kálmán was enlightened before his time, acclaimed as being the most educated king of his era. He was the first European ruler to prohibit the trial or burning of women as witches (on the relief, see him intervening to save the cowering woman in the bottom-right corner). He was also the king who retook Croatia yet again, bringing it into the Hungar-

ian sphere of influence through the early 20th century. Kálmán reminds us that the Hungarians pride themselves on being a highly intellectual people, as demonstrated by the many scientists, economists, and other great minds they've produced. (As you walk through City Park in a few minutes, keep an eye out for chess players.)

András II (c. 1177-1235)

András (Andrew) II is associated with the golden charter he holds in his hand (with the golden medallion dangling from it)—the Golden Bull of 1222. This decree granted some measure of power to the nobility, releasing the king's stranglehold and acknowledging that his power was not absolute. This was the trend across Europe at the time (the Magna Carta, a similarly important document, was signed in 1215 by England's King John).

András demonstrates the importance Hungarians place on self-determination: Like many small Central European nations, Hungary has often been dominated by a foreign power...but has always shown an uncrushable willingness to fight back. (We'll meet some modern-day Hungarian freedom fighters shortly.) It's no surprise that so many place names in Hungary include the word *Szabadság* ("Liberty"). The relief shows that the Hungarians are willing to fight for this ideal for others, as well: András is called "The Jerosolimitan" for his success in the Fifth Crusade, in which his army liberated Jerusalem. Here he is depicted alongside the pope kissing the rescued "true cross."

Despite his achievements, András is far less remembered today than his daughter **Elisabeth** (1207-1231, not depicted here), who was sent away to Germany for a politically expedient marriage. She is the subject of an often-told legend: The pious, kindly Elisabeth was known to sneak scraps of food out of the house to give to poor people on the street. One evening, her cruel confessor saw her leaving the house and stopped her. Seeing her full apron (which was loaded with bread for the poor), he demanded to know what she was carrying. "Roses," she replied. "Show me," he growled. Elisabeth opened her apron, the bread was gone, and rose petals miraculously cascaded out onto the floor. In her short life, Elisabeth went on to found hospitals and carry out other charitable acts, and (unlike her father) became a saint. Elisabeth remains a popular symbol of charity not only in Hungary, but also in Germany. (It's easy to confuse St. Elisabeth with the equally adored Empress Elisabeth, a.k.a. Sisi, the Habsburg monarch, described on page 316.)

Béla IV (1206-1270)

Having governed over one of the most challenging periods of Hungarian history, the defiant-looking Béla—St. Elisabeth's brother—is celebrated as the "Second Founder of the Country" (after Ist-

ván). Béla led Hungary when the Tatars swept in from Central Asia, devastating Buda, most of Hungary, and a vast swath of Central and Eastern Europe. Because his predecessors had squandered away Hungary's holdings, Béla found himself defenseless against the onslaught. In the relief, we see Béla surveying the destruction left by the Tatars. Béla made a deal with God to send his daughter Margaret to a nunnery (on the island that would someday bear her name—see page 75) in exchange for sparing Hungary from complete destruction. After the Tatars left, he rebuilt his ruined nation. It was Béla who moved Buda to its strategic location atop Castle Hill and built a wall around it, to be better prepared for any future invasion. This was the first of many times that Budapest (and Hungary) was devastated by invaders; later came the Ottomans, the Nazis, and the Soviets. But each time, like Béla, the resilient Hungarian people rolled up their sleeves to rebuild.

Károly Róbert (1288-1342)

Everyone we've met so far was a member of the Árpád dynasty—descendants of the tough guys at the base of the big column. But when that line died out in 1301, the Hungarian throne was left vacant. The Hungarian nobility turned to "Charles Robert," a Naples-born prince from the French Anjou (or Angevin) dynasty, which had married into Hungarian royalty. (His shield combines the red-and-white stripes of Hungary with the fleur-de-lis of France.) The Hungarians were slow to accept Robert—he had to

be crowned four different times to convince everybody, and he was actually banned from Buda. (He built his own palace, which still stands, at Visegrád up the Danube—see page 336.) Eventually he managed to win them over and stabilize the country, even capturing new lands for Hungary (see the relief). Károly Róbert represents the many Hungarian people who are not fully, or even partially, Magyar. Today's Hungarians are a cultural cocktail of the various peoples—German, Slavic, Jewish, Roma (Gypsy), and many others—that have lived here and been "Magyarized" to adopt Hungarian language, culture, and names.

Nagy Lajos (1326-1382)

"Louis the Great" built on his father Károly Róbert's successes and presided over the high-water mark of Hungarian history. He expanded Hungarian territory to its historical maximum—including parts of today's Dalmatia (Croatia), Bulgaria, and Bosnia-Herzegovina—and even attempted to retake his father's native Naples (pictured in the relief). Hungarians still look back with great pride on these days more than six centuries ago, when they were a vast and mighty kingdom.

• Now turn your attention to the...

Second (Right) Colonnade

The gap between the colonnades coincides with some dark times for the Hungarians. The invading **Ottomans** swept up the Balkan Peninsula from today's Turkey, creeping deeper and deeper into Hungarian territory...eventually even taking over Buda and Pest for a century and a half. Hungarian nobility retreated to the farthest corners of their lands, today's Slovakia and Transylvania, and soldiered on.

Salvation came in the form of the **Habsburgs,** rulers of a fast-expanding Austrian Empire, who presented Hungary with a classic "good news, bad news" scenario: They forced out the Ottomans, then claimed Hungary as part of their realm. While the Habsburgs eventually granted the Hungarians some leadership in the empire, the Habsburg era was a time of frustration and rebellion. In fact, at the time of this monument's construction—when Budapest was controlled from Vienna—Habsburg rulers stood in the last five slots of the right-hand colonnade. (The statue of Empress Maria Theresa now stands in the lobby of the Museum of

Fine Arts, across the street.) But after the monument was damaged in World War II, locals seized on the opportunity to replace the Habsburgs with Hungarians...who were famous for fighting *against* those slots' former occupants.

János Hunyadi (c. 1387-1456)

A military hero who achieved rare success fighting the Ottomans, Hunyadi won the fiercest-fought skirmish of the era, the Battle of Belgrade (Nándorfehérvár in Hungarian). The relief depicts a particularly violent encounter in that battle. (The guy holding the cross is János Kapisztran, a.k.a. St. John Capistrano, an Italian friar and Hunyadi's right-hand man.) This victory halted the Ottomans' advance into Hungary for decades. Owing largely to his military prowess, Hunyadi was extremely popular among the people and became wealthier than even the king. He led Hungary for a time as regent, when the preschool-age king was too young to rule. After he died of the plague, Hunyadi's reputation allowed his son Mátyás to step up as ruler....

Mátyás Corvinus (1443-1490)

Perhaps the most beloved of all Hungarian rulers, Mátyás (Matthias) Corvinus was a Renaissance king who revolutionized the monarchy. He was a clever military tactician and a champion of the downtrodden, known among commoners as "the people's king." The long hair and laurel wreath (instead of a crown) attest to his knowledge and enlightenment. And most importantly, he was the first (and last) Hungarian-blooded king from the death of the Árpád dynasty in 1301 until today. Building on his father's military success against the Ottomans, Matthias achieved a diplomatic peace with them—allowing him to actually expand his territory while other kings of this era were losing it. (He even had time for some vanity building projects—the relief shows him appreciating a model of his namesake church, which still stands atop Castle Hill.) Matthias' death represented the death of Hungarian sovereignty. After him, Hungary was quickly swallowed up by the Ottomans, then the Habsburgs. For more on King Matthias, see page 204.

Appropriately, Matthias is the final head of state at Heroes' Square. Reflecting the sea change after his death, the rest of the heroes here are freedom-fighters who rallied against Habsburg influence.

István Bocskai (1557-1606), Gábor Bethlen (1580-1629), and Imre Thököly (1657-1705)

After Matthias, the Ottomans took over most of Hungary. Transylvania, the eastern fringe of the realm, was fragmented and in a state of ever-fluctuating semi-independence—sometimes under the firm control of sovereign princes, at other times controlled by the Ottomans. The three Hungarian dukes depicted here helped to unify their people through this difficult spell (see the reliefs): Bocskai and Thököly found rare success on the battlefield against the Habsburgs, while Bethlen made peace with the Czechs and united with them to fight against the Habsburgs.

The next two statues are of Ferenc Rákóczi and Lajos Kossuth, arguably the greatest Hungarian heroes of the Habsburg era and the namesakes of streets and squares throughout the country.

Ferenc Rákóczi II (1676-1735)

Although he was a wealthy aristocrat educated in Vienna, Rákóczi (Thököly's stepson) resented Habsburg rule over Hungary. When his countrymen mobilized into a ragtag peasant army to stage a War of Independence (1703-1711), Rákóczi reluctantly took charge. (The relief depicts an unpleasant moment in Rákóczi's life, when he realizes just how miserable his army will be.) Allied with the French (who were trying to wrest power from the Habsburgs' western territory, Spain), Rákóczi mounted an attack that caught the Habsburgs off-guard. Moving west from his home region of Transylvania, Rákóczi succeeded in reclaiming Hungary all the way to the Danube. But the tide turned when, during a pivotal battle, Rákóczi fell from his horse and was presumed dead by his army. His officers retreated and appealed to the Habsburgs for mercy, effectively ending the revolution. Rákóczi left Hungary in disgrace and rattled around Europe—to like-minded

Habsburg enemies Poland, France, and the Ottoman Empire—in a desperate attempt to gain diplomatic support for a free Hungary. He died in exile in a small Turkish town, but his persistence still inspires Hungarians today.

Lajos Kossuth (1802-1894)

Kossuth was a nobleman and parliamentarian known for his rebellious spirit. When the winds of change swept across Europe

in 1848, the Hungarians began to murmur once again about more independence from the Habsburgs—and Kossuth emerged as the movement's leader (in the relief, he's calling his countrymen to arms). After a bitterly fought revolution, Habsburg Emperor Franz Josef enlisted the help of the Russian czar to put down the Hungarian uprising, shattering Kossuth's dream. (For more on the 1848 Revolution, see page 450.) Kossuth went into exile and traveled the world, tirelessly lobbying foreign governments to support Hungary's bid for independence. He even made his pitch to the US Congress...and today, a bust of Kossuth is one of only three sculptures depicting non-Americans in the US Capitol. After Kossuth died in exile in 1894, his body was returned to Budapest for an elaborate three-day funeral. The Habsburg Emperor Franz Josef—who knew how to hold a grudge—refused to declare the former revolutionary's death a national holiday, so Catholic church bells did not toll...but Protestant ones did.

The less-than-cheerful ending to this survey of Hungarian history is fitting. Hungarians tend to have a pessimistic view of their past...not to mention their present and future. In the Hungarian psyche, life is a constant struggle, and you get points just for playing your heart out, even if you don't win.

• *Two fine museums flank Heroes' Square. As you face the Millennium Monument, to your left is the...*

Museum of Fine Arts (Szépművészeti Múzeum)

This giant collection of mostly European art is the underachieving cousin of the famous Kunsthistorisches Museum in Vienna. Like that collection, it's strong in art from areas in the Habsburgs' cultur-

al orbit: Germanic countries, the Low Countries, and especially Spain. (For the best Hungarian art, head for the National Gallery on Castle Hill—see page 201.) The collection belonged to the noble Eszterházy family, and was later bought and expanded by the Hungarian government.

If you enjoy European art (particularly Spanish Golden Age), consider visiting this museum. After buying your ticket, grab a floor plan and head up the stairs on the right, go to the end of the hall and through the door on the right, and do a clockwise spin through the good stuff: German and Austrian (including some works by Albrecht Dürer); early Dutch and Flemish (including paintings by both Brueghels); and finally Spanish. The Spanish collection features works by Murillo, Zubarán, and Velázquez, along with five El Grecos and several Goyas, including *The Water Carrier*.

• *Across Heroes' Square (to the right as you face the Millennium Monument) is the...*

Műcsarnok ("Hall of Art")

Used for cutting-edge contemporary art exhibits, the Műcsarnok (comparable to a German *"Kunsthalle"*) has five or six temporary exhibits each year. It also houses the Ernst Museum and the Dorottya Gallery (specializing in up-and-coming new artists). While art-lovers enjoy this place, it's more difficult to appreciate than some other Budapest museums.

The Műcsarnok was also the site of a major event in recent history. On June 16, 1989, several anti-communist heroes who had been executed by the regime were finally given a proper funeral on the steps of this building. The Műcsarnok was draped in black-and-white banners, and in front were four actual coffins (including one with the recently exhumed remains of reformist hero Imre Nagy—see page 111), and a fifth, empty coffin to honor others who were lost. The Yugoslav Embassy, which was in the building across the busy ring road from Heroes' Square (on the left-hand corner), was the last place Imre Nagy was seen alive in public.

• *Before continuing into the park, consider an optional 15-minute detour down Dózsa György út, a.k.a...*

"Parade Street"

The area along the busy street beyond the Műcsarnok was once used for communist parades. While the original communist monuments are long gone, two new monuments have replaced them.

As you walk behind the Műcsarnok, first you'll see the giant,

circular **Time Wheel** (Időkerék). Notice
the sand inside the circle, which acts like
a giant hourglass. Unveiled with much
fanfare when Hungary joined the European Union on May 1, 2004, the wheel
is manually rotated 180 degrees to restart
the hourglass every year. Unfortunately,
unexpected condensation has gummed
up the mechanism (hardly an auspicious
kickoff for Hungary's EU membership).

While most Budapesters laugh it off as an eyesore, it's cheaper to
leave it here than to tear it down.

Across the street, notice the
shiny, undulating **ING Bank Headquarters.** ING has invested heavily
in Budapest in recent years, building
both this and the shiny glass mall on
Vörösmarty tér.

Continuing along the parking
lot, you'll soon see the impressive
1956 Monument, celebrating the
historic uprising against the communists (see page 112). During
the early days of the Soviet regime, this was the site of a giant

monument to Josef Stalin that
towered 80 feet high (Stalin
himself was more than 25 feet
tall). While dignitaries stood
on a platform at Stalin's feet,
military parades would march
past. From the inauguration
of the monument in 1951, the
Hungarians saw it as a hated
symbol of an unwanted regime. When the 1956 Uprising broke
out, the removal of the monument was high on the protesters' list
of 16 demands. On the night the uprising began, October 23, some
rebels decided to check this item off early. They came here, cut off
Stalin just below the knees, and toppled him from his platform.
(Memento Park has a reconstruction of the original monument's
base, including Stalin's boots—see page 223.) The current monument was erected in 2006 to commemorate the 50th anniversary
of the uprising. Symbolizing the way Hungarians came together to
attempt the impossible, it begins with scattered individuals at the
back (rusty and humble), gradually coming together and gaining
strength and unity near the front—culminating in a silver ship's
prow boldly plying the ground. To fully appreciate the monument,
walk up the middle of it from the back to the front. Think about

how comforting it is to realize you're not alone, as others like you gradually get closer and closer.

• *Head back to the Műcsarnok at Heroes' Square. The safest way to reach City Park is to begin in front of the Műcsarnok, then use the crosswalk to circle around across the street from the Millennium Monument to reach the bridge directly behind it. (There's no crosswalk from the monument directly to the bridge.)*

Begin walking over the bridge into...

City Park (Városliget)

Budapest's not-so-central "Central Park" was the site of the overblown 1896 Millennium Exhibition, celebrating Hungary's 1,000th birthday. It's still packed with huge party decorations from that bash: a zoo with quirky Art Nouveau buildings, a replica of a

Transylvanian castle, a massive bath/swimming complex, walking paths, and an amusement park. City Park is also filled with unwinding locals.

Orient yourself from the bridge: The huge Vajdahunyad Castle is across the bridge and on your right. Straight into the park and on the left are the big copper domes of the fun, relaxing Széchenyi Baths. And the zoo is on the left, beyond the lake and the recommended waterfront Robinson restaurant. Near the zoo (not quite visible from here) is the world-famous Gundel restaurant, where visiting bigwigs have dined—though it was recently bought out by an international hotel chain and has gone downhill.

The area in front of the castle, used as a boat pond in summer and a skating rink in winter, has been undergoing renovation for years. They can't seem to decide what to do with it—every time I come back to Budapest, it's something different: a parking lot, a staging area for construction, a big sandy beach, and even the site for an aerial dining table where diners were strapped into their seats and hoisted high in the air for a scenic meal (no joking). Work has been delayed several times since the discovery of unexploded Allied bombs dropped here during World War II.

• *Cross the bridge, take the immediate right turn, and follow the path to the entrance of...*

Vajdahunyad Castle (Vajdahunyad Vára)

Many of the buildings for Hungary's Millennial National Exhibition were erected with temporary materials, to be torn down at the

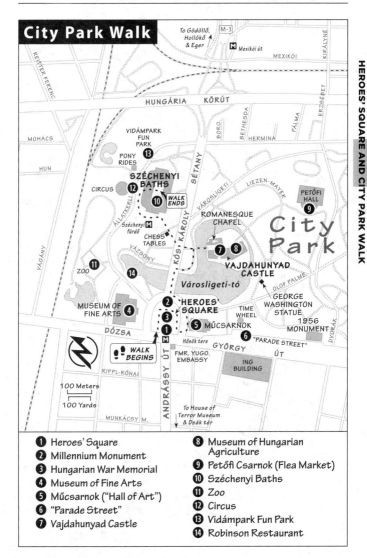

City Park Walk

To Gödöllő,
Hollókő
& Eger

M-3

M Mexikói út

MEXIKÓI

HUNGÁRIA   KÖRÚT

VIDÁMPARK
FUN
PARK   ⑬

PONY
RIDES

SZÉCHENYI
BATHS

CIRCUS   ⑫

⑩   WALK
ENDS

Széchenyi   M
fürdő

CHESS
TABLES

ZOO   ⑪

⑭

ROMANESQUE
CHAPEL

City
Park

PETŐFI
HALL   ⑨

⑦   ⑧

VAJDAHUNYAD
CASTLE

Városligeti-tó

MUSEUM OF
FINE ARTS   ④

②   HEROES'
SQUARE

③

WALK
BEGINS

⑤   MŰCSARNOK

Hősök tere   GYÖRGY

FMR. YUGO.
EMBASSY

ING
BUILDING

TIME
WHEEL

GEORGE
WASHINGTON
STATUE

1956
MONUMENT   ⑥

"PARADE STREET"

ÚT

DÓZSA

RIPPL-RÓNAI

100 Meters
100 Yards

To House of
Terror Museum
& Deák tér

MUNKÁCSY M.

HEROES' SQUARE AND CITY PARK WALK

❶ Heroes' Square
❷ Millennium Monument
❸ Hungarian War Memorial
❹ Museum of Fine Arts
❺ Műcsarnok ("Hall of Art")
❻ "Parade Street"
❼ Vajdahunyad Castle
❽ Museum of Hungarian Agriculture
❾ Petőfi Csarnok (Flea Market)
❿ Széchenyi Baths
⓫ Zoo
⓬ Circus
⓭ Vidámpark Fun Park
⓮ Robinson Restaurant

end of the festival—as was the case for most world fairs at the time. But locals so loved Vajdahunyad Castle that they insisted it stay, so it was rebuilt in brick and stone. The complex actually has four parts, each representing a high point in Hungarian architectural style: Romanesque chapel, Gothic gate, Renaissance castle, and Baroque palace (free and always open to walk around the grounds).

From this direction, the **Renaissance castle** dominates the view. It's a replica of a famous castle in Transylvania that once belonged to the Hunyadi family (János and Mátyás Corvinus—both of whom we met back on Heroes' Square).

Cross over the bridge and through the **Gothic gateway.** Once inside the complex, on the left is a replica of a 13th-century Romanesque **Benedictine chapel.** Consecrated as an actual church, this is Budapest's most popular spot for weddings on summer weekends. Farther ahead on the right is a big Baroque mansion housing the **Museum of Hungarian Agriculture** (Magyar Mezőgazdasági Múzeum). It brags that it's Europe's biggest agriculture museum, but most visitors will find the lavish interior more interesting than the exhibits.

Facing the museum entry is a monument to **Anonymous**—specifically, the Anonymous from the court of King Béla IV who penned the first Hungarian history in the Middle Ages.

For an optional detour to yet another monument (of György—er, George—Washington), consider going for a walk in the park. Continue across the bridge at the far end of Vajdahunyad Castle, then turn right along the main path. **George Washington** (funded by Central European immigrants to the US) is about five minutes down, on the left-hand side.

Deeper in the park is the giant **Petőfi Csarnok,** which is used for big rock concerts (tel. 1/363-3730, www. petoficsarnok.hu) as well as a weekend flea market (see page 276).

• *Time for some fun. Head back out to the busy main road, and cross it. Under the trees, you'll pass some red outdoor tables where you'll likely see elderly locals playing chess. Beyond the tables and a bit to the right, the pretty gardens and copper dome mark the famous...*

Széchenyi Baths (Széchenyi Fürdő)

Budapest's best thermal baths, and (for me) its single best experience, period, the Széchenyi Baths offer a refreshing and culturally enlightening Hungarian experience. Reward yourself with a soak.

○ For all the details, see the Thermal Baths chapter.

• The best entrance to the baths is around the back side. That's also where you'll find...

Attractions Behind Széchenyi Baths

Lining the street behind the baths are three kid-friendly attractions. From the steps of the swimming pool entrance, look through the fence across the street to see the **zoo's** colorful Art Nouveau elephant house (pictured at left), slathered with Zsolnay tiles outside and mosaics inside. To the right are a **circus** (marked *Nagycirkusz*) and the **Vidámpark fun park,** with rides appealing to travelers both big and small. For more details on these attractions, see the Budapest with Children chapter.

• Our walk is over. Your options are endless. Soak in the bath, ride a roller coaster, go for a stroll, rent a rowboat, buy some cotton candy...enjoy City Park any way you like.

If you're ready for some food, cheap snack stands are scattered around the park; for something fancier, consider the recommended Robinson restaurant (see page 260).

When you're ready to head home, the M1/yellow Metró line (with effortless connections to the House of Terror, Opera, the Metró hub of Deák tér, or Vörösmarty tér in downtown Pest) has two handy stops here: The entrance to the Széchenyi fürdő stop is at the southwest corner of the yellow bath complex (easy to miss—to the left and a bit around the side as you face the main entry, just a stairway in the middle of the park); and the Hősök tere stop is back across the street from Heroes' Square, where we began this walk.

GREAT SYNAGOGUE AND JEWISH QUARTER TOUR

Zsinagóga / Zsidónegyed

With an elegant history cut brutally short by the Holocaust, Pest's Jewish Quarter is gradually restoring its once-grand sights and embracing its long-dormant heritage. Today's Jewish Quarter is a ramshackle neighborhood—still quite run-down despite its city-center location—that contains several synagogues, Jewish-themed restaurants, and other remnants of a once-thriving Jewish community. And in the last few years, this neighborhood has emerged as Budapest's most lively nightlife zone. Each year, there seem to be more and more distinctive "ruin pubs" (convivial, youthful bars with ramshackle furniture that sprawls through should-be-condemned buildings and courtyards), art galleries, fashion boutiques, and all the trappings of hipster culture. This means that two very different cultures coexist in these streets: traditional Jewish heritage and cutting-edge, hard-partying trendiness. Somehow, it works.

The area's main attraction is the spectacular Great Synagogue, but some might find it worthwhile to also explore nearby sights, including two other synagogues. This tour explains all three synagogues, plus a few other sights and monuments sprinkled between them.

Orientation

Length of This Tour: 1.5-2 hours.

Dress Code: To visit the interiors of the Great Synagogue and the Orthodox Synagogue, men will need to cover their heads, and women, their shoulders (loaner yarmulkes and scarves are available at the door).

Getting There: The Great Synagogue is at Dohány utca 2, district VII. From M2: Astoria (or the Astoria stop on trams #47 and #49), it's a five-minute walk—but it can be hard to find since the synagogue hides behind a line of modern buildings. Just follow the Small Boulevard (called Károly körút at this point) and keep an eye to the right.

Great Synagogue and Jewish Museum: 2,250 Ft for Great Synagogue and Jewish Museum, 500 Ft to take photos; *Tree of Life* and memorial garden are always free. Open March-Oct Sun-Thu 10:00-17:30, Fri 10:00-15:30; Nov-Feb Sun-Thu 10:00-15:30, Fri 10:00-13:30; always closed Sat and Jewish holidays, last entry 30 minutes before closing, tel. 1/344-5131, www.dohanyutcaizsinagoga.hu.

Hungarian Jewish Archives and Family Research Center: Exhibit covered by Great Synagogue ticket, 1,000 Ft to use archives with some help from the staff. Open Mon-Thu 10:00-17:00, Fri 10:00-15:00, closed Sat-Sun. If you plan to do research here, it's best to contact them in advance to let them know you're coming: tel. 1/413-5547, www.milev.hu, family@milev.hu.

Orthodox Synagogue: 1,000 Ft, Sun-Thu 10:00-15:00, Fri 10:00-12:30, closed Sat.

Printa Café: Mon-Fri 11:00-19:00, Sat-Sun 12:00-18:00—except closed Sun Sept-May, Rumbach 10, www.printa.hu.

Synagogue at Rumbach Street: 500 Ft, Sun-Thu 10:00-15:30, Fri 10:00-13:30, closed Sat.

Tours: Aviv Travel, with a kiosk just outside the synagogue entrance, leads tours of the synagogue, museum, and related sights. You have three options: A quick 45-minute tour combines the Great Synagogue and the *Tree of Life* (2,650 Ft). A longer 80-minute tour covers the above, plus a guided visit to the Jewish Museum (3,000 Ft). The 90-minute version includes the Great Synagogue, *Tree of Life*, and the nearby synagogue on Rumbach Street, but not the museum (3,650 Ft). Since these tours include admission, you're paying only a small price for the guiding—making this an affordable way to really understand the place (tours leave every 30 minutes during the Great Synagogue's open hours—listed above, last tour departs one hour before closing).

Jewish Quarter by Night: This walk—which you'll presumably do during the day (when the sights are open)—leads past several streets that seem decrepit and sleepy in the sunlight, but 12 hours later are hopping with rollicking nightlife. After you get your bearings in this neighborhood during the day, consider returning here at night to experience this fascinating and accessible Budapest phenomenon. My self-guided "Ruin Pub Crawl" (see page 287) passes many of these same streets, but focuses on a very different slice of life.

Starring: Budapest's rich tapestry of Jewish history.

Background

As the former co-capital of an empire that included millions of Jews, Budapest always had a high concentration of Jewish residents. Before World War II, 5 percent of Hungary's population and 25 percent of Budapest's were Jewish (and the city was dubbed "Judapest" by the snide Viennese up the river).

In 1783, the progressive Habsburg Emperor Josef II emancipated the Jews of his empire, allowing them to live and do business in the city of Pest. Because they were still not allowed to purchase property within the city, many settled in the area just outside the city wall (today marked by the Small Boulevard ring road), in what would become the Jewish Quarter. Many of these Jews were eager to win the acceptance of their Catholic neighbors—which is why the Great Synagogue they built here almost feels more like a Christian house of worship than a Jewish one. At the same time, many Jews (like other minorities) were compelled to undergo "Magyarization," taking on Hungarian language and culture, and even adopting Hungarian spellings of their names.

The anti-Semitism that infected Europe around the turn of the 20th century also tainted Budapest. In fact, Hungary—and not Germany—was the first European country to enforce "Jewish laws" in the 1920s. A long tradition of resentment toward Jews had been amplified by a more recent perception of the Jewish connection to the "dangerous" influence of communism. Furious and humiliated after losing two-thirds of their territory in the Treaty of Trianon that ended World War I, the Hungarians sought a handy scapegoat—and Jews filled that role.

When Hitler was on the rise in Germany, Hungary allied with him, allowing local politicians some degree of self-determination. The Hungarians sometimes interned but did not execute their Jewish citizenry, even as the Nazis began to institute their "Final Solution" of Jewish genocide in the lands they controlled. But Hitler grew impatient and invaded Hungary in March of 1944, installing the Arrow Cross regime. Jews were forced to live in a small, walled ghetto surrounding the Great Synagogue, and allowed no contact with the outside world. By May—just two months after the Nazi takeover—trains began heading for Auschwitz; by the middle of July, about 430,000 Hungarian Jews had already been deported. (For more on the Arrow Cross, see the House of Terror Tour chapter.)

As the end of the war neared, Hungarian Nazi collaborators resorted to desperate measures, such as lining up Jews along the

Danube and shooting them into the river (now commemorated by a monument near the Parliament—see page 110). To save bullets, they'd sometimes tie several victims together, shoot one of them, and throw him into the freezing Danube—dragging the others in with him. Hungary lost nearly 600,000 Jews to the Holocaust. Today, only half of 1 percent of Hungarians are Jewish, and most of them live in Budapest.

After the Holocaust, the Great Synagogue sat neglected for 40 years. But since the thawing of communism, Hungarian Jews have taken a renewed interest in preserving their heritage. In 1990, the Great Synagogue was painstakingly rebuilt, partly with financial support from Tony Curtis, the late American actor of Hungarian-Jewish origin (his daughter Jamie Lee Curtis continues to support these causes today). Theodor Herzl, a pioneer of Zionism, was born in a house next door to the Great Synagogue (now gone). Other people of Hungarian-Jewish descent include big names from every walk of life: Harry Houdini (born Erich Weisz), Elie Wiesel, Joseph Pulitzer, Estée Lauder, Goldie Hawn, Peter Lorre, and Eva and Zsa Zsa Gabor. A visit to the Great Synagogue and surrounding Jewish Quarter offers insight into this vital facet of Hungarian history and contemporary life.

The Tour Begins

• *Stand in front of the...*

Great Synagogue (Zsinagóga)

Also called the "Dohány Street Synagogue," Budapest's gorgeous synagogue is the biggest in Europe and the second biggest in the world (after the Temple Emanu-El of New York). A visit here has three parts: touring its ornately decorated interior; exploring the attached museum, which offers a concise lesson in the Jewish faith; and lingering in the evocative memorial garden, with its weeping-willow *Tree of Life* sculpture and other poignant monuments.

• *You might see a long ticket and tour line to the left of the main entrance gate. But since you can also buy tickets and book tours in the courtyard, skip that line and go through the security checkpoint. Once inside the fence, head for the cashier at the end of the courtyard on the right. Then visit the sights in the order described in this tour. (Note that you can visit the* Tree of Life *and memorial garden*

GREAT SYNAGOGUE

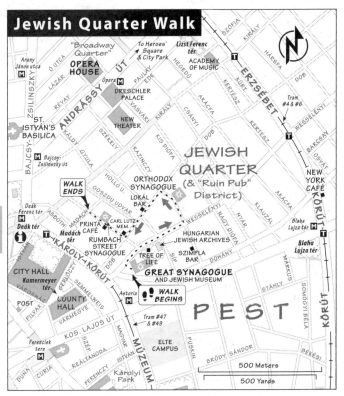

Jewish Quarter Walk

even if you don't buy a ticket for the synagogue. Or, if the synagogue is closed, go around the left side to view the monument through a fence.)

Synagogue Exterior

Before going inside, check out the synagogue's striking facade, and consider the rich history of the building and the people it represents: The synagogue was built in 1859 just outside what was then the city limits. Although Budapest's Jews held fast to their own faith, they also wished to prove their worth, and to demonstrate how well-integrated they were with the greater community. Building this new synagogue was partially an attempt to impress the city's Gentile majority.

The religious leaders commissioned the Austrian (and non-Jewish) architect Ludwig Förster to create a synagogue in Budapest that would top the Stadttempel recently built in Vienna (also designed by a Gentile). The synagogue is loosely based on biblical descriptions of the Temple of Solomon in Jerusalem. This explains the two tall towers, which are not typical of synagogues. The towers—along with the rosette (rose window)—also helped the synagogue resemble Christian churches of the time. In fact, when it was built, the synagogue was cynically dubbed by one onlooker as "the most beautiful Catholic synagogue in the world."

• *Now step inside.*

Synagogue Interior

Notice that the synagogue interior really feels like a church with the symbols switched—with a basilica floor plan, three naves, two pulpits, and even a pipe organ. The organ—which Franz Liszt played for the building's inauguration—is a clue that this synagogue belonged to the most progressive of the three branches of Judaism here at the time. (Orthodox Jews would never be able to do the "work" of playing an organ on the Sabbath.) Of the various synagogues in this district, this one belonged to the Neolog Jewish congregation (close to Conservative Judaism in the US).

The Moorish-flavored decor—which looks almost Oriental—is a sign of the Historicist style of the time, which borrowed eclectic elements from past styles. Specifically, it evokes the Sephardic Jewish culture that flourished in Iberia; many Hungarian Jews are descended from that group, who fled here after being expelled from Spain in 1492.

In the ark, behind the burgundy curtain, 25 surviving Torah scrolls are kept. Catholic priests hid these scrolls during World War II (burying them temporarily in a cemetery). The synagogue itself, while damaged, avoided being completely destroyed in the war. While it might have been luck, or divine intervention, it was likely also because the occupying Nazis protected it for their own uses: They put radio antennas in the two towers, stabled horses in the nave, and (according to some reports) might have even had a Gestapo base in the balcony above the main entrance.

The two biggest chandeliers are typical neither of synagogues nor of churches; they were likely inspired by concert halls of the day. During the war, the chandeliers were melted down and used to make bullets, but have since been recast. The pews are original, as are the kneelers—another Christian feature not typically used in Jewish worship, but added to make the place feel more church-like.

The two-tiered balconies on the sides of the nave were originally for women, who worshipped separately from the men. (These galleries are accessed by separate staircases, from outside.) Today, men and women can sing together in the choir, but they still sit apart: men in the two inner rows, and women in the two outer rows. (Women sit in the balconies only on important holy days.) The service, attended by several hundred local Jews each Sabbath (and a couple thousand on high holidays), is still said in Hebrew. However, due to security concerns, people who are not members of the local congregation are generally not invited to attend.

• *When you're finished inside, exit through the main doors, turn right, and go to the opposite end of the front courtyard. Here you'll find the entrance to the...*

Jewish Museum (Zsidó Múzeum)

This small but informative museum illuminates the Jewish faith, with artifacts and succinct but engaging English explanations. Pick up the audioguide as you enter (included with ticket). You'll find descriptions of **rituals and holidays,** from Rosh Hashanah and Yom Kippur to Passover and Chanukah. The exhibit also explains ancient **symbols** (prayer shawls, the mezuzah, and so on).

The next room focuses on **family life,** tracing the Jewish lifeline from birth to marriage to death. The marriage contracts posted on the wall show the relative equality between the sexes: Like an old-fashioned form of "prenups," they provide for how property would be divided equitably between both spouses in the event of a divorce. In the funeral section, notice the bowl filled with wooden knobs: If a person died without kin, the Jewish community would provide proper burial. This bowl was a sort of lottery system for randomly determining which person was responsible for burying the deceased.

The final room holds a small, powerful exhibit about the **Holocaust.** Follow the exhibit chronologically as it wraps clockwise around the room: The first few panels are a reminder that the roots of the Holocaust existed in Hungary long before the Nazis took over. In one photo, Hungarian leader Miklós Horthy shakes hands with Hitler—the two nations were allied early in World War II. As the war raged on, the Hungarians proved more benevolent toward their Jewish population than the Germans, but some Jews were still forced to leave the cities and move to the countryside.

Then came the horrific time after the Nazis invaded Hungary and installed the Arrow Cross regime, which swiftly began to send Jews to death camps. One display case shows drums made out of Torah scrolls (see photo, facing page). In another is a bar of soap made of human fat—a grotesquely "efficient" use of "resources" from the Nazi concentration-camp system. In the same case is a menorah made by a resourceful inmate out of scraps of bread. Then comes a series of disturbing images of this very neighborhood during World War II, including bodies lined up waiting to be buried in the park next to this synagogue (we'll see that area soon). The final photo shows the hanging of Arrow Cross leader Ferenc Szálasi, who was executed in 1946. In the middle of the room is an exhibit honoring non-Jews who risked everything to rescue Jews during this dark time. (We'll find out more about some of these people later on this tour.) Stairs lead down to a small Holocaust memorial. (For more about this tragic chapter of the Hungarian Jewish experience, don't miss the outstanding Holocaust Memorial Center—see page 71.)

• *Exiting back into the front courtyard, go down the passageway between the synagogue and the museum (straight ahead from the security checkpoint, past the gift shop).*

Tree of Life and Memorial Garden

As you walk alongside the Great Synagogue, notice the small **park** on your left. During the Soviet siege that ended the Nazi occupation of Budapest in the winter of 1944-1945, many Jews in the ghetto here died of exposure, starvation, and disease. Soon after the Soviets liberated the city, a mass grave was dug here for the bodies of an estimated 2,281 Jews. The trees and headstones (donated by survivors) were added later. The pillars you'll pass have historical photos of the synagogue and Jewish Quarter.

At the far end of the cemetery, look for the small, angular **sculpture** on the pedestal by renowned artist Imre Varga (for more on Varga, see page 87). This represents a forced march—with clearly defined figures at  the front, melting into a blocky form at the back. When the Nazi-puppet Arrow Cross regime took over Hungary, they wanted to quickly transport as many Jews as possible to death camps. The trains couldn't take the Jews away fast enough, so the Arrow Cross made them march hundreds of miles to their final destination. Among the victims was a poet named Miklós Radnóti, who was compelled to fight with the Hungarian Army, and then forced to

GREAT SYNAGOGUE

march back to Hungary after a defeat. He died and was buried along the way. A year and a half later, his body was exhumed. In his pocket was a notebook with poignant handwritten poems about his experience. In one poem, Radnóti daydreams about a life to which (he seems to suspect) he would never return:

> *If only once again I heard the quiet hum*
> *Of bees on the veranda, the jar of orchard plums*
> *Cooling with late summer, the gardens half asleep,*
> *Voluptuous fruit lolling on branches dipping deep,*
> *And she before the hedgerow stood with sun-bleached hair,*
> *The lazy morning scrawling vague shadows on the air...*
> *Why not? The moon is full, her circle is complete.*
> *Don't leave me, friend, shout out, and see! I'm on my feet!*

The building just past the garden is the **Heroes' Temple,** built in 1929 to honor Hungarian Jews who had fought in World War I.

In the garden behind the synagogue is the *Tree of Life,* also sculpted by Imre Varga. This was erected in 1990, soon after the fall of communism made it possible to acknowledge the Holocaust. The willow makes an upside-down menorah, and each of the 4,000 metal leaves is

etched with the name of a Holocaust victim. New leaves are added all the time, donated by families of the victims. Notice that at the end of each branch is a Roman numeral, to assist people in finding their relatives' names. The large black-marble gateway represents a temple; the Hebrew inscription reads, "Is there a bigger pain than mine?" The plaques embedded in the base of the sculpture bear messages (many in English) from donors.

In the center of the garden is a **symbolic grave of Raoul Wallenberg** (1912-1947). An improbable hero, this ne'er-do-well Swedish playboy from a prominent family was sent as a diplomat to Hungary because nobody else wanted the post. He was empowered by the Swedish government to do whatever he could—bribe, threaten, lie, or blackmail—to save as many Jews as possible from the Nazis. He surpassed everyone's low expectations by dedicating (and ultimately sacrificing) his life to the cause. By giving Swedish pass-

ports to Jews and admitting them to safe houses, he succeeded in rescuing tens of thousands of people from certain death. Shortly after the Soviets arrived, Wallenberg was arrested, accused of being a US spy, sent to a gulag...and never seen alive again. Russian authorities recently acknowledged he was executed, but have not revealed the details.

The grave is also etched with the names of other "righteous Gentiles" who went above and beyond to save Jews. According to the Talmud, "Whoever saves one life, saves the world entire." The small stones are typical of Jewish cemeteries (evoking the age-old tradition of placing pebbles over desert graves to cover the body and prevent animals from disturbing it). Surrounding the grave are four rose-colored pillars with the names of other non-Jews who saved individuals or families. The list is still growing, with periodic new additions. In the big stained-glass window that stands near the grave, the fire symbolizes the Holocaust (the Hebrew word is *Shoah*, literally, "catastrophe"), and the curling snake represents fascism.

Along the back wall behind the stained glass, find the little **alcoves** labeled for victims, with lights that go on after dark. The alcoves—like other memorials in this garden—are filled with small stones.

• *The building that defines the far end of the memorial garden is the...*

Hungarian Jewish Archives (Magyar Zsidó Levéltár)

This facility, worth a visit only for those with a special interest, has a **prayer room** on the ground floor and, on the first floor, the **Family Research Center**—with birth, marriage, and death records for Jews from Budapest and much of Hungary. For 1,000 Ft, you're welcome to use their archives. They'll point you in the right direction and can help with basic translations. (Ideally, bring not just your family name, but also—if possible—ancestors' birth and death dates, and any other data you have. It's also best to notify them a few days ahead of your visit—see contact information at the beginning of this chapter.)

Upstairs on the second floor of the same building is a small **virtual exhibition** about the Jewish Quarter, with a few historical artifacts from everyday life, touchscreens with maps and documents to help you learn more about topics of your choice, and a screening room for English-subtitled films about the local Jewish experience, past and present.

• *The exit is through the fence, near the* Tree of Life.

Near the Great Synagogue

For most visitors, the Great Synagogue is enough. But if you're interested in exploring the rest of the Jewish Quarter, consider the following sights.

• *Exiting the Great Synagogue grounds by the Tree of Life, turn right up Wesselényi utca. After two blocks, you reach the intersection with the recently spiffed-up Kazinczy utca. If you're curious about Budapest's burgeoning "ruin pub" nightlife scene, you could detour here half a block to the right to see* **Szimpla,** *the first and best of those ramshackle nightspots. (While it's pretty dead—and often closed—during the daytime, the space hosts a farmers market on Sunday mornings.)*

> *To head for the next sight, turn left on Kazinczy utca. Where the road curves, on the right you'll see the...*

Orthodox Synagogue

The Orthodox Synagogue is located on a nondescript urban street two blocks from the Great Synagogue. Built in the Vienna-inspired

Secession style in 1912, damaged and deserted for decades after World War II, and recently renovated, today this temple invites visitors to see its colorful, sumptuously decorated interior (completed in 2006). While grandly opulent, this place is far more typical of synagogue architecture than the Great Synagogue.

To find the entrance, go down the passage that runs along the right side of the building (if nobody's there, ask at the nearby

Hannah Restaurant—a fully kosher eatery). Inside, the green pillars at the front flanking the ark evoke the Torah scrolls, and the red columns (with Zsolnay tile decorations) echo the Temple of Solomon. The seat on the left was filled by the synagogue's first rabbi, Koppel Reich (1838-1929), who was a pillar of the community: He advised Habsburg Emperor Franz Josef and was a member of the Hungarian parliament. Out of deference to him, nobody has sat in this seat since his death. The temple is still used from spring through fall by a small but dedicated local Orthodox congregation of about 50 people.

• *From the Orthodox Synagogue, turn right onto Kazinczy utca. At the end of the block, turn left onto Dob utca. After about a block and a half on your right, just past the Lokál ruin pub, is the easy-to-miss entrance to...*

Gozsdu Udvar

This long series of courtyards burrows through the middle of a city block, between Dob utca 16 and Király utca 13. When this

neighborhood hosted a fast-growing Jewish population and space was at a premium, courtyards like this one were filled with community life: restaurants, shops, and other businesses. After decades of neglect, this one was recently spruced up and opened to the public. This genteel space—which evokes the Golden Age of Jewish life in Budapest—is filled with cafés and bars, and after hours it's a bustling nightlife hub.

• *A few steps down from the courtyard, on the right side of Dob utca (where the street widens), keep an eye out for the...*

Monument to Carl Lutz (1895-1975)

Born in Switzerland and educated in the US, Carl Lutz became a Swiss vice-consul to Hungary during World War II. After the

Nazis invaded and began sending Hungarian Jews to death camps, Lutz set up safe houses around the city (which he formally registered as "Swiss soil"), and issued permission for tens of thousands of Jews to emigrate. In the monument, the figure on the side of the building (representing Lutz) is extending a lifeline to the vulnerable figure lying on the ground below him. Lutz is credited, ultimately, with saving 62,000 Jewish lives.

This monument also marks the edge of the WWII-era Jewish ghetto.

• *A few steps beyond the Lutz monument, on the left at #9, notice another long series of courtyards like Gozsdu Udvar—but this one's still deserted and under lock and key.*

At the end of the block, turn right on Rumbach utca. Just before the synagogue, on the left at #10, is the creative...

Printa Café

This inviting design shop/silkscreen studio/art gallery/coffeehouse offers a perfect glimpse at the hipster culture that's taking over this area of Budapest—designer fair-trade coffee, local artists exhibiting their works, and a wide array of "trashion" accessories made from reused materials (stylish bags made from old leather jackets, belts made from discarded shirts, and so on).

• *A bit further down on the right is the...*

Synagogue at Rumbach Street

This synagogue's colorful but faded Moorish-style interior survives from the Golden Age of Jewish culture in Budapest. The late-19th-

century building was designed by the great Viennese architect Otto Wagner. It was abandoned for years, and rumor has it that Yoko Ono nearly bought it as a studio space—but backed out when she realized its proximity to the tram tracks would cause unacceptable background noise. Today the building awaits a desperately needed renovation. In the meantime, if it's open and you enjoyed the Great Synagogue, it's worth a look. You'll wander through the relatively small but very tall space, and peruse a few scant posted plans (in Hungarian only) about what the renovated synagogue will look like someday.

• *From the synagogue, turn right and walk to the end of the block. On the left, you'll see a giant ceremonial **gateway** built into a drab red-brick apartment building. This was designed to be the entrance of an elaborate boulevard that would connect the Small and Great Boulevards (similar—and parallel—to Andrássy út). But this great road was never built, leaving this impressive gateway to an underwhelming, narrow street with a parking garage and office building.*

Our tour is finished. From here, you can either continue toward Andrássy út (jog right up Király utca, then left on Káldy Gyula utca), or go left on Rumbach utca to return to the Great Synagogue. Or, if you'd like to head into the Town Center, go through the gateway, cross the Small Boulevard and tram tracks, bear right, and you'll find yourself at the Deák tér public-transit hub.

CASTLE HILL WALK

Várhegy

Once the seat of Hungarian royalty, and now the city's highest-profile tourist zone, Castle Hill is a historic spit of land looming above the Buda bank of the Danube. Scenic from afar, but (frankly) a bit soulless from up close, it's best seen quickly. This walk gives you the lay of the land and leads you to the hill's most worthwhile attractions, including grand sights and monuments (the Matthias Church and Fishermen's Bastion) and fine museums (such as the National Gallery and the WWII-era "Hospital in the Rock"). You'll also appreciate the bird's-eye views that a visit to Castle Hill offers across the Danube to Pest.

Orientation

Length of This Walk: Allow about two hours, including quick visits to the National Gallery and Matthias Church; you'll need more time for additional sights (especially the "Hospital in the Rock").

Overview: Castle Hill is manageable for visitors: The major landmarks are the huge, green-domed Royal Palace at the south end of the hill (housing a pair of museums) and the frilly spired Matthias Church near the north end (with the hill's best interior). In between are tourist-filled pedestrian streets and dull but historic buildings.

When to Visit: Castle Hill is packed with tour groups in the morning, but it's much less crowded in the afternoon. Since restaurants up here are touristy and bad-value, Castle Hill is an ideal after-lunch activity. I've suggested a few lunch options up here, but if you want a good meal on this side of the river, it's better to head to Batthyány tér just downhill (see page 260).

Getting There: The Metró and trams won't take you to the top of

Castle Hill. Instead, you can hike, taxi, catch a bus, or ride the funicular.

For most visitors, the easiest bet is to hop on **bus #16,** with handy stops in both Pest (at the Deák tér Metró hub—near the old bus building in Erzsébet tér; and at Széchenyi tér at the Pest end of the Chain Bridge) and Buda (at Clark Ádám tér at the Buda end of the Chain Bridge—across the street from the lower funicular station, and much cheaper than the funicular). Or you can go via Széll Kálmán tér (on the M2/red Metró line or by taking tram #4 or #6 around Pest's Great Boulevard); from here, bus **#16,** as well as buses **#16A** and **#116,** head up the hill (at Széll Kálmán tér, catch the bus just uphill from the Metró station—in front of the red-brick, castle-looking building). All buses stop at Dísz tér, at the crest of the hill, about halfway along its length (most people on the bus will be getting off there, too). From Dísz tér, go past the war-damaged building (the old Ministry of War), walk five minutes along the row of flagpoles toward the green dome, then bear left to find the big Turul bird statue at the start of this walk.

The **funicular** (*sikló*, SHEE-kloh), which lifts visitors from the Chain Bridge to the top of Castle Hill, is a Budapest landmark. Built in 1870 to provide cheap transportation to Castle Hill workers, today it's a pricey little tourist trip. Read the fun first-person history in glass cases at the top station (900 Ft one-way, 1,500 Ft round-trip, not covered by transit pass, daily 7:30-22:00, departs every 5 minutes, closed for maintenance every

other Mon). It leaves you right at the Turul bird statue, where this walk begins.

If you'd like to **hike** up, you'll find a variety of paths and stairways leading up from Víziváros (the residential neighborhood along the Danube at the base of the hill). Just head for the giant dome.

To **leave the hilltop,** most visitors find it easiest just to walk down after their visit (see the end of this tour). But if you'll be taking the bus down, it's smart to buy tickets for the return trip before you ascend Castle Hill, as there are only a few places on top of Castle Hill to buy them, including the TourInform office (near Matthias Church, open daily 10:00-18:00) and the post office near Dísz tér (Mon-Fri until 16:00, closed Sat-Sun).

Changing of the Guard: On the hour, uniformed soldiers do a changing-of-the-guard ceremony at Sándor Palace (the president's residence, near the top of the funicular), with a more elaborate show at 12:00. While not worth planning your day around (it's just a few guys in modern military uniforms slinging rifles), it's fun to watch if you happen to be nearby.

Hungarian National Gallery: 1,200 Ft, may be more for special exhibits, 500 Ft extra to take photos, Tue-Sun 10:00-18:00, closed Mon, Szent György tér 2, mobile 0620-439-7325, www.mng.hu. Note that you're required to check any large bags.

Budapest History Museum: 1,500 Ft, audioguide-1,200 Ft; March-Oct Tue-Sun 10:00-18:00, Nov-Feb Tue-Sun 10:00-16:00, closed Mon year-round; Szent György tér 2, tel. 1/487-8800, www.btm.hu.

Matthias Church: 1,000 Ft, audioguide may be available, Mon-Sat 9:00-17:00—possibly also open 19:00-20:00 in summer, Sun 13:00-17:00, may close Sat after 14:30 for weddings, Szentháromság tér 2, tel. 1/488-7716, www.matyas-templom.hu.

Fishermen's Bastion: 600 Ft, daily mid-March-mid-Oct 9:00-21:00; after closing time and off-season, no tickets are sold but bastion is open and free to enter; Szentháromság tér 5.

Starring: Budapest's most historic quarter, with a palace (and a top collection of Hungarian art), a gorgeous church interior, sweeping vistas over city rooftops, and layers of history.

Background

This hilltop has a history as complex and layered as Hungary's. Originally, the main city of Hungary wasn't Buda or Pest, but Esztergom (just up the river—see page 340). In the 13th century, Tatars swept through Eastern Europe, destroying much of Hungary. King Béla IV, who was forced to rebuild his kingdom, re-envisioned Buda as a fortified hilltop town, and moved the capital to this more protected location in the interior of the country. The city has dominated the region ever since.

Over the years, the original Romanesque fortress here was rebuilt and accentuated with a textbook's worth of architectural styles: Gothic, Renaissance, and Baroque. It was one of Europe's biggest palaces by the early 15th century, when King Mátyás (Matthias) Corvinus made the palace even more extravagant, putting Buda—and Hungary—on the map.

Just a few decades later, the invading Ottomans occupied Buda and turned the palace into a military garrison. When the Habsburgs laid siege to the hill for 77 days in 1686, gunpowder stored in the cellar exploded, destroying the palace. The Habsburgs (with a motley, pan-European army that included few Hungarians) took the hill, but Buda was deserted and in ruins. The town was re-settled by Austrians, who built a new Baroque palace, hoping that the Habsburg monarch would move in—but none ever did. The useless palace became a garrison, then the viceroy's residence. It was damaged again during the 1848 Revolution, but was repaired and continued to grow right along with Budapest's prominence.

As World War II drew to a close, Budapest became the front line between the Nazis and the approaching Soviets. The labyrinth of natural caves under the hill was even adapted for use as a se-cret military hospital (the tourable "Hospital in the Rock"). The Nazis, who believed the Danube to be a natural border for their empire, destroyed bridges across the river and staged a desperate "last stand" on Castle Hill. The Red Army laid siege to the hill for 100 days. They eventually succeeded in taking Budapest...but the city—and the hill—were devastated once again. Since then, the Royal Palace and hilltop town have been rebuilt once more, with a mix-and-match style that attempts, with only some success, to evoke the site's grand legacy.

The Walk Begins

• *Orient yourself from the top of the funicular, enjoying the views over the Danube. (We'll get a full visual tour from a better viewpoint later.) At the top of the nearby staircase, notice the giant bird that looks like a vulture. This is the...*

Turul Bird

This mythical bird of Magyar folktales sup-posedly led the Hungarian migrations from the steppes of Central Asia in the ninth cen-tury. He dropped his sword in the Carpath-ian Basin, indicating that this was to be the permanent home of the Magyar people. While the Hungarians have long since integrated into Europe, the Turul remains a symbol of Mag-yar pride. During a surge of nationalism in the 1920s, a movement named after this bird helped revive traditional Hungarian culture. And today, the bird is invoked by right-wing nationalist politicians.

• *We'll circle back this way later. But for now,*

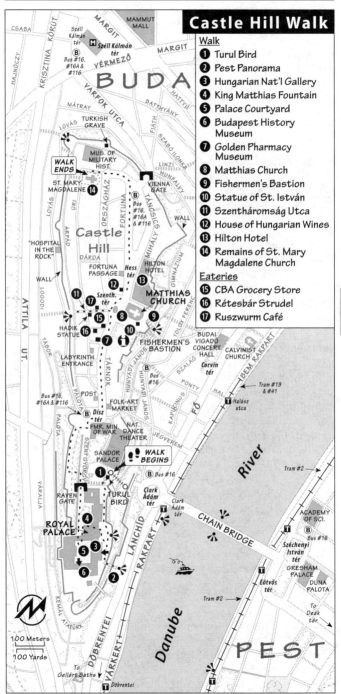

Castle Hill Walk

Walk

1. Turul Bird
2. Pest Panorama
3. Hungarian Nat'l Gallery
4. King Matthias Fountain
5. Palace Courtyard
6. Budapest History Museum
7. Golden Pharmacy Museum
8. Matthias Church
9. Fishermen's Bastion
10. Statue of St. István
11. Szentháromság Utca
12. House of Hungarian Wines
13. Hilton Hotel
14. Remains of St. Mary Magdalene Church

Eateries

15. CBA Grocery Store
16. Rétesbár Strudel
17. Ruszwurm Café

CASTLE HILL WALK

go through the monumental gateway by the Turul and climb down the stairs, then walk along the broad terrace in front of the...

Royal Palace (Királyi Palota)

The imposing palace on Castle Hill barely hints at the colorful story of this hill since the day that the legendary Turul dropped his

sword. It was once the top Renaissance palace in Europe...but that was several centuries and several versions ago. While impressive from afar, the current version of the palace—a historically inaccurate, post-WWII reconstruction—is a loose rebuilding of previous versions, lacking the style and sense of history that this important site deserves. The most prominent feature of today's palace—the green dome—didn't even exist in earlier versions. Fortunately, the palace does house some worthwhile museums (described later), and boasts the fine terrace you're strolling on, with some of Budapest's best views.

Walk all the way down the terrace to the big **equestrian statue** in front of the dome. This depicts Eugene of Savoy, a French general who had great success fighting the Hungarians' hated enemies, the Ottomans. First he helped break the Turkish Siege of Vienna in 1683, and he led the successful Siege of Belgrade in 1717; together, these victories marked the beginning of the end of the Ottoman advance into Europe. Eugene—who fought under three successive Habsburg emperors—was hugely popular across a Europe that was

terrified of the always-looming Ottoman threat. He was the Patton or Eisenhower of his day—a great war hero admired and appreciated by all.

• *With the palace at your back, notice the long, skinny promontory sticking out from Castle Hill (on your right). Walk out to the tip of that promontory to enjoy Castle Hill's best...*

Pest Panorama

From here, you can see how topographically different the two halves of Budapest really are. The hill you're on is considered one of the last foothills of the Alps, which ripple from here all the way to France. But immediately across the Danube, everything is oh so flat. Here begins the so-called Great Hungarian Plain, which comprises much of the country—a vast expanse that stretches all the way to Asia. For this reason, Budapest has historically been thought of as on the bubble between West and East. From the ancient Romans to Adolf Hitler, many past rulers have considered the Danube through Budapest a natural border for Europe.

Scan Pest on the horizon, from left to right. Margaret Island, a popular recreation spot, sits in the middle of the Danube. Following the Pest riverbank, you can't miss the spiny Parliament, with its giant red dome. Straight ahead, you enjoy views of the Chain Bridge, with Gresham Palace and the 1896-era St. István's Basilica lined up just beyond it. (The Parliament and St. István's are both exactly 96 meters tall, in honor of the auspicious millennium celebration in 1896—see page 43.) The Chain Bridge cuts downtown Pest in two: The left half, or "Leopold Town," is administrative, with government ministries, embassies, banks, and so on; the right half is the commercial center of Pest, with the best riverside promenade. (Each of these is covered by a different self-guided walk in this book.) To the right is the white Elisabeth Bridge, named for the Austrian empress ("Sisi") who so loved her Hungarian subjects. Downriver (to the right) is the green Liberty Bridge, formerly named for Elisabeth's hubby Franz Josef. (If you squint, you might be able to see the Turul birds that top the pillars of this bridge.) And the tall hill to the right, named for the martyred St. Gellért (who patiently attempted to convert the rowdy Magyars after their king adopted Christianity), is topped by the Soviet-era Liberation Monument.

• *Head back to the statue on the terrace. Facing Eugene's rear end is the main entrance to the...*

Hungarian National Gallery (Magyar Nemzeti Galéria)

Hungarians are the first to admit that they're not known for their artists. But this collection of Hungarian art—with an emphasis on the 19th and 20th centuries, and an excellent collection of medieval altars—offers even non-art-lovers a telling glimpse into the Magyar psyche.

➊ **Self-Guided Tour:** This once-over-lightly tour touches on the most insightful pieces in this sprawling museum. Note: After a recent reshuffling, some of these pieces may appear in a different order; ask museum attendants for help finding the ones you want to see.

From the atrium, head up two flights on the grand staircase. When you reach the first floor, turn right and walk through a room of gloomy paintings (which we'll return to in a moment). Turn right into the hallway, then take an immediate left to reach the excellent collection of **15th-century winged altars.** The ornately decorated wings could be opened or closed to acknowledge special occasions and holidays. Most of these come from "Upper Hungary," or today's Slovakia—which is more heavily wooded than modern (Lower) Hungary, making woodcarving a popular way to worship there. These date from a time when Hungary was at its peak—before the Ottomans and Habsburgs ruined everything.

Backtrack to the room of **gloomy paintings** from the 1850s and 1860s. We've just gone from one of Hungary's highest points to one of its lowest. In the two decades between the failed 1848 Revolution and the Compromise of 1867, the Hungarians were colossally depressed—and these paintings show it. The best-known, dominating the end of the hall (by the door you just came through), is Viktor Madarász's grim *The Bewailing of László Hunyadi,* which commemorates the death of the Hungarian heir-apparent. (The Hungarians couldn't explicitly condemn their Habsburg oppressors, but invoking this dark event from the Middle Ages had much the same effect.) To the right, *Dobozi* features a Hungarian nobleman who stabs his wife as they're pursued on horseback by Ottomans to prevent her from being raped. While Hungarian culture is generally considered less than upbeat, this period took things to a new low.

Cross through the atrium to another room of depressing canvases, including women valiantly fighting Ottomans at the Siege of Eger, on the right; and, in the next section, the crushing Hungarian defeat at the Battle of Mohács, a pivotal victory for the invading Ottomans. At the far end of this room, we come to a turning point: a painting of St. István (or Vajk, his heathen name) being baptized and accepting European Christianity in the year 1000. Not surprisingly, this was painted at the time of the Compromise of 1867, when Hungary was ceded authority within the Catholic Habsburg Empire. Again, the painter uses a historical story as a tip of the hat to contemporary events.

Continue through the door next to the baptism, then turn left into the hallway and take an immediate right. From here, do a

clockwise spin through this wing. The first hall features Hungarian Impressionists, including the appealing *Picnic in May* by Pál Szinyei-Merse. While this scene is innocent today, the thought of men and women socializing freely was scandalous at the time. The next, large room shows off Hungarian artists who took to the country-side, painting landscapes and peasant life in the 1880s and 1890s.

When you're done here, duck into the hall, turn left, then go through the door on your right (past the elevator) into a long hall filled with works by a pair of Hungarian **Realists:** Mihály Munkácsy and László Paál. Mihály Munkácsy, who lived in France alongside the big-name Impressionists and Post-Impressionists, was

wealthy and popular, so he was frequently hired to paint portraits. (As a mainstream artist, he was much more successful in his lifetime than the avant-garde, fringe painters who have since become far better known.) In the third room, Munkácsy shows his skills by capturing

the intensity of English poet John Milton in the painting of Milton with his family. He did paint the occasional landscape—look for the evocative, Turner-esque *Evening Atmosphere* (to the right of the Milton portrait). Farther along in the room are works by László Paál, who primarily painted murky nature scenes—sun-dappled paths through the forest, pondering the connection between man and nature.

Loop back around to the atrium, then climb up one more flight of stairs. Straight ahead from the landing are three works by **Tivadar Csontváry Kosztka,** the "Hungarian Van Gogh" (for more on Csontváry, see page 382).

Here you see a few of this well-traveled painter's destinations: the giant canvas in the center depicts the theater at Taormina, Sicily; on the left are the waterfalls of Schaffhausen, Germany; and on the right is a cedar tree in Lebanon. Colorful, allegorical, and expressionistic, Csontváry has recently become the most in-demand and expensive of Hungarian

Mátyás (Matthias) Corvinus: The Last Hungarian King

The Árpád dynasty—descendants of the original Magyar tribes—died out in 1301. For more than 600 years, Hungary would be ruled by foreigners...with one exception.

In the middle of the 15th century, Hungary had bad luck hanging on to its foreign kings: Two of them died unexpectedly within seven years. Meanwhile, homegrown military general János Hunyadi was enjoying great success on the battlefield against the Ottomans. When five-year-old László V was elected king, Hunyadi was appointed regent and essentially ruled the country.

Hunyadi defeated the Ottomans in the crucial 1456 Battle of Belgrade, which kept them out of Hungary (at least for another 70 years) and made him an even greater hero to the Hungarian people. But soon afterward, Hunyadi died from the plague, which he had contracted during that fateful battle. When the young king also died (at the tender age of 16), the nobles looked for a new leader. At first their sights settled on Hunyadi's eldest son, László. But the Habsburgs—who were trying to project their influence from afar—felt threatened by the Hunyadi family, and László was killed.

At this dark moment, the Hungarians turned to the younger Hunyadi son, Mátyás (or Matthias in English). At the time, Matthias (whose first wife was a Czech princess) was at court in Prague. According to legend, Matthias' mother sent for him with a raven with a ring in its beak. The raven supposedly flew nonstop from Transylvania to Prague. The raven-with-ring motif became part

artists. If you enjoy Csontváry's works and are headed to his hometown of Pécs, don't miss his museum there (see page 381).

If you like, you can climb up one more flight to explore works from the 20th century (including some smaller canvases by Csontváry, depicting scenes in Athens and in Jajce, Bosnia-Herzegovina).

I'd skip the 300-Ft elevator trip to the **dome**—the views are no better than from the promontory out front (dome elevator included in museum ticket, last entry 30 minutes before museum closing).

• Head back out to the Eugene statue and face the palace. Go through the passage to the right of the National Gallery entrance (next to the café). You'll emerge into a courtyard decorated with the...

of the family crest, as well as the family name: Corvinus (Latin for "raven").

Matthias Corvinus returned to Buda, becoming the first Hungarian-descended king in more than 150 years. Progressive and well-educated in the Humanist tradition, Matthias Corvinus (r. 1458-1490) was the quintessential Renaissance king. A lover of the Italian Renaissance, he patronized the arts and built palaces legendary for their beauty. Also a benefactor of the poor, he dressed up as a commoner and ventured into the streets to see firsthand how the nobles of his realm treated his people.

Matthias was a strong, savvy leader. He created Central Europe's first standing army—30,000 mercenaries known as the Black Army. No longer reliant on the nobility for military support, Good King Matthias was able to drain power from the nobles and make taxation of his subjects more equitable—earning him the nickname the "people's king."

King Matthias was also a shrewd military tactician. Realizing that squabbling with the Ottomans would squander his resources, he made peace with the Ottoman sultan to stabilize Hungary's southern border. Then he swept north, invading Moravia, Bohemia, and even Austria. By 1485, Matthias moved into his new palace in Vienna, and Hungary was enjoying a Golden Age.

Five years later, Matthias died mysteriously at the age of 47, and his empire disintegrated. It is said that when Matthias died, justice died with him. To this day, Hungarians consider him the greatest of all kings, and they sing of his siege of Vienna in their national anthem. They're proud that for a few decades in the middle of half a millennium of foreign oppression, they had a truly Hungarian king—and a great one at that.

King Matthias Fountain

This fountain depicts King Matthias enjoying one of his favorite pastimes, hunting. (Notice the distinctive, floppy-eared Hungarian hound dog, or *vizsla*.) At the bottom of the fountain, the guy on the left is Matthias' scribe, while the woman on the right is Ilonka ("The Beautiful"). While Matthias was on an incognito hunting trip, he wooed Ilonka, who fell desperately in love with him—oblivious to the fact he was the king. When he left suddenly to return to Buda, Ilonka tracked him down and realized who he was. Understanding that his rank meant they could never be together, Ilonka committed suicide. This is typical of many Hungarian legends, which tend to be gloomy and end with suicide.

• *On that cheerful note, go around the right side of the fountain and through the passage, into the...*

Palace Courtyard

This space, while impressive, somehow feels like an empty husk...a too-big office building. The entrance to the Budapest History Museum (described next) is at the far end of the courtyard. But first, duck through the door and down the hallway on your right as you go through the passage (free entry). This hall is lined with minor artifacts from the museum, giving you a free glimpse (and English descriptions) of the evolution of this site over the centuries, including artifacts, paintings, drawings, and photographs of the palace in different eras (plus an ATM). If you like what you see here, consider visiting the museum; if not, skip ahead to "Walk to Matthias Church."

Budapest History Museum (Budapesti Történeti Múzeum)

This good but stodgy museum celebrates the earlier grandeur of Castle Hill. It's particularly strong in early history (prehistoric, ancient, medieval; for modern history, the National Museum is better). If Budapest really intrigues you, this is a fine place to explore its history. Otherwise, skip it.

On the ground floor (back-right corner, in a darkened room), stroll through the collection of 14th-century sculpture fragments. Many have strong Magyar features—notice that they look Central Asian (similar to Mongolians). In a small room at the end of this wing is a tapestry mixing the coats of arms of the Magyar Árpád dynasty (red-and-white stripes) with the French Anjou dynasty (fleur-de-lis)—the first two royal houses of Hungary—which was found balled up in a wad of mud.

One floor up, the good exhibit called "Budapest: Light and Shadow" traces a thousand years of the city's history, with concise English descriptions. The top floor has artifacts of Budapest's prehistoric residents. The cellar illustrates just how much this hill has changed over the centuries—and how dull today's version is by comparison. You'll wander through a maze of old palace parts, including the remains of an original Gothic chapel, a knights' hall, and marble remnants (reliefs and fountains) of Matthias Corvinus' lavish Renaissance palace.

Walk to Matthias Church

Leaving the palace courtyard, walk straight up the slight in-cline. In good weather, you might see an opportunity to try your hand at shooting an old-fashioned bow and arrow. Then you'll pass under a gate with a raven holding a ring in its mouth (a symbol of King Matthias). As you

continue along the line of flagpoles, the big white building on your right (near the funicular station) is the **Sándor Palace.** This mansion underwent a very costly renovation under the previous Hungarian prime minister, who hoped to make it his residence. But in 2002, the same year it was finished, he lost his bid for re-election. The spunky new PM refused to move in. By way of compromise, this is now the president's office. This is where you can see the relatively low-key changing of the guard each hour on the hour, with a special show at noon.

After Sándor Palace is the yellow **National Dance Theater,** where Beethoven once performed (for details, see page 282).

In the field in the middle of this terrace, you'll notice the **ruins** of a medieval monastery and church. Along the left side (past the flagpoles) is the ongoing excavation of the medieval Jewish quarter—more reminders that most of what you see on today's Castle Hill has been destroyed and rebuilt many times over.

Notice the bridge on the left, crossing over some of those ruins, as well as a trench around the castle wall. Go over that bridge to a viewpoint for a look at the **Buda Hills**—the "Beverly Hills" of Budapest, draped with orchards, vineyards, and the homes of the wealthiest Budapesters.

Walk along this outer terrace. The hulking, war-damaged building on your right (at the end of the lawn, partially covered by the huge banner) once housed the **Ministry of War.** Most of the bullet holes are from World War II, while others were left by the Soviets who occupied this hill in response to the 1956 Uprising (see pages 112-113).

The building is a political hot potato—prime real estate, but nobody can decide what to do with it.

You'll pop out onto the street, next to the entrance to the rampart garden. A few steps uphill is **Dísz tér** ("Parade Square"). Here you'll see convenient bus stops for connecting to other parts of Budapest (bus #16, #16A, or #116 to Széll Kálmán tér; or bus #16 to the Pest side of the Chain Bridge).

Cross the street in front of the Ministry of War, noticing the handy post office on your left (bus tickets sold here Mon-Fri before 16:00, closed Sat-Sun). On the right, behind the yellow wall, is a courtyard with an open-air Hungarian **folk-art market.** While it's fun to browse, prices here are high (haggle away). The Great Market Hall has a better selection and generally lower prices (see page 64).

Continue straight uphill on **Tárnok utca** (noticing, on the left, the recommended Vár Bistro—a handy lunch cafeteria). This area often disappoints visitors. After being destroyed by Ottomans, it was rebuilt in sensible Baroque, lacking the romantic time-capsule charm of a medieval old town. But if you poke your head into some courtyards, you'll almost always see some original Gothic arches and other medieval features.

As you continue along, ponder the fact that there are miles of **caves** burrowed under Castle Hill—carved out by water, expanded by the Ottomans, and used by locals during the siege of Buda at the end of World War II. If you'd like to spelunk under Castle Hill, there are two different sightseeing options: To learn about how the caves were used during the 20th century, it's worth going on the lengthy "Hospital in the Rock" tour (see page 80); for just a quick look, you can check out the touristy Buda Labyrinth cave, with a sparse, hokey historical exhibit (see page 81).

As you approach the plague column, on your left is the low-profile entrance to the **Golden Pharmacy Museum** (dark-orange building). Consider dipping into this modest three-room collection of historic pharmaceutical bric-a-brac, including a cute old pharmacy counter and an alchemist's lab (500 Ft, borrow English descriptions, Tue-Sun 10:30-18:00, last entry 30 minutes before closing, closed Mon, Tárnok utca 18).

Finally, you'll come to a little park. The white, circular building in the park, marked *TourInform*, is a **TI** that can answer questions and has a handy pictorial map of the castle area (daily 10:00-18:00). You can also get bus tickets here.

Across the street from the park (on the left), the **CBA grocery store** sells reasonably priced cold drinks, and has a coffee shop upstairs (Mon-Fri 7:00-20:00, Sat 8:00-20:00, Sun 9:00-18:00). Just beyond it, the same store runs a "Szendwics" shop selling cheap and basic sandwiches and sides to go. The little window sells a delicious

CASTLE HILL WALK

Hungarian treat, *kürtőskalács*—a "pastry horn" that's slow-cooked on a rotisserie, then rolled in cinnamon, coconut, or other toppings.

Another good spot for dessert is just around the corner: **Rétes-bár,** selling strudel *(rétes)* with various fillings for 250 Ft each (just down the little lane—Balta köz—next to the grocery store, daily 8:00-20:00).

Just beyond the park, a warty plague column from 1713 marks **Szentháromság tér** ("Holy Trinity Square"), the main square of old Buda.

• *Dominating the square is the...*

Matthias Church (Mátyás-Templom)

Budapest's best church has been destroyed and rebuilt several times in the 800 years since it was founded by King Béla IV. Today's version—renovated at great expense in the late 19th century and restored after World War II—is an ornately decorated lesson in Hungarian history. While it's officially named the "Church of Our Lady," everyone calls it the Matthias Church, for the popular Renaissance king who got married here—twice.

Note: As a result of renovations underway inside the church (likely through 2014), some of the items described here may not be accessible.

❍ Self-Guided Tour: Examine the **exterior.** While the nucleus of the church is Gothic, most of what you see outside—including the frilly, flamboyant steeple—was added for the 1896 celebrations. At the top of the spire facing the river, notice the raven—the ever-present symbol of King Matthias Corvinus.

Buy your ticket across the square, at the ticket windows embedded in the wall. (You can also rent an audioguide for additional information, but this may not be available during the church renovation. The same windows also sell tickets for the Fishermen's Bastion, described later.) Then enter the church.

The sumptuous **interior** is wallpapered with gilded pages from a Hungarian history textbook. Different eras are represented by symbolic motifs. For example, the wall immediately to the left of the main entry door represents the Renaissance, with a giant coat of arms of the beloved King Matthias Corvinus. (The tough guys in armor on either side are members of his mercenary Black Army, the source of his power.) Notice another raven, with a ring in its beak. Meanwhile, the wall across from the entry—with Oriental motifs—commemorates the Ottoman reign of Buda.

Work your way clockwise around the church from the entry. The first chapel (in the back corner, by the closed main doors)—the **Loreto Chapel**—holds the church's prize possession: Peer through the black iron grill to see the 1515 statue of Mary and Jesus. Anticipating Ottoman plundering, locals walled over this precious statue. The occupying Ottomans used the church as their primary mosque—oblivious to the statue plastered over in the niche. Then, a century and a half later, during the siege of Buda in 1686, gunpowder stored in the castle up the street detonated, and the wall crumbled. Mary's triumphant face showed through, terrifying the Ottomans. Supposedly this was the only part of town taken from the Ottomans without a fight.

As you look down the **nave,** notice the banners. They've hung here since the Mass that celebrated Habsburg monarch Franz Josef's coronation at this church on June 8, 1867. In a sly political compromise to curry favor in the Hungarian part of his territory, Franz Josef was "emperor" *(Kaiser)* of Austria, but only "king" *(König)* of Hungary. (If you see the old German phrase "K+K"—still used today as a boast of royal quality—it refers to this *"König und Kaiser"* arrangement.) So, after F. J. was crowned emperor in Vienna, he came down the Danube and said to the Hungarians, "King me." (For more on the K+K system, see page 316.)

Continue circling around the church. Along the left aisle (toward the main altar from the gift shop) is the altar of St. Imre, the son of the great King (and later Saint) István. This heir to the Hungarian throne was mysteriously killed by a boar while hunting when he was only 19 years old. Though he didn't live long enough to do anything important, he rode his father's coattails to sainthood. The next chapel is the tomb of Béla III, utterly insignificant except that this is one of only two tombs of Hungarian kings that still exist in the country. The rest—including all of the biggies—were defiled by the Ottomans. Up next to the main altar is the chapel of László—St. István's nephew, who stepped in as king of Hungary when the rightful heir, St. Imre, was killed.

Along the left aisle is the entrance to the upstairs gallery, which holds the **Museum of Ecclesiastical Art** (Egyházművészeti Gyűjteménye, same ticket and hours as church). The original Hungarian crown is under the Parliament's dome (described on page 107)—but a replica is up here, and worth a peek. The church also hosts concerts (Oct-Feb only, maybe a few in shoulder season, none in summer, may be cancelled during the renovation; ask at ticket windows or church entry, or look for posted schedules).

• *Back outside, at the end of the square next to the Matthias Church, is the...*

Fishermen's Bastion (Halászbástya)

This Neo-Romanesque fantasy rampart offers beautiful views over the Danube to Pest. In the Middle Ages, the fish market was

just below here (in today's Víziváros, or "Water Town"), so this part of the rampart actually was guarded by fishermen. The current structure, however, is completely artificial—yet another example of Budapest sprucing itself up for 1896. Its seven pointy towers represent the seven Magyar tribes. The cone-headed arcades are reminiscent of tents the nomadic Magyars called home before they moved west to Europe.

Paying 600 Ft to climb up the bastion makes little sense. Enjoy virtually the same view through the windows (left of café) for free. (The café offers a scenic break if you don't mind the tour groups.) There's a pay WC to the right of the bastion.

Explore the full length of the bastion, and you'll find that several other sections are also open and free to the public—as well as more scenic cafés, sometimes with live "Gypsy" music. Note that the (free) grand staircase leading down from the bastion offers a handy shortcut to the Víziváros neighborhood and Batthyány tér (for affordable restaurants there, see pages 260-261).

Tucked around the far side of the bastion, at the back of a pastry shop in the modern, glassy building, is the **Szabó Marzipan Museum,** where you can pay 400 Ft to see two rooms crammed full of little sculptures created from this almond-paste confection (daily 9:00-18:00). While it's not as impressive as the similar sight in Eger (see page 358), it's worth a peek if you're curious.

• *Between the bastion and the church stands a statue of...*

St. István (c. 967-1038)

Hungary's first Christian king tamed the nomadic, pagan Magyars and established strict laws and the concept of private property. In the late 900s, King Géza of Hungary lost a major battle against the

forces of Christian Europe—and realized that he must raise his son Vajk as a Catholic and convert his people, or they would be forcefully driven out of Europe. Vajk took the Christian name István (EESHT-vahn, "Stephen") and was baptized in the year 1000. The reliefs on this statue show the commissioners of the pope crowning St. István, bringing Hungary into the fold of Christendom. This put Hungary on the map as a fully European kingdom, forging alliances that would endure for centuries. Without this pivotal event, Hungarians believe that the Magyar nation would have been lost. A passionate evangelist—more for the survival of his Magyar nation than for the salvation of his people—István beheaded those who wouldn't convert. To make his point perfectly clear, he quartered his reluctant uncle and sent him on four separate, simultaneous tours of the country to show Hungarians that Christianity was a smart choice. Gruesome as he was, István was sainted within 30 years of his death.

• *Directly across from Matthias Church is a charming little street called...*

Szentháromság Utca

Halfway down this street on the right, look for the venerable, recommended **Ruszwurm** café—the oldest in Budapest (see page 266). At the end of the street is an equestrian statue of the war hero **András Hadik.** If you examine the horse closely, you'll see that his, ahem, undercarriage has been polished to a high shine. Local students rub these for good luck before a big exam. I guess you could say students really have a ball preparing for tests.

Continue out to the terrace and appreciate more views of the Buda Hills. If you go down the stairs here, then turn right up the street, you'll reach the entrance of the World War II-era **"Hospital in the Rock,"** which you can tour to learn about the Nazi and Cold War era of Castle Hill (excellent tours at the top of each hour, closed Mon, described on page 80).

• *Retrace your steps back to Matthias Church. Some visitors will have had their fill of Castle Hill; if so, you can make a graceful exit down the big staircase below the Fishermen's Bastion. You'll wind up in Víziváros, on the embankment.*

*But if you'd like to extend your walk to the northern part of Castle Hill, start at the plague column, and go up the street next to the modern building, noticing (on the left, at the start of the block) the **House of Hungarian Wines**, which offers wine tastings (see page 79).*

Now turn your attention across the street to that jarringly modern building next to Matthias Church....

Hilton Hotel

Built in 1976, the Hilton was the first plush Western hotel in town. Before 1989, it was a gleaming center of capitalism, offering a cushy  refuge for Western travelers and a stark contrast to what was, at the time, a very gloomy city. To minimize the controversy of building upon so much history, architects thoughtfully incorporated the medieval ruins into their modern design. Halfway down the hotel's facade (after the first set of doors, at the base of the tower), you'll see fragments of a 13th-century wall, with a monument to King Matthias Corvinus. After the wall, continue along the second half of the Hilton Hotel facade. Turn right into the gift-shop entry, and then go right again inside the second glass door. Through yet another glass door, stairs on the left lead down to a reconstructed 13th-century Dominican cloister (now housing a wine cellar). For an even better look at what was here back then, go back up the stairs and turn left. As you enter the lounge, look out the back windows to see fragments of the 13th-century Dominican church incorporated into the structure of the hotel. If you stood here eight centuries ago, you'd be looking straight down the church's nave. You can even see tomb markers in the floor.

Back out on the street, cross the little park and duck into the entryway of the **Fortuna Passage.** Along the passageway to the courtyard, you can see the original Gothic arches of the house that once stood here. In the Middle Ages, every homeowner had the right to sell wine without paying taxes—but only in the passage of his own home. He'd set up a table here, and his neighbors would come by to taste the latest vintage. These passageways evolved into very social places, like the corner pub.

Leaving the passage, turn left down Fortuna utca and walk toward the mosaic roof (passing the recommended 21 Magyar Vendéglő on your right—a good place for an upscale meal). Reaching the end of the street, look right to see the low-profile **Vienna Gate.** If you go through it and walk for about 10 days, you'll get to Vienna. (For now, settle for climbing up to the top for a view of some of Buda's residential neighborhoods.) Just inside the Vienna Gate, notice the bus stop—handy for leaving Castle Hill when you're finished.

• *Now turn left and walk along the hulking, mosaic-roofed National Archive building (with your back to the Danube) until you reach the...*

Remains of St. Mary Magdalene Church

This was once known as the Kapisztrán Templom, named after a hero of the Battle of Belgrade in 1456, an early success in the struggle to keep the Ottomans out of Europe. (King Matthias' father, János Hunyadi, led the Hungarians in that battle.) The pope was so tickled by the victory that he decreed that all church bells should toll at noon in memory of the battle—and, technically, they still do. (Californians might recognize Kapisztrán's Spanish name: San Juan Capistrano.) This church was destroyed by bombs in World War II, though no worse than Matthias Church. But, since this part of town was depopulated after the war, there was no longer a need for a second church. The remains of the church were torn down, the steeple was rebuilt as a memorial, and a carillon was added—so that every day at noon, the bells can still toll...and be enjoyed by the monument of János Kapisztrán, just across the square.

• *Our walk is finished, but there are a few more options nearby. You can walk out to the terrace just beyond the big building for another look at the Buda Hills. From here, just to the right (near the flagpole), is the entrance to the* **Museum of Military History**, *with a mountain of army-surplus artifacts from Hungary's gloriously unsuccessful military past (described on page 80). If you continue around the terrace past the museum, at the northern point of Castle Hill you'll find an old* **Turkish grave**, *honoring a pasha who once ruled here during Ottoman times.*

If you're ready to leave Castle Hill, you can backtrack to the Fishermen's Bastion and walk down the grand staircase there (into the Víziváros neighborhood). Or, from the square just inside Vienna Gate, you can catch bus #16, #16A, and #116 to Széll Kálmán tér—or head out through the gate and follow the road downhill. You'll run into bustling Széll Kálmán tér, which has a handy Metró stop (M2/ red line) and the huge, modern, popular Mammut shopping complex.

CASTLE HILL WALK

MEMENTO PARK TOUR

a.k.a. Statue Park (Szoborpark)

When regimes fall, so do their monuments...literally. Just think of all those statues of Stalin and Lenin that crashed to the ground in late 1989, when people throughout Eastern Europe couldn't wait to get rid of these reminders of their oppressors. But some clever entrepreneur hoarded Budapest's, collecting them in a park in the countryside just southwest of the city—where tourists flock to get a taste of the communist era. Though it can be time-consuming to visit, this collection is worth ▲▲▲ for those fascinated by Hungary's commie past.

Orientation

Name-Change Warning: Confusingly, this attraction—which for years had been called Statue Park—was recently re-branded as Memento Park. The names are still occasionally used interchangeably; they refer to the same sight.
Cost: 1,500 Ft.

Hours: Daily 10:00-sunset.

Getting There: It's in the countryside six miles southwest of the city center, at the corner of Balatoni út and Szabadka út, in district XXII.

The park runs a convenient **direct bus** from Deák tér in downtown Budapest (where all three Metró lines converge; bus stop is at corner of busy Bajcsy-Zsilinszky út and Harmincad utca). The trip takes 2.5 hours total, including a 1.5-hour visit to the park (4,900-Ft fee includes round-trip and park entry, 33 percent discount if you pre-book online at www.mementopark.hu, runs year-round daily at 11:00, July-Aug also at 15:00).

Hiring a **taxi** for the round-trip, including about an hour of waiting time at the park, should cost around 12,000 Ft (ask your hotel to call one for you, and confirm the price before you set out).

While it's possible to reach the park by **public transit** (explained on the park's fliers and website), it's complicated, requiring a number of changes; several of my readers have deemed it more trouble than it's worth. Ideally, take the direct bus noted above or a taxi.

Tours and Information: This chapter's self-guided tour gives you all the information you need. Alternatively, 50-minute English tours depart from the entrance (1,200 Ft, 33 percent discount if you prebook online, daily at 11:45; March-Oct also at 12:45 and 13:45; July-Aug also at 15:45 and 16:45). The 600-Ft English guidebook, while poorly translated, is very informative. Tel. 1/424-7500, www.mementopark.hu.

Starring: Marx, Engels, Lenin, stiff soldiers, passionate patriots... and other ghosts of Hungary's communist past.

Background

Under the communists, creativity was discouraged. The primary purpose of art was to further the goals of the state, with creative expression only an afterthought. This **Socialist Realistic** art served two purposes: It was Realistic, breaking with the "decadent" bourgeois art that came before it (Impres-

sionism, Post-Impressionism, and other modern -isms); and Socialistic, encouraging complicity with the brave new world the communists were forging. From 1949 until 1956, Socialist Realism was legally enforced as the sole artistic style of the Soviet Bloc.

As propaganda was an essential weapon in the Soviet arsenal,

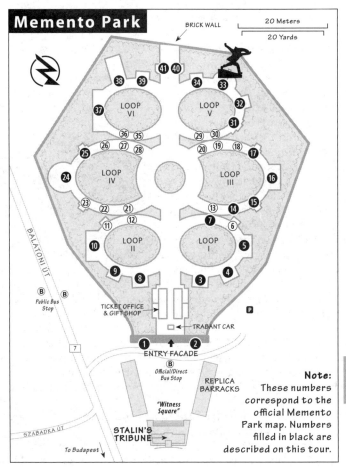

Memento Park

BRICK WALL

20 Meters
20 Yards

LOOP VI
LOOP V
LOOP IV
LOOP III
LOOP II
LOOP I

BALATONI ÚT

Public Bus Stop

TICKET OFFICE & GIFT SHOP

TRABANT CAR

P

ENTRY FACADE

Official/Direct Bus Stop

REPLICA BARRACKS

"Witness Square"

STALIN'S TRIBUNE →

SZABADKA ÚT

To Budapest

Note:
These numbers correspond to the official Memento Park map. Numbers filled in black are described on this tour.

the regime made ample use of Socialist Realistic art. Aside from a few important figureheads, individuals didn't matter. Everyone was a cog in the machine—strong, stoic, doing their job well and proudly for the good of the people. Individual characteristics and distinguishing features were unimportant; people were represented as automatons serving their nation. Artistic merit was virtually ignored. Most figures are trapped in stiff, unnatural poses that ignore the 3,000 years of artistic evolution since the Egyptians. Sculptures and buildings alike from this era were designed to evoke feelings of power and permanence.

The Tour Begins

• *The numbers in the following tour match the statue labels in the park, the official park map, and the map in this chapter.*
As you approach the park, you encounter the imposing red-brick...

Entry Facade

You're greeted by three of the Communist All-Stars: ❶ **Vladimir Lenin,** a leader of Russia's Bolshevik Revolution; and ❷ **Karl Marx** and **Friedrich Engels,** the German philosophers whose *Communist Manifesto* first articulated the principles behind communism

in 1848. (These three figures weren't offensive enough to be destroyed, but very few statues survive anywhere of the biggest "star" of all, the hated Josef Stalin.)

Like the rest of the park, this gate's design is highly conceptual: It looks impressive and monumental...but, like the rotted-out pomp of communism, there's nothing behind it. It's a glossy stage-set with no substance. If you try to go through the main, central part of the gate, you'll run into an always-locked door. Instead, as with the communist system, you have to find another way around (in this case, the side gate to the left). Etched in the door is the Hungarian poem "Where seek out tyranny?", published after the 1956 Uprising.

Inside the gate on the left, buy your ticket and head into the park. Surveying the layout, notice that the main road takes you confidently toward...a dead end (the brick wall). Once again, as with life under the communists, you'll have to deviate from this main axis to actually accomplish anything. Even so, notice that the six walkways branching off the main road all loop you right back to where you started—representing the endless futility of communism. The loops are thematically tied together in pairs: Roughly, the first figure-eight focuses on Hungarian-Soviet friendship; the second figure-eight celebrates the heroes of communism; and the third figure-eight shows off the idealized concepts of communism.
• *Now we'll zigzag back and forth through each of the six loops. Begin with the loop to the right as you enter the park.*

Liberation Monuments (Loop I)

All of these statues celebrate the Soviet Army's triumphant rescue of Hungary from the Nazis in 1945.

Dominating this loop is a ❸ **giant soldier** holding the Soviet flag. This statue once stood at the base of the Liberation Monument that still overlooks the Danube from Gellért Hill (see page 82). Typical of Socialist Realistic art, the soldier has a clenched fist (symbolizing strength) and a face that is inspired by his egalitarian ideology. After the fall of communism, some critics wanted the entire monument torn down. As a compromise, they removed the overt communist themes (the red star and this soldier), covered what remained with a sheet for a while to exorcise the communist mojo, then re-unveiled it.

To the left of this soldier, see the ❹ **two comrades** stiffly shaking hands: the Hungarian worker thrilled to meet the Soviet soldier—protector of the proletariat.

Beyond them is a ❺ **long wall,** with a triumphant worker breaking through the left end—too busy doing his job to be very excited. Just another brick in the wall. (The three big blocks protruding from the wall were for hanging commemorative wreaths.)

The big ❼ **panel** came from an apartment building in a conservative Buda Hills neighborhood. Each neighborhood had a similar monument to the liberation. The nail holes once held letters that proclaimed in Hungarian and Russian: "Everlasting praise for the freedom of the Soviet Union, for its independence, and for its fallen heroes in the battle to liberate Hungary."

• *Cross "main street" to a group of statues commemorating the key communist holiday of...*

April 4, 1945 (Loop II)

On this date, the Soviets forced the final Nazi soldier out of Hungary. The tall panel nearest the entrance shows a Hungarian woman and a Soviet woman setting free the ❽ **doves of peace.** According to the inscription, "Our freedom and peace is founded upon the enduring Hungarian-Soviet friendship." (With friends like these....)

The ❾ **woman holding the palm leaf** is reminiscent of the Liberation Monument back on the Danube—which, after all, celebrates the same glorious day.

At the back of the loop, the ❿ **Hungarian worker and Soviet soldier** (who appear to be doing calisthenics) are absurdly rigid even though they're trying to be dynamic. (Even the statues couldn't muster genuine enthusiasm for communist ideals.)

• *Cross over and head up to the next loop to pay homage to...*

Heroes of the Workers' Movement (Loop III)

Look for the ⓮ bust of the Bulgarian communist leader **Georgi Dimitrov** (ruled 1946-1949)—one of communist Hungary's many Soviet Bloc comrades. During the 1956 Uprising, protesters put a noose around this bust's neck and hung it from a tree. Next is a ⓯ full-size statue of Dimitrov, a gift from "the working people of Sofia." (Talk about a white elephant.)

At the back of this loop are ⓰ three blocky portraits. The middle figure is the granddaddy of Hungarian communism: **Béla Kun** (1886-1938) fought for the Austro-Hungarian Empire in World War I. He was captured by the Russian Army, taken to a prisoner of war camp inside Russia, and became mysteriously smitten with communism. After proving himself too far left even for Lenin, Kun returned to Hungary in 1918 and formed a Hungarian Communist Party at a time when communism was most definitely not in vogue. We'll see more of Kun later in the park.

To the left is one of the park's best-loved, most-photographed, and most artistic statues: ⓱ **Vladimir Lenin,** in his famous "hailing a cab" pose. It once stood at the entrance to the giant industrial complex in Budapest's Csepel district.

• *Cross over—passing the giant red star made of flowers (resembling one that was once planted in the middle of the roundabout at the Buda end of the Chain Bridge)—to meet...*

MEMENTO PARK TOUR

More Communist Heroes (Loop IV)

This group—which includes a ❷❺ statue of an interior minister made a foot shorter at the bottom when the Iron Curtain fell—is dominated by a ❷❹ dramatic, unusually emotive sculpture by a

genuine artist, **Imre Varga** (described on page 87). Designed to commemorate the 100th anniversary of Béla Kun's birth, this clever statue accomplishes seemingly contradictory feats. On the one hand, it reinforces the commu-

nist message: Under the able leadership of Béla Kun (safely overlooking the fray from above), the crusty, bourgeois old regime of the Habsburg Empire (on the left, with the umbrellas and fancy clothes) was converted into the workers' fighting force of the Red Army (on the right, with the bayonets). And yet, those silvery civilians in back seem more appealing than the lunging soldiers in front. And notice the lamppost next to Kun: In Hungarian literature, a lamppost is a metaphor for the gallows. This reminds viewers that Kun—in spite of his groundbreaking and heroic work for the communist movement in Hungary—was ultimately executed by the communists during Stalin's purges of the late 1930s.

• *Zig and head up again, for a lesson in...*

Communist Concepts (Loop V)

Look for a rusty pair of ❸❶ **workers' hands** holding a sphere (which was once adorned with a red star). This represented the hard-won ideals of communism, carefully protected by the hands—but also held out for others to appreciate.

The ❸❷ **monument to Hungarian soldiers** (who look like saluting Rockettes) honors those who fought against the fascist Francisco Franco in the Spanish Civil War.

Dominating this group is a ❸❸ **communist worker** charging into the future, clutching the Soviet flag. Budapesters of the time had a different interpretation: a thermal bath attendant running after a customer who'd forgotten his towel. This is a favorite spot for goofy posed photos.

To the left is a monument to the communist version of the Boy Scouts: the elementary-school-age ❸❹ **Little Drummers** and the older **Pioneers.** While these organizations existed before the communists, they were slowly infiltrated and turned into propaganda machines by the regime. These kids—with their jaunty red and blue neckerchiefs— were sent to camp to be properly raised as good little communists; today, many of them have forgotten

the brainwashing but still have fond memories of the socializing.

• *Now zag once more to learn about...*

More Communist Concepts (Loop VI)

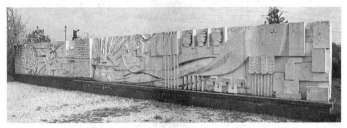

The ❸ long, **white wall** at the back of this section tells quite a story (from left to right): The bullet holes lead up to a jumbled, frightful clutter (reminiscent of Pablo Picasso's *Guernica*) representing World War II. Then comes the bright light of the Soviet system, and by the end everyone's properly regimented and looking boldly to the future (and enjoying a bountiful crop, to boot). The names in the center represent "heroes" who stayed true to the ideology, Party, and nation and died in "defense of proletarian power" in 1956. Some became household names to older locals, who show their age by still referring to places using their communist titles (from 1956 until 1990, many Budapest streets were named in honor of these "heroes").

Next is a ❸ **fallen hero** with arm outstretched, about to collapse to the ground— mortally wounded, yet victorious. This monument to "the Martyrs of the Counter-Revolution" also commemorates those who died attempting to put down the 1956 Uprising.

Finally you'll see a ❸ **plundered monument.** Missing its figures and red star, it was destroyed in 1989 by jubilant Hungarians celebrating their freedom.

• *Now continue down the main drag to, um, a....*

Dead End

The main path dead-ends at the wall, symbolizing life's frustrations under communism. Here stand statues of two Soviet officers who negotiated with the Nazis to end the WWII siege of Budapest. ❹ **Captain Miklós Steinmetz** (on the right) was killed by a Nazi land mine, while ❹ **Ilja Ostapenko** (on the left) was shot under mysterious circumstances as he returned from the successful

summit. Both became heroes for the communist cause. Were they killed by wayward Nazi soldiers, as the Soviets explained—or by their own Red Army, to create a pair of convenient martyrs? These two statues once flanked the road out of Budapest toward the popular resort area at Lake Balaton. Locals eager to get out of town would hitchhike "at Ostapenko."

Heading back out to the entry gate, peruse the fun parade of communist kitsch at the **gift shop.** The stirring music may just move you to pick up the CD of *Communism's Greatest Hits,* and maybe a model of a Trabant (the classic two-stroke commie-mobile). A real **Trabant** is often parked just inside the gate.

• *Now head out across the parking lot to find...*

Stalin's Tribune

This section of the complex is a re-creation of the giant grandstand that once stood along Parade Street (the boulevard next to City

Park; the original site is described on page 177). Hungarian and Soviet leaders stood here, at the feet of a giant Stalin statue, to survey military and civilian processions. But during the 1956 Uprising, protesters cut Stalin off at the knees... leaving only the boots. (The entire tribune was later dismantled, and Stalin disappeared without a trace.)

• *Flanking the lot in front of the tribune are replica...*

Barracks

These are reminiscent of the ramshackle barracks where political prisoners lived in communist-era work camps (sometimes called gulags, described on page 162). These hold special exhibits, often including a good explanation of "Stalin's Boots" (with photos of the original tribune) and the events of 1956. Sit down for the short and creepy film, *The Life of an Agent*, which was actually used to train spies on secret-police methods and policies.

• *Our tour is over. Now, inspired by the bold propaganda of your Hungarian comrades, march proudly into the dawn of a new day.*

SLEEPING IN BUDAPEST

I favor hotels and restaurants that are handy to your sightseeing activities. Rather than list hotels scattered throughout a city, I describe my favorite neighborhoods and recommend the best accommodations values in each, from dorm beds to fancy doubles with all of the comforts.

A major feature of this book is its extensive listing of good-value rooms. I like places that are clean, central, relatively quiet at night, reasonably priced, friendly, small enough to have a hands-on owner and stable staff, run with a respect for Hungarian traditions, and not listed in other guidebooks. Obviously, a place meeting every criterion is rare, and all of my recommendations fall short of perfection—sometimes miserably. But I've listed the best values for each price category. I'm more impressed by a convenient location and a fun-loving philosophy than flat-screen TVs and shoeshine machines.

Book your accommodations well in advance if you'll be traveling during busy times. September is extremely tight (because of conventions), with October close behind. The Formula 1 races (one weekend in late July or early Aug) send rates through the roof; also see page 476 for a list of major holidays and festivals in Hungary. Most rates drop 10-25 percent in the off-season (generally Nov-March). For tips on making reservations, see page 228.

Rates and Deals

I've described my recommended accommodations using a Sleep Code (see sidebar). Prices listed are for one-night stays in peak season, include breakfast (unless specified), and assume you're booking directly (not through a TI or online hotel-booking engine). Using an online booking service costs the hotel about 15 percent and logically closes the door on special deals. Book direct.

Sleep Code

(€1 = $1.30, 200 Ft = about $1, country code: 36, area code: 1)

Price Rankings

To help you easily sort through my listings, I've divided the accommodations into three categories based on the price for a double room with bath during high season:

  $$$ **Higher Priced**—Most rooms €100 or more.

  $$ **Moderately Priced**—Most rooms between €70-100.

  $ **Lower Priced**—Most rooms €70 or less.

    I always rate hostels as $, whether or not they have double rooms, because they have the cheapest beds in town.

    Prices can change without notice; verify the hotel's current rates online or by email.

Abbreviations

To pack maximum information into minimum space, I use the following code to describe the accommodations in this book. Prices listed are per room, not per person. When a price range is given for a type of room (such as double rooms listing for €100-120), it means the price fluctuates with the season, size of room, or length of stay; expect to pay the upper end for peak-season stays.

  S = Single room (or price for one person in a double).

  D = Double or twin room. "Double beds" are often two twins sheeted together and are usually big enough for nonromantic couples.

  T = Triple (generally a double bed plus a single).

  Q = Quad (usually two double beds; adding an extra child's bed to a T is usually cheaper).

  b = Private bathroom with toilet and shower or tub.

  s = Private shower or tub only (the toilet is down the hall).

    According to this code, a couple staying at a "Db-€100" hotel would pay a total of €100 (about $130) for a double room with a private bathroom. Unless otherwise noted, prices include breakfast but not the 3 percent tourist tax, hotel staff speak basic English, and credit cards are accepted.

    There's almost always Wi-Fi and/or Internet access available, either free or for a fee.

In Budapest, most hotels quote their rates in euros (for the convenience of their international guests), and I've followed suit. (Outside of the capital, hotels more often quote rates in forints.) However, most places prefer to be paid in forints (figured at the exchange rate on the day of payment). Unless I note otherwise in the listing, you can assume the hotel accepts credit cards—though smaller places always prefer cash. I've listed prices per room, not per person.

The majority of hotels don't include the 3 percent tourist tax in their rates. Be warned that some big chains also don't include the whopping 22 percent sales tax, which can make your hotel cost nearly a quarter more than you expected. (Independent hotel rates typically do include sales tax.)

While most hotels listed in this chapter cluster at about €70-105 per double, they range from €20 bunks to €500-plus splurges (maximum plumbing and more). (Rooms outside the capital—such as in Eger, Pécs, and Sopron—are much cheaper.) Hoteliers know what their beds are worth, so generally you get what you pay for. Since my €100 listings are substantially nicer than my €85 listings, I'd spring for the extra expense to have a comfortable home base. In general, a triple room is cheaper than the cost of a double and a single. Traveling alone can be expensive: A single room can be close to the cost of a double.

For each hotel in this chapter, I've listed the average price during relatively busy periods (though not peak-of-peak times). At most hotels, you'll find these rates vary dramatically with demand. A few years back, Budapest built a few too many new hotels; with Hungary's recent economic woes, many—including some luxury hotels—routinely offer deeply discounted rates to attract guests. Use my prices as a rough guideline, but check the hotel's own website or try emailing them to ask for their best price. Try comparing several to find the top deal.

In general, prices can soften if you do any of the following: offer to pay cash, stay at least three nights, or mention this book. You can also try asking for a cheaper room or a discount, or offer to skip breakfast.

If you're on a tight budget, consider one of Budapest's many hostels (described on page 230). But don't overlook the good-value **Bellevue B&B** (page 243) and **Mária and István**'s place (page 239). At any hotel, three or four people can save money by requesting one big room.

Types of Accommodations
Hotels
If you're arriving early in the morning, your room probably won't be ready. You can drop your bag safely at the hotel and dive right into sightseeing. When packing, keep in mind that hotel elevators, while becoming more common, are often very small, forcing you to send your bags up separately—another reason to pack light.

Hoteliers can be a great help and source of advice. Most know their city well, and can assist you with everything from public transit and airport connections to finding a good restaurant, the nearest

Making Hotel Reservations

Given the quality of the places I've found for this book, reserve your rooms several weeks in advance (or as soon as you've pinned down your travel dates), particularly if you'll be traveling during peak times. Finding accommodations as you travel is possible, but if you plan ahead, you're less likely to wind up in a poorly located and/or overpriced hotel. Note that some national holidays jam things up and merit your making reservations far in advance (see "Holidays and Festivals" on page 476), and that hotels fill up fast in convention season (mainly September and, to a lesser degree, October).

Requesting a Reservation: It's usually easiest to book your room through the hotel's website; many have a reservation-request form built right in. (For the best rates, be sure to use the hotel's official site and not a booking agency's site.) Just type in your preferred dates and the website will automatically display a list of available rooms and prices. Simpler websites will generate an email to the hotelier with your request. If there's no reservation form, or for complicated requests, send an email. Other options include calling (see "Phoning" later, and be mindful of time zones) or faxing. Most recommended hotels are accustomed to guests who speak only English.

The hotelier wants to know these key pieces of information (also included in the sample request form in the appendix):
- number and type of rooms
- number of nights
- date of arrival
- date of departure
- any special needs (such as bathroom in the room or down the hall, twin beds vs. double bed, air-conditioning, quiet, view, ground floor, etc.)

When you request a room, use the Hungarian style for writing dates: year.month.day. For example, for a two-night stay in July of 2014, I would request: "2 nights, arrive 2014.07.16, depart 2014.07.18." Consider carefully how long you'll stay; don't just assume you can tack on extra days once you arrive. Remember to ask for the hotel's best price—many are eager to offer discounts. It can't hurt to mention this book.

If you don't get a response to your email, it usually means the hotel is already fully booked—but try sending the message again or call to follow up.

Confirming a Reservation: Most places will request your credit-card number to hold the room. To confirm a room using a hotel's secure online reservation form, enter your contact information and credit-card number; the hotel will email a confirmation.

If you sent an email to request a reservation, the hotel will reply with its room availability and rates. This is not a confirmation. You must email back to say that you want the room at the given rate. While you can email your credit-card information (I do), it's safer to share that confidential info by phone call, two emails (splitting your number between them), or the hotel's secure online reservation form.

Canceling a Reservation: If you must cancel your reservation, it's courteous to do so with as much notice as possible—at least three days. Simply make a quick phone call or send an email. Family-run places lose money if they turn away customers while holding a room for someone who doesn't show up. Understandably, many places bill no-shows for one night.

Cancellation policies can be strict: For example, you might lose a deposit if you cancel within two weeks of your reserved stay, or you might be billed for the entire visit if you leave early. Internet deals may require prepayment, with no refunds for cancellations. Ask about cancellation policies before you book.

If canceling via email, request confirmation that your cancellation was received to avoid being accidentally billed.

Reconfirming Your Reservation: Always call to reconfirm your room reservation a few days in advance. Smaller hotels and pensions appreciate knowing your estimated time of arrival. If you'll be arriving late (after 17:00), let them know. On the small chance that a hotel loses track of your reservation, bring along a hard copy of their confirmation.

Reserving Rooms as You Travel: You can make reservations as you travel, calling hotels and pensions a few days to a week before your arrival. If everything's full, don't despair. Call a day or two in advance and fill in a cancellation. If you'd rather travel without any reservations at all, you'll have greater success snaring rooms if you arrive at your destination early in the day. When you anticipate crowds (weekends are worst), call hotels at about 9:00 or 10:00 on the day you plan to arrive, when the receptionist knows who'll be checking out and which rooms will be available. If you encounter a language barrier, ask the fluent receptionist at your current hotel to call for you.

Phoning: To call Hungary from the US or Canada, dial 011-36, and then the numbers listed in this chapter. The 011 is our international access code, and 36 is Hungary's country code. If you're calling Hungary from another European country, dial 00-36, then the area code and number. The 00 is Europe's international access code. To call within Budapest, dial the number direct, omitting the initial 1. For long-distance within Hungary (for example, calling from Budapest to Eger), you have to dial 06 before the number.

The way you dial a Hungarian **mobile number** depends on where you're calling from. I've listed these numbers as you'd dial them from a fixed line in Hungary (generally beginning with 0620, 0630, or 0670). From another country, or from a mobile phone in Hungary, you'll need to omit the initial 06, and replace it with the international access code (011 from the US, 00 from Europe, or + on a mobile phone), then 36, then the number. For example, to dial a number appearing as 0630-370-8678 from outside Hungary, you'd dial the international access code (011, 00, or +), then 36-30-370-8678.

For more tips on calling, see page 463.

launderette, or an Internet café. Of my recommended hotels, all of the places in Budapest (and virtually all those outside of Budapest) have English-speaking staff. In the rare instance where they do not, you'll find a note in my listing.

For environmental reasons, towels are often replaced only when you leave them on the floor. In some cheap hotels, they aren't replaced at all during your stay, so hang them up to dry and reuse. You might be tempted to borrow your hotel towel for your visit to the thermal baths (saving the towel-rental cost). Some hotels frown on this, others forbid it, and a few will loan you a special towel for this purpose.

Most hotels listed here include a buffet breakfast. Some smaller budget places serve no breakfast at all, while larger chain hotels charge (too much) extra for it; in these cases, I've noted it in the listing. Consider having breakfast instead at one of two good cafés I've recommended in the Eating in Budapest chapter: Gerlóczy Café or Callas (see "Budapest's Café Culture" on page 263).

Even at the best places, mechanical breakdowns occur: Air-conditioning malfunctions, sinks leak, hot water turns cold, and toilets gurgle and smell. Report your concerns clearly and calmly at the front desk. For more complicated problems, don't expect instant results.

If you suspect night noise will be a problem (if, for instance, your room is over a nightclub), ask for a quieter room in the back or on an upper floor. To guard against theft in your room, keep valuables out of sight. Some rooms come with a safe, and other hotels have safes at the front desk. I've never bothered using one.

Checkout can pose problems if surprise charges pop up on your bill. If you settle your bill the afternoon before you leave, you'll have time to discuss and address any points of contention (before 19:00, when the night shift usually arrives).

The only tip my recommended accommodations would like is a friendly, easygoing guest. And, as always, I appreciate feedback on your experiences.

Above all, keep a positive attitude. Remember, you're on vacation. If your hotel is a disappointment, spend more time out enjoying the city you came to see.

Hostels

You'll pay about €20 per bed to stay at a hostel. Travelers of any age are welcome if they don't mind dorm-style accommodations and meeting other travelers. Most hostels offer kitchen facilities, Internet access, Wi-Fi, and a self-service laundry. Nowadays, concerned about bedbugs, hostels are likely to provide all bedding, including sheets. Family and private rooms may be available on request.

Independent hostels, which Budapest is full of, tend to be easygoing, colorful, and informal (no membership required); see www.hostelz.com, www.hostelseurope.com, www.hostels.com, and www.hostelbookers.com. **Official hostels** are part of Hostelling International (HI) and share an online booking site (www.hihostels.com); these are fairly rare in Hungary. HI hostels typically require that you either have a membership card or pay extra per night.

Apartments

It's easy, and often cheaper than a hotel room, to rent a furnished apartment in Budapest (I've listed a few in this chapter). Consider this option if you're traveling as a family or with friends, staying at least a few days, and like the option of cooking some of your own meals to save money. Most rental apartments are squirrelled away in big, dank buildings; the proprietors can't do much about a gloomy entrance and stairwell, but the apartments themselves are generally bright and nicely furnished. When you reserve, you'll typically arrange a meeting time with the proprietor, who will greet you in Budapest to hand over the keys. Remember that you'll be basically on your own after that first meeting, so ask any questions up front.

In Pest

Most travelers find staying in Pest more convenient than sleeping in Buda. Most sights worth seeing are in Pest, which also has a much higher concentration of Metró and tram stops, making it a snap to get around. Pest feels more lively and local than stodgy, touristy Buda, but it's also much more urban (if you don't enjoy big cities, sleep in Buda instead). I've arranged my listings by neighborhood, clustered around the most important sightseeing sectors.

Near Andrássy Út

Andrássy Boulevard is handy, local-feeling, and endlessly entertaining. With its ample restaurants, upscale-residential vibe, and easy connection to downtown (via the M1/yellow line), it's the neighborhood where I prefer to sleep. Most of the hotels listed here are within a two-block walk of this main artery. For specific locations, see the map on page 232.

$$$ K+K Hotel Opera is wonderfully situated beside the Opera House in the fun "Broadway Quarter"—my favorite home-base location in Budapest. It's a regal splurge, with 200 classy rooms and helpful, professional service. The published rates are sky-high (Sb-€230, Db-€280), but most of the time you can score a better deal (often Sb-€110, Db-€125 in summer and on weekends; €25 more for bigger and fancier "executive" rooms, non-smoking

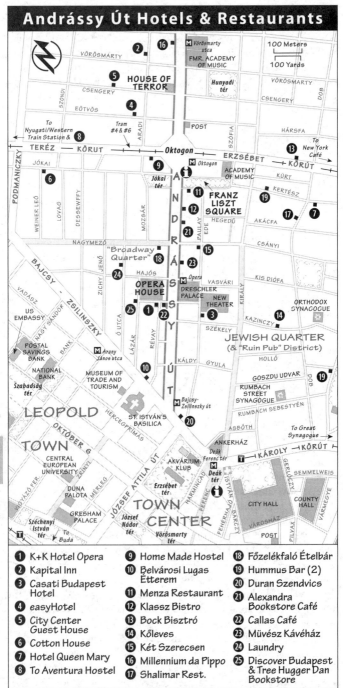

Andrássy Út Hotels & Restaurants

1. K+K Hotel Opera
2. Kapital Inn
3. Casati Budapest Hotel
4. easyHotel
5. City Center Guest House
6. Cotton House
7. Hotel Queen Mary
8. To Aventura Hostel
9. Home Made Hostel
10. Belvárosi Lugas Étterem
11. Menza Restaurant
12. Klassz Bistro
13. Bock Bisztró
14. Kőleves
15. Két Szerecsen
16. Millennium da Pippo
17. Shalimar Rest.
18. Főzelékfaló Ételbár
19. Hummus Bar (2)
20. Duran Szendvics
21. Alexandra Bookstore Café
22. Callas Café
23. Müvész Kávéház
24. Laundry
25. Discover Budapest & Tree Hugger Dan Bookstore

floors, air-con, elevator, free Internet access and Wi-Fi, parking garage-€16/day, Révay utca 24, district VI, M1: Opera, tel. 1/269-0222, fax 1/269-0230, www.kkhotels.com, kk.hotel.opera@kkhotels.hu).

$$$ Kapital Inn is an upscale, gay-friendly boutique B&B tucked behind the House of Terror. Its four rooms are pricey but perfectly stylish—there's not a pillow out of place. Albert, who lived in Boston, gives his B&B a sense of real hospitality (D-€65-89—a particularly good value, Db-€85-125, cheaper Nov-March, air-con, free Internet access and Wi-Fi, pleasant breakfast terrace, free communal minibar, up several flights of stairs with no elevator, Aradi utca 30, district VI, M1: Vörösmarty utca, mobile 0630-915-2029, www.kapitalinn.com, kapitalinn@kapitalinn.com).

$$ Casati Budapest Hotel is a solid value, and conveniently located a block off Andrássy út (across the boulevard from the Opera House, then down a side street—just steps from the edge of the ruin-pub zone). This classy, Swiss-run hotel has 25 rooms in four different styles, ranging from "classic" to "cool" (all the same price—review your options online and choose your favorite). Many rooms surround a peaceful courtyard—in this potentially noisy neighborhood, it's worth requesting one of these (Sb-€88, Db-€98, junior suite-€108, cheaper Nov-mid-March, air-con, elevator, free Internet access and Wi-Fi, free sauna and fitness room, Paulay Ede utca 31, district VI, M1: Opera, tel. 1/343-1198, fax 1/351-9164, www.casatibudapesthotel.hu, info@casatibudapesthotel.hu).

The **$ easyHotel** chain follows a similar model to its parent company, the no-frills easyJet airline: They charge you very little up front, then nickel-and-dime you with optional extras—so you pay only for what you want (pick up the list at entry: TV access-€7.50/24 hours; cable Internet access-€2/hour, €10/24 hours; hairdryer-€1/24 hours; laundry-€10/load; room-cleaning during your stay-€10; €10 extra if arriving before 8:00 or checking out after 14:00, and so on). The 59 rooms feel popped out of a plastic mold, with a nauseating orange color scheme, sterile quasi-linoleum floors, and tiny prefab ship's-head bathrooms. But it's conveniently located (just a block off the busy Great Boulevard and around the corner from the Oktogon), well-run by Zoltán, and the price is right...if you can resist the extras (Sb/Db-€19-69 depending on demand, average rate is €27 for a small room and €31 for a standard room, no breakfast, 24-hour reception, non-smoking, air-con, elevator, two wheelchair-accessible rooms, Eötvös utca 25A, district VI, M1: Oktogon, tel. 1/411-1982, www.easyhotel.com, info@budapestoktogon.easyhotel.com).

$ City Center Guest House is a dreary building on a dreary street, offering 29 surprisingly modern and stylish rooms with bathrooms down the hall. It feels institutional—just one notch above a youth hostel—and is worthwhile mainly because it's very cheap for those who opt to share a bathroom (S-€35, D-€40, suite Db-€69, breakfast-€4, air-con, elevator, free Internet access and Wi-Fi, parking-€10/day, two blocks behind House of Terror at Csengery utca 53, district VI, M1: Oktogon, tel. 1/332-1339, www.citycenterguesthousebudapest.com, ccghbp@gmail.com).

Pest Town Center (Belváros), near Váci Utca

Most hotels on the very central and convenient Váci utca come with overly inflated prices. But these less expensive options—just a block or two off Váci utca—offer some of the best values in Budapest.

$$$ Gerlóczy Café & Rooms, which also serves good meals in its recommended café, is the best spot in central Budapest for affordable elegance. The 19 rooms, set around a classy old spiral-staircase atrium with a stained-glass ceiling, are thoughtfully and stylishly appointed. This gem is an exceptional value (cozy low-beamed attic Db-€99, standard Db-€114, Sb for €12 less, rates include great à la carte breakfast in café, some restaurant noise on lower floors until 23:00, air-con, elevator, free Wi-Fi, 2 blocks from Váci utca, just off Városház utca at Gerlóczy utca 1, district V, M3: Ferenciek tere or M2: Astoria or M1/M2/M3: Deák tér, tel. 1/501-4000, www.gerloczy.hu, info@gerloczy.hu).

$$ Peregrinus Hotel, just a block off Váci utca, has 25 high-ceilinged, spacious, institutional-feeling rooms (most of which lack air-conditioning—in summer, request a room with air-con for the same price). Because it's owned by the big ELTE university, many of its guests are visiting professors and lecturers (Sb-€65, Db-€90, Tb-€105, cheaper June-Aug and Nov-March, rates very soft—email to ask about deals, elevator, free Internet access and Wi-Fi, free loaner bikes, Szerb utca 3, district V; 5-minute walk to M3: Kálvin tér, or tram #47 or #49 to Fövám tér; tel. 1/266-4911, fax 1/266-4913, www.peregrinushotel.hu, peregrinushotel@elte.hu).

$$ Butterfly Home, run with care by Hungarian-Croatian couple Ágnes and Tonči, is a B&B with five spacious, contemporary-style rooms overlooking a pleasantly bustling square a few steps from the happening Egyetem tér (Sb-€72, Db-€92, air-con, free Internet access and Wi-Fi, Képíró utca 3, district V, M3: Kálvin tér, mobile 0670-276-0080, www.butterflyhome.hu, info@butterflyhome.hu).

$$ Kálvin-Ház, a long block up from the Great Market Hall, has quirky management, a nice classic feel, and 38 big rooms with old-fashioned furnishings and squeaky parquet floors. The newer top-floor rooms have a bit less classic character, but are air-conditioned and tidier than the older rooms (all rooms cost the same, slippery rates vary with demand—generally around Sb-€59, Db-€79, extra bed-€20, elevator, free Internet access and Wi-Fi,

Gönczy Pál utca 6, district IX, M3: Kálvin tér, tel. 1/216-4365, fax 1/216-4161, www.kalvinhouse.hu, info@kalvinhouse.hu).

$$ Ibis Hotel Budapest Centrum, with 126 rooms, is part of the no-frills chain that's sweeping Europe, with cookie-cutter predictability and utterly no charm. But it's well-equipped for the price and beautifully located at the start of the Ráday utca outdoor café drag, just up the street from the Great Market Hall and Váci utca (Sb/Db-€80-96 but can flex with demand, lousy breakfast-€10, non-smoking rooms, air-con, elevator, pay Internet access, free Wi-Fi, Ráday utca 6, district IX, M3: Kálvin tér, tel. 1/456-4100, fax 1/456-4116, www.ibis-centrum.hu, h2078@accor. com).

$$ Loft V65 is an apartment right on Váci utca, rented by the family who also run the recommended Bellevue B&B (described later). The large, well-appointed apartment has two double bedrooms, one-and-a-half baths, and a kitchen. You can rent just one bedroom (for 2 people, €85 mid-March-mid-Oct, €60-75 off-season) or both bedrooms (for up to 4 people, €95 mid-March-mid-Oct, €75-85 off-season). After you reserve, Gábor and András will arrange a meeting time to give you the keys (non-smoking, air-con, elevator, free Wi-Fi, Váci utca 65, district V, M3: Kálvin tér or Ferenciek tere, in the mornings call András at mobile 0630-964-7287, in the afternoons call Gábor at US tel. 917-880-3656, www. LoftV65.com, LoftV65@gmail.com).

Near the National Museum

These two places are within a block or two of the National Museum, just across the Small Boulevard from the Town Center, near M3/Blue: Kálvin tér (district VIII).

$$ Brody House fills two spacious floors of a townhouse next door to the National Museum with eight rooms and three apartments that all ooze a funky, idiosyncratic style. The big, artistically decorated public spaces may tempt you to just hang out. Each of the rooms is wildly different and thoughtfully described on their website (Db-€70-110 depending on size, 2-room apartments with kitchenettes-€100, continental breakfast-€5, air-con in half the rooms, free Wi-Fi, two stories up with no elevator, Brody Sándor utca 10, tel. 1/266-1211, www.brodyhouse.com, reception@brodyhouse.com).

$ Budapest Rooms is a great budget option, where the Bodá family rents five simple but surprisingly stylish, nicely appointed rooms in a dreary residential zone (Sb-€48, Db-€62, Tb-€74, Qb-€84, all have en-suite bathrooms except one room with private bathroom across the hall, includes continental breakfast, free Wi-Fi, Szentkirályi 15, tel. 1/630-4743, mobile 0620-569-9513, www. budapestrooms.eu, info@budapestrooms.eu).

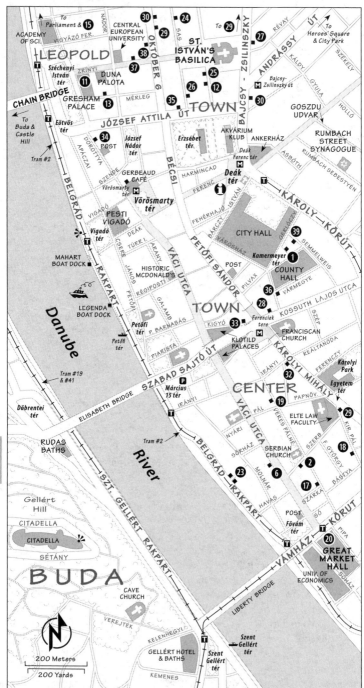

To Parliament & 15

ACADEMY OF SCI.

VIGYÁZÓ FER.

NÁDOR

CENTRAL EUROPEAN UNIVERSITY

30

24

SAS

OKTÓBER 6

29

To 29

RÉVAY

ÚT

To Heroes' Square & City Park

27

ANDRÁSSY

KÁLDY GYULA

SZÉKELY

LEOPOLD

ZRÍNYI

Széchenyi István tér

11

DUNA PALOTA

37

38

ST. ISTVÁN'S BASILICA

25

Bajcsy-Zsilinszky út

GOSZDU UDVAR

HOLLÓ

CHAIN BRIDGE

GRESHAM PALACE

13

MÉRLEG

26

12

TOWN

30

BAJCSY - ZSILINSZKY

To Buda & Castle Hill

Eötvös tér

JÓZSEF ATTILA ÚT

RUMBACH STREET SYNAGOGUE

ASBÓTH

RUMBACH SEBESTYEN

Tram #2

DOROTTYA

APÁCZAI

POST

34

József Nádor tér

SZENDE

BÉCSI

HARMINCAD

AKVÁRIUM KLUB

ANKERHÁZ

Deák Ferenc tér

M

GERBEAUD CAFÉ

Vörösmarty tér M

Vörösmarty tér

FERENC

FEHÉRHAJÓ ISTVÁN

Deák tér

T

i

KÁROLY - KÖRÚT

GERLÓCZY

SEMMELWEIS

PESTI VIGADÓ

DEÁK

ARANY

Vigadó tér

T

CSERE

TÜRR I.

VÁROSHÁZ

CITY HALL

39

MAHART BOAT DOCK

JÁNOS

RÉGIPOSTI

HISTORIC MCDONALD'S

VÁCI UTCA

POST

Kamermeyer tér

1

COUNTY HALL

PILVAX

28

VÁRMEGYE

KOSSUTH LAJOS UTCA

SZÉP

Danube

LEGENDA BOAT DOCK

Petőfi tér

GÁLAMB

P. PÁRNÁBÁS

PETŐFI SÁNDOR

TOWN

36

Ferenciek tere

FRANCISCAN CHURCH

REÁLTANODA

FERENCZY

Károlyi Park

Petőfi tér

PIARISTA

KIGYÓ

33

KLOTILD PALACES

M

KÁROLY MIHÁLY

Egyetem tér

29

Tram #19 & #41

Döbrentei tér

ELISABETH BRIDGE

SZABAD SAJTÓ ÚT

Március 15 tér

P

IRÁNYI

CENTER

32

PAPNÖV.

19

ELTE LAW FACULTY

KIR. PÁL

18

Tram #2

BELGRÁD RAKPART

VÁCI UTCA

NYÁRI

VERES PÁLNÉ

SERBIAN CHURCH

SZERB

F. GYÖRGY

2

RUDAS BATHS

River

SZT. GELLÉRT RAKPART

SÖRHÁZ

23

MOLNÁR

HAVAS

6

17

SZARKA

BÁGYTA

Gellért Hill

CITADELLA

POST

Fővám tér

SÓ

KÖRÚT

PIPA

20

CITADELLA

SÉTÁNY

T

VÁMHÁZ

T

GREAT MARKET HALL

BUDA

CAVE CHURCH

UNIV. OF ECONOMICS

SOHÁZ

N

VEREJTÉK

KELENHEGYI

200 Meters

200 Yards

GELLÉRT HOTEL & BATHS

Szent Gellért tér

T

LIBERTY BRIDGE

Szent Gellért tér

KEMENES

Pest Town Center Hotels & Restaurants

1. Gerlóczy Café & Rooms
2. Peregrinus Hotel
3. Butterfly Home
4. Kálvin-Ház Hotel
5. Ibis Hotel Budapest Centrum
6. Loft V65
7. Brody House
8. Budapest Rooms
9. Danube Guest House
10. BudaBaB
11. Four Seasons Gresham Palace
12. Hotel Central Basilica
13. Starlight Suiten
14. Mária & István Rooms
15. To Guestbed Budapest
16. Marco Polo Hostel
17. Halkakas Halbisztró
18. Borssó Bistro
19. BorLabor Restaurant
20. Great Market Hall
21. Soul Café
22. Café Intenzo
23. Trattoria Toscana & Taverna Dionysos
24. Café Kör
25. DiVino Wine Bar
26. Borkonyha Wine Bar
27. Belvárosi Lugas Étterem
28. Főzelékfaló Ételbár
29. Hummus Bar (4)
30. Duran Szendvics (2)
31. To New York Café
32. Centrál Kávéház
33. Jégbüfé Café
34. Dorottya G. Pharmacy
35. MÁV Train Ticket Office
36. Patyolat G. Laundry
37. CEU Bookshop
38. Bestsellers Bookstore
39. Red Bus Bookstore

Map labels: KIRÁLY, KIS DIÓFA, CSÁNYI, KLAUZÁL, KERTÉSZ, KAZINCZY, AKÁCFA, JEWISH QUARTER (& "Ruin Pub" District), ORTHODOX SYNAGOGUE, WESSELÉNYI, NYÁR, NAGY DIÓFA, DOB, To 31, GREAT SYNAGOGUE AND JEWISH MUSEUM, SIP, DOHÁNY, DOHÁNY ÚT, RÁKÓCZI, PEST, STÁHLY, GYULAI, VAS, Astoria, Tram #47 & #49, TREFORT, MÚZEUM KÖRÚT, ELTE CAMPUS, PUSKIN, BRÓDY SÁNDOR, SZENTKIRÁLYI, HORÁNSZKY, HUNGARIAN NATIONAL MUSEUM, POLLACK MIHÁLY, MÚZEUM, KRÚDY LŐRINC, Kálvin tér, SZABÓ ERV., BAROSS, ÜLLŐI ÚT, ERKEL, KÖZTELEK, KINIZSI, GÖNCZY PÁL, ERKEL, RÁDAY, IMRE, LÓNYAY, MÁTYÁS, CZUCZOR, KÖZRAKTÁR, KINIZSI, BAKÁTS, KNÉZICH, TŰZOLTÓ, FUTÓ, POST, HOLOCAUST MEMORIAL CENTER, APPLIED ARTS MUSEUM, Tram #4 & 6, To Corvin-negyed, To Petőfi Bridge, ÚT, To New York Café

In the Jewish Quarter

District VII—the city's Jewish Quarter—has emerged as one of Budapest's most happening nightlife zones, with ramshackle "ruin pubs" popping up all over. These two budget options offer proximity to the fun, which means they also come with some noise.

$ Danube Guest House's seven basic, gaudily decorated rooms can be noisy for light sleepers (more so in warm weather, as open windows are the only "air-conditioning" here—ask for a quieter courtyard room). But if you want proximity to one of the city's liveliest nightlife areas, this place is a great value (small Sb-€35, bigger Sb-€39, small Db-€49, bigger Db-€59, free Internet access and Wi-Fi, Dohány utca 16-18, district VII, M2/red: Astoria, tel. 1/788-2891, mobile 0620-419-3986, www.danubeguesthouse.com, danube.guesthouse@upcmail.hu).

$ At BudaBaB, thoughtful Americans Ryan and Ron rent two rooms in their apartment. You'll feel like you're a houseguest, as everybody shares the bathrooms and the comfy living room; they appreciate conscientious guests (smaller room: S-€30, D-€45, T-€55; larger room: S-€40, D-€55, T-€70, Q-€85; cash only or prepay with PayPal, Akácfa utca 18, district VII, M2: Blaha Lujza tér, or tram #4 or #6 to Wesselényi stop, tel. 1/267-5240, www.budabab.com, info@budabab.com).

In Leopold Town, near the Chain Bridge

The first listing below is the city's most prestigious address; the next two are business-class options that are nicely located and worth booking if you can get a discounted rate.

$$$ Four Seasons Gresham Palace is Budapest's top hotel—and one of its most expensive. Stay here only if money is truly no object. You'll sleep in what is arguably Budapest's finest Art Nouveau building. Damaged in World War II, the Gresham Palace sat in disrepair for decades. Today it's sparkling from a recent head-to-toe renovation, and every detail in its lavish public spaces and 179 rooms is perfectly in place. Even if you're not sleeping here, dip into the lobby and café to soak in the elegance (non-view Db-€300-400, Danube-view Db-€490-650, prices don't include 22 percent tax—not a typo, breakfast-up to €35, non-smoking rooms, air-con, elevator, free Internet access and Wi-Fi, top-floor spa, Széchenyi tér 5-6, district V, between M1: Vörösmarty tér and M2: Kossuth tér, tel. 1/268-6000, fax 1/268-5000, www.fourseasons.com/budapest, budapest.reservations@fourseasons.com). For more on the building's history, see page 120.

$$ Hotel Central Basilica has 47 forgettable business-class rooms in the heart of the tidy and sane Leopold Town, near St. István's Basilica and the surrounding yuppie dining and nightlife zone. The location makes it worth considering if you can score a good price (Sb-€99, Db-€109, superior Db-€139, but prices very soft—usually more like Db-€89, even cheaper Nov-March, air-con, elevator, pay Wi-Fi but free cable Internet in rooms, Hercegprímás utca 8, district V, M1: Bajcsy-Zsilinszky út, tel. 1/328-5010, www. hotelcentral-basilica.hu, info@hotelcentral-basilica.hu).

$$ Starlight Suiten has 54 spacious suites—each with a living room, bedroom, and kitchenette—on a quiet but dull street directly behind the Gresham Palace (listed earlier). While rates can range widely (€80-130), suites often go for €90—at that price, this place is a great deal (includes breakfast, air-con, elevator, free Internet access, pay Wi-Fi, free fitness room and sauna, Mérleg utca 6, district V, M1: Vörösmarty tér, tel. 1/484-3700, www.starlighthotels.com, manager.merleg@starlighthotels.com).

On or near the Great Boulevard

All of these places are on or near Budapest's Great Boulevard (Nagykörút) ring road—though they are spread far and wide. Tram #4 and #6 travel around the Great Boulevard, connecting all of these, and most are also near a Metró stop. The Queen Mary and Cotton House, which are often mysteriously empty, are likely to have rooms when other hotels are full.

Friendly Budget Beds near Üllői Út: **$ Mária and István,** your chatty Hungarian aunt and uncle, are saving a room for you in their Old World apartment. For warmth and hospitality at youth-hostel prices, consider bunking in one of their two simple, old-fashioned rooms, which share a bathroom. The smaller room is cheaper and quieter; the bigger room gets some street noise on weekends. They may be retiring in 2014—call ahead (S-€20-22, D-€30-34, T-€39-42, price depends on size of room and length of stay—longer is cheaper, no breakfast but guests' kitchen, cash only, elevator plus a few stairs, Ferenc körút 39, district IX, M3 or tram #4/#6: Corvin-negyed, tel. & fax 1/216-0768, www.mariaistvan.hu, mariaistvan@upcmail.hu). From the Corvin-negyed Metró stop, follow signs for the *Ferenc körút 41-45* exit, bear right up the stairs, and walk straight about a block and a half, looking for #39 (on the left, after the post office; dial 19 at the door and ride the elevator to floor 4). Mária and István also rent an apartment that's two Metró stops farther from the center (Db-€42-44, Tb/Qb-€68-72, family apartment, near M3: Nagyvarad tér).

Near Margaret Bridge: **$ Guestbed Budapest** is four apartments—two in a mellow residential zone near the Margaret Bridge and the Great Boulevard, north of downtown Pest, with others near the Opera House and Western/Nyugati train station. The straightforward apartments, all of them with full kitchens, are not luxurious—they're an old-fashioned mix of parquet floors and Ikea furniture. But this place is distinguished by its welcoming and conscientious owners, János and Jószef. When you book, arrange a time to meet them to check in and get oriented. They also rent a "B&B" room in their own apartment (sharing their bathroom)—you'll really feel like you're staying with local friends (B&B room-€45, apartment-€60, 2-bedroom apartment-€65, for best rates reserve direct rather than through a booking site, cheap Wi-Fi, János also offers bike tours, Katona József utca 39, district XIII, tram #4/#6: Jászai Mari tér, mobile 03670-258-5194, www.guestbudapestapartment.com, budapestrentapartment@gmail.com).

Near Nyugati/Western Train Station: **$ Cotton House,** in a semi-seedy zone near the station, has 22 faded but affordable rooms with retro 1930s themes; each one is devoted to a different mobster (Al Capone) or old-time performer (Ella Fitzgerald, Elvis Presley, Frank Sinatra; Sb/Db-€60, €75 with Jacuzzi, rates very soft—often cheaper off-season, air-con, non-smoking rooms but smoky lobby, elevator, free Internet access and Wi-Fi, some street noise on weekends, a few blocks from the Oktogon at Jókai utca 26—for location see map on page 232, district VI, M3 or tram #4/#6: Nyugati pu., tel. 1/354-2600, fax 1/354-1341, www.cottonhouse.hu, info@cottonhouse.hu). The basement jazz club is fun to explore (closes at 24:00, closed June-Aug).

Near the Oktogon: **$ Hotel Queen Mary** (named not for the British monarch, but for the owner's wife) is mysteriously cheap, with impersonal service and 26 unimaginative rooms. The neighborhood is dingy and gloomy (two blocks beyond the end of the happening Franz Liszt Square), but it's affordable for those on a tight budget (Sb-€50, Db-€60, Tb-€70, prices vary with demand, 20 percent cheaper Nov-March, air-con, elevator, free cable Internet, Kertész utca 34—for location see map on page 232, district VII, between M1: Oktogon and M2: Blaha Lujza tér, closer to tram #4/#6: Király utca, tel. 1/413-3510, fax 1/413-3511, www.hotelqueenmary.hu, info@hotelqueenmary.hu).

Hostels

Budapest has seemingly dozens of apartments that have been taken over by young entrepreneurs, offering basic, rough-around-the-edges hostel charm. You'll buzz in at the door and climb up a creaky, dank, and smelly staircase to a funky little enclave of fellow backpackers. Most of these places have just three rooms (one double and two small dorms) and feel more like communes than some of the finely tuned, high-capacity youth-hostel machines common in many other cities. As each of these fills a niche (party, artsy, communist-themed, etc.), it's hard to recommend just one—read reviews on a hostel site (such as www.hostels.com) and find one that suits your hosteling philosophy. Of the places I've seen, I particularly liked Aventura and Home Made; Marco Polo has less personality but more beds.

$ Aventura Hostel is a low-key, colorful, and stylish place in a dreary urban neighborhood near the Nyugati/Western train station. Well-run by friendly Ágnes, it's both homey and tastefully mod, with clean, imaginatively decorated rooms (4 rooms, bunk in 5- to 8-bed dorm-€19, D-€50, price depends on season, breakfast-€2-5, includes sheets, towel rental-450 Ft, free Internet access and Wi-Fi, kitchen, laundry service, massage available, across the busy Great Boulevard ring road and a very long block from Nyugati train station at 12 Visegrádi utca—dial 5 at door, district XIII, M3: Nyugati pu., tel. 1/239-0782, www.aventurahostel.com, reservation@aventurahostel.com). They also rent two apartments—one nearby, the other near Andrássy út (both Db-€70).

$ Home Made Hostel is a fun-and-funky slumbermill artfully littered with secondhand furniture. It's run and decorated with a sense of humor. With 20 beds in four rooms located near the Oktogon, it's another good option (bunk in 8-bed dorm-€18, in 4-bed dorm-€21, D-€50, apartment Db-€53, includes sheets and towels, no breakfast, free Internet access and Wi-Fi, kitchen, laundry service, Teréz körút 22, district VI, M1: Oktogon, tel. 1/302-2103, www.homemadehostel.com, info@homemadehostel.com).

$ Marco Polo Hostel has six 4- to 12-bed dorms and 36 twin rooms (with bathrooms). Although it's a bit dingy and very institutional, and the location is a bit inconvenient, the private rooms are a good deal—and the dorm beds are a steal (dorm bed-€11, Sb-€33, Db-€36, Qb-€60, 20 percent cheaper Nov-Feb, includes sheets, private rooms include towels but dorm-dwellers pay €2 extra, breakfast-€3, elevator, free Internet access, free Wi-Fi in some areas, pay laundry, Nyár utca 6, district VII, M2: Blaha Lujza tér, tel. 1/413-2555, fax 1/413-6058, www.marcopolohostel.com, sales@marcopolohostel.com).

In Buda

Víziváros

The Víziváros neighborhood—or "Water Town"—is the lively part of Buda squeezed between Castle Hill and the Danube, where fishermen and tanners used to live. Víziváros is the most pleasant central area to stay on the Buda side of the Danube, with fine views

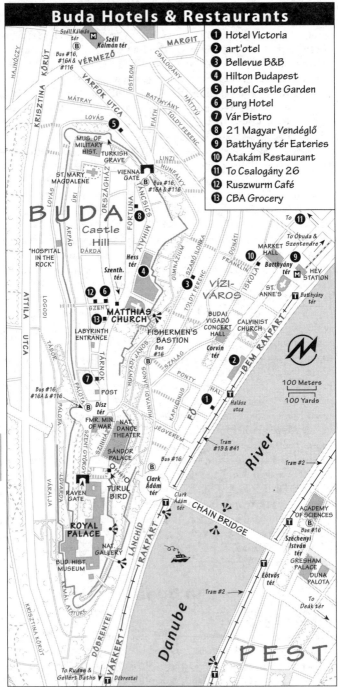

Buda Hotels & Restaurants

1 Hotel Victoria
2 art'otel
3 Bellevue B&B
4 Hilton Budapest
5 Hotel Castle Garden
6 Burg Hotel
7 Vár Bistro
8 21 Magyar Vendéglő
9 Batthyány tér Eateries
10 Atakám Restaurant
11 To Csalogány 26
12 Ruszwurm Café
13 CBA Grocery

across the river toward the Parliament building and bustling Pest. It's expensive and a little less convenient than Pest, but feels less urban.

The following hotels are in district I, between the Chain Bridge and Buda's busy Margit körút ring road. Trams #19 and #41 zip along the embankment in either direction. Batthyány tér, a few minutes' walk away, is a handy center with lots of restaurants (see page 260), a Metró stop (M2/red line), and the HÉV train to Óbuda and Szentendre. All of these places come with professional, helpful staff.

$$$ Hotel Victoria, with 27 stylishly renovated, business-class rooms—each with a grand river view and attention to detail— is a class act. This tall, nar-

row place (three rooms on each of nine floors) is run with pride and attention to detail by on-the-ball manager Zoltán and his friendly staff (Sb-€114, Db-€119, Tb-€149, extra bed-€30, 20 percent cheaper Nov-March, air-con, elevator, free Internet access and Wi-Fi, cheap international phone calls, free sauna, free afternoon tea for guests 16:00-17:00, reserve ahead for €16/day parking garage or park free on street, Bem rakpart 11, tel. 1/457-8080, fax 1/457-8088, www.victoria. hu, victoria@victoria.hu). The painstakingly restored 19th-century Hubay Palace behind the hotel (entrance next to reception) is used for concerts and other events. It feels like a museum, with inlaid floors, stained-glass windows, and stuccoed walls and ceilings— even if you're not staying at Hotel Victoria, drop in and ask to see it.

$$$ art'otel impresses New York City sophisticates. Every detail—from the breakfast dishes to the carpets to the good-luck blackbird perched in each room—was designed by American artist Donald Sultan. This stylish, fun hotel has 165 rooms spread between two attached buildings: The new section fronting the Danube, and a restored older house just behind it (high rack rates, but usually Sb/Db-€99-165 depending on season, figure Sb/Db-€129 in summer, Danube view-€20 more, bigger "executive" rooms-€30 more, deluxe "art suites"-€60 more, breakfast-€14, non-smoking rooms, air-con, elevator, free Internet access, free Wi-Fi, free sauna and mini-exercise room, Bem rakpart 16-19, tel. 1/487-9487, fax 1/487-9488, www.artotel.hu, budapest@artotel.hu).

$ Bellevue B&B is one of Budapest's best deals. It hides in a quiet residential area on the Víziváros hillside just below the Fishermen's Bastion staircase. This gem is run by retired economists

Judit and Lajos Szuhay, who lived in Canada for four years, and their son András; all of them speak flawless English. The breakfast room and some of the six straightforward, comfortable rooms have views across the Danube to the Parliament and Pest. Judit (YOO-deet), Lajos (LIE-yosh), and András (OHN-drash) love to chat, and pride themselves on offering genuine hospitality and a warm welcome (let them know what time you're arriving). As this B&B is understandably popular, book ahead (Sb-€50-65, Db-€60-75, price depends on room size and view, 20-30 percent cheaper mid-Oct-mid-April, cash only, non-smoking, air-con, free Internet access and Wi-Fi; M2: Batthyány tér plus a 10-minute uphill walk, or bus #16 from Deák, Széchenyi, or Adam Clark squares to Dónati utca plus a 2-minute walk uphill, then downhill—they'll email you detailed directions; Szabó Ilonka utca 15/B, mobile 0630-370-8678 or 0630-951-5494, www.bellevuebudapest.com, judit@bellevuebudapest.com). The same family rents the Loft V65 in central Pest (described on page 235).

Castle Hill

Romantics may enjoy calling Castle Hill home (district I). The Hilton and Burg hotels share Holy Trinity Square (Szentháromság tér) with Matthias Church. They couldn't be closer to the Castle Hill sights, but they're in a tourist zone—dead at night, and less convenient to Pest than other listings.

$$$ Hilton Budapest is a 322-room landmark—the first big Western hotel in town, back in the gloomy days of communism. Today, while slightly faded, it still offers a complete escape from Hungary and a chance to be surrounded by rich tourists mostly from Japan, Germany, and the United States (very flexible rates, but usually about Db-€130 in slower times—a great deal, check for better prices online, best rates are for 3-week advance booking with nonrefundable prepayment in full, €30 more for Danube-view rooms, prices do not include 22 percent tax, continental breakfast-€20/person, full breakfast-€28/person, non-smoking floors, elevator, pay Wi-Fi, Hess András tér 1-3 on Castle Hill next to Matthias Church, tel. 1/889-6600, fax 1/889-6644, www.budapest.hilton.com, reservations.budapest@hilton.com).

$$ Hotel Castle Garden, huddled in a tranquil, park-like neighborhood just outside the castle's Vienna Gate (north end), has 39 tastefully appointed, contemporary rooms above an Italian restaurant. As it's roughly on the way between the castle and Széll Kálmán tér, it's relatively handy, though still less convenient than the Víziváros listings (Sb-€74, Db-€89, maybe less June-Aug and Nov-April, "superior" room with terrace for €20 more, air-con, elevator, free Internet access and Wi-Fi, Lovas út 41, M2: Széll Kálmán tér; exit the castle through the Vienna Gate and turn left along the wall, or hike up from Széll Kálmán tér and turn right along the castle wall; tel. 1/224-7420, fax 1/224-7421, www.castlegarden.hu, hotel@castlegarden.hu).

$$ Burg Hotel, with 26 overpriced rooms, is simply efficient: concrete, spacious, and comfy, with a professional staff. You'll find more conveniently located hotels for less money elsewhere, but if you simply *must* stay in a modern hotel across the street from Matthias Church, this is it (official rates: Sb-€105, Db-€115, Db apartment-€134, but rates very soft—usually more like €85-99, extra bed-€15, 10 percent discount on their official online rate if you book direct and mention this book—unless they're very busy, 20 percent cheaper Nov-March, request view room for no extra charge, entirely non-smoking, no elevator, top-floor rooms are extremely long, family rooms, free Internet access and Wi-Fi, Szentháromság tér 7-8, tel. 1/212-0269, fax 1/212-3970, www.burghotelbudapest.com, info@burghotelbudapest.com, Lajos).

EATING IN BUDAPEST

Hungarian cuisine is one of Europe's most delightful—rich, spicy, smooth, and delicious. And Budapest specializes in trendy restaurants that mix Hungarian flavors with international flair, making the food here even tastier. Best of all, the prices are reasonable, especially if you venture off the main tourist trail. This is affordable sightseeing for your palate.

Dining Tips

When restaurant-hunting, choose a spot filled with locals, not the place with the big neon signs boasting, *"We Speak English and Accept Credit Cards."* Most restaurants have an English menu posted (or you can ask to see one). Any restaurant specializing in purely "traditional Hungarian food" is catering almost entirely to tourists. Locals prefer international-slash-Hungarian places, which is what I've emphasized in my listings.

If the place isn't full, you can usually just seat yourself (get a server's attention to be sure your preferred table is OK)—the American-style "hostess," with a carefully managed waiting list, isn't common here.

Once seated, feel free to take your time. In fact, it might be difficult to dine in a hurry. Only a rude waiter will rush you. Hungarian service is polite, but formal; don't expect "Hi, I'm László and I'll be your server—how you folks doin' tonight?" chumminess. At traditional places, your tuxedoed server might bring your food to the table, bow with a formal click of the heels...then go back to the kitchen to apply more wax to his moustache. At any eatery, good service is deliberate (slow to an American).

An *étterem* ("eatery") is a nice sit-down restaurant, while a *vendéglő* is usually more casual (similar to a tavern or an inn). A

söröző ("beer place") is a pub that sells beer and food, ranging from a small selection of snacks to a full menu. A *kávéház* ("coffeehouse"), or café, is where Budapesters gather to meet friends, get a caffeine fix...and sometimes to have a great meal. (I've listed my favorite cafés—including a few that are also some of Budapest's best eateries—on page 263.) Other cafés serve only light food, or sometimes only desserts. But if you want a wide choice of cakes, look for a *cukrászda* (pastry shop—*cukr* means "sugar").

Ethnic restaurants provide a break from Hungarian fare (in the unlikely event you need one). Budapest has abundant vegetarian, Italian, Indian, Chinese, and other non-Hungarian eateries; I've listed my favorites. Once you leave the capital, the options are fewer, and the food gets even heartier and cheaper.

Occasionally, when you order a main course, it includes only the item itself (with no garnishes, side dishes, or starches). In these cases, you can order your choice of sides—listed on a separate page of the menu, and paid for separately. If you see a page listing these extras, ask the server if anything is included with your main dish.

Menus usually list drink prices by the tenth of a liter, or deciliter (dl), not by the glass; this is an honest and common practice, but can trip up visitors.

When the server comes to take your order, he or she might say *"Tessék"* (TEHSH-shayk), or maybe the more formal *"Tessék parancsolni"* (TEHSH-shayk PAW-rawn-chohl-nee)—"Please command, sir." When they bring the food, they will probably say, *"Jó étvágyat!"* (yoh AYT-vah-yawt)—"Bon appétit." When you're ready for the bill, you can simply say, *"Fizetek"* (FEE-zeh-tehk)—"I'll pay."

At any restaurant, it's smart to check the bill and count your change carefully. While most Hungarian restaurateurs are honest, rip-off joints abound in downtown Budapest's tourist zone—especially along the main walking street, Váci utca. (Frankly, I'd never eat on Váci utca, which practically guarantees bad food and service for high prices.) Avoid any place with a menu that doesn't list prices, and tune in to the fine print (such as the service charge—see next).

Tipping

Hungarians tip less than Americans do. Most restaurants in

Budapest automatically add a 10 percent service charge to the bill. (A few of the more tourist-oriented eateries have nudged this up to 12 or even 15 percent, which Hungarian diners consider excessive.) The extra charge should be noted on the menu (if it's not, complain), and appears as a line item after the subtotal on the bill (look for "service," "tip," *felszolgálási díj*, or *szervízdíj*). In these cases, an additional tip is not necessary.

If the service fee is not included, waiters expect a tip of about 10 percent (or a little less; more than 10 percent is reserved for exceptional service).

For more on tipping, see page 13.

Hungarian Cuisine

Most Eastern Europeans dine on a starchy meat-and-potatoes cuisine to maximize calories and carbs through a harsh winter. But, as with many things, Hungary is different in this regard. Hungarians don't just eat to live—they live to eat. This makes Hungarian cuisine the undisputed best in Central Europe. It delicately blends Magyar peasant cooking (with rich spices), refined by the elegance of French preparation, with a delightful smattering of flavors from the vast, multiethnic Austro-Hungarian Empire (including Germanic, Balkan, Jewish, and Carpathian). Everything is heavily seasoned: with paprika, tomatoes, and peppers of every shape, color, size, and flavor.

When foreigners think of Hungarian cuisine, what comes to mind is goulash. But tourists are often disappointed when "real Hungarian goulash" isn't the thick stew that they were expecting. The word "goulash" comes from the Hungarian *gulyás leves*, or "shepherd's soup"—a tasty, rustic, nourishing dish originally eaten by cowboys and shepherds on the Great Hungarian Plain. Here in its homeland, it's a clear, spicy broth with chunks of meat, potatoes, and other vegetables. Elsewhere (such as in the Germanic and Slavic countries that are Hungary's neighbors), the word "goulash" does describe a thick stew.

Aside from the obligatory *gulyás*, make a point of trying another unusual Hungarian specialty: cold fruit soup *(hideg gyümölcs leves)*. This sweet, cream-based treat—generally eaten before the meal, even though it tastes more like a dessert—is usually made with *meggy* (sour cherries), but you'll also see versions with *alma* (apples) or *körte* (pears). Other Hungarian soups *(levesek)* include *bableves* (bean soup), *zöldségleves* (vegetable soup), *gombaleves* (mushroom soup), *halászlé* (fish broth with paprika), *húsleves* (meat or chicken soup), and *pörkölt* (a simmered-meat soup similar to goulash but without the potatoes). The ultimate staple of traditional Hungarian home-cooking, but rarely served in restaurants, is *főzelék*—a simple but tasty wheat flour-thickened stew that can be supplemented with various vegetables and meats (served at cheap restaurants around Budapest—see the Főzelékfaló Ételbár listing on page 262).

Hungarians adore all kinds of meat. *Hús* or *marhahús* is beef,

 *csirke* is chicken, *borjú* is veal, *kacsa* is duck, *liba* is goose, *sertés* is pork, *sonka* is ham, *kolbász* is sausage, *szelet* is schnitzel (*Bécsi szelet* means Wiener schnitzel)—and the list goes on. *Libamáj* is goose liver, which shows up everywhere (for example, anything prepared "Budapest style" is topped with goose liver). Lard is used extensively in cooking, making Hungarian cuisine very rich and filling.

Meat is often covered with delicious sauces or garnishes, from rich cream sauces to spicy pastes to fruit jam. For classic Hungarian flavors, you can't beat chicken or veal *paprikás* (described in the "Paprika Primer" sidebar).

Vegetarians have a tricky time in traditional Hungarian restaurants, many of which offer only a plate of deep-fried vegetables. A traditional Hungarian "salad" is composed mostly or entirely of pickled vegetables (pickles, cabbage, peppers, and others); even many modern restaurants haven't quite figured out how to do a good, healthy, leafy salad. Fortunately, the more modern, trendy eateries in the capital often offer excellent vegetarian options.

Starches *(köretek)*—which you'll sometimes order separate from the meat course—can include *nokedli* (small potato dumplings, a.k.a. *Spätzle*), *galuska* (noodles), *burgonya* (potatoes), *krumpli* (French fries), *krokett* (croquettes), or *rizs* (rice). *Kenyér* (bread) often comes with the meal.

Sometimes your main dish will come with steamed, grilled, or deep-fried vegetables. A common side dish is *káposzta* (cabbage, often prepared like sauerkraut). You may also see *töltött káposzta* (cabbage stuffed with meat) or *töltött paprika* (stuffed peppers). Look for the traditional (and increasingly in-vogue) dish called *lescó* (LEH-chew). Basically the Hungarian answer to ratatouille, this is a mix of tomatoes, peppers, and other vegetables.

Thin, crêpe-like pancakes *(palacsinta)* are sometimes served as a main dish. A delicious traditional Hungarian dish is *Hortobágyi palacsinta* (Hortobágy pancakes, named for the Hungarian Great Plain where the dish originates). This is a savory crêpe wrapped

Paprika Primer

The quintessential ingredient in Hungarian cuisine is paprika. In Hungarian, the word *paprika* can mean both peppers (red or green) and the spice that's made from them. Peppers can be stewed, stuffed, sau-téed, baked, grilled, or pickled. For seasoning, red shakers of dried pa-prika join the salt and pepper on tables.

Locals say paprika is best from the sunny south of Hungary. There are more than 40 variet-ies of paprika spice, with two main types: hot (*csípős* or *erős*) and sweet (*édesnemes* or simply *édes,* often comes in a white can; sometimes also called *csemege*—"delicate"). Hungarians typically cook with sweet paprika to add flavor and color. Then, at the table, they put out hot paprika so each diner can adjust the heat to his or her preferred taste. A can or bag of paprika is a handy and tasty souve-nir of your trip (see the Shopping in Budapest chapter).

On menus, anything cooked *paprikás* (PAW-pree-kash) comes smothered in a spicy, creamy red stew. Most often you'll see this op-tion with *csirke* (chicken) or *borjú* (veal), and it's generally served with dumpling-like boiled egg noodles called *nokedli* (similar to German *Spätzle*). This dish is *the* Hungarian staple—if you sample just one dish in Hungary, make it chicken or veal *paprikás*.

To add even more kick to your food, ask for a jar of the bright-red paste called *Erős Pista* (EH-rewsh PEESH-taw). Lit-erally "Spicy Steve," this Hungarian answer to Tabasco is best used sparingly. Or try *Édes Anna* (AY-desh AW-naw, "Sweet Anna"), a variation that's more sweet than spicy.

around a tasty meat filling and drenched with creamy paprika sauce.

Pancakes also appear as desserts, stuffed and/or covered with fruit, jam, chocolate sauce, walnuts, poppy seeds, or whipped cream. Most famous is the *Gundel palacsinta*, named for *the* top-of-the-line Budapest restaurant—stuffed with walnuts and raisins in a rum sauce, topped with chocolate sauce, and flambéed.

Pastries are a big deal in Hungary. In the late 19th century, pastry-making caught on here in an attempt to keep up with the renowned desserts of rival Vienna. Today Hungary's streets are still lined with *cukrászda* (pastry shops) where you can simply point to which-

ever treat you'd like. Try the *Dobos torta* (a many-layered chocolate-and-caramel cream cake), *somlói galuska* (a dumpling with vanilla, nuts, and chocolate), anything with *gesztenye* (chestnuts), and *rétes* (strudel with various fillings, including *túrós,* curds). And many *cukrászda* also serve *fagylalt* (ice cream, *fagyi* for short), sold by the *gomboc* (ball).

For an excellent glossary of Hungarian cuisine, see www.chew.hu/encyclopedia.

Drinks

Kávé (KAH-vay) and *tea* (TEH-aw) are coffee and tea. (Confusingly, *tej* is not tea—it's milk.) As for water (*víz,* veez) it comes as *szódavíz* (soda water, sometimes just carbonated tap water) or *ásványvíz* (spring water, more expensive).

Hungary is first and foremost a wine country. For the complete rundown on Hungarian wines, see the next section.

Hungary isn't particularly well-known for its beer (*sör,* pronounced "shewr"), but Dreher and Borsodi are two of the better brands. *Villagos* is lager; if you prefer something darker, look for *barna* (brown).

Hungary is almost as proud of its spirits as its wines. Unicum is a unique and beloved Hungarian bitter liquor made of 40 different herbs and aged in oak casks. The flavor is powerfully unforgettable—like Jägermeister, but harsher. A swig of Unicum is often gulped before the meal, but it's also used as a cure for an upset stomach (especially if you've eaten too much rich food—not an uncommon problem in Hungary). Unicum has a history as complicated as its flavor. Invented by a Doctor Zwack in the late 18th century, the drink impressed Habsburg Emperor Josef II, who supposedly declared: *"Das ist ein Unikum!"* ("This is a specialty!"). The Zwack company went on to thrive during Budapest's late-19th-century Golden Age (when Unicum was the subject of many whimsical Guinness-type ads). But when the communists took over after World War II, the Zwacks fled to America—taking their secret recipe for Unicum with them. The communists continued to market the drink with their own formula, which left Hungarians (literally and figuratively) with a bad taste in their mouths.

In a landmark case, the Zwacks sued the communists for infringing on their copyright...and won. In 1991, Péter Zwack—who had been living in exile in Italy—triumphantly returned to Hungary and resurrected the original family recipe. A newer version, called Unicum Next, has a softer cherry flavor; its ads target the new generation of Hungarian drinkers. To get your own taste of this family saga, look for the round bottle with the red cross on the label (www.zwack.hu).

For a more straightforward spirit, try the local firewater, *pálinka,* a powerful schnapps made from various fruits (most often plum, *szilva;* or apricots, *barack*). Also look for the pear-flavored Vilmos brandy.

If you're drinking with some new Magyar friends, impress them with the standard toast: *Egészségedre* (EH-gehs-shay-gehdreh; "to your health").

Hungarian Wines

Wine *(bor)* is an essential part of Hungarian cuisine. Grapes have been cultivated here since Roman times, and Hungarian wines had an excellent reputation (winning raves from the likes of France's King Louis XIV and Ludwig von Beethoven) up until World War II. Under communism, most vineyards were collectiv-

ized, and the quality suffered terribly. But since the end of that era, many wine-growing families have reclaimed their property and gone back to their roots (literally). Today they're attempting to resuscitate the reputation of Hungarian wines. They're off to a great start.

Hungary boasts 22 designated wine-growing regions. The area around Eger is the most famous, but that's only the beginning. The Villány Hills south of Pécs—with a semi-Mediterranean climate at the same latitude as Bordeaux, France—produce full-bodied, tannic reds. The Sopron region near the Austrian border produces both reds and whites. (Northern reds like these tend to be fruity and light.) The Szekszárd area, along the Danube in southern Hungary, also produces wines.

Whites *(fehér)* can be sweet *(édes)*, half-dry *(félszáraz)*, or dry *(száraz)*. Whites include the standards (Riesling, Chardonnay), as well as some wines made from more typically Hungarian grapes: **Leányka** ("Little Girl"), a half-dry, fairly heavy, white table wine; **Cserszegi Fűszeres,** a spicy, light white that can be fruity; the half-dry, full-bodied **Hárslevelű** ("Linden Leaf"); and the dry **Furmint** and **Kéknyelű** ("Blue Stalk").

Reds *(vörös)* include the familiar varieties (Cabernet Sauvignon, Cabernet Franc, Merlot, Pinot Noir), and some that are less familiar. **Kekporto** is better known as Blauer Portugieser in German-speaking countries. In Eger, don't miss **Bull's Blood,** a.k.a. Egri Bikavér, a distinctive blend of reds that comes with a fun local  legend (described on page 362). The spicy, medium-body **Kékfrankos** ("Blue Frankish") supposedly got its name because when Napoleonic soldiers were here, they could pay either with valuable blue-colored bank notes, or unstable white ones...and local vintners wanted the blue francs. (Like most wine origin legends, this story is untrue—Kékfránkos wasn't cultivated here until after Napoleon's time.)

Probably the most famous Hungarian wine is **Tokaji Aszú,** a sweet, late-harvest, honey-colored dessert wine made primarily from Furmint grapes. Known as the "wine of kings, and the king of wines," Tokaji Aszú is a D.O.C. product, meaning that to have that name, it must be grown in a particular region. Tokaj is a town in northeastern Hungary (not far from Eger), while Aszú is a "noble rot" grape. The wine's unique, concentrated flavor is made possible by a fungus *(Botrytis cinerea)* that thrives on the grapes in the late fall. The grapes are left on the vine, where they burst and wither like raisins before they are harvested in late October and November. This sucks the water out of the grape, leaving behind very high sugar content and a deep golden color. Tokaji Aszú wines are numbered, from three to six, indicating how many eight-gallon tubs *(puttony)* of these "noble rot" grapes were added to the base wine—the higher the number, the sweeter the wine. Other variations on Tokaji can be less sweet. (This might sound like another bizarre Hungarian custom, but the French Sauterne and German Beerenauslese wines are also made from "noble rot" grapes. The similarly named French Tokay wine—which derives from the same word—is a different story altogether.)

Finally, note that, except for Bull's Blood and Tokaji Aszú, Hungarian wines are not widely available in the US. Packing home a bottle or two (in your checked luggage) is a unique souvenir.

Restaurants in Budapest

Thanks to Budapest's ever-evolving culinary scene, there's no shortage of places to dine. A few years ago, I had to scrape the bottom of the barrel to recommend eateries here. Now, I can barely keep track of what's new—and scouting new restaurants is the highlight of my research chores. The broad range of options and healthy sense of one-upmanship among local chefs keeps prices reasonable and the quality high. This also means that the foodie scene here is boom-and-bust: A place quickly acquires a huge and enthusiastic following, but soon falls from grace as an even more enticing competitor opens up shop.

While you'll find the standard Hungarian fare, most big-city restaurants like to dabble in international cuisine. Most of my listings feature an international menu with some Hungarian flourishes. (If you want truly traditional Hungarian fare, you'll actually do a bit better in smaller towns.) The good news: Most Hungarian chefs are so skilled that any cuisine is well-executed here.

Most Hungarians dine between 19:00 and 21:00, peaking around 20:00; trendy zones such as Franz Liszt Square and Ráday utca, which attract an after-work crowd, are lively earlier in the evening.

Lunch Specials: Many Budapest restaurants offer lunch specials, called *napimenü*, on weekdays. As these are designed for local office workers on their lunch breaks rather than for tourists, they're often not advertised in English—but if you see the magic word *napimenü*, ask about it. Even at trendy, otherwise pricey eateries, you'll generally pay around 1,000 Ft for a fixed menu (soup and main dish or main dish and dessert; no choices—take it or leave it).

In Pest

I've listed these options by neighborhood, for easy reference with your sightseeing.

In Pest's Town Center (Belváros), near Váci Utca

When you ask natives about good places to eat on Váci utca, they just roll their eyes. Budapesters know that only rich tourists who don't know better would throw their money away on the relatively bad food and service along this high-profile pedestrian drag. But wander a few blocks off the tourist route, and you'll discover alternatives with fair prices and better food. For locations, see the map on pages 236-237.

Gerlóczy Café is tucked on a peaceful little square next to the giant City Hall. This classy café features French, Hungarian, and international cuisine with several seating options (out on the square, in the coffee-house interior, or upstairs). There's a

good permanent menu, seasonal specials, and a charcoal grill for preparing fish fresh from a barrel. The clientele is a mix of tourists and upscale-urban Budapesters, including local politicians and actors from several nearby theaters. With a take-your-time ambience that's arguably more Parisian than Hungarian—and with live harp or piano music most evenings inside—this is a particularly inviting spot (1,100-2,900-Ft light dishes, 1,700-3,500-Ft main dishes, 1,500-Ft two-course or 2,000-Ft three-course lunch specials available Mon-Thu, good breakfasts, fresh-baked pastries and bread, daily 7:00-23:00, 2 blocks from Váci utca, just off Városház utca at Gerlóczy utca 1, district V, M3: Ferenciek tere, tel. 1/501-4000). They rent good rooms, too (see page 234).

Halkakas Halbisztró ("Fishrooster Fish Bistro") is a tight, tidy, cheery, colorful French-style bistro serving up mostly Hungarian fish with a variety of sauces. In this landlocked country, that means freshwater fish (catfish, pikeperch, trout, and so on)—better than it sounds, and very local (1,200-2,000-Ft main dishes, Mon-Sat 12:00-22:00, closed Sun, Veres Pálné utca 33, mobile 0630-226-0638).

Borssó Bistro, in the newly spiffed-up area near University Square (Egyetem tér), is a trendy eatery offering small portions of delicately assembled modern French cuisine with a bit of Hungarian flair. The cozy two-story interior's ambience, like the cuisine, is an elegant yet accessible blend of old and new. They also have outdoor tables and occasional live music. Reservations are smart at this pricey, popular place (3,200-5,900-Ft main dishes, daily 12:00-23:00, Király Pál utca 14, district V, M3: Kálvin tér, tel. 1/789-0975).

BorLabor ("Wine Lab") features traditional, regional, updated Hungarian specialties at reasonable prices in a warm, mod, romantic wine-cellar atmosphere (2,400-2,800-Ft main dishes, daily 12:00-24:00, a block north of Váci utca at Veres Pálné utca 7, district V, M3: Ferenciek tere, tel. 1/328-0382).

Great Market Hall: At the far south end of Váci utca, you can eat a quick lunch on the upper floor of the Great Market Hall (Nagyvásárcsarnok). **Fakanál Étterem**—the glassed-in, sit-down cafeteria above the main entrance—is overpriced and touristy, but offers good seating (1,600-2,900-Ft main dishes, Mon-Fri 10:00-17:00, Sat 10:00-14:00, closed Sun). The sloppy, stand-up stalls along the right side of the building are cheaper, but quality can vary (grab a bar stool or you'll stand while you munch). Locals love the **Lángos** stand, for deep-fried bread slathered with sour cream and cheese (add garlic for some kick). Or you can assemble a **picnic**—produce and butcher stands line the main floor, and there's a big, modern, easy-to-miss grocery store in the basement (the end nearest Váci utca; Mon 6:00-17:00, Tue-Fri 6:00-18:00, Sat 6:00-15:00, closed Sun, Fővám körút 1-3, district IX, M3: Kálvin tér).

Ráday Utca: This pleasant street, just a few blocks away from Váci utca, is less touristy, less expensive, and offers a wider variety of cafés and eateries. While its trendy heyday has largely passed, Ráday utca is still worth a stroll, and the outdoor tables lining the street are inviting on a balmy evening. Just take the M3/blue Metró line to Kálvin tér—a five-minute walk from the Great Market Hall—and head south (district IX). If you can't decide among the many options, consider these: **Soul Café** is one of the best-regarded eateries along this drag, with a spacious yet romantic interior, lively sidewalk tables, and international fare with several traditional Hungarian options. Portions are big enough to split (1,600-3,400-Ft main dishes, 1,500-2,000-Ft salads, open daily 12:00-24:00, Ráday utca 11-13, tel. 1/217-6986). **Café Intenzo** hides around the corner from the start of Ráday utca, where it meets the busy ring road. Low-key and with a loyal local following, they serve Hungarian and international cuisine, either in a nondescript interior or out in a pleasant courtyard garden (1,100-Ft sandwiches, 1,200-1,900-Ft pastas, 1,900-3,300-Ft main dishes, daily 11:00-24:00, closed Sat-Sun if construction is still going on outside, Kálvin tér 9, tel. 1/219-5243).

Danube Promenade

The riverbank facing the castle is lined with hotel restaurants and permanently moored restaurant boats. You'll find bad service, mediocre food, mostly tourists, and sky-high prices...but the atmosphere and people-watching are enticing.

For a more affordable and more local experience, head a bit farther south, near the green Liberty Bridge. Along the embankment road called Belgrád Rakpart, you'll find a cluster of fun and lively ethnic restaurants (including good Italian at **Trattoria Toscana,** #13, and a mini-Santorini with Greek fare at **Taverna Dionysos,** #16).

Various companies run **dinner cruises** along the Danube (including Legenda and Hungária Koncert, both of which offer a discount to Rick Steves readers—see pages 54 and 281). While these can be romantic, Budapest's real restaurants are too tempting to pass up. Instead, dine at your choice of eateries, then take the Legenda nighttime cruise (see page 283).

Near St. István's Basilica

For the locations of these restaurants, see the map on pages 236-237.

On Sas Utca, in Front of St. István's Basilica: The street called Sas utca (sounds like "shush"), running along the bottom of the grand plaza in front of St. István's, is lined with a handful of trendy, pricey, well-regarded, and somewhat snobby restaurants (such as **Mokka** and **Dío;** weekday lunch specials help make these places affordable). For something top-notch but a bit less expensive, head for **Café Kör** ("Circle"). This stylish but unsnooty eatery serves up mostly Hungarian and some Mediterranean fare in a tasteful, tight one-room interior and at a few sidewalk tables. It prides itself on being friendly and providing a good value. Because it's beloved by local foodies, reservations are smart anytime—and essential on weekends (2,100-4,300-Ft main dishes, small portions for 30 percent less, good salads, daily specials, cash only, Mon-Sat 10:00-22:00, closed Sun, Sas utca 17, district V, between M3: Arany János utca and M1: Bajcsy-Zsilinszky út, tel. 1/311-0053).

Wine-Focused Eateries: Two wine bars—one casual, the other upscale—have recently made a name for themselves and helped turn this neighborhood into a happening nightspot. **DiVino** is all about the wine, serving 130 different types of exclusively Hungarian wines, listed by region on the chalkboard—all of them available either by the glass or by the bottle. The well-versed staff can help introduce you to Hungary's underrated wines—just tell them what you like and let them guide you to something to try. While DiVino doesn't do flights or "tastings" per se, couples are invited to share glasses to try several varieties. The interior has a hip black-chalkboard atmosphere, and there's also very inviting seating out on the square (many glasses affordable at around 600-900 Ft, also 1,000-2,000-Ft meals, daily 12:00-24:00, later on weekends, St. István tér 3, mobile 0670-935-3980). Just around the corner, **Borkonyha** ("Winekitchen") focuses both on its list of high-quality (and pricey) Hungarian wines, and on its modern Hungarian cuisine ("Hungarian dishes—but less paprika, less fat"). Because they're enthusiastic about their wines, they sell even pricey bottles by the glass (about 45 types—650-3,000 Ft per glass). The menu—especially the adventurous chalkboard specials—ventures into "nose-to-tail" cooking, using ingredients you won't find everywhere. The decor is sophisticated black, white, and gold—it's a dressy place where wine snobs feel at home (3,200-4,300-Ft main dishes, Mon-Sat 12:00-24:00, closed Sun, Sas utca 3, tel. 1/266-0835).

Behind St. István's Basilica: **Belvárosi Lugas Étterem** is your cheap-and-charming, no-frills option. *Lugas* is a Hungarian word for a welcoming garden strewn with grape vines, and the cozy dining room—with a dozen tables of happy eaters under overhanging vines—captures that spirit. Or sit at one of their sidewalk tables outside on busy Bajcsy-Zsilinszky Boulevard. The food is simply good Hungarian (1,400-2,800-Ft main dishes, order starches separately, daily 12:00-23:30, directly behind and across the street from St. István's Basilica at Bajcsy-Zsilinszky út 15, district VI, M1: Bajcsy-Zsilinszky út, tel. 1/302-5393).

Near Andrássy Út and the Oktogon

Some of Budapest's best eateries are in this area, which is a hotbed for capable chefs and restaurateurs. For the locations of these eateries, see the map on page 232.

Franz Liszt Square (Liszt Ferenc Tér): Franz Liszt Square, a leafy park on the most interesting stretch of Andrássy út, boasts a stylish cluster of pricey, pretentious yuppie restaurants, many with outdoor seating (lively on a summer evening; most places have main dishes around 2,500-4,000 Ft). My favorite Liszt Square eatery, **Menza** (the old communist word for "School Cafeteria"), wins the "Best Design" award. Recycling 1970s-era furniture and an

orange-brown-gray color scheme, it's a postmodern parody of an old communist café—half kitschy-retro, half contemporary-stylish. When locals come in here, they can only chuckle and say, "Yep. This is how it was." With tasty and well-priced updated Hungarian and international cuisine, embroidered leather-bound menus, brisk but efficient service, breezy jazz on the soundtrack, and indoor or outdoor seating, it's a memorable spot (2,000-3,300-Ft main dishes, daily 10:00-24:00, halfway up Andrássy út at Liszt Ferenc tér 2, district VII, tel. 1/413-1482, www.menza.co.hu). If you like the Franz Liszt Square scene, you'll find a similar energy on Kertész utca beyond the end of the square, and in the "Broadway Quarter" near the Opera House (on Hajós utca and Nagymező utca).

Right on Andrássy út: **Klassz** is a trendy bistro with a similarly postmodern "eclectic-mod" aesthetic, both in its decor and its food. Serving surprisingly affordable international/nouvelle cuisine with Hungarian flair, it's a favorite among Budapest's value-seeking foodies (1,900-3,600-Ft main dishes, daily 11:30-23:00, Andrássy út 41, district VI, between M1: Opera and M1: Oktogon, no reservations possible—try to arrive by 19:00).

On the Great Boulevard: **Bock Bisztró,** run by a prominent Hungarian vintner from Villány, offers traditional Hungarian staples presented with modern flourish—almost "deconstructed" but still recognizable. The ambience is that of an unpretentious wine bar, with cork-filled tables. Pricey and well-regarded, with 250 different wines on the menu (including 60 by the glass), it's a good opportunity to sample food and wine from around the country. Reservations are essential—try to call a few days in advance (3,100-4,700-Ft main dishes, Mon-Sat 12:00-24:00, closed Sun, in the Corinthia Grand Royal Hotel, a couple of blocks west of the Oktogon on the Great Boulevard, Erzsébet körút 43-49, district VII, M1: Oktogon, right by Király utca stop on trams #4 and #6, tel. 1/321-0340).

In the "Ruin Pub" Zone: **Kőleves** ("Stone Soup"), a couple of blocks east of Andrássy út, is a hybrid—a cross between a ruin pub garden and a funky local eatery. Serving up international fare, including several Jewish (though not kosher) dishes, it's an accessible way to get a taste of the ruin-pub vibe at mealtime rather than party time (2,000-3,000-Ft main dishes, daily 12:00-24:00, Kazinczy utca 41, mobile 0620-213-5999).

On Nagymező utca: **Két Szerecsen** ("Two Saracens"), named for a historic coffee shop at this location a century ago that a trader filled with exotic goods, features eclectic and well-executed international cuisine—including Mediterranean and Asian. With good indoor and outdoor seating, reasonable prices, and relatively small portions, it's a reliable choice (800-1,700-Ft tapas, 1,600-1,900-Ft pastas, 1,400-2,000-Ft salads, 2,000-3,200-Ft main dishes, daily 9:00-24:00, a block off Andrássy út at Nagymező utca 14, district VI, M1: Opera, tel. 1/343-1984).

Italian: **Millennium da Pippo,** run by a Sicilian who speaks only Italian, greets you with a robust *"Buona sera!"* A neighborhood favorite for pasta and pizza, it's a handy choice near the House of Terror (1,900-2,600-Ft pizza and pastas, 2,800-4,700-Ft meat dishes, daily 12:00-24:00, Andrássy út 76, district VI, M1: Vörösmarty utca, tel. 1/374-0880).

Indian: Hungarians seem to have an affinity for Indian cuisines, which, like Hungarian cuisine, smooth together powerful spices. **Shalimar** hides in a stuffy cellar in a dreary neighborhood two blocks beyond the end of Franz Liszt Square. Everything about this place is unexceptional...except the food, which is my favorite for a break from pork and kraut. I can never resist the *murg makhani*...and I'm never disappointed (1,500-2,500-Ft main dishes, half-portions for 40 percent less, daily 12:00-16:00 & 18:00-24:00, reservations smart on weekends, Dob utca 50, district VII, between M1: Oktogon and M2: Blaha Lujza tér, tel. 1/352-0297).

In City Park

I wouldn't go out of my way to eat in City Park, but if you're enjoying a day here and would like a scenic meal, consider this place. For the location, see the map on page 179.

Robinson, stranded on an island in City Park's lake, is a hip, playful, mellow theme restaurant. With island-castaway ambience and more outdoor seating than indoor, it's made to order for lazing away a sunny afternoon at the park. The terrace and elegant, glassed-in dining room feature pricey international and Hungarian cuisine—or you can just sip a coffee or have a slice of cake on the terrace (2,600-4,000-Ft main dishes, 1,100-1,500-Ft desserts, daily 12:00-16:00 & 18:00-23:00, reserve ahead and ask for lakefront seating, Városligeti tó, district XIV, M1: Hősök tere, tel. 1/422-0222).

In Buda

Eateries on Castle Hill are generally overpriced and touristy—as with Váci utca, locals never eat here. The Víziváros ("Water Town") neighborhood, between the castle and the river, is a bit better. Even if sleeping in Buda, try to dine in Pest—that's where you'll find the city's best restaurants. All of the restaurants listed below (except Szent Jupát) are in district I.

Castle Hill

If you must eat atop Castle Hill, and just want a quick bite, visit the handy, affordable **CBA** grocery store and its sandwich shop (see page 242).

Vár Bistro is a convenient, affordable cafeteria that makes for an easy and quick way to grab a meal between sightseeing; best of all, it has delightful outdoor seating overlooking a pretty park (1,500-Ft main dishes, daily 8:00-22:00, Dísz tér 8, mobile 0630-237-0039).

For coffee and cakes, try the historic **Ruszwurm** (described later, under "Budapest's Café Culture"). If you'd rather have a meal—and don't want to head down to Víziváros—try the following choice:

21 Magyar Vendéglő ("21 Hungarian Kitchen") features traditional Hungarian fare in a mod environment, with seating indoors or outside on pretty Fortuna utca (near the north end of the hill). While touristy and overpriced—as you'd expect in this location—it's well-regarded (2,300-3,600-Ft light meals, 3,500-5,000-Ft bigger meals, chalkboard specials, daily 11:00-24:00, Fortuna utca 21, tel. 1/202-2113).

Batthyány Tér and Nearby

This bustling square—the transportation hub for Víziváros—is overlooked by a recently renovated, late-19th-century market hall (today housing a supermarket and various shops). Several worthwhile, affordable eateries cluster around this square. Survey your options before settling in.

Atakám, just around the corner, is a notch above the other options here. Serving well-prepared Hungarian dishes infused with French flair, this bistro has a stylish interior as well as sidewalk seating (2,800-3,400-Ft main dishes, 2,150-Ft three-course lunch special, open daily 10:00-22:00, Iskola utca 29, tel. 1/781-4129).

Nagyi Palacsintázója ("Granny's Pancakes")—just to the right of the market hall entrance—serves up cheap and tasty crêpes *(palacsinta)* to a local crowd (200-400-Ft sweet or savory crêpes, communication can be challenging—ask for English menu, open 24 hours daily, Batthyány tér 5).

As you face the market hall, go up the street that runs along its left side (Markovits Iván utca) to reach more good eateries: On the left, **Coyote Café** has good, affordable sandwiches and light meals. At the end of the block on the right is **Édeni Végan,** a self-service, point-and-shoot vegetarian cafeteria (main dishes around 1,000 Ft, Mon-Thu 8:00-21:00, Fri 8:00-18:00, Sun 11:00-21:00, closed Sat, tel. 1/375-7575). And tucked behind the market hall is **Bratwursthäusle/Kolbászda,** a fun little beer hall/beer garden with specialties and blue-and-white checkerboard decor from Bavaria. Sit outside, or in the woody interior (900-1,200-Ft sausages, daily 11:00-23:00, Gyorskocsi utca 6, tel. 1/225-3674).

Fine Dining near Batthyány Tér: **Csalogány 26** is a stylish, upscale bistro a few short blocks from Batthyány tér in an otherwise dull urban neighborhood. Its modern international cuisine, served in a classy contemporary dining room, has earned it raves as one of the best eateries in this part of town. You can order à la carte (2,400-4,000-Ft main dishes), or go for one of their *menus:* 8,000 Ft/four courses, 12,000 Ft/eight courses (Tue-Sat 12:00-15:00 & 19:00-22:00, closed Sun-Mon, Csalogány utca 26, tel. 1/201-7892).

Snacks and Light Meals

When you're in the mood for something halfway between a restaurant and a picnic meal, look for take-out food stands, bakeries (with sandwiches to go), grocers willing to make you a sandwich, and simple little eateries for fast and easy sit-down restaurant food.

A popular snack is *lángos*—a savory deep-fried doughnut (similar to an elephant ear or Native American fry bread). Sold at stands on the street, the most typical versions are spread with cheese and sour cream, and sometimes topped with garlic. Some restaurants serve a fancier version (often with meat) as an entrée.

The Lángos stand upstairs in the Great Market Hall is a local favorite (see page 64).

For quick, inexpensive, and very local grub, head for the chain called **Főzelékfaló Ételbár** (roughly, "Soup Slurper Eating Bar"). This self-service cafeteria dishes up simple fare to businesspeople on their lunch break. *Főzelék*, a simple soup that's thickened with roux (wheat flour mixed into lard or butter) and can be supplemented with various vegetables, is a staple of Hungarian home cooking. Go to the counter, choose your *főzelék* soup (various flavors, 400 Ft), then choose from a variety of basic meat dishes (chicken, pork, meatballs, and more for 500-1,000 Ft apiece; some English spoken, but pointing also works). A filling meal here typically runs 1,000-2,000 Ft. Because of the limited seating, most people get their grub to go (though the location near Andrássy út has fine outdoor tables). There are two locations in central Pest: One is just off Andrássy út in the "Broadway Quarter" (Mon-Fri 9:00-21:00, Sat 10:00-21:00, Sun 11:00-18:00, Nagymező utca 22, a block north of the Opera House, district VI, M1: Opera); the other is in a big building along the busy highway at Ferenciek tere (Mon-Fri 10:00-21:30, Sat 12:00-20:00, closed Sun, Kossuth Lajos utca 2A, district V, M3: Ferenciek tere). You'll also find them in the WestEnd City Center and Arena Plaza shopping malls.

Hummus Bar, while not authentically Hungarian, is a popular expat-run local chain that offers cheap Middle Eastern vegetarian meals to grateful backpackers and young locals. Their falafel is tasty (600-800 Ft for a pita-wrapped sandwich, combination plates for 900-1,800 Ft). I'd get it to go and enjoy it on a park bench to avoid the cramped interior (locations include: in the Town Center on Egyetem tér at Kecskeméti utca 1, district V, M3: Kálvin tér; in Leopold Town at Alkotmány utca 20, district V, M2: Kossuth tér; near Szabadság tér on Oktober 6 utca 19; and in the ruin pub district at the corner of Síp and Wesselényi; all are open roughly the same hours: Mon-Fri 10:00-22:00, Sat-Sun 12:00-22:00).

All around town, you'll see cheery **open-face sandwich shops,** each displaying a dozen or so tempting little treats in its front window—thin slices of bread piled with egg salad, veggies, cold cuts, cream spreads, cheese, salmon, affordable caviar, or other toppings for 180-300 Ft apiece. There's no English menu—just point at what looks good. Two sandwiches and a drink make a quick and healthy meal for less than $5 (they'll also box things to go for a classy picnic). There are various chains, but **Duran Szendvics** is the dominant operation (convenient location near the start of Andrássy út at Bajcsy-Zsilinszky út 7, district VII, M1: Bajcsy-Zsilinszky út, tel. 1/267-9624; also in Leopold Town at Október 6 utca 15, district V, M3: Arany János utca). These shops are generally open for lunch or an early dinner (Mon-Fri 8:00-19:00, Sat 8:00-15:00, Sun 8:00-12:00).

For a fast snack, you'll see **Fornetti** stands everywhere (on street corners and Metró underpasses). This Hungary-based chain, which is becoming wildly popular across Central and Eastern Europe, sells small, tasty, freshly baked phyllo dough-based pastries by weight. They have both sweet and savory varieties. For a bite on the go, just point to what you want and hold your fingers up for how many you'd like of each type (150 Ft/100 grams). If you smell something heavenly in the Metró passages...it's probably a Fornetti.

Cooking Class

Chefparade's cooking classes offer a fun, if pricey, way to delve into Hungarian cuisine. A local chef walks you through preparing a traditional Hungarian menu of your choosing. Not a stuffy cooking school, they use fun, casual teachers with lively personalities; it's more about the experience of cooking and eating together, rather than just learning how to cook. Sign up for a class, and they'll set you up with others interested in the same menu. Their modern studio also has a well-stocked shop with cookbooks, spices, and cooking tools (€69 for one person, €129 for two people, 3-hour class; "premium package" for €40 extra gets you an apron, cookbook, bottle of wine, and taxi transfer to the class; add a tour of the Great Market Hall to shop for ingredients for €19; Páva utca 13 in Pest, district IX, M3: Corvin-negyed; occasionally you might go instead to second location at Bécsi út 27 in Buda, district II, HÉV suburban train from Batthyány tér to Szépvölgyi út stop; tel. 1/210-6042, www.cookingbudapest.com).

Budapest's Café Culture

In the late 19th century, a vibrant café culture boomed here in Budapest, just as it did in Vienna and Paris. The *kávéház* ("coffeehouse") was a local institution. By 1900, Budapest had more than 600 cafés. In this crowded and fast-growing cityscape, a neighborhood café allowed urbanites to escape their tiny flats (or get a jolt of caffeine to power them through a 12-

hour workday). Local people (many who'd moved to the city from the countryside) didn't want to pay to heat their homes during the day. So instead, for the price of a cup of coffee, they could come to a café to enjoy warmth, companionship, and loaner newspapers.

Realizing that these neighborhood living rooms were breeding grounds for dissidents, the communists closed the cafés or converted them into *eszpresszós* (with uncomfortable stools instead of easy chairs) or *bisztrós* (stand-up fast-food joints with no chairs at all). Today, nostalgia is bringing back the *kávéház* culture—both as a place to get coffee and food, and as a social institution. While some serve only coffee and cakes, most serve light meals, and some serve full meals (as noted below).

On the Great Boulevard: New York Café makes the others listed here look like Starbucks. Originally built in 1894 as part of the "New York Palace" (and it

really is palatial), this fanciful, over-the-top explosion of Neo-Baroque and Neo-Renaissance epitomizes the "mix and match, but plenty of everything" Historicist style of the day. In the early 20th century, artists, writers, and musicians came here to sip overpriced coffee and bask in opulence. After decades of neglect, Italian investors completely restored it in 2006, and now it once again welcomes guests. You'll be met at the door and asked if you want a table; they'll typically let you gape at the inside for a few minutes if you ask nicely, but only paying customers may take photos. If you're up for a coffee break, this place might actually be worth an $8 cup of coffee or an overpriced meal. Read the fun history on the placemat. While it's a few blocks beyond the tourist zone, it's worth the trip out here for the ultimate in turn-of-the-20th-century Budapest elegance (450-1,500-Ft coffee and hot chocolate drinks, 1,800-2,300-Ft desserts, 3,000-4,000-Ft pastas and light dishes, 4,000-6,500-Ft main dishes, 1,500-1,800-Ft à la carte breakfast items served 9:00-12:00, open daily 9:00-24:00, Erzsébet körút 9-11, district VII, tel. 1/886-6167). Take the M2/red Metró line to Blaha Lujza tér, and exit toward *Erzsébet körút pártalan oldal/6É Margit híd*. Bear left up the stairs, then turn right and walk a block. You can also take tram #4 or #6 from the Oktogon (at Andrássy út) around the Great Boulevard to the Wesselényi utca stop.

Two blocks up from Váci utca: Gerlóczy Café, listed as a restaurant on page 254, nicely recaptures Budapest's early-1900s ambience, with loaner newspapers on racks and a management that encourages loitering. Nearby, another good choice for coffee and cakes is the similarly old-fashioned **Centrál Kávéház**. While the food here is pricey and hit-or-miss (don't bother having a meal), it has an enjoyable and atmospheric two-story interior and a handy central location (daily 8:00-23:00, Károlyi Mihály utca 9, district V, M3: Ferenciek tere, tel. 1/266-2110).

Near Ferenciek tere: **Jégbüfé** is where Pest urbanites get their quick, cheap, stand-at-a-counter fix of coffee and cakes. And for those feeling nostalgic for the communist days, little has changed at this typical *bisztró*. First, choose what you want at the counter. Then try to explain it to the cashier across the aisle. Finally, take your receipt back to the appropriate part of the counter (figure out the four different zones: coffee, soft drinks, ice cream, cakes), trade your receipt for your goodie, go to the bar, and enjoy it standing up (cakes for under 300 Ft, Mon-Sat 7:00-21:30, Wed until 20:30, Sun 8:00-21:30, Ferenciek tere 10, district V, M3: Ferenciek tere). If you're not sure what to get, consider these traditional Hungarian favorites: *krémes* (KRAY-mesh) is custard sandwiched between delicate wafers. *Rákóczi turós* (RAH-koh-tsee TOO-rohsh) is a cake of sweet cottage cheese (a Hungarian dessert staple) with jam on top. *Dobos torta* (DOH-bohsh TOR-taw) has alternating layers of chocolate and vanilla cake topped with caramelized sugar. *Somlói galuska* (SHOM-lowee GAW-losh-kaw) is made of pieces of moist sponge cake soaked in rum and drizzled with chocolate. And *flódni* (FLOHD-nee)—in the pie section (in this area, you can pay directly at the counter)—has layers of nut paste and poppy seeds... another Hungarian dessert staple. For a simpler procedure, get in line at the waffle *(gofry)* window facing the street, where you can pay cash for a steaming-hot Belgian waffle with toppings (window open daily 10:00-18:00).

On Andrássy út, near the Opera House: Three fine and very different cafés are within a block of the Opera. The **Alexandra** bookstore—in the Lotz Hall of the newly refurbished Párisi Nagy Áruház (Paris Department Store)—hides a spectacular gilded café that immerses you in turn-of-the-century splendor (walk straight in and go up the escalator). Because this prominent local chain encourages loitering, the service here is no-pressure, and the drinks and desserts are bargain-priced (400-600-Ft  coffee drinks and cakes). Rounding out this café's appeal are the occasional live piano music, periodic evening concerts, and mirrors at either end that make the hall seem to go on forever (daily 10:00-22:00, Andrássy út 39, district VI, M1: Opera, tel. 1/461-5835).

Callas features ideal outdoor seating facing the Opera House, and one of the finest Art Nouveau interiors in town, with gorgeous *Jugendstil* chandeliers. While their full meals are pricey (3,000-6,000 Ft; cheaper 1,800-3,000-Ft "bistro" dishes available 12:00-19:00), this is a wonderful spot on Andrássy út for a coffee break, a tasty dessert, or breakfast (ham and eggs plus coffee for around 2,000 Ft, 800-Ft pastries; daily 10:00-24:00, Andrássy út 20, district VI, M1: Opera, tel. 1/354-0954). Across the street and a block toward the Oktogon, **Művész Kávéház** ("Artists Coffee House") is a classic café with 19th-century elegance, a hoity-toity high-ceilinged interior, snobby staff, and fine outdoor seating on Andrássy út. True to its name, this institution in the "Broadway Quarter" is a favorite after-rehearsal haunt of famous-to-Hungarians actors and musicians (700-900-Ft cakes, 1,400-Ft sandwiches, 3,400-Ft main dishes, 900-1,600-Ft breakfasts, Mon-Sat 9:00-22:00, Sun 10:00-22:00, Andrássy út 29, district VI, M1: Opera, tel. 1/333-2116).

In Buda, atop Castle Hill: **Ruszwurm** lays claim to being Budapest's oldest café (since 1827). Tiny but classy, with old-style Biedermeier furnishings, it carries on its venerable reputation with pride. Its dead-central location—a block in front of St. Matthias' Church in the heart of the castle district—means that it has become a popular tourist spot (though it remains dear to locals' hearts). Look for gussied-up locals chatting here after the 10:00 Sunday-morning Mass at the church (700-Ft coffees, 300-600-Ft desserts, daily 10:00-19:00, Szentháromság utca 7, district I, tel. 1/375-5284).

BUDAPEST WITH CHILDREN

Despite its reputation as a big, gloomy metropolis, Budapest is surprisingly kid-friendly. Many of the city's best experiences—such as splashing around in a warm-water whirlpool at Széchenyi Baths, or ogling giant monuments from the communist days at Memento Park—bring out the kid in any traveler.

Trip Tips

Eating

Try these tips to keep your kids content throughout the day.

- Hungarian food is generally flavorful, filling, and easy to enjoy. But a few ingredients (like liver and spicy paprika) are liberally used and may gross out finicky eaters.
- Start the day with a good breakfast (at hotels, kids sometimes eat free).
- Picnic lunches and dinners work well. Supermarkets and grocery stores abound in the city center, and assembling a picnic at one of the city's many turn-of-the-century market halls (especially the Great Market Hall) is a cultural experience. Having snacks on hand can prevent meltdowns.
- Choose easy eateries. All of the places listed under "Snacks and Light Meals" on page 261—including cafeterias, open-face sandwich shops, hummus bars, and Fornetti pastry kiosks—are quick and easy, and kids can see what they're getting before they order. If you're browsing the Great Market Hall, the food stands upstairs are another easy choice. Eating al fresco is great with kids.
- Eat dinner relatively early (around 18:00) to miss the romantic crowd. Skip the fancy or famous places, which are too formal for kids to really enjoy.

Discounts

- While I haven't listed kids' prices in this book, most sights charge much less for children than for adults—always ask.
- Budapest's hotels often give price breaks for kids (and when it's hot, air-conditioning is worth the splurge).
- If you're taking the train outside of the city, ask about family or child discounts.

Sightseeing

The key to a successful Budapest family vacation is to slow down. Tackle one or two key sights each day, mix in a healthy dose of pure fun at a park or thermal bath, and take extended breaks when needed.

- Incorporate your child's interests into each day's plans. Let your kids make some decisions: choosing lunch spots or deciding which stores to visit. Turn your kid into your personal tour guide and navigator of the Metró system. Deputize your child to lead you on my self-guided walks and museum tours.
- Public WCs can be hard to find. Try shopping malls, museums, cafés, and restaurants, particularly fast-food places.
- Follow this book's crowd-beating tips to a T—kids hate lines even more than you do.
- Since a trip is a splurge for parents, the kids should enjoy a larger allowance, too. Provide ample money and ask your kids to buy their own treats, postcards, and trinkets within that daily budget.
- Even if you have the most well-behaved kids in the world, mix-ups happen. It's good to have a "what if" procedure in place in case something goes wrong, such as getting separated in the Metró. Be sure to give each child a business card from your hotel so they have local contact information.

Top Sights and Activities

Thermal Baths

The top attraction for kids is the same as it is for adults: thermal baths (❷ see the Thermal Baths chapter). **Széchenyi Baths**—with colorful outdoor pools and mostly mixed-gender areas—are fun for families (though children under 14 are not allowed in the indoor thermal pools). **Gellért Baths'** sprawling outdoor area and fun wave pool offer the best thermal bath thrills for kids in Budapest; unfortunately, major sections of Gellért (such as the thermal bath rooms) are gender-segregated on weekdays, potentially interfering with family togetherness (if you're headed to Gellért, aim for Sat or Sun, when most areas are mixed). At both of these baths, children over two years old pay full price. I'd skip the **Rudas Baths** with kids.

There are also fun-for-kids thermal baths in and near **Eger** (see page 360).

Playgrounds

Local parents filled me in on their favorite playgrounds. Many of these are in parks also described in more detail in this book, and are fun for moms and dads, too.

Szabadság Tér—A pair of inviting playgrounds flank the bottom (south) end of this square, which is ringed with some of Budapest's grandest buildings. Nearby is a fun interactive fountain, where kids step on panels to make the fountains start and stop. The café in the middle of the park is perfect for parents to sit out in the sun and sip a coffee. (This square is described in detail on page 114.)

City Park—Enjoyable playgrounds are scattered throughout this park, as well as other attractions listed below.

Millenáris Park—This highly conceptual park is tucked behind the Mammut shopping center (near M2: Széll Kálmán tér). In addition to a fun playground, entertaining exhibits called "House of the Future" and "Palace of Miracles" might appeal to older kids.

Gellért Hill—Kids with hill-climbing stamina might enjoy the trails that twist up this peak overlooking the Danube to great views.

Parks

On a sunny day, there's no better place to have fun than in City Park or on Margaret Island.

City Park

The fun, dynamic statues at Heroes' Square help bring Hungarian history to life. The fairy-tale Vajdahunyad Castle—a striking ensemble of Hungarian buildings—also captures young imaginations. You can rent bikes, bike carts, and rowboats for the lake (once the lake renovation is finished). Or just spread out a picnic blanket and enjoy the park like a local. With a little more energy, tackle one of the following attractions. (For more on this area, ✪ see the Heroes' Square and City Park Walk.)

Zoo (Állatkert)—This modest but enjoyable zoo is entertaining, with a "safari park," butterfly house, petting zoo, baby rhino,

and more. It also has redeeming sightseeing value: Many of its structures are playful bits of turn-of-the-20th-century Art Nouveau. (To reach the beautiful Art Nouveau elephant house, turn right inside the main entry, then right again at the fork, and look for the white-and-turquoise tower.) Sometimes on summer weekends, kids can feed the animals.

Cost and Hours: Adults-2,400 Ft, kids 2-14-1,700 Ft, 6,900-Ft family ticket covers two adults and two kids; May-Aug Mon-Thu 9:00-17:30, Fri-Sun 9:00-18:00; April and Sept Mon-Thu 9:00-16:30, Fri-Sun 9:00-17:00; March and Oct Mon-Thu 9:00-16:00, Fri-Sun 9:00-16:30; Nov-Feb daily 9:00-15:00; these are last entry times—zoo stays open one hour later; Állatkerti körút 6-12, district XIV, M1: Hősök tere, tel. 1/364-0109, www.zoobudapest.com.

Circus (Nagycirkusz)—This old-fashioned big-top act includes clowns, gymnasts, and animals.

Cost and Hours: Adults-1,900-4,500 Ft, kids-1,500-3,300 Ft, show schedule changes depending on season but 2-3 shows per day on weekends, directly across from swimming pool entrance at Széchenyi Baths, M1: Széchenyi fürdő, tel. 1/343-8300, www.fnc.hu.

Fun Park (Vidámpark)—This amusement park, filled with thrill rides and fun-seeking Hungarians, includes modern rides as well as a rickety old wooden roller coaster and a beautifully restored, century-old merry-go-round. While none of it will thrill American kids who've been to Six Flags, it's good fun and has a section with attractions for younger visitors. Purchasing a wristband covers the cost of almost everything.

Cost and Hours: Price based on height—kids under 3 feet tall are free, 3 feet to 4.5 feet-3,500 Ft, over 4.5 feet-4,900 Ft; get park map in English as you enter, in summer Mon-Fri 11:00-19:00, Sat-Sun 10:00-20:00, shorter hours off-season, closed early Nov-March, Állatkerti körút 14-16, M1: Széchenyi fürdő, www.vidampark.hu.

Between the circus and the Vidámpark, look for the **Pónipark,** where kids can see and ride ponies (300 Ft entry, free entry with zoo or Vidámpark ticket, 500 Ft extra to ride, Mon-Thu 12:00-17:00, Fri-Sun 10:00-18:00).

Játék Mester Playhouse—Wedged down a narrow path between the back end of the zoo and the circus (just across from Széchenyi Baths entry), this is a fun indoor play area where kids can climb around and meet Hungarian rugrats.

Cost and Hours: Weekdays—1,200 Ft/child, or 900 Ft with zoo ticket; weekends—1,500 Ft, or 1,100 with zoo ticket; adults free, limited to 80 kids at a time, daily 9:00-20:00, M1: Széchenyi fürdő, www.jatek-mester.hu.

Margaret Island

This delightful island in the Danube is filled with diversions, including baths/swimming pools, a small petting zoo, great bike trails, and fun bike-cart rentals. For details, see page 75.

Károlyi Park

Right in the heart of Pest's Town Center, this inviting garden is a favorite place for local urbanites to simply relax with their children. Small but beautifully landscaped, it's a popular after-school hangout for local kids. For a full description, see page 132.

Children's Railway (Gyermekvasút)

This unusual attraction in the Buda Hills is a holdover from the communist days, when kids were primed from an early age to eagerly work for the betterment of their society. While the commies are long gone, their railway's kid-friendly message of "work is fun!" is full steam ahead—and the line is still manned entirely by children (aside from driving the engines, of course). Children get a kick out of seeing fellow kids selling tickets, acting as conductor, and so on.

The only drawback is that it's on the outskirts of town and requires a few transit changes, but if you (and your kids) have a spirit of adventure, it's a fun ride through the Buda Hills. The easiest trip is this: From Buda's Széll Kálmán tér (on the M2/red Metró line), hop on tram #59 or #61 and ride two stops to Városmajor (or simply walk 10 minutes along the busy road called Szilágyi Erzsébet fasor away from the Danube). Here you can switch to the rack railway *(fogaskerekű vasút)*, which climbs up in about 15 minutes to the end of the line at Széchenyi-hegy. From this stop, it's a short walk to the starting station of the Children's Railway line, which putters seven miles in about 40 minutes through the hills (part of a national park) to the other end at Hűvösvölgy. Near this station is a stop for tram #61 back to Széll Kálmán tér.

Cost and Hours: Public transit covered by regular transit tickets; Children's Railway tickets: free for kids under 6, 350 Ft one-way for kids 6-14, 700 for adults; 3,500-Ft "family day ticket" covers two adults and three kids or one adult and four kids; train runs about hourly, sometimes 2/hour on summer weekends; May-Aug daily 9:00-19:00; Sept-April Tue-Sun 9:00-17:00, closed Mon; old-fashioned steam engine runs occasionally for an extra charge, confirm schedules on website: www.gyermekvasut.hu.

Other Activities

Memento Park, with its gigantic statues, captures kids' imaginations—and offers a good springboard for a lesson about the communist days. (Teenagers might enjoy learning more at the **House of Terror**—though that engaging exhibit is too powerful for most young children.)

The **Puppet Theater** (Bábszínház) offers frequent morning and afternoon performances. The playful "children" shows feature light Hungarian folk tales (800 Ft weekdays, 1,000 Ft weekends), while the "youth/adult" shows can include weightier opera performances and avant-garde modern puppetry (1,000 Ft weekdays, 1,000-1,600 Ft weekends). The performances are typically not in English, but the puppets still entertain (across from the House of Terror at Andrássy út 69, district VI, M1: Vörösmarty utca, tel. 1/342-2702, www.budapest-babszinhaz.hu).

Kids might also enjoy the touristy, crowd-pleasing Hungarian folk music and dancing shows presented by **Hungária Koncert** (see page 281).

The **Labyrinth of Buda Castle,** while a bit too hokey for serious adults, might entertain children with the opportunity to explore the caves beneath Castle Hill. It's especially enjoyable (and a bit spooky) after 18:00, when it's lit only by lanterns. For details, see page 81.

SHOPPING IN BUDAPEST

While it's not quite a shopper's mecca, Budapest does offer some enjoyable opportunities to hunt for that perfect Hungarian souvenir.

For a look at local life and a chance to buy some mementos, Budapest's single best shopping venue is the **Great Market Hall** (described in detail on page 64). In addition to all the colorful produce downstairs, the upstairs gallery is full of fiercely competitive souvenir vendors. There's also a **folk-art market on Castle Hill** (near the bus stop at Dísz tér), but it's generally more touristy and a little more expensive. And, while **Váci utca** has been Budapest's main shopping thoroughfare for generations, today it features the city's highest prices and worst values.

Although Budapest isn't a top destination to browse for fashion or big-ticket items, several city-center streets are being redeveloped as pedestrian malls. So far, you'll find most of the top shops on or near **Deák utca** (connecting Vörösmarty tér and Deák tér), or along **Andrássy út.**

To see how Hungarian urbanites renovate their crumbling concrete flats, don't miss the home-improvement shops that line **Király utca,** which runs parallel to Andrássy út (two short blocks south). For a taste of the good old days—which somehow just feels right, here in nostalgic Budapest—wander up the city's **"antique row,"** Falk Miksa utca, just north of the Parliament (described later).

Budapesters do most of their shopping in big, American-style **shopping malls**—three of which (WestEnd City Center, Mammut, and Arena Plaza) are downtown and described later.

Budapest has several excellent **English bookstores.** For details, see page 44.

Hours: Smaller shops tend to be open Mondays through Fridays from 10:00 to 18:00 (sometimes later—until 20:00 or 21:00—on Thu), Saturdays from 10:00 to 13:00 or 14:00, and are closed Sundays. Big malls have longer hours.

Bargaining: At touristy markets (but not established shops), haggling is common for pricier items (more than about 4,000 Ft)—but you'll likely get the merchant to come down only about 10 percent (maybe down to 20 percent for multiple items). If you pay with a credit card, you're less likely to snare a discount.

VAT Refunds and Customs Regulations: For tips on getting a VAT (value-added tax) refund, and getting your purchases through customs, see page 14.

Souvenir Ideas

The most popular souvenir is that quintessential Hungarian spice, **paprika.** Sold in metal cans, linen bags, or porcelain vases—and often accompanied by a tiny  wooden scoop—it's a nice way to spice up your cooking with memories of your trip. (But remember that only sealed containers will make it through customs on your way back home.) For more, see "Paprika Primer" on page 250.

If you want a top-notch Hungarian **cookbook,** the pricey *Culinaria Hungary* beautifully describes and illustrates Hungary's culinary tradition (though a cheaper paperback edition is available online or at bookstores in North America).

Special drinks are a fun souvenir, though they're tricky to bring home (you'll have to wrap them very carefully and put them in your checked luggage—not permitted in carry-on; for customs regulations, see page 15). Consider the unique Hungarian spirit **Unicum** (described on page 251), or a bottle of Hungarian **wine** (see page 252).

Another popular local item is a hand-embroidered **linen tablecloth.** The colors are often red and green—the national colors of Hungary—but white-on-white designs are also available (and classy). If the thread is thick and the stitching is very even, it was probably done by machine, and obviously is less valuable.

Other handicrafts to look for include **chess sets** (most from Transylvania) and **nesting dolls.** While these dolls have more to do with Russia than with Hungary, you'll see just about every modern combination available: from classic girl dolls, to Russian heads of state, to infamous terrorists, to American presidents. Tacky...but fun.

Fans of **communist kitsch** can look for ironic T-shirts that poke fun at that bygone era. But remember that the best selection is at the Memento Park gift shop, which also sells communist memorabilia and CDs of commie anthems (see page 223).

Music-lovers can shop for a CD of **Hungarian music** at the Opera House gift shop (see pages 284-285).

Hungarian Porcelain

Hungary has two major porcelain manufacturers. While very pricey, their works might interest collectors.

Herend, arguably the best (and most expensive) of all, produces tableware with intricately detailed color patterns on a white base.  They've created porcelain for Queen Victoria, Emperor Maximilian of Mexico, and other historic heads of state. Herend, produced in a town of the same name near Lake Balaton, is also exported (including to the US). In Budapest, the main shop—with the best selection—is in central Pest, just off Vörösmarty tér (go around the right side of Gerbeaud café, József Nádor tér 11, tel. 1/317-2622, www.herend.com). There are also locations at Castle Hill (in front of the Matthias Church, Szentháromság utca 5, tel. 1/225-1051) and on Andrássy út (at #16, tel. 1/374-0006).

Zsolnay also produces tableware, but it's better known for its decorative tiles, which adorn the facades and roofs of many major Budapest buildings. You can buy Zsolnay pieces at several shops in Budapest (see www.zsolnay.hu). For more about Zsolnay, see the sidebar on page 388 in the chapter on the city of Pécs, where the porcelain originates.

For **antique porcelain,** check the several shops along Pest's "antique row" (described later). However, don't buy porcelain (or any glass) at the Great Market Hall, as it will include a significant mark-up.

Modern Shopping Malls

Budapest has a range of modern, American-style shopping malls in the city center (most shops generally open Mon-Sat 10:00-21:00, Sun 10:00-18:00). The biggest and most convenient options include **WestEnd City Center**, next door to Nyugati/Western train station (Váci út 1-3, district VI, M3: Nyugati pu., tel. 1/374-6573, www.westend.hu); **Mammut** ("Mammoth"), two separate malls a few steps from Buda's Széll Kálmán tér (Lövőház utca 2-6, district II, M2: Széll Kálmán tér, tel. 1/345-8020, www.mammut.hu); and **Arena Plaza**, near Keleti/Eastern train station (Kerepesi út 9, district XIV, M2: Keleti pu., tel. 1/880-7000, www.arenaplaza.hu).

Pest's "Antique Row": Falk Miksa Utca

Get into the nostalgic spirit of Budapest with a stroll down Falk Miksa utca, which extends from Kossuth tér (behind the Parliament) four blocks north to the Great Boulevard (near the end point of tram #2; also at Jászaí Mari tér stop for trams #4 and #6 around the Great Boulevard). Browse your way up and down this drag, with several hole-in-the-wall shops selling furniture, porcelain, and other antiques (most shops generally open Mon-Fri 10:00-18:00, Sat 10:00-13:00 or 14:00, closed Sun). Look for signs that say *antik* or *antikvitás*. At the Great Boulevard end of Falk Miksa utca are a pair of particularly interesting shops, both facing the Great Boulevard. On the left is **BÁV**, the state-run antique shop. On the right, look for **Kieselbach Galéria**, which specializes in top-notch modern and contemporary works by Hungarian artists. The hulking building on the east side of the street is the Defense Ministry—sort of the "Hungarian Pentagon."

Flea Markets (Bolhapiac)

The gigantic **Ecseri Flea Market** (sometimes called "Tangó"), on the outskirts of town, is an authentic, down-and-dirty scene where the fringes of society meet to swap goods (free entry, Mon-Fri 8:00-16:00, Sat 6:00-15:00, Sun 8:00-13:00, best on Sat-Sun, mostly under cover, entrance at Nagykörösi út 156, district XIX). The public transit connection is tricky (from Boráros tér, at the Pest end of the Petőfi Bridge, catch bus #54 or #55 and ride it for about 25 minutes, get off at Autópiac stop); it's easier to take a taxi. This is prime pickpocket territory—keep an eye on your valuables.

For something smaller but much more central, drop by the **Petőfi Csarnok** (or "Pecsa," PEH-chaw, for short) concert venue in City Park, which hosts a flea market on weekend mornings (cheap entry fee, Sat-Sun 8:00-14:00, www.bolhapiac.com).

ENTERTAINMENT IN BUDAPEST

Budapest, the cultural capital of Hungary (and much of Central Europe), is endlessly entertaining. Whether it's opera, folk music and dancing, a twilight stroll or boat trip, raving at a nightclub 'til the break-a break-a dawn, or holing up in one of the city's uniquely ramshackle "ruin pubs," Budapest offers something for everybody. While you may not associate Budapest with nightlife, the scene that's emerging is starting to grab international attention; a 2012 poll of Lonely Planet readers ranked two Budapest nightspots as the first and third "great bars in the world" (the A38 party ship and Szimpla ruin pub, respectively).

For **event schedules,** pick up the free, monthly *Budapest Panorama,* which makes things easy—listing performances with dates, venues, performers, and contact information for getting tickets (get it at the TI, or visit www.budapestpanorama.com). The TI also hands out two other helpful guides with a more youthful slant: *Servus* and *Budapest Funzine* (www.funzine.hu). Other helpful websites include www.wherebudapest.hu (general), www.budapestsun.hu (the local English-language newspaper), and www.muzsikalendarium.hu (classical). Hungarian-only websites include www.pestiest.hu (nightlife) and www.pestimusor.hu (cutting-edge arts).

To buy **tickets,** I've given strategies for the top options (Opera House and Hungária Koncert), and listed telephone numbers and (where possible) websites for others. Resources such as *Budapest Panorama* usually explain how you can get tickets for specific performances. You can search for information about—and buy tickets for—many Budapest events at www.kulturinfo.hu and www.jegymester.hu.

What's on can vary by **season.** Some of the best nightclubs and bars are partly or entirely outdoors, so they're far more enjoyable

Entertainment in Pest

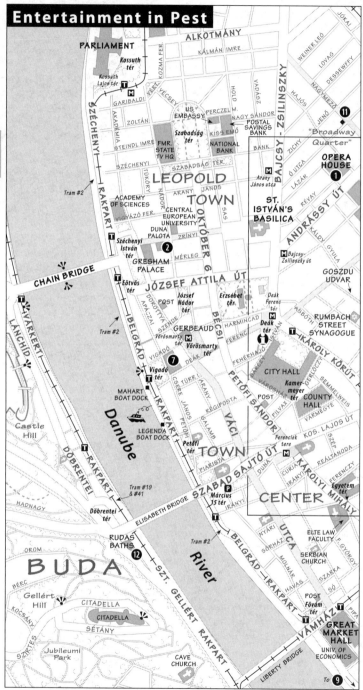

1 Hungarian State Opera House

2 Duna Palota Concert Hall & Hungária Koncert Ticket Office

3 Erkel Színház Opera House

4 Franz Liszt Academy of Music

5 Former Academy of Music

6 Operett Színház

7 Pesti Vigadó Concert Hall

8 Puppet Theater

9 To "Millennium City Center" Venues & Petőfi Bridge Clubs

10 To Petőfi Csarnok & Budapest Sportaréna

11 Instant Ruin Pub

12 Rudas Baths & Romkert

in the summer. Meanwhile, the Hungarian State Opera and other indoor cultural events tend to take a summer break from late June into early September (though that's prime time for outdoor music and Hungária Koncert's touristy shows).

For a list of some local **festivals,** which often include excellent live music, see page 476 in the appendix.

Budapest's Music Scene

Budapest is a great place to catch a good—and inexpensive—musical performance. In fact, music-lovers from Vienna often make the three-hour trip here just to take in a fine opera in a luxurious setting at a bargain price. Options range from a performance at one of the world's great opera houses to light, touristy Hungarian folk concerts. The tourist concerts are the simplest option—you'll see the fliers everywhere—but you owe it to yourself to do a little homework and find something that really appeals to you. See the resources listed earlier, including the good classical music schedules at www.muzsikalendarium.hu.

Locals dress up for the more "serious" concerts and opera, but many tourists wear casual clothes—as long as you don't show up in shorts, sneakers, or flip-flops, you'll be fine.

A Night at the Opera

Consider taking in an opera by one of the best companies in Europe, in one of Europe's loveliest opera houses, for bargain prices.

The Hungarian State Opera performs almost nightly, both at the main Opera House (Andrássy út 22, district VI, M1: Opera, see page 144) and in the Erkel Színház theater (not nearly as impressive—described under "Other Venues," later). If you want classical opulence, be careful to get a performance in the Opera House—not the Erkel Színház. Note that there are generally no performances from late June into early September. Most performances are in the original language with Hungarian supertitles.

Ticket prices range from 1,200 to 16,500 Ft, but the best music deal in Europe may be the 500-Ft, obstructed-view tickets (easy to get, as they rarely run out—even when other tickets are sold out). If you buy one of these $2.50 opera tickets, you'll get a seat in one of two places: If you're sitting at the back of one of the boxes along the side of the theater, you can either sit comfortably, and see nothing; or stand and crane your neck to see about half the stage. If you sit on the top of the side balcony, you can stand near the door for a view of the stage. If the seats in front of you don't fill up, scooting up to an empty seat when the show starts is less than a capital offense. Either way, you'll hear every note along with the big spenders. If a full evening of opera is too much for you, you can leave early or come late (but buy your ticket ahead of time, since the box office closes when the performance starts).

To get tickets, book online (www.opera.hu or www.jegymester.hu), print your e-ticket, and waltz right in. Or you can book by phone with a credit card (tel. 1/332-7914, phone answered Mon-Fri 10:00-17:00), then pick up your ticket at the Opera House before the performance. Maybe best of all, just drop by in person and see what's available during your visit. There are often a few tickets for sale at the door, even if it's supposedly "sold out" (box office open Mon-Sat from 11:00 until show time—generally 19:00, or until 17:00 if there's no performance; Sun open 3 hours before the performance—generally 16:00-19:00, or 10:00-13:00 if there's a matinee; second ticket office around the left side as you face the main entrance, open Mon-Fri 10:00-17:00, closed Sat-Sun).

Tourist Concerts by Hungária Koncert

Hungária Koncert offers a wide range of made-for-tourists performances of traditional music. These take place in one of two historic venues: the Budai Vigadó ("Buda Concert Hall," on Corvin tér in Víziváros, be

tween Castle Hill and the Danube, district I, M2: Batthyány tér—for location, see the map on page 199); or in the former Budapest Ritz, now called the Duna Palota ("Danube Palace," 3 long blocks north of Vörösmarty tér in Pest, behind Széchenyi tér and the Gresham Palace at Zrínyi utca 5, district V, M1: Vörösmarty tér).

While highbrow classical music buffs will want a more serious concert, these shows are crowd-pleasers. The most popular options are Hungarian folk music-and-dance shows by various interchangeable troupes (3,600-6,200 Ft, June-Oct Sun-Fri at 20:00, can be at either theater) and classical "greatest hits" by the Danube Symphony Orchestra (with some traditional Hungarian instruments as well; 6,400-8,900 Ft, June-Oct Sat at 20:00, always at Duna Palota). Or you can take in an organ concert (usually mixing Bach and Mozart with Liszt or Bartók) in the impressive **St. István's Basilica** (4,500-7,800 Ft, May-Oct Thu at 20:00; see page 61).

If you book direct, you'll get a 10 percent Rick Steves discount on anything they offer (must book in person, by phone, or by email; on their website, you can book the "student rate"; discount may not be honored if you buy your tickets through your hotel). The main office is in the Duna Palota at Zrínyi utca 5 (daily April-Dec 8:00-21:00, Jan-March 8:00-18:00, open later during concerts, tel. 1/317-2754 or 1/317-1377, www.ticket.info.hu, hunkonc@ticket.info.hu). Hungária Koncert also offers lunch and dinner cruises on the Danube, in-depth tours of the Jewish Quarter, and (pointless) advance tickets for the baths.

Other Venues

Budapest has many other grand spaces for enjoying a performance. Notice that *Színház* ("scene house") means "Theater."

As noted earlier, the modern **Erkel Színház** is the State Opera's "second venue" (near the Keleti/Eastern train station at Köztársaság tér 30, district VIII, M2: Keleti pu., tel. 1/333-0540, www.opera.hu).

The **Franz Liszt Academy of Music** (Liszt Ferenc Zeneművészeti Egyetem, a.k.a. Zeneakadémia), on Franz Liszt Square, hosts occasional free concerts by its students and pay concerts by professional groups (fewer performances when school's out July-Aug, performance schedule may be sporadic during planned renovation—call first, Liszt Ferenc tér 8, just off of Andrássy út, district VI, M1: Oktogon, tel. 1/342-0179, www.lfze.hu). The **Former Academy of Music** (Régi Zeneakadémia), up Andrássy út near the House of Terror, also hosts performances on Saturday mornings at 11:00 (Vörösmarty utca 35, tel. 1/322-9804, www.lfze.hu).

In the heart of the "Broadway Quarter," the **Operett Színház** specializes in operettas and modern musical theater performances, but these are usually in Hungarian (just off Andrássy út at Nagymező utca 17, district VI, M1: Opera, tel. 1/312-4866, www.operettszinhaz.hu).

The **Pesti Vigadó** ("Pest Concert Hall"), gorgeously restored and sitting proudly on the Pest embankment, will reclaim its status as a fine venue when its interior renovation is complete in the near future (Vigadó tér 1, district V, M1: Vörösmarty tér, tel. 1/266-6177, www.pestivigado.hu).

The **National Dance Theater** (Nemzeti Táncszínház)—with performances ranging from ballet to folk to contemporary—sits on top of Castle Hill, near the upper station for the funicular (Színház utca

1-3, district I, for location see map on page 199, tel. 1/201-4407, www.dancetheatre.hu).

For something a bit more playful, consider the **Puppet Theater** (Bábszínház; across from the House of Terror), which offers puppet performances that please old and young alike (see page 272).

The **"Millennium City Center"** complex, sitting on the Pest riverbank near the Rákóczi Bridge south of downtown (district IX), is a state-of-the-art facility with multiple venues. The **Palace of Arts** (Művészetek Palotája) features art installations as well as musical performances in two venues: the 1,700-seat Béla Bartók National Concert Hall and the 460-seat Festival Theater (tel. 1/555-3001, www.mupa.hu). The **National Theater** (Nemzeti Színház) presents mostly Hungarian-language drama and lectures (tel. 1/476-6868, www.nemzetiszinhaz.hu). For more information on this complex, including how to ride the tram there from downtown, see page 73.

Major rock acts perform at the **Petőfi Csarnok** (in City Park, district XIV, M1: Széchenyi fürdő, tel. 1/363-3730, www.petoficsarnok.hu; also hosts a flea market—see page 276), or at the newly renovated **Budapest Sportaréna** (a.k.a. Papp László Sportaréna; southeast of City Park at intersection of Hungária körút and Kerepesi út, district XIV, M2: Stadionok, www.budapestarena.hu).

Nightlife in Budapest

Budapest is a youthful and lively city, with no shortage of after-hours fun. I've listed these roughly in increasing order of edginess, from "asleep by 10:00 (p.m.)" to "asleep by 10:00 (a.m.)."

Low-Impact Nightlife

This beautiful city is gorgeously lit after dark. Strolling along either the Buda or the Pest **promenade** along the Danube rewards you with wonderful views.

Nighttime Danube Cruise

For a different angle on Budapest, consider joining one of these fun, romantic, crowd-pleasing boat trips. **Legenda**'s cruises include two drinks and evocative commentary about the floodlit buildings you pass (for details, see page 54).

Hungarian Music

As a leading city of the music-loving Habsburg Empire, where so many great composers thrived, Budapest has seen a steady parade of great musical talent waltz through its streets. And, for such a small country, Hungary boasts an exceptional musical tradition. The local music is typified by a unique mingling of powdered-wig classical influences and down-home campfire hoedowns. Even the great classical Hungarian composers freely admitted to drawing inspiration from their humble Magyar heritage.

Hungary's traditional music—like its language, cuisine, and everything else—still shows the influence of its Central Asian roots. Almost hauntingly discordant to foreign ears, it makes ample use of stringed instruments, especially violins and the cimbalom (*czembalom*, similar to a hammered dulcimer). These soulful melodies seem to pluck the strings of the Hungarian soul; more than once I've seen Hungarians (especially after sipping some local wine) spontaneously break into a traditional *csárdás* or *verbunkos* dance, with the womenfolk periodically punctuating the proceedings with an excited little yelp. Popular tunes include the lively "Az a Szép" ("He Is Handsome") and the downbeat "Virágom, Virágom" ("My Flower, My Flower").

Another Asian-descended group, the Roma (Gypsies), have also had a strong influence on Hungarian music. Because of the similarities in these two peoples' music, and the convergence of their cultures in the Hungarian countryside, "Hungarian folk" music and "Gypsy" music are virtually indistinguishable to the casual listener. For example, Roma composer Grigoraș Dinicu's "The Lark"—

a high-speed violin piece that replicates a bird's chirp—is a favorite show-off song for Hungarian violin virtuosos. The rollicking high spirits that accompany a lively music session are described with the Roma term *mulatság*.

The "big three" Hungarian composers all borrowed tunes from their Magyar ancestors:

Franz Liszt (pronounced "list," 1811-1886) was raised speaking German, but had a Hungarian surname and ancestry, and loved what he considered his homeland of Hungary. This master composer, conductor, pedagogue, and (above all) pianist was prodigiously talented and traveled far and wide to share his skill ("Liszt played here" signs are plastered on buildings all over Hungary). He died never having mastered the Magyar tongue, but his countrymen embrace him anyway. Liszt composed what's probably the definitive piece of Magyar music, Hungarian Rhapsody No. 2 in D Minor (famously employed by various cartoons, most notably conducted by Bugs Bunny). His former Budapest apartment now hosts a modest museum to the composer (see page 148).

Béla Bartók (BAR-tohk, 1881-1945), from Transylvania, was as much an ethnomusicologist as a composer. He collected and catalogued folk songs from the distant corners of the Hungarian realm and beyond. In addition to composing the well-known choral work *Cantata Profana* and the symphonic *Concerto for Orchestra*, he penned the opera *Bluebeard's Castle*. His erotic ballet, *The Miraculous Mandarin*, caused a scandal at its 1926 debut; after that he wrote only concert pieces. Bartók is particularly well-known to Americans because he fled to New York City during World War II. He never again set foot in Hungary, dying of leukemia before the war ended.

Zoltán Kodály (KOH-dye, 1882-1967) was also an ethnomusicologist, who strove to analyze folk music on a scientific basis. Like Bartók, he harvested many songs in the fertile soil of rustic Transylvania, where rural traditions thrived. But unlike Bartók, Kodály focused on understanding and forging a uniquely Hungarian folk sound. Kodály was also a composer, but he's best-known today as the namesake of the solfège sight-singing method called the "Kodály Method"—the principle behind "do, re, mi..."

Other (non-Hungarian) composers were also inspired by Magyar music. For example, Johannes Brahms (1833-1897), from Germany, composed a series of Hungarian Folk Dances (the most famous is No. 5/Allegro, which the Hungarians have adopted as an anthem).

Traditional Hungarian music was discouraged by the communists because it stoked Magyar patriotism, but it was kept alive by the underground *tánchaz* ("dance house") movement. Today, traditional music thrives once more out in the open—not only becoming a draw for visitors (touristy Budapest restaurants often have live "Gypsy music"), but also popular among locals. Muzsikás is a well-respected band that performs classic folk music with a very old-fashioned sound (www.muzsikas.hu), while the Roma bands Ando Drom (www.andodrom.com) and Besh o droM each have a following of their own.

If you're in the market for some Hungarian music, you'll find music stores around town (including in the Opera House gift shop). For a good local recording, look for the well-regarded Hungaroton label.

Bathing After Dark

If you need some rejuvenation after a busy day of sightseeing, soak and splash at **Széchenyi Baths.** The indoor thermal baths close down at 19:00, but the outdoor pools—which are the best part anyway—stay open until 22:00 (last entry at 21:00). And both Széchenyi and the mysterious, Turkish-style **Rudas Baths** become nightclubs each weekend until the wee hours (22:00-4:00 in the morning; at Széchenyi it's

only during summer—late June-early Sept—and only on Sat; at Rudas it's Fri and Sat year-round; at either, wear your bathing suit). ۞ See the Thermal Baths chapter.

Yuppie Drinking Zones

Young locals meet up for happy hour after work at the many trendy bars in two areas: on **Franz Liszt Square** (Liszt Ferenc tér, on page 146) and along **Ráday utca** (described on page 256). Many of these places also serve food.

The plaza in front of **St. István's Basilica** has recently become another fashionable locale for a glass of wine. Of the many upscale restaurants and bars in this area, DiVino—a bar with contemporary decor and a wide range of Hungarian wines by the glass—is a good choice (see page 257).

For something a bit more genteel—evocative of this city's late-19th-century Golden Age—locals pass their evenings sipping wine or nibbling dessert at a **café** (see "Budapest's Café Culture" on page 263).

In the "National Ditch"

Akvárium fills the foundation for the never-completed new National Theater, in the very center of Pest at Erzsébet tér (next to Deák tér, where the three Metró lines converge). It's a café by day and a music club by night, when the sprawling subterranean space (which is faintly visible below the surface of the park's shallow pond) hosts an eclectic range of concerts (from DJs and rock bands to folklore shows and electronica). In the summer, people fill the tables on the terraces that lead down into the club, and hang out on the lawn nearby—creating a fun and engaging local scene (concert tickets generally 1,000 Ft, doors open at 21:00, music starts at 22:00, also open earlier for drinks, Erzsébet tér, district V, M1/M2/M3: Deák tér, mobile 0630-860-3368, www.akvariumklub.hu). For more on the history of this odd site—nicknamed the "National Ditch"—see page 141.

Ruin Pubs

If you're looking for memorable, lively, smoke-filled, trendy pubs crammed with twentysomething Budapesters and backpackers, explore the dingy streets of the Jewish Quarter, behind the Great Synagogue. (This area is between the Small and Great Boulevards, south of Király utca and north of Rákóczi út.) Damaged (like most of the city) in World War II, this neighborhood sat, dilapidated and forgotten, for decades—and remained neglected even when other parts of town were rejuvenated in the 1990s and early 2000s. Now it's finally getting a little attention—though it retains a certain scruffiness, still lacking the spit and polish of central neighborhoods just across the Small Boulevard. This unusual combination of a very central location and low rents has attracted a funky new breed of bars, dubbed "ruin pubs" *(romkocsma)*; some also bill themselves as *kert* (garden), *mulató* (club), or *kávézó* (coffeehouse). The low-profile entryways look abandoned, but once you walk back through a maze of hallways, you'll emerge into large halls and open-air courtyards filled with people huddled around ramshackle tables...rickety-chic.

Most of the clientele is in their 20s or 30s, but hip oldsters feel welcome; there's a wide variety of ruin pubs, ranging from rollicking to mellow, so survey several to find your favorite. While dingy and gloomy, this neighborhood is generally considered safe by locals. And at night, the streets can be jammed with bar-hoppers. But it's always smart to be prudent; stick to well-lit streets. Note that most ruin pubs have vast outdoor zones, but small interiors—so they're better in good weather. In addition to the places noted below, you can find a partial listing at www.ruinpubs.com.

Ruin Pub Crawl in the Jewish Quarter

I've connected several of Budapest's most interesting ruin pubs on this pub crawl through the core of Budapest's Jewish Quarter. While this area has several synagogues and other Jewish heritage sights (see the Great Synagogue and Jewish Quarter Tour), it has also emerged in the last few years as *the* hottest place for Budapest nightlife. This walk is designed to give you your bearings, leading you past several of the most appealing streets. If you try to stop at each place, you'll never make it to the end—pace yourself, keeping in mind that the first, best, and quintessential ruin pub is Szimpla, near the end of this walk. This area can be very lively any night of the week (especially in good weather), but it's best Thursday through Saturday. During the peak of summer (July-Aug), most Budapesters are out of town on holiday, so you'll encounter mostly tourists here; at other times, it has a largely local vibe.

Begin by making your way to **Király utca** (it runs parallel to Andrássy út, two blocks south; for this tour, it's handiest to ride

ENTERTAINMENT IN BUDAPEST

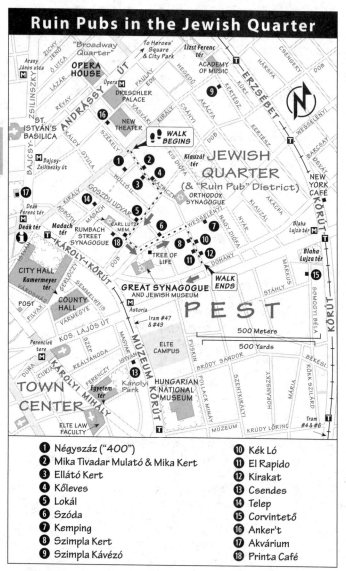

Ruin Pubs in the Jewish Quarter

1 Négyszáz ("400")
2 Mika Tivadar Mulató & Mika Kert
3 Ellátó Kert
4 Kőleves
5 Lokál
6 Szóda
7 Kemping
8 Szimpla Kert
9 Szimpla Kávézó
10 Kék Ló
11 El Rapido
12 Kirakat
13 Csendes
14 Telep
15 Corvintető
16 Anker't
17 Akvárium
18 Printa Café

the M1 Metró line to the Opera stop, then walk south). Király utca itself is lined with a few bars and ruin-pub-type nightspots, but the best scene is just south and east of here.

From Király utca, head down **Kazinczy utca,** at the intersection with a delightful little urban park made much bigger by a cheery parklands mural painted on the adjacent wall. Heading down Kazinczy, after one short block, poke down the unnamed alley on the right (after Piritós). This strip is lined with several enticing places, the best of which is probably **Négyszáz ("400")**, flanking the alley (officially at Kazinczy 52). Continuing straight ahead to the end of the lane, you'll find that you can enter right into the middle of the long series of courtyards called **Gozsdu Udvar**, which is packed with less characteristic bars and cafés.

Head back out to Kazinczy. Directly across the street from the alley is **Mika Tivadar Mulató** (Kazinczy 47)—fun, but with a little less personality. Continuing (to the right) along Kazinczy, however, you'll quickly spot its adjacent and much more characteristic **Mika Kert**, filling a vacant lot with happy drinkers. Across the street is **Ellátó Kert** ("Supplier," Kazinczy 48), a mostly outdoor pub with mismatched furniture under tents, and with Latino flair and food. A bit farther down on the left (at #41), **Kőleves** ("Stone Soup") is another fine garden, this one also well-regarded for its food (see page 259).

Just after Kőleves, Kazinczy utca crosses **Dob street**. Turn right onto Dob, which is lined with more ruin pubs. A block and a half down, on the right (at #18, facing the intersection with Síp street), **Lokál** is another place expertly combining cool and ramshackle, with tables made of repurposed shipping pallets. It has a few indoor rooms, but most of the action happens in the cool graffitied garden. Just past Lokál, also on the right, is the entrance to the **Gozsdu Udvar** passageway mentioned earlier. (While the passageway is worth a stroll to appreciate the nicely restored space, most of the actual bars here lack the appeal of other ruin pubs I've listed.)

Continuing past Gozsdu Udvar on Dob utca, turn left when you reach Rumbach utca (if you went right on Rumbach, it's a one-block detour to the lively **Telep** pub, described later). You'll take Rumbach utca one short block, which leads you right to the gate of the memorial garden for the **Great Synagogue** (and an evocative view of the floodlit weeping-willow Holocaust monument).

Turn left at the gate and head up **Wesselényi utca,** which is also lined with appealing bars and cafés. One of the best, a block and a half up Wesselényi utca on the left (at #18), is **Szóda**—named for the seltzer bottles that line the wall. It's lively and maintains a healthy reverence for the Red old days, with secondhand communist furniture and a sprawling open-air courtyard in good weather (dance floor in cellar, www.szoda.com). More fun bars are farther up Wesselényi utca, including the camping-themed **Kemping** (at #21, on the right).

But before you get that far, take the first right turn after Szóda, putting you back on **Kazinczy utca.** This next block, which has been nicely renovated in recent years, is the home of the first and still the best of the ruin pubs, Szimpla (described next). Now, at least a half-dozen copycats have sprung up around the same area. Feel free to explore the other options, but first head for the top dog.

Szimpla Kert ("Simple Garden," on the right at #14) sprawls through an old building that ought to be condemned, and spills

out into an equally shoddy courtyard. It oozes nostalgia for young Budapesters who have fond memories of their communist-era childhoods. Even the snacks are communist kitsch, and along with a full range of alcohol, they serve the old commie soft drinks (such as grape-flavored Traubiszóda and sour cherry Meggymárka). Although it's on the route of the tourist pub-crawls, Szimpla is still mostly frequented by locals (www.szimpla.hu). This space also hosts a farmers market on Sunday mornings (9:00-14:00). They have a second, smaller, far less impressive café, Szimpla Kávézó, a few blocks north (Kertész utca 48).

Across the street from Szimpla, **Kék Ló** ("Blue Horse," at #10) combines a fashion boutique with a low-key bar. A few doors down on the same side of the street as Szimpla, the *Tacos on Grill* sign (at #11) marks **El Rapido,** a small ruin pub-slash-taquería with a bodega upstairs and a junk-crammed cellar. A few doors down, across the street on the left (at #3), **Kirakat** ("Shop Window") has a white, minimalist, open-feeling interior and a crowded sidewalk out front.

If you're still vertical, head back to the place(s) that caught your eye. Or, to see a different side of the ruin-pub scene, venture to the options listed below; each one is within about a 10- to 15-minute walk from this area.

More Ruin Pubs in Other Parts of Town

Csendes ("Silent"), with two adjacent branches, is a mellower, more grown-up-feeling (but still artistically ramshackle) ruin pub tucked behind Károlyi Park, right in the heart of the Town Center (across the Small Boulevard from the heart of the ruin-pub zone). The junk-cluttered main "art bar" is at Ferenczy István utca 7, while the Csendes Társ ("Silent Partner") wine bar—a bit more upmarket and snooty—has delightful outdoor tables across the street at the gate to the park (Magyar utca 16; both open Mon-Fri 8:00-1:00 in the morning, Sat-Sun 14:00-1:00 in the morning).

Instant—a few blocks away, closer to the Opera House and the "Little Broadway" quarter—fills three floors and a warren of dozens of rooms and alcoves in a historic-feeling (but appropriately run-down) building. Each room is decorated differently, but always

creatively (I like the upside-down room, with furniture on the ceiling). Find your own little private room, and just chill. Choose between the louder dance halls or the quieter café vibe. While there is an outdoor garden, the real appeal here is all those little rooms (daily 16:00 until late, Nagymező utca 38, www.instant.co.hu).

Telep ("Site") is a tumble-down second-hand bar incongruously located in a residential and office-block neighborhood just around the corner from the heart of the ruin-pub scene. There's an art gallery upstairs, they often host live music, and the semi-rowdy crowd out front gives this otherwise sleepy street a lively ambience (Madách Imre utca 8, just off Rumbach utca, http://telepgaleria.tumblr.com).

Corvintető ("Corvin Roof") isn't exactly a ruin pub, and isn't quite as widely accessible as the ones listed above. However, it's got a memorable location at the top floor of an old department store. You'll hike up several flights of stairs to a maze of bars and dance halls, eventually emerging onto an outdoor terrace looking out over the rooftops of Pest (good weather only; nightly 20:00-5:00 in the morning; a bit farther away from the others, on top of the Corvin department store, across from New York Café at Blaha Lujza tér 1-2, enter on Somogyi Béla utca, district VII, M2: Blaha Lujza tér; www.corvinteto.hu).

Anker't, a trendy-feeling, mostly outdoor, summer-only offshoot of a popular night-club (Anker), has a mini-malist charm and a sandy "beach bar" in the back. It's conveniently located a short block off Andrássy út—look for the |A| sign (across the street from the Opera House at Paulay Ede utca 33).

Nightclubs and Discos

Budapest has a thriving nightlife scene for twentysomethings. In general, places are hopping Wednesday through Saturday nights—and pretty dead Sunday through Tuesday. Remember, in the summer, many Budapesters head to nearby Lake Balaton for the weekend (which has its own share of nightspots)—leaving Budapest's clubs mostly for tourists. To mingle with Hungarians, Thursday nights are best. Many of the places I mention here are outdoor and summer-only—look for the words *kert* (garden), *terasz* (terrace), *udvar* (courtyard), or "beach." Off-season (Oct-April) or in questionable weather, skip the trip. Note that some clubs charge a cover (usually for men only). While this scene is constantly changing, the places listed here are well-established. But before venturing to any specific place, ask around for the latest advice (youth hostels and backpackers are a great source of tips). Look around town (including at some TIs and hotels) for the free weeklies *Budapest Funzine* (in English, www.funzine.hu) and *Pesti Est* (in Hungarian, www.pestiest.hu). *Time Out Budapest* is also helpful (sold at newsstands).

In Buda: At the foot of Gellért Hill, **Romkert** is a very posh option, sexy and filled with plastic-surgery success stories. This is where Budapest's beautiful people go to see and be seen; it's more popular for its aesthetics than for its music (next to Rudas Baths at Buda end of Elisabeth Bridge, Döbrentei tér 9, district I, www.rudasromkert.hu). Near Széll Kálmán tér, **Jam Pub** often features live performances by has-been bands from the 1990s (otherwise "retro disco," in the second building of the giant Mammut shopping mall, Lövőház utca 1-3, district II, M2: Széll Kálmán tér, www.jampub.hu).

On Margaret Island: Budapest's playground island has several summer-only clubs near the southern tip of the island (within a 5-minute walk of Margaret Bridge, district XIII). The mod and classy **Holdudvar** is in the courtyard of an old mansion (www.holdudvar.net).

On "Dockyard Island" (Hajógyári Sziget): One of the most happening zones—especially in the summer—is the island in the Danube just north of Margaret Island (near Óbuda, a.k.a. Óbudai Island, district III). However, this area can be dangerous and is known for its drug scene. Several clubs keep this island throbbing. Some of the best-established are **Mokka Cukka** (alternative, www.mokkacuka.com), **Club Studio** (swanky, techno, with muscle guys and plastic-surgery girls, www.clubstudio.hu), **Bling** (funk, R&B, hip-hop, www.blingclub.hu), and **Budai Sláger Terasz** (pop hits). This is a thriving and sprawling scene, with imported beaches, rental boats, and a meat-market vibe. You can take the HÉV suburban railway from Batthyány tér and get off at the Filatorigát stop, then walk across the bridge to the island—or just take a taxi from downtown. This island is also the site of Budapest's biggest bash, the **Sziget Festival,** which attracts huge-name, mid-name, and small-name acts for a week each August (www.sziget.hu). This "Hungarian Lollapalooza," typically attended by nearly 400,000 people, is one of Europe's top parties.

On the Southern Edge of Downtown Budapest, near the Petőfi Bridge (Petőfi Híd): More summer-only options cluster just south of downtown, next to the Petőfi Bridge (near Boráros tér, district IX, take tram #2 south from Pest Town Center, or tram #4 or #6 around the Great Boulevard). Floating in the river on the Pest side is the party barge/live music venue called **A38** (generally a 3,000-Ft ticket, known for its big-name local acts, www.a38.hu).

Warning: Gentlemen, read and heed my warning about the extremely attractive women nicknamed *konzumlány* who hit on green and goofy tourists in order to lure them into dangerously overpriced bars (see page 41). In general, be highly suspicious if a very attractive local woman fawns all over you. (Sorry, you're not *that* handsome, even here in upside-down Hungary.) Many of the city's strip clubs—whether recommended by *konzumlány* or ones you find on your own—are expert at semi-legally extorting enormous sums of cash from out-of-towners. Even if you're accustomed to visiting strip clubs back home, it's best to steer clear here. (If you're looking for advice on which specific strip clubs are better than others...you bought the wrong book, buddy.)

BUDAPEST CONNECTIONS

Budapest is the hub of transportation for all of Hungary; from here, train lines and expressways fan out like spokes on a wheel. This chapter covers arrivals and departures by train, bus, plane, car, and riverboat.

By Car or Public Transportation?

If you're focusing on Budapest, you definitely don't want a car. Even for side-trips into the countryside, virtually all of the attractions listed in this book (with the possible exception of Hollókő) are easily reachable by public transit. Even so, some areas—such as the Danube Bend and Hollókő—can be done more efficiently by car. Instead of hassling with a car of your own, consider splurging by hiring a local guide (see page 52) or a driver (see page 45).

By Train

Hungary's train network is run by MÁV (Magyar Államvasutak). From centrally located Budapest, train lines branch out across Hungary. Most connections between outlying cities aren't direct—you often end up having to go back through Budapest. While Hungary's trains are generally good, many are old and fairly slow; major routes

(especially those connecting to international destinations such as Bratislava or Vienna) use faster, newer, and slightly more expensive InterCity trains (marked with an "IC" or a boxed "R" on schedules).

To ride an InterCity train, you must pay extra for a required reservation (which is printed on a separate ticket). Warning: Trains can be very crowded on weekends, when it's smart to book a reservation for any train trip.

For timetables, the first place to check is Germany's excellent all-Europe site, www.bahn.com. You can also check Hungary's own timetable website at http://elvira.mav-start.hu. For general rail information in Hungary, call 0640-494-949 (from outside Hungary, dial +36-1-444-4499).

Ticket prices are reasonable (1,500 Ft per 100 kilometers/62 miles). While **railpasses** can be a good deal in other countries, the low cost of point-to-point tickets in Hungary makes passes a lesser value here. However, if you're connecting multiple countries, a railpass might be worth considering. For details on railpasses, see www.ricksteves.com/rail.

It's best to buy your ticket in advance at the MÁV ticket office in downtown Pest (see page 42). Be aware that ticket lines can be very long at the train stations; if you're buying a ticket there, it's smart to arrive with plenty of time to spare.

Train Stations in Budapest

Budapest has three major train stations (*pályaudvar*, abbreviated *pu.*): Keleti ("Eastern") Station, Nyugati ("Western") Station, and Déli ("Southern") Station. A century ago, the name of the station indicated which part of Europe it served. But these days, there's no correlation: Trains going to the east might leave from the Western Station, and vice versa. Even more confusing, the station used by a particular train can change from year to year. Before departing from Budapest, it's essential to carefully confirm which station your train leaves from.

The Keleti/Eastern train station and the Nyugati/Western train station are both cavernous, slightly run-down, late-19th-century Erector-set masterpieces in Pest. The Déli/Southern train station, behind Castle Hill in Buda, mingles its dinginess with modern flair.

All three stations are seedy and overdue for renovation. This makes them a bit intimidating—not the most pleasant first taste of Budapest. But once you get your bearings, they're easy to navigate. A few key words: *pénztár* is ticket window, *vágány* is track, *induló vonatok* is departures, and *érkező vonatok* is arrivals. At all stations, access to the tracks is monitored—you might have to show your ticket to reach the platforms (though this is very loosely enforced).

The taxi stands in front of each train station are notorious for ripping off tourists; it's better to call for a taxi (or, better yet, stick to public transit). For tips on this—and on using the Metró system

BUDAPEST CONNECTIONS

Hungary Transportation

to connect into downtown Budapest—see "Getting Around Budapest" on page 45.

Here's the rundown, station by station:

Keleti/Eastern Station

Keleti train station (Keleti pu.) is just south of City Park, east of central Pest. The area in front of the station has been undergoing renovation (as they build the new M4/green Metró line), so things might be chaotic for your visit.

On arrival, go to the front of long tracks 6-9 to reach the exits and services. Several travel agencies masquerading as TIs cluster near the head of the tracks. There is no official TI at the station, but the railroad runs an information

office with train advice and basic city info (near the front of track 9).

Along track 6, you'll likely see lockers, money-exchange booths (avoid Interchange, which has bad rates), and a narrow passage between gyro stands (faintly marked *Exit*). Following this passage leads you to a broad hallway leading (to the left) to pay WCs and the Baross Restaurant (described later), and (to the right) to an Internet café and international information and ticket windows (look for *nemzetközi pénztár*, and take a number).

Back in the main hall, domestic ticket windows and lockers are across the tracks, near track 9. The big staircase at the head of the tracks leads down to more domestic ticket windows, WCs, telephones, and more lockers.

You should be able to get money from an **ATM** just inside the main door, on the left (at the head of tracks 6-9). If it's not working, don't worry; another one is a five-minute walk away: Go out the front door and look straight ahead and a bit to the right to find the yellow sign for Raffeisen Bank, which has a cash machine.

To get **into the city center,** the easiest option is to take the Metró (M2/red line). To find the Metró entrance, exit straight out the front door of the train station and turn left; at the corner of the building, you'll see stairs leading down to the Metró. (Once construction is completed, you'll probably be able to walk from inside the station straight down the main staircase to the Metró.) In front of the train station (or nearby), a cluster of suspicious-looking, unmarked taxis await. You can try to negotiate with these goons—the fair rate to downtown is about 1,500 Ft—but it's far more reliable and less of a hassle to phone for a taxi (buy phone card at newsstand, go to the phone bank downstairs, call 211-1111 or 266-6666, tell the English-speaking dispatcher where you are, and go out front to meet your taxi).

Eating at Keleti Station: **Baross Restaurant,** at the head of track 6, captures some of the turn-of-the-20th-century gentility that this grand station once enjoyed. A time warp with dingy woodwork, chandeliers, and fake marble, it serves up tired Hungarian classics worth considering if you want a meal while waiting for your train (2,500-3,900-Ft main dishes, daily 8:00-20:00). Your other eating options inside the station are unappealing gyro stands.

Shopping near Keleti Station: Roughly across the street from the station is the **Arena Plaza** shopping mall (Mon-Sat 10:00-21:00, Sun 10:00-18:00, Kerepesi út 9, tel. 1/880-7000, www.arenaplaza.hu).

Nyugati/Western Station

Nyugati train station (Nyugati pu.) is the most central of Budapest's stations, facing the Great Boulevard on the northeast edge of downtown Pest. Most international arrivals use tracks 1-9, which are set back from the main entrance. From the head of these tracks, exit straight ahead into a parking lot with taxis and buses, or use the stairs or escalator just inside the doors to reach an underpass and the Metró (M3/blue line). Note that the taxi drivers  here are often crooked—it's far better to call for your own cab (see instructions and phone numbers above).

Ticket windows are through an easy-to-miss door across the tracks by platform 13 (marked *cassa* and *információ;* once you enter the ticket hall, international windows are in a second room at the far end—look for *nemzetközi jegypénztár,* daily 7:30-19:00). Lockers are down the hall next to the international ticket office, on the left (400-600 Ft). An ATM is just inside the main door, on the right.

From the head of tracks 10-13, exit straight ahead and you'll be on Teréz körút, the very busy Great Boulevard. (Váci utca, at the center of Pest, is dead ahead, about 20 minutes away by foot.) In front of the building is the stop for the handy trams #4 and #6 (which zip around Pest's Great Boulevard ring road); to the right you'll find stairs leading to an underpass (use it to avoid crossing this busy intersection, or to reach the Metró's M3 line); and to the left you'll see the classiest Art Nouveau McDonald's on the planet. (Seriously. Take a look inside.)

Shopping near Nyugati Station: Next door is the huge, American-style **WestEnd City Center** mall (complete with a Starbucks; most shops open Mon-Sat 10:00-21:00, Sun 10:00-18:00, entrance next to track 1, tel. 1/374-6573, www.westend.hu).

Déli/Southern Station

In the late 19th century, local newlyweds caught the train at Déli train station (Déli pu.) for their honeymoon in Venice. Renovated by the heavy-handed communists, today the station—tucked behind Castle Hill on the Buda side—is dreary, dark-stone, smaller, and more modern-feeling than the other train stations. From the tracks, go straight ahead into the vast, empty-feeling main hall, with well-marked domestic and international ticket windows at opposite ends. A left-luggage desk is outside beyond track 1. Downstairs, you'll find several shops and eateries, and access to the very convenient M2/red Metró line, which takes you to several key points in town: Batthyány tér (on the Buda embankment, at the north end of the Víziváros neighborhood), Deák tér (the heart of Pest, with connections to other Metró lines), and Keleti train station.

Train Connections from Budapest

There's no telling which station any given train will use, especially since it can change from year to year—always confirm carefully which station your train leaves from. Remember, for specific schedules, check www.bahn.com or http://elvira.mav-start.hu.

From Budapest by Train to Destinations in Hungary: Eger (5/day direct, 2.5 hours, more with transfer in Füzesabony, usually from Budapest's Keleti/Eastern Station), **Pécs** (8/day direct, 2.75 hours; a few more connections possible with transfer at the suburban Budapest-Kelenföld station), **Sopron** (6/day direct, 2.5 hours, more with a transfer in Győr), **Visegrád** (trains arrive at Nagymaros-Visegrád station, across the river—take shuttle boat to Visegrád; hourly, 40-50 minutes, usually from Budapest's Nyugati/

Western Station), and **Esztergom** (hourly, 1.5 hours, usually from Budapest's Nyugati/Western Station).

Note that Nagymaros (the station for Visegrád) and Esztergom are on opposite sides of the river—and on different train lines. To reach **Szentendre** and **Gödöllő,** take the suburban HÉV line (see "By HÉV," below).

By Train to International Destinations: Bratislava (that's **Pozsony** in Hungarian, 7/day direct, 2.75 hours; more with transfers), **Vienna** (that's **Bécs** in Hungarian, every 2 hours direct, 2.75 hours; more with transfers), **Prague** (5/day direct, 7 hours, more with transfers in Győr and Vienna; plus 1 night train/day, 8 hours), **Kraków** (1 direct night train/day, 10.75 hours; otherwise transfer in Břeclav, Czech Republic), **Zagreb** (2/day direct, 6.25-6.5 hours), **Ljubljana** (1/day direct, 8.75 hours; plus 2/day with a transfer in Zagreb, 9.5 hours; also possible in 8.5 hours with changes at Vienna/Wien Meidling and Maribor; no convenient night train), **Munich** (4/day by express RailJet, 7.5 hours, plus 2/day on slower InterCity connection, 8.75 hours; plus 1 direct night train/day, 9 hours; otherwise transfer in Vienna and Salzburg), and **Berlin** (2/day, 11.75 hours; plus 1 night train/day, 13 hours).

By HÉV: Budapest has its own suburban rail network, called HÉV. For tourists, this is mostly useful for reaching **Szentendre** (from M2: Batthyány tér) and **Gödöllő** (from M2: Örs vezér tere). For more on the HÉV system, see page 49.

By Bus

Buses can be relatively inexpensive, but are typically slower and less convenient than trains. You can search bus schedules at the (Hungarian-only) website www.menetrendek.hu (click on "VOLÁN Menetrend"). Budapest lacks a single, consolidated bus station; instead, buses fan out from several points around town, each one next to—and named for—a Metró stop. (While these aren't all "bus stations" in the strict sense, they are handy transit hubs.) A few are particularly useful for tourists:

From the **Újpest-Városkapu** bus station (on the M3/blue line), buses depart about hourly to trace the Danube Bend around to **Szentendre** (30 minutes), **Visegrád** (1.25 hours), and **Esztergom** (2 hours).

The **Stadionok** bus station (on the M2/red line) serves **Eger** (2/hour, 1.75-2.25 hours).

The **Árpád híd** bus station (on the M3/blue line) has buses taking the faster overland route to **Esztergom** (1-2/hour, 1.25 hours).

The **Népliget** bus station (on the M3/blue line) is mostly used by international buses (including to **Bratislava:** 1/day, 4.25 hours), as well as buses to **Pécs** (5/day direct, 3.5-4.5 hours) and **Sopron** (2/day direct, 3.75 hours). Trains are faster to these three destinations.

Orange Ways Buses: For long-distance international journeys, consider Orange Ways buses, which offer affordable express connections from Budapest to **Bratislava** (1-4/day, 2.5 hours), **Vienna** (3-4/day, 3 hours), **Kraków** (5/week, 6.5 hours), **Prague** (1-4/day, 6.5-7.5 hours; this same bus sometimes continues to **Dresden** and **Berlin**), and more (www.orangeways.com).

By Plane

Budapest Liszt Ferenc Airport

Budapest's airport is 10 miles southeast of the center (airport code: BUD, tel. 1/296-7000, www.bud.hu). Many Hungarians still call the airport by its former name, "Ferihegy." The airport's lone passenger terminal is, oddly, called "Terminal 2" (there once was a "Terminal 1," but it closed in 2012). The terminal has two adjacent parts: 2A is for flights from EU/Schengen countries (no passport control required), while 2B is for flights from other countries. The terminal has ATMs and TI desks in both areas (open daily 8:00-23:00 in 2A, and daily 10:00-22:00 in 2B).

From the Airport to Budapest: The fastest door-to-door option is to take a **taxi.** Zóna Taxi has a monopoly at the taxi stand out front, with a fixed off-meter price depending on where you're going (about 4,600-5,100 Ft to downtown, 1,000 Ft less from downtown to the airport, about 30 minutes, tel. 1/365-5555, www.zonataxi.eu). You may be able to get a cheaper ride by calling another taxi company to take you to or from the airport (see "Getting Around Budapest—By Taxi" on page 51).

The **airport shuttle** minibus is cheaper for solo travelers, but two people will pay only a few dollars more to share a taxi (3,200 Ft/1 person, 4,790 Ft/2 people for minibus ride to any hotel in the city center, about 30-45 minutes depending on hotel location; tel. 1/296-8555, www.airportshuttle.hu; if arranging a minibus transfer *to* the airport, call at least 24 hours in advance). Because they prefer to take several people at once, you may have to wait awhile at the airport for a quorum to show up (about 20 minutes in busy times, up to an hour when it's slow—they can give you an estimate).

Finally, there are two cheap **public-transportation options.** Both begin with a ride on **public bus #200E** (which you can catch at Terminal 2A or 2B). Once on this bus, you can transfer either to a fast train (handy for reaching downtown Pest) or to the slower Metró (slightly cheaper). To take the train, ride bus #200E only as far as the airport's now-closed Terminal 1; out front you'll find a station where you can catch the **train** to Nyugati/Western train station near downtown Pest (365 Ft, plus 520 Ft supplement for

InterCity trains, 3-7/hour depending on the day and time, 25 minutes). It's also possible to take a taxi between Terminals 2A/2B and the airport train station (1,700 Ft). Or, to save money, stay longer on bus #200E and ride it all the way to the Kőbánya-Kispest station on the M3/blue Metró line, then take the Metró the rest of the way into town (covered by basic 320-Ft transit ticket, allow about an hour total for the trip to the center).

To Eger: Eger makes an enjoyable small-town entry point in Hungary for getting over your jet lag. Unfortunately, there is no direct connection there from Budapest's airport. The easiest plan is to ride the airport shuttle minibus to Budapest's Keleti/Eastern train station, then catch the Eger-bound train from there. Or, to save a little money, you could take public bus #200E to Kőbánya-Kispest, ride the M3/blue Metró line to Deák tér, and transfer to the M2/red Metró line, which stops at both Keleti Station (for the train to Eger) and Stadionok (for the bus to Eger).

Flights from Budapest

If you're considering a train ride that's more than five hours long, a flight may save you both time and money. When comparing your options, factor in the time it takes to get to the airport and how early you'll need to arrive to check in.

The best comparison search engine for both international and intra-European flights is www.kayak.com. For inexpensive flights within Europe, try www.skyscanner.com or www.hipmunk.com. If you're not sure who flies to your destination, check that destination's airport website for a list of carriers.

Malév Hungarian Airlines went bust in 2012—leaving Hungary without an official national airline. But many major international lines (such as Lufthansa and Austrian Airlines) still serve Budapest, and the void has been capably filled by various low-cost airlines. The most prominent of these  is Budapest-based **Wizz Air** (www.wizzair.com)—which also has hubs in the Polish cities of Warsaw, Gdańsk, and Katowice (near Kraków). Also consider budget-carrier standbys **easyJet** (www.easyjet.com), **Ryanair** (www.ryanair.com), and **germanwings** (www.germanwings.com).

If you're not finding the flight you want out of Budapest, consider flying out of **Bratislava**, Slovakia, instead—just a 2.75-hour train ride away (see the Bratislava chapter). Bratislava is served by several daily flights on the budget carriers Ryanair and Danube

Wings (www.danubewings.eu). **Vienna,** Austria—just three hours from Budapest by train—has cheap flights on germanwings.

Be aware of the potential drawbacks of flying on the cheap: nonrefundable and nonchangeable tickets, minimal or nonexistent customer service, stingy baggage allowances with steep overage fees, and treks to airports far outside town. For example, Wizz Air's flights to Kraków actually arrive at Katowice, 50 miles away. If you're traveling with lots of luggage, a cheap flight can quickly become a bad deal. To avoid unpleasant surprises, read the small print before you book.

By Car

Renting a Car

If you're planning to rent a car in Hungary, bring your driver's license. You're also required to have an International Driving Permit—an official translation of your driver's license (sold at your local AAA office for $15 plus the cost of two passport-type photos; see www.aaa.com). While that's the letter of the law, I've often rented cars in Hungary without having—or being asked to show—this permit. If all goes well, you'll likely never be asked to show this permit—but it's a must if you end up dealing with the police.

Rental companies require you to be at least 21 years old to drive in Hungary and to have held your license for one year. Drivers under the age of 25 may incur a young-driver surcharge, and some rental companies do not rent to anyone 75 and over.

Research car rentals before you go. It's cheaper to arrange most long-term car rentals from the US. Call several companies and look online to compare rates, or arrange a rental through your hometown travel agent.

All of the major US rental agencies (including National, Avis, Budget, Hertz, and Thrifty) have offices in Budapest. Also consider the two major Europe-based agencies, Europcar and Sixt. It can be cheaper to use a consolidator, such as Auto Europe (www.autoeurope.com) or Europe by Car (www.ebctravel.com), which compares rates at several companies to get you the best deal. However, my readers have reported problems with consolidators, ranging from misinformation to unexpected fees; because you're going through a middleman, it can be more challenging to resolve disputes that arise with the rental agency.

Regardless of the car-rental company you choose, always read the contract carefully. The fine print can conceal a host of common add-on charges—such as one-way drop-off fees, airport surcharges, or mandatory insurance policies—that aren't included in the "total price," but can be tacked on when you pick up your car. You may need to query rental agents pointedly to find out your actual cost.

For the best deal, rent by the week with unlimited mileage. To save money on fuel, ask for a diesel car. I normally rent the smallest, least-expensive model with a stick shift (cheaper than an automatic). An automatic transmission adds about 50 percent to the car-rental cost over a manual transmission. Almost all rentals are manual by default, so if you need an automatic, you must request one in advance; be aware that these cars are usually larger models (not as maneuverable on narrow, winding roads).

Allow roughly $100 per day for a short-term rental of just a few days, or less per day for longer stretches. Be warned that international trips—say, picking up in Budapest and dropping in Vienna—can be expensive (it depends partly on distance, but the extra fee averages a few hundred dollars).

As a rule, always tell your car-rental company up front exactly which countries you'll be entering. Some companies levy extra insurance fees for trips taken in certain countries with certain types of cars (such as BMWs, Mercedes, and convertibles). Double-check with your rental agent that you have all the documentation you need before you drive off (especially if you're crossing borders into non-Schengen countries, such as Croatia, where you might need to present proof of insurance). For more on borders, see page 9.

You can sometimes get a GPS unit with your rental car or leased vehicle for an additional fee (around $15/day; be sure it's set to English and has all the maps you need before you drive off). Or, if you have a portable GPS device at home, consider taking it with you to Europe (buy and upload European maps before your trip). GPS apps are also available for smartphones, but downloading maps on one of these apps in Europe could lead to an exorbitant data-roaming bill (for more details, see the sidebar on page 468).

Big rental companies have offices in most cities; ask whether they can pick you up at your hotel. Small local companies can be cheaper but aren't as flexible.

Compare pickup costs (downtown can be less expensive than the airport) and explore drop-off options. When selecting a location, don't trust the agency's description of "downtown" or "city center." In some cases, a "downtown" branch can be on the outskirts of the city—a long, costly taxi ride from the center. Before choosing, plug the addresses into a mapping website. You may find that the "train station" location is handier. Returning a car at a big-city train station or downtown agency can be tricky; get precise details on the car drop-off location and hours, and allow ample time to find it. Note that rental offices usually close from midday Saturday until Monday morning.

When you pick up the rental car, check it thoroughly and make sure any damage is noted on your rental agreement. Find out how your car's lights, turn signals, wipers, and fuel cap function, and know what kind of fuel the car takes. When you return the car, make sure the agent verifies its condition with you.

Car Insurance Options

When you rent a car, you are liable for a very high deductible, sometimes equal to the entire value of the car. Limit your financial risk by choosing one of these three options: Buy Collision Damage Waiver (CDW) coverage from the car-rental company, get coverage through your credit card (free, if your card automatically includes zero-deductible coverage), or buy coverage through Travel Guard.

CDW includes a very high deductible (typically $1,000-1,500). Though each rental company has its own variation, basic CDW costs $15-35 a day (figure roughly 30 percent extra) and reduces your liability, but does not eliminate it. When you pick up the car, you'll be offered the chance to "buy down" the basic deductible to zero (for an additional $10-30/day; this is sometimes called "super CDW").

If you opt for **credit-card coverage,** there's a catch. You'll technically have to decline all coverage offered by the car-rental company, which means they can place a hold on your card (which can be up to the full value of the car). In case of damage, it can be time-consuming to resolve the charges with your credit-card company. Before you decide on this option, quiz your credit-card company about how it works.

Finally, you can buy collision insurance from **Travel Guard** ($9/day plus a one-time $3 service fee covers you for up to $35,000, $250 deductible, tel. 800-826-4919, www.travelguard.com). It's valid everywhere in Europe except the Republic of Ireland, and some Italian car-rental companies refuse to honor it. Note that various states differ on which products and policies are available to their residents.

For more on car-rental insurance, see www.ricksteves.com/cdw.

Driving

Avoid driving in Budapest if you can. Especially during rush hour (7:00-9:00 and 16:00-18:00), congestion is maddening, and since there are no expressway bypasses, any traffic going through the city

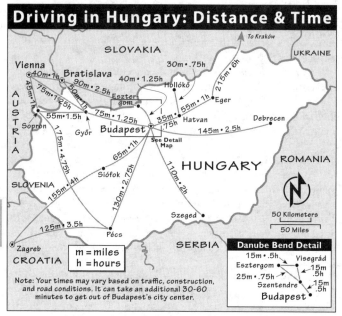

Driving in Hungary: Distance & Time

Note: Your times may vary based on traffic, construction, and road conditions. It can take an additional 30-60 minutes to get out of Budapest's city center.

m = miles
h = hours

has to go *through* the city—sharing the downtown streets with local commuters. The recent wave of roadwork and other construction around Budapest only complicates matters. Signage can be confusing. Do not drive down roads marked with a red circle, or in lanes marked for buses; these can be monitored by automatic traffic cameras, and you could be mailed a ticket.

There are three concentric ring roads, all of them slow: the Small Boulevard (Kiskörút), Great Boulevard (Nagykörút), and outermost Hungária körút, from which highways and expressways spin off to other destinations. The new, desperately needed fourth ring—the M-0 expressway—is partly finished (south and east of downtown); when it's complete in a few years, it will have a huge impact on traffic, diverting freight trucks away from the city center and other ring roads.

Parking: While in Budapest, unless you're heading to an out-of-town sight (such as Memento Park), park the car at your hotel and take public transportation. Public parking costs 150-600 Ft per hour (pay in advance at machine and put ticket on dashboard—watch locals and imitate; free parking Mon-Fri 18:00-8:00 and all day Sat-Sun—but you'll always have to pay in tourist zones). Be careful to park within the lines—otherwise, your car is likely to get "booted" (I've seen more than one confused tourist puzzling over the giant red brace on his or her wheel). A guarded parking lot is safer, but more expensive (figure 3,000-4,000 Ft/day, ask your hotel or look for the blue *P*s on maps). As rental-car theft can be a problem, ask at your hotel for advice. For driving info in Budapest, visit www.fovinform.hu.

Toll Stickers: Hungary has a fine network of expressways, which always begin with "M" (e.g., the M-3 expressway runs east of Budapest toward Eger). To drive on Hungarian expressways, you'll need a toll sticker, called an *autópálya matrica* (also called a "vignette"; 2,975 Ft/week, 4,780 Ft/month, www.motorway.hu). Ask about this when you rent your car (if it's not already included, you'll have to buy one). It's not uncommon to be pulled over at an on- or off-ramp to be checked for a toll sticker; those caught without one are subject to a hefty fine. If you drive into Slovakia or Austria, you'll also need to buy a toll sticker to use their highways (Slovakia—*úhrada*, €10/10 days; Austria—*Vignette*, €8/10 days, €24/2 months). You don't need a toll sticker if you'll be dipping into the country on minor roads—only for major highways.

Road Rules: Be aware of typical European road rules; for example, many countries, including Hungary, require headlights to be turned on at all times (the lights of many newer cars automatically turn on and off with the engine). Seatbelts are mandatory in Hungary, and it's illegal to drink any alcohol at all before driving. As in most other European countries, it's also illegal to drive while using your mobile phone without a hands-free headset. In Europe, you're not allowed to turn right on a red light, unless there is a sign or signal specifically authorizing it. Ask your car-rental company about these rules, or check the US State Department website (www.travel.state.gov, click on "International Travel," then specify your country of choice and click "Traffic Safety and Road Conditions").

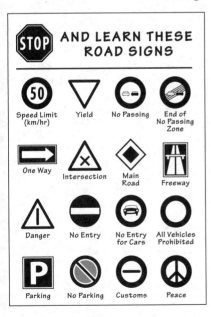

Route Tips for Drivers

To Eger and Other Points East: Head out of the city center on Andrássy út, circling behind Heroes' Square to access Kós Károly sétány through the middle of City Park. You'll pass Széchenyi Baths on the left, then (exiting the park) go over the Hungária körút ring road, before getting on M-3. This expressway zips you conveniently to Eger (exit #114 for Füzesabony; go north on road 33, then follow 3, then 25 into Eger). Between Budapest and Eger, M-3 also passes Gödöllő (with its Royal Palace) and to Hatvan (where you can exit for Hollókő).

To Bratislava, Vienna, and Other Points West: From central Pest, head over the Danube on the white, modern Elisabeth Bridge (Erzsébet híd). Once in Buda, the road becomes Hegyalja út; simply follow *Wien* signs to get on M-1.

To the Danube Bend: For tips on driving around the Danube Bend (Szentendre, Visegrád, and Esztergom), see page 344.

By Boat

BUDAPEST CONNECTIONS

In the summer, Mahart runs daily high-speed hydrofoils up the Danube to **Vienna.** It's not particularly scenic, and it's slower than the train, but it's a fun alternative for nautical types. The boat leaves Budapest at 9:00 and arrives in Vienna at 15:30; on the return trip, a boat leaves from Vienna at 9:00 and reaches Budapest at 14:30 (May–late Sept only, departs from Budapest Mon and Wed, from Vienna Tue and Thu). The trip costs €99 one-way between Budapest and Vienna (or €109 the other direction); you can also ride between Budapest and the Slovak capital, **Bratislava.** To confirm times and prices, and to buy tickets, contact Mahart in Budapest (tel. 1/484-4010, www.mahartpassnave.hu) or DDSG Blue Danube in Vienna (tel. 01/58880, www.ddsg-blue-danube.at).

For details on taking the boat to **Danube Bend** towns (Szentendre, Visegrád, and Esztergom), see page 327.

NEAR
BUDAPEST

DAY TRIPS FROM BUDAPEST

Gödöllő Palace • Hollókő • Szentendre • Visegrád • Esztergom

The most rewarding destinations outside Budapest are Eger, Pécs, Sopron, and Bratislava (Slovakia). But each of those (covered in their own chapters) is more than two hours away; for a shorter visit, the region immediately surrounding Budapest offers some enticing options for a break from the big city. Just outside Budapest, Gödöllő Palace is the best spot in Hungary to commune with its past Habsburg monarchs, the larger-than-life Franz Josef and Sisi. The tiny village of Hollókő, tucked in the hills northeast of Budapest, combines a living community with an open-air folk museum. And three river towns along the Danube Bend offer an easy escape: the charming town of Szentendre is an art colony with a colorful history to match; the castles of Visegrád boast a sweeping history and equally grand views over the Bend; and Esztergom is home to Hungary's top church.

Planning Your Time

Of this chapter's five attractions, Gödöllő Palace and Szentendre are the easiest to reach from Budapest (each one is a quick ride away on the suburban train, or HÉV). These sights—which are also the best attractions in this chapter—can be done in just a few hours each. The other sights (Hollókő, Visegrád, and Esztergom) are farther afield and less rewarding; do these only if you have extra time or they're on the way to your next stop.

For efficient sightseeing, you can cluster your visits to these sights strategically. If you have a car, Gödöllő Palace and Hollókő can be done in a day (round-trip from Budapest, or on a long day driving between Budapest and Eger; for details, see page 307). The Danube Bend sights (Szentendre, Visegrád, and Esztergom) also go well together if you have a car, and line up conveniently between Budapest and Bratislava or Vienna.

Day Trips from Budapest

SLO-
VAKIA   HUNGARY
To
Bratislava   Nagymaros-
Visegrád
See The Danube Bend Map   Station

Hollókő   To
Salgótarján

•Rétság   Pásztó
21

Štúrovo 11
•Esztergom   •Vác   Zagyvaszántó
•Dorog   Visegrád
Pilisszent-
kereszt   Hatvan
To
Vienna   Szentendre•   E-77   M-3
To
Pomáz   Eger
10   •Bag
To
Győr,   Gödöllő
Sopron &   3
Vienna   ÓBUDA
M-1   — • — Rail
BUDAPEST   +++++ HÉV
MEMENTO
PARK   Ferihegy   M-0
To   N
Lake Balaton   M-7   4   10 Kilometers
& Zagreb   To   Danube   M-5   To   10 Miles
Pécs M-6   Szeged &
Belgrade

DAY TRIPS

Gödöllő Palace

Holding court in an un-
assuming town on the
outskirts of Budapest,
Gödöllő Royal Palace
(Gödöllői Királyi Kas-
tély; pronounced roughly
"GER-der-ler") is Hunga-
ry's most interesting royal
interior to tour. Once the
residence of Habsburg

Emperor Franz Josef and his wife, Empress Elisabeth (known as
Sisi), Gödöllő has recently been restored to its *"K und K"* (royal and
imperial) splendor. The pink-and-white, U-shaped Baroque complex looks like just another midsized palace from the outside, but
it's haunted by Habsburg ghosts...with an unmistakably Hungarian
twist. Compared to other Habsburg properties, it's compact and
pleasantly uncrowded. If you want a Habsburg fix and aren't going
to Vienna (or if you're a Habsburg completist), Gödöllő is worth a
half-day visit from Budapest.

Budapest Day Trips at a Glance

If you only have a day or two to venture outside of Budapest, this overview might help you decide where to go. I've listed these sights roughly in order of worthiness.

▲▲▲**Eger** This appealing midsized town, packed with gorgeous Baroque architecture, has one of Hungary's most historic castles, some pleasantly quirky museums, excellent local wines, and fine thermal baths (including the excellent Salt Hill Thermal Spa in the nearby countryside). Eger is the best look at workaday Hungary outside Budapest. Allow a full day or overnight. See the Eger chapter.

▲▲▲**Pécs** A medium-sized city in southern Hungary, Pécs features a rich history (typified by the unique mosque-turned-church on its main square), surprisingly top-notch museums, and beautiful buildings slathered with colorful local Zsolnay tiles. Allow a full day or overnight. See the Pécs chapter.

▲▲**Bratislava**, **Slovakia** The Slovak capital—conveniently situated between Budapest and Vienna—is worth a look for its increasingly rejuvenated Old Town, taste of Slovak culture, and evocative sea of construction cranes, which are hard at work reinventing the city as an economic capital of the New Europe. Allow a half-day to a full day (most convenient on the way to Vienna). See the Bratislava chapter.

▲▲**Sopron** A small-town alternative that's also between Budapest and Vienna, Sopron has a charmingly well-preserved Old Town peppered with dusty museum and historic buildings. Allow a half-day to a full day (most convenient on the way to Vienna). See the Sopron chapter.

Orientation

Cost and Hours: 2,000 Ft; April-Oct daily 10:00-18:00; Nov-March Tue-Sun 10:00-17:00, closed Mon; last entry one hour before closing, tel. 28/410-124, www.kiralyikastely.hu.

Getting There: Gödöllő Palace is an easy side-trip from Budapest, by HÉV suburban train or by car. By **public transit,** take the M2/red Metró line to the end of the line at Örs vezér tere, then go under the street to the HÉV suburban train green line and hop a train marked for Gödöllő (2/hour). Once in Gödöllő, get off at the Szabadság tér station (about an hour total from central Budapest). The palace is across the street, kitty-corner from the station. **Drivers** will find the palace 17

▲▲**Gödöllő Palace** This summer palace of the Habsburg monarchs is the best place in Hungary to get to know the "royal and
imperial" couple, Franz Josef and Sisi. It's easy to see in a half-day
from Budapest (or, by car, combine with Hollókő for a full day).
See page 311.

▲▲**Szentendre** This colorful, Balkan-feeling artist colony is the
easiest (and most touristy) small town to visit from Budapest.
Allow a half-day from Budapest, or combine with a full-day trip
around the Danube Bend. See page 328.

▲▲**Esztergom Basilica** Hungary's biggest and most important
church, packed with history, looms above the Danube. Allow a full
day combined with other Danube Bend sights (Szentendre and
possibly Visegrád). See page 340.

▲**Hollókő** This intriguing village-meets-open-air folk museum
hides in the middle of nowhere an hour and a half northeast of
Budapest. Visit only if you have a car and are interested in Hungarian countryside culture and architecture. Allow a full day (by
car, it can be combined with Gödöllő Palace for a full-day side-
trip, or visited en route between Budapest and Eger). See page
319.

Visegrád The least engaging of the Danube Bend sights, Visegrád offers a small riverside palace museum and a dramatic hilltop
castle with fine views over the Bend. Visit only if it's on the way of
your Danube Bend day. See page 336.

DAY TRIPS

miles east of Budapest, just off the M-3 expressway (on the
way to Eger and other points east).

Audioguide: You can rent a 600-Ft audioguide, but my self-guided
tour (next page) covers the basics and enough English descriptions are posted throughout to bring meaning to each of the
rooms and exhibits.

Services: The palace houses a café that Sisi would appreciate.
There's also baggage storage (no bags are allowed within the
tourable parts of the palace).

Expect Changes: As renovation work at the palace continues, you
may find some details to be different than described here.

Time to Allow: By public transportation, figure an hour each way
from central Budapest, plus another hour or so to tour the pal-

ace. You'll need additional time to visit the other sights at the palace (such as the Baroque theater).

Starring: The royal and imperial couple, Franz Josef and Sisi.

Background

The palace was built in the 1740s by Count Antal Grassalkovich, a Hungarian aristocrat who was loyal to Habsburg Empress Maria Theresa (at a time when most Hungarians were chafing under her rule). When the Compromise of 1867 made Habsburg rulers Franz Josef and Sisi "king and queen of Hungary" (see page 316), the couple needed a summer home where they could relax in their Hungarian realm—and Gödöllő Palace was the place. Later it became the home of Admiral Miklós Horthy, who led Hungary as regent between the World Wars. After falling into disrepair during the communist period (when the Soviets gutted it of period furniture and used it as military barracks, then a nursing home), the palace was recently rehabilitated to Habsburg specifications and opened to the public. Renovations are ongoing, and more parts of the palace open each year.

The most interesting part of the palace is its permanent exhibit, which fills two wings: the Franz Josef wing (to the right as you enter) and the Sisi wing (to the left), which you'll visit in that order. Pleasant gardens stretch behind the palace. Various other parts of the palace—such as a Baroque theater, the stables, and Admiral Horthy's bunker—are also tourable, but not really geared for English-speakers.

Self-Guided Tour

• *After buying your ticket, pick up the free floor plan and check out the model next to the ticket desk to see how the palace was gradually expanded from its original U-shaped core.*

Head upstairs and go right, following the marked tourist route into the...

Franz Josef Wing

You'll walk down a long hallway and view a series of rooms celebrating the palace's construction and its original builders, the aristocratic **Grassalkovich family.** If this obscure blue blood doesn't thrill you, take the opportunity to simply appreciate the opulent apartments. As in other palaces of the day, servants actually scurried around inside the walls like mice, serving their masters unseen and unheard. Look for "secret" access doors to these servant spaces, and notice that the stoves have no doors—they were fed from behind, inside the walls.

At the end of the Grassalkovich exhibit, the **oratory** gives you a peek into the chapel. This room allowed the royal couple to "attend" Mass without actually mingling with the rabble. Soon after the oratory, keep an eye out for the hideaway toilet and the access to the servants' crawlspace.

In the **coronation chamber,** we finally catch up with the Habsburgs. Look for the giant painting of Franz Josef being crowned at Matthias Church, on top of Buda's Castle Hill. (On the right side, hat in hand, is Count Andrássy. He gestures with the air of a circus ringmaster—which makes sense, as he was a kind of MC of both this coronation and the Hungarian government in general. Andrássy is the namesake of Pest's main drag—and was the reputed lover of Franz Josef's wife Sisi.) Across the room is a painting of another Franz Josef coronation, this time at today's Széchenyi tér in Pest. Back then, Buda and Pest were separate cities—so two coronations were required.

In the **study of Franz Josef,** we see a portrait of the emperor, with his trademark bushy 'stache and 'burns. The painting of the small boy depicts Franz Josef's great-great-nephew Otto von Habsburg, the Man Who Would Be Emperor, if the empire still existed. Otto (1912-2011), was an early proponent of the creation of the European Union (whose vision for a benevolent, multiethnic state bears eerie similarities to the Habsburg Empire of Franz Josef's time). Otto celebrated his 90th birthday (in 2002) here at Gödöllő Palace. The statue depicts Otto's father, Charles IV. He was the last Habsburg emperor, ruling from the death of Franz Josef in 1916 to the end of World War I (and the end of the great dynasty) in 1918. Sisi looks on from across the room. And her son, Rudolf (who committed suicide), is between Franz Josef and the statue of Charles IV.

Franz Josef's salon (a.k.a. the reception room) displays a map of the Habsburg Empire at its peak, flanked by etchings featuring 12 of the many different nationalities it ruled. Notice the very colorful reconstructed stove.

The lavishly chandeliered **grand ballroom** still hosts concerts. Above the main door, notice the screened-in loft where musicians could play—heard, but not seen.

• *At the far end of the grand ballroom, you enter the...*

Sisi Wing

This wing—where the red color scheme gives way to violet—is dedicated to the enigmatic figure that most people call "Empress

Franz Josef (1830-1916) and Sisi (1837-1898): Emperor and Empress of Austria, King and Queen of Hungary

In a unique power-sharing compromise, the emperor and empress of the Austrian realm were only the "king" and "queen" of Hungary. (This was known as *"K und K"* in German, for *König und Kaiser*, king and emperor...same guy.) From the beginning of this "K+K" arrangement in 1867 through World War I, this "royal and imperial" couple was Franz Josef and Sisi.

Franz Josef I—who ruled for 68 years (1848-1916)—was the embodiment of the Habsburg Empire as it finished its six-century-long ride. Born in 1830, Franz Josef had a stern upbringing that instilled in him a powerful sense of duty and—like so many men of power—a love of all things military.

His uncle, Ferdinand I, suffered from profound epilepsy, which prevented him from effectively ruling. As the revolutions of 1848 (including Hungary's) were rattling royal families throughout Europe, the Habsburgs forced Ferdinand to abdicate, and put 18-year-old Franz Josef on the throne. Ironically, as one of his first acts as emperor, Franz Josef—whose wife would later become closely identified with Hungarian independence—marched into Budapest to put down the 1848 Revolution. He spent the beginning of his long reign understandably paranoid, as social discontent continued to simmer.

Franz Josef was very conservative. But worse, he wrongly believed that he was a talented military tactician, and led Austria into catastrophic battles. Wearing his uniform to the end, he couldn't see what a dinosaur his monarchy was becoming, and never thought it strange that the majority of his subjects didn't even speak German. Like Queen Victoria, his contemporary, Franz Josef was the embodiment of his empire—old-fashioned but sacrosanct. His passion for low-grade paperwork earned him the nickname "Joe Bureaucrat." Mired in these petty details, he missed the big picture. In 1914, he helped start a Great War that ultimately ended the age of the divine monarchs.

Empress **Elisabeth**—Franz Josef's mysterious, narcissistic, and beautiful wife—has been compared to Princess Diana because of her beauty, bittersweet life, and tragic death.

Sisi, as she's lovingly called, was mostly silent. Her main goals in life seem to have been preserving her reputation as a beautiful empress, maintaining her Barbie-doll figure, and tending to her fairy-tale, ankle-length hair. In the 1860s, she was considered one of the most beautiful women in the world. But, in spite of severe dieting and fanatic exercise, age took its toll. After turning

30, she allowed no more portraits to be painted of her and was generally seen in public with a delicate fan covering her face (and bad teeth).

Complex and influential, Sisi was adored by Franz Josef, whom she respected. Although Franz Josef was supposed to marry her sister Helene (in an arranged diplomatic marriage), he fell in love with Sisi instead. It was one of the Habsburgs' few marriages for love. (The family was famously adept at strategic marriages.) Still, Sisi never felt fully accepted by her mother-in-law...which made the Hungarians—who also felt misunderstood and not taken seriously by the Habsburgs—appreciate her even more.

Sisi's personal mission and political cause was promoting Hungary's bid for autonomy within the empire. While she was married to Emperor Franz Josef, she spent seven years in Budapest and at Gödöllő, enjoying horseback riding, the local cuisine... and the company of the dashing Count Gyula Andrássy. (For more on the Count, see page 143.) Hungarians, who call Sisi their "guardian angel," partly credit her for the Compromise of 1867, which elevated their status within the Habsburg Empire.

Sisi's personal tragedy was the death of her son Rudolf, the crown prince, in an apparent suicide. Disliking Vienna and the confines of the court, Sisi traveled more and more frequently. As years passed, the restless Sisi and her hardworking husband became estranged. In 1898, while visiting Geneva, Switzerland, she was murdered by an Italian anarchist.

A final note: While for simplicity in this book I've referred to these figures as history knows them—"Emperor Franz Josef" and "Empress Sisi"—Hungarians might bristle at these imperial titles. After all, they (and *only* they) called the couple "King Franz Josef" and "Queen Sisi."

DAY TRIPS

Elisabeth," but whom the Hungarians call "our Queen Elisabeth." Sisi adored her Hungarian subjects, and the feeling was mutual. At certain times in her life, Sisi spent more time here at Gödöllő Palace than in Vienna. While the Sisi obsession is hardly unusual at Habsburg sights, notice that the exhibits here are particularly doting...and always drive home Sisi's Hungarian affinities.

In the **reception room,** along with the first of many Sisi portraits, you'll see the portrait of Count Gyula Andrássy. Sisi's enthusiasm for all things Hungarian reportedly extended to this dashing aristocrat, who enjoyed riding horses with Sisi...and allegedly sired her third daughter, Marie Valerie—nicknamed the "Little Hungarian Princess."

In Sisi's **study,** see the engagement portraits of the fresh-faced Franz Josef (age 23) and Sisi (age 16). While they supposedly married for love, Sisi is said to have later regretted joining the imperial family. The book by beloved Hungarian poet Sándor Petőfi, from Sisi's bedside, is a reminder that Sisi could read and enjoy the difficult Magyar tongue. (It's also a reminder of Sisi's courageous empathy for the Hungarian cause, as Petőfi was killed—effectively by Sisi's husband—in the Revolution of 1848.)

You'll then pass through Sisi's **dressing room** (with small family portraits) and **bedroom,** before reaching three more rooms with...more exhibits on Sisi. Look for the letter in Hungarian, written in Sisi's own hand (#17, in the case) and an invitation to her wedding (set with the fancy lace collar). The third room is filled with images of edifices throughout Hungary that are dedicated to Sisi (such as Budapest's Elisabeth Bridge).

Other Sights at Gödöllő Palace

Though the royal apartments are the most important thing to see at Gödöllő, while you're here consider these additional options (all open the same hours as the palace). Note that the theater and bunker tours and falconry show are all usually in Hungarian only; an English version of each one is possible if you contact them to arrange it in advance.

The newly opened **Gisella Wing** fills six rooms with a permanent exhibit about the history of the building (included in palace ticket).

The **Baroque Theater** can only be visited with a 30-minute guided tour (1,400 Ft, 1,100 Ft with palace ticket).

The **stables** have an exhibit about the beloved equestrian culture of European aristocrats (1,200 Ft, 900 Ft with palace ticket).

A 15-minute **3-D movie** with English subtitles narrates the history of the palace (1,200 Ft, 900 Ft with palace ticket).

The WWII-era **bunker** that remains from the time when this was a summer residence of Admiral Miklós Horthy (who led Hungary between the World Wars) can be seen only on a 30-minute tour (800 Ft, 700 Ft with palace ticket).

On summer Sundays (May-Oct at 11:00 and 16:00), the palace hosts a 30-minute **falconry and archery show** (1,300 Ft).

Hollókő

Worth ▲, remote, miniscule Hollókő (HOH-loh-ker), nestled in the hills a 1.5-hour drive from Budapest, survives as a time capsule of Hungarian tradition.

This proud village is half living hamlet, half open-air folk museum; unlike many such places around Europe, people actually reside in quite a few of Hollókő's old buildings. To retain its "real village" status, Hollókő has its own mayor, elementary school, general store, post office, and doctor (who visits twice a week). Hollókő is worth a visit for those who are interested in Hungarian folk culture, especially if you have a car. Note that most of the village shuts down off-season (mid-Oct-Easter) and on Mondays; at these times, skip Hollókő.

Getting There

Hollókő is in a distant valley about 60 miles northeast of Budapest. By **car,** it's about a 1.5-hour drive (assuming light traffic): Take the M-3 expressway east, exit at Hatvan (exit 55), and follow road #21 north toward Salgótarján. Keep an eye out (on the left) for the turnoff for Hollókő and Szécsény, then carefully track *Hollókő* signs. From Eger, figure about 1.5 hours (fastest via the M-3 expressway west, then follow the directions above).

In the summer, and on Sundays year-round, it's possible (but more time-consuming) to reach Hollókő by public transportation: A **bus** leaves from Budapest's Stadionok bus station daily year-round at 15:15; on weekends only (Sat-Sun), a second bus departs at 8:30. Buses return to Budapest on a similar schedule (May-Aug daily at 14:00; year-round Sat-Sun at 16:00; plus one early-morning departure at 5:00 on weekdays). The trip takes about two hours each way. Notice that this schedule makes a same-day round-trip from Budapest impossible on weekdays.

Planning Your Time

Hollókő deserves at least a couple of hours; a half-day is about right for most visitors. With a car, consider detouring to Hollókő between Budapest and Eger. Remember, Gödöllő Palace (which is also off the M-3 expressway) combines well with Hollókő; for example, see them both as a side-trip from Budapest, or on the way between Budapest and Eger.

The village is particularly worthwhile on festival days (listed on its website—www.holloko.hu). Don't bother on a Monday or off-season, when nearly everything is closed.

If choosing what to visit at Hollókő, the Village Museum is the most worthwhile, followed by the Doll Museum. The others sights are skippable, but it's worth poking into several shops. Hike up to the castle only if you've got time and energy to burn.

Orientation to Hollókő

Hollókő (total population: about 350) is a village squeezed into a dead-end valley overlooked by a castle. The hamlet is divided into two parts: the Old Village (with all the protected old houses, shops, and museums, and about 35 residents) and the New Village. The bus stop and big parking lot are just above the entry point to the Old Village. There's an ATM and a WC behind the pub that overlooks the entrance to the Old Village.

Tourist Information

Hollókő's useful TI is along the main street in the middle of the Old Village. They can give you a brochure and help you find a room (summer daily 8:00-18:00, sometimes until 20:00; winter Mon-Fri 8:00-16:00, Sat-Sun open only briefly or closed entirely; Kossuth utca 68, tel. 32/579-011, www.holloko.hu).

Local Guide: Since English-speakers get little respect at Hollókő (only a few borrowable translations in some museums), you owe it to yourself to hire a local guide. **Ádám Kiss** is a young city slicker who fell in love with Hollókő and moved here with his wife and kids to become part of the community. Ádám, who lived in Montana and speaks good English, will enthusiastically make your time here more meaningful, and he's a great value (6,500 Ft/2-hour tour, does not include entrance fees—figure 10,000 Ft total for two people, mobile 0620-379-6132, adamtheguide@gmail.com).

Self-Guided Tour

Hollókő's Old Village

The Old Village at Hollókő is a perfectly preserved enclave of the folk architecture, dress, and traditions of the local Palóc culture.

Because it's in a dead-end valley, Hollókő's folk traditions survived here well into the 20th century. (Only when villagers began commuting to other towns for work in the 1950s did they realize how "backward" they seemed to other Hungarians.)

It's free to enter the Old Village, but each sight inside has its own modest entry fee (generally around 250 Ft). Unless otherwise noted, sights here are open Easter-mid-Oct Tue-Sun 10:00-17:00, closed Mon; off-season, most places close entirely or are only open Sat-Sun in good weather. Assume that no English is spoken, but at most places you can ask to borrow English translations.

• *Start at the entry point into the Old Village, which begins where the cobbles do. Get oriented with the big wooden map posted nearby. Across the street is the...*

Barnyard (Pajtakert): A local agency coordinates special events here for visiting groups. If you see the ladies in their colorful folk dresses (generally a few times each day in summer), feel free to gawk from over the fence. Hollókő's men, who tended to go elsewhere for work, abandoned their old-fashioned outfits earlier; but the women, who remained in the valley, kept wearing traditional dress much longer. Their costume is marked by a big, round abdomen (a sign of fertility, created by layering many petticoats), an embroidered vest, and a colorful headdress. In this courtyard, you can pay 300 Ft to enter the weaving room and see an old loom.

• *Now head down the village's main street. As you walk, don't be afraid to poke into any shop. (I'll mention only a few.) One of the best (on the right) is the...*

Handicraft Workshop: Here you can buy some local crafts, or English-speaking Tunde will teach you how to make them yourself (same price, takes 5-30 minutes depending on craft, closed Mon-Tue; may be closed).

On the left, the **Waxworks** (Panoptikum) is a tiny exhibit illustrating local legends (400 Ft, daily).

• *As you continue, take a closer look at the...*

Traditional Houses: The exteriors of these houses cannot be changed without permission, but interiors are modern (with plumbing, electricity, Internet access, phones, and so on). They once had thatched roofs with

no chimneys (to evade a chimney tax), but a devastating fire in 1909 compelled residents to replace the thatch with tiles and add little chimneys. The thick walls are made of a whitewashed, adobe-type mix of mud and dung (which keeps things cool in summer and warm in winter). Thick walls, small doors (watch your head), small windows...small people back then. The big, overhanging roof (nicknamed the house's "skirt") prevents rain from damaging this fragile composition. Most began as one simple house along the road; as children grew and needed homes of their own, a little family compound evolved around a central courtyard.

• *After passing two of the town's restaurants (on the right), you'll reach the TI on the left. As you continue, at the fork in the road is Hollókő's...*

Church: A traveling priest says Mass here twice weekly. This is a popular wedding spot for Budapest urbanites charmed by its simplicity.

• *Take the fork to the right (Petőfi út) and wander past a few more shops until the road rejoins (at the town's third restaurant). Continue a few yards down the street. On the left, you'll see a vár/castle sign leading very steeply up to the town's castle (which is prominent overhead; for a more gradual approach, read on). Across the street is the...*

People and Landscape Museum: This little collection displays photos of Hollókő in the olden days—with thatched roofs and dirt roads...but otherwise looking much the same (250 Ft, closed Mon and Wed).

• *Now backtrack and head back up on the other road (Kossuth út). On the right, across from the restaurant, is the...*

Doll Museum: Step inside to see some 200 dolls dressed in traditional costumes of the area. Each is labeled with the specific place of origin and a basic English description, allowing you to see the subtle changes from village to village (250 Ft, daily 10:00-17:00).

• *Farther up on the right is...*

Grandma's Shop: Here you can browse a wide range of locally produced Hungarian foods in jars—pickles, jams, honey, *pálinka* (schnapps), and more. Next door is a basket-maker's shop.

• *A few steps up on the right is the...*

Village Museum: The Old Village's highlight, this is the only house here with an authentic interior (250 Ft, March-mid-Dec daily 10:00-18:00, closed off-season). Take a trip back a hundred years as you stroll through the house.

You enter into the **kitchen.** Most of the family (including piles of kids) would sleep on the floor here, near the warmth of the stove. The doors on the back wall (behind the stove) lead to a smoker. This very efficient design allowed them to heat the house, cook, bake, and smoke foods all at the same time.

Then head into the **main room** (to the left as you enter). Even

today, many older Hungarians have a "nice room" where they keep their most prized possessions and decorations. They let visitors peek in to see their treasures...then make them sit in the kitchen to socialize. In here you'll see plates and clocks proudly displayed. Looking around this room also gives you clues to the family's status. The pillows and linens piled on the bed (stored there during the day, as most family members bunked on the floor) indicate that this was a middle-class home. The linens were traditionally given by the bride's father as a dowry to the groom, allowing the couple to start their life together. The matching furniture is delicately painted. The dresser is well-built and intricate, indicating that a carpenter was paid to make it (other furniture would have been more roughly built by the head of the household). The glass in the windows is not authentic; back then, they would have stretched pig bladders over the windows instead. Turn your attention to the ceiling: The rafters are painted blue to ward off flies (the blue hue contains copper sulfate, a natural insecticide). People would hang their boots (their most expensive item of clothing) up high to prevent mice from ruining them.

Now cross back over to the **third room,** used for storing tools and food. The matriarch of the house slept in here (on the uncomfortable-looking rope bed) and kept the key for this room, doling out the family's ration of food—so in many ways, Grandma was the head of the household. While the rest of the family slept elsewhere in the house, a young woman of courting age could come here to meet up with a suitor, who'd sneak in through the window (The Hungarians even have a verb for these premarital

interactions—roughly, "storaging.") Find the crude crib, used to bring a baby along with adults working the fields (notice it could be covered to protect from the sun's rays). In other parts of Hungary, peasants were known to partially bury their babies in the ground to prevent them from moving around while they worked. (These days, we use TV—is that really so much more humane?) Look up to find the bread rack suspended from the ceiling—again, to rescue the bread from those troublesome mice. Out back, you'll see the old wine press.

• *Continue up the street. A bit farther up on the right, look for the...*

DAY TRIPS

Post Office Museum: This shows off old postal uniforms, equipment, stamps, and currency (700 Ft).

• *A few more steps up, and you've completed your circle—you're back at the town church. There's one more sight in town. If you're up for a 15-20-minute uphill hike, consider going up to the...*

Castle: First hike up to the big parking lot; from there, follow the rough path marked *vár/castle* (a bit uphill at first, then mostly level).

Hollókő's castle originally dates from the 13th century. By the 16th century, it was on the frontier between Habsburg-held Hungary and the Ottoman invaders (who eventually conquered the castle and used it for their own defense for a century and a half). After the Habsburgs had retaken Hungary, Emperor Leopold I destroyed the castle prophylactically (in 1711, just after the failed War of Independence) to ensure his Hungarian subjects wouldn't use it against him. It sat in ruins until 1966, when it underwent an extensive, 30-year-long renovation. There are only a few small exhibits to see inside, but it's enjoyable enough to hike around to ever-higher and better panoramas

(700 Ft, daily 10:00-17:30, in winter on good-weather Sat-Sun only). Views over the Old Village give you a sense of how miniscule the town is. The nearby fields are used to graze Hollókő's livestock, which stay out to pasture at all times rather than being stabled. The high hills on the horizon are across the border, in Slovakia.

The castle is also tied to the legend of how Hollókő ("Hill of the Ravens") got its name: Supposedly the owner of a castle that stood on the hill above this one once kidnapped a girl from the village. The girl's nanny, who was a witch, sent ravens to pick the castle apart, stone by stone.

Sleeping in Hollókő

This is a very sleepy place to spend the night, but those who really want to delve into village Hungary might enjoy it (and its accommodations are far cheaper than other cities or towns in this book).

The **TI** rents several rooms in nine traditional buildings right in the Old Village (figure Db-12,000 Ft including breakfast; see contact information under "Tourist Information," earlier).

Tugári Vendégház, run by local guide Ádám Kiss and his wife, has four rooms in a nicely restored old building in the New Village, a five-minute walk from the main sights (8,500-10,500 Ft depending on room size, breakfast-1,200 Ft, cheaper for stays of longer than one night, Rákóczi út 13, tel. 32/379-156, mobile 0620-379-6132, www.holloko-tugarivendeghaz.hu, tugarivende-ghaz@gmail.com).

Eating in Hollókő

There are three restaurants in the Old Village of Hollókő, each one slinging traditional, well-priced Hungarian food: **Muskátli Restaurant** and **Katalin Csárda** (near the entrance to the village), and **Vár Restaurant** (at the bottom of the village). Be warned that all of these close early (by 18:00 or 19:00, just after the day-trippers go home), so don't wait too long for dinner. At the start of the village, you'll also see a **pub.** A humble **grocery store** is upstairs above the pub (Mon-Sat 7:30-15:30, closed Sun).

DAY TRIPS

The Danube Bend

The Danube, which begins as a trickle in Germany's Black Forest, becomes the Mississippi River of Central Europe—connecting 10 countries and four capitals (Vienna, Bratislava, Budapest, Belgrade) as it flows southeast through the Balkan Peninsula toward the Black Sea. Just south of Bratislava, the river gets squeezed between mountain ranges, which force it to loop back on itself—creating the scenic "Danube Bend" (Dunakanyar). Here Hungarians sunbathe and swim along the banks of the Danube, or hike in the rugged hills that rise up from the river. Hungarian history hides around every turn of the Bend: For centuries, Hungarian kings ruled not from Buda or Pest, but from Visegrád and Esztergom. And during the Ottoman occupation of Hungary, this area was a buffer zone between Christian and Muslim Europe.

Today, three river towns north of Budapest on the Danube Bend offer a convenient day-trip getaway for urbanites who want

The Danube Bend

a small-town break. Closest to Budapest is Szentendre, whose colorful, storybook-cute Baroque center is packed with tourists. The ruins of a mighty castle high on a hill watch over the town of Visegrád. Esztergom, birthplace of Hungary's first Christian king, has the country's biggest and most important church. All of this is within a one-hour drive of the capital, and also reachable (up to a point) by public transportation.

Planning Your Time

Remember, Szentendre is the easiest Danube Bend destination—just a quick suburban-train (HÉV) ride away, it can be done in a few hours. Visegrád and Esztergom are more difficult to reach by public transportation; either one can require a substantial walk from the train or bus stop to the town's major sight.

By **public transportation,** don't try to see all three towns in one day; focus on one or two. (I'd skip Visegrád, whose fine castle is a headache to reach without a car.) If you want to do the whole shebang, take a tour, rent a car, or hire a driver (see page 45) or local guide (page 52).

With a **car,** try this ambitious one-day plan:

      9:00 Leave Budapest.

    9:30   Arrive at Szentendre and see the town.
  12:00   Leave Szentendre.
  12:30   Lunch in Visegrád.
  13:30   Tour Visegrád Royal Palace and Citadel.
  15:30   Leave Visegrád.
  16:00   Visit Esztergom Basilica.
  17:00   Head back to Budapest.

With extra time, add a visit to the Hungarian Open-Air Folk Museum ("Skanzen") near Szentendre.

If you're driving between Budapest and Vienna (or Bratislava), the Danube Bend towns are a fine way to break up the journey, but seeing all three en route makes for a very long day—get an early start, or skip one.

Getting Around the Danube Bend

Going north from Budapest, the three towns line up along the same road on the west side of the Danube—Szentendre, Visegrád, Esztergom—each spaced about 15 miles apart.

By Car: It couldn't be easier. Get on road #11 going north out of Buda, which will take you through each of the three towns—the road bends with the Danube. As you approach Szentendre (just before the train station), watch for signs for *Centrum Szentendre* to branch off to the right, toward the old center and the river promenade. To return from Esztergom to Budapest, see "Route Tips for Drivers" at the end of this chapter.

By Boat: From early April to late October, Mahart runs boats from Budapest up the Danube Bend. The slower **riverboats** (1.5 hours to Szentendre, 3 hours to Visegrád, 4.75 hours to Esztergom) run daily except Mondays in the peak of the summer (May-Sept for Szentendre, until Aug for Visegrád and Esztergom), and less frequently (generally Sat only) in the shoulder season. The faster **hydrofoils** (none to Szentendre, 1 hour to Visegrád, 1.5 hours to Esztergom) run only on summer weekends (May-Sept Sat-Sun). No boats run off-season (Oct-April). Check schedules and buy tickets at Mahart in Budapest (dock near Vigadó tér in Pest, tel. 1/484-4010, www.mahartpassnave.hu).

By Train: The three towns are on three separate train lines. Szentendre is truly handy by train, while Visegrád and Esztergom are less convenient.

Getting to **Szentendre** is a breeze by train—the HÉV, Budapest's suburban rail, zips you right there (catch train at Batthyány tér in Buda's Víziváros neighborhood, easy connection via M2/red Metró line; 4-7/hour, 40 minutes each way, last train returns from Szentendre around 23:00).

The nearest train station to **Visegrád** is actually across the river in Nagymaros (this station is called "Nagymaros-Visegrád";

don't get off at the station called simply "Nagymaros"). From the station, you'll walk five minutes to the river and take a ferry across to Visegrád (see "Arrival in Visegrád" on page 337). Trains run hourly between Nagymaros-Visegrád and Nyugati/Western Station in Budapest (trip takes 40-50 minutes).

To **Esztergom,** trains run hourly from Budapest's Nyugati/ Western Station (1.5 hours), but the Esztergom train station is a 45-minute walk from the basilica.

By Bus: Without a car, buses are the best way to hop between the three towns. They're as quick as the train if you're coming from Budapest, but can be standing room only. There are two main routes. The **river route** runs hourly from Budapest along the Danube through Szentendre (30 minutes) and Visegrád (1.25 hours), then past Esztergom Basilica (2 hours, Iskola Utca stop) to the Esztergom bus station (more frequent during weekday rush hours). This bus leaves from Budapest's Újpest-Városkapu bus station (at the M3/blue line Metró station of the same name). A different bus takes the **overland shortcut** (skipping Szentendre and Visegrád) to directly connect Budapest and Esztergom (1-2/hour, 1.25 hours, departs from Budapest's Árpád híd station on the M3/blue Metró line). Buses make many stops en route, so you'll need to pay attention for your stop (ask driver or other passengers for help).

By Tour from Budapest: If you want to see all three towns in one day but don't have a car and don't want to shell out for a private driver, a bus tour is the most convenient way to go. All of the companies are about the same (all 3 towns in about 10 hours, including lunch and shopping stops, plus return by boat, for around 20,000 Ft); look for fliers at the Budapest TI or in your hotel's lobby.

Szentendre

Worth ▲▲, the Old Town of Szentendre (SEHN-tehn-dreh, "St. Andrew" in English) rises gently from the Danube, a postcard-pretty village with a twisty Mediterranean street plan filled with Habsburg Baroque houses. Arguably the most "Balkan-feeling" town of Hungary—thanks to the many diverse immigrants who settled the community—Szentendre promises a taste of Hungarian village life without having to stray far from Budapest...

but it sometimes feels like too many other people have had the same idea. Szentendre is where Budapesters bring their wives or girlfriends for that special weekend lunch. The town has a long tradition as an artists' colony, and it still has more than its share of museums and

DAY TRIPS

galleries. It's also packed with corny, gimmicky museums—a few of which (such as the Micro Art collection) are actually worthwhile. But the best plan is this: Venture off the souvenir-choked, tourist-clogged main streets...and you'll soon have the quiet back lanes under colorful Baroque steeples all to yourself.

Orientation to Szentendre

Little Szentendre (pop. 23,000) is easy to navigate. It clusters along a mild incline rising from the Danube, culminating at the main square (Fő tér) at the foot of Church Hill (Templomdomb). From the embankment—where most tourists arrive—various streets lead up to Fő tér, none more touristy than the souvenir gauntlet of Bog-dányi utca.

Tourist Information

The TI is on the riverside, below the main square, where Bercsényi utca hits the promenade. Pick up the good town map, with sights and services well-marked (mid-June-Aug Mon-Fri 9:00-16:30, Sat-Sun 10:00-16:00, less off-season, tel. 26/317-965, www.szen-tendreprogram.hu).

Arrival in Szentendre

By Train or Bus: The combined **train/HÉV and bus station** is at the southern edge of town. To reach the town center from the station (about a 10-minute walk), go through the pedestrian un-derpass at the head of the train tracks. (A handy map of town is posted by the head of the tracks.) The underpass funnels you onto the small Kossuth Lajos utca. After a long block, you'll pass the yellow Pozsarevacska Serbian Orthodox church, then cross the bridge; the TI is on the right, and the main square is three blocks straight ahead.

By Boat: Some boats arrive right near the main square, but most come to a pier about a 15-minute walk north of the center. After you get off the boat, take the first path to your left; stay on it, and it'll lead you straight into town.

By Car: Approaching on road #11 from Budapest, turn right at signs for *Centrum Szentendre* (as you enter the outskirts of town, just before the train station), then park anywhere along the em-bankment road. Look for a blue parking pay station (pay at meter, then put ticket in window—300 Ft/hour), or pay the parking at-tendant, if there is one. If you can't find parking here, continue on to the large bus parking lot near the boat dock. From the embank-ment, it's an easy uphill walk into town; all roads lead to the main square.

A Taste of the Balkans: Szentendre's History

While it's in Hungary, Szentendre is hardly a Hungarian town. In fact, it's a melting pot for all the Balkan peoples—built by Serbs, Greeks, and Dalmatians who were on the lam from the Ottomans.

After the Habsburgs succeeded in pushing the Ottomans out of Hungary in the late 17th century, the Ottomans began to claim lands farther south on the Balkan Peninsula. Especially after their successful 1690 siege of Belgrade, a flood of some 40,000 refugee families sought shelter up the Danube. Many settled here in Szentendre. Most were Serbs, but the diaspora also included Dalmatians (from today's Croatia) and Greeks.

At first, these Balkan trans-plants expected that their settle-ment here would be short-lived. They built temporary houses and shops, following the narrow-al-ley street plan of their homeland (where skinny streets protected pedestrians from the hot sun). They tended to settle in regional enclaves, each of which maintained its heritage and traditions: four neighborhoods representing different regions of Serbia, and two from other ethnic backgrounds (Greeks and Dalmatians). Each of the six neighborhoods had its own church. Add to that the original, medieval Catholic church, and Szentendre has seven very different houses of worship.

While they were waiting to return home, the Balkan refugees supported the Habsburgs (who were facing down the Hungarians in Ferenc Rákóczi's War of Independence). This earned Szenten-dre the favor of the emperor, who rewarded the town with spe-cial trade privileges, including the right to make and sell wine—a tradition still evidenced by the vineyards blanketing the hillsides around town.

Sights in Szentendre

Sightseeing in Szentendre is low-impact. While there are museums and churches to visit, the best plan for most is to simply stroll and people-watch through town and along the elevated Danube river-bank. Head off to the back streets, and you'll be surprised at how quickly you'll find yourself alone with Szentendre.

▲Main Square (Fő Tér)

Szentendre's top sight is the town itself. Start at the main square (Fő tér). Take a close look at the **cross,** erected in 1763 to give

Gradually the Ottomans were forced out of the Balkans. But by this time, the Balkan settlers of Szentendre had decided to stick around. They benefited from the increased trade flowing up the Danube (from lands recently liberated from the Ottomans), and replaced their temporary houses and churches with permanent ones (but still following the same Mediterranean street plan)—mostly in the snazzy, colorful Baroque and Rococo styles popular in Habsburg lands at the time. This explains why so many churches in town look like any old Hungarian Baroque Catholic church from the outside, but have strikingly different Orthodox interiors.

The fortunes of the people here began to change in the 1770s, when the reformist Emperor Josef II took back the special rights Szentendre had enjoyed. The town's prominence declined, as commerce shifted down the Danube to Buda and Pest. The final nail in the coffin came with a phylloxera pest infestation in the 1880s, which devastated the town's vineyards.

By the late 19th century, Szentendre was a semi-ghost town, still populated by the now-poor descendants of those original Balkan immigrants. Artists began to discover the village, and were inspired by its colorful cultural pastiche, unusual-for-Hungary narrow lanes, low rents, and closeness to nature—all within close proximity to the bustling metropolis of Budapest. A "Szentendre School" of artists emerged, putting the town on the map of art history and luring art-loving Budapesters to come for a visit. Today Szentendre has six different museums dedicated to local artists, with many more starving art students who toil away, hoping to fill their own gallery someday. (While art-lovers can browse to their heart's content, the best single museum is dedicated to Margit Kovács.)

Today's Szentendre remains a thriving art colony and tourist town, but also a bedroom community for wealthy Budapesters—near the big city, but still in a tranquil and beautiful setting.

DAY TRIPS

thanks for surviving the plague. Notice the Cyrillic lettering at the monument's base. This is a reminder that in many ways, Szentendre is more of a Serbian town than a Hungarian one (see sidebar).

Face the cross and get oriented: Behind the cross, the square narrows as it curls around Church Hill, with its hilltop Catholic church; just behind that is the Orthodox Cathedral. Through a narrow alley to the left (between the red and yellow houses) is the fun Micro Art

Museum. The street to the left (Dumtsa Jenő utca) leads to the Marzipan Museum and TI. To the right, the church fronting the square is Orthodox (called Blagovestenszka); it's been closed for a lengthy restoration, but might reopen as a museum. And directly behind you (facing the cross) is the ticket office for Szentendre's top art collection, the Margit Kovács Museum. All of these sights are described below.

On or near Fő Tér

Margit Kovács Museum (Kovács Margit Múzeum)—The best of Szentendre's small art museums celebrates the local artist Margit Kovács, highly regarded for her whimsical, primitive, wide-eyed pottery sculptures. Kovács (1902-1977) was the first female Hungarian artist to be accepted as a major talent by critics and by her fellow artists. She came from a close-knit family, and had a religious upbringing, both themes that would appear frequently in her work. The down-to-earth Kovács, who never married, lived with her mother—her best friend and most constructive critic. This collection of her ceramic sculptures, displayed on several floors and explained in English, is organized by theme. You'll see Christian, mythological, and folkloric subjects depicted side by side; even in many biblical scenes, the subjects wear traditional Hungarian clothing. Look for the room of sorrowful statues dating from after her mother's death. On the top floor, in the replica of Kovács' study, find the gnarled tree stump. This tree, which once stood on Budapest's Margaret Island, had been struck by lightning, and its twisted forms inspired Kovács.

Cost and Hours: 1,000 Ft, daily 10:00-18:00, www.pmmi.hu. First buy your tickets at the office at the bottom of Fő tér (at #2-5). Then, you might be able to pass directly into the museum, or you might have to go around the block to get there (jog down Görög utca and take your first right to Vastagh György utca 1).

Micro Art Museum (Mikro Csodák Múzueuma)—This charming and genuinely fascinating "Micro Miracles" collection, while a bit of a tourist trap, is worth a squint. Ukrainian artist Mikola "Howdedoodat" Szjadrisztij has crafted an array of 15 literally microscopic pieces of art—a detailed chessboard on the head of a pin, a pyramid panorama in the eye of a needle, a swallow's nest in half a poppy seed, a golden lock on a single strand of hair, and even a miniscule portrait of Abe Lincoln. You'll go from microscope to microscope, peering at these remarkably detailed sculptures.

Cost and Hours: 500 Ft, English descriptions, daily 10:00-18:00, down the appropriately tiny alley called Török főz at Fő tér 18-19, tel. 26/313-651.

On Dumtsa Jenő Utca

This street, which leads away from Fő tér, is where you'll find the...

Marzipan Museum—This collection (attached to a popular candy and ice-cream store) features two floors of sculptures made of marzipan. Feast your eyes on Muppets, cartoon characters, Russian nesting dolls, an over-the-top wedding cake, a life-size Michael Jackson, and, of course, Hungarian patriotic symbols (the Parliament, the Turul bird, and so on). While fun for kids, this is skippable for adults. Note that there are similar marzipan museums in Eger and on Budapest's Castle Hill; visiting more than one is redundant.

Cost and Hours: Shop—free, upper floor—400 Ft, daily 10:00-18:00, Dumtsa Jenő utca 12, enter from Batthyány utca, tel. 26/311-931, www.szamosmarcipan.hu.

Church Hill Loop

For a representative look at Szentendre's seven churches, visit these two, connected by a loop walk.

• *Begin on the main square (Fő tér). Go a few steps up the street at the top of the square (behind the cross). Just before the white Town Hall, climb the stairs on your right, and work your way up to the hilltop park, called...*

Church Hill (Templomdomb)—This hill-capping perch offers some of the best views over the jumbled, Mediterranean-style roofline of old Szentendre. (See how many steeples you can count in this church-packed town.) Looking down on Fő tér, you can see how the town's market square evolved at the place where its three trade roads converged.

• *The hill's centerpiece is...*

St. John Catholic Church (Keresztelő Szent János)—This was the first house of worship in Szentendre, around which the Balkan settlers later built their own Orthodox churches. If it's open, step into the humble interior (free, sporadic hours, 100 Ft to take pictures). Pay special attention

to the apse, which was colorfully painted by starving artists in the early 20th century.

• *Exiting the church, take the downhill lane toward the red-and-yellow steeple. Find the gate in the wall (along Alkotmány street) to enter the yard around this church. Pay a visit to the...*

▲Belgrade Serbian Orthodox Cathedral (Belgrádi Székesegyház)—This offers perhaps Szentendre's best opportunity to dip into an Orthodox church.

Cost and Hours: 600 Ft, also includes museum; May-Sept Tue-Sun 10:00-18:00, closed Mon; Oct-Nov and March-April Tue-Sun 10:00-16:00, closed Mon; Dec-Feb Fri-Sun 10:00-16:00, closed Mon-Thu; during winter, go to the museum first, then they'll let you into the church.

Visiting the Church: Standing in the gorgeous **church interior,** ponder the Orthodox faith that dominates in most of the Balkan Peninsula (starting just south and east of the Hungarian border). Keep in mind that these churches carry on the earliest traditions of the Christian faith. Notice the lack of pews—worshippers stand through the service, with men separate from women, as a sign of respect before God. The Serbian Orthodox Church uses essentially the same Bible as Catholics, but it's written in the Cyrillic alphabet (which you'll see displayed around many Orthodox churches). Following Old Testament Judeo-Christian tradition, the Bible is kept on the altar behind the iconostasis—the big screen in the middle of the room covered with icons (golden paintings of saints), which separates the material world from the spiritual one.

Orthodox icons are typically not intended to be lifelike. Packed with intricate symbolism, and cast against a shimmering golden background, they're meant to remind viewers of the metaphysical nature of Jesus and the saints rather than their physical form. However, this church, which blends pure Orthodoxy with Catholic traditions of Hungary, features some Baroque-style statues that are unusually fluid and lifelike.

Orthodox services generally involve chanting (a dialogue that goes back and forth between the priest and the congregation), and the church is filled with the evocative aroma of incense. The incense, chanting, icons, and standing up are all intended to heighten the experience of worship. While many Catholic and Protestant services tend to be more of a theoretical and rote consideration of religious issues, Orthodox services are about creating an actual religious experience.

Don't miss the adjacent **museum,** covered by the same ticket. You'll see religious objects, paintings, vestments, and—upstairs—icons, with good English descriptions.

• *For a scenic back-streets stroll before returning to the tourist crush, go*

through the yard around the church, exit through the gate, turn left up the little alley, and then turn right at the T-junction, which takes you through what was the Dalmatian neighborhood to charming Rab-Ráby tér. The lanes between here and the waterfront are among the most appealing and least crowded in Szentendre.

Near Szentendre

Hungarian Open-Air Folk Museum (Szabadtéri Néprajzi Múzeum, a.k.a. Skanzen)—Three miles northwest of Szentendre is an open-air museum featuring examples of traditional Hungarian architecture from all over the country. As with similar museums throughout Europe, these aren't replicas—each building was taken apart at its original location, transported piece by piece, and reassembled here. The museum is huge and spread out, so a thorough visit could take several hours. The admission price includes a map in English, and the museum shop sells a good English guidebook for 1,000 Ft. Because it's so large, the museum is worth visiting only if you can give it the time it deserves. Skip it unless you can arrange your visit to coincide with one of their frequent special-events-laden "festival days" (listed on their website).

Cost and Hours: 1,500 Ft, 100 Ft more on "festival days"; April-Oct Tue-Sun 9:00-17:00, closed Mon; mid-Feb-March Sat-Sun only 10:00-16:00, closed Mon-Fri; closed Nov-mid-Feb; last entry 30 minutes before closing, Sztaravodai út, tel. 26/502-500, www.skanzen.hu.

Getting There: It takes about five minutes to **drive** from Szentendre to Skanzen (parking-500 Ft). **Bus** #7 heads from Szentendre to Skanzen when the museum's open (departs HÉV station on the hour, stops along the river at Szentendre's ferry dock at :10 past; return bus departs Skanzen at :30 past, last return bus departs Skanzen at 17:30; 400 Ft one-way, 600 Ft round-trip). A **taxi** from Szentendre to the museum should cost no more than 2,000 Ft; the TI can call one for you (mobile 0626-311-111).

Eating in Szentendre

Interchangeable, touristy restaurants abound in Szentendre. I enjoy the ambience at **Promenade Vendéglő,** with charming courtyard or indoor seating. They serve Hungarian and Balkan cuisine with take-your-time service (2,000-3,000-Ft main dishes, daily 10:00-22:00, Futó utca 4, along the Dunakorzó embankment, tel. 26/312-626).

DAY TRIPS

Visegrád

Visegrád (VEE-sheh-grahd, Slavic for "High Castle," pop. 1,600) is a small village next to the remains of two major-league castles: a hilltop citadel and a royal riverside palace. While the town itself disappoints many visitors, others enjoy the chance to be close to these two chapters of history.

The Romans were the first to fortify the steep hill overlooking the river. Later, Károly Róbert (Charles Robert), from the French/Neapolitan Anjou dynasty, became Hungary's first non-Magyar king in 1323. He was so unpopular with the nobles in Buda that he had to set up court in Visegrád, where he built a new residential palace down closer to the Danube. (For more on this king, see page 171.) Later, King Mátyás (Matthias) Corvinus—notorious for his penchant for Renaissance excess—ruled from Buda but made Visegrád his summer home, and turned the riverside palace into what some called a "paradise on earth." Matthias knew how to party; during his time here, red-marble fountains flowed with wine. (To commemorate these grand times, the town hosts a corny Renaissance restaurant, with period cookware, food, costumed waitstaff, and live lute music—you can't miss it, by the palace and Hotel Vár.)

Today, both citadel and palace are but a shadow of their former splendor. The citadel was left to crumble after the Habsburg reoccupation of Hungary in 1686, while the palace was covered by a mudslide during the Ottoman occupation, and is still being excavated. The citadel is more interesting, but difficult to reach by public transport. Non-drivers who don't want to make the steep hike to the citadel are probably better off skipping this town.

Orientation to Visegrád

The town of Visegrád is basically a wide spot in the riverside road, squeezed between the hills and the riverbank. At Visegrád's main intersection (coming from Szentendre/Budapest), the crossroads leads to the left through the heart of the village, then hairpins up the hills to the citadel. To the right is the dock for the ferry to Nagymaros (home to the closest train station, called Nagymaros-Visegrád—see "Arrival in Visegrád," next page).

The town has two sights. The less-interesting, riverside Royal Palace is a 15-minute walk downriver (toward Szentendre/Budapest) from the village center. The hilltop citadel, high above the village, is the focal point of a larger recreational area best explored by car.

Tourist Information

The town does not have an official TI. You can get information at the giant **Hotel Visegrád** complex, which caters to passing tour groups at the village crossroads. They answer basic questions, sell maps, and hand out a few free leaflets. In summer, check in at the **Visegrád Tours** travel agency (May-Oct daily 8:00-17:30, generally closed Nov-April, Rév utca 15, tel. 26/398-160, www.visegrad. hu or www.visegradtours.hu); at other times, ask at the hotel reception desk (at the opposite end of the complex, through the unappealing Sirály restaurant).

Arrival in Visegrád

Train travelers arrive across the river at the Nagymaros-Visegrád station (don't get off at the station called simply "Nagymaros"). Walk five minutes to the river and catch the ferry to Visegrád, which lands near the village's main crossroads (hourly, usually in sync with the train, last ferry around 20:30). **Buses** to Visegrád make several stops: the Királyi Palota stop is most convenient for the Royal Palace near the entrance to town, while the Nagymarosi Rév stop is at the main crossroads in the heart of town.

Sights in Visegrád

Visegrád Citadel (Fellegvár)

The remains of Visegrád's hilltop citadel, while nothing too exciting, can be fun to explore. Only a few exhibits have English labels, but headsets allow you to hear information in English. Perhaps best of all, the upper levels of the citadel offer commanding views over the Danube Bend—which, of course, is exactly why they built it here.

Cost and Hours: 1,400 Ft, plus 300 Ft more for waxworks; daily May-Sept 10:00-18:00, mid-March-April and Oct 9:00-17:00, Nov and Jan-mid-March 9:00-16:00, Dec 9:00-15:00, closed in icy winter weather, last entry 30 minutes before closing, tel. 26/398-101, www.parkerdo.hu/visegradi_var.

Getting There: To **drive** to the citadel, follow *Fellegvár* signs down the village's main street and up into the hills (parking-300 Ft). Otherwise, you have two options: Get a map at Visegrád Tours/Hotel and **hike** 45 steep minutes up from the village center; or take the **taxi service** misleadingly called "City Bus." This minivan trip costs 2,600 Ft one-way, no matter how many people ride along (ask at Visegrád Tours/Hotel, or call 26/397-372, www.city-bus.hu).

Visiting the Castle: Buy your ticket and hike up the path toward the castle entry. On the way up, you can pay extra to try your hand with a bow and arrow, or pose with a bird of prey perched on your arm.

Belly up to the viewpoint for sweeping **Danube Bend views.** From here, you can see that the Danube actually does a double-bend—a smaller one (upstream), then a bigger one (downstream)—creating an S-shaped path before settling into its southward groove. It's easy to understand why the Danube, constricted between mountains, is forced to bend here. The river narrows as it passes through this gorge, then widens again below the castle, depositing sediment that becomes the islands just downstream. Just upstream from Visegrád, the strange half-lake on the riverbank is all that's left of an aborted communist-era dam project to tame the river.

Climb up to the top of the complex. In the **castle museum,** you'll see a replica of the Hungarian crown. The real one (now safely stored under the Parliament dome in Budapest) was actually kept here, off and on, for some 200 years, when this was Hungary's main castle.

Deeper into the complex, you reach the **waxworks** *(panoptikum).* Here you can pay 300 Ft extra to see a scene from an important medieval banquet: In 1335, as Habsburg Austria was rising to the west, the kings of Hungary, Poland, and Bohemia converged here to strategize against this new threat. Centuries later, history repeated itself: In February of 1991, after the fall of the Iron Curtain, the heads of state of basically the same nations—Hungary, Poland, and Czechoslovakia—once again came together here, this time to compare notes about Westernization. To this day, Hungary, Poland, the Czech Republic, and Slovakia are still sometimes referred to collectively as the "Visegrád countries."

Continue up to the very top of the complex, the **inner castle.** Here you'll find a hunting exhibit (dioramas with piles of stuffed animals) and the armory (with a few weapons, and coats of arms of knights). To conquer the castle, climb up to the very top tower, where you can scramble along the ramparts.

Near the Citadel: Around the citadel is a recreational area that includes restaurants, a picnic area, a luge and toboggan run, a network of hiking paths, a Waldorf school, and a children's nature-education center and campground.

Eating near the Citadel: Eating options in Visegrád are limited; most restaurants are big operations catering to tour groups. By the luge run (a lengthy-but-doable walk from the citadel), the **Nagyvillám restaurant** is elegant, with breathtaking views from the best tables (2,000-3,300-Ft main dishes, Mon-Thu 12:00-18:00, Fri-Sun 12:00-22:00, tel. 26/398-070). Only drivers can reach the **picnic area** (called Telgárthy-rét), in a shady valley with paths and waterfalls.

Royal Palace (Király Palota)

Under King Matthias Corvinus, this riverside ruin was one of Europe's most elaborate Renaissance palaces. During the Ottoman occupation, it was deserted and eventually buried by a mudslide. For generations, the palace's existence faded into legend, so its rediscovery in 1934 was a surprise. Today, the partially excavated remains are tourable, with sparse English descriptions.

The palace courtyard, decorated with a red-marble fountain, evokes its Renaissance glory days. Upstairs, look for the giant green ceramic stoves, and at the top level, find the famous canopied fountain with lions. This "Hercules Fountain"—pictured on the back of the 1,000-Ft note—once had wine spouting from the lions' mouths, which Matthias used to ply visiting dignitaries to get the best results.

The small Solomon's Tower up the hill from the Royal Palace (not worth the 700-Ft admission) once held a vampire... sort of. Vlad the Impaler, a nobleman who terrorized villagers in Transylvania (back when it was part of Hungary), was arrested and imprisoned here during the time of Matthias. Centuries later, Bram Stoker found inspiration in Vlad's story while writing his novel *Dracula*.

Cost and Hours: 1,100 Ft, Tue-Sun 9:00-17:00, closed Mon, tel. 26/398-026, www.visegradmuzeum.hu.

Esztergom

Esztergom (EHS-tehr-gohm, pop. 29,000) is an unassuming town with a big Suzuki factory. You'd never guess it was the first capital of Hungary—until you see the towering 19th-century Esztergom Basilica, built on the site where István (Stephen) I, Hungary's first Christian king, was crowned in A.D. 1000.

Arrival in Esztergom

Esztergom's **boat dock** is more convenient to the basilica than the bus or train stations are (can't miss the basilica as you disembark—hike on up).

If arriving on the **riverside bus** from Visegrád, get off by the basilica (Iskola Utca stop)—not at the bus station.

If you're coming by **train,** or on the **overland bus** from Budapest, you're in for a longer walk. To reach the basilica on foot from the train station, allow at least 45 minutes. Continue in the same direction as the train tracks, and when the street forks, go straight along the residential Ady Endre utca. After a few minutes, you'll pass the bus station, from which it's 30 minutes farther to the basilica. Local buses run between the train station and the basilica roughly hourly. On Wednesdays and Fridays, an open-air market enlivens the street between the bus station and the center.

Sights in Esztergom

▲▲Esztergom Basilica (Esztergomi Bazilika)

This basilica, on the site of a cathedral founded by Hungary's beloved St. István, commemorates Hungary's entry into the fold of Western Christendom. St. Ist-

ván was born in Esztergom, and on Christmas Day in the year 1000—shortly after marrying the daughter of the king of Bavaria and accepting Christianity—he was crowned here by a representative of the pope (for more on St. István, see page 211). Centuries later, after Esztergom had been retaken from the retreating Ottomans, the Hungarians wanted to build a "small Vatican" complex to celebrate the Hungarian

Cardinal József Mindszenty
(1892-1975)

József Mindszenty was a Hungarian priest who rose through the ranks to become Archbishop of Esztergom, cardinal, and head of the Hungarian Catholic Church. This outspoken cleric was arrested several times, by very different regimes: in 1919 for defying the early Hungarian communist leader Béla Kun; during World War II, for criticizing the Arrow Cross's deportation of Jews; and again in 1948, for speaking out against the communist regime.

Upon his arrest in 1948, Mindszenty was relentlessly tortured to extract a confession. He became the subject of a high-profile "show trial," and was convicted to life in prison. (An enraged Pope Pius XII excommunicated those who had tried and convicted Mindszenty.) Mindszenty's plight was dramatized in the 1955 film *The Prisoner,* starring Alec Guinness as the cardinal.

During the 1956 Uprising, Mindszenty was freed for a brief time. But when the uprising was put down with violence, he sought refuge in the US Embassy on Budapest's Szabadság tér—where he stayed for 15 years, unable to leave for fear of being recaptured. Many Catholic Americans who grew up during this time remember praying for Cardinal Mindszenty every day when they were kids. In 1971, he agreed to step down from his position, then fled to Austria.

On his deathbed, in 1975, Mindszenty said that he did not want his body returned to Hungary as long as there was a single Russian soldier still stationed there. As the Iron Curtain was falling in 1989, Mindszenty emerged as an important hero to post-communist Hungarians, who wanted to bring his remains back to his homeland. But Mindszenty's secretary, in accordance with the cardinal's final wishes, literally locked himself to the coffin—refusing to let the body be transported as long as any Soviet soldier remained in Hungary. In May of 1991, when only a few Russians were still in Hungary, Mindszenty's remains were finally brought to the crypt in the Esztergom Basilica.

DAY TRIPS

Catholic Church and their triumphant return to the region. The Habsburgs who controlled the area at the time (and were also good Catholics) agreed, but did not want to be upstaged, so progress was sluggish. The Neoclassical basilica was erected slowly between 1820 and 1869, on top of the remains of a ruined hilltop castle. With a 330-foot-tall dome, this is the tallest building in Hungary.

Cost and Hours: Basilica—free, daily April-Oct 8:00-18:00, Nov-March 8:00-16:00. Tower climb—600 Ft, same hours as basilica. Crypt—200 Ft, daily March-Oct 9:00-16:30, Nov-Feb 10:00-15:30. Treasury—800 Ft; March-Oct daily 9:00-16:30;

Nov-mid-Jan Tue-Sun 10:00-15:30, closed Mon; closed mid-Jan-Feb, tel. 33/402-354, www.bazilika-esztergom.hu.

Ø Self-Guided Tour: Approaching the church is like walking toward a mountain—it gets bigger and bigger, yet you never quite reach it. In front of the church is a **statue of Mary,** the "Head, Mother, and Patron" of the Hungarian Church.

Enter through the side door (on the left as you face the front of the basilica, under the arch). In the foyer, the stairway leading down to the right takes you to the **crypt.** This frigid space, with tree-trunk columns, culminates at the tomb of Cardinal József Mindszenty, revered and persecuted for standing up to the communist government (see sidebar on previous page). Also in the main chamber, look for original tombstones of 15th-century archbishops.

Back upstairs in the foyer, a stairway leads up to the church **tower,** which has fine views.

Enter the cavernous **nave.** Take in the enormity of the third-biggest church in Europe (by square footage). The lack of supporting pillars in the center of the church further exaggerates its vastness. This space was consecrated in 1856—before the entire building was finished—at a Mass with music composed by Franz Liszt.

As you face the altar, find the chapel on the left before the transept. This Renaissance **Bakócz Chapel,** part of an earlier church that stood here, predates the basilica by 350 years. It was commissioned by the archbishop during King Matthias Corvinus' reign. The archbishop imported Italian marble-workers to create a fitting space to house his remains. Note the typically Renaissance red marble—the same marble that decorates Matthias' palace at Visegrád. When the basilica was built, the chapel was disassembled into 1,600 pieces and rebuilt inside the new structure. The heads around the chapel's altar were defaced by the Ottomans, who, as Muslims, believed that only God—not sculptors—can create man.

Continue to the **transept.** On the right transept wall, St. István offers the Hungarian crown to Mary—seemingly via an angelic DHL courier. There's a depiction of this very church towering on the horizon. Mary is particularly important to Hungarians, because István—the first Christian king of Hungary—had no surviving male heir, so he appealed to Mary for help. (Eventually one of István's cousins, András I, took the crown and managed to keep his kingdom in the fold of Christianity.)

And one more tour-guide factoid: Above the **altar** is what's reputed to be the biggest single-canvas oil painting in the world. (It's of the Assumption, by Michelangelo Grigoletti.)

Finish your visit with the **treasury,** to the right of the main altar (do this last, as you'll exit outside the building; no English descriptions—pick up the illustrated listing at the entrance or, if they're out, at the gift shop at the end). Head up the spiral staircase to view the impressive collection. After a display of vestments, you'll wander a long hall tracing the evolution of ecclesiastical art styles: Gothic, Renaissance, Baroque, Rococo, and Modern. In the first (Gothic) section, find the giant drinking horns, used by kings at royal feasts. The second (Renaissance) section shows off some intricately decorated chalices. A close look at the vestments here shows that they're embroidered with 3-D scenes, and slathered with gold and pearls. In the case on the wall, find the collection's prized possession: an incredibly ornate example of Christ on the cross—but Jesus here bears an unmistakable likeness to King Matthias Corvinus. In the third (Baroque) and fourth (Rococo) sections, notice things getting frilly—and bigger and bigger, as the church got more money. The fifth (Modern) section displays an array of kissable bishop rings.

The exit takes you out to a **Danube-view terrace.** For the best river-bend view, walk a hundred yards or so downstream (right) to the modern statue of St. István. It shows Hungary's favorite saint being crowned by the local bishop after converting to Christianity; St. István symbolically holds up the arches of the Hungarian Church. (Until this statue was built in 2003, this was *the* choice spot for Esztergom teens to kiss.) Between the statue and the river, you can see the ruins of an Ottoman bath and the evocative stub of a ruined minaret, with its spiral staircase exposed and going nowhere.

That's **Štúrovo, Slovakia,** across the river, connected to Hungary by the Mária Valéria Bridge—destroyed in World War II and rebuilt only a decade ago. Before its reconstruction, no bridges spanned the Danube between Budapest and Bratislava. When they rebuilt the bridge in 2001, they included border checkpoints; less than seven years later, these became obsolete, when in December of 2007 Hungary and Slovakia—fellow members of the open-borders Schengen Agreement—did away with passport checks. If you have time, you can walk or drive across the bridge to Slovakia (for the best views back to this basilica) without even having to stop or flash your passport.

Near the Basilica

This hilltop was once heavily fortified, and some ruins of its castle survive—now part of the **Castle Museum** next to the basilica (opposite side from the István statue). In 2007, restorers discovered a fresco of the four virtues, likely by Sandro Botticelli. The complex also includes the chapel where St. István was supposedly born. Unfortunately, both of these areas are closed for restoration (work has stalled due to lack of funding). For now, all there is to see is lots of dusty old exhibits about arcane Hungarian history, from the Stone Age through the Ottoman period (500-Ft "walking ticket" to tour the grounds, 1,800-Ft for English tour—4/day, April-Oct Tue-Sun 10:00-18:00, Nov-March Tue-Sun 10:00-16:00, closed Mon year-round, www.mnmvarmuzeuma.hu).

Eating in Esztergom

A few restaurants cluster near the basilica (including one built into the fortifications underneath it), but these cater to tour groups and serve mediocre food. It's more interesting to venture down the hill to the **Víziváros** ("Water Town") neighborhood on the riverbank below the basilica. This area has a pleasant, old-town ambience and some fine local-style eateries. You can either walk down on the path from the basilica, or (in summer) catch a handy tourist train for 500 Ft.

Esztergom Connections

By Bus

For connections, see "Getting Around the Danube Bend" on page 327. When choosing between the riverside bus and the direct overland bus, note that the overland bus—while faster and offering different scenery—departs much farther from the basilica than the riverside bus.

Route Tips for Drivers: Returning from Esztergom to Budapest

The easiest choice is to retrace your route on road #11 around the Bend to Budapest. But to save substantial time and see different scenery, I prefer "cutting the Bend" and taking a shortcut through the Pilis hills (takes just over an hour total, depending on traffic).

To Cut the Bend: From the basilica in Esztergom, continue along the main road #11 (away from Budapest) to the roundabout with the round, yellow, Neoclassical church (built as a sort of practice before they started on the basilica). Here you can choose your exit: If you exit toward **Budapest/Dorog,** it'll take you back on road #11 for a while, then route you onto the busier road #10 (which can have heavy traffic—especially trucks—on weekdays). Better yet, if you head for **Dobogókő,** you'll follow a twistier but faster route via the town of Pilisszentkereszt to Budapest. After about 30 minutes on this road, in the town of Pomáz, follow signs to road #11 to the left, then turn right toward Budapest at the next fork to join road #11 into the city. (Don't follow signs at the Pomáz intersection for Budapest, which takes you along a more heavily trafficked road.)

EGER

Eger (EH-gehr) is a county-seat town in northern Hungary, with about 60,000 people and a thriving teacher-training college. While many travelers have never heard of Eger, among Hungarians, the town has various claims to fame. It's a bishopric whose powerful bishops have graced it with gorgeous churches. It has some of the best and most beloved spas in this hot-water crazy country (including the excellent Salt Hill Thermal Spa in the nearby countryside). And, perhaps most of all, Eger makes Hungarians proud as the town that, against all odds, successfully held off the Ottoman advance into Europe in 1552. This stirring history makes Eger the mecca of Hungarian school field trips. If the town is known internationally for anything, it's for the surrounding wine region (its best-known red wine is Bull's Blood, or Egri Bikavér).

And yet, refreshingly, enchanting Eger remains mostly off the tourist trail. Egerites go about their daily routines amidst lovely Baroque buildings, watched over by one of Hungary's most important castles. Everything in Eger is painted with vibrant colors, and even the communist apartment blocks seem quaint. The sights are few but fun, the ambi-ence is great, and strolling is a must. It all comes together to make Eger an ideal introduction to small-town Hungary.

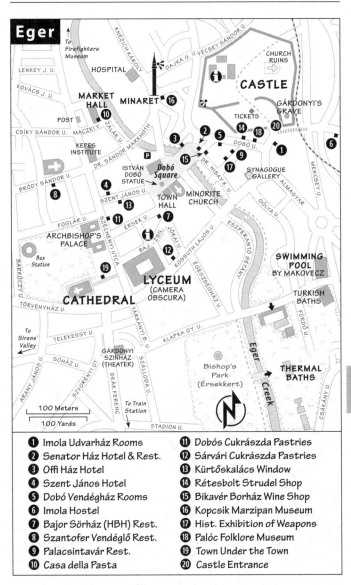

Eger

To Firefighters Museum

LENKEY J. U.
KOVÁCS J. U.
HOSPITAL
KNEZICH KÁROLY
DAJKA G. U. VÉCSEY SÁNDOR U.
CHURCH RUINS
CASTLE
MARKET HALL
MINARET ❶❻
GÁRDONYI'S GRAVE
POST
TICKETS
CSÍKY SÁNDOR U.
MACZKI V.
ZALÁR U.
❶⓪
KEPES INSTITUTE
DR. SÁNDOR MARKHOTH
❸
❷❺
DOBÓ U.
❶❹ ❶❽ ⓶⓪
❶
❻
P
❶❺
DR. HIBAY K. U.
❾
BRÓDY SÁNDOR U.
ISTVÁN DOBÓ STATUE
Dobó Square
SYNAGOGUE GALLERY
❶❼
MENCSEY U.
ALMAGYAR
❽
❹
SZENT JÁNOS U.
TOWN HALL
MINORITE CHURCH
ESZPERANTÓ U.
GÖLYA U.
FOGLÁR U.
SZÉCHENYI UTCA
❶❶
ÉRSEK U.
❶❸
❼
BAJ. ZSIL.
JÓKAI U.
KOSSUTH LAJOS U.
ESZPERANTÓ SÉTÁNY
ARCHBISHOP'S PALACE
Bus Station
BARKÓCZY U.
❶❾
❶❷
LYCEUM (CAMERA OBSCURA)
EGERSZEGHÁZ U.
SWIMMING POOL BY MAKOVECZ
TURKISH BATHS
CATHEDRAL
TÖRVÉNYHÁZ U.
Eger Creek
FÜRDŐ U.
To Sirens' Valley
TELEKESSY U.
SÓHÁZ U.
GÁRDONYI SZÍNHÁZ (THEATER)
DEÁK FERENC
SZÁLLODA U.
TÁRKÁNYI B. U.
KLAPKA GY. U.
Bishop's Park (Érsekkert)
THERMAL BATHS
ARANY JÁNOS U.
SZIVÓRÁNYI ÚT
To Train Station
STADION U.
N
CSÁKÁNY U.

100 Meters
100 Yards

EGER

❶ Imola Udvarház Rooms
❷ Senator Ház Hotel & Rest.
❸ Offi Ház Hotel
❹ Szent János Hotel
❺ Dobó Vendégház Rooms
❻ Imola Hostel
❼ Bajor Sörház (HBH) Rest.
❽ Szantofer Vendéglő Rest.
❾ Palacsintavár Rest.
❿ Casa della Pasta
⓫ Dobós Cukrászda Pastries
⓬ Sárvári Cukrászda Pastries
⓭ Kürtőskalács Window
⓮ Rétesbolt Strudel Shop
⓯ Bikavér Borház Wine Shop
⓰ Kopcsik Marzipan Museum
⓱ Hist. Exhibition of Weapons
⓲ Palóc Folklore Museum
⓳ Town Under the Town
⓴ Castle Entrance

Planning Your Time

Mellow Eger is a fine side-trip from Budapest. It's doable round-trip in a single day (about two hours by train or bus each way), but it's much more satisfying and relaxing to spend the night.

A perfect day in Eger begins with a browse through the very local-feeling market and a low-key ramble on the castle ramparts. Then head to the college building called the Lyceum to visit the library and astronomy museum, and climb up to the thrillingly low-tech camera obscura. Take in the midday organ concert in the cathedral across the street from the Lyceum (mid-May-mid-Oct only). In the afternoon, unwind on the square or, better yet, at a thermal bath (in Eger, or at the Salt Hill Thermal Spa in nearby Egerszalók). If you need more to do, consider a drive into the countryside (including visits to local vintners—get details at TI). Round out your day with dinner on Little Dobó Square, or a visit to Eger's touristy wine caves in the Sirens' Valley.

In July and August (when Hungarians prefer to go to Lake Balaton), Eger is busy with international visitors; in September and October, around the wine harvest, most of the tourists are Hungarians.

Orientation to Eger

Eger Castle sits at the top of the town, hovering over Dobó Square (Dobó István tér). This main square is divided in half by Eger Creek, which bisects the town. Two blocks west of Dobó Square is the main pedestrian drag, Széchenyi utca, where you'll find the Lyceum and the cathedral. A few blocks due south from the castle (along Eger Creek) are Eger's various spas and baths.

Tourist Information

Eger's TI (TourInform) offers a free brochure and town map, as well as piles of other brochures about the city and region. They can help you find a room and are eager to answer any questions you have (mid-June-mid-Sept Mon-Fri 9:00-18:00, Sat-Sun 9:00-13:00; mid-Sept-mid-June Mon-Fri 9:00-17:00, Sat 9:00-13:00, closed Sun; Bajcsy-Zsilinszky utca 9, tel. 36/517-715, www.eger.hu or www.mheger.hu).

Arrival in Eger

By Train: Eger's tiny train station is a 20-minute walk south of the center. The baggage-deposit desk is out along the platform by track 1, between the WCs (500 Ft/day, daily 7:00-19:00, attendant often waits in the adjacent *büfé*). For those in need of Hungarian cash, the closest ATM is at the Spar grocery store just up the street (turn left out of station, walk about 100 yards, and look for red-and-white supermarket on your right; the ATM is next to the main door, around front).

Taxis generally wait out front to take new arrivals into town (1,000-1,200 Ft). Even in little Eger, it's always best to take a taxi with a company name and number posted.

To catch the **bus** toward the center, go a block straight out of the station. Buses #11, #12, and #14 cut about 10 minutes off the walk into town (300 Ft if you buy ticket from driver; 240 Ft if you buy it at the train station newsstand facing track 1—ask for *helyijárat buszjegy*). Get off the bus when you reach the big yellow cathedral.

To **walk** all the way, leave the station straight ahead, walk one block, take the hard right turn with the road, and then continue straight (on busy Deák Ferenc utca) about 10 minutes until you run into the cathedral. With your back to the cathedral entry, the main square is two blocks ahead of you, then a block to the left.

By Car: In this small town, most hotels will provide parking or help you find a lot. For a short visit, the most central lot is behind the department store on Dobó Square.

By Plane: Low-impact Eger is a pleasant place to get over jet lag. For tips on coming to Eger from Budapest's airport, see page 302.

Getting Around Eger

Everything of interest in Eger is within walking distance. But a taxi can be helpful to reach outlying sights, including the Sirens' Valley wine caves and the Salt Hill Thermal Spa in Egerszalók (taxi meter starts at 250 Ft, then around 250 Ft/km; try City Taxi, tel. 36/555-555 or toll-free tel. 0680-622-622).

Helpful Hints

Phoning: Confusingly, Hungary's country code is the same as Eger's city code (36). This means that if you're calling from another country, you'll have to dial 36 twice. For example, to call my favorite Eger hotel from the US, I'd dial 011-36-36-411-711.

Blue Monday: Note that the castle museums and the Lyceum are closed on Mondays. But you can still visit the cathedral (and enjoy its organ concert), swim in the thermal bath, explore the market, see the castle grounds, and enjoy the local wine.

Organ Concert: Daily from mid-May to mid-October, Hungary's second-biggest organ booms out a glorious 30-minute concert in the cathedral (800 Ft, Mon-Sat at 11:30, Sun at 12:45).

Internet Access: The town's many Internet cafés come and go—ask the TI or your hotelier for current options.

Local Guide: The TI can arrange a private guide to give you a tour of town (8,000 Ft/hour, arrange through TI, tel. 36/517-715, eger@tourinform.hu).

Tourist Train: A variety of hokey little tourist trains leave the main square regularly (at least at the top of each hour, and often other times when it's busy). These trains do a circuit around town, then head out to the Sirens' Valley wine caves (700 Ft, 50-minute trip).

Sights in Eger

▲▲Dobó Square (Dobó István Tér)

Dobó Square is the heart of Eger. In most towns this striking, the main square is packed with postcard stalls and other tourist traps. Refreshingly, Eger's square seems mostly packed with Egerites. Ringed by pretty Baroque buildings, decorated with

vivid sculptures depicting the city's noble past, and watched over by Eger's historic castle, this square is one of the most pleasant spots in Hungary.

The statue in the middle is **István Dobó** (EESHT-vahn DOH-boh), the square's namesake and Eger's greatest hero, who defended the city—and all of Hungary—from an Ottoman invasion in 1552 (see his story in the sidebar). Next to Dobó is his cocommander, István Mekcsey. And right at their side is one of the brave women of Eger—depicted here throwing a pot down onto the attackers.

Dominating the square is the exquisitely photogenic pink **Minorite Church**—often said to be the most beautiful Baroque church in Hungary. The shabby interior is

less interesting, but has some appealing details (free entry, daily 9:30-17:30). Notice that each of the hand-carved wooden pews has a different motif. Pay close attention to the side altars that flank the nave: The first set (left and right) are 3-D illustrations, painted to replicate the wood altars that burned in a fire; the next set are real. And looking up at the faded ceiling frescoes, you'll see (in the second one from the entrance) the church's patron: St. Anthony of Padua, who's preaching God's word to the fishes after the townspeople refused to hear him.

Next to the Minorite Church is the Town Hall, then an old-fashioned pharmacy. The **monument** in front of the Town Hall also commemorates the 1552 defense of Eger: one Egerite against two Ottoman soldiers, reminding us of the townspeople's bravery despite the odds.

Use the square to orient yourself to the town. Behind the statue of Dobó is a bridge over the stream that bisects the city. Just before you reach that bridge, look to the left and you'll see the northernmost Ottoman **minaret** in Europe—once part of a mosque, it's

István Dobó and the Siege of Eger

In the 16th century, Ottoman invaders swept into Hungary. They easily defeated a Hungarian army—in just two hours—at the Battle of Mohács in 1526. When Buda and Pest fell to the Ottomans in 1541, all of Europe looked to Eger as the last line of defense. István Dobó and his second-in-command, István Mekcsey, were put in charge of Eger's forces. They prepared the castle (which still overlooks the square) for a siege and waited.

On September 11, 1552—after a summer spent conquering more than 30 other Hungarian fortresses on their march northward—40,000 Ottomans arrived in Eger. Only about 2,000 Egerites (soldiers, their wives, and their children) remained to protect their town. The Ottomans expected an easy victory, but the siege dragged on for 39 days. Eger's soldiers fought valiantly, and the women of Eger also joined the fray, pouring hot tar down on the Ottomans...everyone pitched in. A Hungarian officer named Gergely Bornemissza, sent to reinforce the people of Eger, startled the Ottomans with all manner of clever and deadly explosives. One of his brilliant inventions was a "fire wheel"—a barrel of gunpowder studded with smaller jars of explosives, which they'd light and send rolling downhill to wreak havoc until the final, deadly explosion. Ultimately, the Ottomans left in shame, Eger was saved, and Dobó was a national hero.

The unfortunate epilogue: The Ottomans came back in 1596 and, this time, succeeded in conquering an Eger Castle guarded by unmotivated mercenaries. The Ottomans sacked the town and then controlled the region for close to a century.

In 1897, a castle archaeologist named Géza Gárdonyi moved from Budapest to Eger, where tales of the siege captured his imagination. Gárdonyi wrote a book about István Dobó and the 1552 Siege of Eger called *Egri Csillagok* ("Stars of Eger," translated into English as *Eclipse of the Crescent Moon*, available at local bookstores and souvenir stands). The book—a favorite of many Hungarians—is taught in schools, keeping the legend of Eger's heroes alive today.

now a tourist attraction. Across the bridge is the charming **Little Dobó Square** (Kis-Dobó tér), home to the town's best hotels, its outdoor dining zone, and a handy and atmospheric opportunity to sample local wines at the Bikavér Borház wine shop (see page 363). Hovering above Little Dobó Square is Eger Castle; to get there, hang a right at the Senator Ház Hotel and go up Dobó utca. (All of these places are described later in more detail.)

Now face in the opposite direction, with the castle at your back. On your right is a handy department store (with an ATM by the door). At the bottom end of this square, various pedestrian shopping lanes lead straight ahead two short blocks to Eger's main "walking street," Széchenyi utca (with the cathedral and the Lyceum at its left end). To reach the TI, jog left at the end of this square, then right onto Bajcsy-Zsilinszky utca (TI one block ahead on right). The market hall is in the opposite direction: Leave Dobó Square to the right (on Zalár József utca, with department store on your right-hand side; you'll see the market hall on the left).

▲Dobó Utca

This street, which leads to the entrance of the castle (up the street to the right of Senator Ház Hotel), is lined with colorful shops and attractions. You'll encounter these sights in the following order as you head from the main square toward the castle:

The **antique shop** (Régiségbolt, at #24) is worth a peek. If musty old things from the communist era—a painting of Lenin or a classic old radio—are cluttering your attic, you can sell them here.

The **wine-tasting courtyard** (#18) features a different local winery each week from May through October. Pop into the brightly lit, vaulted tasting room in the back to try a glass (300-600 Ft/glass).

A few steps down Fazola Henrik (on the right), the **Historical Exhibition of Weapons** (Törteni Tárház) features centuries of Eger armaments: clubs, rifles, and everything in between (400 Ft, Tue-Sun 10:00-18:00 except in winter 12:00-17:00, closed Mon, 300-Ft booklet labels weapons in English, 1,000-Ft English book gives a full weapon-by-weapon tour).

The **Palóc Folklore Museum** (#12) displays a handful of traditional tools, textiles, ceramics, costumes, and pieces of furniture (200 Ft, no English information, sporadically open—likely May-Sept Tue-Sun 11:00-15:00, closed Mon and Oct-April).

The **Rétesbolt** strudel shop (#10) offers a delightful chance to watch them make mouthwatering strudel...and then eat one (360 Ft, daily 10:00-17:00).

▲Eger Castle (Egri Vár)

The great St. István—Hungary's first Christian king—founded a church on this hill a thousand years ago. The church was destroyed by Tatars in the 13th century, and this fortress was built to repel another attack. Most importantly, this castle is Hungary's Alamo, where István Dobó defended Eger from the Ottomans

EGER

in 1552—as depicted in the relief just outside the entry gate. These days, it's usually crawling with schoolchildren on field trips from all over the country. Every Hungarian sixth grader reads and enjoys the thrilling *Eclipse of the Crescent Moon*, which explains the heroic siege of Eger. While the exhibits are humble and the history is obscure to foreign visitors, a visit here provides a fun "king of the castle" stroll along the ramparts with fine views over Eger's rooftops.

Cost: While an 800-Ft "walking ticket" gets you into the castle grounds only, the 1,400-Ft ticket includes the big castle sights (history museum, art gallery, casements tour—see next). At times when the museums are closed (see hours below) and only the casements tour is open, the ticket is reduced to 1,100 Ft—but since the tour is only in Hungarian, on those days you might as well just get a walking ticket.

Tours: The underground casements and Heroes' Hall are only accessible by a one-hour tour in Hungarian (included in ticket price, tours depart frequently in summer, sporadically off-season).

Hours: Castle grounds—April-Aug daily 8:00-20:00, Sept until 19:00, March and Oct until 18:00, Nov-Feb until 17:00; castle museums—April-Oct Tue-Sun 10:00-17:00, Nov-March Tue-Sun 10:00-16:00, closed Mon year-round. General castle info: tel. 36/312-744, www.egrivar.hu.

Getting There: To reach the castle from Dobó Square, cross the bridge toward Senator Ház Hotel, then jog right around the hotel, turning right onto Dobó utca (with its own set of attractions, described earlier). Take this street a few blocks until it swings down to the right; the ramp up to the castle is across the little park to your left.

Visiting the Castle: For those of us who didn't grow up hearing the legend of István Dobó, the complex is hard to appreciate, and English information is sparse. Most visitors find that the most rewarding plan is to stroll up, wander around the grounds, and enjoy the view overlooking the town (find the minaret and other landmarks).

The castle grounds feature two small museums, which are both in the pink buildings surrounding the central courtyard. The **history museum** (in the top floor of the main building of the garrison) is the best of its kind in town, with lots of artifacts and good English descriptions. The **picture gallery** (top floor of building to the left as you enter the courtyard) is worth a few minutes, with paintings giving you a look at traditional life in Hungary.

On the **grounds,** you'll see the remains of a once-grand cathedral and a smaller rotunda dating from the days of St. István (10th or 11th century; at the far-right corner as you enter). The underground **casements** (tunnels through the castle walls, which include the Heroes' Hall with the symbolic grave of István Dobó) are accessible only by guided tour (explained earlier), but you can dip into the **dungeon** anytime with the museum ticket.

Other Castle Sights: The castle hosts a few privately run exhibits (with sporadic hours and prices).

The **waxworks,** or "Panoptikum" (500 Ft, daily April-Oct 9:00-17:00, Nov-March 9:00-16:00, along the wall on the left as you enter), while kind of silly, is fun for kids or those who never really grew up. Think of it as a very low-tech, walk-through *Ottomans of the Caribbean*. You'll see a handful of eerily realistic heroes and villains from the siege of Eger (including István Dobó himself and the leader of the Ottomans sitting in his colorful tent). Notice the exaggerated Central Asian features of the Egerites—a reminder that the Magyars were more Asian than European. A visit to the waxworks lets you scramble through a segment of the tunnels that run inside the castle walls (a plus since it's not really worth it to wait around through the similar, Hungarian-language casements tour).

Additional sights include an **archery** exhibit (look for archers just inside inner gate in summer, and pay them for the chance to shoot old-fashioned bows and crossbows); the **mint,** with a display of former currencies and a chance to make your own souvenir (in the cellar of the Gothic palace); and **temporary exhibits** in the pink round tower.

On Széchenyi Utca

▲▲Lyceum (Líceum)—In the mid-18th century, Bishop Károly Eszterházy wanted a university in Eger, but Habsburg Emperor Josef II refused to allow it. So instead, Eszterházy built the most impressive teacher-training college on the planet, and stocked it with the best books and astronomical equipment that money could buy. The

Lyceum still trains local teachers (enrollment: about 2,000). The halls of the Lyceum are also roamed by tourists who have come to visit its classic old library, and its astronomy museum, with a fascinating camera obscura. The library and museum are tucked away

in the big, confusing building; a flier that comes with your ticket helps you find your way.

Cost and Hours: Library-800 Ft, museum-1,000 Ft; both open April-Sept daily 9:30-15:30; Oct-March Tue-Sun 9:30-15:30, closed Mon; Eszterházy tér 1, at south end of Széchenyi utca at intersection with Kossuth utca, enter through main door across from cathedral and buy tickets just inside and to the left.

Visiting the Lyceum: First, visit the old-fashioned **library** one floor up (from the main entry hall, cut through the middle of the courtyard, go up the stairs to the next floor, and look for room 223, marked *Bibliothek*—it's on the right side of the complex as you face it from the entrance). This library houses 60,000 books (here and in the two adjoining rooms, with several stacked two deep). Dr. Erzsébet Löffler and her staff have spent the last decade cataloging these books. This is no easy task, since they're in over 30 languages—from Thai to Tagalog—and are shelved according to size, rather than topic. Only one percent of the books are in Hungarian—but half of them are in Latin. The ticket-taker can give you an English information sheet highlighting the collection's most prized pieces. The shelves are adorned with golden seals depicting some of the great minds of science, philosophy, and religion. Marvel at the gorgeous ceiling fresco, dating from 1778. To thank the patron of this museum, say *köszönöm* to the guy in the second row up, to the right of the podium (above the entry door, second from left, not wearing a hat)—that's Bishop Károly Eszterházy.

Turn right as you leave the library to find the staircase that leads up the **Astronomical Tower** (*Varázstorony*, follow signs several flights up) to the **Astronomical Museum.** Some dusty old stargazing instruments occupy one room, as well as a meridian line in the floor (a dot of sunlight dances along this line each day around noon). Across the hall is a fun, interactive **magic room,** where you can try out scientific experiments—such as using air pressure to make a ball levitate or sending a mini "hot-air balloon" up to the ceiling.

A few more flights up is the Lyceum's treasured **camera obscura**—one of just two originals surviving in Europe (the other is in Edinburgh). You'll enter a dark room around a big, bowl-like canvas, and the guide will fly you around the streets of Eger (presentations about 2/hour, maybe more when busy). Fun as it is today, this camera must have astonished viewers when it was built in 1776—well before anyone had seen "moving pictures." It's a bit of a huff to get up here (nine flights of stairs, 302 steps)—but the camera obscura, and the actual view of Eger from the outdoor terrace just outside, are worth it.

▲▲**Eger Cathedral**—Eger's 19th-century bishops peppered the city with beautiful buildings, including the second-biggest church in Hungary (after Esztergom's—

see page 340). With a quirky, sumptuous, Baroque-feeling interior, Eger's cathedral is well worth a visit.

Cost and Hours: Free entry (except before and during organ concert, 11:00-12:00), open Mon-Sat 8:30-18:00, Sun 13:00-18:00. The cathedral is the big, can't-miss-it yellow building at Pyrker János tér 1, facing the start of Széchenyi utca.

Visiting the Cathedral: Eger Cathedral was built in the 1830s by an Austrian archbishop who had previously served in Venice, and who thought Eger could use a little more class. The colonnaded Neoclassical **facade,** painted a pretty Habsburg yellow, boasts some fine Italian sculpture. As you walk up the main stairs, you'll pass saints István and László—Hungary's first two Christian kings—and then the apostles Peter and Paul.

Enter the cathedral and walk to the first collection box, near the start of the nave. Then, turning back to face the door, look up at the ornate **ceiling fresco:** On the left, it shows Hungarians in traditional dress; and on the right, the country's most important historical figures. At the bottom, you see this cathedral, celestially connected with St. Peter's in Rome (opposite). This symbol of devotion to the Vatican was a brave statement when it was painted in 1950. The communists were closing churches in other small Hungarian towns, but the Eger archbishop had enough clout to keep this one open.

Continue to the transept, stopping directly underneath the main dome. The **stained-glass windows** decorating the north and south transepts were donated to the cathedral by a rich Austrian couple to commemorate the 1,000th anniversary of Hungary's conversion to Christianity—notice the dates 1000 (when St. István converted the Magyars to Christianity) and 2000.

As you leave, notice the enormous **organ**—Hungary's second-largest—above the door. In the summer, try to catch one of the cathedral's daily half-hour organ concerts (800 Ft, mid-May–mid-Oct Mon-Sat at 11:30, Sun at 12:45, no concerts off-season).

Near the back-right corner, look for the statue of **Szent Rita,** a local favorite; the votive plaques that say *köszönöm* and *hálából* are offering "thanks" and "gratitude" for prayers answered.

Nearby: If you walk up Széchenyi utca from here, you'll see the fancy Archbishop's Palace on your left—still home to Eger's archbishop.

Just to the right of the steps leading up to the cathedral is the entrance to the...

Town Under the Town (Város a Város Alatt)—Here you can take a 45-minute guided tour of the archbishop's former wine-cellar network, which honeycombs the land behind the Archbishop's Palace.

Cost and Hours: 950 Ft, departs at the top of each hour, 5-person minimum, you'll get a little English sprinkled in with the Hungarian, daily April-Sept 9:00-19:00, Oct-March 10:00-17:00, last tour departs one hour before closing, www.varosavarosalatt.hu.

North of Dobó Square

▲Market Hall (Piaccsarnok)—Wandering Eger's big indoor market will give you a taste of local life—and maybe some samples of local food, too. This ramshackle hall is a totally untouristy scene, with ugly plastic tubs piled high with an abundance of fresh local produce. Tomatoes and peppers of all colors and sizes are plentiful—

magic ingredients that give Hungarian food its kick.

Hours: Opens daily at 6:00; while open weekday afternoons, it's best in the mornings.

Minaret—Once part of a mosque, this slender, 130-foot-tall minaret represents the century of Ottoman rule that left its mark on Eger and all of Hungary. The little cross at the top symbolizes the eventual Christian victory over Hungary's Ottoman invaders. You can climb the minaret's 97 steps for fine views of Eger, but it's not for those scared of heights or enclosed spaces. Because the staircase was designed for one man to climb to call the community to prayer, it's very tight. To avoid human traffic jams, they allow groups of visitors in about twice an hour.

Cost and Hours: 250 Ft, April-Oct daily

10:00-18:00, closed Nov-March; if it's locked, ask around for the key.

▲**Kopcsik Marzipan Museum (Kopcsik Marcipánia)**—Lajos Kopcsik is a master sculptor who has found his medium: marzipan.

Kopcsik can make this delicate mixture of sugar dough, ground almonds, egg whites, and tempera paints take virtually any form. Pass through the entryway, filled with awards, to enter this surprisingly engaging little museum. You'll see several remarkable, colorful examples of Kopcsik's skill: sword, minaret, gigantic wine bottle, suitcase, Russian stacking dolls, old-timey phonograph, grandfather clock, giant bell...and paintings galore (including Van Gogh's sunflowers and Picasso's musicians). Who'd have thought you could do so much with candy? Don't miss the European map celebrating May 1, 2004, when much of Eastern Europe joined the EU; and the "Baroque room"—furnished and decorated entirely in marzipan.

Cost and Hours: 600 Ft, no English information, daily 9:00-18:00, shorter hours off-season, Harangöntő utca 4, tel. 36/412-626, www.kopcsikmarcipania.hu.

▲**Kepes Institute (Kepes Intézet)**—Hungarian-born György Kepes (1906-2001) later moved to the US, where he was a university professor in Chicago and at MIT in Boston. A painter and photographer, Kepes followed the very Hungarian, left-brained artistic tradition of Op Artist Viktor Vasarely, drawing inspiration from geometry—except that Kepes ventured deeper into abstraction (producing canvases reminiscent of fuzzy Abstract Expressionism). And, naturally for a Hungarian artist, he combined art with practical purpose as he helped design effective camouflage for the US military. This beautifully renovated, minimalist building—sitting proudly on Eger's main walking street, Széchenyi utca—has a permanent collection of Kepes' works upstairs, and fills several other halls with good temporary exhibits of contemporary artwork.

Cost and Hours: 1,200 Ft, Tue-Sat 10:00-18:00, Sun 10:00-16:00, closed Mon, Széchenyi utca 16, tel. 36/440-044, www.kepeskozpont.hu.

Other Museums

Eger has a variety of other, small museums that may be worthwhile for those with a special interest. Though Eger's Jewish population was wiped out during the Holocaust, one of its synagogues has been converted into the **Synagogue Gallery** (Zsinagóga Galéria), allowing you to see the roughly restored interior and peruse temporary exhibits on various topics (exhibits are generally not Jewish-focused; 500 Ft, Tue-Sun 10:00-18:00, closed Mon, two short blocks straight ahead from castle ramp at Kossuth Lajos utca 17). Additionally, the TI can give you information about the **Firefighters Museum** (Egri Tűzoltó Múzeum, a long walk north of downtown on Széchenyi utca, www.tuzoltomuzeum.hu), the **Sport Museum**, and more.

Experiences in Eger

Aqua Eger

Swimming and water sports are as important to Egerites as good wine. They're proud that many of Hungary's Olympic medalists in aquatic events have come from this county. The men's water polo team took the gold for Hungary at three Olympiads in a row (2000-2008), and swimmer László Cseh might have been a multiple gold medal-winner at Beijing in 2008 if he hadn't been swimming next to Michael Phelps. The town's Bitskey Aladár swimming pool—arguably the most striking building in this part of Hungary—is practically a temple to water sports.

Eger also has two of the most appealing thermal bath complexes outside of Budapest: one right in town, and the other a few miles away (near the village of Egerszalók). Budapest offers classier bath experiences, but the Eger options are more modern and a bit more accessible, and allow you to save your Budapest time for big-city sights. Before you go, be sure to read the Thermal Baths chapter.

In Eger

Note that you can't rent a swimsuit or a towel at either of these places; bring both with you, along with shower sandals for the locker room (if you've got them).

Bitskey Aladár Pool—This striking swimming pool was designed by Imre Makovecz, the father of Hungary's Organic architectural style. Some Eger taxpayers resented the pool's big price tag, but it left the city with a truly distinctive building befitting its love of water sports. You don't need to be an architecture student to know that the pool is special.

It's worth the five-minute walk from Dobó Square just to take a look. Oh, and you can swim in it, too.

Cost and Hours: 970 Ft, Mon-Fri 6:00-21:30, Sat-Sun 7:30-18:00, follow Eger Creek south from Dobó Square to Frank Tivadar utca, tel. 36/511-810, www.egertermal.hu.

▲Eger Thermal Bath (Eger Thermálfürdő)—For a refreshing break from the sightseeing grind, consider a splash at the spa. This is a fine opportunity to try a Hungarian bath: relatively accessible (men and women are clothed and together most of the time), but frequented mostly by locals.

Cost and Hours: 1,700 Ft, 1,100 Ft extra gives you access to sauna and Turkish bath for two hours; June-Aug Mon-Wed 8:30-19:00, Thu-Fri 8:30-23:00, Sat 8:00-23:00, Sun 8:00-19:00; Sept Mon-Wed 8:30-19:00, Thu-Fri 8:30-21:00, Sat 8:00-21:00, Sun 8:00-19:00; Oct-May Mon-Wed 9:00-19:00, Thu-Sat 9:00-21:00, Sun 9:00-19:00; Petőfi tér 2, tel. 36/510-558, www.egertermal.hu.

Getting There: It's easy to reach and within a 10-minute walk of most hotels. From Dobó Square, follow the stream four blocks south (look for signs for *Strand*). You'll come first to the main entrance (on the left after crossing busy street, roughly facing the fancy swimming-pool building on Petőfi tér). However, as this entrance is a bit more confusing and farther from the best pools, I'd use the side entrance instead: Continue following the stream as it runs along the side of a park (to the right of the main entrance building). Soon you'll see the side entrance to the bath on your left over a bridge.

Entry Procedure: You'll enter and be given a little barcode bracelet, which acts as your ticket (keep it on until you leave). At the better side entrance, you'll show your bracelet to get a key to a locker (1,000-Ft deposit per key, which will be refunded; private changing cabins available in the locker room for no extra charge). After you change and stow your stuff, put the key around your wrist, then join the fun. If you use the main entrance, you'll change in the blocky white buildings just inside the entry (get a hanger from the desk, change in one of the free little cabins, then bring your clothes-laden hanger back for them to store it, 400 Ft extra to use safe-deposit box).

Taking the Waters: There's a sprawling array of different pools, each one thoughtfully described in English and labeled with its depth and temperature. The best part is the green-domed, indoor-outdoor adventure bath, right at the side entrance. Its cascades, jets, bubbles, geysers, and powerful current pool will make you feel like a kid again. Exploring the complex, you'll also find big and small warm pools, a very hot sulfur pool (where Egerites sit peacefully, ignore the slight stink, and supposedly feel their ar-

Hungary's Organic Architecture

In recent years, a unique, eye-catching style of architecture has caught on in Hungary: Organic. The Hungarian brand of Organic was developed and championed by Imre Makovecz (1935-2011). After being blacklisted by the communists for his nationalistic politics, Makovecz was denied access to building materials, so he taught himself to make impressive structures with nothing more than sticks and rocks. Makovecz was inspired by Transylvanian village architecture: whitewashed walls with large, overhanging mansard roofs to maximize attic space (resembling a big mushroom).

After the fall of the regime, Makovecz became Hungary's premier architect—but he still kept things simple. He believed that a building should be a product of its environment, rather than a cookie-cutter copy. Organic buildings use indigenous materials (especially wood) and take on unusual forms—often inspired by animals or plants—that blend in with the landscape. Organic buildings look like they're rising up out of the ground, rather than plopped down on top of it. You generally won't find this back-to-nature style in big cities like Budapest; Makovecz preferred to work in small communities such as Eger (see photo on page 359) instead of working for corporations. For more on Makovecz, visit www.makovecz.hu.

Organic architecture has become *the* post-communist style in Hungary. Even big supermarket chains are now imitating Makovecz—a sure sign of architectural success.

EGER

thritis ebb away), a kids' pool with splashy slide fun, and a lap pool (some of these are closed off-season).

Near Eger, in Egerszálok

▲▲**Salt Hill Thermal Spa**—This spa complex, in the hills about four miles outside of Eger, is the most modern and accessible thermal bath I've visited in Hungary. While it lacks the old-fashioned class of the Budapest options, it trumps them in user-friendliness and overall soggy fun.

For decades, Egerites would come to this "salt hill" (a natural terraced formation caused by mineral-rich spring water running

down the hillside) in the middle of nowhere and cram together to baste in pools of hot water. Then the developers arrived. Today, those same simple pools are still used by local purists, but a giant new hotel and spa complex has been built nearby. With 12 indoor pools and five outdoor ones—many cleverly overlapping one another on several levels—these cutting-edge baths are worth the trip outside of Eger.

Ideal for kids but fun for anyone, the complex has pools with mineral water as well as plain old swimming-pool water.

Cost and Hours: 4,900 Ft, discounted to 1,500 Ft after 17:00 on Mon-Fri. You'll pay 1,500 Ft extra to access "sauna world," with five different saunas. Towel rental is 1,000 Ft; massages and other treatments also available. Open June-Aug daily 10:00-20:00, likely less off-season—call ahead to check. Tel. 36/688-500, www.egerszalokfurdo.hu.

Getting There: It's about a mile outside the village of Egerszalók, which is itself about three miles from Eger. You can take a public **bus** from Eger's bus station to the baths (take bus going toward Demjén, you want the *Egerszalók Gyógyfürdő* stop—tell the bus driver "EH-gehr-sah-lohk FEWR-dur"—just after leaving the town of Egerszalók, 9/day Mon-Sat, only 4/day Sun, 17-minute trip, 400 Ft). Check the return bus information carefully (especially on weekends, when frequency plummets). Or you can take a **taxi** from Eger (about 3,000 Ft; tel. 36/555-555 for a return taxi from Egerszalók). Here's a fun and very hedonistic afternoon plan: Take the bus or taxi to the spa, taxi back to Eger's Sirens' Valley for some wine-cave hopping, then taxi back to your Eger hotel.

Note: The humble little baths beside the parking lot are a whole other story—fun but very traditional (just sitting in hot water). Don't mistake these for the new complex. To find the big one, continue walking about five minutes beyond the parking lot to the hotel.

Entry Procedure: You pay and are given a watch-like wristband, which serves as your ticket, locker key, and credit card. Press it against a nearby computer screen to find out which locker you've been assigned. Find that locker in the common locker room (you can change in one of the private cabins), stow your stuff there, and have fun. Take some time to explore the sprawling complex. Everything is labeled in English, and each pool is clearly marked with the depth and temperature (in Celsius). You can buy food or drinks with the wristband, too—it's keeping tabs so you can be charged when you leave.

Eger Wine

Eger is at the heart of one of Hungary's best-known wine regions, internationally famous for its **Bull's Blood** (Egri Bikavér). You'll likely hear various stories as to how Bull's Blood got its name during the Ottoman siege of Eger. My favorite version: The Ottomans were amazed at the ferocity displayed by the Egerites, and wondered what they were drinking that boiled their blood and stained their beards so red...it must be potent stuff. Local merchants, knowing that the Ottomans were Muslim and couldn't drink alcohol, told them it was bull's blood. The merchants made a buck, and the name stuck.

Creative as these stories are, they're all bunk—the term dates only from 1851. Egri Bikavér is a blend (everyone has their own recipe), so you generally won't find it at small producers. Cabernet Sauvignon, Merlot, Kékfránkos, and Kékoportó are the most commonly used grapes.

Of course, there's so much more to Hungarian wines than Bull's Blood—and the Eger region produces many fine options. For all the details, see "Hungarian Wines" on page 252.

While it would be enjoyable to drive around the Hungarian countryside visiting wineries, the most accessible way to get a quick taste of local wine is at a wine shop in town. I like the Kenyeres family's **Bikavér Borház,** right on Little Dobó Square (across from Senator Ház Hotel). In addition to a well-stocked (if slightly overpriced) wine shop, they have a wine bar with indoor and outdoor seating (six tastings and two cheeses for less than 2,000 Ft, wine also sold by the glass, some English spoken, menu lists basic English description for each wine, daily 10:00-22:00, possibly later in busy times, Kis-Dobó tér 10, tel. 36/413-262).

Sirens' Valley (Szépasszony-völgy)—When the Ottoman invaders first occupied Eger, residents moved into the valley next door, living in caves dug into the hillside. Eventually the Ottomans were driven out, the Egerites moved back to town, and the caves became wine cellars. (Most Eger families who can afford it have at least a modest vineyard in the countryside.) There are more than 300 such caves in the valley to the southwest of Eger, several of which are open for visitors.

The best selection of these caves (about 50) is in the Sirens' Valley (sometimes also translated as "Valley of the Beautiful Women"—or, on local directional signs, the less poetic "Nice Woman Valley"). While the valley can feel vacant and dead (even sometimes in the summer), if you visit when it's busy it can be a fun scene—locals showing off their latest vintage, with picnic tables and tipsy tourists spilling out into the street. At some places, you'll be offered free samples; others have a menu for tastes or glasses of wine. While you're not expected to buy a bottle, it's a nice gesture to buy one if you've spent a while at one cave (and it's usually very cheap). Most caves offer something light to eat with the wine, and you'll also see lots of non-cave, full-service restaurants. Some of

EGER

the caves are fancy and finished, staffed by multilingual waiters in period costume. Others feel like a dank basement, with grandpa leaning on his moped out front and a monolingual granny pouring the wine inside. (The really local places—where the decor is cement, bottles don't have labels, and food consists of potato chips and buttered Wonder bread—can be the most fun.)

This experience is a strange mix of touristy and local, but not entirely accessible to non-Hungarian-speakers—it works best with a bunch of friends and an easygoing, social attitude. Hopping from cave to musky cave can make for an enjoyable evening, but be sure to wander around a bit to see the options before you dive in (cellars generally open 10:00-21:00 in summer, best June-Aug in the late afternoon and early evening, plus good-weather weekends in the shoulder season; it's sleepy and not worth a visit off-season, when only a handful of cellars remain open for shorter hours).

Getting to the Sirens' Valley: The valley is on the southwest outskirts of Eger. Figure no more than 1,000 Ft for a **taxi** between your hotel and the caves. During the summer, you can take a 700-Ft **tourist train** from Eger's main square to the caves (see "Helpful Hints" on page 349), then catch a later one back.

You can **walk** there in about 25 minutes: Leave the pedestrian zone on the street next to the cathedral (Törvényház utca), with the cathedral on your right-hand side. Take the first left just after the back end of the cathedral (onto Trinitárius utca), go one long block, then take the first right (onto Király utca). At the fork, bear to the left. You'll stay straight on this road—crossing busy Koháry István utca—for several blocks, passing through some nondescript residential areas (on Szépasszony-völgy utca). When you crest the hill and emerge from the houses, you'll see the caves (and tour buses) below you on the left—go left (downhill) at the fork to get there. First you'll come to a stretch of touristy non-cave restaurants; keep going past these, and eventually you'll see a big loop of caves on your left.

Nightlife in Eger

Things quiet down pretty early in this sedate town. Youthful student bars and hangouts cluster along the main "walking street," Széchenyi utca. Older travelers feel more at home on Little Dobó Square, with schmaltzy live music until 21:00 or 22:00 in summer.

Sleeping in Eger

Eger is a good overnight stop, and a couple of quaint, well-located hotels in particular—Senator Ház and Offi Ház—are well worth booking in advance. The TI can help you find a room; if you're stumped, the area behind the castle has a sprinkling of cheap guesthouses *(vendégház)*. Elevators are rare—expect to climb one or two flights of stairs to reach your room. A tax of 400 Ft per person will be added to your bill (not included in the prices listed here). Parking is generally free and easy.

$$$ Imola Udvarház rents six spacious apartments—with kitchen, living room, bedroom, and bathroom—all decorated in modern Ikea style. They're pricey for this small town, but roomy and well-maintained, with a great location near the castle entrance (Sb-19,000 Ft, Db-23,000 Ft, 1,000 Ft more July-Aug, 3,000 Ft less in winter, extra person-3,000 Ft, air-con, free Wi-Fi, enter through restaurant courtyard at Dózsa György tér 4, tel. & fax 36/516-180, www.imolaudvarhaz.hu, udvarhaz@imolanet.hu).

$$ Senator Ház Hotel is one of my favorite small, family-run hotels in Eastern Europe. Though the 11 rooms are a bit worn, this place is cozy and well-run by András Cseh and his right-hand man, Viktor. With oodles of character, all the right quirks, and a picture-perfect location just under the castle on Little Dobó Square, it's a winner (Sb-13,200 Ft, Db-18,000 Ft, extra bed-6,000 Ft, 1,000 Ft more in July-Aug, less in winter, András offers 10 percent cash dis-

count for Rick Steves readers who book direct and mention this book, air-con, free Internet access and Wi-Fi, Dobó István tér 11, tel. & fax 36/411-711, www.senatorhaz.hu, info@senatorhaz.hu). The Cseh family also runs **Pátria Vendégház**—two doubles (same prices as main hotel) and four luxurious apartments (Db-20,000 Ft, Tb-27,000 Ft).

$$ Offi Ház Hotel shares Little Dobó Square with Senator Ház. Its five rooms are classy and romantic, but a bit tight, with slanted ceilings. Communication can be tricky (German helps), but the location is worth the hassle (Sb-14,000 Ft, Db-17,500 Ft, Db suite-19,500 Ft, Tb suite-23,000 Ft, extra bed-5,000 Ft, 15 percent cheaper Nov-March, non-smoking, air-con, free Wi-Fi, Dobó István tér 5, tel. & fax 36/518-210, www.offihaz.hu, offihaz@t-online. hu, Offenbächer family).

$$ Szent János Hotel, less charming and more businesslike than the Senator Ház and Offi Ház, offers a good but less atmospheric location, 11 straitlaced rooms, and a pleasant winter garden to relax in. Choose between the newly renovated rooms, which face a busy pedestrian street and can be noisy on weekend nights, or the still good older rooms, which face the quieter back side—both for

Sleep Code

(200 Ft = about $1, country code: 36, area code: 36)
S = Single, **D** = Double/Twin, **T** = Triple, **Q** = Quad, **b** = bathroom. Unless otherwise noted, English is spoken, breakfast is included, and credit cards are accepted.

To help you sort easily through these listings, I've divided the accommodations into three categories, based on the price for a standard double room with bath:

$$$ Higher Priced—Most rooms 20,000 Ft or more.
$$ Moderately Priced—Most rooms between 15,000-20,000 Ft.
$ Lower Priced—Most rooms 15,000 Ft or less.

Prices can change without notice; verify the hotel's current rates online or by email.

Phone Tip: Remember, if calling or faxing Eger internationally, you'll have to dial 36 twice (once for the country code, again for the area code).

the same price (Sb-13,000 Ft, Db-15,000 Ft, extra bed-5,000 Ft, cheaper Nov-April, non-smoking, air-con, free Wi-Fi, a long block off Dobó Square at Szent János utca 3, tel. 36/510-350, fax 36/517-101, www.hotelszentjanos.hu, hotelszentjanos@hotelszentjanos.hu).

$ Dobó Vendégház, run by warm Marianna Kleszo, has seven basic but colorful rooms just off Dobó Square. Marianna speaks nothing but Hungarian, but gets simple reservation emails and faxes translated by a friend (Sb-9,000 Ft, Db-13,500 Ft, extra bed-4,000 Ft, cash only, no air-con, free Wi-Fi, Dobó utca 19, tel. 36/421-407, fax 36/515-715, www.dobovendeghaz.hu, info@dobovendeghaz.hu).

$ Imola Hostel, a big, modern, and comfy hostel, is basically a college dormitory that welcomes travelers of any age into its dorm rooms in summer (July-Aug only). As there are 400 beds, finding a place should be easy (bunk in 2-3-bed room-3,300 Ft, includes sheets but no breakfast; a short hike up behind the castle or a 5-minute walk from the Old Town at Leányka utca 2; tel. 36/520-430, www.imolanet.hu/imolahostel, hostel@imolanet.hu).

Eating in Eger

Bajor Sörház (known to locals as "HBH" for the brand of beer on tap) is favored by tourists and locals alike for its excellent Hungarian cuisine. Everything's good here. You could make a meal of the giant 700-Ft bowl of their spicy *gulyás leves* soup (that's *real* Hungarian goulash, described on page 248)—but it's fun to supplement it with some other well-prepared Hungarian dishes. This is a good place for two or more people to split several dishes. They also feature some Bavarian specialties...but with a Hungarian accent (1,000-1,500-Ft light meals, 1,500-3,000-Ft main dishes, daily 11:30-22:00, outdoor tables in summer, right at the bottom of Dobó Square at Bajcsy-Zsilinszky utca 19, tel. 36/515-516). Say hello to animated István "Call Me Steve Miller" Molnár, one of my favorite Hungarians.

Restaurant Senator Ház, at the top end of Dobó Square, offers the best setting for al fresco dining in town, with good Hungarian and international food (1,200-2,000-Ft light meals, 1,700-2,600-Ft main dishes). Sure, you're paying a bit extra for the setting—but it's worth it. With its postcard-perfect outdoor seating from which to survey the Little Dobó Square action, and cheesy live music pouring from their gazebo on summer evenings, this place might just tempt you to savor an after-dinner glass of wine (open daily 10:00-22:00). Neighboring restaurants (such as Offi Ház) offer the same ambience.

Szantofer Vendéglő serves traditional Hungarian food at local prices to both Egerites and tourists. The good, unpretentious, fill-the-tank grub is designed for the neighborhood gang (1,800-2,500 Ft main dishes, daily 11:30-22:00, Bródy Sándor utca 3, tel. 36/517-298).

Palacsintavár ("Pancake Castle"), near the ramp leading up to the castle, isn't your hometown IHOP. This cellar bar (which also has pleasant sidewalk seating) serves up inventive, artfully presented crêpe-wrapped main courses to a mostly student clientele. It's decorated with old cigarette boxes, and cutting-edge rock music plays on the soundtrack (1,800-1,900-Ft main dishes, daily 12:00-23:00, Dobó utca 9, tel. 36/413-980).

Casa della Pasta, above the market hall, has a pleasant treehouse ambience. As it's outside of the cute zone, it attracts more locals than tourists. Sit indoors or enjoy covered terrace seating that's delightful in warm weather. The menu is mostly Italian, with pasta and pizzas (1,000-1,700 Ft) and main dishes (2,000-3,000 Ft), and a few Hungarian standbys thrown in (1,800-2,300 Ft; daily 12:00-22:00, Katona István tér 2, tel. 36/412-452).

Dessert: Cukrászda (pastry shops) line the streets of Eger. For deluxe, super-decadent pastries of every kind imaginable, drop by **Dobós Cukrászda** (400-600-Ft cakes, daily 9:30-20:00, point to what you want inside and they'll bring it out to your table, Széchenyi utca 6, tel. 36/413-335). For a more local scene, find the tiny **Sárvári Cukrászda,** a block behind the Lyceum. Their pastries are good, but Egerites line up here for homemade gelato (200 Ft/scoop, Mon-Fri 7:00-19:00, Sat-Sun 10:00-19:00, Kossuth utca 1, between Jókai utca and Fellner utca). You'll spot several ice-cream parlors in this town, where every other pedestrian seems to be licking a cone. Another good option is the *kürtőskalács* **window** on Szent János utca, where you can step up and grab a piping-hot "pastry horn" that's slow-cooked on a rotisserie, then rolled in toppings (small-300 Ft, large-400 Ft, daily 9:00-19:30, Szent János utca 10).

Eger Connections

By Train

The only major destination you'll get to directly from Eger's train station is **Budapest** (5/day direct to Budapest's Keleti/Eastern Station, 2.5 hours, 2,200 Ft; more frequent and faster with a change in Füzesabony—see next). For other destinations, you'll connect through Füzesabony or Budapest.

Eger is connected to the nearby junction town of **Füzesabony** (FOO-zesh-ah-boyn) by frequent trains (13/day, 17 minutes). The very rustic Füzesabony station does not have lockers or an ATM; to find an ATM, exit straight from the station, walk about two blocks, and you'll find one on your right (just past the *Napcentrum*).

In Füzesabony, you can transfer to Budapest on either a slower milk-run train or a speedier InterCity train (a little pricier, as it requires an extra supplement, but get you to Budapest in just under 2 hours total).

Night Train to Kraków: If you're connecting to Poland, it may be possible to use a night train between Budapest and Kraków that stops at Füzesabony. If you want to start (or end) your Hungarian trip in Eger, this allows you to sleep into (or out of) Eger with a handy change at Füzesabony, rather than backtracking to Budapest. However, recently this train has run sporadically (summer only, or maybe not at all); sometimes the Budapest-Kraków night train is routed through the Czech Republic instead. If this option intrigues you, investigate your options carefully at www.bahn.com.

By Bus

Eger's bus station (unlike its train station) is right in town, a five-minute uphill walk behind Eger's cathedral and the Archbishop's Palace: Go behind the cathedral and through the park, and look for the modern, green, circular building. Blue electronic boards in the center of the station show upcoming departures.

From Eger to Budapest: The direct Eger-Budapest bus service is about the same price as the train, and can be a bit faster (2,500 Ft, 2/hour, tickets generally available just before departure). Express buses depart Eger at :15 after each hour and make the trip in one hour and 50 minutes; slower regular buses leave at :45 after each hour and take 20 minutes longer. While Eger's bus station is closer to the town center than its train station, this bus takes you to a less central point in Budapest (near Budapest's Stadionok bus station, on the M2/red Metró line).

To Salt Hill Thermal Spa: Buses from the same station also connect Eger to the Salt Hill Thermal Spa near Egerszalók (see "Getting There" on page 362). However, buses marked for *Egerszalók* do not actually go to the spa; instead, you need a bus going *beyond* Egerszalók, marked for *Demjén*.

PÉCS

An established settlement for nearly 2,000 years, Pécs (pronounced "paych") is a historic, museum-packed, and oh-so-pretty city near Hungary's southern frontier. Cheerful, inviting Pécs, with colorful buildings dripping with lavish Zsolnay porcelain decoration, feels unusually proud and prosperous. Of course, it's a relative backwater, and compared to Budapest, its charms are modest...but they're also delightfully accessible. Pécs offers an unusually satisfying day of sightseeing for a city its size. And you'll hardly see another tourist, as this place is rarely visited by Americans.

Pécs' position as the major city of southern Hungary often placed it at the crossroads of cultures. Owing to the city's illustrious history, museum-going is fun and enlightening here. You'll gradually peel back the many layers of Pécs' past: Walk in the footsteps of Romans through ancient crypts, stroll the medieval trade-town street plan, explore some rare surviving artifacts of the Ottoman occupation, ogle colorful Baroque and Art Nouveau buildings...and enjoy the energetic bustle of one of Hungary's leading cities. The city's symbol—a mosque-turned-church—says it all.

The Mecsek Hills gently cradle the city, blocking out the colder weather from the north to give Pécs a mild Mediterranean climate closer to Croatia's than to Budapest's. It's no surprise that this bright and invigorating city has earned a reputation as a leading art colony. Its streets are lined with museums devoted to local artists both obscure and well-known (including Vasarely and Csontváry, considered the two great figures of Hungarian art). Students love it, too. Hungary's first university was founded here in 1367, and today's U. of Pécs rivals Budapest's ELTE as the country's biggest university. More than 30,000 students give Pécs a youthful buzz.

Pécs was a European Capital of Culture in 2010; it used the occasion as an opportunity to spiff up its townscape, renovate many of its buildings, resurface its streets, and pedestrianize much of its urban core. The city is proud and gleaming—and there's never been a better time to visit.

Planning Your Time

One full day is plenty to get your fill of Pécs. It's barely doable as a long day trip from Budapest (three hours each way by train)—so it's worth spending the night. With the better part of a day in Pécs, go for a walk through town following my self-guided commentary, dipping into the museums that appeal to you. Nearly everything is within a few minutes' walk of the main square. The one exception—the Zsolnay Cultural Quarter, a 15- to 20-minute walk east—is interesting but skippable, or can be squeezed into any remaining time you have on a busy day (or the next morning).

Orientation to Pécs

With about 170,000 people, Pécs is Hungary's fifth-largest city. But it feels like a small town, right down to the convivial strolling atmosphere that combusts along its pedestrian zone. The Belváros, or Inner Town, is hemmed in by a ring road (the site of the former town wall, some of which still stands). You can walk from one end of this central tourist zone to the other in about 15 minutes. All roads lead to the main square, Széchenyi tér, marked by the palatial yellow Town Hall and giant mosque/church. Because Pécs is nestled up against a gentle hillside, you'll go gradually uphill as you head north.

Tourist Information

The main TI—Pécs Infopoint—is in the pedestrian zone just below the main square, facing the yellow Town Hall building (June-Aug Mon-Fri 9:00-17:00, Sat 9:00-15:00, Sun 9:00-13:00; April-May and Sept-Oct Mon-Fri 9:00-17:00, Sat 9:00-15:00, closed Sun; Nov-March Mon-Fri 9:00-17:00, possibly closed Sat-Sun; Széchenyi tér 7, tel. 72/213-315, www.iranypecs.hu). A second, seasonal branch is in a kiosk just below the cathedral, where Dom tér meets István tér (June-Sept Tue-Sun 10:00-18:00, closed Mon and Oct-May).

Arrival in Pécs

By Train: The Pécs train station is three-quarters of a mile due south of the city center's Széchenyi tér. Inside, the station is long but straightforward (with ATM, lockers, and all the usual amenities).

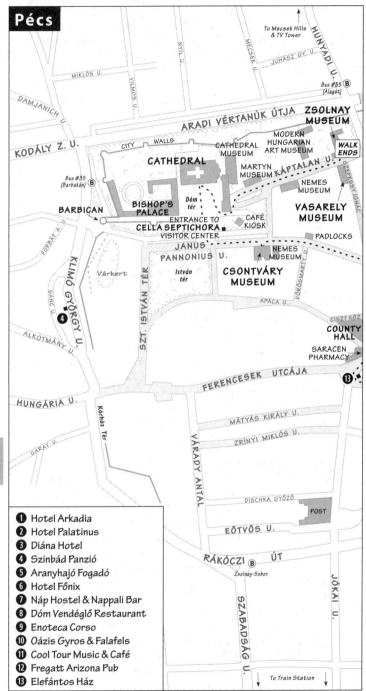

Pécs

To Mecsek Hills & TV Tower

Bus #35 (Alagút) Ⓑ

ZSOLNAY MUSEUM

MODERN HUNGARIAN ART MUSEUM

CATHEDRAL MUSEUM

CATHEDRAL

MARTYN MUSEUM

WALK ENDS

NEMES MUSEUM

Bus #35 (Barbakán) Ⓑ

BISHOP'S PALACE

Dóm tér

VASARELY MUSEUM

BARBICAN

ENTRANCE TO CELLA SEPTICHORA VISITOR CENTER

CAFÉ KIOSK

PADLOCKS

Várkert

NEMES MUSEUM

CSONTVÁRY MUSEUM

István tér

COUNTY HALL

SARACEN PHARMACY

❹

FERENCESEK UTCAJA

⓭

POST

To Train Station

Zsolnay-Sobor

PÉCS

❶ Hotel Arkadia
❷ Hotel Palatinus
❸ Diána Hotel
❹ Szinbád Panzió
❺ Aranyhajó Fogadó
❻ Hotel Főnix
❼ Náp Hostel & Nappali Bar
❽ Dóm Vendéglő Restaurant
❾ Enoteca Corso
❿ Oázis Gyros & Falafels
⓫ Cool Tour Music & Café
⓬ Fregatt Arizona Pub
⓭ Elefántos Ház

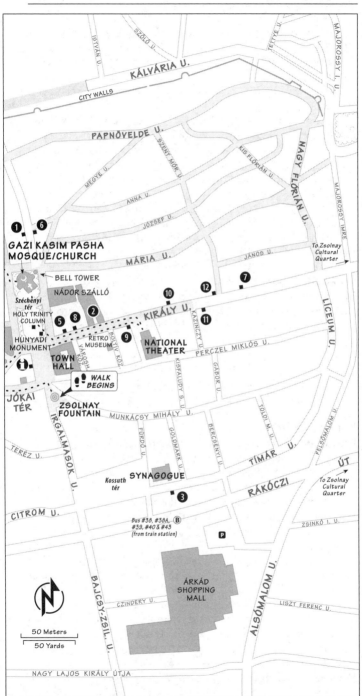

A **taxi** to any of my recommended hotels should cost no more than 1,000 Ft.

You can **walk** from the train station to the town center in about 15 minutes: Exit straight ahead from the station and walk up the tree-lined, slightly angled Jókai út, which funnels you directly to Széchenyi tér.

Various **bus** lines (#38, #38A, #39, #40, and #43) shave a few minutes off the walk downtown, taking you to the Árkád shopping center just south of the pedestrianized old center. As you exit the station, head down to the left end of the bus stops; you'll find these buses at the second row of bus stops (out in the parking lot, marked *VI*; buy 360-Ft ticket from driver, ride two stops to Árkád). From the Árkád bus stop, it's about a five-minute walk to the main square (backtrack a few steps up Rákóczi street, then angle diagonally through the long square called Kossuth tér and turn right up Irgalmasok utcája).

Getting Around Pécs

In compact Pécs, you could easily get by without using local buses—but they may come in handy for getting into the town center from the train station, reaching the Zsolnay Cultural Quarter, or heading up into the hills. A single ticket is 280 Ft when purchased in advance at a kiosk, or 360 Ft when bought on the bus (www.pkrt.hu). If you buy it on the bus, the driver will likely stamp it to validate it for you. Otherwise, you'll need to validate it yourself: Stick the ticket in the slot, then pull the slot toward you.

Helpful Hints

Pécs Outdoor Festival (Pécsi Szabadtéri Játékok): Each July through mid-August, the city hosts a festival with lots of concerts at reasonable prices (www.pecsinyariszinhaz.hu). If visiting in the summer, ask about it. The kiosk at the National Theater sells tickets to all festival events.

Internet Access: Internet cafés with long hours and fair prices are easy to find and well-signed from the main walking zone.

Shopping: The big, American-style **Árkád** shopping mall—with a supermarket, food court, and lots more—is just a block beyond the synagogue and Kossuth tér, at the southern edge of the Inner Town (shops open Mon-Sat 9:00-20:00, Sun 10:00-18:00, Bajcsy-Zsilinszky utca 11, www.arkadpecs.hu).

Tourist Train: A hokey tourist train does a 40-minute loop through the city center, and heads out to the Zsolnay Cultural Quarter (1,350 Ft, departs from bottom of Széchenyi tér, May-Sept only).

Local Guide: Brigitta Gombos is a knowledgeable guide who leads good tours of her hometown (15,000 Ft/3 hours, mobile 0670-505-3531, gerluc@freemail.hu).

Sights in Pécs

I've arranged these sights roughly in the order of a handy self-guided orientation walk through town.

Note that most museums in Pécs (except the cathedral and the Roman crypts) have similar **hours:** Tue-Sun 10:00-18:00 in summer (May-Sept), 10:00-16:00 in winter (Oct-April). Everything but the cathedral is closed on Monday.

The 3,500-Ft **day ticket** *(napijegy)*—saves you a little money if you're seeing the three main museums downtown (Csontváry, Vasarely, and Zsolnay). Simply buy it at the first museum you visit. Note that it does not cover the mosque/church, cathedral, Roman crypts, or Zsolnay Cultural Quarter.

• *Begin in front of the little church next to the Town Hall, at the...*

▲Zsolnay Fountain (Zsolnay-kút)

This fountain, an icon of Pécs, was a gift from the beloved local Zsolnay (ZHOL-nay) family. The family created an innovative

type of ceramics called pyrogranite that allowed colorful, delicate-seeming porcelain to be made frost-proof and hard as steel—ideal for external building decoration. The ox heads—modeled after an ancient drinking vessel found in Pécs—are specially glazed with another Zsolnay invention, eosin. Notice how the eosin glaze glimmers with a unique range of colors. (Since this glaze compromises the pyrogranite, the fountain must be covered in winter.) Above the oxen heads are traditional symbols of Pécs. One is the shield with five tall churches, dating from the Middle Ages. (Germans still call the town Fünfkirchen.) This seal was appropriated by the Zsolnay family as a symbol of their porcelain. The other seal is Pécs' coat of arms: a walled city under vineyard-strewn hills.

This is the first of many gorgeous Zsolnay decorations we'll see all over town. But Pécs is just the beginning. In the late 19th and early 20th centuries, Budapest and cities all over Europe covered their finest buildings with decorations from this city's Zsolnay Porcelain Manufacture. (For all the details, see the "Zsolnay Porcelain" sidebar on page 388.)

• *Basically across the pedestrian street from the fountain, and 20 yards uphill, is the entrance to an enjoyable zone called...*

Jókai Tér

At the start of the street, notice the **game boards** on top of the little pillars. When this street was renovated in 2000—with funky benches and other playful elements—the designers wanted to remind locals to take time to relax.

On the right (a few doors down, at #2), notice the **Zsolnay porcelain shop.** Although the company was reduced to an industrial supplier under the communists, today Zsolnay is proudly reclaiming its role as a maker of fine art. Dipping into the shop, notice that some of the decorative items use the same distinctive eosin glaze as the fountain's oxen heads...and are priced accordingly (Mon-Fri 10:00-18:00, Sat 9:00-13:00, closed Sun).

Continuing to the corner, you enter a fine little square with a kid-pleasing fountain. At the far end of the square, look left down the street called **Ferencesek utcája.** When Pécs was a walled market town, this street—and Király utca to the east, also now pedestrianized—made up the main east-west road. At the house on the uphill corner, notice the elephant. This used to be a grocery store, which likely imported exotic Eastern goods, symbolized by the then-mysterious pachyderm.

Hang a right around the elephant house, noticing the former tram tracks preserved in the street. The yellow bricks were pretty standard in 20th-century Hungary. Imagine how unappealing this drag was when it was choked with tram and car traffic. At the corner (on the left), look for the old-time **Saracen Pharmacy** (marked with the words *Sipöcz István* and an African prince over the door). Its interior features gorgeous woodwork, little porcelain medicine pots, and a Zsolnay fountain. Now it's a tourist shop, selling wine, candy, soaps, and other local artisan products (Tue-Sat 10:00-18:00, closed Sun-Mon).

• *Continuing up the street, you'll emerge into the main square...*

▲▲Széchenyi Tér

In the Middle Ages, Pécs was a major trading crossroads, located at the intersection of two Byzantine trade routes. Széchenyi tér was a natural meeting point and market zone. Today the market is gone, but this square remains the bustling city center, where both political demonstrations and the annual New Year's Eve festivities percolate.

Let's get oriented. Stand at the base of the square (across from the McDonald's). Face the green-domed **Gazi Kasim Pasha Mosque** at the top of the square (described in detail later). On the

right (housing the McDonald's), the giant yellow-and-white building with the tower is the **Town Hall** (Városház, 1908), strategically located here since the olden days to watch over the market activities. The Town Hall's tower plays laid-back organ ditties throughout the day. (The **TI** is directly across the pedestrian street from the Town Hall.) Across the square is the gorgeous, red-roofed **County Hall** (Megyháza, 1898), frosted like a wedding cake with sumptuous Zsolnay decorations. Because the building was originally a bank, it's adorned with beehives (one at the very peak of the building, and two more between the top-floor windows). Industrious bees, who carefully collect and store away their golden deposits, are a common symbol for banking. Farther up the square on the right is the pink **Nádor Szálló.** In the early 20th century, this hotel was a popular gathering place for artists and intellectuals (but now it's awaiting a massive renovation).

The square has two monuments. On the right is an equestrian statue of **János Hunyadi,** the war hero who fended off the Ottoman invaders at the 1456 Battle of Belgrade (described on page 173). Later those Ottomans took Pécs and built the mosque at the top of the square. But Hunyadi gets the last laugh: If you position yourself just right, it appears that Hunyadi's club is smashing the crescent at the top of the mosque. (Try it.) This statue is a popular meeting point: Locals say, "I'll meet you under the horse's...tail." With perhaps unintended irony, Hunyadi—who died of the plague soon after that battle—shares the square with the **Holy Trinity Plague Column,** which townspeople built to give thanks to God after surviving a nasty bout of the plague in the late 17th century. Around its base are three saints known for protecting against disease or injury: Sebastian, who was killed by arrows (on left); Rocco, with his trusty dog and trademark leg wound (on right); and Anthony of Padua, who offers help recovering that which is lost—including health (behind the pillar).

• *We'll visit the mosque/church soon. But first, head down the street branching off to the right, next to the Town Hall...*

▲The Walking Street: Király Utca

This vibrant Technicolor people zone—combined with Jókai tér and Ferencesek utcája, across the square—bisects the city center. Király utca ("Royal Street") is a delight to stroll. Walk its entire length, simply enjoying street musicians and people-watching, and noting its personality-filled architecture.

There are several recommended **restaurants** along this street (see "Eating in Pécs," later)—as you stroll, peruse the posted menus and scope out a place for a meal later.

About a block down (on the left, at #5), keep an eye out for the gorgeous, horseshoe-shaped **Hotel Palatinus;** step into its lobby for a taste of genteel Secession architecture. A few steps farther (down the alley on the right, at #10), you'll see signs for the silly but intriguing **Retro Museum,** displaying shelves of old communist-era kitsch with no explanations (500 Ft, daily 10:00-18:00).

Soon you'll reach the square in front of the **National Theater,** built (along with most of the other houses on this square) for the Hungarian millennial celebrations of 1896 (see page 43). The decorations on the theater—including the stone-like statues—are all made of Zsolnay pyrogranite. This is a popular venue in this city of culture, and hosts the local philharmonic (their season runs Sept-May). Duck into the box office here any time of year to see what's on, either here or elsewhere in town.

Farther along, you'll find a good ice-cream parlor (at #15, on the left); the recommended **Oázis "Keleti Étterem"** ("eastern eatery")—a good spot for a quick gyro or falafel snack (at #17, on the left); a very cool "ruin pub" (the recommended **Cool Tour**—a play on words from the formal "Kultur" label for local cultural centers, with an inviting garden out back; at #26, on the right); and, finally, a contemporary Hungarian painting gallery (at #31, on the left).

While this part of Pécs appears wealthy and manicured, the region is struggling. In the early 1950s, Pécs had only about 50,000 residents. Coal and uranium mines kick-started the economy, causing the population to more than triple over the last 50 years. However, both mines are now closed, and while Pécs' university and business center continue to thrive, outlying communities are grappling with 30 percent unemployment.

• *Head back to Széchenyi tér to visit the...*

▲▲Gazi Kasim Pasha Mosque (Gázi Kászim Pasa Dzsámija)/Inner Town Parish Church

It's rare to find such a well-preserved Ottoman structure in Hungary. The Ottomans—who began their 150-year stay in Pécs in 1543—lived here in the Inner Town, while the dwindling Hungarian population moved to the outskirts. The Ottomans tore down the church that stood on this spot and used the stones to build the structure you see today. After the Ottomans were forced out, the Catholic Church reclaimed this building and turned it into a church—which is why it's still intact today. Despite renovations over the years, it remains an offbeat hybrid of the Islamic and Christian faiths.

Cost and Hours: 400 Ft; mid-April-mid-Oct Mon-Sat 9:00-17:00, Sun 12:00-17:00; mid-Oct-mid-April Mon-Sat 10:00-14:00, Sun 12:00-17:00.

◒ Self-Guided Tour: From the **outside,** notice the crescent moon of Islam capping the dome—but it's topped by the victorious Christian cross. The only decorations on the austere facade are the striped ogee arches over the windows. Before entering, notice the fig trees; locals are proud that their mild climate can support these heat-seekers.

Go **inside** and let your eyes adjust to the low light. Are you in a church, or a mosque... or both? The striped arches over the windows are even more apparent inside. Notice the colorful Islamic-style stalactite decorations at the tops of the corners. The painting on the underside of the dome seems to combine Christian figures with the geometric designs of Islam. To the right of the main altar is a verse from the Quran translated into Hungarian and used for Christian worship (a reminder that Islam and Christianity are founded on many of the same principles).

Looking back to where you entered, scan the back wall for gray patches with faint Arabic script peeking through—most were whitewashed over during the church-ification. In the middle of the wall, next to the door, is a large **prayer niche** (mihrab). This niche, which faces Mecca (southeast from here), indicated to Muslim worshippers the direction they had to face to pray. The holy water basin in the niche and the crucifix suspended above it make it clear who's in charge now.

Mentally erase these and other Christian elements, and imagine worshipping here during the Ottoman period. There were no pews, and carpets covered the floor. Worshippers—men in front, women segregated in back—stood and knelt as they prayed toward the mihrab. A step-stair pulpit, called a mimber, likely stood off to one side of the mihrab.

When the Christians reclaimed this building, they flipped it around, creating an entrance near the mihrab, and an altar at the former entrance. Much later, in 1940, they added the giant **apse** (semicircular area behind the altar). Explore this area, with its striking 1930s-style murals. The modern paintings depict Bible scenes and events in Hungary's Christian history. And the giant organ is an Angster (made by a local Hungarian organ-maker). In the corners, you'll see small stone basins. These once stood outside the building, where the Ottoman worshippers performed their ablution, or ritual washing before prayer.

Exiting the building, head around back to find the latest addition to this constantly evolving structure: the modern **bell tower** and a concrete footprint that recalls the original church that preceded the mosque. The statue is St. Bartholomew, the patron of this church. Depicted (as he always is) with his skin peeling away, he steps on a serpent, representing victory over evil (Islam?). Every day at 12:00 and 19:00, the bell tower mechanically rises 40 feet into the air to play a tune. Viewing the church from back here, you can also appreciate how jarringly ugly the 1940 concrete addition is.

• *While interesting, this is not Pécs' main church. To see that (and a lot more), go down the street at the upper-left corner of the square...*

Janus Pannonius Utca

About a block down this street, watch (on the right) for a railing that's completely covered in **padlocks.** Nobody knows for sure how this local tradition began, back in the 1980s. Some say it was a clever way for graduating students to get rid of the padlocks from their lockers.

These days, the padlocks mostly belong to lovers who want to pledge themselves to each other. You can see that many of the locks are marked (or even engraved) with couples' names. Farther down the same block, the tradition continues at the padlock-covered gate. (Not missing a sales opportunity, guess what the nearby shop sells.)

• *Continue along the street until you emerge into the little square. In the pretty off-white building on the left (with the gray roof), you'll find Pécs' best art museum...*

▲▲Csontváry Museum (Csontváry Múzeum)

This small but delightful collection showcases the works of beloved Hungarian painter Tivadar Csontváry Kosztka. Csontváry produced only 100 paintings and 20 drawings, and about half are collected here. For a crash course in this enigmatic painter, read the sidebar before visiting; the paintings are also described in English.

Cost and Hours: 1,200 Ft, covered by 3,500-Ft day ticket, borrow the English information sheet, May-Oct Tue-Sun 10:00-18:00, Nov-April Tue-Sun 10:00-16:00, closed Mon year-round, Janus Pannonius utca 11, tel. 72/224-255.

Visiting the Museum: The museum is divided into five rooms. In Room 1 are Csontváry's art-school sketches, which capture people at unguarded moments and show the work of a budding genius. Rooms 2, 3, and 4 are mostly dedicated to Csontváry's many travel canvases. Room 2 has "postcards" from his trips to Sicily (Castellammare, Taormina) and Bosnia-Herzegovina (Mostar, Jajce), but the best canvas in here is from Hungary: *Storm over the Great Hortobágy* is a dynamic snapshot of life on the Great Hungarian Plain, where cowherds tend longhorn cattle. A storm brews on the horizon as a horseman races across the bridge. Notice the balance between movement and stillness, and between the yellow sky and the blue clouds. Room 3 covers Baalbek, the High Tatras (where Csontváry first had the epiphany that drove him to paint, and to madness), and a historical scene of Mary's well in Nazareth. In Room 4, along with Jerusalem, is Csontváry's most acclaimed work, *Solitary Cedar:* a windblown tree on a ridge above the sea. The tree seems boldly independent even as it longs for companionship. The last room (5) displays Csontváry's final major painting, *Riders on the Seashore.* This haunting valedictory canvas, with an equestrian party pausing by an eerily deep-blue cove, hints at the troubled depths of Csontváry's own psyche. Other works in this room date from Csontváry's final days, when—in his worsening mental state—he sketched large-scale, absurdist scenes.

• *Leaving the museum, cross the street and continue left down the tree-lined, pedestrian-only path. Soon you'll see a beautiful yellow kiosk (on the right)—an inviting place for a coffee break. A few steps beyond that, look for the modern entrance to the...*

Tivadar Csontváry Kosztka
(1853-1919)

Adored by Hungarians, but virtually unknown outside his home-land, Tivadar Csontváry Kosztka had a life as fascinating as his paintings. Because of the time in which he lived and his struggles with mental illness (schizophrenia)—if not for his talent—Csontváry (CHONT-vah-ree) is often compared to Van Gogh. While that's a bit of a stretch, viewing Csontváry's works gives you a glimpse into the Hungarian psyche, and into his own fractured mind.

Tivadar Kosztka was born to an up-per-class family, seemingly bound for a humdrum lot in life. He didn't pick up a paintbrush until his 27th year. Then one day, idly sketching sleeping oxen while recovering from an illness in the High Ta-tras, he had a revelation (or, perhaps, a psychotic episode): A voice told him that he was destined to become "the world's greatest *plein air* painter, greater even than Raphael."

He adopted the pseudonym "Csontváry" and became driv-en by an almost pathological compulsion to prepare himself for what he believed to be his destiny. He figured it would take him 20 years, working as a pharmacist to finance his quest. By age 41, he had saved enough to attend art school (in Munich and In Paris). Seeking the ideal subjects for his outdoor style, he trav-eled extensively around Europe and the Middle East: Italy, Croa-tia, Bosnia-Herzegovina, Greece, Egypt, Lebanon, Jerusalem, and

▲Cella Septichora Visitor Center (Roman Crypts)

This unique, modern, well-presented museum allows visitors to take a peek inside some remarkably preserved Roman crypts. (Note: If you skip this museum, sneak a free look at the some of the ruins through the glass behind the yellow kiosk.)

Cost and Hours: 1,200 Ft; April-Oct Tue-Sun 10:00-18:00, Nov-March Tue-Sun 10:00-16:00, closed Mon year-round; Dóm tér, tel. 72/224-755, wwww.pecsorokseg.hu.

Discount with Zsolnay Cultural Quarter: If you'll definitely be visiting some of the museums in the Zsolnay Cultural Quarter, ask about combo-tickets that let you save more the more sights you visit (see museum descriptions and discount details on page 390).

Nearby: If you're interested in these sorts of ruins, ask about the three nearby sights managed by the same office; a 1,620-Ft combo-ticket covers everything.

Tours: For an extra 400 Ft/person, you can join a 45-minute

the Tatra Mountains of his own homeland. By the time he began painting in earnest, he had only six productive years (1903-1909).

Csontváry's rough, autodidactic (self-taught) style reveals his untrained origins, but contains a depth of meaning and of composition that exceeded his technical skill. While classified as a Post-Impressionist, Csontváry forged a style all his own. Like his contemporary Marc Chagall, he worked in almost childlike bright colors and often reverted to big, bold themes. His most common subjects are the destinations to which he traveled—they were his main inspiration.

After exhibitions in 1909 and 1910 failed to win him the praise he so desperately sought, he became consumed by his schizophrenia and created only bizarre, surrealistic works. He died in obscurity in 1919.

After Csontváry's death, his family planned to sell his works to wagon-makers, who wanted the valuable canvas to stretch over their wagons. Fortunately, a Budapest art collector bought them instead, preserving the legacy of this important figure in Hungarian art history.

Csontváry remained largely unappreciated until the 1960s, when art-lovers began to take notice. But one discerning eye for talent knew greatness when he saw it, before many others did: Pablo Picasso reportedly discovered Csontváry's canvases at a 1949 exhibition, and proceeded to lock himself in the room with them for an hour. Finally emerging, he told his friend Marc Chagall that Chagall could never produce a work half as good as Csontváry's.

English tour (for details, call 72/224-755 or email info@pecso-rokseg.hu). For a brief visit, my self-guided tour (next page)—and the good posted English descriptions—will guide you through the basics.

Background: There was a Roman settlement in today's Pécs from the year A.D. 30, and by the second century it was a provincial capital called Sopinae. During that time, this part of town was a vast cemetery, which included the graves of early Christian martyrs. Later, after Christianity became the state religion in the early fourth century, these tombs attracted pilgrims from afar. Wealthy Christian families were now free to build a double-decker structure to hold the remains of their relatives: a sealed crypt below ground (painted with Bible scenes and floral motifs), with a chapel directly above for remembering and praying for the dead. About a century later, Rome fell. Nomadic invaders lived in the chapels and raided the crypts (then carefully re-covered them). Today the remains of some of these crypt-chapels have been discovered, excavated, and opened to visitors.

◐ Self-Guided Tour: Buy your ticket, borrow the English map of the sprawling underground complex, and head into the first area (under the glass roof), the foundation of a **giant chapel with seven apses.** (The exhibit is named for this—Cella Septichora means "seven-apsed chapel.") Experts believe that the crypt of a different martyr would have been placed in each apse, and pilgrims would come here to worship. However, the structure was never finished.

From here, follow signs (and your map) as you climb up and down through the subterranean exhibit to the highlights. Unlike Rome's famous catacombs, these crypts were not originally connected underground; modern archaeologists built the tunnels you'll pass through to allow visitors easier access to all the tombs.

Find the **Wine Pitcher Burial Chamber.** The model shows the two-tiered structure. Peer through the window to see the paintings that decorate the crypt. Its nickname comes from the wine jug and glass painted in the niche above the body. Romans used wine to toast to the memory of the departed (the Roman version of "pour one out for the homies who ain't here"). Climb up the stairs to what was ground level, where you can view the foundation of the chapel and look down into the crypt. From here, you'll see other paintings (representing paradise), as well as the drain at the bottom of the sarcophagus. The Romans, ever the clever engineers, provided drainage so that accumulating groundwater would not defile the body.

Retrace your steps back up the long hallway, then follow signs to the Peter and Paul crypt. Along the way, you'll pass through an area with several **smaller crypts.** Notice that these didn't have large chapels up top; rather, worshippers would kneel and look inside a small decorative chapel. In one, a hole in the floor of the chapel indicates where tomb raiders broke in to search for valuables. Turn right into the **octagonal chapel,** which—like the seven-apsed chapel—was likely designed to be a pilgrim church. Finally you'll pass another small crypt that's more intact, showing the barrel vaulting that once covered all of these.

Take the spiral stairs all the way down to the bottom to enter the **Peter and Paul Burial Chamber.** Standing under the painted tomb, you'll see faded Sts. Peter and Paul flanking the Christogram (an ancient Christian symbol). The side walls are painted with biblical scenes, while the ceiling features another Christogram, four portraits (possibly the Four Evangelists), and more nature motifs—plants and birds. (An artist's rendering of the original version is nearby.) Notice the little window above the body. Experts believe that a ribbon tied to the sarcophagus led through this window up into the chapel, so the faithful could have a tangible connection to the dead.

Retracing your steps on your way out, you'll pass through even more crypts (they've unearthed more than 20), as well as some simple brick sarcophagi used by poorer families to bury their dead.

• *Exiting the exhibit, turn right and continue down Janus Pannonius utca, which deposits you at...*

István Tér and Dóm Tér

These two squares—the lower István Square, which belonged to the people, and the upper Cathedral Square, which was the bishop's—used to be separated by a wall and moat. But later, the enlightened **Bishop Szepesy** turned them into one big park. In the statue that dominates the square, the bishop is stepping down from the pulpit clutching a Bible—a reminder that he's believed to have been the first priest to use Hungarian.

Walk up the stairs and into Cathedral Square. The brown, Neo-Renaissance building on the left is the Bishop's Palace. At the corner of this building, notice the engaging statue of **Franz Liszt** by popular 20th-century sculptor Imre Varga. Liszt was a friend of the bishop, and Liszt's visit here in 1846 is still the stuff of legend.

• *Now turn your attention to the massive, four-towered...*

▲▲Cathedral

With an imposing exterior and an elaborately decorated interior, Pécs' cathedral merits a close look. St. István established a bishopric in Pécs in the year 1009, and this church building grew in fits and starts from then on. By the 14th century, it had roughly the same floor plan as today, and gradually morphed with the styles of the day: Romanesque, Gothic, Renaissance. The Ottomans preserved the building, using it first as a mosque and later as a stable, a grain store, and a library. Later, when it became the cathedral again, it got a Baroque makeover. Finally, in the 1880s, a bishop

(likely hoping to be remembered as a visionary) grew tired of the architectural hodgepodge, gutted the place, and turned it into the Neo-Romanesque fortress of God you see today. The 12 apostles stand along the roofline, and the four distinctive corner towers anchor and fortify the massive structure.

Cost and Hours: 800 Ft; April-Oct Mon-Sat 9:00-17:00, Sun 13:00-17:00; Nov-March Mon-Sat 10:00-16:00, Sun 13:00-16:00; can close for weddings Sat afternoons—especially in summer, tel. 72/513-057.

Nearby: You could pay 400 Ft extra to visit the cathedral's lapidary museum and bishop's wine cellar for a tasting (both nearby, but outside the church), but I'd skip them.

Visiting the Cathedral: Outside, study the symbolic **bronze gate** from 2000. The vines, grapes, and branches are all connected, symbolizing our connection to God. If you look closely, you'll find animals representing good (birds) and evil (snake, scorpion, frog). On the left, St. István gives Pécs to the first bishop; on the right, Jesus offers his hand to St. Peter.

Stepping inside, you're struck by the rich Neo-Romanesque, 19th-century decor. It's clear that the renovating bishop did not subscribe to the "less is more" school of church decoration. Like the Matthias Church in Budapest (see page 78)—renovated at about the same time—every square inch is covered by a thick and colorful layer of paint. Along the **nave** are paintings depicting the lives of the church's patrons, Sts. Peter and Paul. Above the arches are biblical scenes. The coffered ceiling of the nave depicts the 12 apostles and (near the organ) John the Baptist.

The **altar,** with its highly decorated canopy, is a replica of the 13th-century original. The mosaic on the apse dome (behind the altar, not entirely visible from here) features Jesus flanked by Peter and Paul (on the right) and, on the left, Mary and István (the patron saint of Hungary).

Turn 180 degrees and face the back of the church. To the right of the organ is the **bishop's treasury,** inside the Chapel of Mary. (This is the only one of the cathedral's four such chapels open to tourists.) Pop in to see vestments, goblets, and monstrances, all surrounded by paintings of events from the Christian history of Hungary. At the far end of the chapel is a remarkably detailed 16th-century alabaster sculpture, done by a Dutch sculptor for an Italian family who decided they didn't want it after all (so the Pécs bishop bought it instead).

Back in the main church, to the right of the altar are the stairs down to the **crypt**. This 11th-century forest of columns (redecorated like the rest of the church) is part of the original church building on this site. The bust at the front depicts the bishop who decided to renovate the church.

• *From in front of the cathedral, if you want to take a look at part of the old city wall, you can go down the stairs and turn right at the wide path, which will take you to a barbican (round tower) that helped fortify the walls. (For more on these walls, see page 390.) If you decide to visit the wall, on your way there—but just before the barbican and busy street—watch on the left for the gateway at #5 (marked Várkert), which leads to a pleasant series of sleepy parks along the inside of the town wall, and some modest views of the four cathedral steeples. (If you're interested in all these ruins, ask around about the excavations of a medieval university building, scheduled to go on display behind the cathedral sometime in 2013.)*

Otherwise, after you exit the cathedral, walk about halfway down the square, turn left before the steps, pass through the archway, walk over the glassed-in Roman ruins, and head down...

Káptalan Utca: Pécs' "Museum Row"

A cluster of museums line tranquil Káptalan utca ("Chapterhouse Street," where priests once lived). A few of the smaller museums are skippable, but the Zsolnay and Vasarely museums are worthwhile (www.jpm.hu). Remember, all of these have the same hours and are covered by the same 3,500-Ft day ticket (explained on page 375).

▲**Viktor Vasarely Museum (Vasarely Múzeum)**—You might not know Viktor Vasarely (1908-1997), but you know his work. Think optical illusions, and the dizzying Op Art that inspired the psychedelic 1960s. Here in his hometown, you can see a museum of Vasarely's eye-popping creations. Inspired by nature, Vasarely discovered that the repetition

Zsolnay Porcelain

Thanks to the pioneering Zsolnay (ZHOL-nay) family of Pécs, buildings all over Hungary are slathered with gorgeously colorful porcelain.

Miklós Zsolnay (1800-1880) opened a porcelain factory in Pécs in 1853. But the real breakthrough came at the hands of his innovative son, Vilmos Zsolnay (1828-1900), who experimented with glazes and additives, and revolutionized the use of porcelain in building materials. He invented a type of ceramic called pyrogranite to create porcelain decorative elements that were as resilient as steel and weatherproof, but could still be delicately sculpted and painted any color of the rainbow. Zsolnay pyrogranite made a splash at the 1873 World

Exhibition in Vienna, winning an avalanche of orders from all over Europe. The twists and curves that Zsolnay porcelain allowed for were a perfect fit for the slinky, organic Art Nouveau style of the day. Exhibits at further world fairs added to the Zsolnay family's renown and wealth.

In 1893, Vilmos Zsolnay unveiled his latest innovation: eosin, a shimmering—almost metallic—iridescent glaze. Named for the Greek word for "dawn," it has an otherworldly way of making porcelain resemble light striking a precious gemstone or the glistening surface of a soap bubble. This eosin technique is exemplified by Pécs' Zsolnay Fountain (described on page 375).

Boom time for the Zsolnays also coincided with the 1896

and slight variation of lines and forms can play with the viewer's brain to create illusions of depth and movement. In other words, black-and-white lines undulating across a canvas are trippy, baby. It's easy to get lost in Vasarely's mind-bending designs—such as, in the first room, a pair of carpets with zebras—which make you go cross-eyed before you stumble up the stairs to see him add more color to the mix.

Cost: 1,200 Ft, covered by 3,500-Ft day ticket, Káptalan utca 3, mobile 0630-539-8069.

▲**Zsolnay Porcelain Museum (Zsolnay Múzeum)**—This museum, situated in the former mansion of the Zsolnay family, is as much a shrine to the family as a showcase of their work. (For more on the family and their legacy, see the "Zsolnay Porcelain" sidebar.) The collection is divided into two parts: architectural elements and decorative ware. Each room is well-described in English. In the architectural elements section (on the ground floor), you'll see im-

millennial celebrations in Budapest (see page 43). The city's architects, who had ample resources and imagination, were striving to create a unique Hungarian national style. Many of them adopted colorful pyrogranite tiles and other decorations as an integral part of that style. In Buda-

pest alone, the Great Market Hall, Matthias Church and National Archives on Castle Hill, and Ödön Lechner's Postal Savings Bank and Museum of Applied Arts are roofed with Zsolnay pyrogranite tiles. Zsolnay decorative elements also adorn the Hungarian Parliament, Gellért Baths, and many other buildings. To this day, Zsolnay tiles are synonymous with Budapest (and Hungarian) architecture.

All of that porcelain generated a lot of work for the Pécs factory. By the time World War I broke out, the Zsolnay family business was the Austro-Hungarian Empire's biggest company (unlikely but true). But the stripped-down modern styles that emerged in the 20th century had little use for the fanciful Zsolnay decorations. The factory was nationalized by the communists, the Zsolnay name was abandoned, and quality plummeted.

In the 1990s, private investors took over and have made great strides toward rehabilitating the Zsolnay name. All over Hungary, you'll see shops selling beautiful Zsolnay tableware, some with designs as innovative as ever. But to keep up with our modern economy, Zsolnay also creates everyday items. In fact, they recently signed a big deal to make dishes for Ikea.

pressively detailed and colorful decorations for the many buildings the Zsolnays were involved in renovating (including Budapest's Matthias Church and Parliament). You'll also see a playful duck fountain, with its colorful eosin glaze, and some beautiful pieces of the destroyed István Stove that once warmed Budapest's Royal Palace. Upstairs, the decorative-ware collection displays vases, sculptures, and other objects that demonstrate the evolution of porcelain style. Notice how trends came and went over time. A spinning table allows you to easily inspect each place setting of Zsolnay dinnerware. The "memorial room" is furnished as it would have been during the Zsolnays' day.

Cost: 1,200 Ft, covered by 3,500-Ft day ticket, Káptalan utca 4, tel. 72/514-045.

Other Museums—Nearby are museums that showcase the work of yet two more local artists, Ferenc Martyn and Endre Nemes, and the Modern Hungarian Art Museum.

• *From Káptalan utca, you're just a block above the main square and our starting point. If you have more time, consider some of these sights...*

Elsewhere in Pécs

City Walls—Several segments of the city walls around the northern part of Pécs are still standing (most notably around the cathedral area). Built after the Tatar invasions of the 13th century, and beefed up in the 15th century, the walls were no match for the Ottoman invaders who took the town in 1543. Still standing just west of the cathedral area is the round, stout barbican defensive gate, which you can actually climb.

Synagogue (Zsinagóga)—Just south of the old center, overlooking the modern, beautifully renovated Kossuth tér, is Pécs' colorful synagogue. Dating from the 1860s but recently restored, this building is a powerful reminder of Pécs' Jewish heritage. The city had a thriving population of 4,000 Jews; only a few hundred survived the Holocaust.

Cost and Hours: 500 Ft, May-Sept Sun-Fri 10:00-12:00 & 12:45-17:00, closed Sat and Oct-April, Kossuth tér, tel. 72/315-881.

Mecsek Hills—Pécs is picturesquely nestled in the Mecsek (MEH-chek) Hills, a popular place to go for a hike. To get an aerial view of Pécs, ride bus #35 about 30 minutes up to the TV tower overlooking the city and surrounding region (catch this bus at the train station, or at the northern entrance to city center). Ascend the 580-foot-tall TV tower for views over the town and region (790 Ft, daily 9:00-20:00).

Zsolnay Cultural Quarter (Zsolnay Kulturális Negyed)

The first and last name in Pécs industry, the Zsolnay porcelain-making family operated their major factory on the eastern edge of town. Tucked in the middle of the sprawling brick industrial center were some fine villas and houses and a leafy park. A few years ago, this facility was thoroughly restored and converted into

a community cultural center with indoor and outdoor events venues, cafés, restaurants, children's play zones, and—of course—a collection of small museums celebrating the Zsolnay clan and their works. While it's a bit out on the edge of things—a dull 15- to 20-minute walk or quick bus ride from downtown—and it's slightly better in concept than execution (while the facilities are beautiful, it lacks a workaday vitality), the center is worth the trip if you've exhausted your in-town sightseeing interests and are curious to see another side of Pécs. And those taken with Zsolnay tiles may enjoy a pilgrimage to where they were created. (For more on the family and their legacy, see the "Zsolnay Porcelain" sidebar.)

Cost: It's free to enter the complex and explore the grounds. You'll pay individually for each of the museums (prices listed later), and buy tickets at a ticket desk rather than at the museum entrances. The more sights you visit, the bigger a discount you get (2 sights—10 percent off, 3 sights—15 percent off, 4 sights—20 percent off, 5 sights—25 percent off, 6 sights—30 percent off). Think carefully about which places you'll visit to maximize your discount. Of the major sights in downtown Pécs, only the excellent Cella Septichora Visitor Center participates in this discount deal.

Hours: While the grounds are open daily 9:00-1:00 in the morning, the individual sights are open substantially shorter hours (most open April-Oct Tue-Sun 10:00-18:00, Nov-March Tue-Sun 10:00-16:00, closed Mon year-round). A few exceptions are noted later. Tel. 72/500-350, www.zsn.hu.

Getting There: It's due east of the town center. You can **walk** there in about 15-20 minutes. The slightly more interesting route is to follow Király utca (the main walking street) to its end, then continue straight (as the road becomes Felsővámház utca) through residential neighborhoods about 10 minutes farther to the complex. Alternatively, from the Árkád shopping center at the south end of the Inner Town, walk east on the busy, bus-clogged Rákóczi út, which becomes Zsolnay Vilmos út. On either route, head for the many tall smokestacks of the complex.

Multiple **buses** run to the complex. From in front of Árkád shopping center, catch bus #20, #20A, #21, #27, #31, #31A, #43, #901, or #902, and get off at the Zsolnay Negyed stop. From Búza tér, at the end of the traffic-free section of Király utca, catch bus #27 or #40 for the short trip to the Bóbita Bábszínház stop near the complex (though this saves you only an easy 10-minute walk). From the train station, take bus #31, #31A, #40, or #43; all stop at Zsolnay Negyed (except #40, which goes to Bóbita Bábszínház).

You could also hop on the corny **tourist train** from Széchenyi tér, but it's pricey (see "Helpful Hints," earlier).

Orientation: There are two main gates to the complex: the lower gate (just up from Zsolnay Vilmos út) and the upper gate (on Felsővámház utca). Once inside, you'll find a lower complex of buildings surrounding a small park with a short, colorful chimney. The modern building just uphill houses the **Visitors Center** (with ticket office, open daily April-Oct 9:00-19:00, Nov-March 9:00-17:00), a planetarium, a kids' play zone with hands-on scientific exhibits, and (downstairs) a funky café and the Pécsi Galéria (contemporary art installations). At the lower end of the park are the **E78 Pyrogranite Courtyard** (a modern indoor theater and outdoor live music venue, plus a tall smokestack with colorful Zsolnay tiles embedded in the base). Nearby is the Sikorski Villa, which houses the **Gyugyi Collection.**

More sights cluster up the small hill, in a long, sprawling mansion—here you'll find (in the right half of the building) the **Pink Zsolnay Exhibition** and the **Zsolnay Live Manufactory,** and (in the left half) the **Zsolnay Family and Factory History Exhibition.** The building also contains various eateries and, tucked back in a little courtyard (follow the signs), the **American Corner**—a service of the US Embassy that strives to educate Hungarians about American culture with an English lending library, special events on American holidays, English conversation clubs, and other resources.

Finally, up a few more steps to the top of the hill is another ticket office and the **"street of shops"**—basically a row of candy, chocolate, wine, and handicraft shops (generally open Tue-Sun 10:00-12:30 & 13:00-18:00, closed Mon). Leaving the gate by the ticket office, you'll turn right on Felsővámház utca and walk 200 yards to find the **Zsolnay Mausoleum.** If you turn left on Felsővámház utca, you'll find the **Bóbita Puppet Theater** (Bóbita Bábszínház), which offers periodic performances for kids.

And, of course, the grounds are studded with pretty Zsolnay decorations—fountains, pillars, and statues. Posted maps and directional signs help you find your way.

Planning Your Time: While it sounds like a lot—and Zsolnay enthusiasts could spend hours here—for the casual visitor, it's enough to simply stroll the colorful grounds; the only sights I'd pay to enter are the Gyugyi Collection (if you didn't get your fill at the Zsolnay Museum downtown) and the mausoleum. Those fascinated by all things Zsolnay may find it worth paying for the whole shebang. Below are brief descriptions of each sight to help you decide.

▲**Gyugyi Collection (Gyugyi-gyűjtemény)**—Dr. László Gyugyi fled Hungary after the 1956 Uprising and settled in the US,

where he gradually amassed a breathtaking collection of sumptuous decorative Zsolnay objects. Now he has donated them to their hometown of Pécs, where they are displayed in a fine old villa at the heart of the complex. With a remarkable collection of Historicist and Art Nouveau items, beautifully displayed and well-described in English on two floors, this is a better collection of decorative works than the Zsolnay Museum downtown (though unless you're a connoisseur, it may feel like a rerun, and it lacks the Zsolnay Museum's impressive collection of architectural features).

Cost and Hours: 1,200 Ft, April-Oct Tue-Sun 10:00-18:00, Nov-March Tue-Sun 10:00-16:00, closed Mon year-round.

Pink Zsolnay Exhibition (Rózsaszín Zsolnay Kiállítás)— Early on, the Zsolnay factory focused on producing everyday items

in the then-in-vogue hue of pink. This modest collection shows off as much pink porcelain as you'll see anywhere in one place. Unlike the finely detailed showpieces of the Gyugyi Collection, these are practical, unglamorous objects that were handmade, making them a bit rougher and each one with its own subtle imperfections. If it's fancy vases and plates you're hoping to see, skip it.

Cost and Hours: 800 Ft, daily April-Oct 10:00-18:00, Nov-March 10:00-16:00.

Zsolnay Live Manufactory (Látványmanufaktúra)—This lets you peer through windows at Zsolnay potters hard at work. Posted English information briefly outlines the manufacture process, but it's tricky to appreciate and there's no practical English tour option.

Cost and Hours: 500 Ft, Mon-Sat 10:00-15:00; it's free Mon-Sat 15:00-18:00 and Sun 10:00-18:00 because you won't see craftspeople at work.

Zsolnay Family and Factory History Exhibition (Család-és Gyártörténeti Kiállítás)—Displayed on two floors (factory downstairs, family upstairs), this exhibit traces—with dry English descriptions—the history of this complex and the people who built it. The exhibit doesn't add much to your visit here, and the few pieces on display are less striking than those in the Gyugyi Collection or the Zsolnay Museum downtown. For me, the offbeat highlight was the Zsolnay porcelain bust of Lenin dating from just after the factory was nationalized by the communists.

Cost and Hours: 1,200 Ft, April-Oct Tue-Sun 10:00-18:00, Nov-March Tue-Sun 10:00-16:00, closed Mon year-round.

▲**Zsolnay Mausoleum (Zsolnay Mauzóleum)**—A short walk from the rest of the complex, this hilltop perch is home to the final resting place of Vilmos Zsolnay, who founded the factory and enjoyed sitting on this hill to survey the family business. After his death in 1900, Vilmos' son Miklós commissioned this fine mausoleum (Miklós and his mother Terézia are also buried here)—entirely decorated in Zsolnay tiles, of course. Everything is now carefully restored and gleaming. From the road, you'll climb a staircase lined with 42 resting lions to reach the mausoleum itself. The entry doors (with eosin-glazed plaques depicting the 12 apostles) lead into a structure beautiful in its simplicity: a cylinder turned on end. Inside are an eosin altar and chandelier

above an opening in the floor where you can peer down at Vilmos' monumental tomb. Back outside, you can circle around back to find stairs down for a better look (through a grate).

Cost and Hours: 800 Ft, April-Oct Tue-Sun 10:00-19:00, Nov-March Tue-Sun 10:00-16:00, closed Mon year-round, possibly closed in bad weather.

Sleeping in Pécs

Most of Pécs' city-center accommodations are affordable pensions with simple but sleepable rooms. Elevators are rare.

$$$ Hotel Arkadia is a new, minimalist, concrete place with 25 modern rooms—the most stylish I've seen in Pécs—wonderfully located just a few steps above the mosque/church on the main square (Sb-16,500 Ft, Db-19,900 Ft, cheaper mid-Oct-mid-April, air-con, elevator, free Internet access and Wi-Fi, Hunyadi út 1, tel. 72/512-550, www.hotelarkadiapecs.hu, info@hotelarkadiapecs.hu).

$$$ Hotel Palatinus is your impersonal big-hotel option, with 194 rooms perfectly located right on the main walking street. You'll rarely find a more impressive facade, lobby, and breakfast room; the showpiece 1915 building (although not all of its bedrooms) has been painstakingly restored to its turn-of-the-20th-century glory. Though it's overpriced and less than charming (it's run by a big company), the location and public areas help compensate. Choose among the three room types: small, simple, communist-vintage "economy" (Db-18,500 Ft); lightly renovated "standard" with balconies on the walking street (Db-21,500 Ft); and nicely renovated and air-conditioned, but still not quite luxurious, "superior" (24,500 Ft; these are average prices—can vary with demand, elevator, free Wi-Fi in lobby, free sauna, underground parking nearby-3,200 Ft/day, Király utca 5, tel. 72/889-400,

www.danubiushotels.com/palatinus, palatinus.reservation@danubiushotels.com).

$$ Diána Hotel has 22 simple but comfortable-enough rooms just up the street from the synagogue, between the town center and the Árkád shopping mall (Sb-11,000 Ft, Db-15,000 Ft, rates about 1,000 Ft cheaper if you pay cash, air-con-1,500 Ft, some street noise, free Internet access and Wi-Fi, limited free parking or pay 2,000 Ft/24 hours to park at nearby garage, Tímár utca 4a, tel. 72/328-594, www.hoteldiana.hu, info@hoteldiana.hu).

$$ Szinbád Panzió is on a busy street in a dull urban area just outside the city wall. Though it has a labyrinthine floor plan, it feels more hotelesque than the other mid-range options in town:

Its public areas are classy, the 27 rooms are nice and woody, and it's a short walk from the cathedral area (Sb-9,500 Ft, Db-12,500 Ft, Tb-15,500 Ft, request quieter courtyard room, air-con, free Internet access and Wi-Fi, free parking, Klimó György utca 9, tel. 72/221-110, www.szinbadpanzio.hu, info@szinbadpanzio.hu).

$$ Aranyhajó Fogadó ("Golden Ship Inn"), a lesser value, is ideally situated at the start of the Király utca pedestrian zone. In operation since the 18th century, the hotel's 18 rooms are old and a bit musty, with once-classy furniture. The front "deluxe" rooms are a bit bigger, noisier, and more expensive (Sb-11,000, Db-15,000); I'd request a quieter back "standard" room (Sb-9,500 Ft, Db-12,500 Ft; free Internet access and Wi-Fi, Király utca 3, tel. 72/210-685, www.aranyhajo.hu, hotel@aranyhajo.hu).

$$ Hotel Fönix has 13 dated-feeling rooms ideally located just beyond the mosque/church at the top of the main square (Sb-7,500 Ft, Db-12,000 Ft, Tb-15,000 Ft, reception open 8:00-20:00, only 2 rooms with air-con, free Wi-Fi, no parking, Hunyadi János út 2, tel. 72/311-680, www.fonixhotel.com, sales@fonixhotel.com).

$ Náp Hostel ("Sun") is colorful and well-run by Tamás. Hiding upstairs in an apartment building on the main walking street, its four bedrooms share three WCs and two showers. Enter through the Nappali bar on the main street and head up through the graffiti-slathered atrium (D-13,000 Ft, bunk in 8-bed dorm-3,000 Ft, in 6-bed dorm-4,300 Ft, in 6-bed dorm with balcony-4,800 Ft, à la carte breakfast in the bar, free Internet access and Wi-Fi, kitchen, laundry service, Király utca 23-25, mobile 0630-277-0733, tel. 72/950-684, www.naphostel.com).

Eating in Pécs

On the Pedestrian Drag, Király Utca

The walking streets branching off from the main square are lined with restaurants and cafés that feature outdoor tables with ideal people-watching. Király utca (described earlier, under "Sights in Pécs") is Pécs' "restaurant row," with a fine variety of eating options. While there are other good eateries in town, none is worth going out of your way for—you might as well pick the low-hanging fruit and enjoy the people-watching on Király. Window-shop for your favorite, considering the following choices (listed in the order you'll pass them on this street):

Dóm Vendéglő serves traditional Hungarian cuisine along with pizzas and other international dishes. It has both indoor and outdoor seating (1,800-3,000-Ft main dishes, 700-1,500-Ft pizzas, daily 10:00-24:00, Király utca 3, tel. 72/210-088).

Enoteca Corso, serving modern international cuisine for locals and modern Hungarian dishes for tourists, considers itself the finest dining establishment in town. Its upstairs dining room defines Hungarian pretense, with shag carpet, trendy music, a flatscreen monitor showing the chefs hard at work in the kitchen, an adult-contemporary vibe, and fine views on the National Theater. The food is tasty, and the prices are surprisingly reasonable (2,200-3,200-Ft main dishes, daily 11:00-24:00, Király utca 14, tel. 72/525-198). Its street-level Étkező ("eatery") serves cheaper meals.

Oázis is the place for a simple, cheap, fast, and good gyro or falafel. Grab one to go, or enjoy it at their outdoor tables on this main street (600-Ft sandwiches, daily 10:00-23:00, Fri-Sat until late, Király utca 17).

Cool Tour Music & Café is a "ruin pub" with a bohemian vibe and rickety tables strewn around its hidden garden, draped with twinkling Christmas lights. It's a fine place for a toasted sandwich, pastry, coffee, or drink (Király utca 26). Consider dropping by after dinner for a cocktail or beer (nightly until wee hours).

Fregatt Arizona Pub is an enthusiastically American steak-house considered by locals to be a fine value. Choose from three dining zones: a Buffalo Bill interior, a cool back courtyard, or streetside seating ideal for people-watching (2,100-4,500-Ft main dishes, pricier steaks, daily 11:00-24:00, Király utca 21, tel. 72/511-068).

Nappali Bar, on the ground floor of a gorgeously restored townhouse, is a mecca for Pécs' hipsters and hipster tourists. While they serve only light food (basic sandwiches), this is a fine place for a pre- or after-dinner drink; they host live bands or DJs two nights a week in their bohemian interior (which displays works by local artists), and their outdoor seating is delightful (daily 9:00-2:00 in the morning, Király utca 23-25, mobile 0630-277-0733).

Elsewhere in Pécs

Elefántos Ház ("House at the Elephant") features good Italian fare in its ho-hum interior or at its inviting outdoor tables on a delightful shopping square in the town center (1,200-2,500-Ft pizzas and pastas, 2,600-4,600-Ft meat dishes, daily 11:30-23:30, Jókai tér 6, tel. 72/216-055).

Pécs Connections

From Pécs by Train: For destinations in this book (including **Eger, Sopron,** and **Bratislava**), you'll generally change trains in Budapest. Direct trains connect Pécs and **Budapest** (8 fast IC trains/day, every 2 hours, 2.75 hours; a few additional connections are possible with a transfer at the suburban Budapest-Kelenföld station). One handy train each afternoon (departing at 15:30) follows a different route, near the Croatian border, connecting Pécs directly to **Sopron** (5.5 hours), then **Vienna** (6.75 hours).

SOPRON

Sopron (SHOH-prohn), nestled in the foothills of the Alps a stone's throw from Austria, is a picture-perfect little Baroque town jam-packed with historic buildings. Its square—watched over by the town's symbol, the Fire Tower—is one of the most romantic in Hungary. Because Austrians flock over the border to sightsee, sample the local wine, and get dental work done (at a fraction of the cost back home), then stumble home, the town's streets are lined with modest museums and dentist's offices.

Sopron, populated since Roman times, was a stop on the Amber Route of trade between the Adriatic and Baltic Seas. As a Hungarian backwater of Austria's Vienna, the town has long been a unique bilingual mix of Hungarian and Germanic culture. But it's always remained true to Hungary, most famously after World War I, when residents voted to stick with the Magyars rather than becoming part of Austria—earning it the nickname "the most loyal town." Even so, its proximity to Austria keeps Sopron in touch with its Germanic heritage. Today Sopron caters almost entirely to its German-speaking tourists (while English is in short supply).

Sopron is sleepy...sometimes *too* sleepy, in fact. After dark, the Main Square is magical—but deserted. Museum attendants react to your visit as though they've never seen a tourist before. With a little more restoration and liveliness in the Old Town, it could become a major draw. For now, this not-quite-ready-for-prime-time Hungarian burg is a delightful hidden secret.

Planning Your Time

Sopron deserves a half-day. A few hours is more than enough time to exhaust its sightseeing options, and its sleepiness makes the initial "Oh, wow!" wear off quickly. Sopron fits perfectly on a trip between Budapest and Vienna (adding about an hour to your total train time between those cities). Consider arriving at midday, spending the afternoon here, then either taking a late train out, or spending the night and leaving the next morning.

On a brief visit, lock up your bag at the station and do a spin through the Old Town. With a little more time, explore the Ikva neighborhood northeast of town. If you're here for a while, head into the Lővér Hills.

Orientation to Sopron

Sopron, with about 60,000 in-habitants, is a manageable small city. The compact tourist zone of the Old Town (Belváros) con-tains most of Sopron's attrac-tions, and you can walk from one end to the other in less than 10 minutes. The retail district along the ring road (Várkerület) that follows the former outer walls surrounding the Old Town is much livelier, and the gently rolling Lővér Hills embrace the entire city.

Tourist Information

Sopron's TI (called TourInform) hands out maps and brochures about the town and has free Internet access. It's in the big, yellow Franz Liszt Cultural Center at the southwest corner of the Old Town (Mon-Fri 9:00-17:00, Sat 9:00-12:00, closed Sun, Liszt Fe-renc utca 1, tel. 99/517-560, www.sopron.hu). The TI is next to the city's central box office, which has tickets and information on local cultural events. Plans call for a second TI to open at the Fire Tower when renovation work there is complete.

Arrival in Sopron

By Train: Sopron's compact little train station is situated an easy half-mile walk south of the Old Town. Stepping into the main lobby with your back to the tracks, you'll find luggage lockers (on left), an ATM (on right), an international ticket window (ahead on left), and a domestic ticket window (ahead on right).

Outside on the left is a **taxi** stand (about 1,000 Ft to hotels at the far end of town, taxi tel. 99/333-333). You can also hop a **bus** heading into town (#1, #2, #3Y, #10, #10Y, #12, and #12A); all of them go directly to the Várkerület ring road that encircles the Old Town. Note: As you exit the station, the bus stop directly to your left is for buses going *away from* town; for buses *into* town, walk a half-block straight ahead and look for the stop on the right side of the street. You can buy a ticket for 300 Ft from a kiosk, or pay 350 Ft to the driver.

It's a 10-minute **walk** into the Old Town—just go straight out of the station and head four blocks up Mátyás király utca toward the big yellow building in the distance (halfway there, you'll cross the long, skinny park called Deák tér). When you reach the park-like Széchenyi tér, cross into it, turn left at the flagpole (commem-orating Hungarian uprisings throughout history), and look for the big, yellow building on the right (the Franz Liszt Cultural Center). The TI is inside, and the street next to it—Templom utca—is the main drag through the Old Town.

Sights in Sopron

Old Town (Belváros)

Sopron's Old Town is peppered with museums, but only a few are worthwhile (if tight on time or money, visit the Storno House and climb the Fire Tower, but skip the rest). Notice that these sights are listed in order of a handy orientation walk (which begins where the "Arrival in Sopron" directions, earlier, leave off). While the Old Town is charming, it can feel pretty dead. The main business street, Várkerület, which arcs around the Old Town, makes up for this, and the square around the Fidelity Monument at the far side of town can be full of energy.

• *Begin exploring the town in front of the TI and the yellow...*

Franz Liszt Cultural Center—The huge building holds Sopron's main concert hall, TI, and central box office. The side facing Széchenyi tér is boldly marked with the words *Magyar Művelődés Háza* ("House of Hungarian Culture") to show up their Germanic rivals. Its current name honors the composer who was born in So-pron county (back when it was part of Austria) and performed his first-ever public concert here in Sopron in 1820, when he was only nine years old. Notice the bust (to the right of the entrance) honoring this favorite son. You'll see "Liszt played here" signs all over town.

• *Now head into the Old Town on...*

Templom Utca ("Church Street")—This was where impor-tant local bigwigs lived: mayors, lawyers, and intelligentsia. The town's sturdy wall spared it from being devastated by the Tatar and Ottoman invaders that reshaped much of Hungary. However, a fire, quickly spread by the strong winds that blow through this valley, consumed the town in 1676. Sopron was rebuilt in Baroque style (often over earlier Gothic cellars), which has left it color-ful and tidy-looking. You'll notice that every other building has a *MŰEMLÉK* ("historical monument") plaque. Although lots of locally important people and events have graced Sopron, very little

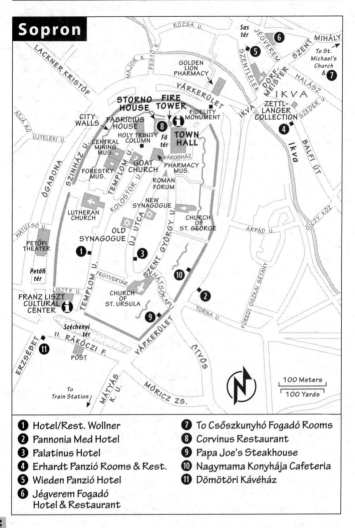

Sopron

1 Hotel/Rest. Wollner

2 Pannonia Med Hotel

3 Palatinus Hotel

4 Erhardt Panzió Rooms & Rest.

5 Wieden Panzió Hotel

6 Jégverem Fogadó
Hotel & Restaurant

7 To Csőszkunyhó Fogadó Rooms

8 Corvinus Restaurant

9 Papa Joe's Steakhouse

10 Nagymama Konyhája Cafeteria

11 Dömötöri Kávéház

of it is meaningful to visitors. Don't worry about the nitty-gritty of the town's history—just enjoy its ambience.

Notice the many fine passages leading to noble courtyards. For example, near the end of the first, very long block, at #12 (on the left), go into the Gothic passage (with pointy arches), which goes into a little courtyard with a Renaissance porch (with rounded arches), showing the evolution of the local architecture.

Back on the main street and a few steps down, the big church on the left is Lutheran. Because the local mayor protected the rights of religious minorities, Sopron was unusually tolerant, attracting groups who were persecuted elsewhere (such as Lutherans at the time of the Reformation). The first Lutheran congregation here was established in 1565, and the current building dates from 1782. Inside, the fine 1884 pipe organ and stately pulpit emphasize the Lutheran emphasis on preaching the word of God. The white-marble 1946 monument just outside the door memorializes the boarded-up windows of Sopron's Jewish ghetto; the local Jewish population was decimated during the Holocaust (we'll learn more about this dark time later).

• *When the road forks at the green building, stay left. In the next block on the left are two very modest museums, dedicated to Sopron's major industries. First, at #4, is the...*

Forestry Museum (Erdészeti Gyűjtemény)—While most of Hungary's geography consists of rolling plains and farmland, the area around Sopron is heavily wooded. This museum, part of the local Forestry College, celebrates that heritage, but has virtually no English information and is worthwhile only if you have a special interest. A second collection, upstairs, features the big- and small-game hunting trophies of Béla Hidvégi, a Hungarian sportsman who has traveled the world (a touchscreen provides information in English).

After the 1956 Uprising, there was an exodus of teachers and students from Sopron's Forestry College to Vancouver, British Columbia. To this day, Hungarians play a major role in the Canadian timber industry.

Cost and Hours: 800 Ft for each collection or 1,300 Ft for both; May-Oct Thu-Tue 10:00-17:00, Nov-April Thu-Tue 10:00-13:00—possibly later, closed Wed year-round; Templom utca 4, tel. 99/338-870.

• *Next door at #2 is the slightly more interesting...*

Central Mining Museum (Központi Bányászati Múzeum)—Displayed around a courtyard in the beautiful town house of a powerful local family, this museum explains the lives of miners and the history of Hungarian mining and coinage. It also features a life-size replica of a mineshaft and small-scale working models of mining equipment. Collections include decorative items made of metal, and rock and mineral samples. Look for the little dioramas-in-bottles, created by miners.

Cost and Hours: 700 Ft; April-Oct Tue-Sun 10:00-18:00, Nov-March Tue-Sun 10:00-16:00, closed Mon year-round; Templom utca 2, tel. 99/312-667.

• *At the end of the block, the street opens into the main square. Before exploring the square, visit the Gothic church on the right...*

Goat Church (Kecske Templom)—So nicknamed for the goat on the coat of arms over its door, this prominent Benedictine church is a Sopron landmark. While much of the rest of Hungary was occupied by the Ottomans, this region remained in Hungarian hands—and this church was actually used for a few royal coronations and parliament sessions. The Gothic interior is adorned with wood-carved Baroque altars and a Rococo pulpit. Notice how the once-clean Gothic apse has been obliterated by the retrofitted Baroque altar—illustrating how little regard each age had for the previous era's art. On the right, find the plaque listing the ancestors of István Széchenyi who are buried here. (Széchenyi was a powerful 18th-century aristocrat who championed the rights of the poor and built,

among other things, Budapest's Chain Bridge.) By the door, you can pop in a coin to light things up: 200 Ft for a little light, or 400 Ft for lots of light.

Other parts of the church require an additional admission fee (not worth it): the crypt, where various old graves and tombs have been consolidated into a tasteful modern mausoleum; a series of touchscreen terminals that offer additional information about specific church features; and the little cloister and chapter hall, where the carvings that top the columns represent human sins.

Cost and Hours: The church is open daily 8:00-19:00 (likely closes earlier in winter). During certain times when the touchscreen exhibition is open (Tue-Sun 10:00-12:00 & 13:00-17:00), you'll pay 200 Ft for the church or 700 Ft to also enter the crypt and chapter house; at other times, it's free to enter the church but the exhibition is closed.

• *Leaving the church, you're in the middle of Sopron's...*

▲▲**Main Square (Fő Tér)**—One of the most appealing Old World squares in Hungary, this area is dominated by the giant **Holy Trinity Column,** erected in 1701 to commemorate the 1695 plague. The wealthy local couple who survived the plague and commissioned the column kneel in thanksgiving at its base.

Above them, the column corkscrews up to heaven, marked by Jesus, God the Father, and a dove representing the Holy Spirit. Gleeful cherubs, as if celebrating life after the plague, ride back down the column like kids on a waterslide.

Grand buildings surround the column. Orient yourself with the Goat Church to your back: On the left is the big, white Neoclassical County Hall. To the right of it are three historic houses, two of which contain museums. The tall **Fire Tower** (described later) is the town's main landmark. Next to it is the vast, off-white 19th-century Town Hall, in the eye-pleasing Historicist style of the day. (Those interested in ancient history can walk behind the Town Hall to see fragments of Roman-era Sopron, with posted English information.) Across from the Town Hall, the little yellow building sticking out into the square houses a small **Pharmacy Museum** (Patika-Ház), which was a working pharmacy from 1642 to 1967 (you can see most everything from the door with a sweep of your head, or pay 500 Ft to examine the exhibits up close; Tue-Sun 10:00-14:00, closed Mon). In the early 16th century, local officials wanted to tear down this house to enlarge the square. But the king, who had visited Sopron earlier and enjoyed the square the way it was, decreed that it not be touched...making it Hungary's first government-protected building.

• *If you're ready for some museum-going, consider the two collections in the pretty Baroque house with the corner turret overlooking the square.*

▲▲**Storno House (Storno-Ház)**—This prime real estate is marked with plaques celebrating visits by two big-league Hungarians: King Mátyás (Matthias) Corvinus and Franz Liszt. Today the building houses two exhibits: the Storno Collection and the "History without Borders" exhibition.

Cost and Hours: Storno Collection-1,000 Ft, history exhibit-700 Ft; both open April-Sept Tue-Sun 10:00-18:00, Oct-March Tue-Sun 14:00-18:00, closed Mon year-round; Fő tér 8, tel. 99/311-327.

Visiting the Museum: Sopron's best museum is the **Storno Collection** (Storno-Gyűjtemény), upstairs. Franz Storno, the son of a poor 19th-century Swiss family of chimney sweeps, showed prodigious talent as an artist at a young age and ultimately became

quite a Renaissance man. He moved here to Sopron, married a chimney-sweep master's widow, and became a restorer of buildings for the Habsburg Empire. Today, in his creaky old house, charming attendants direct visitors through a series of jam-packed rooms to look at a random but fun grab-bag of paintings, decorative items, and other bric-a-brac that Franz collected in his renovation work. While you can borrow an English leaflet for a room-by-room description, renting the cheap audioguide (200 Ft) makes the place much more meaningful—well worth the 30 minutes

its narration takes. Following this forces you to take time to look around, and it highlights wonderful little details. In the entrance hall, check out the panorama painting of 18th-century Sopron (high up on the wall). Later, the balcony room boasts a gorgeously painted, light-filled alcove with table and chairs (as well as more paintings of old Sopron). The old iron box in the middle of this room has a complicated secret-locking system. Passing through the painted door into the bedroom, look for the Biedermeier paintings on the ceilings. The antler chandelier shows a 3-D version of the family seal: chimney-sweeping brush in one hand, compass (for restoration work) in the other. In the final room (the salon), you'll see square tables with hinged edges that can be brought up to make them circular. These were practical but also superstitious: It was considered bad luck for a young woman to sit at the corner of a table (either she'd never marry or have a difficult mother-in-law, depending on the legend), so this design ensured that would never happen.

Downstairs, the well-presented **"History without Borders"** (Határtalan Történet) exhibit, which traces the history of Sopron, is also worth a look (no audioguide, but good English information posted). In the final room, find the exhibit about the post-World War I referendum in which Sopron elected to remain part of Hungary instead of Austria. The referendum, which took place in December of 1921, asked citizens to vote with color-coded ballots whether they would join Austria or Hungary. As you can see from the bilingual posters announcing the results, Hungary won 15,334 votes to Austria's 8,227. This cemented Sopron's already-established reputation as being the "most loyal town." (Maybe it was because other Austrians would never let them live down the town's German name, Ödenburg, which roughly means "Dullsville.") Nearby, you'll see propaganda trying to convince locals to vote one way or another—such as the unsettling poster of the skeleton, clad in traditional Hungarian folk costume, menacingly serenading the town on his violin.

• *Two buildings to the left of the Storno House is the...*

Fabricius House (Fabricius-Ház)—This historic mansion, once belonging to Sopron's most beloved mayor, is home to a pair of dull, skippable museums. The **Civic Apartments** (Polgári Lakások), basically a collection of old furniture, will appeal only to antique-lovers. The **Archaeological Exhibit** (Régészet-Kőtár) is a very dry overview of the history of Sopron, especially relating to the Amber Road trade route that put the town on the map. The best part is the Roman Lapidarium in the cellar (same ticket)—a collection of Roman tombstones unearthed here, as well as the shattered fragments of three larger-than-life Roman statues.

Cost and Hours: Apartments-800 Ft, archaeological exhibit-700 Ft; both open April-Sept Tue-Sun 10:00-18:00, Oct-March Tue-Sun 10:00-14:00, closed Mon year-round; Fő tér 6.

• *Dominating the Main Square is Sopron's symbol, the...*

Fire Tower (Tűztorony)—A Roman watchtower once stood here, but the current version was gradually expanded from the 13th to the 18th centuries. Fire watchmen would survey the town from the top of the tower, then mark the direction of a fire with colorful flags (by day) or a bright light (at night) to warn townspeople. The tower recently completed an extensive restoration, so some details may differ from what's described here.

Cost and Hours: Likely 1,000 Ft; May-mid-Sept daily 10:00-20:00; April and mid-Sept-Oct Tue-Sun 10:00-18:00, closed Mon; closed Nov-March; Fő tér 1.

Visiting the Tower: Just above the passage through the gate is a stone carving depicting Hungária, the female embodiment of Hungary—given to the city to thank them for choosing Hungary during the 1921 referendum.

Buy your ticket and climb the 120 steps to the top. On the way up, pause at the landings to check out the exhibits. There are historic photos and drawings of the tower, and the original double-headed Habsburg eagle—with an "L" for the Emperor Leopold—that topped the tower's spire.

At the top, do a clockwise spin: First is a great view over the rooftops of the Old Town; beyond that, you can see the Lőver Hills,

Sopron's playground. (While the name sounds romantic, *lőver* refers to master archers who defended the border from Tatar invasions in the 13th century.) Continuing around the tower and looking down, you'll see remains of the city wall defining the Old Town; an outer wall was once located on the outside of today's ring road. Beyond the stadium lights is Austria. A bit farther to the right, the big steeple in the distance is St. Michael's, one of Sopron's historic churches. Farther to the right, the oddly shaped bulbous tower on the hill is a windmill missing its blades. This was used to garrison Habsburg troops after the 1848 Revolution.

• *Descending from the tower, continue through the gateway.*

Outside the Walls—Just on the other side of the tower, look for the giant **key monument** on the left, commemorating a "key" event in this loyal town's history. After presenting the Hungarian king with the key to their city when his rival was planning an invasion, Sopron was rewarded with free royal town status, which came with special privileges (in 1277). Just beyond is the entrance to the **City**

Wall Walk (Várfal Sétány), where you can walk along part of the course of the surviving wall (not particularly scenic since it's outside the wall rather than on top of it; free, Mon-Fri 9:00-20:00, Sat-Sun 9:00-18:00).

Just outside the Old Town, you reach the ring road and a livelier zone. Look (on your left) for a modern **sculpture** with three figures, each one representing a time when Sopron demonstrated its fidelity: 1277, when the town sided with the Hungarian king (described earlier); 1921, when they voted to remain part of Hungary; and 1989, when the Iron Curtain fell (symbolized by the woman breaking the barbed wire). In August of that fateful year—before the communists had officially given up the ghost—the "Pan-European Picnic" took place in the hills near Sopron. Residents of various Central European countries—East Germany, Austria, and Hungary—came together for the first time in decades, offering a tantalizing taste of freedom.

Across the busy ring road from this sculpture, look for the **Golden Lion Pharmacy** (Gyógyszertár Apotheke sign), which has beautiful Art Nouveau Zsolnay porcelain decorations.

Looking back toward the Old Town, notice the **colorful little shops** that cling like baby animals to the protective town walls.

• From here, you can backtrack to the Main Square and head down New Street to more sights (described next). Or keep going beyond the walls into the Ikva neighborhood (described in the "Ikva Neighborhood" section on next page).

To see more of the **Old Town**, take the street to the left of the Pharmacy Museum (as you face it). This is...

New Street (Új Utca)—This misnamed street is actually one of the oldest in town. Near the start of the street (a few steps down from the Main Square), the building at the fork has remains of the original **forum** of Sopron's Roman settlement in its basement (likely closed to the public except by prior reservation—but if you see a museum here and are interested in ancient ruins, drop in).

Continue to the right, down New Street—which used to be

called **"Jewish Street"** (Zsidó utca) until the Jews were kicked out in 1526. After the 1848 Revolution, they finally returned...but for less than a century. When the Nazis took control of Hungary, they walled off both ends of this street and turned it into a ghetto. Some 1,840 Sopron Jews were eventually sent to concentration camps... where 1,650 of them died. Along the street, about one block down, are two synagogues. The first is the **New Synagogue** (Új Zsinagóga), in a modern office on the left at #11. It's not a museum, but if the door is open you can peek inside.

A few steps down, on the right at #22, is the **Old Synagogue** (Ó Zsinagóga), dating from the early 14th century (800 Ft, borrow English descriptions, May-Oct Tue-Sun 10:00-18:00, closed Mon and Nov-April, Új utca 22, tel. 99/311-327). Rediscovered in 1968, it has been renovated but still retains a few of its original elements (such as the Torah holder). Notice the two adjacent rooms, separated by narrow windows: Men worshipped in the main room, with the women in the smaller room. In the courtyard is a reconstruction of a ritual bath.

• *New Street ends at Ursula Square (Orsolya tér), watched over by the Church of St. Ursula and a statue of Mary that stands in the center of the square. If you double back to the left, you can head up the third of old Sopron's three parallel streets...*

St. George's Street (Szent György Utca)—This street is named for the red-and-white **Church of St. George** (halfway down the street on the right, free, daily 8:00-18:00). The beautiful, stuccoed Baroque interior hosted Lutheran services for a time, but the Lutherans were evicted during the Counter-Reformation. Head across the street and into the fine Renaissance courtyard at #12, where the Lutherans were forced to worship al fresco. Notice the stone pulpit carved into the upper balcony, and the metal rings used to secure a tarp that covered the service in bad weather.

• *St. George's Street will take you right back up to the Main Square, where—if you haven't already—you can head into...*

The Ikva Neighborhood, Northeast of the Old Town

With a little more time, venture into the workaday streets northeast of the Old Town—beyond the ring road and the Ikva brook (hidden here beneath the road). While lacking the storybook charm of the Old Town, this area is also historic. Back when wealthy aristocrats populated the Old Town, farmers and craftsmen lived here—giving it a rustic, lived-in ambience that's fun to explore. (It's also home to several recommended accommodations, and the good Jégverem restaurant—see "Sleeping in Sopron" and "Eating in Sopron," later.)

The main drag changes names as it twists through this neighborhood (first called Ikva híd, then Dorfmeister utca, then Szent Mihály utca). Eventually it leads up a hill to **St. Michael's Church** (Szent Mihály Templom) and the adjacent little Romanesque chapel. The church complex is surrounded by a cemetery.

• *Closer to the Belváros, but still in the Ikva neighborhood, is one final Sopron sight, the...*

▲Zettl-Langer Collection (Zettl-Langer Gyűjtemény)—A Bavarian art lover named Gustav Zettl came to Sopron in the late 19th century, set up a distillery, and became a pillar of the community. Today his descendants (usually his great-granddaughter,

Ágnes Langer, who speaks English) lead tours of this fine old townhouse that's jammed with Gustav's eclectic private collection of furniture, porcelain, paintings, knickknacks, and more. Ágnes will show you everything from a collection of ancient Roman vessels to fine inlaid furniture (find out why a "money changer's table" has a marble top) to delicately decorated windows to all manner of clever cupboards with hidden panels and drawers. It's similar in many ways to the excellent Storno Collection on the Main Square, but because the family still resides here, this is a unique opportunity to see a very lived-in home that feels like a museum (or vice versa). Each item on display has been in the family for generations, and Ágnes relishes telling their stories in as much detail as you'd like to hear. Near the end is Gustav's death announcement, in a frame that also holds a stack of dozens more. It must be both sobering and comforting for Gustav's descendants to know that their death notices will be added to the family stack someday. The public can only visit with a tour (generally about 40 minutes); it's smart to call ahead to let Ágnes know you're coming.

Cost and Hours: 1,000 Ft per person to enter, plus 2,000 Ft for the group for the mandatory tour; April-Oct Tue-Sun 10:00-12:00, closed Mon; Nov-Jan and March, Fri-Sun 10:00-12:00, closed Mon-Thu; closed Feb; Balfi utca 11, tel. 99/311-136.

Hiking

With its forested hillsides and fresh air, Sopron is popular with hikers. To get to the best trailhead, take bus #1 or #2 from the Old Town to Lőver Körút, and get off at the giant-domed bath complex. From here, several trails lead through the hills. Before setting out, get advice from the TI (they can give you a free map, or sell you a better one).

Sleeping in Sopron

Few places have air-conditioning; even fewer have an elevator (I've noted those that do).

In or near the Old Town

You'll pay a bit extra to be right in the Old Town. But it's worth it—not for the convenience, but for the romance of calling those floodlit cobbles home after dark.

$$$ Hotel Wollner, a top option in Sopron, is classy. This 300-year-old Baroque townhouse on the Old Town's main street is thoroughly renovated and rents 18 tastefully appointed rooms. A good restaurant and an inviting terraced garden in the rear round out its appeal (Sb-17,000 Ft, Db-20,000 Ft, bigger superior Db-23,000 Ft, Tb-26,000 Ft, entirely non-smoking, free Wi-Fi, Templom utca 20, tel. 99/524-400, www.wollner.hu, wollner@wollner.hu).

$$$ Pannonia Med Hotel, a Best Western, rents 87 rooms on the ring road just across from the Old Town. The large public areas recall Sopron's faded elegance, while the rooms are straightforward business-class and charmless. As you're paying a premium for its big-hotel services (such as a swimming pool and fitness center), it's a bit overpriced (smaller "classic" Db with older furnishings-16,000-29,000 Ft depending on demand, 2,000 Ft more for bigger and newer "comfort" Db with air-con, elevator, free Internet access and Wi-Fi, street noise—ask for quieter room, Várkerület 75, tel. 99/312-180, www.pannoniahotel.com, sopron@hotelpannonia.com).

$$ Palatinus Hotel is a soulless, tour-oriented place with 31 rooms. But it's a good value—modern, well-priced, and ideally located in the heart of the Old Town (rates vary but typically Sb-9,000 Ft, Db-13,000 Ft, three floors with no elevator, non-smoking rooms, free Wi-Fi, parking-1,000 Ft/day—reserve ahead, Új utca 23, tel. 99/523-816, www.palatinussopron.com, info@palatinussopron.com).

Northeast of the Old Town

These four accommodations are just outside the ring road. While not as romantic as the Old Town, this appealing residential zone is

Sleep Code

(200 Ft = about $1, country code: 36, area code: 99)
S = Single, **D** = Double/Twin, **T** = Triple, **Q** = Quad, **b** = bathroom. Unless otherwise noted, English is spoken, breakfast is included, and credit cards are accepted. The hotel tax (350 Ft per person, per night) is not included in these rates.

To help you sort easily through these listings, I've divided the accommodations into three categories, based on the price for a standard double room with bath:

$$$ Higher Priced—Most rooms 15,000 Ft or more.
$$ Moderately Priced—Most rooms between 10,000-15,000 Ft.
$ Lower Priced—Most rooms 10,000 Ft or less.

Prices can change without notice; verify the hotel's current rates online or by email.

also historic. The first three places are a five-minute, slightly uphill walk from the Old Town, while the fourth (the best value) is about five minutes farther up.

$$ Erhardt Panzió rents nine rooms above their upscale-feeling restaurant, in a nicely restored house on a quiet, if dingy, street (Sb-10,000 Ft, Db-12,500 Ft, air-con, free Wi-Fi, Balfi utca 10, tel. 99/506-711, www.erhardtpanzio.hu, info@erhardtpanzio.hu).

$$ Wieden Panzió, run by the Fazekas family, has 15 basic but crisp, recently renovated rooms (Sb-8,000 Ft, Db-11,000 Ft, Tb-14,000 Ft, some very large rooms also available, free Wi-Fi, some street noise—request quiet room on the courtyard, Sas tér 13, tel. 99/523-222, www.wieden.hu, wieden@fullnet.hu).

$ Jégverem Fogadó ("Ice House Inn"), with a recommended restaurant, rents five cheap, simple, well-worn rooms upstairs from its busy eatery (Sb-7,000 Ft, Db-9,000 Ft, extra bed-2,000 Ft, breakfast extra, free Wi-Fi, Jégverem utca 1, tel. 99/510-113, www.jegverem.hu, jegverem@jegverem.hu).

$ Csőszkunyhó Fogadó ("Field Guard's Shelter") sits across the street from St. Michael's Church, on a small hill near the Old Town. Above this local restaurant are two beautiful, spacious, woody rooms—the nicest I've seen in Sopron in this price range. The catch: Limited English is spoken (Sb-5,900 Ft, Db-6,900 Ft, Tb-9,300 Ft, cash only, free Wi-Fi, Szent Mihály utca 35, tel. 99/506-588, www.csoszkunyho.hu, csoszkunyho@gmail.com).

SOPRON

Eating in Sopron

You might notice lots of bean dishes on the menu in Sopron. The thrifty Germans—who were responsible for most of the winemaking in the surrounding hills—would plant beans in the earth between their rows of vines. In fact, in local dialect, German residents are called "bean farmers." Sopron is also known for its local beer (called Soproni) and for its local wines.

Jégverem Fogadó ("Ice House Inn") serves up heaping plates of reliably tasty Hungarian food from a clever, descriptive menu. It's worth the five-minute walk outside the Old Town (near several recommended accommodations). The circular table in the middle of the cozy dining room peers down into a pit where ice was stored to be sold through the hot summer months. In good weather, sit out on the inviting terrace. As portions are huge, consider sharing or ordering a smaller dish (1,700-2,800-Ft meals, daily 11:00-23:00, Jégverem utca 1, tel. 99/510-113).

Corvinus, across from the City Hall and in the shadow of the Fire Tower, is a no-brainer for a romantic al fresco dinner on the Main Square. With a traditional menu of good Hungarian classics and a few international dishes, the place sprawls into a wine cellar and its sister restaurant next door, the Generális café (1,000-2,200-Ft main dishes, also indoor seating, daily 11:30-22:00, Fő tér 7-8, tel. 99/505-035).

Papa Joe's, an American-style steakhouse, had my travel sensibilities crying, "No!"—but my stomach saying, "Hmmmm... maybe." Here's your chance to experience the Old West through Hungarian eyes. Done up to the nines like a cowboy saloon (including six-shooter-handle doorknobs and saddle barstools), this theme restaurant grills up steaks and other Tex-Mex dishes (such as baked beans). When Hungarians want a break from Hungarian food, they come here (2,000-4,000-Ft main dishes, daily 11:00-24:00, Várkerület 108, tel. 99/340-933).

Erhardt Restaurant, in the Ivka neighborhood just outside the Old Town (a 5-minute walk away), serves Hungarian and international fare in a sophisticated-feeling, white-tablecloth, mellow dining room (2,300-2,900-Ft main dishes, daily 11:30-23:00, Balfi utca 10, tel. 99/506-711).

Hotel Wollner, nicely located in the center of the Old Town, has a good restaurant with indoor or outdoor courtyard seating, serving up crowd-pleasing Hungarian and international dishes (1,900-2,400-Ft main dishes, daily 12:00-22:00, Templom utca 20, tel. 99/524-400).

Fast and Cheap: **Nagymama Konyhája** ("Grandma's Kitchen") is your best option for a quick, no-frills meal. This small self-service cafeteria, filled with locals, specializes in savory and

sweet crêpes (*palacsinta*, 600-900 Ft), but also offers other traditional Hungarian dishes. Just point to what you want, or ask to see
the clear English menu (1,000-1,200 Ft for most meals, Mon-Sat
10:00-21:00, Sun 12:00-21:00, Várkerület 104, mobile 0620-315-
8730).

Coffee and Cake: **Dömötöri Kávéház** is a pastry and coffee
shop slinging a wide array of cakes and fancy ice-cream dishes—
with seating in a classy interior, in an aristocratic upstairs, and out
on a pretty square across from the big, yellow Franz Liszt Center. It's where locals satisfy their sweet tooth (400-500-Ft desserts, Mon-Thu 7:00-22:00, Fri-Sat 7:00-23:00, Sun 8:00-22:00,
Széchenyi tér 13, tel. 99/506-623).

Sopron Connections

From Sopron by Train to: Budapest (6/day direct, 2.5 hours, more
with a transfer in Győr), **Eger** (about every 2 hours, 5-6 hours,
transfer in Budapest and sometimes also in Füzesabony), **Pécs**
(1/day direct in the morning, 5.5 hours; otherwise about every 2
hours, 5.25 hours, most transfer at Budapest's suburban Kelenföld
station), **Bratislava,** Slovakia (at least hourly, 2.5-3 hours, usually
two transfers—often at stations in downtown and/or suburban
Vienna), **Vienna,** Austria (1-2/hour, 1.5 hours, transfer in Weiner
Neustadt).

BRATISLAVA, SLOVAKIA

Pozsony / Pressburg

The Slovak capital, Bratislava (brah-tee-SLAH-vah), enjoys a priceless location—on the Danube (and the tourist circuit) smack-dab between Budapest and Vienna—that helps make it a worthwhile "on the way" destination.

Long a drab lesson in the failings of the communist system, Bratislava is turning things around. A decade ago, the city center was grim, deserted, and dangerous—a place where only thieves and fools dared to tread. Today it's downright charming, bursting with colorfully restored facades, lively outdoor cafés, swanky boutiques, in-love-with-life locals, and (on sunny days) an almost Mediterranean ambience.

The rejuvenation doesn't end in the old town. The ramshackle quarter to the east is gradually being flattened and redeveloped into a new forest of skyscrapers. Bratislava is working together with its neighbor Vienna to forge a new twin-city relationship for trade and commerce, bridging the former Eastern Europe and the former Western Europe. The hilltop castle is getting a facelift. And even the glum commie suburb of Petržalka is undergoing a Technicolor makeover. Before our eyes, Bratislava is becoming the quintessential post-communist Central European city—showing what can happen when government and business leaders make a concerted effort to jump-start a failing city.

And yet, it's still a city in transition, with sometimes striking contrasts. Tucked between the quaint old town and super-modern Euro-commerce zones, large pockets of post-communist decrepitude remain. (There's a reason why moviemakers wanting to show the stereotypically gloomy "communist Eastern Europe" decide to film here.)

You get the feeling that workaday Bratislavans—who strike some visitors as gruff—are being pulled to the cutting edge of the

21st century kicking and screaming. But many Slovaks embrace the changes and fancy themselves as the yang to Vienna's yin: If Vienna is a staid, elderly aristocrat sipping coffee, then Bratislava is a vivacious young professional jet-setting around Europe. Bratislava at night is a lively place; its very youthful center thrives. While it has tens of thousands of university students, there are no campuses as such—so the old town is the place where students go to play.

Frankly, Bratislava used to leave me cold. But all the changes are positively inspiring. While they still have a long way to go, the Slovaks have made the city well worth a quick visit to get a glimpse of a country in transition.

Planning Your Time

A few hours are plenty to get the gist of Bratislava. Head straight to the old town and follow my self-guided walk, finishing with a stroll along the Danube riverbank to the thriving, modern Eurovea development. With more time, take advantage of one or more of the city's fine viewpoints: Ascend to the "UFO" observation deck atop the funky bridge, ride the elevator up to the Sky Bar for a peek (and maybe a drink), or hike up to the castle for the views (but skip the ho-hum museum inside). There's little reason to spend the night here, but if you do, you'll find Bratislava lively with students, busy cafés, and nightlife.

Note that all museums and galleries are closed on Monday. That said, it's not a big deal if you're here on a Monday, since none of these sights is worth planning a trip around (the Primate's Palace is the best, but even that is skippable). Bratislava is more about wandering and catching the town's vibe than seeing specific sights.

Day-Tripping Tip: Bratislava is perfect for a side-trip from Vienna, or as a stopover on the way from Vienna to Budapest. But pay careful attention to train schedules, as the Vienna connection alternates between Bratislava's two train stations (Hlavná Stanica and Petržalka). If checking your bag at the station, be sure that your return or onward connection will depart from there.

Orientation to Bratislava

Bratislava, with nearly a half-million residents, is Slovakia's capital and biggest city. It has a small, colorful old town *(Staré Mesto)*, with the castle on the hill above. This small area is surrounded by a vast construction zone of new buildings, rotting residential districts desperately in need of beautification, and some colorized communist suburbs (including Petržalka, across the river). The northern and western parts of the city are hilly and cool (these "Little Carpathians" are draped with vineyards), while the southern and eastern areas are flat and warmer.

You've dropped in to visit Bratislava just as the city is trying to undo the brutally ugly infrastructure inflicted upon it by the communists. Eventually, the highway that barrels between the old town and the castle will be diverted underground (through a tunnel beneath the Danube); the TGV bullet train from Paris will swoosh to a stop at a slick new train station; and a new six-station subway line will lace the city together. The entire riverfront is being transformed into a people-friendly park (to match the new zone beyond the old iron bridge, in Eurovea). But Europe's economic situation has substantially slowed progress. Expect lots of construction (and possible public-transit and traffic headaches) during your visit.

Tourist Information

The TI is on **Primate's Square** behind the Old Town Hall (daily May-Sept 9:00-19:00, Oct-April 9:00-18:00, tel. 02/16186 or 02/5935-6661, www.bratislava.sk). Pick up the free *Bratislava Guide* (with map) and browse their brochures; they can help you find a room in town for a small fee. They also have a branch at the airport.

Discount Card: The TI sells the €10 **Bratislava City Card,** which includes free transit and sightseeing discounts for a full day—but it's worthwhile only if you're doing the old town walking tour (€14 without the card—see "Tours in Bratislava," later; also available for €12/2 days, €15/3 days).

Arrival in Bratislava

By Train

Main Train Station (Hlavná Stanica): This glum and depressing station is about a half-mile north of the old town. It was still standing on my last visit—but barely. In the next few years the city plans to tear it down and start from scratch (to accommodate, among other things, a new high-speed rail line connecting Bratislava to Paris). Therefore, these arrival instructions are likely to change; just look for signs.

As you emerge from the tracks, the left-luggage desk is to your right (€1-2, depending on size; look for *úschovňa batožín;* there are no lockers, and the check desk closes for 30-minute lunch and dinner breaks).

Getting from the Station to Downtown: It's an easy 15-minute **walk** to the town center. Leave the station straight ahead, take the overpass across the busy cross street, and continue straight on Štefánikova. This once-elegant old boulevard is lined with rotting facades from Bratislava's high-on-the-hog Habsburg era. After about 10 minutes, you'll pass the nicely manicured presidential gardens on your left, then the Grassalkovich Palace, Slovakia's "White House." Continue straight through the busy intersection onto

Welcome to Slovakia

In many ways, Slovakia is the "West Virginia of Europe"—relatively poor and undeveloped, but spectacularly beautiful in its own rustic way. Sitting quietly in the very center of Central Europe, wedged between bigger and stronger nations (Hungary, Austria, the Czech Republic, and Poland), Slovakia was brutally disfigured by the communists, then overshadowed by the Czechs. But in recent years, this fledgling republic has found its wings.

With about 5.5 million people in a country of 19,000 square miles (similar to Massachusetts and New Hampshire combined), Slovakia is one of Europe's smallest nations. Recent economic reforms have caused two very different Slovakias to emerge: the modern, industrialized, flat, affluent west, centered on the capital of Bratislava; and the remote, poorer, mountainous, "backward" east, with high unemployment and traditional lifestyles. Slovakia is ethnically diverse: In addition to the Slavic Slovaks, there are Hungarians (about 10 percent of the population, "stranded" here when Hungary lost this land after World War I) and Roma (Gypsies, also about 10 percent). Slovakia has struggled to incorporate both of these large and often-mistreated minority groups.

Slovakia has spent most of its history as someone else's backyard. For centuries, Slovakia was ruled from Budapest and known as "Upper Hungary." At other times, it was an important chunk of the Habsburg Empire, ruled from neighboring Vienna. But most people think first of another era: the 75 years that Slovakia was joined with the Czech Republic as the country of "Czechoslovakia." From its start in the aftermath of World War I, this union of the Czechs and Slovaks was troubled; some Slovaks chafed at being ruled from Prague, while many Czechs resented the financial burden of their poorer neighbors to the east.

After they gained their freedom from the communists during 1989's peaceful "Velvet Revolution," the Czechs and Slovaks

---

Súche Mýto, and head for the green onion-domed steeple (take the narrow street next to the mod, green, white-capped building). This is St. Michael's Gate, at the start of the old town (and the beginning of my self-guided walk, described later).

If you want to shave a few minutes off the trip, go part of the way by tram or bus. The **tram** is a bit easier (but may be closed for reconstruction): From the train station's main hall, with the tracks at your back, look left for signs to *električky*; take the escalator down, buy a ticket from the machine, hop on tram #13, and ride

began to think of the future. The Slovaks wanted to rename the country Czecho-Slovakia, and to redistribute power to give themselves more autonomy within the union. The Czechs balked, relations gradually deteriorated, and the Slovak nationalist candidate Vladimír Mečiar fared surprisingly well in the 1992 elections. Taking it as a sign that the two peoples wanted to part ways, politicians pushed through (in just three months) the peaceful separation of the now-independent Czech and Slovak Republics. (The people in both countries never actually voted on the change, and most opposed it.) The "Velvet Divorce" became official on January 1, 1993.

At first the Slovaks struggled. Communist rule had been particularly unkind to them, and their economy was in a shambles. Visionary leaders set forth bold solutions, including the 2003 implementation of a flat tax (19 percent), followed by EU membership in 2004. Before long, major international corporations began to notice the same thing the communists had: This is a great place to build stuff, thanks to a strategic location (300 million consumers live within a day's truck drive), low labor costs, and a well-trained workforce. Not surprisingly, multiple foreign automakers have plants here. Today Slovakia produces one million cars a year, making the country the world's biggest car producer (per capita) and leading the *New York Times* to dub Slovakia "the European Detroit."

The flat tax and other aggressively pro-business policies have not been without their critics—especially in the very impoverished eastern half of the country, where poor people feel they're becoming even poorer. With the rollback of social services and the proverbial cracks widening, many seem to have been left behind by Slovakia's bold new economy.

Even so, particularly if you zoom in on its success story around Bratislava, the evidence is impressive. Bratislava has only 3 percent unemployment. The standard of living (as it relates to local costs) puts Bratislava in 10th place among European cities. Slovakia joined the EU in 2004; in 2009, it adopted the euro currency. While most of Europe is struggling through difficult economic times, much of Slovakia seems poised for its brightest future yet.

it to the Poštová stop, then walk straight down Obchodná street toward St. Michael's Gate. If the tram isn't running, you can take **bus** #X13 or #93: Walk out the front station door and find the bus stops lining the road to the right. Ride two stops to Hodžovo Námestie, across the street from Grassalkovich Palace. Facing the palace, turn left and curve with the busy street past the pink-and-white church and toward the onion-topped tower. Both the tram and bus are covered by a €0.70/15-minute ticket (buy from a kiosk or one of many machines, select *základný lístok—latí 15 minút,* then insert coins—change given).

Petržalka Train Station (ŽST Petržalka): About half the trains from Vienna arrive at Bratislava's other train station, in the Petržalka suburb. From this station, walk out front and ride bus #80, #93, or #94 to the Zochova stop (near St. Michael's Gate), or bus #91 or #191 to the Nový Most stop (at the old town end of the New Bridge). Buses #93 (by day) and #N93 (by night) also connect the two stations. Any of these rides is covered by the same €0.70/15-minute ticket described earlier.

By Boat or Plane

For information on Bratislava's riverboats and airport, see "Bratislava Connections," at the end of this chapter.

Helpful Hints

Money: Slovakia uses the euro currency (€1 = about $1.30). You'll find ATMs at the train stations and airport.

Language: While many people in Bratislava speak English, the official language is Slovak (closely related to Czech and Polish). The local "ciao"—used informally for both "hi" and "bye"—is easy to remember: *ahoj* (pronounced "AH-hoy," like a pirate). "Please" is *prosím* (PROH-seem), "thank you" is *ďakujem* (DYAH-koo-yehm), "good" is *dobrý* (DOH-bree), and "Cheers!" is *Na zdravie!* (nah ZDRAH-vyeh).

Phone Tips: When calling locally (such as within Bratislava), dial the number without the area code. To make a long-distance call within Slovakia, start with the area code (which begins with 0). Slovakia's country code is 421. To call from Hungary to Slovakia, dial 00-421, then the area code minus the initial zero, then the number (from the US, dial 011-421-area code minus zero, then the number). To call from Slovakia to Hungary, you'd dial 00-36, then the area code (minus the initial zero) and number.

Internet Access: You'll see signs advertising Internet cafés around the old town. If you have a laptop or other Wi-Fi-enabled device, you can get online for free at the three major old town squares (Main Square, Primate's Square, and Hviezdoslav Square).

Local Guidebook: For in-depth suggestions on Bratislava sightseeing, dining, and more, look for the excellent and eye-pleasing *Bratislava Active* guidebook by Martin Sloboda (see "Tours in Bratislava," next; around €10, sold at every postcard rack).

Tours in Bratislava

Walking Tour—The **TI** offers a one-hour old town walking tour in English every day in the summer at 14:00 (€14, or free with €10 Bratislava City Card; you must book and pay at least two hours in advance). Those arriving by boat will be accosted by guides selling their own 1.5-hour tours (half on foot and half in a little tourist train, €10, in German and English).

Local Guide—MS Agency, run by **Martin Sloboda** (can-do entrepreneur and tireless Bratislava booster, and author of the great local guidebook described earlier), can set you up with a good guide (€130/3 hours, €150/4 hours); he can also help you track down your Slovak roots. Martin, whose expertise has made much of this chapter possible, is a fine example of the youthful energy and leadership responsible for Bratislava's success story (mobile 0905-627-265, tel. 02/5464-1467, www.msagency.sk, info@msagency.sk).

Self-Guided Walk

Bratislava's Old Town

This orientation walk passes through the heart of delightfully traffic-free old Bratislava and then down to its riverside commercial zone (figure 1.5 hours, not including stops, for this walk). If you're coming from the station, make your way toward the green onion-domed steeple of St. Michael's Gate (explained in "Arrival in Bratislava," earlier). Before going through the passage into the old town, peek over the railing on your left to the inviting garden below—once part of the city moat.

• *Step through the first gate, walk along the passageway, and pause as you come through the onion-domed...*

St. Michael's Gate (Michalská Brána)

This is the last surviving tower of the city wall. Just below the gate, notice the "kilometer zero" plaque in the ground, marking the point from which distances in Slovakia are measured.

• *You're at the head of...*

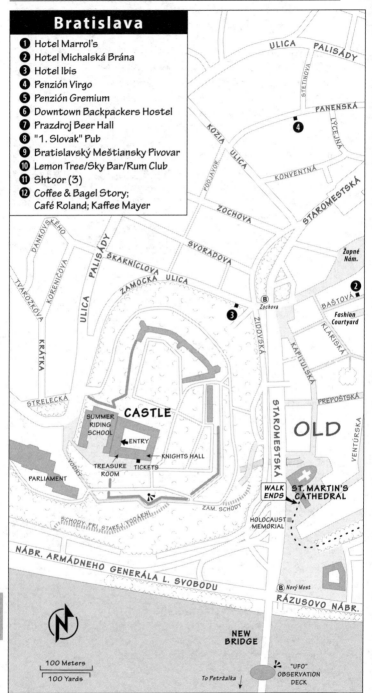

Bratislava

1. Hotel Marrol's
2. Hotel Michalská Brána
3. Hotel Ibis
4. Penzión Virgo
5. Penzión Gremium
6. Downtown Backpackers Hostel
7. Prazdroj Beer Hall
8. "1. Slovak" Pub
9. Bratislavský Meštiansky Pivovar
10. Lemon Tree/Sky Bar/Rum Club
11. Shtoor (3)
12. Coffee & Bagel Story;
    Café Roland; Kaffee Mayer

ULICA PALISÁDY
ŠTETINOVA
PANENSKÁ
LYCEJNÁ
KOZIA ULICA
PODJAVOR
KONVENTNÁ
STAROMESTSKÁ

DANKOVSKÉHO
KORENIČOVA
ULICA PALISÁDY
ŠKARNÍCLOVA
ZOCHOVA
SVORADOVA
Župné Nám.

TVAROŽKOVA
ZÁMOCKÁ ULICA
ZOCHOVA
B Zochova
BAŠTOVÁ
Fashion Courtyard

KRÁTKA
ŽIDOVSKÁ
KLARISKÁ
KAPITULSKÁ

STRELECKÁ
PREPOŠTSKÁ

CASTLE
SUMMER RIDING SCHOOL
ENTRY
KNIGHTS HALL
TREASURE ROOM
TICKETS
STAROMESTSKÁ
OLD
VENTÚRSKA

PARLIAMENT
VODNÝ
WALK ENDS
ST. MARTIN'S CATHEDRAL
ZÁM. SCHODY
HOLOCAUST MEMORIAL

SCHODY PRI STAREJ VODÁRNI
NÁBR. ARMÁDNEHO GENERÁLA L. SVOBODU

B Nový Most
RÁZUSOVO NÁBR.

N

100 Meters
100 Yards

NEW BRIDGE

To Petržalka

"UFO" OBSERVATION DECK

BRATISLAVA

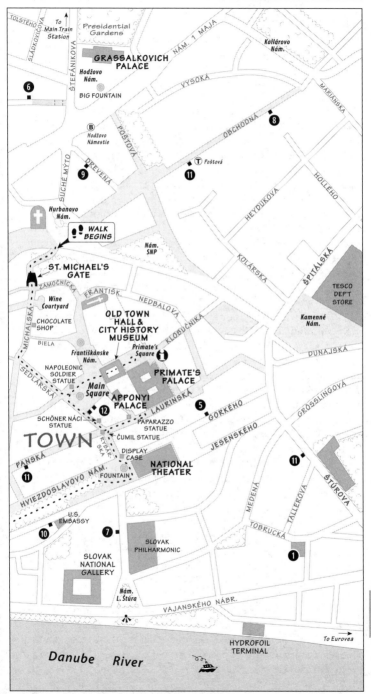

TOLSTÉHO

To Main Train Station

Presidential Gardens

SLÁDKOVIČOVA

ŠTEFÁNIKOVA

NÁM. 1 MÁJA

Kollárovo Nám.

GRASSALKOVICH PALACE

Hodžovo Nám.

❻

BIG FOUNTAIN

VYSOKÁ

MARIÁNSKA

OBCHODNÁ

❽

POŠTOVÁ

Ⓑ Hodžovo Námestie

HOLLÉHO

DREVENÁ

❾ SUCHÉ MÝTO

Ⓣ Poštová

❶❶

HEYDUKOVA

ŠPITÁLSKA

KOLÁRSKA

Hurbanovo Nám.

👣 **WALK BEGINS**

Nám. SNP

TESCO DEP'T STORE

ST. MICHAEL'S GATE

ZÁMOČNÍCKA

Wine Courtyard

FRANTIŠK.

NEDBALOVA

Kamenné Nám.

MICHALSKÁ

CHOCOLATE SHOP

BIELA

OLD TOWN HALL & CITY HISTORY MUSEUM

KLOBUČNÍKA

DUNAJSKÁ

Františkánske Nám.

Primate's Square ℹ

SEDLÁRSKA

Napoleonic Soldier Statue

Main Square

PRIMATE'S PALACE

APPONYI PALACE

❺

LAURINSKÁ

GORKÉHO

GRÖSSLINGOVA

SCHÖNER NÁCI STATUE

❶❷

PAPARAZZO STATUE

JESENSKÉHO

TOWN

RYBÁRSKA

ČUMIL STATUE

PANSKÁ

DISPLAY CASE

❶❶

NATIONAL THEATER

❶❶

FOUNTAIN

ŠTÚROVA

HVIEZDOSLAVOVO NÁM.

MEDENÁ

TALLEROVA

U.S. EMBASSY

❿

❼

TOBRUCKÁ

SLOVAK PHILHARMONIC

❶

SLOVAK NATIONAL GALLERY

Nám. L. Štúra

VAJANSKÉHO NÁBR.

HYDROFOIL TERMINAL

To Eurovea

Danube River

Michalská Street

Pretty as it is now, the old town was a decrepit ghost town during the communist era. Bratislava was a damaged husk after World War II. The communist regime cared only for the future—they had no respect for the town's heritage. In the 1950s, they actually sold Bratislava's original medieval cobbles to cute German towns that were rebuilding themselves with elegant Old World character. Locals avoided this desolate corner of the city, preferring to spend time in the Petržalka suburb across the river.

With the fall of communism in 1989, the new government began a nearly decade-long process of restitution—sorting out who had the rights to the buildings, and returning them to their original owners. During this time, little repair or development took place (since there was no point investing in a property until ownership was clearly established). By 1998, most of these property issues had been sorted out, and the old town was made traffic-free. The city replaced all the street cobbles, spruced up the public buildings, and encouraged private owners to restore their buildings. (If you see any remaining decrepit buildings, it's likely that their ownership is still in dispute.)

The cafés and restaurants that line this street are inviting, especially in summer. But if you don't look beyond the facades and outdoor tables, you'll miss much of Bratislava's charm. Poke around. Courtyards and galleries—most of them open to the public—burrow through the city's buildings. For example, a half-block down Michalská street on the left, the gallery at #12 was once home to vintners who lived within the walls for safety; their former cellars are now coffee shops, massage parlors, crafts boutiques, and cigar shops. Across the street, on the right, the gallery at #7 is home to several fashion designers.

Speaking of fashion...are you noticing a lot of skin? Tight jeans? Low-cut tops? Slovak women are known for their provocative dress. When pressed for a reason for this, one male resident of "Leg-islava" smirked and told me, "Women like to show what they have. Why should they hide it?"

On the left (at #6), the **Čokoládovňa pod Michalom** chocolate shop is highly regarded among locals for its delicious hot chocolate and creamy truffles (Mon-Thu 9:00-21:00, Fri-Sat 9:00-22:00, Sun 10:00-21:00, tel. 02/5443-3945).

Above the shop's entrance, the **cannonball** embedded in the wall commemorates Napoleon's two sieges of Bratislava, which together caused massive devastation—even worse than the city suffered during World War II. Keep an eye out for these cannonballs all over town...somber reminders of one of Bratislava's darkest times.

• *Two blocks down from St. Michael's Gate, the street jogs slightly right*

and its name changes to Ventúrska. At the jog, detour left (along Sedlár-
ska) and head for the...

Main Square (Hlavné Námestie)

This is the bustling centerpiece
of Old World Bratislava. Cute
little kiosks, with old-time
cityscape engravings on their
roofs, sell local handicrafts and
knickknacks (Easter through
October). Similar stalls fill the
square from mid-November
until December 23, when the
Christmas market here is a big
draw (www.vianocnetrhy.sk).

Virtually every building around this square dates from a different architectural period, from Gothic (the yellow tower) to Art
Nouveau (the fancy facade facing it from across the square). When
these buildings were restored a few years ago, great pains were
taken to achieve authenticity—each one matches the color most
likely used when it was originally built.

Extremely atmospheric cafés line the bottom of the square.
You can't go wrong here. Choose the ambience you like best (indoors or out) and sip a drink with arguably Slovakia's best urban
view. **Café Roland** is known for its 1904 Klimt-style mosaics and
historic photos of Pressburg/Pozsony. The barista stands where a
different kind of bean counter once did, guarding a vault that now
holds coffee (€2-3 coffee drinks and beer, full menu, daily 8:30-
23:00, Hlavné Námestie 5, tel. 02/5443-1372). The classic choice is
the kitty-corner **Kaffee Mayer.** This venerable café, an institution
here, has been selling coffee and cakes to a genteel clientele since
1873. You can enjoy your pick-me-up in the swanky old interior or
out on the square (€2-3 cakes, Mon-Fri 9:30-22:00, Sat-Sun 9:30-
23:00, Hlavné Námestie 4, tel. 02/5441-1741).

Peering over one of the benches on
the square is a cartoonish statue of a **Napoleonic officer** (notice the French flag
marking the embassy right behind him).
With bare feet and a hat pulled over his
eyes, it's hardly a flattering portrait—
you could call it the Slovaks' revenge for
the difficulties they faced at Napoleon's
hands. Across the square, another soldier from that period stands at attention.
At the top of the Main Square is

the impressive **Old Town Hall** (Stará Radnica), marked by a bold yellow tower. Near the bottom of the tower (to the left of the window), notice the cannonball embedded in the facade—yet another reminder of Napoleon's impact on Bratislava. Over time, the Old Town Hall gradually grew, annexing the buildings next to it and creating a mishmash of architectural styles along this side of the square. (A few steps down the street to the right are the historic apartments and wine museum at the **Apponyi House**—described later, under "Sights in Bratislava.")

Step through the passageway into the Old Town Hall's gorgeously restored **courtyard,** with its Renaissance arcades. (The **City History Museum**'s entrance is here—described later.)

Then, to see another fine old square, continue through the other end of the courtyard into **Primate's Square** (Primaciálne Námestie). The pink mansion on the right is the **Primate's Palace,** with a fine interior decorated with six English tapestries (described later). Do you see a lot of people using laptops? In a progressive move befitting its status as an emerging European business center, Bratislava provides free Wi-Fi on three squares in the old town. The huge student population (not to mention tourists) happily surfs in this beautiful setting. At the far end of this square is the **TI.**

• *Backtrack to the Main Square. With your back to the Old Town Hall, go to the end of the square and follow the street to the left (Rybárska Brána). Soon you'll pass a pair of...*

Whimsical Statues

Playful statues (such as the Napoleonic officer we met earlier) dot Bratislava's old town. Most date from the late 1990s, when city leaders wanted to entice locals back into the newly prettied-up center.

A half-block down this street (on the left), you'll come to a jovial chap doffing his top hat. This is a statue of **Schöner Náci,** who lived in Bratislava until the 1960s. This eccentric old man, a poor carpet cleaner, would dress up in his one black suit and top hat, and go strolling through the city, offering gifts to the women he fancied. (He'd often whisper *"schön"*—German for "pretty"—to the women, which is how he got his nickname.) Schöner Náci now gets to spend eternity greeting visitors outside his favorite café, Kaffee Mayer. Schöner is missing an arm: A bunch of drunks broke it off. As Prague gets more expensive, Bratislava is becoming the cheaper alternative for weekend "stag parties," popular with Brits lured here by cheap flights and cheap beer. Locals hope this is

a short-lived trend, and that those rowdy louts will move farther east before long.

• *Continue down Rybárska.*

At the end of this block, at the intersection with Panská, watch out on the right for **Čumil** ("the Peeper"), grinning at passersby from a manhole. This was the first and is still the favorite of Bratislava's statues. There's no story behind this one—the artist simply wanted to create a fun icon and let the townspeople make up their own tales. Čumil has survived being driven over by a truck—twice—and he's still grinning.

For a peek at a third statue—a nosy **Paparazzo**—you can take a side-trip left up Panská and go one block, watching the corner on the left.

• *Back at Čumil, continue along Rybárska to reach the long, skinny square called...*

Hviezdoslav Square (Hviezdoslavovo Námestie)

The landscaped park in the center of this square is particularly inviting. At this end is the impressive, silver-topped Slovak National Theater (Slovenské Národné Divadlo). Beyond that, the opulent yellow Neo-Baroque building is the Slovak Philharmonic (Slovenská Filharmónia). The prominence of these two venues is evidence of Bratislava's strong performing arts tradition.

Right in front of the theater (by the McDonald's), look down into the glass **display case** to see the foundation of the one-time Fishermen's Gate into the city. Surrounding the base of the gate is water. This entire square was once a tributary of the Danube, and the Carlton Hotel across the way was a series of inns on different islands. The buildings along the old town side of the square mark where the city wall once stood.

Stroll down the long art-and-people-filled park, nicknamed "**The Promenade**." Each summer, as part of an arts festival, the park is ornamented with entertaining modern art. After passing a statue of the square's namesake (Pavol Országh Hviezdoslav, a beloved Slovak poet), you'll come upon an ugly fence and barriers on the left, which mark the fortified US Embassy. Just past the embassy is the entrance to the Sky Bar, offering excellent views over this square, the cathedral, and the castle (ride elevator to seventh

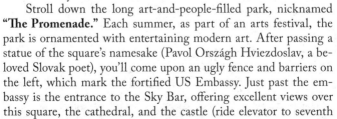

City of Three Cultures: Pressburg, Pozsony, Bratislava

Historically a Hungarian and Austrian city as much as a Slovak one, Bratislava has always been a Central European melting pot. The Hungarians used Pozsony (as they called it) as their capital during the century and a half that Buda and Pest were occupied by Ottoman invaders. Later, the city was a retreat of Habsburg Empress Maria Theresa (who used its German name, Pressburg). Everyone from Hans Christian Andersen to Casanova sang the wonders of this bustling burg on the Danube.

By its late-19th-century glory days, the city was a rich intersection of cultures. Shop clerks had to be able to greet customers in German, Hungarian, and Slovak. It was said that the mornings belonged to the Slovaks (farmers who came into the city to sell their wares at market), the afternoons to the Hungarians (diplomats and office workers filling the cafés), and the evenings to the Austrians (wine producers who ran convivial neighborhood wine pubs where all three groups would gather). In those wine pubs, the vintner would listen to which language his customers used, then automatically bring them the correct size glass: 0.3 liters for Hungarians, 0.25 liters for Austrians, and 0.2 liters for Slovaks (a distinction that still exists today). Jews (one-tenth of the population), Romanians, and Roma (Gypsies) rounded out the city's ethnic brew.

When the new nation of Czechoslovakia was formed from the rubble of World War I, the city shed its German and Hungarian names, proudly taking the new Slavic name Bratislava. The Slovak population—which had been at only about 10 percent—was on the rise, but the city remained tri-cultural.

World War II changed all of that. With the dissolution of Czechoslovakia, Slovakia became an "independent" country under the thumb of the Nazis—who all but wiped out the Jewish

floor; see "Eating in Bratislava," later). Farther along, after the giant chessboard, the glass pavilion is a popular venue for summer concerts. On the right near the end of the park, a statue of Hans Christian Andersen is a reminder that the Danish storyteller enjoyed his visit to Bratislava, too.

• *Reaching the end of the square, you run into the barrier for a busy highway. Turn right and walk one block to find the big, black marble slab facing a modern monument—and, likely, a colorful wooden reconstruction of a synagogue.*

Holocaust Memorial

This was the site of Bratislava's original synagogue. To echo ages past, a replica of the building was recently erected here (with painted plywood). If the reconstruction is gone, you should still be able to see an etching of the building in the big slab.

population. Then, at the end of the war, in retribution for Hitler's misdeeds, a reunited Czechoslovakia expelled people of Germanic descent (including all of those Austrians). And finally, a "mutual exchange of populations" sent the city's ethnic Hungarians back to Hungary.

Bratislava suffered terribly under the communists. The historic city's multilayered charm and delicate cultural fabric were ripped apart, then shrouded in gray. For example, the communists were more proud of their ultramodern New Bridge than of the historic Jewish quarter they razed to make way for it. Now the bridge and its highway slice through the center of the old town, and the heavy traffic rattles the stained-glass windows of St. Martin's Cathedral.

But Bratislava's most recent chapter is one of great success. Over the last few decades, the city has gone from gloomy victim of communism to thriving economic center and social hub. Its population of 450,000 includes some 70,000 students (at the city's six universities), creating an atmosphere of youthful energy and optimism. Its remarkable position on the Danube, a short commute from Vienna, is prompting its redevelopment as one of Europe's up-and-coming cities.

Bratislava and Vienna have realized that it's mutually beneficial to work together to bring the Slovak capital up to snuff. They're cooperating as a new "twin city" commerce super-zone. In the coming years, foreign investors plan to erect a skyline of 600-foot-tall skyscrapers and a clutch of glittering new megamalls. You'd never have guessed it a few years ago, but today calling Bratislava "the next Berlin on a smaller scale" is only a bit of a stretch.

Turn your attention to the memorial. The word "Remember" carved into the base in Hebrew and Slovak commemorates the 90,000 Slovaks who were deported to Nazi death camps. Nearly all were killed. The fact that the town's main synagogue and main church (to the right) were located side by side illustrates the tolerance that characterized Bratislava before Hitler. Ponder the modern statue: The two pages of an open book, faces, hands in the sky, and bullets—all under the Star of David—evoke the fate of 90 percent of the Slovak Jews.

• *Now head toward the adjacent church, up the stairs.*

St. Martin's Cathedral (Dóm Sv. Martina)

This historic church isn't looking too sharp these days—and the highway thundering a few feet in front of its door doesn't help matters. If it were any closer, the off-ramp would go through the nave.

Sad as it is now, the cathedral has been party to some pretty important history. While Buda and Pest were occupied by Ottomans for a century and a half, Bratislava was the capital of Hungary. Nineteen Hungarian kings and queens were crowned in this church—more than have been crowned anywhere in Hungary. In fact, the last Hungarian coronation (not counting the Austrian Franz Josef) was not in Budapest, but in Bratislava. A replica of the Hungarian crown still tops the steeple.

It's worth walking up to the cathedral's entrance to observe some fragments of times past (circle around the building, along the busy road, to the opposite, uphill side). Directly across from the church door is a broken bit of the 15th-century town wall. The church was actually built into the wall, which explains its unusual north-side entry. In fact, notice the fortified watchtower (with a WC drop on its left) built into the corner of the church just above you.

There's relatively little to see inside the cathedral—I'd skip it (€2, Mon-Sat 9:00-11:30 & 13:00-18:00, Thu until 17:00, Sun 13:30-16:00). If you do duck in, you'll find a fairly gloomy interior, some fine carved-wood altarpieces (a Slovak specialty), a dank crypt, a replica of the Hungarian crown, and a treasury in the back with a whimsical wood carving of Jesus blessing Habsburg Emperor Franz Josef.

Head back around the church for a good view (looking toward the river) of the **New Bridge** (Nový Most, a.k.a. Most SNP), the communists' pride and joy. As with most Soviet-era landmarks in former communist countries, locals aren't crazy about this structure— not only for the questionable star-

ship *Enterprise* design, but also because of the oppressive regime it represented. However, the restaurant and observation deck up top has been renovated into a posh eatery called (appropriately enough) "UFO." You can visit it for the views, a drink, or a full meal.

• *You could end the walk here. Two sights (both described later, under "Sights in Bratislava") are nearby. You could hike up to the **castle** (take the underpass beneath the highway, go up the stairs on the right marked by the* Hrad/Castle *sign, then turn left up the stepped lane marked* Zámocké Schody*). Or hike over the New Bridge (pedestrian walkway on lower level) to ride the elevator up the* **UFO** *viewing platform.*

*But to really round out your Bratislava visit, head for the river and stroll downstream (left) to a place where you get a dose of modern development in Bratislava—**Eurovea.** Walk about 10 minutes downstream, past the old town, boat terminals, and iron bridge, until you come to a big, slick complex with a grassy park leading down to the riverbank.*

Eurovea

Just downstream from the old town is the futuristic Eurovea, with four vibrant layers, each a quarter-mile long: a riverside park, luxury condos, a thriving modern shopping mall, and an office park. Walking out onto the view piers jutting into the Danube and surveying the scene, it looks like a computer-generated urban dreamscape come true. Exploring the old town gave you a taste

of where this country has been. But wandering this riverside park, enjoying a drink in one of its chic outdoor lounges, and then browsing through the thriving mall, you'll enjoy a glimpse of where Slovakia is heading.

• *Our walk is finished. If you haven't already visited them, consider circling back to some of the sights described next.*

Sights in Bratislava

If Europe had a prize for "city with the most underwhelming museums," I'd cast my vote for Bratislava. You can easily have a great day here without setting foot in a museum, instead focusing on Bratislava's charming, fun-to-stroll streets and grand views from the castle and UFO restaurant. But if you're feeling particularly driven to visit a museum, the Primate's Palace (with its cheap admission and fine tapestries) ranks slightly above the rest.

On or near the Old Town's Main Square

All three of these museums are within a few minutes' walk of one another, on or very near the Main Square.

City History Museum (Mestské Múzeum)—Delving into the bric-a-brac of Bratislava's past, this museum includes ecclesiastical art on the ground floor and a sprawling, chronological look at local history upstairs. The displays occupy rooms once used by the town council—courthouse, council hall, chapel, and so on. Everything is described in English, and the included audioguide tries hard, but nothing quite succeeds in bringing meaning to the place. On your way upstairs, you'll have a chance to climb up into the Old Town

Hall's tower, offering so-so views over the square, cathedral, and castle.

Cost and Hours: €5 includes dry audioguide, covered by Apponyi House ticket, Tue-Fri 10:00-17:00, Sat-Sun 11:00-18:00, closed Mon, in the Old Town Hall—enter through courtyard, tel. 02/5920-5130, www.muzeum.bratislava.sk.

Apponyi House (Apponyiho Palác)—This nicely restored mansion of a Hungarian aristocrat is meaningless without the included audioguide (dull but informative). The museum has two parts. The cellar and ground floor feature an interesting exhibit on the vineyards of the nearby "Little Carpathian" hills, with historic presses and barrels, and a replica of an old-time wine-pub table.

Upstairs are two floors of urban apartments from old Bratislava, called the Period Rooms Museum. The first floor up shows off the 18th-century Rococo-style rooms of the nobility—fine but not ostentatious, with ceramic stoves. The second floor up (with lower ceilings and simpler wall decorations) illustrates 19th-century bourgeois/middle-class lifestyles, including period clothing and some Empire-style furniture.

Cost and Hours: €6, includes City History Museum admission, Tue-Fri 10:00-17:00, Sat-Sun 11:00-18:00, closed Mon, last entry 30 minutes before closing, Radničná 1, tel. 02/5920-5135, www.muzeum.bratislava.sk.

▲Primate's Palace (Primaciálny Palác)—Bratislava's most interesting museum, this tastefully restored French-Neoclassical mansion (formerly the residence of the archbishop, or "primate") dates from 1781. The religious counterpart of the castle, it filled in for Esztergom—the religious capital of the Hungarians—when that city was taken by the Ottomans. Throughout the Ottoman occupation, from 1543 to the late 1800s, this was the winter residence of Hungary's archbishops.

Cost and Hours: €2, Tue-Fri 10:00-17:00, Sat-Sun 11:00-18:00, closed Mon, Primaciálne Námestie 3, tel. 02/5935-6394.

Visiting the Museum: The palace features one fine floor of exhibits. Walk up the grand staircase, then turn left into the Mirror Hall, used for concerts, city council meetings, and other important events.

From here, do a U-turn and progress through the large public rooms—designed to impress. Displayed in several of these rooms is the museum's collective highlight: a series of six English **tapestries,** illustrating the ancient Greek myth of the tragic love between Hero and Leander. The tapestries—the only complete cycle of royal English tapestries in existence—were woven in England by Flemish weavers for the court of King Charles I (in the 1630s). They were kept in London's Hampton Court Palace until Charles was deposed and beheaded in 1649. Cromwell sold them to France to help fund his civil war, but after 1650, they disappeared. Centuries later, in 1903, restorers broke through a false wall in this mansion and discovered the six tapestries, neatly folded and perfectly preserved. Nobody knows how they got there (perhaps they were squirreled away during the Napoleonic invasion, and whoever hid them didn't survive). The archbishop—who had just sold the palace to the city, but emptied it of furniture before he left—cried foul and tried to get the tapestries back...but the city said, "A deal's a deal."

After traipsing through the grand rooms, find the hallway that leads through the smaller rooms of the archbishop's private quarters, now decorated with Dutch, Flemish, German, and Italian paintings. At the end of this hall, a bay window looks down into the archbishop's own private marble chapel. When the archbishop became too ill to walk down to Mass, this window was built for him to take part in the service.

Bratislava Castle (Bratislavský Hrad)

This imposing fortress, nicknamed the "upside-down table," is the city's most prominent landmark. There surely has been a castle on

this spot for centuries. The oldest surviving chunk is the 13th-century Romanesque watchtower (the one slightly taller than the other three). When Habsburg Empress Maria Theresa took a liking to Bratislava in the 18th century, she transformed the castle from a military fortress to a royal residence suitable for holding court. She added a summer riding school (the U-shaped complex next to the castle), an enclosed winter riding school out back, and lots more. Maria Theresa's favorite daughter, Maria Christina, lived here with her husband, Albert, when they were newlyweds. Locals nicknamed the place "little Schönbrunn," in reference to the Habsburgs' summer palace on the outskirts of Vienna.

But M.T.'s castle burned to the ground in an 1811 fire, and it was left as a ruin for 150 years before being reconstructed in 1953. Unfortunately, the communist rebuild was drab and uninviting; the inner courtyard feels like a prison exercise yard.

A more recent renovation has done little to improve things, and the museum exhibits inside aren't really worth the cost of admission (described next). The best visit is to simply hike up (it's free to enter the grounds), enjoy the views over town, and take a close-up look at the stately old building (the big, blocky, modern building next door is the Slovak Parliament).

For details on the best walking route to the castle, see page 430.

Castle Museum—The newly restored castle has a few sights inside, with more likely to open in the future. Two small exhibits are skippable: the misnamed **Treasure Room** (a sparse collection of items found at the castle site, including coins and fragments of Roman jugs) and the **Knights Hall** (offering a brief history lesson in the castle's construction and reconstruction). You can also enter the **palace** itself. A blinding-white staircase with gold trim leads to the Music Hall, with a prized 18th-century *Assumption* altarpiece by Anton Schmidt (first floor); a collection of historical prints depicting Bratislava and its castle (second floor); and temporary exhibits (third/top floor). From the top floor, a series of very steep, modern staircases take you up to the Crown Tower (the castle's oldest and tallest) for views over town—though the vista from the terrace in front of the castle is much easier to reach and nearly as good.

Cost and Hours: €4 for all-inclusive "Road A" ticket, €2 for pointless "Road B" (covers only the less interesting parts of palace—the Treasure Room and Knights Hall); April-Oct Tue-Sun 10:00-18:00, Nov-March Tue-Sun 9:00-17:00, closed Mon year-round; ticket office is right of main riverfront entrance—enter exhibits from passage into central courtyard, tel. 02/2048-3110, www.snm.sk.

▲▲The UFO at New Bridge (Nový Most)

The bizarre, flying-saucer-capped bridge near the old town—completed in 1972 in heavy-handed communist style—has been reclaimed by capitalists. It's now a spruced-up, overpriced café/restaurant, with an observation deck allowing sweeping 360-degree views of Bratislava from about 300 feet above the Danube. Think of it as the "Slovak Space Needle."

Cost and Hours: €6.50, daily 10:00-23:00, elevator free if you have a meal reservation or order food at the restaurant—main courses steeply priced at €22-30, tel. 02/6252-0300, www.u-f-o.sk.

BRATISLAVA

Getting There: Walk across the New Bridge from the old town (there's a pedestrian walkway on the lower level)—the elevator entrance is underneath the tower on the Petržalka side.

❂ Self-Guided Tour: The "elevator" that takes you up is actually a funicular—you'll notice you're moving at an angle. At the top, walk up the stairs to the observation deck.

Begin by viewing the **castle** and **old town.** The area to the right of the old town, between and beyond the skyscrapers, is a massive construction zone. A  time-lapse camera set up here over the next few years would catch skyscrapers popping up like dandelions. International investors are throwing lots of money at Bratislava. (Imagine having so much prime, undeveloped real estate available downtown in the capital of an emerging European economic power...and just an hour down the road from Vienna, no less.) Most of the development is taking place along the banks of the Danube. In a decade, this will be a commercial center.

The huge TV tower caps a forested hill beyond the old town. Below and to the left of it, the pointy monument is **Slavín,** where more than 6,800 Soviet soldiers who fought to liberate Bratislava from the Nazis are buried. A nearby church had to take down its steeple so as not to draw attention away from the huge Soviet soldier on top of the monument.

Now turn 180 degrees and cross the platform to face **Petržalka,** a planned communist suburb that sprouted here in the 1970s. The site was once occupied by a village, and the various districts of modern Petržalka still carry their original names (which now seem ironic): "Meadows" *(Háje),* "Woods" *(Lúky),* and "Courtyards" *(Dvory).* The ambitious communist planners envisioned a city laced with Venetian-style canals to help drain the marshy land, but the plans were abandoned after the harsh crackdown on the 1968 Prague Spring uprising. Today, one in four Bratislavans lives in Petržalka. A few years ago, this was a grim and decaying sea of miserable concrete apartment *panelák* ("panel buildings," so called because they're made of huge prefab panels). But things are changing fast. Many of the *panelák* are being retrofitted with new layers of insulation, and the apartments inside are being updated. And, like Dorothy opening the door to Oz, the formerly drab buildings are being splashed with bright new colors. Far from being a slum, Petržalka is a popular neighborhood for Bratislavan yuppies who can't yet afford to build their dream houses. Locals read the Czech-

language home-improvement magazine *Panel Plus* for ideas on how to give their *panelák* apartments some style (www.panelplus.cz).

Still facing Petržalka, notice that construction is also happening along this riverbank (such as the supermall down below). But there's still history here. The **park** called Sad Janka Kráľa, a.k.a. "Aupark"—just downriver from the bridge—was technically the first public park in Europe and is still a popular place for locals to relax and court.

Scanning the **horizon** beyond Petržalka, two things stick out: on the left, the old communist oil refinery (which has been fully updated and is now state-of-the-art); and on the right, a sea of modern windmills. These are just over the border, in Austria...and Bratislava is sure to grow in that direction quickly. Austria is about three miles that way, and Hungary is about six miles farther to the left.

Before you leave, consider a drink at the café (€3-4 coffee or beer, €7-20 cocktails). If nothing else, be sure to use the memorable WCs (guys can enjoy a classic urinal photo).

Sleeping in Bratislava

I'd rather sleep in Budapest (or in Vienna)—particularly since good-value options in central Bratislava are slim, and service tends to be surly. But if Bratislava entices you to stay longer than a day trip, these options are all inside or within a short walk of the old town. Business-oriented places charge more on weekdays than on weekends. Hotel Michalská Brána is right in the heart of the old town, while the others are just outside of it—but still within a 5-10-minute walk.

$$$ Hotel Marrol's is the town's most enticing splurge. Although it's in a drab urban neighborhood, it's a five-minute walk from the old town, and its 54 rooms are luxurious and tastefully appointed Old World country-style. While pricey, the rates drop on weekends (prices flex, but generally Mon-Thu: Db-€160, Fri-Sun: Db-€120, Sb-€10 less, non-smoking rooms, elevator, air-con, free Internet access and Wi-Fi, loaner laptops, free minibar, gorgeous lounge, Tobrucká 4, tel. 02/5778-4600, www.hotelmarrols. sk, rec@hotelmarrols.sk).

BRATISLAVA

Sleep Code

(€1 = about $1.30, country code: 421, area code: 02)
S = Single, **D** = Double/Twin, **T** = Triple, **Q** = Quad, **b** = bathroom. English is spoken at each place. Unless otherwise noted, breakfast is included and you can pay by credit card.

To help you sort easily through these listings, I've divided the accommodations into three categories, based on the price for a standard double room with bath:

$$$ **Higher Priced**—Most rooms €100 or more.
$$ **Moderately Priced**—Most rooms between €50-100.
$ **Lower Priced**—Most rooms €50 or less.

Prices can change without notice; verify the hotel's current rates online or by email.

$$$ Hotel Michalská Brána is a charming boutique hotel just inside St. Michael's Gate in the old town. The 14 rooms are sleek, mod, and classy, and the location is ideal—right in the heart of town, but on a relatively sleepy lane just away from the hubbub (Mon-Thu: Db-€105, Fri-Sun: Db-€90, pricier suites also available, €5 less in July-Aug, non-smoking, air-con, elevator, free Wi-Fi in lobby, free cable Internet in rooms, Baštová 4, tel. 02/5930-7200, www.michalskabrana.com, reception@michalskabrana.com).

$$ Hotel Ibis, part of the Europe-wide chain, offers 120 nicely appointed rooms just outside the old town, overlooking a busy tram junction—request a quieter room (Mon-Thu: Sb/Db-€85, Fri-Sun: Sb/Db-€69, rates flex with demand, you'll likely save €20 or more with advance booking on their website, breakfast-€10, elevator, air-con, free Wi-Fi, Zámocká 38, tel. 02/5929-2000, fax 02/5929-2111, www.ibishotel.com, h3566@accor.com).

$$ Penzión Virgo sits on a quiet residential street, an eight-minute walk from the old town. The 11 boutiqueish rooms are classy and well-appointed (Sb-€61, Db-€74, breakfast-€6, free Wi-Fi, Panenská 14, tel. 02/2092-1400, www.penzionvirgo.sk, reception@penzionvirgo.sk).

$$ Penzión Gremium has eight nondescript rooms and two apartments in a very central location, just a block behind the National Theater and a few steps from the old town. It's on a busy street with good windows but no air-conditioning, so it can be noisy on rowdy weekends (Sb-€60, Db-€70, Db apartment-€90, prices soft—cheaper in slow times, breakfast-€5, free Wi-Fi, Gorkého 11, tel. 02/070-4874, www.penziongremium.sk, recepcia@penziongremium.sk).

$ Downtown Backpackers Hostel is a funky but well-run

place located in an old-fashioned townhouse. Rooms are named for famous artists and decorated with reinterpretations of their paintings (61 beds in 12 rooms, D-€54, bunk in 7-8-bed dorm-€20, bunk in 10-bed dorm-€18, breakfast-€3-5, free Wi-Fi, laundry facilities, kitchen, bike rental nearby, Panenská 31—across busy boulevard from Grassalkovich Palace, five-minute walk from old town, tel. 02/5464-1191, www.backpackers.sk, info@backpackers.sk).

Eating in Bratislava

Slovak cuisine shows some Hungarian and Austrian influences, but it's closer to Czech—lots of starches and gravy, and plenty of pork, cabbage, potatoes, and dumplings. Keep an eye out for Slovakia's national dish, *bryndzové halušky* (small potato dumplings with sheep's cheese and bits of bacon). Like the Czechs, the Slovaks produce excellent beer (*pivo*, PEE-voh). One of the top brands is Zlatý Bažant ("Golden Pheasant"). For a fun drink and snack that locals love, try a Vinea grape soda and a sweet *Pressburger* bagel in any bar or café. Long a wine-producing area, the Bratislava region makes the same wines that Vienna is famous for. But, as nearly all is consumed locally, most people don't think of Slovakia as wine country.

Bratislava is packed with inviting new eateries. In addition to the heavy Slovak staples, you'll find trendy new bars and bistros, and a smattering of ethnic offerings. The best plan may be to stroll the old town and keep your eyes open for the setting and cuisine that appeals to you most. Or consider one of these options.

Beer Halls

While not quite as famous as their Czech cousins, Slovak beers are well regarded by connoisseurs. Bratislava's beer halls are good places to sample Slovak and Czech beers, and to get a hearty, affordable meal of stick-to-your-ribs pub grub. Here are several options around town.

Prazdroj ("Urquell") is a Czech-style, copper-vats-and-pipes beer hall with lively ambience and good, hearty traditional food. It sprawls through several rooms of a building just off Hviezdoslav Square at the edge of the old town, with outdoor seating facing the Philharmonic. Pilsner Urquell is on tap (€7-15 main courses, Mon-Fri 10:00-24:00, Sat-Sun 11:00-24:00, Mostová 8, tel. 02/5441-1108).

1. Slovak Pub (as in "the first") is the Slovak equivalent of Prazdroj, attracting a younger crowd. Enter from a bustling modern shopping street just outside the old town, and climb the stairs into a vast warren of rustic, old countryside-style pub rooms with uneven floors. While enjoying the lively, loud, almost chaotic ambience, you'll dine on affordable and truly authentic Slovak fare, made with products from the pub's own farm. This is a good place to try the Slovak specialty, *bryndzové halušky*. It feels like a tourist trap, but it's filled with locals—go figure (€5-12 main courses, Mon-Sat 10:00-24:00, Sun 12:00-24:00, Obchodná 62, tel. 02/5292-6367).

Bratislavský Meštiansky Pivovar ("Bratislava Town Brewpub"), in a modern zone just outside the old town, brews its own beer and also sells a variety of others. Seating stretches over several levels in the new-meets-old interior (€6-10 meals, daily 11:00-24:00, Drevená 8, mobile 0944-512-265).

Upscale Dining Neighborhoods

As this scene is changing fast, I've suggested two neighborhoods worth exploring for good-quality eateries. These zones feel jammed with visiting European businessmen looking for good-quality, expense-account meals of international fare.

Hviezdoslav Square (Hviezdoslavovo Námestie): This long square, running along the bottom of the old town, is a delightful people zone with several fine restaurants offering al fresco tables. The highest concentration, including some splurgy steakhouses, is near the silver-roofed National Theater building. But for one of the best views in town, walk just past the US Embassy to find the low-profile door for **Lemon Tree/Sky Bar/Rum Club**. This three-in-one place features the same Thai-meets-Mediterranean menu throughout (€8-11 pasta and noodle dishes, €14-16 main courses). But the real reason to come here is for the seventh-floor Sky Bar, with fantastic views. It's smart to reserve a view table in advance if you want to dine here—or just drop by for a pricey vodka cocktail on the small terrace (daily 11:00-late, Sun from 12:00, Hviezdoslavovo Námestie 7, mobile 0948-109-400).

Eurovea: Huge outdoor terraces rollicking with happy eaters line this swanky riverfront residential and shopping-mall complex, about a 10-minute walk downstream from the old town. You'll pay high prices for the great atmosphere and views at international eateries—French, Italian, Brazilian—and a branch of the Czech beer-hall chain Kolkovna.

Fast and Cheap

Two local chains, with branches throughout the old town and beyond, offer a good, quick bite. The hip, rustic-chic **Shtoor** (named for a beloved 19th-century champion of Slovak culture, Ľudovít Štúr) is a "home made café" with coffee drinks and €3-5 sandwiches and quiches (takeaway or table service, open long hours daily).

BRATISLAVA

They have three locations: in the heart of the old town at Panská 23; just east of the old town (near Eurovea) at Štúrova 8; and inside a Barnes & Noble-type bookstore, Martinus.sk, at Obchodná 26. Also in the old town, the **Coffee & Bagel Story** chain sells...coffee and €3-5 bagel sandwiches (handiest location on Main Square at Hlavné Námestie 8).

Bratislava Connections

By Train

Bratislava has two major train stations. The main train station (Hlavná Stanica, abbreviated "Bratislava hl. st." on schedules) is closer to the old town, while the Petržalka station (ŽST Petržalka) is in the suburb across the river. When checking schedules (www.bahn.com is helpful), pay attention to which station your train uses. Bus #93 connects these two Bratislava stations (5-12/hour, 10 minutes; take bus #N93 at night).

From Bratislava by Train to: Budapest (7/day direct, 2.5 hours to Keleti Station, more with transfers; also doable—and possibly cheaper—by Orange Ways bus, 1-4/day, 2.5 hours, www.orangeways.com), **Vienna** (2/hour, 1 hour, round-trip ticket is cheaper than one-way fare—simply buy it moments before and hop on; departures alternate between the two stations—half from main station, half from Petržalka), **Sopron** (at least hourly, 2.5-3 hours, usually 2 transfers—often at stations in downtown and/or suburban Vienna), **Prague** (5/day direct, 4.25 hours). To reach other Hungarian destinations (including **Eger** and **Pécs**), it's generally easiest to change in Budapest; for Austrian destinations (such as **Salzburg** or **Innsbruck**), you'll connect through Vienna.

By Bus

Two different companies run handy buses that connect Bratislava, **Vienna,** and the **airports** in each city: Blaguss (www.eurolines.at) and Slovak Lines/Post Bus (tel. 0810-222-3336, www.slovaklines.sk). You can pre-book online, or (if arriving at the airport) just take whichever connection is leaving first. The bus schedules are handily posted at www.airportbratislava.sk (find the "Navigation—From the Airport" tab).

The buses run about hourly from Bratislava's airport to Bratislava (15 minutes, stops either at the main bus station east of the old town or at the New Bridge), continue on to Vienna's airport (1 hour), and end in Vienna (1.25 hours, Erdberg stop on the U-3 subway line). They then turn around and make the reverse journey (€7.50-10, depending on route).

By Boat

Riverboats connect Bratislava to Budapest and Vienna. Conveniently, these boats dock right along the Danube in front of Bratislava's old town. While they are more expensive, less frequent, and slower than the train, some travelers enjoy getting out on the Danube. Passports are not required.

To Budapest: For details on the Mahart boats to and from Budapest, see page 308 in "Budapest Connections."

To Vienna: The **Twin City Liner** offers several daily boat trips between downtown Bratislava and Vienna's Schwedenplatz (where Vienna's town center hits the canal; €29 each way, 1.25-hour trip; daily April-Oct only, Austrian tel. 01/58880, www.twincityliner.com).

Two competing lines, the Slovak **LOD** (www.lod.sk) and the Hungarian **Mahart** (www.mahartpassnave.hu) connect the cities a little more cheaply, but only once a day. These boats are slower (1.5-1.75 hours), as they use Vienna's Reichsbrücke dock on the main river, and therefore need to go through the locks.

By Plane

You have two options for reaching Bratislava: You can fly into its own airport, or into the very nearby Vienna Airport. Both options are outlined below.

Bratislava Airport (Letisko Bratislava)

This airport (airport code: BTS, www.letiskobratislava.sk) is six miles northeast of downtown Bratislava. The airport offers budget flights on low-cost carriers Ryanair (www.ryanair.com) and Danube Wings (www.danubewings.eu). Some airlines market it as "Vienna-Bratislava," thanks to its proximity to both capitals. The airport is officially named for Milan Rastislav Štefánik, who worked toward the creation of Czechoslovakia at the end of World War I. It's compact and manageable, with all the usual amenities (including ATMs).

From the Airport to Downtown Bratislava: The airport has easy **public bus** connections to Bratislava's main train station (€1.30, bus #61, 4-5/hour, 30 minutes). To reach the bus stop, exit straight out of the arrivals hall, cross the street, buy a ticket at the kiosk, and look for the bus stop on your right. For directions from the train station into the old town, see "Arrival in Bratislava," earlier. A **taxi** from the airport into central Bratislava should cost less than €20.

To Budapest: Take the bus or taxi to Bratislava's train station (described earlier), then hop a train to Budapest.

To Vienna: A slow option is to connect through Bratislava's train station (described above). More direct and still affordable,

BRATISLAVA

you can take a Eurolines bus from Bratislava Airport to the Erd-berg stop on Vienna's U-3 subway line (described earlier, under "By Bus"). A taxi from Bratislava Airport directly to Vienna costs €60-90 (depending on whether you use a cheaper Slovak or more expensive Austrian cab).

Vienna International Airport

This airport, 12 miles from downtown Vienna and 30 miles from downtown Bratislava, is well-connected to both capitals (airport code: VIE, airport tel. 01/700-722-233, www.viennaairport.com). As you exit baggage claim, all the terminals lead into a single ar-rivals hall with an array of services: shops, ATMs, TI, and restau-rants. This is also where you'll find the various connections.

To reach **Bratislava** from the airport, the easiest option is to take the Blaguss or Slovak Lines bus described earlier (under "By Bus"). Ask the TI which bus is leaving first, then head straight out the door and hop on. After about 45 minutes, the bus drops off in downtown Bratislava, then heads to its airport. I'd skip the train connection, which takes longer and involves complicated changes (airport train to Wien-Mitte Bahnhof in downtown Vienna, S-Bahn/subway to Südbahnhof, train to Bratislava, figure 1.75 hours total).

HUNGARY: PAST AND PRESENT

The Hungarian story—essentially the tale of a people finding their home—is as epic as any in Europe. Over the course of a millennium, a troublesome nomadic tribe that was the scourge of Europe gradually assimilated with its neighbors and—through a combination of tenacity and diplomacy—found itself controlling a vast swath of Central and Eastern Europe. Since arriving in Europe in 896, the Hungarians adopted Christianity; fended off Tatars and Turks; lost, regained, then lost again two-thirds of their land; and built one of the world's great 19th-century cities. Today, the Hungarians still perplex and amuse their neighbors with their bizarre Asian language, lovably quirky customs, and spicy cuisine. And yet, despite their mysterious origins and idiosyncrasies, the Hungarians have carved out a unique and vital niche in European life. Hungary is a place worth grappling with, and the persistent reap grand rewards here. Locals toss around the names of great historical figures such as Kossuth, Széchenyi, and Nagy as if they're talking about old friends. Take this crash course so you can keep up.

The story begins long, long ago and far, far away....

Welcome to Europe

The land we call Hungary today has long been considered the place—culturally, if not geographically—where the West (Europe) meets the East (Asia). The Roman province of Pannonia extended to the final foothills of the Alps that constitute the Buda Hills, on the west side of the Danube. Across the river, Rome ended and the barbarian wilds began. From here, the Great Hungarian Plain stretches in a long, flat expanse all the way to Asia—hemmed in to the north by the Carpathian Mountains. (Geologists consider this prairie-like plain to be the westernmost steppe in Europe—

Who Were the Magyars?

The ancestors of today's Hungarians, the Magyars, are a mysterious lot. Of all the Asian invaders of Europe, they were arguably the most successful—integrating more or less smoothly with the Europeans, and thriving well into the 21st century. Centuries after the Huns, Tatars, and Ottomans retreated east, leaving behind only fragments of their culture, the Hungarians remain a fixture in contemporary Europe.

The history of the Magyars before they arrived in Europe in A.D. 896 is hotly contested. Because their language is related only to Finnish and Estonian, it's presumed that these three peoples were once a single group, which likely originated east of the Ural Mountains (in the steppes of present-day Asian Russia).

After the Magyars' ancestors spent some time in Siberia, climatic change pushed them south and west, eventually (likely around the fifth century A.D.) crossing the Ural Mountains and officially entering Europe. They settled near the Don River (in today's southwestern Russia) before local warfare pushed them farther and farther west. The Magyars began raiding European lands, eventually setting up camp in the Carpathian Basin—today's Hungary—in A.D. 896.

resembling the terrain that covers much of Central Asia.) After Rome collapsed and Europe fell into the Dark Ages, Hungary became the territory of Celts, Vandals, Huns, and Avars...until some out-of-towners moved into the neighborhood.

The seven Magyar tribes, led by the mighty Árpád (and, according to legend, guided by the mythical Turul bird), thundered into the Carpathian Basin in A.D. 896. They were a rough-and-tumble nomadic people from Central Asia who didn't like to settle down in one place. (For more on this mysterious clan, see the "Who Were the Magyars?" sidebar.) And yet, after their long and winding westward odyssey, the Great Hungarian Plain felt comfortingly like home to the Magyars—reminiscent of the Asian steppes of their ancestors.

The Magyars would camp out in today's Hungary in the winters, and in the summers, they'd go on raids throughout Europe.

After the Magyars settled down and began to intermarry with Germans, Slavs, and other European peoples, their Asian features and customs mostly faded away. But the Europeans also took on the Hungarian language and some elements of the culture ("Magyarization"). Hungary became Central Europe's melting pot. After all these centuries, most Hungarians have lost track of the many tangled strains of their personal family history. In fact, a recent genetic study found that Hungarians are the most ethnically diverse nationality on the planet.

But even though certain aspects of their Magyar heritage have been lost to time, the Hungarians have done a remarkable job of clinging to their Asian roots. They still do things their own way, making Hungary subtly but unmistakably different from its neighboring countries. And people of German-Hungarian, Slavic-Hungarian, and Jewish-Hungarian descent still speak a language that's not too far removed from the Asian tongue of those original Magyars.

Were the Hungarians (Magyars) descended from the Huns, a similarly violent nomadic tribe that lived in the same area centuries earlier? It has long been a popular romantic notion—for historians, but also in legends and among everyday people—to speculate a tie between these two groups. But modern historians strongly doubt that the two ever had anything to do with each other. Even so, many Hungarians still take pride in the legendary link to the Huns...and Attila remains a popular name even today.

They were notorious as incredibly swift horsemen, whose use of stirrups (an eastern innovation largely unknown in Europe at the time) allowed them to easily outmaneuver foes and victims. Italy, France, Germany's Rhine, the Spanish Pyrenees, all the way to Constantinople (modern-day Istanbul)—the Magyars had the run of the Continent.

For half a century, the Magyars ranked with the Vikings as the most feared people in Europe. To Europeans, this must have struck a chord of queasy familiarity: a mysterious and dangerous eastern tribe running roughshod over Europe, speaking a gibberish language, and employing strange, terrifying, relentless battle techniques. No wonder they called the new arrivals "Hun-garians."

Now planted in the center of Europe, the Hungarians effectively drove a wedge in the middle of the sprawling Slavic populations of the Great Moravian Kingdom (basically today's "Eastern Europe"). The Slavs were split into two splinter groups, north and south—a division that persists today: Czechs, Slovaks, and Poles to the north; and Croats, Slovenes, Serbs, and Bosniaks to the south. (You can still hear the division caused by the Magyars in the language: While Czechs and Russians call a castle *hrad*, Croats and Serbs call it *grad*.)

After decades of terrorizing Europe, the Magyars were finally defeated by a German and Czech army at the Battle of Augsburg in 955. The Magyars' King Géza—realizing that if they were to survive, his people had to put down roots and get along with their neighbors—made a fateful decision that would forever shape Hungary's future: He adopted Christianity; baptized his son, Vajk; and married him to a Bavarian princess at a young age.

On Christmas Day in the year 1000, Vajk changed his name to István (Stephen) and was symbolically crowned by the pope (for more on István, see page 169). The domestication of the nomadic Magyars was difficult, thanks largely to the resistance of István's uncles, but was ultimately successful. Hungary became a legitimate Christian kingdom, welcomed by its neighbors. Under kings such as László I, Kálmán "the Book-Lover," and András II, Hungary entered a period of prosperity. (For more on these three kings, see pages 169-170.)

The Tatars, the Ottomans, and Other Outsiders (A.D. 1000-1686)

One of Hungary's earliest challenges came at the hands of fellow invaders from Central Asia. Through the first half of the 13th century, the Tatars—initially led by Genghis Khan—swept into Eastern Europe from Mongolia. In the summer of 1241, Genghis Khan's son and successor, Ögedei Khan, broke into Hungarian territory. The Tatars sacked and plundered Hungarian towns, laying waste to the kingdom. It was only Ögedei Khan's death in early 1242—and the ensuing dispute about succession—that saved the Hungarians, as Tatar armies rushed home and the Mongolian Empire contracted. The Hungarian king at the time, Béla IV, was left to rebuild his ruined kingdom from the rubble—creating for the first time many of the stout hilltop castles that still line the Danube. (For more on Béla IV, see page 171.)

Each of Béla's successors left his own mark on Hungary, as the Magyar kingdom flourished. They barely skipped a beat when the original Árpád dynasty died out in 1301, as they imported French kings (from the Naples-based Anjou, or Angevin, dynasty) to continue building their young realm. King Károly Róbert (Charles Robert) won over the Magyars, and his son Nagy Lajos (Louis the Great) expanded Hungarian holdings (for more on these two, see pages 171 and 172).

This was a period of flux for all of Central and Eastern Europe, as the nearby Czech and Polish kingdoms also saw their long-standing dynasties expire. For a time, royal intermarriages juggled the crowns of the region between various ruling families. Most notably, for 50 years (1387-1437) Hungary was ruled by Holy Roman Emperor Sigismund of Luxembourg, whose holdings also included the Czech lands, parts of Italy, much of Croatia, and more.

For more than 150 years, Hungary did not have a Hungarian-blooded king. This changed in the late 15th century, when a shortage of foreign kings led to the ascension to the throne of the enlightened King Mátyás (Matthias) Corvinus. The son of popular military hero János Hunyadi, King Matthias fostered the arts, sparked a mini-Renaissance, and successfully balanced foreign threats to Hungarian sovereignty (the Habsburgs to the north and west, and the Ottomans to the south and east). Under Matthias, Hungarian culture and political power reached a peak. (For more on this great Hungarian king, see page 173.)

But even before the reign of "good king Mátyás," the Ottomans (from today's Turkey) had already begun slicing their way through the Balkan Peninsula toward Central Europe. (It's ironic that the two greatest threats to the Magyar kingdom came in the form of fellow Asian invaders: Tatars and Turks. Or maybe it's not surprising, as these groups all found the steppes of Hungary so familiar and inviting.) In 1526, the Ottomans entered Hungary when Sultan Süleyman the Magnificent killed Hungary's King Lajos II at the Battle of Mohács. By 1541, they took Buda. The Ottomans would dominate Hungarian life (and history) until the 1680s—nearly a century and a half.

The Ottoman invasion divided Hungary into thirds: Ottoman-occupied "Lower Hungary" (more or less today's Hungary); rump "Upper Hungary" (basically today's Slovakia), with its capital at Bratislava (which they called "Pozsony"); and the loosely independent territories of Transylvania (in today's Romania), ruled by Hungarian dukes. During this era, the Ottomans built many of the thermal baths that you'll still find throughout Hungary.

Ottoman-occupied Hungary became

severely depopulated, and many of its towns and cities fell into ruins. While it was advantageous for a Hungarian subject to adopt Islam (for lower taxes and other privileges), the Ottomans rarely resorted to forced conversion—unlike the arguably more oppressive Catholics who controlled other parts of Europe at the time (such as the monarchs of Spain, who expelled the Jews and conducted the Spanish Inquisition). Ottoman rule meant that Hungary took a different course than other parts of Europe during this time. The nation fully enjoyed the Renaissance, but missed out on other major European historical events—both good (the Age of Discovery and Age of Reason) and bad (the devastating Catholic-versus-Protestant wars that plagued much of the rest of Europe).

Crippled by the Ottomans and lacking power and options, Hungarian nobles desperately offered their crown to the Austrian Habsburg Empire, in exchange for salvation from the invasion. The Habsburgs instead used Hungary as a kind of "buffer zone" between the Ottoman advance and Vienna. And that was only the beginning of a very troubled relationship between the Hungarians and the Austrians.

Habsburg Rule, Hungarian National Revival, and Revolution (1686-1867)

In the late 17th century, the Habsburg army, starting from Vienna, began a sustained campaign to push the Ottomans out of Hungary in about 15 years. They finally wrested Buda and Pest from the Ottomans in 1686. The Habsburgs repopulated Buda and Pest with Germans, while Magyars reclaimed the countryside. Even 25 years after the Ottomans were kicked out, the combined population of Buda and Pest was less than 20,000—and most of them were Germans from other parts of the Habsburg Empire. As recently as the early 19th century, Hungary was considered practically beyond Europe; Vienna marked the end of the "civilized" European world. But that would soon change. The population of Buda and Pest grew nearly tenfold from the beginning to the end of the 19th century. The new Austrian rulers rebuilt Hungary in their favored colorful, frilly Baroque style. Even today, it seems every Hungarian town has a cheerfully painted church with a Habsburg-style onion dome.

The Habsburgs governed the country as an outpost of Austria. The Hungarians—who'd had enough of foreign rule—fought them tooth and nail. Countless streets, squares, and buildings throughout the country are named Rákóczi, Széchenyi, or Kossuth—the "big three" Hungarian patriots who resisted the Habsburgs during this time.

Transylvanian prince Ferenc Rákóczi led Hungarians in the first major rebellion against the Habsburgs, the War of Independence (1703-1711). While Rákóczi initially enjoyed great territorial

Top 10 Dates That Changed Hungary

A.D. 896—The nomadic Magyars (a tribe from Central Asia) arrive in the Carpathian Basin and begin to terrorize Europe.

1000—King István (Stephen) accepts Christianity, marking the domestication of the Magyars.

1541—Invading Ottomans take Buda and Pest...and build thermal baths.

1686—The Austrian Habsburgs drive out the Ottomans, making Hungary part of their extensive empire (despite occasional rebellions from nationalistic Hungarians).

1867—A Golden Age begins, as Hungary gains semi-autonomy from Austria; Budapest, the new co-capital of a vast empire, booms.

1920—A loser in World War I, Hungary is stripped of two-thirds its territory and half its population in the Treaty of Trianon...and they're still angry about it.

1945—Hungary allies with Germany for most of World War II. After the war, the Soviet Union "liberates" the country and establishes a communist state.

1956—Hungarians bravely revolt. A massive invasion of Soviet tanks and soldiers brutally suppresses the rebellion, killing 2,500.

1989—Hungary is the first Soviet satellite to open its borders to the West, sparking similar reforms throughout the Eastern Bloc.

2004—Hungary joins the European Union.

gains, his war ultimately failed, he went into exile in the Ottoman Empire, and Habsburg rule continued. (For more on Rákóczi, see page 174.)

The early 19th century saw a thawing of Habsburg oppression. Here as throughout Europe, "backward" country traditions began to trickle into the cities, gaining more respect and prominence. It was during this time of reforms that Hungarian (rather than German) became the official language. It also coincided with a Romantic Age of poets and writers (such as Mihály Vörösmarty and Sándor Petőfi) who began to use the Hungarian tongue to create literature for the first time. By around 1825, the Hungarian National Revival was under way, as the people began to embrace the culture and traditions of their Magyar ancestors. Like people across Europe—from Ireland to Italy, and from Prague to Scandinavia—the Hungarians were becoming aware of what made them a unique people.

In Hungary, the movement was spearheaded by Count István Széchenyi, who had a compelling vision of a resurgent Hungarian nation...and the wealth and influence to make it happen. Széchenyi funded grand structures in Budapest (such as the iconic Chain Bridge) to give his Magyar countrymen something to take pride in. But even as Széchenyi spurred Hungarian patriotism, he was savvy enough not to push for total Hungarian independence—knowing that the volatile combination of strong Habsburg rule and a complicated ethnic mix would make an independent Hungarian state unlikely. Rather, he sought some degree of autonomy within the empire. And it began to work, as the Habsburgs gave in to some Hungarian demands.

And yet, despite the "Reform Age" that was already brewing, the gradual progress was too little, too late for many Hungarians. In March of 1848, a wave of Enlightenment-fueled nationalism that began in Paris spread like wildfire across Europe, igniting a revolutionary spirit in cities such as Vienna, Milan...and Budapest.

In Hungary, it inspired a revolt against the Habsburgs. Széchenyi's slowly-but-surely patriotism was eclipsed by the militarism of popular orator Lajos Kossuth (pictured) and patriotic poet Sándor Petőfi. On March 15, the Revolution of 1848 began on the steps of the National Museum in Pest (see page 65).

For several tense months, the uprising led to little more than diplomatic wrangling (as the Habsburgs were distracted elsewhere). Meanwhile, minority groups inside Hungarian territory—most notably the Croats, led by Josip Jelačić—began to rise up against the Hungarians. That winter, Habsburg Emperor Ferdinand I abdicated, replaced by his young and dynamic nephew, Franz Josef. One of his first acts was to officially condemn Hungarian independence.

In the spring of 1849, the Hungarians mounted a bloody but successful offensive to take over a wide swath of territory, including Buda and Pest. But in June, Franz Josef enlisted the aid of his fellow divine monarch, the Russian czar, who did not want the Magyars to provide an example for his own independence-minded subjects. Some 200,000 Russian reinforcements flooded into Hungary, crushing the revolution by August. After the final battle, the Habsburgs executed 13 Hungarian generals, then celebrated by clinking mugs of beer. To this very day, clinking beer mugs is, for many traditional Hungarians, just bad style.

For a while, the Habsburgs cracked down on their unruly Hungarian subjects. It was a time of shame for Hungary. Lajos Kossuth, now in exile, traveled the world to convince foreign leaders to take an interest in Hungary's plight (for more on him, see page 175). The now-forgotten Count Széchenyi spent his final years in a mental hospital, before committing suicide in 1860. The poet Sándor Petőfi—sort of the Hungarian Lord Byron—disappeared while participating in an 1849 battle, and is presumed to have been killed in the fighting.

In the 1860s, a clever elder statesman named Ferenc Deák—in an attempt to seize on the spirit of reform and the liberalization of the time—began to advocate for a power-sharing arrangement with the Habsburgs. Deák believed that diplomacy, rather than unilateral military action, could be most effective. Deák's often-repeated motto: "Quiet persistence can succeed where violence fails." (In some ways, this could be the slogan for the whole of Hungarian history.)

After an important military loss to Bismarck's Prussia in 1866, Austria began to agree that it couldn't control its rebellious Slavic holdings all by itself. The Habsburgs found themselves governing a vast, sprawling empire in which their own ethnic/linguistic group—Germans—were a tiny minority. In order to balance out the huge Slav population, they took Deák's advice and teamed up with the Hungarians.

And so, just 18 years after crushing the Hungarians in a war, the Habsburgs handed them the reins. With the Compromise *(Ausgleich)* of 1867, Austria granted Budapest the authority over the eastern half of their lands, creating the so-called Dual Monarchy of the Austro-Hungarian Empire. Hungary was granted their much-prized "home rule," where most matters (except finance, foreign policy, and the military) were administered from Budapest rather than Vienna. The Habsburg emperor, Franz Josef, agreed to a unique "king and emperor" *(König und Kaiser)* arrangement, where he was emperor of Austria, but only king of Hungary. In 1867, he was crowned as Hungarian king in both Buda (at Matthias Church) and Pest (on today's Széchenyi tér). The insignia "K+K" *(König und Kaiser,* king and emperor)—which you'll still see everywhere—evokes these grand days. (For more on Franz Josef and his wife Sisi, see page 316.)

Budapest's Golden Age (1867-1918)

The *Ausgleich* marked a precipitous turning point for the Hungarians, who once again governed their traditional holdings: large parts of today's Slovakia, Serbia, and Transylvania (northwest Romania), and smaller parts of today's Croatia, Slovenia, Ukraine, and Austria. To better govern their sprawling realm, in 1873, the cities of Buda, Pest, and Óbuda merged into one mega-metropolis: Budapest. But each part retained (and still retains) its unique character. Buda, which was more Germanic, Catholic, and pro-Habsburg, remains the traditional, conservative part of town. And Pest (with three times Buda's population), which was a hotbed of Magyar pride and the crucible of the uprisings of the mid-19th century, remains the more liberal, youthful, forward-looking part of town.

Serendipitously, Budapest's new prominence coincided with the 1,000th anniversary of the Hungarians' ancestors, the Magyars, arriving in Europe...one more excuse to dress things up. Budapest's long-standing rivalry with Vienna only spurred them to build bigger and better. The year 1896 saw an over-the-top millennial celebration, for which many of today's greatest structures were created (see page 43).

It was clearly Budapest's Golden Age. No European city grew faster in the second half of the 19th century than Budapest; in the last quarter of the 19th century alone, Budapest doubled in size, building on the foundation laid by Széchenyi and other patriots. By 1900, the city was larger than Rome, Madrid, or Amsterdam. During this time, among other claims to fame, Budapest was the world's biggest mill city—grinding grains from across Hungary and throughout the Balkans. The speedy expansion of the city garnered comparisons with Chicago, another boomtown of that era.

Budapest's most characteristic and most impressive architecture dates from this era. Today's palatial mansions and administrative buildings—whether sooty and crumbling, or newly restored and gleaming—hint at this era of unbridled prosperity. Compelled to adopt the trends of the Habsburgs, but eager to distinguish their own, uniquely Hungarian style, local architects made creative use of Historicism—borrowing bits and pieces of past styles, injecting a healthy dose of bigger-is-better modernity, and finishing it all off with striking, unique flourishes. Miklós Ybl and Ödön Lechner were two of the most prominent architects of this era, designing banks, museums, churches, and municipal buildings around Budapest. It was during this time that many buildings were first decorated with the colorful Zsolnay tiles—pretty as porcelain but hard as stone—invented in the city of Pécs (see page 388). To this day, these colorful adornments are a defining characteristic of Hungarian architecture.

It was also a period of great artistic and creative achievement.

Composers Franz Liszt (more Germanic than Magyar) and, later, Béla Bartók and Zoltán Kodály incorporated the folk and Roma (Gypsy) songs of the Hungarian and Transylvanian countryside into their music. As Magyar culture thrived, the traditions of the countryside flowed into the music salons of Budapest. (For more on these great musicians, see "Hungarian Music" on page 284.)

Observers at the time saw Hungarians as characterized by a strange combination of pessimism and optimism: pessimistic about their future, especially relating to the Habsburgs; and optimistic (or maybe even chauvinistic) about the influence of their culture—which, while thriving, remained on the fringe of mainstream Europe. Hungarian historians proposed outrageous boasts about Magyar heritage (including suggesting that Adam and Eve must have been Magyars, and "proving" connections between the Magyars and the Huns and ancient Greeks).

During its time of plenty, Hungary—which had for so long been an oppressed minority under the Habsburgs—became known for trampling its own minorities' rights. (Only a little more than half of the people in Hungarian territory were ethnic Hungarians.) Most signs were in Hungarian only, and the Magyar tongue was taught in every school in the realm. Minorities—who were given virtually no say in government—staged uprisings and revolts, and in 1868 Croatia was even granted semi-autonomy. (It wasn't enough—as early as 1890, Croats began grumbling with Serbs and other South Slavs to create their own Yugo-Slavia.)

However, this did have the intended effect of "Magyar-ization"—people from all ethnic backgrounds adopted the Hungarian language and culture, giving it an uncanny persistence for something so very foreign and so very old. Germans and Jews adapted their names to Hungarian. For example, the Hungarian communist leader Béla Kun was born Aaron Kohn.

Before long, the optimist in every Hungarian would be proven very wrong indeed—as the Golden Age came crashing to an end, and Hungary plunged into its darkest period.

The Crisis of Trianon (1918-1939)

World War I marked the end of the age of divine monarchs, as the Romanovs of Russia, the Ottomans of Asia Minor, and, yes, the Habsburgs of Austria-Hungary saw their empires break apart. Hungary, which had been riding the Habsburgs' coattails to power and prominence for the past half-century, now paid the price. As retribution for their role on the losing side of World War I, the 1920 Treaty of Trianon (named for the palace on the grounds of Versailles where it was signed) reassigned two-thirds of Hungary's former territory and half of its population to Romania, Ukraine, Czechoslovakia, and Yugoslavia (Slovenia, Croatia, and Serbia).

Pre-Trianon Hungary

Pre-Trianon Hungary (1920)

Current Hungarian Border

It is impossible to overstate the impact of the Treaty of Trianon on the Hungarian psyche—and on Hungarian history. Not unlike the overnight construction of the Berlin Wall, towns along the new Hungarian borders were suddenly divided down the middle. Many Hungarians found themselves unable to visit relatives or commute to jobs that were in the same country the day before. This sent hundreds of thousands of Hungarian refugees—now "foreigners" in their own towns—into Budapest, sparking an enormous but bittersweet boom in the capital.

To this day, the Treaty of Trianon is regarded as one of the greatest tragedies of Hungarian history. Like the Basques and the Serbs, the Hungarians feel separated from each other by circumstances outside their control. Today, more than two million ethnic Hungarians live outside Hungary (mostly in Romania)—and many Hungarians claim that these lands still belong to the Magyars. The sizeable Magyar minorities in neighboring countries have often been mistreated—particularly in Romania (under Ceauşescu), Yugoslavia (under Milošević), and Slovakia (under Mečiar). You'll see maps, posters, and bumper stickers with the distinctive shape of a much larger, pre-WWI Hungary...patriotically displayed by Magyars who feel as strongly about Trianon as if it happened yesterday. Some Hungarians see the enlargement of the European Union as a happy ending in the big-picture sense: They have finally been reunited with Slovakia, Romania, and (as of July 2013) Croatia.

After Trianon, the newly shrunken Kingdom of Hungary had to reinvent itself. The Hungarian crown sat unworn in the Royal Palace, as if waiting for someone worthy to claim it. The WWI hero Admiral Miklós Horthy had won many battles with the Austro-Hungarian navy. Though the new Hungary had no sea and no navy, Horthy retained his rank and ruled the country as a regent. A popular joke points out that during this time, Hungary was a "kingdom without a king" and a landlocked country ruled by a sea admiral. This sense of compounded deficiency pretty much sums up the morose attitude Hungarians have about those gloomy post-Trianon days.

Adding insult to injury, in the mid-1940s Hungary's currency (the *pengő*) underwent the worst inflation in the history of money. At the lowest point of the crisis, the government issued a 100,000,000,000,000,000,000-*pengő* note. Their plan for a 1,000,000,000,000,000,000,000-*pengő* bill fell through when the note became worthless after they printed it, but before they had a chance to circulate it.

The mounting financial crisis, and lingering resentment about the strict post-WWI reparations, made Hungary fertile ground for some bold new fascist ideas.

World War II and the Arrow Cross (1939-1945)

As Adolf Hitler rose to power in Germany, some other countries that had felt unfairly treated in the aftermath of World War I—including Hungary—saw Nazi Germany as a vehicle to greater independence. Admiral Horthy joined forces with the Nazis with the hope that they might help Hungary regain the crippling territorial losses of Trianon. In 1941, Hungary (reluctantly) declared war on the Soviet Union in June—and against the US and Britain in December.

Being an ally to the Nazis, rather than an occupied state, also allowed Hungary a certain degree of self-determination through the war—temporarily saving its sizeable Jewish population from immediate deportation. Winning back chunks of Slovakia, Transylvania, and Croatia in the early days of World War II also bolstered the Nazis' acceptance in Hungary.

As Nazism took hold in Germany, the Hungarian fascist movement—spearheaded by the Arrow Cross Party (Nyilaskeresztes Párt)—gained popularity within Hungary. As Germany increased its demands for Hungarian soldiers and food, Admiral Horthy resisted...until Hitler's patience wore thin. In March of 1944, the Nazis invaded and installed the Arrow Cross in power. The Arrow Cross made up for lost time, immediately beginning a savage campaign of executing Hungary's Jews—not only sending them to death camps, but butchering them in the streets. Almost 600,000 Hungarian Jews were murdered. (For more on this dark era of Hungarian history, see the Great Synagogue and Jewish Quarter Tour chapter.)

The Soviet Army eventually "liberated" Hungary, but at the

expense of Budapest: A months-long siege, from Christmas of 1944 to mid-February of 1945, reduced the proud city to rubble. One in 10 Hungarian citizens perished in the war.

Communism...with a Pinch of Paprika (1945-1989)

After World War II, Hungary was gradually compelled to adopt Moscow's system of government. The Soviet-puppet hardliner Mátyás Rákosi ruled Hungary with an iron fist. Everyday people were terrorized by the KGB-style secret police, called the ÁVO and ÁVH, to accept the new regime. Non-Hungarians were deported, potential and actual dissidents disappeared into the horrifying gulag system of Siberia, food shortages were epidemic, people were compelled to spy on their friends and families, and countless lives were ruined. Coming on the heels of Trianon and two devastating world wars, communist rule was a blow that Hungary is still recovering from. (For much more on life in Soviet-controlled Hungary, see the House of Terror Tour chapter.)

Beginning on October 23, 1956, the Hungarians courageously staged a monumental uprising, led by Communist Party reformer Imre Nagy. Initially, it appeared that one of the cells on the Soviet Bloc might win itself the right to semi-autonomy. But Moscow couldn't let that happen. In a Tiananmen Square-style crackdown, the Soviets sent in tanks to brutally put down the uprising and occupy the city. When the dust settled, 2,500 Hungarians were dead, and 200,000 fled to the West. (If you know any Hungarians in the US, their families more than likely fled there in 1956.) Nagy was arrested, given a sham trial, and executed in 1958. For more on these events, see the "1956" sidebar on page 112.

The Hungarians were devastated, in every sense. They were frustrated that the Suez Canal crisis distracted the world from their uprising. Many felt betrayed that the US—which spoke so boldly against the Soviet Union—did not offer them military support (contrary to the promises of the US-based Radio Free Europe). While the US and its Western allies understandably did not want to turn the Cold War hot, the Hungarians (also understandably) felt abandoned.

Weeks after the uprising came the now-legendary "Blood in the Water" match at the Melbourne Olympics. Soviet satellite states were often ordered to "throw" matches to allow the USSR's athletes to prevail. On December 6, 1956, Moscow issued such a decree to the Hungarian men's water polo team in their semifinal against the Soviet Union. The Hungarians refused and played their hearts out, much to the delight of their fans (and the rest of the world). The game turned violent, and in one indelible image, a Hungarian athlete emerged from the pool with blood pouring from a gash above his right eye. The Hungarians won, 4-0, and went on to take the gold.

After the uprising, the USSR installed János Kádár—a colleague of Nagy's who was also loyal to Moscow—to lead Hungary. For a few years, things were bleak, as the secret police ratcheted up their efforts against potential dissidents. But in the 1960s, Kádár's reformist tendencies began to cautiously emerge. Seeking to gain the support of his subjects (and avoid further uprisings), Kádár adopted the optimistic motto, "If you are not against us, you are with us." While still mostly cooperating with Moscow, Kádár gradually allowed the people of Hungary more freedom than citizens of neighboring countries had—a system dubbed "goulash communism." The "New Economic Mechanism" of 1968 partly opened Hungary to foreign trade. People from other Warsaw Pact countries—Czechs, Slovaks, and Poles—flocked to Budapest's Váci utca to experience "Western evils" unavailable to them back home, such as Adidas sneakers and Big Macs. People half-joked that Hungary was the happiest barrack in the communist camp.

In the late 1980s, the Eastern Bloc began to thaw. And Hungary—which was always skeptical of the Soviets (or any foreign rule)—was one of the first satellite states that implemented real change. In February of 1989, the Hungarian communist parliament, with little fanfare, essentially voted to put an expiration date on their own regime. There were three benchmarks in that fateful year: May 2, when Hungary was the first Soviet Bloc country to effectively open its borders to the West (by removing its border fence with Austria); June 16, when communist reformer Imre Nagy and his comrades were given a proper, ceremonial reburial on Heroes' Square; and August 19, when, in the first tentative steps toward the reunification of Europe, Hungarians and Austrians came together in a field near the town of Sopron for the so-called "Pan-European Picnic." (Some 900 East Germans seized this opportunity to make a run for the border...and slipped into the West when Hungarian

What Do Stephen Colbert, Chuck Norris, and Miklós Zrínyi Have in Common?

In 2006, the Hungarian government announced an online contest to choose a name for a new bridge in northern Budapest. While Hungarians tend to be proud of their rich history, a spirit of irreverence permeated this particular contest. The name "Chuck Norris Bridge"—for the American action star, popularized in a series of campy Hungarian ads—shot out to an early lead. The government, nervous about the unexpected irreverence, lobbied hard to win votes for the name "Miklós Zrínyi Bridge," for a 17th-century Croatian military leader who defended Hungary from invading Ottomans.

But then, on August 11, American television satirist Stephen Colbert implored his viewers to visit the website to name the bridge for himself. When the voting was complete a week and a half later, Colbert had trounced his competitors with 17 million votes—that's 7 million more than the entire population of Hungary—with Zrínyi finishing a distant second with 2 million votes. The Hungarian ambassador to the US was a good sport, appearing on Colbert's show to tell him he'd won, but was ineligible (since he neither spoke Hungarian nor was deceased).

A few weeks later, the bridge was unimaginatively christened "Megyeri Bridge," since it connects two suburbs called Megyer (Káposztásmegyer and Békásmegyer)—a name that hadn't even been in the running. Today it's a crucial link in Budapest's M-0 beltway. If nothing else, the bridge-naming contest demonstrated that democracy and the Internet don't always combine for serious results.

border guards refused their orders to shoot defectors.) On October 23—the anniversary of the 1956 Uprising—the truly democratic Republic of Hungary triumphantly replaced the People's Republic of Hungary.

Hungary's first post-communist president, Árpád Göncz, was a protester from the 1950s who was famous for learning English while in prison...a skill that later came in handy when he translated *The Lord of the Rings* into Hungarian. Fantasy was becoming a reality in Hungary. Change was in the air.

Hungary Today (1989-Present)

The transition from communism to capitalism has been rocky in Hungary. While many Hungarians were eager for the freedom to travel and pursue the interests that democracy allowed them, many others struggled to cope with the sudden reduction of government-provided services. Hungary seems to have had an even more difficult transition than some of its neighbors, as post-communist governments have attempted to preserve as many social services as possible while stepping down taxation—leaving Hungary with rampant inflation unmatched in Europe (and bringing back unpleasant memories of the *pengő* debacle of the 1940s).

The process of privatization (handing property once seized by the communist government back over to private owners) has been messy. When possible, the government attempted to find the original owners of the property, and allow them to purchase it at a low price. But it was often difficult, or impossible, to find someone who was the owner of a property before World War II (especially considering that one in 10 Hungarians did not survive that war). And so, in other cases, people were simply given the opportunity to purchase the apartment or house where they were living on the day of the transition. If you had a good apartment, this was good news; if not, you were out of luck.

The transition has manifested itself in sometimes surprising ways. For example, under communism, the medical profession was prestigious but not very lucrative. In the new capitalist era, things have not changed much, and Hungarians carry on an unusual tradition: It's expected that a patient will tip his or her doctor after the appointment. While this is a largely unspoken agreement, it follows a carefully prescribed routine: The money, always cash, is inserted into a blank white envelope and handed to the doctor at the end of the session. The amount that's expected varies by procedure, which can cause a lot of anxiety for a patient who doesn't know how much to pay (as if going to the doctor wasn't stressful enough).

In 2004, Hungary took the monumental step of joining the European Union (along with nine other, mostly former-communist nations). Many of the new members demonstrated great ambivalence about joining the EU, fearing that they would lose their hard-fought autonomy. And EU membership has come with its share of heavy-handed regulation and convoluted bureaucracy. But even the most ardent Euroskeptics now agree that the EU has done more good than harm.

Still, the EU hasn't solved all of Hungary's problems. In the 21st century, Hungary's leaders have struggled with how to afford the generous social-welfare network its people have come to expect.

The Hungarian Socialist Party, which took control of parliament in 2002, stubbornly maintained and even extended some social programs, prompting experts to worry that the mounting public debt would bankrupt the country. After they won re-election in April of 2006, Prime Minister Ferenc

Gyurcsány gave a shockingly frank "wake-up call" speech to his party's leaders. Although his remarks were intended to be kept secret, someone recorded it. And, a few months later, on September 17, Hungarians turned on their TVs to hear their prime minister detailing the ways he and his party had driven their country to the brink of ruin: "We have screwed up. Not a little but a lot. No country in Europe has screwed up as much as we have...We did not actually do anything for four years. Nothing...We lied morning, noon, and night." The release of the tape sparked protests—which occasionally turned violent—as furious demonstrators demanded Gyurcsány's resignation. He refused.

Rampant inflation continued to wrack the country. In late 2008, with Gyurcsány warning of "state bankruptcy" and a currency collapse, Hungary received a $25 billion bailout package from the EU, International Monetary Fund, and World Bank. Gyurcsány finally resigned in early 2009, acknowledging that he was getting in the way of Hungary's economic recovery.

Viktor Orbán, of the right-of-center Fidesz Party, became prime minister in May of 2010. Fidesz took its huge two-thirds majority as a mandate to completely remake Hungary. Fidesz quickly passed a law extending Hungarian citizenship to people of Hungarian descent living in neighboring countries (stoking age-old Hungarian resentment about the post-World War I Treaty of Trianon territorial losses). This strained the always-tense relations with Slovakia. In early 2011, Orbán's party created a new FCC-like media authority with broad latitude for suppressing material that it considers inappropriate. Attacked by both Hungarian and international critics for its potential to infringe on free press, this new media law has been submitted to EU authorities for review. Fidesz has also pursued reforming the government in ways that, both the US and European governments have stated, may place alarming limits on Hungary's democracy.

The party's also gone on a renaming binge; in 2011, more than two dozen streets, squares, and other features of Budapest were re-christened with more Fidesz-friendly names (creating headaches for mapmakers everywhere).

Fortunately, tourists visiting today's Hungary are scarcely aware of its economic and political woes. The Hungarian people—relieved to be free of oppression, and allowed to pursue their lovably quirky customs with a renewed vigor—enthusiastically welcome and charm visitors. It's been a long road for the Hungarians from those distant, windblown steppes of Central Asia...but today they seem to be doing better than ever.

APPENDIX

Contents

Tourist Information

The Hungarian National Tourist Office **in the US** is a wealth of information. Before your trip, contact their office to request brochures on topics or regions that interest you. Call 212/695-1221 or visit www.gotohungary.com.

In Hungary, Budapest has its own tourism organization, called Budapest Info (www.budapestinfo.hu), with several branches in the city (for details, see page 39). Other towns have their own local tourist information offices, which all belong to a large government agency called "TourInform"; these are marked by a white *i* in a green rectangle (www.tourinform.hu). Tourist offices vary in quality; those in some of the smaller towns (including Eger's) can be excellent, while Budapest's are hit-or-miss. Remember that tourist information offices are abbreviated "TI" in this book.

Communicating

Hurdling the Language Barrier

The language barrier in Hungary is no bigger than elsewhere in Europe. In fact, as a monolingual visitor, I find that it's actually easier to communicate in Hungary than in places such as Italy or France. Since Hungary is small and not politically powerful, the people here realize that it's unreasonable to expect visitors to learn Hungarian (which has only 12 million speakers worldwide). It's essential for them to find a common language with the rest of the world—so they learn English early and well. You'll find that most people in the tourist industry—and virtually all young people—speak fine English.

Of course, not *everyone* speaks English. You'll run into the most substantial language barriers in situations when you need to deal with a less highly educated clerk or service person (train station and post-office counters, maids, museum guards, bakers, and so on)—especially outside of Budapest. Be reasonable in your expectations. Museum ticket-sellers in Hungary are every bit as friendly and multilingual as they are in the US.

Luckily, it's relatively easy to get your point across in these places. I've often bought a train ticket simply by writing out the name of my destination; the time I want to travel (using the 24-hour clock); and the date I want to leave (year first, then month, then day). Here's an example of what I'd show a ticket-seller at a train station: "Eger, 10:30, 2013.8.15."

Hungarians, realizing that their language intimidates Americans, often invent easier nicknames for themselves—so András becomes "Andrew," Erzsébet goes by "Elisabeth," and István tells you, "Call me Steve."

There are certain universal English words all Hungarians know: "hello," "please," "thank you," "super," "pardon," "stop," "menu," "problem," and "no problem." While Hungarians don't expect you to be fluent in their tongue, they definitely appreciate it when they can tell you're making an effort to pronounce Hungarian words correctly or to use the local pleasantries. For pronunciation tips, see page 24. For survival phrases in Hungarian, see page 483.

Don't be afraid to interact with locals. Hungarians might initially seem shy, overly formal, or even brusque (a holdover from the closed communist society), but usually a simple smile is the only icebreaker you need to make a new friend. You'll find that doors open a little more quickly when you know a few words of the language. Give it your best shot. The locals will appreciate your efforts.

Telephones

Smart travelers use the telephone to reserve or reconfirm rooms, get tourist information, reserve restaurants, confirm tour times, or phone home. This section covers dialing instructions, phone cards, and types of phones (for more in-depth information, see www.ricksteves.com/phoning).

How to Dial

Calling from the US to Europe, or vice versa, is simple—once you break the code. The European calling chart in this chapter will walk you through it.

APPENDIX

Dialing Domestically Within Hungary

Like many things in Hungary, making domestic calls is uniquely confusing. You must dial different codes depending on whether you're calling locally or long distance within the country.

The following instructions apply to dialing from a landline (such as a pay phone or your hotel-room phone) or a Hungarian mobile phone. If you're dialing within Hungary using your US mobile phone, you may need to dial as if it's a domestic call, or you may need to dial as if you're calling from the US (see "Dialing Internationally," next). Try it one way, and if it doesn't work, try it the other way.

To dial a number in the same city, simply dial direct, with no area code.

To dial long-distance within Hungary, add the prefix 06, followed by the area code (e.g., Budapest's area code is 1, so you dial 06-1, then the rest of the number).

For example, to call a hotel in Eger, I'd dial 411-711 if I'm calling from within Eger; but from Budapest, I'd have to dial 06, then 36 (Eger's area code), then 411-711.

Dialing Internationally to or from Hungary

If you want to make an international call, follow these steps:

Calling to Hungary: Dial the international access code (00 if calling from Europe, 011 from the United States or Canada), then Hungary's country code (36), then the area code (but not the 06) and number.

Calling from Hungary: Dial 00, the country code of the country you're calling, the area code, if applicable (many countries require dropping the initial zero), and the local number. For specifics per country, see the European calling chart in this chapter.

Calling from any European country to the US: To call my office in Edmonds, Washington, from anywhere in Europe, I dial 00 (Europe's international access code), 1 (the US country code), 425 (Edmonds' area code), and 771-8303.

European Calling Chart

Just smile and dial, using this key:
AC = Area Code, LN = Local Number.

European Country	Calling long distance within...	Calling from the US or Canada to...	Calling from a European country to...
Austria	AC + LN	011 + 43 + AC (without the initial zero) + LN	00 + 43 + AC (without the initial zero) + LN
Belgium	LN	011 + 32 + LN (without initial zero)	00 + 32 + LN (without initial zero)
Bosnia-Herzegovina	AC + LN	011 + 387 + AC (without initial zero) + LN	00 + 387 + AC (without initial zero) + LN
Britain	AC + LN	011 + 44 + AC (without initial zero) + LN	00 + 44 + AC (without initial zero) + LN
Croatia	AC + LN	011 + 385 + AC (without initial zero) + LN	00 + 385 + AC (without initial zero) + LN
Czech Republic	LN	011 + 420 + LN	00 + 420 + LN
Denmark	LN	011 + 45 + LN	00 + 45 + LN
Estonia	LN	011 + 372 + LN	00 + 372 + LN
Finland	AC + LN	011 + 358 + AC (without initial zero) + LN	999 (or other 900 number) + 358 + AC (without initial zero) + LN
France	LN	011 + 33 + LN (without initial zero)	00 + 33 + LN (without initial zero)
Germany	AC + LN	011 + 49 + AC (without initial zero) + LN	00 + 49 + AC (without initial zero) + LN
Gibraltar	LN	011 + 350 + LN	00 + 350 + LN
Greece	LN	011 + 30 + LN	00 + 30 + LN
Hungary	06 + AC + LN	011 + 36 + AC + LN	00 + 36 + AC + LN
Ireland	AC + LN	011 + 353 + AC (without initial zero) + LN	00 + 353 + AC (without initial zero) + LN

European Country	Calling long distance within ...	Calling from the US or Canada to ...	Calling from a European country to ...
Italy	LN	011 + 39 + LN	00 + 39 + LN
Montenegro	AC + LN	011 + 382 + AC (without initial zero) + LN	00 + 382 + AC (without initial zero) + LN
Morocco	LN	011 + 212 + LN (without initial zero)	00 + 212 + LN (without initial zero)
Netherlands	AC + LN	011 + 31 + AC (without initial zero) + LN	00 + 31 + AC (without initial zero) + LN
Norway	LN	011 + 47 + LN	00 + 47 + LN
Poland	LN	011 + 48 + LN	00 + 48 + LN
Portugal	LN	011 + 351 + LN	00 + 351 + LN
Slovakia	AC + LN	011 + 421 + AC (without initial zero) + LN	00 + 421 + AC (without initial zero) + LN
Slovenia	AC + LN	011 + 386 + AC (without initial zero) + LN	00 + 386 + AC (without initial zero) + LN
Spain	LN	011 + 34 + LN	00 + 34 + LN
Sweden	AC + LN	011 + 46 + AC (without initial zero) + LN	00 + 46 + AC (without initial zero) + LN
Switzerland	LN	011 + 41 + LN (without initial zero)	00 + 41 + LN (without initial zero)
Turkey	AC (if there's no initial zero, add one) + LN	011 + 90 + AC (without initial zero) + LN	00 + 90 + AC (without initial zero) + LN

APPENDIX

- The instructions above apply whether you're calling to or from a European landline or mobile phone.

- If calling from any mobile phone, you can replace the international access code with "+" (press and hold 0 to insert it).

- The international access code is 011 if you're calling from the US or Canada.

- To call the US or Canada from Europe, dial 00, then 1 (country code for US and Canada), then the area code and number. In short, 00 + 1 + AC + LN = Hi, Mom!

Note: If you're dialing from a mobile phone, you can replace the international access code with +, which works regardless of where you're calling from. (On many mobile phones, you can insert a + by pressing and holding the 0 key.)

Dialing Mobile Phones and Other Unusual Numbers

Certain Hungarian phone numbers are particularly confusing to dial. Numbers beginning with 0620, 0630, or 0670 are mobile phones; those beginning with 0680 are toll-free; and 0681 and 0690 are expensive toll lines. The way you dial these numbers depends on where you're calling from, and whether you're calling from a fixed line or a mobile phone.

To call these numbers **from a fixed line within Hungary,** simply dial them direct, as they appear in this book.

To dial them **from a fixed line outside of Hungary,** you need to replace the initial 06 with other numbers: From the US, replace the 06 with 011-36. From other European countries, replace the 06 with 00-36. Then dial the rest of the number.

To dial them **from a mobile phone** (whether within or outside of Hungary), replace the initial 06 with +36, then dial the rest of the number.

So, to call my favorite Budapest guide from a fixed line inside Hungary, you'd dial 0620-926-0557; from North America, you'd dial 011-36-20-926-0557; and from another European country, you'd dial 00-36-20-926-0557. From any mobile phone, you'd dial +36-20-926-0557.

Mobile Phones

Traveling with a mobile phone is handy and practical. Whether you're using a smartphone or a conventional cell phone, the basics for how to make calls and send texts are the same. For specifics on using your smartphone to get online, see the sidebar.

Roaming with Your Mobile Phone: Your US mobile phone works in Europe if it's GSM-enabled, tri-band or quad-band, and on a calling plan that includes international calls. Phones from AT&T and T-Mobile, which use the same GSM technology that Europe does, are more likely to work overseas than Verizon or Sprint phones (if you're not sure, ask your service provider). Most US providers will charge you $1.29-1.99 per minute to make or receive calls while roaming internationally, or 20-50 cents to send or receive text messages. If you sign up for an international calling plan with your provider, you'll save a few dimes per minute. Though pricey, roaming on your own phone is easy and can be a cost-effective way to keep in touch—especially on a short trip or if you won't be making many calls.

Buying and Using SIM Cards in Europe: You'll pay much

cheaper rates if you put a European SIM card in your mobile phone; to do this, your phone must be electronically "unlocked" (ask your provider about this, buy an unlocked phone before you leave, or get one in Europe—see "Other Mobile-Phone Options," next). Then, in Europe, you can buy a fingernail-sized **SIM card,** which gives you a European phone number. SIM cards are sold at mobile-phone stores for around 1,500-2,000 Ft, and often include at least that much prepaid domestic calling time (making the card itself almost free). When you buy a SIM card, you may need to show ID, such as your passport.

Insert the SIM card in your phone (usually in a slot behind the battery or on the side) and it'll work like a European mobile phone. Before purchasing a SIM card, always ask about fees for domestic and international calls, roaming charges, and how to check your credit balance and buy more time. When you're in the SIM card's home country, domestic calls average 10-20 cents per minute, and incoming calls are free. Rates are higher if you're roaming in another country, and you may pay more to call a toll number than you would dialing from a fixed line.

Other Mobile-Phone Options: Many travelers like to carry two phones: both their own US mobile phone (allowing them to stay reachable on their own phone number) and a second, unlocked European phone (which lets them do all their local calling at far cheaper rates). You could either bring two phones from home, or get one in Europe. If you have an old mobile phone sitting around, ask your provider for the "unlock code" so it can be used with European SIM cards. Or buy a cheap, basic phone before you go (search your favorite online shopping site for "unlocked quad-band GSM phone").

In Europe, basic phones are sold at mobile phone stores, at hole-in-the-wall vendors at many airports and train stations, and at phone desks within larger department stores. Phones that are "locked" to work with a single provider start around $40; "unlocked" phones (which work with any SIM card) start around $60. Regardless of how you get your phone, remember that you'll need a SIM card to make it work.

Car-rental companies and mobile-phone companies offer the option to rent a mobile phone with a European number. While this seems convenient, hidden fees (such as high per-minute charges or expensive shipping costs) can really add up—which usually makes it a bad value. One exception is Verizon's Global Travel Program, available only to Verizon customers.

Calling over the Internet

Some things that seem too good to be true...actually are true. If you're traveling with a laptop, tablet, or smartphone, you can make

Smartphones and Data Roaming

I take my smartphone to Europe, using it to make phone calls (sparingly) and send texts, but also to check email, listen to audio tours, and browse the Internet. If you're clever, you can do all this without incurring huge data-roaming fees. Here's how.

Many smartphones, such as the iPhone, Android, and BlackBerry, work in Europe (though some older Verizon iPhones don't). For voice calls and text messaging, smartphones work like any mobile phone (as described under "Roaming with Your Mobile Phone," earlier)—unless you're connected to free Wi-Fi, in which case you can use Skype, Google Talk, or FaceTime to call for free (or at least very cheaply; see "Calling over the Internet," earlier).

The (potentially) *really* expensive aspect of using smartphones in Europe is not voice calls or text messages, but sky-high rates for using data: checking email, browsing the Internet, streaming videos, using certain apps, and so on. If you don't proactively adjust your settings, these charges can mount up even if you're not actually using your phone—because the phone is constantly "roaming" to update your email and such. (One tip is to switch your email settings from "push" to "fetch," so you can choose when to download your emails rather than having them automatically "pushed" over the Internet to your device.)

The best solution: Disable data roaming entirely, and use your device to access the Internet only when you find free Wi-Fi (at your hotel, for example). Then you can surf the net to your heart's content, or make free (or extremely cheap) phone calls via Skype. You can manually turn off data roaming on your phone's menu (check under the "Network" settings). For added security, you can call and ask your service provider to temporarily suspend your data account entirely for the length of your trip.

Some travelers enjoy the flexibility of getting online even when they're not on free Wi-Fi. But be careful. If you simply switch on data roaming, you'll pay exorbitant rates of about $20 per megabyte (figure around 40 cents per email downloaded, or about $3 to view a typical web page)—much more expensive than it is back home. If you know you'll be doing some data roaming, it's far more affordable to sign up for a limited international data-roaming plan through your carrier (but be very clear on your megabyte limit to avoid inflated overage charges). In general, ask your provider in advance how to avoid unwittingly roaming your way to a huge bill.

free calls over the Internet to another wireless device, anywhere in the world, for free. (Or you can pay a few cents to call from your computer to a telephone.) The major providers are Skype, Google Talk, and (on Apple devices) FaceTime. You can get online at a Wi-Fi hotspot and use these apps to make calls without ringing up expensive roaming charges (though call quality can be spotty on slow connections). You can make Internet calls even if you're traveling without your own mobile device: Many European Internet cafés have Skype, as well as microphones and webcams, on their terminals—just log on and chat away.

Landline Telephones

As in the US, these days most make the majority of their calls on mobile phones. But you'll still encounter landlines in hotel rooms and at pay phones.

Hotel-Room Phones: Calling from your hotel room can be great for local calls and for international calls if you have an international phone card (described later). Otherwise, hotel-room phones can be an almost criminal rip-off for long-distance or international calls. Many hotels charge a fee for local and sometimes even "toll-free" numbers—always ask for the rates before you dial. Incoming calls are free, making this a cheap way for friends and family to stay in touch (provided they have a good long-distance plan with good international rates—and a list of your hotels' phone numbers).

Public Pay Phones: Coin-op phones are virtually extinct in Europe. To make calls from public phones, you'll need a prepaid phone card, described next.

Types of Telephone Cards

There are two types of phone cards: insertable (for pay phones) and international (cheap for overseas calls and usable from any type of phone). A phone card works only in the country where you bought it, so you have a live card at the end of your trip, give it to another traveler to use—most cards expire three to six months after the first use.

Insertable Phone Cards: These cards can only be used at pay phones. They're sold at post offices, tobacco shops, newsstands, and train stations (sold in several denominations starting at 1,000 Ft). To make a call, physically insert the card into a slot in the pay phone. While you can use these cards to call anywhere in the world, they're only a good deal for making quick local calls from a phone booth. Be aware that with the prevalence of mobile phones, public phones are getting harder to find.

International Phone Cards: While these cards are popular and easy to buy in some parts of Europe, they are still relatively rare (and more expensive) in Hungary. With these cards, phone calls from Hungary to the US can cost around 25-50 cents per minute. The cards can also be used to make local calls, and they work from any type of phone, including your hotel-room phone or a mobile phone with a European SIM card. To use a card, dial a toll-free access number, then enter your scratch-to-reveal PIN code. If the prompts are in Hungarian, experiment: Dial your code, followed by the pound sign (#), then the number, then the pound sign again, and so on, until it works.

Look for fliers advertising long-distance rates, or ask about the cards at Internet cafés, newsstands, souvenir shops, youth hostels, and post offices. Before buying a card, make sure the access number you dial is toll-free, not a local number (or else you'll be paying for a local call *and* deducting time from your calling card).

US Calling Cards: These cards, such as the ones offered by AT&T, Verizon, and Sprint, are a rotten value, and are being phased out. Try any of the options outlined earlier.

Useful Phone Numbers
Emergency Needs
Any Emergency: Tel. 112
Police: Tel. 107
Ambulance: Tel. 104
Fire: Tel. 105

Directory Assistance
Operator/Directory Assistance for Hungary: Tel. 198
Operator/Directory Assistance for International Calls: Tel. 199

Embassies in Budapest
United States: Tel. 1/475-4400, emergency tel. 1/475-4703 or 1/475-4924 (Mon-Fri 8:00-17:00, closed Sat-Sun, Szabadság tér 12, district V, www.usembassy.hu).
Canada: Tel. 1/392-3360 (Mon-Thu 8:30-12:30 & 13:00-16:30, Fri 8:00-13:30, closed Sat-Sun, Ganz utca 12-14, district II, www.hungary.gc.ca); for after-hours emergencies, call collect to Canadian tel. 613/996-8885.

Embassies/Consulates in Bratislava, Slovakia
United States: Tel. 02/5443-0861 (Mon-Fri 8:00-11:45 & 14:00-15:15, closed Sat-Sun, Hviezdoslavovo Námestie 4, http://slovakia.usembassy.gov).
Canada: Tel. 02/5920-4031 (Mon-Fri 8:30-12:30 & 13:30-16:30, closed Sat-Sun, Mostová 2, www.czechrepublic.gc.ca); for after-hours emergencies, call collect to Canadian tel. 613/996-8885.

APPENDIX

Travel Advisories
US Department of State: Tel. 888-407-4747, from outside US tel. 1-202-501-4444, www.travel.state.gov.
Canadian Department of Foreign Affairs: Canadian tel. 800-267-8376, from outside Canada tel. 1-613-996-8885, www.voyage.gc.ca.
US Centers for Disease Control and Prevention: Tel. 800-CDC-INFO (800-232-4636), www.cdc.gov/travel.

Internet Access

It's useful to get online periodically as you travel—to confirm trip plans, check train or bus schedules, get weather forecasts, catch up on email, blog or post photos from your trip, or call folks back home (explained earlier, under "Calling over the Internet").

Your Mobile Device: The majority of accommodations in Hungary offer Wi-Fi, as do many cafés, making it easy for you to get online with your laptop, tablet, or smartphone. Access is often free, but sometimes there's a fee.

Some hotel rooms and Internet cafés have high-speed Internet jacks that you can plug into with an Ethernet cable (sometimes called "WLAN"). A cellular modem—which lets your device access the Internet over a mobile network—provides more extensive coverage, but is much more expensive than Wi-Fi.

Public Internet Terminals: Many accommodations offer a computer in the lobby with Internet access for guests. If you ask politely, smaller places may let you sit at their desk for a few minutes just to check your email. If your hotelier doesn't have access, ask to be directed to the nearest place to get online. Internet cafés are easy to find in Budapest.

Security: Whether you're accessing the Internet with your own device or at a public terminal, using a shared network or computer comes with the potential for increased security risks. Be careful about storing personal information online, such as passport and credit-card numbers. If you're not convinced a connection is secure, avoid accessing any sites that could be vulnerable to fraud (e.g., online banking).

Mail

You can mail one package per day to yourself worth up to $200 duty-free from Europe to the US (mark it "personal purchases"). If you're sending a gift to someone, mark it "unsolicited gift." For details, visit www.cbp.gov and search for "Know Before You Go."

The Hungarian postal service works fine, but for quick transatlantic delivery (in either direction), consider services such as DHL (www.dhl.com). Get stamps at the neighborhood post office, newsstands within fancy hotels, and some mini-marts and card shops.

Resources

Resources from Rick Steves

Rick Steves' Budapest is one of many books in my series on European travel, which includes country guidebooks (including Eastern Europe), city and regional guidebooks (including Prague & the Czech Republic and Vienna, Salzburg & Tirol), Snapshot guides (excerpted chapters from my country guides), Pocket guides (full-color little books on big cities), and my budget-travel skills handbook, *Rick Steves' Europe Through the Back Door*. My phrase books—for German, French, Italian, Spanish, and Portuguese—are practical and budget-oriented. My other books include *Europe 101* (a crash course on art and history), *Mediterranean Cruise Ports* (how to make the most of your time in port), and *Travel as a Political Act* (a travelogue sprinkled with tips for bringing home a global perspective). A more complete list of my titles appears near the end of this book.

Video: My public television series, *Rick Steves' Europe,* covers European destinations in 100 shows, including one on Budapest. To watch episodes online, visit www.hulu.com; for scripts and local airtimes, see www.ricksteves.com/tv.

Audio: My weekly public radio show, *Travel with Rick Steves,* features interviews with travel experts from around the world, including Hungary. All of this free audio content is available at Rick Steves Audio Europe, an extensive online library organized by destination. Choose whatever interests you, and download it via the Rick Steves Audio Europe smartphone app, www.ricksteves.com/audioeurope, iTunes, or Google Play.

Maps

The black-and-white maps in this book are concise and simple, designed to help you locate recommended places and get to local TIs, where you can pick up a more in-depth map of cities and regions (usually free).

Better maps are sold at newsstands and bookstores all over Hungary. Before you buy a map, look at it to be sure it has the

Begin Your Trip at www.ricksteves.com

At our travel website, you'll find a wealth of free information on European destinations, including fresh monthly news and helpful tips from thousands of fellow travelers. You'll also find my latest guidebook updates (www.ricksteves.com/update) and my travel blog.

Our **online Travel Store** offers travel bags and accessories specially designed by me to help you travel smarter and lighter. These include my popular carry-on bags (roll-aboard and rucksack versions), money belts, totes, toiletries kits, adapters, other accessories, and a wide selection of guidebooks, journals, planning maps, and DVDs.

Choosing the right **railpass** for your trip—amid hundreds of options—can drive you nutty. We'll help you choose the best pass for your needs, plus give you a bunch of free extras.

Want to travel with greater efficiency and less stress? We offer **tours** with more than three dozen itineraries and more than 500 departures reaching the best destinations in this book...and beyond. We offer an 8-day Prague and Budapest tour, and a 16-day Best of Eastern Europe tour that visits Budapest and Eger, along with highlights of the Czech Republic, Poland, Croatia, and Slovenia. You'll enjoy great guides, a fun bunch of travel partners (with small groups of 20-24), and plenty of room to spread out in a big, comfy bus. You'll find European adventures to fit every vacation length. For all the details, and to get our Tour Catalog and a free Rick Steves Tour Experience DVD (filmed on location during an actual tour), visit www.ricksteves.com or call the Tour Department at 425/608-4217.

level of detail you want. The Hungarian-produced maps by Cartographia are best (www.cartographiaonline.com). Train travelers can usually manage fine with the freebies they get at the local tourist offices. Hikers will find no shortage of excellent, very detailed maps locally. For drivers, I'd recommend a 1:450,000-scale map of Hungary.

Other Guidebooks

If you're like most travelers, this book is all you need. But if you're heading beyond my recommended neighborhoods and destinations, $40 for extra maps and books can be money well spent. For more extensive coverage of Hungary's neighboring countries, consider *Rick Steves' Eastern Europe; Rick Steves' Vienna, Salzburg & Tirol; Rick Steves' Prague & the Czech Republic;* and *Rick Steves' Croatia & Slovenia.*

The following books are worthwhile, though not updated annually; check the publication date before you buy. The Rough Guides are packed with historical and cultural insight. The Lonely Planet guides are similar, but are designed more for travelers than for intellectuals. Both of these publish books on Hungary and on Budapest. If choosing between competing books by these two companies, I buy the one that was published most recently.

Students, backpackers, and nightlife-seekers should consider the Let's Go guides (by Harvard students, with the best hostel listings; look for their Eastern Europe title). Dorling Kindersley (DK) publishes snazzy Eyewitness Guides on Budapest and on Hungary. While pretty to look at, these guides weigh a ton and are skimpy on actual content.

Recommended Books and Movies

To learn more about Hungary past and present, check out a few of these books and films.

Nonfiction

Lonnie Johnson's *Central Europe: Enemies, Neighbors, Friends* is the best history overview of Hungary and the surrounding nations. John Lukacs' *Budapest 1900* is a scholarly but readable cultural study that captures Budapest at its turn-of-the-20th-century zenith. Patrick Leigh Fermor's *Between the Woods and the Water* is the vividly recounted memoir of a young man who traveled by foot and on horseback across the Balkan Peninsula (including Hungary) in 1933. András Török's irreverent *Budapest: A Critical Guide,* while technically a guidebook, offers more local insight (and wit) than any other source. Timothy Garton Ash has written several good "eyewitness account" books analyzing the transition in Central and Eastern Europe over the last two decades, including *History of the Present* and *The Magic Lantern*. Tina Rosenberg's dense but thought-provoking *The Haunted Land* asks how individuals who actively supported communist regimes should be treated in the post-communist age. For information on Eastern European Roma (Gypsies), consider the textbook-style *We Are the Romani People* by Ian Hancock, and the more literary *Bury Me Standing* by Isabel Fonseca. And for a look at life during communist times—albeit not in Hungary—Croatian journalist Slavenka Drakulić has written a pair of insightful essay collections from a woman's perspective: *Café Europa: Life After Communism* and *How We Survived Communism and Even Laughed*.

Fiction

Imre Kertész, a Hungarian-Jewish Auschwitz survivor who won the Nobel Prize for Literature in 2002, is best known for his semi-autobiographical novel *Fatelessness (Sorstalanság)*, which chronicles the experience of a young concentration-camp prisoner. Arthur Phillips' confusingly titled novel *Prague* tells the story of American expats negotiating young-adult life in post-communist Budapest, where they often feel one-upped by their compatriots doing the same in the Czech capital (hence the title). Joseph Roth's *The Radetzky March* details the decline of an aristocratic family in the Austro-Hungarian Empire. The Newbery Honor book *Zlateh the Goat* (Isaac Bashevis Singer) includes seven folktales of Jewish Eastern Europe.

Films

One of the more accessible films for an introduction to Budapest is *Sunshine* (1999, starring Ralph Fiennes, directed by István Szabó; not to be confused with Danny Boyle's very different 2007 film of the same name). Tracing three generations of an aristocratic Jewish family in Budapest—from the Golden Age, through the Holocaust, to the Cold War—*Sunshine* is an enlightening if melodramatic look at recent Hungarian history.

For Hungarian-language films, one of the biggest crossover hits of recent years is the surreal dark comedy *Kontroll* (2003), about ticket inspectors on the Budapest Metró whose lives are turned upside down by a serial killer lurking in the shadows. *Fateless*, the 2005 adaptation of Imre Kertész's Nobel Prize-winning novel about a young man in a concentration camp, was scripted by Kertész himself. The 1998 Oscar-winning documentary *The Last Days* chronicles the fate of Jews when the Nazis took over Hungary in 1944. *The Witness* (*A Tanú*, a.k.a. *Without a Trace*, 1969), a cult classic about a simple man who mysteriously wins the favor of communist bigwigs, is a biting satire of the darkest days of Soviet rule. *Time Stands Still (Megáll Az Idö)*, a hit at the 1982 Cannes Film

Festival, tells the story of young Hungarians in the 1960s. *Children of Glory* (*Szabadság, Szerelem*, 2006) dramatizes the true story of the Hungarian water polo team that defiantly trounced the Soviets at the Olympics just after the 1956 Uprising.

Many American studios have taken advantage of Hungary's low prices to film would-be blockbusters in Budapest (such as the 2002 Eddie Murphy/Owen Wilson action-comedy *I Spy*—a terrible film that makes wonderful use of many real Budapest settings). More often, Budapest stands in for other cities—for example, as Buenos Aires in Madonna's 1996 film *Evita,* and as various European locales in Stephen Spielberg's 2005 film *Munich.*

Two recent German movies—while not about Hungary—are still excellent for their insight into the surreal and paranoid days of the Soviet Bloc. The Oscar-winning *The Lives of Others* (2006) chronicles the constant surveillance that the communist regime employed to keep potential dissidents in line. For a funny and nostalgic look at post-communist Europe's fitful transition to capitalism, *Good Bye Lenin!* (2003) can't be beat.

Holidays and Festivals

This list includes selected festivals in Budapest, plus national holidays observed throughout Hungary. While nominally a Catholic country, most Hungarians are not very devout. Catholic holidays (such as Epiphany, Ascension, Corpus Christi, and the Assumption of Mary) are observed, but with less impact than in some other countries. Before planning a trip around a festival, verify its dates by checking the festival's website or TI sites (www.gotohungary.com). Many of Budapest's top festivals share a website (www.fesztivalvaros.hu); www.whatsonwhen.com also lists many festival dates.

Jan 1	New Year's Day
Jan 6	Epiphany
March 15	National Day (celebrates 1848 Revolution)
Late March	Budapest Spring Festival (2 weeks, March 22-April 7 in 2013)
Early April	Budapest Fringe Festival (last weekend of Spring Festival)
Good Friday	(March 29 in 2013, April 18 in 2014)
Easter	(March 31 in 2013, April 20 in 2014)
May 1	Labor Day (and anniversary of joining the EU)
Ascension	(May 9 in 2013, May 29 in 2014)
Pentecost	("Whitsunday"; May 19 in 2013, June 8 in 2014)

Whitmonday	(May 20 in 2013, June 9 in 2014)
Corpus Christi	(May 30 in 2013, June 19 in 2014)
June-mid-Aug	Outdoor Festival, Pécs (outdoor performances in the evenings, www.pecsiszabadteri.hu)
Late June-late Aug	Summer on the Chain Bridge, Budapest (bridge is closed to traffic on weekends, lined with food stalls and performers)
Late June-late Aug	Szentendre Summer Festival, Szentendre (art festival with theater, concerts, film, activities)
Late June	Early Music Days, Sopron (1 week, www.filharmoniabp.hu)
Late July	Formula 1 races, Budapest (July 27-29 in 2013, www.hungaroinfo.com/formel1)
Early Aug	Sziget Festival, Budapest (1 week, rock and pop music, www.sziget.hu)
Aug 15	Assumption of Mary
Aug 20	St. István's Day (fireworks, celebrations)
Late Aug-early Sept	Jewish Summer Festival, Budapest (2 weeks, Aug 26-Sept 4 in 2013, www.zsidonyarifesztival.hu)
Oct 23	National Day (remembrances of 1956 Uprising)
Mid-Oct	Budapest Autumn Festival (1 week, music)
Nov 1	All Saints' Day/Remembrance Day (religious festival, some closures)
Dec 24-25	Christmas Eve and Christmas Day
Dec 26	Boxing Day

Conversions and Climate

Numbers and Stumblers

- Europeans write a few of their numbers differently than we do. 1 = 1, 4 = 4, 7 = 7.
- In Hungary, dates appear as year/month/day, so Christmas is 2014/12/25 (or sometimes using dots: 2014.12.25).
- Commas are decimal points and decimals commas. A dollar and a half is 1,50, and there are 5.280 feet in a mile.
- Hungarians usually list their surname first (for example, Bartók Béla instead of Béla Bartók).
- When counting with fingers, start with your thumb. If you hold up your first finger to request one item, you'll probably get two.

- What Americans call the second floor of a building is the first floor in Europe.
- On escalators and moving sidewalks, Europeans keep the left "lane" open for passing. Keep to the right.

Metric Conversions (approximate)

A kilogram is 2.2 pounds and 1 liter is about a quart, or almost four to a gallon. A kilometer is six-tenths of a mile. I figure kilometers to miles by cutting them in half and adding back 10 percent of the original (120 km: 60 + 12 = 72 miles, 300 km: 150 + 30 = 180 miles).

APPENDIX

1 foot = 0.3 meter	1 square yard = 0.8 square meter
1 yard = 0.9 meter	1 square mile = 2.6 square kilometers
1 mile = 1.6 kilometers	1 ounce = 28 grams
1 centimeter = 0.4 inch	1 quart = 0.95 liter
1 meter = 39.4 inches	1 kilogram = 2.2 pounds
1 kilometer = 0.62 mile	32°F = 0°C

Clothing Sizes

When shopping for clothing, use these US-to-European comparisons as general guidelines (but note that no conversion is perfect).

- Women's dresses and blouses: Add 30
  (US size 10 = European size 40)
- Men's suits and jackets: Add 10
  (US size 40 regular = European size 50)
- Men's shirts: Multiply by 2 and add about 8
  (US size 15 collar = European size 38)
- Women's shoes: Add about 30
  (US size 8 = European size 38-39)
- Men's shoes: Add 32-34
  (US size 9 = European size 41; US size 11 = European size 45)

Climate

First line, average daily high; second line, average daily low; third line, average days with some rain. For more detailed weather statistics for destinations in this book (as well as the rest of the world), check www.worldclimate.com.

J	F	M	A	M	J	J	A	S	O	N	D
HUNGARY • Budapest											
34°	39°	50°	62°	71°	78°	82°	81°	74°	61°	47°	39°
25°	28°	35°	44°	52°	58°	62°	60°	53°	44°	38°	30°
13	12	11	11	13	13	10	9	7	10	14	13

Temperature Conversion: Fahrenheit and Celsius

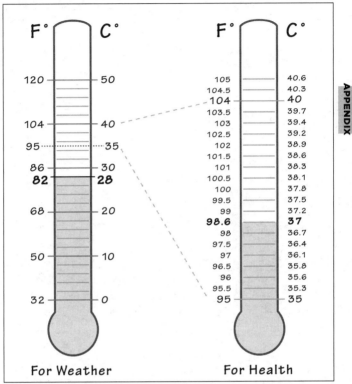

Europe takes its temperature using the Celsius scale, while we opt for Fahrenheit. For a rough conversion from Celsius to Fahrenheit, double the number and add 30. For weather, remember that 28°C is 82°F— perfect. For health, 37°C is just right.

Packing Checklist

Whether you're traveling for five days or five weeks, here's what you'll need to bring. Pack light to enjoy the sweet freedom of true mobility. Happy travels!

- ❑ 5 shirts: long- and short-sleeve
- ❑ 1 sweater or lightweight fleece
- ❑ 2 pairs pants
- ❑ 1 pair shorts
- ❑ 1 swimsuit
- ❑ 5 pairs underwear and socks
- ❑ 1 pair shoes
- ❑ 1 rainproof jacket with hood
- ❑ Tie or scarf
- ❑ Money belt
- ❑ Money—your mix of:
  - ❑ Debit card (for ATM withdrawals)
  - ❑ Credit card
  - ❑ Hard cash (in easy-to-exchange $20 bills)
- ❑ Documents plus photocopies:
  - ❑ Passport
  - ❑ Printout of airline eticket
  - ❑ Driver's license
  - ❑ Student ID and hostel card
  - ❑ Railpass/car rental voucher
  - ❑ Insurance details
- ❑ Daypack
- ❑ Electronics—your choice of:
  - ❑ Camera (and related gear)
  - ❑ Computer/mobile devices (phone, MP3 player, ereader, etc.)
  - ❑ Chargers for each of the above
  - ❑ Plug adapter
- ❑ Empty water bottle

- ❑ Wristwatch and alarm clock
- ❑ Earplugs
- ❑ Toiletries kit
  - ❑ Toiletries
  - ❑ Medicines and vitamins
  - ❑ First-aid kit
  - ❑ Glasses/contacts/sunglasses (with prescriptions)
- ❑ Sealable plastic baggies
- ❑ Laundry soap
- ❑ Clothesline
- ❑ Small towel
- ❑ Sewing kit
- ❑ Travel information (guidebooks and maps)
- ❑ Address list (for sending postcards)
- ❑ Postcards and photos from home
- ❑ Notepad and pen
- ❑ Journal

If you plan to carry on your luggage, note that all liquids must be in 3.4-ounce or smaller containers and fit within a single quart-size sealable baggie. For details, see www.tsa.gov/travelers.

Hotel Reservation

To: _____   _____
            hotel   *email or fax*

From: _____   _____
            name   *email or fax*

Today's date: _____ /_____ /_____
                     day   *month*   *year*

Dear Hotel _____ ,
Please make this reservation for me:

Name: _____

Total # of people: _____   # of rooms: _____   # of nights: _____

Arriving: _____ /_____ /_____   My time of arrival (24-hr clock): _____
                day *month* *year*   (I will telephone if I will be late)

Departing: _____ /_____ /_____
                 day *month* *year*

Room(s): Single____   Double ____   Twin ____   Triple ____   Quad____

With: Toilet _____   Shower_____   Bath _____   Sink only_____

Special needs: View____   Quiet____   Cheapest____   Ground Floor____

Please email or fax confirmation of my reservation, along with the type of room reserved and the price. Please also inform me of your cancellation policy. After I hear from you, I will quickly send my credit-card information as a deposit to hold the room. Thank you.

_____
Name

_____
Address

_____
City   *State*   *Zip Code*   *Country*

Before hoteliers can make your reservation, they want to know the information listed above. You can use this form as the basis for your email, or you can photocopy this page, fill in the information, and send it as a fax (also available online at www.ricksteves.com/reservation).

Hungarian Survival Phrases

Remember, the letter *a* is pronounced "aw," while *á* is a brighter "ah." In the phonetics, *dj* is pronounced like the j in "jeans."

Hello. (formal)	Jó napot kívánok.	yoh NAH-pot KEE-vah-nohk
Hi. / Bye. (informal)	Szia. or Hello.	SEE-yaw, "Hello"
Do you speak English?	Beszél angolul?	BEH-sayl AWN-goh-lool
Yes. / No.	Igen. / Nem.	EE-gehn / nehm
I (don't) understand.	(Nem) értem.	(nehm) AYR-tehm
Please.	Kérem.	KAY-rehm
You're welcome.	Szívesen.	SEE-veh-shehn
Thank you (very much).	Köszönöm (szépen).	KUR-sur-nurm (SAY-pehn)
Excuse me. / I'm sorry.	Bocsánat.	BOH-chah-nawt
No problem.	Semmi gond.	SHEH-mee gohnd
Good.	Jól.	yohl
Goodbye.	Viszontlátásra.	VEE-sohnt-lah-tahsh-raw
one / two	egy / kettő	edj / KEH-tur
three / four	három / négy	HAH-rohm / naydj
five / six	öt / hat	urt / hawt
seven / eight	hét / nyolc	hayt / nyolts
nine / ten	kilenc / tíz	KEE-lehnts / teez
hundred / thousand	száz / ezer	sahz / EH-zehr
How much?	Mennyi?	MEHN-yee
local currency	forint (Ft)	FOH-reent
Where is it?	Hol van?	hohl vawn
Is it free (no charge)?	Ingyen van?	een-JEHN vawn
Is it included?	Benne van az árban?	BEH-neh vawn oz AHR-bawn
Where can I find / buy...?	Hol találok / vehetek...?	hohl TAW-lah-lohk / VEH-heh-tehk
I'd like...	Kérnék...	KAYR-nayk
We'd like...	Kérnénk...	KAYR-naynk
...a room	...egy szobát	edj SOH-baht
...a ticket (to ___)	...egy jegyet (___-ig)	edj YEHDJ-eht (___-ig)
Is it possible?	Lehet?	leh-HEHT
Where is the...?	Hol van a...?	hohl vawn aw
big train station (in Budapest)	pályaudvar	PAH-yood-vawr
small train station (elsewhere)	vasútállomás	VAW-shoot-ah-loh-mahsh
bus station	buszpályaudvar	BOOS-pah-yood-vawr
tourist information office	turista információ	TOO-reesh-taw EEN-for-maht-see-yoh
toilet	toalet or WC	TOH-aw-leht, VAYT-say
men	férfi	FAYR-fee
women	női	NUR-ee
left / right	bal / jobb	bawl / yohb
straight	egyenesen or előre	EDJ-eh-neh-shehn, EH-lew-reh
At what time...	Mikor...	MEE-kohr
...does this open / close?	...nyit / zár?	nyit / zahr
Just a moment.	Egy pillanat.	edj PEE-law-nawt
now / soon / later	most / hamarosan / később	mohsht / HAW-maw-roh-shawn / KAY-shurb
today / tomorrow	ma / holnap	maw / HOHL-nawp

In the Restaurant

I'd like to reserve a table for one / two people.	Szeretnék foglalni egy asztalt egy / két fő részére.	SEH-reht-nayk FOG-lawl-nee edj AWS-tawlt edj / kayt few RAY-say-reh
Non-smoking.	Nem dohányzó.	nehm DOH-hayn-zoh
Is this table free?	Ez az asztal szabad?	ehz oz AWS-tawl saw-BAWD
Can I help you?	Tessék.	TEHSH-shayk
The menu (in English), please.	Kérem az (angol) étlapot.	KAY-rehm oz (AWN-gohl) AYT-law-poht
service (not) included	a számla a felszolgálási díjat (nem) tartalmazza	aw SAHM-law aw FEHL-sohl-gah-lah-shee DEE-yawt (nehm) TAWR-tawl-maw-zaw
cover charge	belépő	BEH-lay-pur
"to go"	elvitelre	EHL-vee-tehl-reh
with / without	___-val / nélkül	___-vawl / NAYL-kewl
and / or	és / vagy	aysh / vawdj
fixed-price meal (of the day)	(napi) menü	(NAW-pee) MEH-new
specialty of the house	a ház specialitása	aw hahz SHPEHT-see-aw-lee-tah-shaw
half portion	fél adag	fayl AW-dawg
daily special	napi ajánlat	NAW-pee AW-yahn-lawt
fixed-price meal (for tourists)	(turista) menü	(TOO-reesh-taw) MEH-new
main courses	főételek	FUR-ay-teh-lehk
appetizers	előételek	EH-lur-ay-teh-lehk
bread / cheese	kenyér / sajt	KEHN-yayr / shayt
sandwich	szendvics	SEND-veech
soup / salad	leves / saláta	LEH-vehsh / SHAW-lah-taw
meat / poultry	hús / szárnyasok	hoosh / SAHR-nyaw-shohk
fish	halak	HAW-lawk
seafood	tengeri halak	TEHN-geh-ree HAW-lawk
fruit	gyümölcs	JEWM-urlch
vegetables	zöldség	ZULRD-shayg
dessert	desszert	DEH-sehrt
vegetarian	vegetáriánus	VEH-geh-tah-ree-ah-noosh
(tap) water	(csap) víz	(chawp) veez
mineral water	ásványvíz	ASH-vawn-veez
milk	tej	TAYee
(orange) juice	(narancs) lé	(NAW-rawnch) lay
coffee / tea	kávé / tea	KAH-vay / TEH-aw
beer / wine	sör / bor	shohr / bohr
red / white	vörös / fehér	VUR-rursh / FEH-hayr
sweet / dry / semi-dry	édes / száraz / félszáraz	AY-dehsh / SAH-rawz / FAYL-sah-rawz
glass / bottle	pohár / üveg	POH-hahr / EW-vehg
Cheers!	Egészségedre!	EH-gehs-shay-geh-dreh
More. / Another.	Még. / Másikat.	mayg / MAH-shee-kawt
The same.	Ugyanazt.	OODJ-aw-nawst
Bill, please. (literally, "I'll pay.")	Fizetek.	FEE-zeh-tehk
tip	borravaló	BOH-raw-vaw-loh
Bon appétit!	Jó étvágyat!	yoh AYT-vah-yawt
Delicious!	Finom!	FEE-nohm

INDEX

MAP INDEX

Audio Europe

RICK STEVES AUDIO EUROPE

Rick's Free Travel App

Get your FREE **Rick Steves Audio Europe**™ app to enjoy…

- Dozens of self-guided tours of Europe's top museums, sights and historic walks

- Hundreds of tracks filled with cultural insights and sightseeing tips from Rick's radio interviews

- All organized into handy geographic playlists

- For iPhone, iPad, iPod Touch, Android

With Rick whispering in your ear, Europe gets even better.

Find out more at ricksteves.com

Join
a Rick
Steves
tour

Enjoy Europe's
warmest welcome...
with the flexibility and
friendship of a small group
getting to know Rick's
favorite places and people.
It all starts with our free
tour catalog and DVD.

Great guides, small
groups, no grumps.

See more than three dozen itineraries throughout Europe
ricksteves.com

Start your trip at

Free information and great gear to

▸ Plan Your Trip

Browse thousands of articles and a wealth of money-saving tips for planning your dream trip. You'll find up-to-date information on Europe's best destinations, packing smart, getting around, finding rooms, staying healthy, avoiding scams and more.

▸ Eurail Passes

Find out, step-by-step, if a railpass makes sense for your trip—and how to avoid buying more than you need. Get free shipping on online orders

▸ Graffiti Wall & Travelers Helpline

Learn, ask, share—our online community of savvy travelers is a great resource for first-time travelers to Europe, as well as seasoned pros.

Rick Steves' Europe Through the Back Door, Inc.

NOW AVAILABLE:
eBOOKS, DVD & BLU-RAY

TRAVEL CULTURE

Europe 101
European Christmas
Postcards from Europe
Travel as a Political Act

eBOOKS

*Nearly all Rick Steves guides
are available as eBooks. Check
with your favorite bookseller.*

RICK STEVES' EUROPE DVDs

10 New Shows 2011–2012
Austria & the Alps
Eastern Europe
England & Wales
European Christmas
European Travel Skills & Specials
France
Germany, BeNeLux & More
Greece & Turkey
Iran
Ireland & Scotland
Italy's Cities
Italy's Countryside
Scandinavia
Spain
Travel Extras

BLU-RAY

Celtic Charms
Eastern Europe Favorites
European Christmas
Italy Through the Back Door
Mediterranean Mosaic
Surprising Cities of Europe

PHRASE BOOKS & DICTIONARIES

French
French, Italian & German
German
Italian
Portuguese
Spanish

JOURNALS

Rick Steves' Pocket Travel Journal
Rick Steves' Travel Journal

PLANNING MAPS

Britain, Ireland & London
Europe
France & Paris
Germany, Austria & Switzerland
Ireland
Italy
Spain & Portugal

Rick Steves books and DVDs are available at bookstores
and through online booksellers.

Credits

Contributor
Gene Openshaw

Gene, the co-author of a dozen Rick Steves books, specializes in Europe's art and history. When not traveling, Gene enjoys composing music, recovering from his 1973 trip to Europe with Rick, and living every day life with his daughter.

Acknowledgments

Many thanks to our Hungarian friends for sharing their invaluable insights: Péter Pölczman, Andrea Makkay, and Elemér Boreczky. *Köszönjük szépen!*